Drug Abuse

Origins & Interventions

Drug Abuse
Origins & Interventions

Edited by

Meyer D. Glantz
and Christine R. Hartel

American Psychological Association
Washington, DC

Published by
American Psychological Association
750 First Street, NE
Washington, DC 20002

Copies may be ordered from
APA Order Department
P.O. Box 92984
Washington, DC 20090-2984

In the U.K., Europe, Africa, and the Middle East, copies may be ordered from
American Psychological Association
3 Henrietta Street
Covent Garden, London
WC2E 8LU England

Typeset in Goudy by EPS Group Inc., Easton, MD

Printer: United Book Press, Inc., Baltimore, MD
Jacket Designer: Design Concepts, San Diego, CA
Technical/Production Editor: Eleanor Inskip

Library of Congress Cataloging-in-Publication Data
Drug abuse : origins and interventions / edited by Meyer D. Glantz and
    Christine R. Hartel.
        p.   cm.
    Includes bibliographical references and index.
    ISBN 1-55798-601-0 (case : alk. paper)
    1. Drug abuse—Government policy—United States.   2. Drug abuse—
Treatment—United States.   3. Drug abuse—Research—United States.
I. Glantz, Meyer D., 1952–   II. Hartel, Christine R., 1947–   .
HV5825.D7736   1999
326.29—DC21   99-27656
                                                                   CIP

British Library Cataloguing-in-Publication Data
A CIP record is available from the British Library.

Printed in the United States of America
First Edition

For our spouses, Linda and Frank,
Who supported us in this project as they do in all else.

CONTENTS

List of Contributors ix

Foreword xiii
    Alan I. Leshner

Preface xxi

I. ORIGINS

1. The Etiology of Drug Abuse: Mapping the Paths 3
    Meyer D. Glantz, Naimah Z. Weinberg, Lucinda L. Miner,
    and James D. Colliver

2. Frontline Surveillance: The Community Epidemiology
    Work Group on Drug Abuse 47
    Zili Sloboda and Nicholas J. Kozel

3. The Impact of Public Attitudes on Drug Abuse Research
    in the Twentieth Century 63
    David F. Musto

4. Explaining Attitudes About Public Policy on Drug
    Availability: The Role of Expectancies About Drinking
    and Drug Effects 79
    Robin Room and Angela Paglia

5. A Developmental Psychopathology Perspective on
    Drug Abuse 97
    Dante Cicchetti

6. Why People Use, Abuse, and Become Dependent on
    Drugs: Progress Toward a Heuristic Model 119
    Robert J. Pandina and Valerie L. Johnson

7. Prevention and Treatment of Drug Abuse: Use of Animal
   Models to Find Solutions 149
   Marilyn E. Carroll

8. Neurobiology of Drug Addiction 161
   George F. Koob, S. Barak Caine, Petri Hyytia,
   Athina Markou, Loren H. Parsons, Amanda J. Roberts,
   Gery Schulteis, and Friedbert Weiss

9. Ethnic Minority Women, Health Behaviors, and
   Drug Abuse: A Continuum of Psychosocial Risks 191
   Kathy Sanders-Phillips

II. INTERVENTIONS

10. The Prevention of Drug Abuse: Interrupting the Paths ... 223
    Zili Sloboda

11. The Treatment of Drug Abuse: Changing the Paths 243
    Christine R. Hartel and Meyer D. Glantz

12. Adolescent Drug Abuse Prevention: Current Findings
    and Future Directions 285
    Gilbert J. Botvin

13. HIV Prevention: We Don't Need to Wait for a Vaccine .. 309
    Thomas J. Coates and Chris Collins

14. An Ecodevelopmental Framework for Organizing the
    Influences on Drug Abuse: A Developmental Model of
    Risk and Protection 331
    José Szapocznik and J. Douglas Coatsworth

15. Development, Evaluation, and Dissemination of Effective
    Psychosocial Treatments: Levels of Disorder, Stages of
    Care, and Stages of Treatment Research 367
    Marsha M. Linehan

16. Therapeutic Communities: Research and Applications 395
    George De Leon

17. Scientific Basis for Tobacco Policy: Nicotine Research
    Travails 431
    Jack E. Henningfield and Christine R. Hartel

Author Index 447

Subject Index 473

About the Editors 491

CONTRIBUTORS

Gilbert J. Botvin, PhD, Professor and Director, Institute for Prevention Research, Cornell University Medical College

S. Barak Caine, PhD, Alcohol and Drug Abuse Research Center, McLean Hospital, Harvard Medical School

Marilyn E. Carroll, PhD, Professor of Psychiatry and Neuroscience, University of Minnesota

Dante Cicchetti, PhD, Professor, Departments of Psychology, Psychiatry, and Pediatrics, University of Rochester, Director, Mt. Hope Family Center

Thomas J. Coates, PhD, Director, UCSF AIDS Research Institute and Director, Center for AIDS Prevention Studies, Department of Medicine, University of California, San Francisco

J. Douglas Coatsworth, PhD, Research Assistant Professor, Center for Family Studies, Department of Psychiatry and Behavioral Sciences, University of Miami School of Medicine

Chris Collins, MPP, UCSF AIDS Research Institute and Center for AIDS Prevention Studies, Department of Medicine, University of California, San Francisco

James D. Colliver, PhD, Acting Branch Chief, Epidemiology Research Branch, Division of Epidemiology and Prevention Research, National Institute on Drug Abuse, National Institutes of Health

George De Leon, PhD, Director, Center for Therapeutic Community Research, Clinical Professor of Psychiatry, New York University School of Medicine

Meyer D. Glantz, PhD, Associate Director for Science and Acting Deputy Director, Division of Epidemiology and Prevention Research, National Institute on Drug Abuse, National Institutes of Health

Christine R. Hartel, PhD, Associate Executive Director for Science, American Psychological Association

Jack E. Henningfield, PhD, Associate Professor, Department of Psychiatry and Behavioral Sciences, The John Hopkins University School of Medicine and Vice President, Research and Health Policy, Pinney Associates

Petri Hyytia, PhD, Department of Alcohol Research, National Public Health Institute, Helsinki, Finland

Valerie L. Johnson, PhD, Associate Research Professor, Center of Alcohol Studies, Rutgers University

George F. Koob, PhD, Professor and Director, Division of Psychopharmacology, Department of Neuropharmacology, The Scripps Research Institute

Nicholas J. Kozel, MS, Associate Director, Program Development and Intergovernmental Coordination, Division of Epidemiology and Prevention Research, National Institute on Drug Abuse, National Institutes of Health

Alan I. Leshner, PhD, Director, National Institute on Drug Abuse, National Institutes of Health

Marsha M. Linehan, PhD, Professor, Department of Psychology, Director, Behavioral Research and Therapy Clinics, University of Washington

Athina Markou, PhD, Assistant Professor, Division of Psychopharmacology, Department of Neuropharmacology, The Scripps Research Institute

Lucinda L. Miner, PhD, Office of Science Policy and Communications, National Institute on Drug Abuse, National Institutes of Health

David F. Musto, MD, Professor, Child Psychiatry and the History of Medicine, Yale University

Angela Paglia, MA, Addiction Research Foundation Division, Centre for Addiction and Mental Health, Toronto, Ontario, Canada

Robert J. Pandina, PhD, Professor and Director, Center of Alcohol Studies, Rutgers University

Loren H. Parsons, PhD, Assistant Professor, Division of Psychopharmacology, Department of Neuropharmacology, The Scripps Research Institute

Amanda J. Roberts, PhD, Staff Scientist, Division of Psychopharmacology, Department of Neuropharmacology, The Scripps Research Institute

Robin Room, PhD, Professor and Director, Centre for Social Research on Alcohol and Drugs, Stockholm University, Stockholm, Sweden

Kathy Sanders-Phillips, PhD, Director, Research and Evaluation, The California Endowment, Department of Pediatrics, University of California School of Medicine

Gery Schulteis, PhD, Senior Research Associate, Division of Psychopharmacology, Department of Neuropharmacology, The Scripps Research Institute

Zili Sloboda, ScD, Director, Division of Epidemiology and Prevention Research, National Institute on Drug Abuse, National Institutes of Health

José Szapocznik, PhD, Professor and Director, Center for Family Studies, Department of Psychiatry and Behavioral Sciences, University of Miami School of Medicine

Naimah Z. Weinberg, MD, Medical Officer, Division of Epidemiology and Prevention Research, National Institute on Drug Abuse, National Institutes of Health

Friedbert Weiss, PhD, Associate Professor, Division of Psychopharmacology, Department of Neuropharmacology, The Scripps Research Institute

FOREWORD

ALAN I. LESHNER

For decades, drug abuse and addiction have ranked highly among the most complex, costly, and widely misunderstood problems facing the United States. These disorders exact an enormous toll on the health, well-being, and safety of our citizens, and their study presents challenges unparalleled in most other fields of scientific inquiry. Fortunately, the phenomenal advances made in behavioral science and neuroscience in recent years have virtually revolutionized the fundamental views of drug abuse and addiction and have led to the development of effective strategies for their prevention and treatment. Likewise, the remarkable gains made in the science of drug abuse and addiction have helped to propel the behavioral science and neuroscience fields dramatically forward.

The National Institute on Drug Abuse (NIDA) is the component of the National Institutes of Health whose mission it is to conduct and support drug abuse research. In fact, NIDA provides over 85% of the world's support for investigations into the health aspects of drug abuse and addiction. Basic research and an even longer history of clinical experience affirm that drug abuse is a preventable behavior and drug addiction is a treatable disease. Scientists in virtually every area of psychology have helped to build the current scientific knowledge base about these intriguingly complex disorders. In fact, recent research has made major advances in key priority areas, including neuroscience, behavioral science, protective–resilience factors and epidemiology, prevention, treatment, and HIV infection and AIDS.

NEUROSCIENCE

Among the impressive breakthroughs made in neuroscience have been the identification and genetic specification of receptors for all the major drugs of abuse, including cocaine, marijuana, and a whole variety of opiate receptors within the brain. Extraordinary progress also has been made in mapping the intricate network of neural circuitry and neurotransmitter systems involved in drug addiction. Although each drug class may have its own specific mode of action, in tracing the pathways through which a variety of drugs exert their effects, certain commonalities for all drugs of abuse have emerged. The convergence of a series of recent basic science discoveries suggests one common reward pathway in the brain where all drugs of abuse act. Regardless of their initial site of action, every known drug of abuse—be it nicotine, cocaine, heroin, or amphetamine—has been found to increase levels of the neurotransmitter dopamine in the neural pathways that control pleasure. The knowledge that is being generated about dopamine and the integral role it plays in addiction is paving the way toward the development of medications to treat addiction.

Recent advances in biomedical research technologies also have provided the means to explore the molecular and cellular underpinnings of the addictive process. For example, new noninvasive brain-imaging technologies are affording unprecedented opportunities for assessing the effects of acute and chronic drug administration on the anatomy, chemistry, and physiology of the brain. By combining the use of these valuable tools with a variety of sophisticated assessment techniques derived from behavioral science, we can concurrently monitor brain function and neuropsychological status. Integration of these technologies is enabling us to relate changes in the patterns of biologic activity in the human brain to the subjective experiences of individuals exposed to drugs of abuse. Researchers now are able to explore the connections between behaviors and underlying neurobiological and neurochemical changes and to demonstrate correlations between alterations in specific brain regions and subjective behavioral states related to drug abuse and addiction.

Knowledge gained from studies using such innovative technologies are helping us to better understand the biological and behavioral bases of many aspects of the addictive process, including drug-seeking behavior, craving, euphoria, and drug tolerance. Imaging technology also has enormous utility in diagnostic assessment and is playing an important role in the development of effective medications, nonpharmacological therapies, and their combination, for use in treating addiction.

BEHAVIORAL SCIENCE

Behavioral research has produced an outstanding foundation on which many of today's drug abuse and addiction prevention and treatment strategies are built. The science of psychology has advanced understanding about the behavioral effects of these disorders; has assessed the abuse liability and potential toxicity of abused pharmacological compounds; and has developed useful tools to aid behavioral scientists, as well as scientists in other areas, in exploring the biological, behavioral, social, and environmental origins of drug abuse and addiction.

For example, the self-administration or behavioral reinforcement model and a variety of other techniques founded on learning theory have provided a window through which scientists have been able to study the nature and course of such drug abuse transition states as initiation, abstinence, and withdrawal. They also have helped to demonstrate empirical evidence of drug-induced changes in motivational states and to delineate the role of tolerance and physical dependence in drug craving and drug seeking.

Perhaps the most significant outcome of studies using these technologies has been to underscore the importance of a confluence of variables that underlie drug-taking behavior. Such knowledge has been instrumental in broadening the perspective of clinicians as to the large number and the wide variety of factors that may be involved in drug abuse.

Until recently, basic behavioral research investigations have relied extensively on the behavioral reinforcement model to determine why animals and humans abuse drugs, which drugs have the potential to be abused, and the ways in which drugs of abuse affect an organism's behavior. These studies continue to generate a wealth of useful information about drug abuse and addiction, but their findings also have made it abundantly clear that there is still a great deal more to be learned about other behavioral processes and phenomena that play a role in drug abuse and addiction.

During the past several years, intensive efforts on the part of behavioral scientists have expanded to include the investigation of cognitive, motivational, and social processes of health behavior. Broadening the scope of the basic behavioral science explorations will help to better address questions of underlying behavioral mechanisms, determinants, and correlates of drug abuse as well as to better characterize the harmful sequelae of drug use and abuse. Some areas in which more research is needed include the following:

- cognitive processes (e.g., learning and memory, language and information processing, perception, problem solving, concept formation, spatial ability, and animal cognition);
- social and personality factors (e.g., dominance hierarchies, social influence, social values, social attitudes and cognition, persuasion, conformity and compliance, group and interpersonal processes, conflict and resolution, sex roles, sexual behavior, risk taking, and HIV and AIDS);
- behavior-change models (e.g., self-control, self-management, incentive motivation theory, and behavioral alternatives);

- developmental processes (e.g., cognitive, perceptual, motor and language development, psychosocial and personality development, and life span studies);
- health-related behavioral processes (e.g., stress-coping strategies, health decision models, placebo effects, self-medication, and comorbidity, including sleep and eating disorders);
- biological bases of behavior (e.g., aggression; behavioral genetics; animal learning and behavior; physiology and behavior; stress; pain and analgesia; and diurnal, circadian, and ultradian rhythms).

PROTECTIVE–RESILIENCE FACTORS AND EPIDEMIOLOGY

The patterns of drug use and abuse in this country are continually changing. Variations in the availability of drugs, new or changing modes of drug administration, and fluctuating levels of social acceptance and perceived risk of drug use all contribute to the dynamic and sometimes elusive nature of the problem. Epidemiologic research is essential in describing these changing patterns and in better understanding their underlying factors and processes. Epidemiologic research can also help to forecast and study emerging forms or patterns of abuse and to identify variables that alter an individual's vulnerability to drug abuse.

Researchers have made great progress in assessing trends in drug abuse patterns nationwide, describing patterns of drug abuse in certain at-risk subpopulations, identifying and understanding relevant risk and protective factors, and characterizing the consequences of drug abuse. Increasingly sophisticated epidemiologic methods, developed and used through research, can be credited with much of this progress. For example, information provided by the Monitoring the Future study, a survey supported by NIDA and conducted annually since 1975 by scientists at the University of Michigan on the values, preferences, lifestyles, and levels of drug abuse of a nationally representative sample of youth has alerted us, in recent years, to the significant upward trends in drug use that have been occurring among 12th, 10th, and even 8th graders and the reciprocal decline in their perception of the risk associated with drug use. Such information has prompted increased efforts in conveying to the public the science-based facts about drug use.

Psychologists also have played a lead role in elucidating the origins and pathways to drug abuse. By identifying many of the risk factors that are often associated with individuals who develop drug abuse problems— including shy, aggressive, and impulsive personality traits; chaotic family environments; poor academic performance; and deviant peer influences— behavioral scientists have made major contributions in defining levels of risk for initial drug use. In addition, researchers have identified many of the protective or resiliency factors, such as positive parental involvement in the life of a child, that typically reduce the chance of an individual becoming a substance abuser. Advances in understanding both risk and protective factors, as well as how to balance their relative contributions in any given situation, have served as the basis for developing increasingly effective and targeted prevention strategies.

PREVENTION

The process of prevention, basically one of education and behavior change, is another important area of study within the purview of psychologists. In recent years, researchers have successfully demonstrated that a variety of specific interventions can have both short- and long-term positive outcomes in preventing initial drug use and in interrupting the progression from drug abuse to addiction. Much of the focus of prevention research has been on the development and assessment of theory-based universal prevention strategies directed at the general population. Interventions developed to date have used a variety of integrated activities, including social resistance education in the schools, antidrug media campaigns, parent skills training, antidrug coalitions at the neighborhood level, and anti-drug-use policies and enforcement practices.

Insights being generated through current prevention intervention efforts suggest that a comprehensive approach to drug abuse prevention offers the best chance of positively affecting this complex problem. Conversely, simplistic strategies do not work. The premise of comprehensive drug prevention is that program activities should focus both on the individual and on his or her social environment. Multicomponent, community-based prevention programs that use schools, parents, media, community, and public policy to prevent drug abuse among youth have reported significant long-term reductions in marijuana and cocaine use. Research has shown that effective drug abuse prevention programs for young teenagers must address a wide range of interpersonal skills, including building self-esteem, developing personal relationships, managing anxiety, and resisting social pressure. Recent data also suggest that optimal effectiveness is achieved when repeated rather than single exposures are provided. And, of course, prevention messages must be accurate and credible, as well as delivered in a way appropriate to the target audience.

TREATMENT

Drug addiction is most accurately characterized as a chronic, relapsing disease characterized by compulsive drug seeking and use. The chronic nature of this disease often results in addicts experiencing multiple cycles of treatment, abstinence, and relapse. More than one treatment episode is frequently required for addicts to sustain healthy lifestyles over the long term. Even in cases where pharmacological interventions are used to treat addiction, behavioral interventions also must be included, to address the concomitant psychological, social, and environmental problems associated with drug abuse.

Behavioral and psychosocial treatment research—much of which is being conducted by psychologists—is focusing on the development, refinement, and efficacy testing of such behavioral and psychosocial therapeutic approaches as individual and group psychotherapy, psychodynamic and interpersonal psychotherapy, behavior therapy, cognitive psychotherapy, family therapy, drug abuse counseling, vocational rehabilitation, skills training, and relapse-prevention strategies. Behavioral techniques derived from learning theory, such as contingency management, are showing promise in their ability to reduce drug use. Although pharmacological and behavioral treatments work for some individuals, integrating pharmacological and behavioral–psychosocial approaches to treatment in ways that are specific for different subgroups and for different drugs of abuse is often the most promising way to develop effective treatments for addictive disorders.

Addiction is the quintessential biobehavioral disorder. Because drug abuse and addiction can profoundly impact the biological, behavioral, and social functioning of a person, the treatments that will ultimately be most effective are those that attend to all of these aspects: the biological, behavioral, and social context in which the drug use occurs.

HIV INFECTION AND AIDS

Behavioral science also is critical in the fight against another drug-abuse-related condition: HIV/AIDS. AIDS is currently the most rapidly increasing fatal consequence of drug abuse. For adults, drug abuse, either directly or indirectly, is now the leading risk factor for acquiring HIV infection. Perhaps even more tragic is the fact that drug abuse is the primary risk factor for HIV/AIDS in infants and children born to mothers who are HIV infected as a result of their own drug use or drug use by sexual partners, accounting for more than half of all pediatric cases reported. Research has shown that drug abuse treatment is among the best ways to stop the spread of HIV. Numerous studies show HIV seroconversion rates for those engaged in treatment to be dramatically lower than those not in treatment.

Significant progress has been made in reducing the risk of HIV infection in drug abusers not engaged in treatment; behavioral change interventions currently are the most promising strategy. AIDS outreach programs have been very successful in helping to foster changes in behavior related to needle sharing and high-risk sex and in encouraging drug users to enroll in drug treatment.

Efforts also are under way to evaluate the effectiveness of controlled experimental interventions to reduce HIV-risk behaviors among injecting drug users, crack cocaine users, and others at risk for drug use. Programs in 23 sites around the country have been reaching individuals who had never before been tested for HIV infection or who had never before been in treatment for drug abuse.

Although we have come a long way in advancing our understanding of drug abuse and addiction and what to do about these problems, there are still a number of major gap areas involving behavioral science that need to be filled. For example, better, more accurate models of addiction are needed, as is a better understanding of the behavioral effects of drugs and the many factors that can modulate these effects.

Some existing models of drug use do come close to approximating drug addiction. However, more behavioral sophistication must be brought to bear, to fully address the many facets of this complex process. For example, models are needed that more closely approximate the clinical condition of addiction, that is, the compulsive drug seeking and use that an addict engages in, for no medical benefit and in the face of negative consequences. There is also a need to gain a better understanding of the cognitive and motivational aspects of the effects of drugs and the role of craving in maintaining drug use or relapsing to drug abuse after periods of abstinence. In addition, there are opportunities for doing translational research, that is, moving the findings that are being generated through basic research to their clinical application in preventing and treating drug abuse and addiction.

Like research into many other diseases, drug abuse and addiction research can yield improvements in the quality of life for millions of affected individuals; dramatic reductions in social, criminal justice, and health care costs; and decreases in the transmission of serious communicable disorders like tuberculosis, hepatitis, and AIDS. This field offers a wealth of both research and clinical possibilities, as well as providing the perfect opportunity to make significant contributions both to science and to society. Now more than ever it is critical to bring the full power of science to bear on drug abuse and addiction.

CONCLUSION

What you are about to read within the body of this book will demonstrate how far we have come in our understanding of and approaches to drug abuse and addiction, as well as attempting to identify some of the research gaps that need to be filled as we travel the remaining journey in finding solutions to this complex problem. The authors in this book provide the reader with a thoughtful summary of the science in their area of expertise. Readers will come away with a better understanding of basic and applied knowledge in research, prevention, education, and treatment. In the end, there will be no magic bullet that is going to make drug abuse and addiction go away, but as the information in this book conveys, there is great cause for hope that we will continue to make progress in dealing with this, the most complex and compelling issue facing modern day society.

PREFACE

Throughout recorded history, and most likely even before that, people have ingested substances that changed their experience of the world. Modern chemical techniques have made it possible to isolate and refine the psychoactive components of natural and some synthetic substances, creating eminently transportable, extraordinarily potent, easy to market, and easy to self-administer doses of drugs. This wholesale transformation of the availability, purity, and potency of illicit drugs has outstripped our human ability to control the deleterious effects of these drugs on our own neurochemistry and our social behavior.

And the costs are staggering. In the United States alone, the economic costs are estimated at $109.8 billion during 1995 (Harwood, Fountain, & Livermore, 1998). This includes the costs of the health consequences of alcohol and drug use to the health care system, the costs of criminal behavior and violence related to alcohol and drug use, and the costs related to job loss and family impoverishment, including welfare. The costs in human misery and pain remain inestimable.

Science and its applications have played an extraordinary role in drug abuse research, prevention, and treatment interventions, and in the making of public policy about drug abuse. However, it can be difficult to grasp the main concepts of the field and the societal implications amid the wealth of detail that is available. For this reason, *Drug Abuse: Origins and Interventions* provides a comprehensive introduction to the current state of research on the etiology or causes of drug abuse and its prevention and treatment. The book is divided into two parts, etiology and interventions, and each part begins with a thorough overview of its main topic. These overviews provide the necessary background for the speculative and descriptive chapters that follow, although the book is not intended to be encyclopedic.

Thus, we expect that this book will be read by people with a variety of levels of technical background in drug abuse. It is not intended for use solely by drug abuse researchers or therapists. Many of the chapters could provide supplementary readings for a college or graduate level course on drug abuse. We believe that the book will be useful to graduate students, psychologists, addiction counselors, and policymakers, as well as to those who simply want to know more about one of the most pressing social problems of our times.

We have tried to include chapters that the majority of readers, regardless of their knowledge of drug abuse, will find both understandable and informative. We know that some readers will find a few chapters too esoteric for their needs, and others will wish for a greater depth of coverage. We hope that all will find the extensive lists of references useful, if they wish to learn more about some particular aspect of the field. It is unlikely that anyone will find all the chapters equally useful, but it is our hope that the broad coverage they provide will make picking and choosing what to read both enjoyable and interesting.

This book is unique in that it has a dual purpose: to provide a general description of the state of drug abuse research and practice today and to present the views of 14 scientists who have something new to say about their special areas of interest. These range from new ideas about neurobiology to a revitalized version of therapeutic communities as a treatment modality. The chapter authors were invited specifically to use this opportunity to speculate about the future of their fields of interest and to present new theoretical formulations that might drive additional research or new prevention or treatment protocols.

Part I treats the etiology of drug abuse. In chapter 1, Glantz, Weinberg, Miner, and Colliver, discuss the epidemiology and patterns of drug abuse, the complexity of interactions in the causality of drug abuse, comorbidity with other psychiatric disorders, and other psychological aspects of the reasons why some people are either more vulnerable or more resistant to drug abuse. Some of the chapters that follow provide detailed information to help the reader to understand the broad range of the etiology field better (Sloboda & Kozel, chap. 2, on epidemiology; Koob, chap. 8, on neurobiology; Sanders-Phillips, chap. 9, on the etiology of drug use among ethnic minority women). Two authors present new observations about public attitudes and expectancies about drug abuse (Musto, chap. 3; Room, chap. 4). Other chapter authors present new or less familiar theoretical formulations of drug abuse etiology (Cicchetti, chap. 5, developmental psychopathology; Pandina, chap. 6, dependence; Carroll, chap. 7, animal models).

Part II describes the prevention and treatment interventions that have been developed to meet the challenges of drug addiction. There are two overviews, one on prevention (Sloboda, chap. 10), the other on treatment (Hartel & Glantz, chap. 11). Both provide extensive references to research in the areas of prevention and of drug abuse treatment, including psychopharmacology and psychosocial interventions. Three of the chapters that follow (Botvin, chap. 12, adolescent drug abuse prevention; Coates & Collins, chap. 13, HIV/AIDS prevention; De Leon, chap. 16, therapeutic communities) describe some new approaches to current interventions in detail, whereas two others (Szapocznik & Coatsworth, chap. 12, an eco-developmental model of adolescent drug abuse prevention and treatment; Linehan, chap. 14, the development and evaluation of treatment programs) present new theoretical ideas in prevention and treatment. The final chapter in this section (Henningfield & Hartel, chap. 17) describes how drug abuse research had a profound effect on current policy on tobacco and nicotine.

In 1996, the National Institute on Drug Abuse (NIDA) and the American Psychological Association (APA) co-sponsored a special conference on drug abuse held in conjunction with the APA annual convention in Toronto, Canada. Leaders in their fields were invited to present not just their latest research, but some new and forward-looking observations, as well as theoretical speculations about their fields. That meeting served as a springboard for this volume.

We are very grateful to the authors of the chapters in this volume for their many efforts on behalf of this project and in the field of drug abuse research. We also wish to thank our many colleagues at APA and at NIDA, who, as individuals, were encouraging and enthusiastic about this book. We particularly thank Lula Beatty, Timothy Condon, Harold Gordon, Sander Genser, Steven Heishman, Virginia Holt, Arthur M. Horton, Eleanor Inskip, Theresa Levitin, Robin Mackar, Edward Meidenbauer, Carolyn Mosher, Richard Needle, Joan Nolan, Lisa Onken, Sangeeta Panicker, Elizabeth Rahdert, David Shurtleff, Jaylan Turkkan, and Candy Won. As institutions, both APA and NIDA provided an atmosphere of cooperation and support for this project that is as unusual as it is gratifying.

REFERENCE

Harwood, H., Fountain, D., & Livermore, G. (1998). *The economic costs of alcohol and drug abuse in the United States, 1992* (NIH Publication Number 98-4327). Rockville, MD: National Institute on Drug Abuse.

I

ORIGINS

1

THE ETIOLOGY OF DRUG ABUSE: MAPPING THE PATHS

MEYER D. GLANTZ, NAIMAH Z. WEINBERG, LUCINDA L. MINER, AND
JAMES D. COLLIVER

Understanding the origins and development of drug abuse is the critical foundation for developing the most effective interventions to prevent and treat it. Given the prevalence of drug abuse and the harm that it causes, bringing about this understanding is a goal of paramount importance.

This overview will focus on the etiology of higher levels of drug involvement, including chronic prolonged use, drug abuse, and drug use disorders. Obviously there is a strong relationship between the etiological factors associated with initial involvement with illegal psychoactive drugs and higher levels including drug abuse. However, the factors that determine the initiation of a behavior are not necessarily the same as those that account for its maintenance and escalation, and this appears to be the case with drug-using behaviors. Several other points should be noted. Although alcohol and nicotine use often appear to play a role in the development of illicit drug abuse, and even though there is likely to be significant overlap in the etiologies of the abuse of different psychoactive substances, this overview will concentrate on the etiology of illegal-drug abusing behaviors.

3

Most research on the origins of drug abuse and drug abuse disorders has focused on risk or vulnerability characteristics and has not considered protective factors. Thus, this approach neglects a critical component of drug abuse etiology. The limited research that is available has primarily investigated resilience factors in the early stages of drug involvement and as such it will not be discussed. Lastly, the overview does not include a discussion of gender and ethnic group findings. This is primarily because most of the etiological studies on population groups have concentrated on earlier stages of drug involvement.

THE EPIDEMIOLOGY OF DRUG ABUSE

The sanctioned use of at least some psychoactive substances is found in most societies, and this is certainly true of contemporary American society. Caffeinated beverages are almost ubiquitous and often consumed by adolescents and preteenagers as well as adults. Alcohol and tobacco are widely available; prescription and over-the-counter psychoactive drugs are used appropriately by many people as aids in dealing with psychological and behavioral difficulties. Although most individuals do not lose control of their use of these substances, some do, and some escalate to the use of nonsanctioned—illegal—psychoactive substances. Unfortunately, drug abuse is not a rare behavior.

The epidemiological study of drug abuse over a period of years clearly shows that drug abuse is a constantly evolving phenomenon. The use of different illegal drugs seems to wax and wane over time. This is apparently related to any number of factors such as changes in drug availability, drug laws and enforcement, new drugs and new forms of administration which become available, and so forth. There are changes in secular trends, social attitudes, and beliefs about the harmful consequences of drug use. The development and growth of drug prevention and treatment programs are also likely to be factors in the changing epidemiology of drug abuse. Differences in drug use patterns have varied sufficiently over a number of generations to suggest that drug abuse is in many ways a cohort phenomenon requiring constant reexamination of each new cohort, and probably continuous monitoring.

Illegal Drug Use

The use of illegal drugs is a prevalent phenomenon in late-20th-century America. Almost 77 million people—35.6% of the population 12 years of age and older—are estimated to have used drugs illicitly at least once in their lifetime (Substance Abuse and Mental Health Services Administration [SAMHSA], 1999), and 14 million—6.4%—report current (i.e., past month) illicit drug use. These findings are from the *National Household Survey on Drug Abuse Main Findings 1997* (NHSDA), the latest in a series of cross-sectional, self-reporting personal interview surveys begun in 1971 to track drug abuse. Among cohorts followed sequentially, illicit drug use tends to begin in the teen years, reach a high point in young adulthood, and decrease in later years. This pattern is reflected in the 1997 cross-sectional prevalence rates in Table 1, which shows that current illicit drug use is reported by 11.4% of youth 12 to 17 years old, 14.7% of young adults 18 to 25 years old, 7.4% of those 26 to 34 years old, and 3.6% of adults 35 years of age and older. The table also shows rates for individual substances, with marijuana clearly the most common illicit drug in each age group. "Hard-core" drug abuse, including use of heroin, is not well

TABLE 1
Percent of U.S. Household Population 12 Years of Age and Older Reporting Past 30 Day Illicit Drug and Alcohol Use According to Age Group: 1997

Drug	Age group				
	12 to 17 years	18 to 25 years	26 to 34 years	35 years & older	Total 12 years & older
Any illicit drug[a]	11.4	14.7	7.4	3.6	6.4
Marijuana and hashish	9.4	12.8	6.0	2.6	5.1
Cocaine (including crack)	1.0	1.2	0.9	0.5	0.7
Crack	0.4	0.4	0.3	0.2	0.3
Inhalants	2.0	1.0	0.4	*	0.4
Hallucinogens	1.9	2.5	0.5	0.3	0.8
Heroin	0.3	0.5	0.2	0.2	0.3
Nonmedical use of psychotherapeutics[b]	2.1	2.4	1.4	0.8	1.2
Stimulants	0.6	0.7	0.2	0.2	0.3
Sedatives	.01	0.2	0.1	0.1	0.1
Tranquilizers	0.5	1.0	0.7	0.2	0.4
Analgesics	1.3	1.3	0.6	0.5	0.7
Any alcohol use	20.5	58.4	60.2	52.8	51.4
Binge alcohol use[c]	8.3	28.0	23.1	11.7	15.3
Heavy alcohol use[c]	3.1	11.1	7.5	4.0	5.4

*Low precision; no estimate reported.
[a]"Any illicit drug" indicates use at least once of marijuana or hashish, cocaine (including crack), inhalants, hallucinogens (including PCP and LSD), heroin, or any prescription-type psychotherapeutic used nonmedically.
[b]Nonmedical use of any prescription-type stimulant, sedative, tranquilizer, or analgesic; does not include over-the-counter-drugs.
[c]"Binge alcohol use" is defined as drinking five or more drinks on the same occasion on at least one day in the past 30 days. "Occasion" means at the same time or within a couple hours of each other. "Heavy alcohol use" is defined as drinking five or more drinks on the same occasion on each of 5 or more days in the past 30 days; all Heavy Alcohol Users are also Binge Alcohol Users.
Source: *1997 National Household Survey on Drug Abuse Main Findings* (Substance Abuse and Mental Health Services Administration, 1999)

measured by the NHSDA because of difficulties in sampling rare, hard-to-reach populations.

The rate of illicit drug use has increased among youth in recent years, but the rate in the overall population has remained stable (SAMHSA, 1999). NHSDA trend data show that current drug use among 12 to 17-year-olds doubled from 5.3% in 1992 to 10.9% in 1995, declined to 9.0% in 1996, then increased to 11.4% in 1997. This recent increase followed several years of decline from a high of 16.3% in 1979. Current illicit drug use among all ages, 12 years and older, also reached a record high in 1979, at 14.1%, declined through 1992, and has remained at about 6.0% since that time.

The NHSDA trends for youth are generally corroborated by findings from the school-based *Monitoring the Future* (MTF) Study. Clear increases in current use of illicit drugs were observed from 1992 through 1996 for students in the three grades in the MTF study; among 10th graders, for example, use increased from 11.0% to 23.4%. From 1996 to 1998, rates appear to have leveled off and, in some cases, to have declined. In 1998, 12.1% of 8th graders, 21.5% of 10th graders, and 25.6% of 12th graders reported past-month illicit drug use (Table 2). Trend data from MTF and the NHSDA are usually similar, but MTF tends to find higher rates of drug use than the NHSDA. Although the NHSDA includes school dropouts, who are not sampled in MTF and have a higher rate of drug abuse than students who stay in school, the effects of this are outweighed by greater underreporting of illicit drug use in the household setting as compared with the classroom (Gfroerer, Wright, & Kopstein, 1997).

Substance Use Disorders

Substance use is a necessary but not sufficient condition for the development of substance use disorders (SUD), and only a subset of users go on to develop symptoms of SUD. Although studies of clinical populations are a rich source of information, such studies may be biased by selection factors associated with receiving treatment. Understanding the nature and extent of SUD therefore requires studies of the general population. In North America, general population studies of SUD epidemiology fall into two categories: household surveys by lay interviewers, and controlled-environment structured interviews by clinically trained professionals.

In addition to ascertaining rates of use, the NHSDA monitors the prevalence of self-reported drug problems using questions that reflect components of dependent and nondependent abuse described in the American Psychiatric Association's (APA) *Diagnostic and Statistical Manual of Mental Disorders*, 3rd revised edition, (*DSM-III-R*; American Psychiatric Association, 1987) and its more recent fourth edition (*DSM-IV*; American Psychiatric Association, 1994). Although the questions in the NHSDA do

TABLE 2
Percent of Students Reporting Use of Selected Substances in the Past
30 Days in 1998

Substance and pattern of use in past 30 days	Grade		
	Eighth	Tenth	Twelfth
Any illicit drug—any use	12.1	21.5	25.6
Marijuana—any use	9.7	18.7	22.8
Cocaine (including crack)—any use	1.4	2.1	2.4
Hallucinogens—any use	1.4	3.2	3.8
Stimulants (excluding medical use)—any use	3.3	5.1	4.6
Cigarettes—any use	19.1	27.6	35.1
Cigarettes—1/2 pack or more per day	3.6	7.9	12.6
Alcohol—any use	23.0	38.8	52.0
Alcohol—"been drunk" at least once	8.4	21.1	32.9

Source: University of Michigan, 1998 Monitoring the Future Study.

not address all the *DSM* diagnostic criteria, the findings are nevertheless informative. Table 3 shows 1997 NHSDA (SAMHSA, 1999) estimates of the proportion of persons reporting each of seven past-year problems attributed to marijuana use among those who used the drug 12 times or more in the past year (monthly users). The majority (57.9%) of monthly users reported at least one problem, and more than one quarter (27.6%) reported three or more problems. The most frequently reported problem was having a period of a month or more during the past year when the user spent a

TABLE 3
Rate of Problems (Components of Dependence) Attributed to
Marijuana Use Experienced in the Past Year by Monthly Users, by Age
Group: 1997

Problems attributed to marijuana use	12 to 17 years	18 to 25 years	26 to 34 years	35 years & older	Total 12 years & older
Wanted or tried to cut down but could not	23.4	19.7	16.2	8.5	16.5
Built up tolerance	45.9	41.6	21.0	*	31.8
Spent month or more on drug	52.9	44.5	40.0	*	41.1
Used drug more than intended	44.5	34.1	22.9	*	30.0
Reduced important activities	16.9	11.9	9.2	2.2	9.5
Caused emotional or psychological problems	25.7	18.8	14.7	*	15.8
Caused health problems	17.2	9.9	4.6	*	9.2
Any of these problems	74.0	65.2	53.7	*	57.9
2 or more of these problems	56.7	49.0	32.8	*	40.7
3 or more of these problems	42.3	32.3	23.1	*	27.6

*Low precision; no estimate reported.
Note. Denominator is persons reporting using marijuana on 12 or more days in the past year.
Source: *1997 National Household Survey on Drug Abuse Main Findings* (Substance Abuse and Mental Health Services Administration, 1999)

great deal of time getting the drug, using it, and recovering from its effects; this problem was acknowledged by 41.1% of monthly users. Considered by age group, 74.0% of monthly users 12 to 17 years old reported at least one problem they attributed to marijuana; comparable rates for monthly users 18 to 25 and 26 to 34 years old were 65.2% and 53.7%, respectively.

The only nationally representative general population study that provides estimates of the prevalence of SUD based on all relevant *DSM-III-R* criteria is the National Comorbidity Survey (NCS), which was conducted between 1990 and 1992 and used a structured diagnostic interview administered to persons 15 to 54 years of age (Warner, Kessler, Hughes, Anthony, & Nelson, 1995). Among the overall NCS sample, 51.0% reported illicit drug use at least once in their life, and 15.4% acknowledged past year use; these use rates are similar to those reported in the NHSDA. Persons meeting criteria for drug dependence in their lifetime comprised 7.5% of the overall 15 to 54-year-old population and 14.7% of lifetime drug users—one in seven. Table 4 shows lifetime and past-year rates of drug dependence according to sex and age. With few exceptions, dependence rates are higher among men than women and, across age groups, the dependence rates are highest among people 12 to 24 years old.

The roughly inverse relationship between age and drug dependence (Table 4) and drug problems (Table 3) is consistent with observations that initiation of substance use at an earlier age is associated with greater likelihood of subsequent development of dependence (Anthony & Petronis, 1995; Grant & Dawson, 1998; Robins & Przybeck, 1985), because the youngest age group can be inferred to include a higher proportion of early-onset users than the other age groups.

In summary, drug abuse is a prevalent phenomenon, and the resurgence of drug use among youth in the 1990s may foreshadow an increasing problem among adults in the next decade. The most commonly abused

TABLE 4

Percent of Experiencing Drug Dependence by Sex and Age Based on Two Reference Time Periods for Drug Users in those Time Periods

Age Group	Lifetime dependence rates among lifetime users			Past 12 month dependence among past 12 month users		
	Men	Women	Total	Men	Women	Total
15–24	19.7	14.1	17.3	13.0	10.6	12.2
25–34	17.8	11.7	14.7	9.9	8.1	9.1
35–44	16.7	12.5	14.9	9.7	11.1	10.3
45–54	5.8	13.8	9.2	11.9*	0.4*	6.1
Total	16.4	12.6	14.7	11.3	9.0	10.3

*Low precision.
Note. Drug use includes any use of marijuana/hashish, cocaine/crack, heroin, hallucinogens; any use of inhalants; and nonmedical use of sedatives, tranquilizers, stimulants, and analgesics.
Source: National Comorbidity Survey (Warner, Kessler, Hughes, Anthony, & Nelson, 1995).

illicit drug is marijuana. About 15% of persons who use drugs at some time in their life develop symptoms that qualify them for a clinical diagnosis of drug dependence. Among users, drug dependence rates are higher for men than for women and higher for younger people, this is consistent with findings of increased risk of dependence among early-onset users.

THE COMPLEXITY OF DRUG ABUSE

Drug abuse has often been thought of as a relatively simple undifferentiated phenomenon. Historically, it has been seen as an extremely serious problem, but many have viewed it as a problem with a single primary cause, a fairly unidimensional nature, and a typical course and presentation. In other words, the tacit assumption has often been that drug abusers are more or less alike in most critical ways and that the development of their drug abuse is fundamentally the same as the etiology of other abusers' drug using behavior. In reality, drug abuse is more accurately characterized by diversity and complexity. This has made drug abuse not only difficult to study and understand, but also difficult to prevent and treat.

Drug abusers are highly heterogeneous as a group and drug abuse patterns are diverse. Although typologies of drug abusers can be constructed and different groups of individuals are associated with different risks for and patterns of drug involvement, drug abuse is highly individualized. No known characteristics allow the certain prediction of an individual's risk for drug abuse. At best, assessments of risk are derived from percentages of population groups demonstrating certain characteristics and then attributed as probabilities to individuals. Even the behavior of initiating illicit drug use allows only limited prediction of future drug abuse, because the large majority of those who initiate some drug use do not escalate to clinically defined drug abuse. Despite the importance of understanding individual differences in drug abuse etiology, research has tended to focus on commonalities and group comparisons.

Numerous studies support the assertion that the initiation of drug abuse is more associated with social and environmental factors, whereas higher levels of involvement and abuse are more associated with biological and psychiatric factors (see Glantz & Pickens, 1992). Although biological views of drug abuse seem to compete at times with environmental ones, drug abuse is the result of the interaction between the individual and his or her environment (e.g., Blackson, 1994; Cadoret, Yates, Troughton, Woodworth & Stewart, 1996). The multifactorial nature of drug abuse has further implications. The interaction of biological–psychiatric factors with social–environmental ones takes place over time through multiple interactions. This implies that drug abuse does not simply occur, it evolves and it does so according to developmental principles (see Cicchetti, chap. 5, this volume; Glantz, 1992). Furthermore, it must be understood in terms of the interactive system of the individual in his or her particular environment. The nature of that synergy will change over time, and because it will be in the context of developmental stages, the person–environmental interactions will probably vary in accordance with the individual's developmental stage. There is almost certainly more than one path leading to drug abuse and drug use disorders (e.g., Cadoret et al., 1995), and despite the many obvious similarities common to different individuals' drug abuse patterns, there are also likely to be critical dimensions on which they vary.

DRUG ABUSE PROGRESSIONS

The full course of a typical drug abuse disorder evolves through a series of transitions that begins with the initial onset of drug use, the maintenance or continuation and eventual escalation of use, progression from one drug class to another, escalation of use within that drug class, multiple drug use (in many cases), spontaneous discontinuation or cessation aided by treatment, and, frequently, relapse. Drug abuse disorders are chronic relapsing disorders, and as such their course often takes on a cyclical quality. Explaining the transitions involved in the course of drug abuse is critical to understanding the nature of the behavior and the associated disorders. Some models of drug abuse assume that the primary causal influences for the different transitions and stages of drug abuse are basically the same. As indicated above, current research argues against this assumption of unvarying determinants; in all likelihood, different transitions are primarily influenced by different factors or different combinations of factors (e.g., Newcomb & Felix-Ortiz, 1992). Most etiological research focuses on adolescent onset of use and escalation. It is possible that the onset or the escalation or both that occurs later in life are associated with different factors or follow other patterns.

The transition from lower levels of involvement with a given illicit psychoactive drug to higher levels of involvement, possibly including chronic prolonged abuse and/or a drug abuse disorder, is one of the defining characteristics of drug abuse. Generally, escalation within a drug class or type is attributed primarily to increasing physical and/or psychological tolerance and dependence. Environmental influences probably play a causal role, but the nature of their contributions is unclear, although drug availability, social pressure, exposure to cues associated with use, and so forth are assumed to be relevant to all drug abuse stages and transitions. Although the relative contribution of biological and psychological factors to escalation is debated and although it probably varies with different drugs and different individuals, the basic concepts are widely accepted. Considerably more controversial is the explanation of the transition from the use of one substance to another. Neither tolerance nor dependence would be adequate explanations, although intensity of use may be a marker of subsequent transitions and problems and perhaps a contributing factor.

THE GATEWAY HYPOTHESIS

A frequent research finding is that there is a common seemingly hierarchical and often cumulative sequence for individuals becoming involved with illicit drugs. This assertion, usually referred to as the "gateway" or "stepping stone" hypothesis, originally proposed that there is a "developmental progression" to drug involvement in which most adolescents begin using substances in a particular common sequence of drug use "stages." An early form of the gateway theory originated in the 1930s and described the belief that marijuana use led to heroin use as well as immoral and criminal behaviors. Despite the lack of an empirical basis at the time, the public's belief influenced public policies contributing to the 1937 Marijuana Tax Act making it effectively illegal to sell marijuana. Although there continued to be sporadic research, the theory received less attention until it reemerged with a more scientific basis when Johnson (1972) reported finding that there was a relationship between marijuana and heroin use, although the association was interpreted as occurring through the intermediary of drug using friends. In 1975, there were two independent proposals of a more rigorous stage model by Kandel and by Hamburg, Kraemer, and Jahnke. The model has evolved over time as research has provided a more detailed description (for a more complete discussion of the history of the gateway hypothesis see Etz, Robertson, Glantz, & Colliver, 1999).

As discussed by Kandel and Yamaguchi (1999), there is considerable support for the general model that adolescents' involvement with drugs typically begins with alcohol use, cigarette use, or both. Although these are not scheduled or controlled substances, it is important to remember that use of alcohol and tobacco by teenagers is usually underage use and therefore legally prohibited (or at least the sale of these substances to teenagers is illegal). The next "stage" is marijuana use followed by the use of other illicit drugs, such as cocaine or heroin. The research clearly shows that there is not an inevitable progression. In fact, the majority of individuals at one stage do not "progress" to the next. However, the sequence is very common at least in the United States for those who do use illegal drugs. Most illegal drug users have previously used the drugs described as being earlier in the gateway sequence. This finding has been replicated in a number of studies both in the United States and in some other countries. There is some variation by gender, by subgroup, geographical area cohort, and in other cultures, but the general model has been found fairly consistently. One possibly important exception was demonstrated in Golub and

Johnson's work (1994a, 1994b). They have reported that among serious drug users alcohol often does not precede the use of marijuana or other illicit drugs.

Other than the affirmation that there is a common sequence, there is no consensus in the research field on the definition of the gateway hypothesis. There is also no consensus on the nature or mechanism of the sequence, or on the relationship among the steps. There is clearly little justification for the old assertion that any step or stage in the sequence is the "cause" of subsequent steps; for example, marijuana use does not appear to be the "cause" of cocaine or heroin use. However, it is equally untenable to assume that behaviors are not critically influenced by significant behaviors and experiences that precede them, including the illicit use of psychoactive substances. The importance of these earlier experiences with psychoactive drugs is potentially even greater, because the population of concern consists of pre-adolescents and adolescents, and their development may be impaired by drug use, perhaps in ways that predispose them to greater drug involvement.

For the most part, it is the explanation and implications of the gateway sequence that are controversial, rather than the finding of a common sequence or the specifics of the sequence. It may be that there is more than one sequence and that sequences vary over time, in different environments, or for different groups. Variability of the substances and order in the sequence may be less important than the finding that drug abuse commonly involves a seemingly meaningful sequence of increasing involvement and transitions to other drugs. There may be multiple factors that determine the sequence and the transitions, and the driving factors may vary for different transitions and different individuals. Some of the factors are likely to be neuropharmacological, but psychological and environmental factors are also probably involved.

Some concepts implied by the gateway model seem to be readily plausible. First, it is likely that any psychoactive drug use facilitates further drug use including the use of other substances. Second, it is reasonable that drug abuse would parallel the development of most deviant behaviors in moving from the less deviant to the more deviant. Perhaps one of the most important questions related to the gateway phenomenon is the extent to which it has the characteristics of a developmental series of steps. There is obviously neither inevitability to the typical drug involvement sequence nor any teleological impetus. There is no predetermined endpoint such as in the case of the development of a normal ability such as walking or speech nor the inexorable course of an untreated disease. Nevertheless, a common meaningful sequence in which the steps strongly influence subsequent ones does imply some developmental qualities. A greater understanding of the gateway phenomenon, the extent to which it is a developmental process, and the nature of the contributions of each step to the next would greatly increase understanding of drug abuse etiology. One of the most important related questions is why most individuals who use substances earlier in the sequence do not progress to the use of substances later in the sequence. Despite the current limited understanding of the nature of the gateway sequence, it is an important phenomenon, and many prevention programs are based on the idea of delaying, preventing, or interrupting the gateway sequence.

CO-OCCURRING BEHAVIORS

Another consistent finding in drug abuse research is that adolescents' drug abuse often co-occurs with other problem behaviors, particularly delinquency and precocious sexual behavior. This frequent finding has led some researchers to propose a general deviance model in which individuals are believed to have a "problem behavior proneness" (Jessor & Jessor, 1977) or a "deviance syndrome" (Robins, 1966). Although there is little question that there is some clustering of deviant behaviors, the nature of the relationships among them is unclear as is the possibility that drug abuse is caused by a general deviance factor.

White and Labouvie (1994), Loeber, Farrington, Stouthamer-Loeber, and Van Kammen (1998), and others have argued against a common-cause general deviance model at least in part because of the variability of the association among deviant behaviors, the heterogeneity of adolescents' manifestation of deviant behavior, and the complicating influence of psychopathology. They believe that the data do not support the hypothesis that the expression of deviance is predominantly undifferentiated or the assertion that there is a single common factor underlying adolescent problem behaviors. Those researchers espousing the specificity of behavior problems are supported by studies finding a multifactorial nature to adolescent deviant behaviors as well as studies demonstrating their other concerns.

Alternatively, Jessor, Donovan, and Costa (1991), Donovan (1996), Elliott, Huizinga, and Menard (1989), and others have argued for a common-cause general deviance model. They emphasize the phenomena of multiple problem co-occurrence among deviant adolescents and the predictability of other co-occurring and subsequent problem behaviors from a current deviant behavior. They propose that there is a set of common underlying causes rather than a single underlying cause and point to studies that have found a single common factor reflecting a set of common underlying causes. They tend to include mental health problems in their models and therefore they do not consider them to disconfirm the general deviance theory. Some of the disagreement about the generality or specificity of deviance seems to relate to differences in definition, criteria, and emphasis, but even taking these inconsistencies into account, the research does not give a clear answer.

At this time, the evidence does not justify the assertion that adolescent deviant behaviors—including drug abuse—are essentially alternate manifestations of a single determinative underlying general deviance factor. However, deviant behaviors do not seem to be independent, nor is there adequate evidence to support the idea that deviant behaviors are the product of multiple specific and basically unrelated deviance factors. Although more research will be needed to resolve the question, it ultimately seems likely that research will show that there is some degree of generality to deviant behaviors but, at the same time, that different deviant behaviors are at least partially determined by different specific factors (e.g., Brook, Whiteman, & Cohen, 1995). It may also be that some of the ostensible generality of deviance is related to the facilitation of additional deviant behaviors by existing deviant behaviors rather than exclusively to a common underlying antecedent factor (see Kaplan, 1995).

Donovan, Jessor, and Costa (1991) have extended problem behavior theory to include the dimension of conventionality–unconventionality and have found that conventionality is associated with at least some health-related behaviors, and that unconventionality is associated with at least some problem behaviors (Costa, Jessor, Donovan, & Fortenberry, 1995). They have also investigated the role of various protective factors in adolescent problem behaviors. They found that protective factors can have direct effects and can also serve as moderators of risk factors associated with alcohol and drug abuse, delinquency, and sexual precocity (Jessor, Van Den Bos, Vanderryn, Costa, & Turbin, 1995). This illustrates the importance of going beyond a simple risk factor approach to the etiology of drug abuse and considering the influence of protective factors. It is further advisable to approach etiological questions in terms of a system of dynamic interactions of predisposing and protective factors rather than simple linear additive models (see Glantz & Sloboda, 1999).

COMORBIDITY

Population-based epidemiologic studies have verified the clinical observation that substance use disorders are frequently comorbid with other psychiatric disorders, in both adolescents and adults (Cohen et al., 1993; Greenbaum, Foster-Johnson, & Petrila, 1996; Kessler et al., 1994; Kessler, Nelson, McGonagle, Edlund, et al., 1996; Lewisohn, Hops, Roberts, Seeley, & Andrews, 1993; Regier et al., 1990). Some studies have in fact shown that the majority of individuals diagnosed with one type of disorder will also meet diagnostic criteria for the other type. The high prevalence of this co-occurrence has many implications, because comorbid individuals have more severe illnesses, require more intensive treatment, demonstrate worse psychosocial problems, and often have a worse clinical course (Brooner, King, Kidorf, Schmidt & Bigelow, 1997; Kessler, Nelson, McGonagle, Liu, et al., 1996).

Although this phenomenon is now empirically well established, the reason for it is not clear (Kessler, 1995). Three models are often put forward: (a) that mental disorders result in substance abuse (e.g., self-medication of depression [Khantzian, 1997] or impaired judgment in antisocial personality disorder or mania), (b) that substance abuse results in mental disorders (e.g., through brain changes), or (c) that common risk factors result in both. In fact, there are reports that provide support for each of these models, and the relationships between drug use disorders and mental disorders are more complex, transactional, and multifactorial than any of these individual models captures. A fourth model incorporating these concerns and describing at least some instances of comorbidity is that for some individuals, drug abuse and particular psychopathologies develop together, each exacerbating the etiologic steps of the other through multiple interactions, increasing the likelihood of and worsening the outcome of both disorders.

Although the correlational associations between substance use and other psychiatric disorders is very strong, causal inferences regarding these relationships must be approached very cautiously. For one thing, certain variables have not been measured in many of these studies, particularly genetic and other biologic factors. Many studies rely on retrospective report of the temporal onset of disorders, which can be biased and inaccurate. Furthermore, symptoms and prodromes of disorders often precede the manifestation of the full set of symptoms required for diagnosis of a clinical disorder. The tendency of drug use and drug withdrawal states to mimic psychiatric disorders is a further complication. The following is a synopsis of the relationship between drug abuse and a number of relevant psychopathologies.

Conduct Disorder and Antisocial Personality Disorder

These disorders are very strongly and consistently associated with drug use disorders, as demonstrated in several studies. The population-based National Comorbidity Survey (NCS) of 15- to 54-year-olds found that 59.5% of those with a lifetime history of conduct disorder, and 78.7% of participants with adult antisocial behavior, also had a lifetime history of at least one addictive disorder (Kessler, Nelson, McGonagle, Edlund, et al., 1996). Using *DSM-III* criteria, the Epidemiologic Catchment Area (ECA) study (Regier et al., 1990) found that 83.6% of individuals with antisocial personality disorder met criteria for a substance abuse disorder of a severe nature, the odds ratio for any substance use disorder was 29.6, and the odds ratio for substance dependence was 21.1. As part of the Oregon Youth Study, boys from a metropolitan high crime area were assessed originally in fourth grade and followed longitudinally. Assessing the boys when they were 18 to 20 years old, Capaldi and Stoolmiller (1999) found that early conduct problems were a strong predictor of young adult substance use, an even stronger predictor than early adolescent substance use. Biederman, Wilens, Mick, and Faraone (1997), in a follow-up study of children with and without attention deficit hyperactivity disorder (ADHD), found that conduct disorder was a significant predictor of later drug use disorders, regardless of ADHD status. Cadoret (1992) found in a sample of male adopted twins who were separated at birth that antisocial personality was an important factor in the transition from drug use to drug abuse.

Bipolar Disorder

Bipolar disorder is also strongly associated with drug use disorders. The NCS (Kessler, Nelson, McGonagle, Edlund, et al., 1996) found that 71% of participants with a history of mania met criteria for an alcohol or drug use disorder. On the other hand, 1.2% of those with substance use disorders reported a history of mania, probably because of the low base rates of bipolar disorder. Adolescent-onset mania also appears to confer significant risk for substance use disorders. A clinic-based study by Wilens et al. (1999) found that patients with adolescent bipolar disorder had almost three times the risk for substance use disorders in comparison with other adolescent patients, and the risk was even higher when comparisons were limited to adolescents without conduct disorder. This association between early-onset bipolar disorder and risk for substance use disorder was investigated in a different sample reported by Biederman et al. (1997). They also found that a history of bipolar disorder strongly predicted later drug use problems. On the other hand, Wilens et al. (1999) reported that childhood onset bipolar disorder did not confer increased risk for substance use disorders.

Depressive Disorders

The NCS found that 41.4% of those with a lifetime diagnosis of major depressive episode also had a lifetime diagnosis of drug use disorder; 26.6% of those with a drug use disorder history met the criteria for a major depressive episode in their past. Several studies of adolescents have also found an association between depression and drug use disorders (e.g., Bukstein, Glancy, & Kaminer, 1992). However, it is difficult to differentiate the temporal onset of these disorders. Establishing a common sequence is complicated further by the neurodepressive effects of many abused substances (Clark & Neighbors, 1996). Although depression may occur independently of substance use, and may prove to be a risk factor for drug use disorder, it must be recognized that depression often occurs as a secondary disorder to other comorbid disorders (Kessler, Nelson, McGonagle, Liu, et al., 1996).

Anxiety Disorders

In the NCS data, the lifetime co-occurrence of addictive disorders with anxiety disorders ranged from 36.5% for agoraphobia to 45.2% for posttraumatic stress disorder (PTSD). These coefficients represent the proportion of persons with any addictive disorder who also met criteria for the respective anxiety disorders (Kessler, Nelson, McGonagle, Edlund, et al., 1996). The ECA study, using *DSM III* diagnostic criteria, found substance abuse rates of 35.8% for panic disorder and 32.8% for obsessive–compulsive disorder, with notably higher rates of drug rather than alcohol diagnoses (Regier et al., 1990). Swendsen et al. (1998) found that phobic conditions typically precede the onset of alcoholism, and Merikangas, Mehta, et al. (1998) found that even though there was no specific consistent temporal pattern of onset for mood disorders in relation to substance disorders, the onset of anxiety disorders was more likely to precede the onset of substance use disorders. There is increasing evidence that onset patterns and etiology of comorbid anxiety and substance disorders may vary with subtypes of anxiety (Merikangas, Stevens, et al., 1998), but more data is needed to clarify the picture. In their prospective study, Kushner, Sher, and Erickson (1999) found a reciprocal causal relationship over time between alcohol use disorders and anxiety disorders and found that either can lead to the other. It seems likely that a similar pattern occurs between anxiety disorders and drug abuse disorders.

Trauma and PTSD

Numerous retrospective studies of clinical populations have found high rates of childhood trauma and other adverse life events in the histories of alcohol and drug use disordered patients. One study found much higher rates of physical and sexual abuse histories among adolescents in treatment for alcohol dependence in comparison with non-alcohol-abusing community controls (Clark, Lesnick, & Hegedus, 1997); females had a more common history of sexual abuse and males of violent victimization. Several theories have been suggested: that drug use is an effort to self-medicate the anxiety following a trauma; that those with drug use disorders are more likely to be exposed to traumatic events through their risk-taking or other activities; that a common factor (e.g., family history of drug use, depression) may increase the risk of both trauma exposure and drug use. None have yet been proved or disproved, and some combination may operate in many cases. As noted by Chilcoat and Breslau (1998), it is important to distinguish between exposure to trauma and PTSD, as trauma does not usually result in PTSD. They studied adults enrolled in health maintenance organizations, ages 21 to 30 at baseline, and followed them over 5 years for trauma exposure, PTSD, and drug use, including prescription drug use. They found that PTSD was associated with an increased risk for later drug and/or alcohol use disorder, even when controlling for conduct disorder history and depression, whereas trauma exposure without PTSD did not increase substance use disorder risk. The substances most likely to be abused were prescription medications. They further found that trauma was equally likely to occur to those with or without substance use disorders, and that substance use disorders were associated with a small increase in risk of PTSD following trauma.

Attention Deficit Hyperactivity Disorder (ADHD)

The evidence associating ADHD with drug abuse is mixed. Although retrospective studies of substance use disorder patients find high rates of reported childhood ADHD, prospective studies have generally found that the association can be accounted for by the relationship of each disorder (ADHD and substance use disorder) with conduct disorder (e.g., Barkley, Fischer, Edelbrock, & Smallish, 1990; Mannuzza et al., 1991; Mannuzza, Klein, Bessler, Malloy, & LaPadula, 1998). It may be that other comorbid disorders, frequently seen in ADHD (Biederman, Faraone, & Kiely, 1996), and social skills deficits (Greene, Biederman, Faraone, Sienna, & Garcia-Jetton, 1997) also contribute to this seeming association; these factors have not been controlled for in most of the studies in this area. Other study limitations include the use of clinically referred samples (which tend to represent the more challenging cases of ADHD) and the failure to take into account family history of drug use, which could confound findings through association with both ADHD and substance use disorder.

Particular subgroups of individuals with ADHD may face increased risk for substance use disorders. For example, children diagnosed with ADHD frequently demonstrate co-occurring psychiatric disorders (Biederman et al., 1996), and this comorbidity may itself increase risk for substance abuse disorders, particularly when an externalizing disorder such as ADHD is combined with an internalizing disorder (Windle & Windle, 1993). Another high-risk group is people whose ADHD persists into adulthood (Biederman et al., 1995). At least in some cases, there may be an interactive effect of ADHD with conduct disorder, and it may be important to differentiate the impulsivity characteristics of ADHD from those related to attention and distractibility (Molina, Smith, & Pelham, 1999).

One question that has been raised is whether the treatment of ADHD with stimulant medications might alter the subsequent risk for drug abuse.

At this time, data are insufficient to answer this question. However, a study by Biederman, Wilens, Mick, Faraone, and Spencer (1999) found no increased substance abuse risk associated with stimulant treatment, and a possible protective effect. This area of study is complicated by significant differences between treated and untreated children on other salient variables. Of note, no preference for stimulant drugs over other drugs of abuse has been found in drug-abusing ADHD subjects (Biederman, Wilens, Mick, & Faraone, 1997; Klein, 1998).

Psychosis

The ECA found that nearly half of the individuals diagnosed with schizophrenia met criteria for a substance abuse or dependence disorder in their lifetime (Regier et al., 1990). The rate of substance use disorder in this group was 4.6 times that in the general population, confirming the clinical impression of high rates of comorbidity. Moreover, as with other disorders, the co-occurrence is associated with higher illness severity, more numerous hospitalizations, treatment non-compliance, and significantly higher rates of relapse (Swofford, Kasckow, Scheller-Gilkey, & Inderbitzin, 1996). The relationship between the two types of disorders is very complex, however, and currently unclear (Buckley, 1998). On one hand, drug use (including nicotine use) by individuals with schizophrenia may represent an effort at self-medication of negative symptoms or of medication side effects. On the other hand, drug exposure has been found to precede the onset of psychotic symptoms in some individuals with schizophrenia, and may hasten or precipitate the development of schizophrenia in vulnerable individuals (Buckley, 1998). In a 10-year longitudinal study, Kwapil (1996) found that proneness to psychosis identified in early adulthood was predictive of subsequent drug and alcohol abuse problems. The difficulties distinguishing drug-induced psychosis from schizophrenia, and the fact that drug experimentation and psychotic breaks occur at similar ages, make both temporal ordering and causal inferences extremely difficult.

Eating Disorders

Several clinical studies, reviewed by Holderness, Brooks-Gunn, and Warren (1994), have documented associations between eating disorders, particularly bulimia nervosa or the bulimic form of anorexia, and both substance use and abuse. However, these reviewers concluded that the studies are too few and varied to draw conclusions about rates, and there is insufficient evidence to clarify the mechanisms of this association.

Personality Disorders

The major epidemiological surveys have not assessed personality disorders (Rounsaville et al., 1998); the exception is antisocial personality disorder, which was discussed above. The studies that do exist, of clinical samples, are complicated by several factors: sampling bias, overlap of substance use behaviors with personality disorder criteria, the personality-altering effects of drugs, recall bias, and distortion. Despite these limitations, the clinical impression remains strong that substantial numbers of substance abusers, at least those who seek treatment, have comorbid personality disorders. Rounsaville et al. (1998) found that a majority of substance use disorder patients met criteria for at least one comorbid personality disorder, as defined by the *DSM III-R*, the majority of which were antisocial personality disorder or borderline personality disorder (cluster B). In a study of comorbidity among treatment-seeking opioid abusers, Brooner et al. (1997) found high rates of antisocial personality disorder, particularly in men, and of borderline personality disorder in women; other personality disorders occurred at significantly lower rates. In their study of patients referred for treatment of personality disorders, Skodol, Oldham, and Gallagher (1999) found that 50% had a lifetime substance use disorder, with particularly high rates of substance abuse disorders among those diagnosed with borderline personality disorder.

The research data on comorbidity leaves little doubt that the clinical presentation of drug abuse is intertwined with other psychopathologies. However, despite the consistently found association of drug abuse with other psychopathologies, the etiological relationships are not at all clear. It is important to remember that regardless of the etiological chain or causal influences, once the comorbid disorders are established, not only is the clinical course of each likely to be worse, but the disorders may become independently self-perpetuating. An additional consideration is that even if a given psychopathology does not antedate the onset of drug use or disorder, in some cases a subclinical or subsyndromal level of a psychopathology might not only precede but might predispose some individuals to drug abuse; the subclinical impairments might or might not be the earlier manifestation of a later emerging psychopathology. The patterns for the possible predisposing or diathetic effects of subclinical problems would parallel the patterns previously described for psychopathologies: (a) Some subclinical conditions related to psychopathologies might predispose individuals to initial drug involvement and make them more vulnerable to escalation and dependence, (b) the drug abuse may exacerbate the subclinical condition to a full psychopathology, and (c) the comorbid conditions may reinforce both pathologies, making their consequences more severe and making them more resistant to treatment.

OTHER PSYCHOLOGICAL CHARACTERISTICS

It is also possible that a third underlying as yet undetermined psychopathological factor leads to both the substance use disorder and the comorbid psychopathology. A related hypothesis is that, at least in some cases, a third nonpsychopathological factor characterized by some form or level of problematic function is involved in the etiology of drug abuse. There are many nonpsychopathological individual characteristics that can, at least in certain circumstances, contribute to problematic outcomes. Although not specifically a psychopathology, one or more of these function-related characteristics might predispose some people to problem behaviors including drug abuse. A general deviance factor, as previously discussed, might be one such characteristic. Several other possible vulnerability characteristics, particularly characteristics related to cognitive function and temperament, are being researched.

EXECUTIVE COGNITIVE FUNCTION

Clinical observation and cross-sectional studies have found that individuals who abuse or are dependent on drugs frequently demonstrate weaknesses in executive cognitive functions (ECF). These self-regulatory, information-processing, and problem-solving functions are thought to be controlled largely by the frontal lobe of the cerebral cortex and include attention, planning, organization, concept formation, abstract reasoning, cognitive flexibility, self-monitoring, motor programming, and motor control (Giancola, Martin, Tarter, Pelham, & Moss, 1996). Research has yet to clarify the extent to which these impairments precede or follow the exposure to drugs (Scheier & Botvin, 1996). Although there is some evidence for brain changes resulting from drug use, a growing body of literature suggests that deficits in executive cognitive functions predate, and perhaps predispose to, drug abuse and dependence in some individuals.

Although the suspicion that ECF deficits constitute a risk factor for drug abuse is strong and conceptually appealing, the evidence is currently indirect, deriving from the following findings. First, deficits in ECF have been shown to relate to antisocial personality disorder, conduct disorder, and aggression in males (see Giancola et al., 1996, for a review), and to disruptive, delinquent, and aggressive behavior in adolescent girls (Giancola, Mezzich, & Tarter, 1998). As discussed earlier, these conduct problems are strongly related to substance use disorders. Second, difficulties with behavioral self-regulation (Dawes, Tarter & Kirisci, 1997) and aggression (Giancola et al., 1996) have been found significantly elevated in offspring of substance abusers, who are at high risk for substance use disorders themselves. Third, some findings are beginning to emerge that deficits in ECF may indeed predict substance use disorders. One study has found that substance use in early adolescence was predicted by poor ECF function two years earlier (Aytaclar, Tarter, Kirisci, & Lu, 1999). Another study of college students found that tests of executive functioning predicted alcohol consumption three years later, in individuals with a positive family history for alcoholism (Deckel & Hesselbrock, 1996). Giancola and colleagues (1996) have also found that ECF predicted reactive aggression only in boys with a family history of substance abuse. The interaction between family history and cognitive risk factors for substance use disorders is intriguing but as yet unexplained.

TEMPERAMENT AND PERSONALITY

The possibility that individuals with particular temperament characteristics are predisposed to substance abuse disorders is also compelling. The constellation of characteristics that make up individual temperament are thought to be at least partially heritable, largely stable through life, and to interact significantly with the environment, contributing to the formation of personality and perhaps, at least to some extent, psychopathology. Although temperament constellations do not represent psychiatric disorders, these characteristics may underlie some psychiatric syndromes, and perhaps help explain some of the variation in functional outcomes among similarly diagnosed children.

Behavioral Disinhibition

Several temperament clusters have been studied in association with later drug abuse. The strongest and most consistent predictors of later drug abuse are the disinhibited or "behaviorally activated" characteristics, which may manifest as aggressivity, nonconforming impulsivity, or externalizing disorders such as conduct disorder. In a review of the literature, Windle and Windle (1993) found that externalizing behaviors show considerable stability over time and are predictive of poor behavioral outcomes, including substance use. A longitudinal study in New Zealand has found that boys who were classified as undercontrolled at age 3 demonstrated significantly increased rates of alcohol dependence at age 21 (Caspi, Moffitt, Newman, & Silva, 1996). A high level of behavioral activation has also been shown to be associated with higher rates of substance abuse in male U.S. military veterans (Windle, 1994), and poor behavioral self-regulation occurs at high rates in sons of substance abusing fathers, who are at risk for substance abuse themselves (Dawes et al., 1997). Despite using different labels and studying different populations, these studies tend to support the idea that disinhibited temperament characteristics increase the risk for substance abuse.

Novelty–Sensation Seeking

Novelty seeking, or sensation seeking, is another of the temperament constellation that has shown salience in predicting risk for drug abuse. Although different studies have defined the features somewhat differently, this dimension is characterized by disinhibition, seeking novel experiences, and susceptibility to boredom (Bardo & Mueller, 1991). Studies of adolescents (Wills, Vaccaro, & McNamara, 1994), adults (Cloninger, 1987), and animals (Bardo, Donohew, & Harrington, 1996) have related high sensation seeking to greater use of alcohol and drugs. A prospective study by Masse and Tremblay (1997) measured novelty seeking in boys at ages 6 and 10 and found it to be predictive of early onset of substance use during ages 10 to 15. It is likely that high sensation seeking characterizes a subset of substance abusers, rather than all substance abusers, and may be more determinative for males (Bardo & Mueller, 1991).

Mixed Internalizing and Externalizing Patterns

A strong body of evidence demonstrates that the co-occurrence of internalizing and externalizing traits is highly associated with risk. As reviewed by Windle and Windle (1993), these "mixed subtypes" demonstrate both disruptive or aggressive and socially avoidant or withdrawn behaviors, and are often found to have the highest risk for substance abuse. These children, characterized by Kellam, Brown, Rubin, and Ensminger (1983) and by McCord (1988) in their studies as shy and aggressive, did very poorly on longitudinal follow-up and were found to be at higher risk for substance abuse. Peer rejection may play a significant role in these outcomes, and a "mixed type" temperament may be a predisposing pattern.

Difficult Temperament

The "difficult temperament" constellation (see Thomas and Chess, 1977) has been hypothesized to be part of a noteworthy pattern of drug abuse vulnerability (e.g., Blackson, 1994; Glantz, 1992), and it has received some study. Individuals with a difficult temperament are identifiable as infants and demonstrate high activity level, social withdrawal, arrhythmicity, rigidity, negative withdrawal responses to new stimuli, and distractibility. These characteristics have been shown to relate strongly to other risk factors for drug abuse in 10- to 12-year-olds (Blackson, 1994), and to substance use and delinquency in adolescence (Windle, 1991). Lerner and Vicary (1984) found that subjects in the New York Longitudinal Study assessed at 5 years of age as having a difficult temperament were more likely than "easy" children to become regular users of alcohol, tobacco and marijuana in adulthood. Determining the potential role of difficult temperament is complicated and difficult. For example, difficult temperament may be associated with other potentially contributive characteristics such as conduct disorder. Furthermore, it has been proposed that difficult temperament is a risk factor for substance involvement particularly in the context of certain environments such as particular parenting patterns (see Glantz, 1992; also, Blackson, Tarter, & Mezzich, 1996). This follows the "goodness of fit" model proposed by Chess and Thomas (1989), which proposes that it is not the absolute quality of the individual's temperament that influences the behavioral outcomes but the "fit" or "lack of fit" between the individual and the demands of his or her environment. It has also been recommended that temperament be considered from a developmental perspective subject to developmental transformations and differing stage-appropriate manifestations (Glantz, 1992). Although there is some evidence to support the assertion that difficult temperament constellation is an important factor in some patterns of drug abuse etiology, the empirical support at this time is suggestive rather than conclusive.

Inhibition

Least studied have been the inhibited temperament traits. Although this may prove to be an important pathway to drug abuse, thus far studies of inhibited or anxious individuals have resulted in mixed findings. The longitudinal study by Caspi et al. (1996) cited above also followed inhibited youth; boys categorized as inhibited at age 3 were significantly more likely to have experienced alcohol-related problems by age 21 in comparison with well adjusted controls. Windle (1994) found a slightly increased risk for alcohol and substance abuse and dependence in male U.S. military veterans who were characterized as behaviorally inhibited. Some authors have cited Khantzian's self-medication hypothesis (1997) to explain an increased risk for individuals with inhibited temperament.

However, there is also evidence that inhibited individuals do not experience increased risk for drug abuse, and perhaps are even protected from drug abuse, at least in adolescence (see Windle & Windle, 1993). For example, longitudinal studies by Kellam et al. (1983) and by McCord (1988) found that individuals characterized as shy in childhood were least likely to develop alcohol and drug problems in adulthood. In a study by Masse and Tremblay (1997), harm avoidance (characterized by caution, apprehension, and inhibition) was negatively associated with later risk for substance use. Wills, Windle, and Cleary (1998) conclude that inhibitory dimensions are inversely related to substance use, when other affective dimensions are statistically controlled. Thus, it remains unclear whether behavioral inhibition constitutes either a risk or a protective factor for drug abuse.

Affectivity

Research to date provides some support for the possibility that negative affect is a risk factor in some patterns of drug abuse vulnerability. Pandina, Johnson, and Labouvie (1992), in a longitudinal study of adolescents, found that negative affectivity, characterized by distress, nervousness, tension, and hyperreactivity, was a risk factor for problematic alcohol and drug use. Wills, McNamara, Vaccaro, and Hirky (1996) report that anger, among factors from a variety of domains, was associated with escalated substance use in their longitudinal study. Drawing on data from the New York Longitudinal Study, Tubman, Vicary, von Eye, and Lerner (1990) found that negative emotional behavior states in middle childhood preceded problematic substance use in young adulthood. Brook, Brook, Gordon, Whiteman, and Cohen (1990) and Block, Block, and Keyes (1988) also reported associations between emotionality–volatility and later involvement with drugs. Chassin, Pillow, Curran, Molina, and Barrera (1993) and Blackson, Tarter, Martin, and Moss (1994) reported finding that emotional reactivity is associated with early age onset of alcohol and drug use; early onset is a risk factor for subsequent greater drug involvement. Tarter, Blackson, Brigham, Moss, and Caprara (1995) reported that traits later found to be strongly associated with irritability in boys (low behavioral self-control, stress, and family dysfunction), in conjunction with family discord, were associated with subsequent substance use 2 years later as a coping response in early adolescence. Further research will be needed to clarify the etiological role of affectivity. It may be helpful to consider subtypes of affectivity, affective dysregulation, and emotional reactivity in future investigations and to differentiate subtypes related to negative affectivity and behavioral dysregulations. The consideration of affectivity in the context of the social environment of the individual is also important.

Personality

Closely related to temperament characteristics are personality characteristics. An often-asked question is whether there is an "addictive personality" that leads to drug abuse. The empirical literature clearly does not support the existence of a specific cluster of personality traits that "cause" addiction or an addictive personality (Chiauzzi & Liljegren, 1993; Kerr, 1996; Nathan, 1988). Some personality traits may be more frequently associated with the development of drug dependence, but these same traits may relate in other individuals to adaptive pathways and outcomes. Many studies have looked at personality characteristics of drug and alcohol users, but these cross-sectional findings are confounded by behavior changes and personality distortions that are secondary to use (Nathan, 1988; Vaillant, 1983), the overlap of criteria between substance abuse and antisocial personality disorder (Nathan, 1988), and the interference of long-term substance use with maturation and normal development. To date, no individual personality characteristics have been shown to be either necessary or sufficient for the development of drug abuse or dependence.

INTERMEDIATING CHARACTERISTICS

The above discussion of the etiological influences of co-occurring deviant behaviors, psychopathologies, and other psychological conditions has not, for the most part, distinguished between direct and indirect influences, and, in fact, few research findings make this differentiation. However, the most significant drug abuse related contributions of some predisposing and protective factors may be as intermediaries; the most heuristically useful models and approaches may be ones that incorporate concepts of mediating influences. Chess and Thomas (1989) and others have proposed that in general, temperament may act as one of a number of mediating variables "between environmental stimuli and demands and patterns of neurobiological organization" (p. 180). A number of researchers, including several whose findings were discussed earlier, have conceptualized particular etiological influences as operating through a mediating role (e.g., Cadoret et al., 1995). Others, for example Pandina and Johnson chapter 6, this volume, have raised the question of how the biological factors associated with drug abuse etiology exercise their influence, particularly in the early stages of drug abuse before physical dependence develops. In some cases it may be through the intermediaries of psychopathology, temperament, and so forth. Future research and theoretical formulation will need to further delineate the relationship between the biological and behavioral aspects of drug abuse. To date, biologically oriented research on drug abuse has focused primarily on the nature and mechanisms of drug use reinforcement, escalation, physical tolerance, and dependence, and on the neurological consequences of prolonged drug use (see Koob, chapter 8, this volume). However, some biologically based information is available on the premorbid etiological influences of biological factors, and they clearly demonstrate that neurological and genetic factors play a critical role in drug abuse etiology.

NEUROBIOLOGICAL FACTORS

Research has shown that drugs of abuse target the evolutionarily oldest parts of the brain that regulate pain, pleasure, and emotion, making their initial effects very powerful. This brain circuitry, known as the mesolimbic dopamine reward system, extends from the ventral tegmentum to the nucleus accumbens with projections to areas such as the limbic system and the orbitofrontal cortex. Dopamine is the primary neurotransmitter, the brain chemical that mediates neuronal communication in this circuitry. Pleasurable events, such as eating, drinking, and sex, have all been shown to trigger a release of dopamine in this circuitry. It is the powerful pleasurable feelings associated with these activities that serve to reinforce them, making them more likely to be repeated, in these cases to the benefit of the individual's survival (Schultz, Dayan, & Montague, 1997).

Similarly, drugs of abuse are also able to trigger large releases of dopamine in these same brain regions and, as a result, are also very strong positive reinforcers. Although each drug that has been studied has its own unique mechanisms and actions on the brain, research has shown that dopamine release is critical in the acute reinforcing actions of cocaine, amphetamine, and nicotine (see Pontieri, Tanda, Orzi, & DiChiara, 1996; Wise & Rompre, 1989, for reviews). In addition, dopamine has been shown to contribute to the reinforcing actions of many opiates (Bozarth & Wise, 1981), and it has also been implicated in the positive reinforcing actions of tetrahydrocannabinol (THC), the major psychoactive component of marijuana (Tanda, Pontieri, & DiChiara, 1997).

It is generally agreed that it is the positive reinforcing effects of drugs that are critical for the early stages of illegal psychoactive drug use. However, there is also evidence accumulating for another motivational aspect to taking drugs. Negative reinforcement refers to the increase in the probability of a response by the removal of an aversive stimulus (see Koob, 1992, 1996, for reviews). For example, an individual might have a genetic vulnerability for a pathology, such as anxiety, that is relieved by self-administering a drug such as alcohol or nicotine to reduce the anxiety. Thus, in a sense, some individuals' drug using behavior may be attempts to self-medicate.

Whether an individual is primarily motivated by the positive reinforcing effects of drugs (the initial "rush"), or is self-medicating to achieve a feeling of "normalcy," the neurotransmitter dopamine plays a key role in the addiction process. However, the exact nature of its role is still not clear. Whether the surges of dopamine elicited by drugs directly produce feelings of pleasure and euphoria or more subtly draw the individual's attention to significant stimuli is an area of important research interest. Emerging data are suggesting that dopamine may actually signal the presence or coming of a reward (Schultz et al., 1997). This attentional role for dopamine suggests that it plays an important role in learning, which may explain why drug use continues long after the initial euphoric effects have diminished or worn off (see Wickelgren, 1997, for review).

Although many people experiment with drugs of abuse, many do not continue using drugs, and only a small percentage develop an addiction or a dependence. Several lines of research have demonstrated that there are long-lasting physical changes in the brain after chronic drug use. Significant effects of chronic use have been identified both in animal models and in human drug abusers for many drugs at all levels: molecular, cellular, structural, and functional (Hyman, 1996; Melega et al., 1997; Nestler, 1996; Ortiz et al., 1995; Volkow et al., 1990). Using modern neuroimaging technology, research is showing that in human drug abusers, the addicted brain is distinctly different from the nonaddicted brain, as manifested by changes in brain metabolic activity, receptor availability, gene expression, and responsiveness to environmental cues. It has not been determined whether these difference between addicted and nonaddicted brains precede and possibly lead to drug use or, alternatively, result from chronic drug use. However, data from animal models including nonhuman primates show dramatic changes in brain activity and function after chronic drug exposure (Melega et al., 1997). Therefore, it is possible that prolonged drug use leads to changes in the brain that in turn further predispose the individual to further drug abuse. Drug using behavior that was initially voluntary becomes compulsive drug seeking and use.

Some of the neuroadaptive changes that occur after chronic drug exposure are specific to specific drugs. For example, long-term nicotine exposure results in an increase in the actual numbers of nicotinic acetylcholine receptors (Marks, Stitzel, & Collins, 1985), the proteins to which nicotine attaches to cause its initial effects. Chronic morphine treatment results, among other effects, in an increase in the activity of the enzyme adenylate cyclase (Nestler, 1996), which is involved in intracellular information processing. Other neuroadaptive changes may be common to all drugs of abuse. For example, drug withdrawal is accompanied by a decrease in dopamine function (Koob, 1996). These findings raise the possibility of a common substrate for addiction.

Other neurotransmitter systems, such as the serotonin system, also appear to play significant roles in the reinforcing and addictive effects of drugs. Recently, Rocha et al. (1998) reported that a new, genetically altered strain of mice that are deficient in the serotonin 1B receptor were more motivated to self-administer cocaine than their normal, wild-type (non-genetically altered) littermates. In other words, in a drug self-administration paradigm where the animals had to press a lever to obtain drugs, the genetically altered mice would work harder, that is, press the lever more times, to obtain cocaine than their normal siblings. Other behavioral and biochemical characterizations of these "knockout" mice also showed that they were indistinguishable from wild-type mice that had been sensitized to cocaine by repeated exposure to the drug. Thus, the researchers had created a strain of mice that were genetically more vulnerable to the addictive properties of cocaine than were normal mice. These results also suggest that one role that the serotonin system may play in the development of addiction is that of a braking system on the brain's craving system.

One of the most significant breakthroughs is in the identification of areas of the brain that are specifically involved in the phenomenon of craving. Research converging from many laboratories using positron emission tomography (PET) scans shows that when addicts experience craving for a drug there is a high level of activation in specific areas of the brain, particularly in the amygdala, an area of the brain that appears to be involved in all emotional memories (Breiter et al., 1997; Childress et al., 1999; Volkow et al., 1997). Because craving is probably the single most important factor that can lead to relapse, understanding the systems that mediate this phenomenon provides the foundation for developing effective interventions to prevent or reverse the addiction process.

GENETIC FACTORS

Numerous well-conducted studies have reported a very considerable familial aggregation of substance abuse. For example, Merikangas, Stolar, et al. (1998) found an eightfold increased risk of drug disorders among first-degree relatives of probands with drug disorders compared with controls. The familial aggregation of drug and alcohol abuse seems in part to include an association with other characteristics such as certain psychopathologies. The extent to which drug and alcohol abuse clusters in families implies significant intergenerational transmission, and the mechanisms of this transmission are the subject of research and speculation. There is little question that some of the aggregation is related to social and environmental factors. Parents who use drugs model and implicitly sanction drug using behavior. They probably facilitate the availability of drugs, are more tolerant of deviant behavior including the abuse of psychoactive substances and the early consequences of that abuse, have coping and other problems, and provide a poorer quality of parenting.

Findings related to premorbid and concomitant neurobiological influences implicate a genetic contribution to drug abuse etiology. Individual vulnerability to experiment with, use, and possibly become addicted to drugs is influenced by both genetic and environmental factors, as well as the interaction between those factors. Accumulating evidence from family histories and twin and adoption studies points toward genetic factors playing a significant role in an individual's vulnerability to addiction.

Data from family studies can give an indication of whether the occurrence of a disorder has some genetic influence. Simply, if a disorder does not run in families, genetic influence is not likely. However, if a disorder appears within families at a higher rate than in unrelated individuals, there is some indication, although not absolute proof, that there may be genetic influence. Although there have been a number of family studies of alcoholism, there have been relatively few looking specifically at drug abuse. In one study of opioid abuse, investigators found that there were higher rates of opioid dependence among the relatives of opioid-dependent individuals than in the relatives of nondependent individuals, suggestive of some genetic influences (Rounsaville et al., 1991). Parents and siblings of cocaine abusers also tend to show excessive rates of drug abuse, alcoholism, and antisocial personality (Kosten, Anton, & Rounsaville, 1992), suggesting not only a genetic involvement in drug abuse but also a possible genetic link between drug abuse and alcoholism and some psychopathologies.

Although family studies can show that genes may be involved, twin and adoption studies can provide investigators with actual estimates of the extent of the genetic effects, a measure that is termed "heritability." Studies of these types have demonstrated convincingly that genetic factors are important and, depending on the type of drug, can account for up to 60% to 70% of the total variability in the phenotype, that is, the trait being examined. For example, by comparing the rates and amount of drug use in identical or monozygotic twins (who share 100% of their genetic information) and fraternal or dizygotic twins (who on average share 50% of their genetic information), researchers can estimate the extent to which genes are influencing a trait. If a trait is highly heritable, identical twins will be much more alike on that trait than fraternal twins. However, even in twin and adoption studies the degree of environmental influence is unclear. For example, monozygotic twins may have different experiences than dizygotic twins, and adopted children may be placed in families in nonrandom ways, creating more of a similarity between the biological parent and adoptive parent than is being taken into account by the heritability estimates. A survey of the literature of twin studies on substance abuse reveals that heritabilities range from 33% for marijuana use in males (Tsuang et al., 1996) to 79% for cocaine use in females (Kendler & Prescott, 1998a). Nevertheless, in no case is heritability 100%, which reinforces the assertion that the environment always plays a role in drug abuse etiology. Table 5 shows the heritability estimates for dependence, as defined by *DSM III* or heavy use criteria for a number of drugs of abuse.

When considering the heritability estimates presented in Table 5, it is important to note the variability of the estimates. This illustrates the complexity of addiction. The larger heritabilities for dependence in females suggest that genes play a greater role in development of dependence in females than males, and environmental factors appear to play a greater role in the development of dependence in males. The range of heritabilities among these drugs also indicates that dependence on one drug is influenced to some extent by genes specific for that drug, as well as genes influencing a more global addiction phenotype. These and other findings (e.g., Tsuang

TABLE 5
Heritability Estimates for Drug Dependence

Drug	Males	Females
Cocaine	44% (Tsuang et al., 1996)	79% (Kendler & Prescott, 1998a)
Heroin (opiates)	54% (Tsuang et al., 1996)	—
Marijuana	33% (Tsuang et al., 1996)	79% (Kendler & Prescott, 1998b)
Nicotine	53% (Carmelli, Swan, Robinette, & Fabsitz, 1990)	72% (Kendler et al., 1999)

et al., 1996) indicate that the genetic influence on the etiology of drug abuse operates both in terms of drug-specific and a less differentiated—more general—vulnerability.

Heritabilities can also differ depending on the stage of addiction being studied. A recently published twin study of tobacco use by Kendler and colleagues examined risk factors for smoking initiation and nicotine dependence (Kendler et al., 1999). They found in their sample of female twins that although the genetic factors that influence these two stages of tobacco use are correlated, they are not identical. It appears that there are some genes that influence dependence through their effects on smoking initiation. However, there appear to be other genes that play an important role only in the vulnerability to nicotine dependence. Information acquired from behavioral genetic studies can be helpful in guiding future efforts at identifying the genes underlying addiction. Phenotypes that give the highest heritabilities are likely to be the first to be successfully defined genetically. However, to fully understand the genetic risk factors underlying addiction, several stages of addiction, from initiation of drug use to dependence, will eventually have to be explored.

The data from family and twin studies have consistently demonstrated the importance of genes in determining an individual's vulnerability to drug abuse and addiction. Data from the animal literature also support the critical role that genes play in determining sensitivity to the acute and chronic effects of drugs of abuse as well as the willingness for animals to self-administer a wide variety of drugs. With the advent of powerful new molecular genetic mapping techniques, researchers have been able to combine classical behavioral genetic breeding strategies with gene mapping technology to identify chromosomal locations, termed *quantitative trait loci* (QTL), that are associated with drug-related phenotypes. A review article recently compiled all QTL associated with drug-related phenotypes (Crabbe, Belknap, & Buck, 1994). These QTL contain genetic information that makes an animal either more or less sensitive to a particular drug response. Given the large degree of conservation of genetic information (or synteny) between the mouse and human chromosomes, these data can point to chromosomal regions that may contain either risk or protective genes for addiction. No specific genes have yet been linked definitively with any drug phenotype, but the data thus far demonstrate that sensitivity to drugs of abuse in animal models is influenced by a number of genes. There are likely to be genes that are specifically linked to one particular drug or drug class, and there are genes that underlie a more general sensitivity to drugs.

The accumulation of evidence from human and animal behavioral genetic studies to date indicates that there is no single gene for drug abuse, no single gene that makes individuals more or less vulnerable to addiction. It is almost certain that to whatever extent drug addiction is a genetic disorder, like many other psychiatric diseases, it is a complex genetic disorder. Vulnerability is likely influenced by a number of genes (polygenic) that are manifested in varying degrees in different individuals (heterogeneity). In addition, those genes that may be operating at one stage of development to enhance vulnerability may not be as important at earlier or later stages of development. Adding to the complexity is the possibility that the expression of addiction vulnerability may be through other intermediary traits such as temperament or psychopathology. For example, Slutske et al. (1998) recently reported that conduct disorder is an important genetically influenced risk factor for alcohol dependence. Therefore, there is probably no simple correspondence between the phenotype and the genotype or genetic make-up of the individual. Furthermore, the definition of the phenotype is absolutely crucial in this research. There is currently no consensus on the specific behaviors, disorder characteristics, and/or biological characteristics that should be used to denote drug abuse phenotypes, and this further complicates the search for the genetic contribution to drug abuse.

CONCLUSIONS

It is not possible for a single chapter overview of drug abuse etiology to discuss all of the relevant topics, findings, or issues. This chapter has limited its focus by concentrating on the development of higher levels of drug involvement and emphasizing the intrapersonal—the biological, psychological, and psychiatric—rather than the social and environmental influences. Although this reflects the research fields' emphasis, it may be that the influence of social and environmental factors is greater in the earlier stages of drug involvement. The scientific research reviewed in this chapter shows that a great deal of progress has been made in understanding the factors, patterns, and phenomena associated with the development of drug abuse and drug abuse disorders. Several important general points emerge from this review.

Multifactorial Influences

This overview has identified many etiological factors for drug abuse. Not only are there multiple etiological factors for drug abuse in general, but also for individual cases. In other words, drug abuse is a multiply determined behavior; it is not "caused" by a single antecedent factor. Furthermore, different stages and transitions involved in the full course of drug abuse are likely to be primarily influenced by different factors. Some factors seem to exercise their influence directly, and others appear to have an indirect influence, for example, as mediators. Etiologic factors are not static; they are dynamic and evolving, varying in their influence, changing over time and circumstance, probably differently with different individuals. The different contributive factors are associated with multiple domains, including the biological, the psychological–psychiatric, and the social–environmental. Zucker and Gomberg (1986) discussed the importance of considering the etiology of alcoholism as a "biopsychosocial" process, and the same heuristic would apply to the etiology of drug abuse.

Interactive Systems

A number of researchers have reported that the greater the number and severity of any of the prodromal risk factors, the greater the risk for subsequent drug abuse (Bry, 1983, 1989; Bry, McKeon, & Pandina, 1982; Maddahian, Newcomb, & Bentler, 1988). However, this should not be taken as evidence that risk is a simple, additive, linear sum of etiological factors. The contribution of any given risk is likely to depend in part on the other risk factors that are present. At the very least, the degree of a person's vulnerability to drug involvement results from the interaction of predisposing factors with protective factors. Other interactions are equally important.

As discussed above, many etiological factors must be considered as person–environmental interactions that will lead to varying outcomes over time and circumstance. The influence of other risk factors may vary depending on the developmental level of the individual. Drug use has many consequences, but these consequences are not final end points. At each step, the consequences of drug use/abuse become part of the system of influences determining subsequent behavior, and thus, the consequences of drug involvement become etiologic factors themselves. In short, risk factors are interactive and cannot be considered in isolation from other relevant influences. The determinants of drug abuse and drug abuse disorders are highly complex, and they constantly interact in a dynamic system. An etiological theory or investigation that is not based on the model of an interactive system is likely to be inadequate.

Multiple Paths

As previously discussed, there is clear evidence of many factors that appear to have a contributive role in the development of drug abuse. However, different factors may combine or interact to increase an individual's vulnerability, but it is not possible for all of the etiological factors to be involved in the etiology of all drug abuse outcomes. Clearly there is more than one etiological pattern of factors or paths leading to drug abuse. Although this may not seem like a very controversial perspective, it is in fact different from the tacit assumptions and heuristics of many investigations and models of the nature of drug abuse and its etiology.

Multiple Behaviors and Disorders

A parallel and probably noncontroversial point, although one that is very important, is that there is a great deal of heterogeneity to drug abuse behaviors and to drug abuse disorders (see Zucker, Fitzgerald, & Moses, 1995, for a discussion of this and associated issues related to alcoholism). Neglect of the differences in the manifestations of drug abuse may lead to a failure to recognize important differences in etiology and factors related to effective interventions. Even if it is the case that there are critical factors common to all cases of drug abuse and related disorders (for example, the involvement of certain neurological processes), the variabilities remain critical.

Developmental Etiology

In many cases, drug abuse is a behavior that has its roots in childhood and emerges in adolescence. As such, its etiology and manifestation is in the context of child and adolescent development, and the previous discussion has noted some of the implications of this. For example, not only might the influence of a potential risk factor vary with the developmental level of the individual, but drug use may interfere with normal development, limiting adaptive coping and functioning, perhaps in ways that predispose the person to more drug involvement. The study of psychiatric disorders and their etiology in the context of maturation and developmental processes is associated with the field of developmental psychopathology. This orientation is clearly appropriate for the study of drug abuse etiology.

It would be useful in many ways to conceptualize drug abuse etiology in some ways as a developmental process. Consideration of developmental context, emphasizing systems such as person–environmental interactions, stressing the influence of both protective and predisposing factors and many of the other points discussed above, is intrinsic to considering a phenomenon as developmental. Perhaps one of the most helpful aspects of viewing drug abuse etiology from a developmental perspective would be the encouragement to think of it as the evolution of a behavior. Drug abuse and drug abuse disorders are not a quantitative extension of initial drug use behaviors; drug abuse is not just a lot of drug use. Drug abuse is not just a bad habit that escalates and gets out of control, an inchoate disease that unfolds, or the results of a psychological or biological system that abruptly becomes dysfunctional. Any model that depicts drug abuse etiology as a simple linearly increasing or sharply discontinuous phenomenon is probably inadequate. Drug abuse evolves according to developmental principles over multiple interactions and drug use occasions, and as it does, the drug user changes in important ways, all too often including some that predispose individuals to more drug use.

REFERENCES

American Psychiatric Association. (1987). *Diagnostic and statistical manual of mental disorders* (3rd ed., revised). Washington, DC: Author.

American Psychiatric Association. (1994). *Diagnostic and statistical manual of mental disorders* (4th ed.). Washington, DC: Author.

Anthony, J. C., & Petronis, K. R. (1995). Early-onset drug use and risk of later drug problems. *Drug and Alcohol Dependence, 40*(1), 9–15.

Aytaclar, S., Tarter, R. E., Kirisci, L., & Lu, S. (1999). Association between hyperactivity and executive cognitive functioning in childhood and substance use in early adolescence. *Journal of the American Academy of Child and Adolescent Psychiatry, 38*(2), 172–178.

Bardo, M. T., Donohew, R. L., & Harrington, N. G. (1996). Psychobiology of novelty seeking and drug seeking behavior. *Behavioural Brain Research, 77*(1–2), 23–43.

Bardo, M. T., & Mueller, C. W. (1991). Sensation seeking and drug abuse prevention from a biological perspective. In L. Donohew, H. E. Sypher, & W. Bukoski (Eds.), *Persuasive communication and drug abuse prevention: Communication* (pp. 195–207). Hillsdale, NJ: Erlbaum.

Barkley, R. A., Fischer, M., Edelbrock, C. S., & Smallish, L. (1990). The adolescent outcome of hyperactive children diagnosed by research criteria: I. An 8-year prospective follow-up study. *Journal of the American Academy of Child and Adolescent Psychiatry, 29*(4), 546–557.

Biederman, J., Faraone, S. V., & Kiely, K. (1996). Comorbidity in outcome of attention-deficit/hyperactivity disorder. In L. Hechtman (Ed.), *Do they grow out of it? Long-term outcomes of childhood disorders* (pp. 39–75). Washington, DC: American Psychiatric Press.

Biederman, J., Wilens, T. E., Mick, E., & Faraone, S. V. (1997). Is ADHD a risk factor for psychoactive substance use disorders: Findings from a four-year prospective followup study. *Journal of the American Academy of Child and Adolescent Psychiatry, 36*(1), 21–29.

Biederman, J., Wilens, T. E., Mick, E., Faraone, S. V., & Spencer, T. (1999). Protective effects of ADHD pharmacotherapy on subsequent substance abuse: A longitudinal study. *Pediatrics.*

Biederman, J., Wilens, T., Mick, E., Milberger, S., Weber, W., Curtis, S., Thornell, A., Pfister, K., Jetton, J. G., & Soriano, J. (1995). Psychoactive substance use disorders in adults with attention deficit hyperactivity disorder (ADHD): Effects of ADHD and psychiatric comorbidity. *American Journal of Psychiatry, 152*(11), 1652–1658.

Blackson, T. C. (1994). Temperament: A salient correlate of risk factors for alcohol and drug abuse. *Drug and Alcohol Dependence, 36*(3), 205–214.

Blackson, T., Tarter, R., Martin, C., & Moss, H. (1994). Temperament mediates the effects of family history of substance abuse on externalizing and internalizing child behavior. *American Journal on Addictions, 3*(1), 58–66.

Blackson, T. C., Tarter, R. E., & Mezzich, A. C. (1996). Interaction between childhood temperament and parental discipline practices on behavioral adjustment in preadolescent sons of substance abuse and normal fathers. *American Journal of Drug and Alcohol Abuse, 22*(3), 335–348.

Block, J., Block, J. H., & Keyes, S. (1988). Longitudinally foretelling drug stage in adolescence: Early childhood personality and environmental precursors. *Child Development, 52,* 336–355.

Bozarth, M. A., & Wise, R. A. (1981). Heroin reward is dependent on a dopaminergic substrate. *Life Sciences, 29,* 1881–1886.

Breiter, H. C., Gollub, R. L., Weisskoff, R. M., Kennedy, D. N., Makris, N., Berke, J. D., Goodman, J. M., Kantor, H. L., Gastfriend, D. R., Riorden, J. P., Mathew, R. T., Rosen, B. R., & Hyman, S. E. (1997). Acute effects of cocaine on human brain activity and emotion. *Neuron, 19,* 591–611.

Brook, J. S., Brook, D. W., Gordon, A. S., Whiteman, M., & Cohen, P. (1990). The psychosocial etiology of adolescent drug use: A family interactional approach. *Genetic, Social, and General Psychology Monographs, 116,* 111–267.

Brook, J. S., Whiteman, M., & Cohen, P. (1995). Stage of drug use, aggression, and theft/vandalism: Common and uncommon risks. In H. Kaplan (Ed.), *Drugs, crime, and other deviant adaptations: Longitudinal studies* (pp. 83–96). New York: Plenum Press.

Brooner, R. K., King, V. L., Kidorf, M., Schmidt, C. W., Jr., & Bigelow, G. E. (1997). Psychiatric and substance use comorbidity among treatment-seeking opioid abusers. *Archives of General Psychiatry, 54*(1), 71–80.

Bry, B. (1983). Predicting drug abuse: Review and reformulation. *International Journal of the Addictions, 18,* 223–233.

Bry, B. (1989). The multiple risk factor hypothesis: An integrating concept of the etiology of drug abuse. In S. Einstein (Ed.), *Drug and alcohol use: Issues and factors* (pp. 37–43). New York: Plenum Press.

Bry, B., McKeon, P., & Pandina, R. (1982). Extent of drug use as a function of number of risk factors. *Journal of Abnormal Psychology, 91,* 273–279.

Buckley, P. F. (1998). Substance abuse in schizophrenia: A review. *Journal of Clinical Psychiatry, 59,* 26–30.

Bukstein, O. G., Glancy, L. J., & Kaminer, Y. (1992). Patterns of affective co-morbidity in a clinical population of dually diagnosed adolescent substance abusers. *Journal of the American Academy of Child and Adolescent Psychiatry, 31*(6), 1041–1045.

Cadoret, R. J. (1992). Genetic and environmental factors in initiation of drug use and the transition to abuse. In M. Glantz, & R. Pickens (Eds.), *Vulnerability to drug abuse* (pp. 99–114). Washington, DC: American Psychological Association.

Cadoret, R. J., Yates, W. R., Troughton, E., Woodworth, G., & Stewart, M. (1995). Adoption study demonstrating two genetic pathways to drug abuse. *Archives of General Psychiatry, 52*(1), 42–52.

Cadoret, R. J., Yates, W. R., Troughton, E., Woodworth, G., & Stewart, M. A. (1996). An adoption study of drug abuse/dependency in females. *Comparative Psychiatry, 37*(2), 88–94.

Capaldi, D. M., & Stoolmiller, M. (1999). Co-occurrence of conduct problems and depressive symptoms in early adolescent boys: III. Prediction to young-adult adjustment. *Development and Psychopathology, 11,* 59–84.

Carmelli, D., Swan, G. E., Robinette, D., & Fabsitz, R. R. (1990). Heritability of substance use in the NAS-NRC twin registry. *Acta Genetica, 39,* 91–98.

Caspi, A., Moffitt, T. E., Newman, D. L., & Silva, P. A. (1996). Behavioral observations at age 3 years predict adult psychiatric disorders. Longitudinal evidence from a birth cohort. *Archives of General Psychiatry, 53*(11), 1033–1039.

Chassin, L., Pillow, D., Curran, P., Molina, B., & Barrera, M. (1993). Relation of parental alcoholism to early adolescent substance use: A test of three mediating mechanisms. *Journal of Abnormal Psychology, 102,* 3–19.

Chess, S., & Thomas, A. (1989). Temperament and its functional significance. In S. I. Greenspan & G. H. Pollock (Eds.), *The course of life: Volume II. Early childhood* (pp. 163–227). Madison/CT: International Universities Press.

Chiauzzi, E. J., & Liljegren, S. (1993). Taboo topics in addiction treatment: An empirical review of clinical folklore. *Journal of Substance Abuse Treatment, 10*(3), 303–316.

Chilcoat, H. D., & Breslau, N. (1998). Posttraumatic stress disorder and drug disorders: Testing causal pathways. *Archives of General Psychiatry, 55*(10), 913–917.

Childress, A. R., Mozley, P. D., McElgin, W., Fitzgerald, J., Reivich, M., O'Brien, C. P. (1999). Limbic activation during cue-induced cocaine craving. *American Journal of Psychiatry, 156,* 11–18.

Clark, D. B., Lesnick, L., & Hegedus, A. M. (1997). Traumas and other adverse life events in adolescents with alcohol abuse and dependence. *Journal of the American Academy of Child and Adolescent Psychiatry, 36*(12), 1744–1751.

Clark, D. B., & Neighbors, B. (1996). Adolescent substance abuse and internalizing disorders. *Child and Adolescent Psychiatric Clinics of North America, 5*(1), 45–57.

Cloninger, C. R. (1987). Neurogenetic adaptive mechanisms in alcoholism. *Science, 236,* 410–416.

Cohen, P., Cohen, J., Kasen, S., Velez, C. N., Hartmark, C., Johnson, J., Rojas, M., Brook, J., & Streuning, E. L. (1993). An epidemiological study of disorders in late childhood and adolescence: I. Age and gender specific prevalence. *Journal of Child Psychology and Psychiatry, 34*(6), 851–867.

Costa, F. M., Jessor, R., Donovan, J. E., & Fortenberry, J. D. (1995). Early initiation of sexual intercourse: The influence of psychosocial unconventionality. *Journal of Research on Adolescence, 5*(1), 93–121.

Crabbe, J. C., Belknap, J. K., & Buck, K. J. (1994). Genetic animal models of alcohol and drug abuse. *Science, 264,* 1715–1723.

Dawes, M. A., Tarter, R. E., & Kirisci, L. (1997). Behavioral self-regulation: Correlates and 2-year follow-ups for boys at risk for substance abuse. *Drug and Alcohol Dependence, 45*(3), 165–176.

Deckel, A. W., & Hesselbrock, V. (1996). Behavioral and cognitive measurements predict scores on the MAST: A 3-year prospective study. *Alcoholism, Clinical and Experimental Research, 20*(7), 1173–1178.

Donovan, J. E. (1996). Problem-behavior theory and the explanation of adolescent marijuana use. *Journal of Drug Issues, 26*(2), 379–404.

Donovan, J. E., Jessor, R., & Costa, F. M. (1991). Adolescent health behavior and conventionality/unconventionality: An extension of problem-behavior theory. *Health Psychology, 10*(1), 52–61.

Elliott, D. S., Huizinga, D., & Menard, S. (1989). *Multiple problem youth. Delinquency, substance use, and mental health problems.* New York: Springer-Verlag.

Etz, K., Robertson, E., Glantz, M. D., & Colliver, J. (1999). *The gateway model of adolescent substance abuse: An historical perspective.* Manuscript in preparation.

Gfroerer, J., Wright, D., & Kopstein, A. (1997). Prevalence of youth substance use: The impact of methodological differences between two national surveys. *Drug and Alcohol Dependence, 47*(1), 19–30.

Giancola, P. R., Martin, C. S., Tarter, R. E., Pelham, W. E., & Moss, H. B. (1996). Executive cognitive functioning and aggressive behavior in preadolescent boys at high risk for substance abuse/dependence. *Journal of Studies on Alcohol, 57*(4), 352–359.

Giancola, P. R., Mezzich, A. C., & Tarter, R. E. (1998). Disruptive, delinquent and aggressive behavior in female adolescents with a psychoactive substance use disorder: Relation to executive cognitive functioning. *Journal of Studies on Alcohol, 59*(5), 560–567.

Glantz, M. D. (1992). A developmental psychopathology model of drug abuse vulnerability. In M. Glantz & R. Pickens (Eds.), *Vulnerability to drug abuse* (pp. 389–418). Washington, DC: American Psychological Association.

Glantz, M. D., & Pickens, R. W. (1992). Vulnerability to drug abuse: Introduction and overview. In M. D. Glantz & R. Pickens (Eds.), *Vulnerability to drug abuse* (pp. 1–14). Washington, DC: American Psychological Association.

Glantz, M. D., & Sloboda, Z. (1999). Analysis and reconceptualization of resilience. In M. D. Glantz, & J. Johnson (Eds.), *Resiliency and development: Positive life adaptations* (pp. 108–126). New York: Plenum Press.

Golub, A., & Johnson, B. D. (1994a). The shifting importance of alcohol and marijuana as gateway substances among serious drug abusers. *Journal of Studies on Alcohol, 55*(5), 607–614.

Golub, A., & Johnson, B. D. (1994b). Cohort differences in drug-use pathways to crack among current crack abusers in New York City. *Criminal Justice and Behavior, 21*(4), 403–422.

Grant, B. F., & Dawson, D. A. (1998). Age of onset of drug use and its association with *DSM-IV* drug abuse and dependence: Results from the National Longitudinal Alcohol Epidemiologic Survey. *Journal of Substance Abuse, 10*(2), 163–173.

Greenbaum, P. E., Foster-Johnson, L., & Petrila, A. (1996). Co-occurring addictive and mental disorders among adolescents: Prevalence research and future directions. *American Journal of Orthopsychiatry, 66*(1), 52–60.

Greene, R. W., Biederman, J., Faraone, S. V., Sienna, M., & Garcia-Jetton, J. (1997). Adolescent outcome of boys with attention-deficit/hyperactivity disorder and social disability: Results from a 4-year longitudinal follow-up study. *Journal of Consulting and Clinical Psychology, 65*(5), 758–767.

Hamburg, B. A., Kraemer, H. C., & Jahnke, W. (1975). A hierarchy of drug use in adolescence: Behavioral and attitudinal correlates of substantial drug use. *American Journal of Psychiatry, 132*, 1155–1163.

Holderness, C. C., Brooks-Gunn, J., & Warren, M. P. (1994). Co-morbidity of eating disorders and substance abuse review of the literature. *International Journal of Eating Disorders, 16*(1), 1–34.

Hyman, S. E. (1996). Addiction to cocaine and amphetamine. *Neuron, 16*(5), 901–904.

Jessor, R., Donovan, J. E., & Costa, F. M. (1991). *Beyond adolescence: Problem behavior and young adult development.* New York: Cambridge University Press.

Jessor, R., & Jessor, S. (1977). *Problem behavior and psychosocial development: A longitudinal study of youth.* New York: Academic Press.

Jessor R., Van Den Bos, J., Vanderryn J., Costa, F. M., & Turbin, M. S. (1995). Protective factors in adolescent problem behavior: Moderator effects and developmental change. *Developmental Psychology, 31*(6), 923–933.

Johnson, B. D. (1972). *Social determinants of the use of dangerous drugs by college students.* New York: Wiley.

Kandel, D. B. (1975). Stages in adolescent involvement in drug use. *Science, 190*, 912–914.

Kandel, D., & Yamaguchi, K. (1999). Development stages of involvement in substance use. In P. Ott, R. Tarter, & R. Ammerman (Eds.), *Sourcebook on sub-*

stance abuse: Etiology, epidemiology, assessment, and treatment (pp. 50–74). Boston: Allyn & Bacon.

Kaplan, H. B. (1995). Drugs, crime, and other deviant adaptations. In H. Kaplan (Ed.), *Drugs, crime, and other deviant adaptations: Longitudinal studies* (pp. 33–46). New York: Plenum Press.

Kellam, S., Brown, C., Rubin, B., & Ensminger, M. (1983). Paths leading to teenage psychiatric symptoms and substance use: Developmental epidemiological studies in Woodlawn. In S. Guze, F. Earls, & J. Barrett (Eds.), *Childhood psychopathology and development* (pp. 17–51). New York: Raven.

Kendler, K. S., & Prescott, C. A. (1998a). Cocaine use, abuse and dependence in a population-based sample of female twins. *British Journal of Psychiatry, 173,* 345–350.

Kendler, K. S., & Prescott, C. A. (1998b). Cannabis use, abuse, and dependence in a population-based sample of female twins. *American Journal of Psychiatry, 155,* 1016–1022.

Kendler, K. S., Neale, M. C., Sullivan, P., Corey, L. A., Gardener, C. O., & Prescott, C. A. (1999). A population-based twin study in women of smoking initiation and nicotine dependence. *Psychological Medicine, 29,* 299–308.

Kerr, J. S. (1996). Two myths of addiction: The addictive personality and the issue of free choice. *Human Psychopharmacology, 11* (Suppl. 1), S9–S13.

Kessler, R. C. (1995). Epidemiology of psychiatric comorbidity. In M. T. Tsuang, M. Tohen, & G. E. P. Zahner (Eds.), *Textbook in psychiatric epidemiology* (pp. 179–197). New York: Wiley-Liss.

Kessler, R. C., McGonagle, K. A., Zhao, S., Nelson, C. B., Hughes, M., Eshleman, S., Wittchen, H. U., & Kendler, K. S. (1994). Lifetime and 12-month prevalence of *DSM-III-R* psychiatric disorders in the United States. Results from the National Comorbidity Survey. *Archives of General Psychiatry, 51*(1), 8–19.

Kessler, R. C., Nelson, C. B., McGonagle, K. A., Edlund, M. J., Frank, R. G., & Leaf, P. J. (1996). The epidemiology of co-occurring addictive and mental disorders: Implications for prevention and service utilization. *American Journal of Orthopsychiatry, 66*(1), 17–31.

Kessler, R. C., Nelson, C. B., McGonagle, K. A., Liu, J., Swartz, M., & Blazer, D. G. (1996). Comorbidity of *DSM-III-R* major depressive disorder in the general population: Results from the U.S. National Comorbidity Survey. *British Journal of Psychiatry* Suppl. 30, 17–30.

Khantzian, E. J. (1997). The self-medication hypothesis of substance use disorders: A reconsideration and recent applications. *Harvard Review of Psychiatry, 4*(5), 231–244.

Klein, R. G. (1998, November). *Alcohol, nicotine, stimulants, and other drugs.* Paper presented at the NIH Consensus Development Conference: Diagnosis and Treatment of Attention Deficit Hyperactivity Disorder, Washington, DC.

Koob, G. F. (1992). Drugs of abuse: Anatomy, pharmacology and function of reward pathways. *Trends in Pharmacological Science, 13,* 177–184.

Koob, G. F. (1996). Drug addiction: The yin and yang of hedonic homeostasis. *Neuron, 16,* 893–896.

Kosten, T. A., Anton, S. F., & Rounsaville, B. J. (1992). Ascertaining psychiatric diagnoses with the family history method in a substance abuse population. *Journal of Psychiatric Research, 26,* 135–147.

Kushner, M. G., Sher, K. J., & Erickson, D. J. (1999). Prospective analysis of the relation between *DSM-III* anxiety disorders and alcohol use disorders. *American Journal of Psychiatry, 156,* 723–732.

Kwapil, T. R. (1996). A longitudinal study of drug and alcohol use by psychosis-prone and impulsive-nonconforming individuals. *Journal of Abnormal Psychology, 105*(1), 114–123.

Lerner, J. V., & Vicary, J. R. (1984). Difficult temperament and drug use: Analyses from the New York Longitudinal Study. *Journal of Drug Education, 14,* 1–8.

Lewisohn, P. M., Hops, H., Roberts, R. E., Seeley, J. R., & Andrews, J. A. (1993). Adolescent psychopathology: I. Prevalence and incidence of depression and other *DSM-III-R* disorders in high school students. *Journal of Abnormal Psychology, 102*(1), 133–144.

Loeber, R., Farrington, D., Stouthamer-Loeber, M., & Van Kammen, W. B. (1998). Multiple risk factors for multiproblem boys: Co-occurrence of delinquency, substance use, attention deficit, conduct problems, physical aggression, covert behavior, depressed mood, and shy/withdrawn behavior. In R. Jessor (Ed.), *New perspectives on adolescent risk behavior* (pp. 90–149). Cambridge, England: Cambridge University Press.

Maddahian, E., Newcomb, M., & Bentler, P. (1988). Risk factors for substance use: Ethnic differences among adolescents. *Journal of Substance Abuse, 1,* 11–23.

Mannuzza, S., Klein, R. G., Bessler, A., Malloy, P., & LaPadula, M. (1998). Adult psychiatric status of hyperactive boys grown up. *American Journal of Psychiatry, 155*(4), 493–498.

Mannuzza, S., Klein, R. G., Bonagura, N., Malloy, P., Giampino, T., & Addalli, K. (1991). Hyperactive boys almost grown up: V. Replication of psychiatric status. *Archives of General Psychiatry, 48*(1), 77–83.

Marks, M. J., Stitzel, J. A., & Collins, A. C. (1985). Time course study of the effects of chronic nicotine infusion on drug response and brain receptors. *Journal of Pharmacology and Experimental Therapeutics, 235*(3), 619–628.

Masse, L. C., & Tremblay, R. E. (1997). Behavior of boys in kindergarten and the onset of substance use during adolescence. *Archives of General Psychiatry, 54*(1), 62–68.

McCord, J. (1988). Identifying developmental paradigms leading to alcoholism. *Journal of Studies on Alcohol, 49*(4), 357–362.

Melega, W. P., Raleigh, M. J., Stout, D. B., Lacan, G., Huang, S. C., & Phelps, M. E. (1997). Recovery of striatal dopamine function after acute amphetamine and methamphetamine induced neurotoxicity in the vervet monkey. *Brain Research, 766,* 113–120.

Merikangas, K., Mehta, R., Molnar, B., Walters, E., Swendsen, J., Aguilar-Gaziola, S., Bijl, R., Borges, G., Caraveo-Anduaga, J., Dewitt, D., Kolody, B., Vega, W., Wittchen, H., & Kessler, R. (1998). Comorbidity of substance use disorders with mood and anxiety disorders: Results of the international consortium in psychiatric epidemiology. *Addictive Behaviors, 23*(6), 893–907.

Merikangas, K. R., Stevens, D. E., Fenton, B., Stolar, M., O'Malley, S., Woods, S. W., & Risch, N. (1998). Co-morbidity and familial aggregation of alcoholism and anxiety disorders. *Psychological Medicine, 28*, 773–788.

Merikangas, K. R., Stolar, M., Stevens, D. E., Goulet, J., Preisig, M. A., Fenton, B., Zhang, H., O'Malley, S. S., & Rounsaville, B. J. (1998). Familial transmission of substance use disorders. *Archives of General Psychiatry, 55*(11), 973–979.

Molina, B. S. G., Smith, B. H., & Pelham, W. E. (1999). Interactive effects of ADHD and CD on early adolescent substance use. *Psychology of Addictive Behaviors.*

Nathan, P. E. (1988). The addictive personality is the behavior of the addict. *Journal of Consulting and Clinical Psychology, 56*(2), 183–188.

Nestler, E. J. (1996). Under siege: The brain on opiates. *Neuron 16*(5), 897–900.

Newcomb, M. D., & Felix-Ortiz, M. (1992). Multiple protective and risk factors for drug use and abuse: Cross-sectional and prospective findings. *Journal of Personality and Social Psychology, 63*(2), 280–96.

Ortiz, J., Fitzgerald, L. W., Charlton, M., Lane, S., Trevisan, L., Guitart, X., Shoemaker, W., Duman, R. S., & Nestler, E. J. (1995). Biochemical actions of chronic ethanol exposure in the mesolimbic dopamine system. *Synapse, 21*(4), 289–298.

Pandina, R. J., Johnson, V., & Labouvie, E. W. (1992). Affectivity: A central mechanism in the development of drug dependence. In M. D. Glantz & R. Pickens (Eds.), *Vulnerability to drug abuse* (pp. 179–209). Washington, DC: American Psychological Association.

Pontieri, F. E., Tanda, G., Orzi, F., & DiChiara, G. (1996). Effects of nicotine on the nucleus accumbens and similarity to those of addictive drugs. *Nature, 382*, 55–57.

Regier, D. A., Farmer, M. E., Rae, D. S., Locke, B. Z., Keith, S. J., Judd, L. L., & Goodwin, F. K. (1990). Comorbidity of mental disorders with alcohol and other drug abuse: Results from the Epidemiologic Catchment Area (ECA) study. *Journal of the American Medical Association, 264*(19), 2511–2518.

Robins, L. N. (1966). *Deviant children grow up: A sociological and psychiatric study of sociopathic personality.* Baltimore: Williams & Wilkins.

Robins, L. N., & Przybeck, T. R. (1985). Age of onset of drug use as a factor in drug and other disorders. In C. L. Jones & R. J. Battjes (Eds.), *Etiology of drug abuse: Implications for prevention* (NIDA Research Monograph No. 56, pp. 178–192). Rockville, MD: National Institute on Drug Abuse.

Rocha, B. A., Scearce-Levie, K., Lucas, J. J., Hiroi, N., Castanon, N., Crabbe,

J. C., Nestler, E. J., & Hen, R. (1998). Increased vulnerability to cocaine in mice lacking the serotonin-1B receptor. *Nature, 393,* 175–178.

Rounsaville, B. J., Kosten, T. R., Weissman, M. M., Prusoff, B., Pauls, D. L., Anton, S. F., & Merikangas, K. (1991). Psychiatric disorders in relatives of probands with opiate addiction. *Archives of General Psychiatry, 48,* 33–42.

Rounsaville, B. J., Kranzler, H. R., Ball, S., Tennen, H., Poling, J., & Triffleman, E. (1998). Personality disorders in substance abusers: Relation to substance use. *Journal of Nervous and Mental Disease, 186*(2), 87–95.

Scheier, L. M., & Botvin, G. J. (1996). Cognitive effects of marijuana. *Journal of the American Medical Association, 275*(20), 1547.

Schultz, W., Dayan, P., & Montague, P. E. (1997). A neural substrate of prediction and reward. *Science, 275,* 1593–1595.

Skodol, A. E., Oldham, J. M., & Gallagher, P. E. (1999). Axis II comorbidity of substance use disorders among patients referred for treatment of personality disorders. *American Journal of Psychiatry, 156,* 733–738.

Slutske, W. S., Heath, A. C., Dinwiddie, S. H., Madden, P. A. F., Bucholz, K. K., Dunne, M. P., Statham, D. J., & Martin, N. G. (1998). Common genetic risk factors for conduct disorder and alcohol dependence. *Journal of Abnormal Psychology, 107*(3), 363–374.

Substance Abuse and Mental Health Services Administration. (1999). *National Household Survey on Drug Abuse Main Findings 1997* (DHHS Publication No. SMA 99-3295). Rockville, MD: U.S. Government Printing Office.

Swendsen, J. D., Merikangas, K. R., Canino, G. J., Kessler, R. C., Rubio-Stipec, M., & Angst, J. (1998). The comorbidity of alcoholism with anxiety and depressive disorders in four geographic communities. *Comprehensive Psychiatry, 39*(4), 176–184.

Swofford, C. D., Kasckow, J. W., Scheller-Gilkey, G., & Inderbitzin, L. B. (1996). Substance use: A powerful predictor of relapse in schizophrenia. *Schizophrenia Research, 20*(1–2), 145–151.

Tanda, G., Pontieri, F. E., & DiChiara, G. (1997). Cannabinoid and heroin activation of mesolimbic dopamine transmission by a common mu$_1$ opioid receptor mechanism. *Science, 276,* 2048–2050.

Tarter, R. E., Blackson, T., Brigham, J., Moss, H., & Caprara, G. V. (1995). The association between childhood irritability and liability to substance use in early adolescence: A 2-year follow-up study of boys at risk for substance abuse. *Drug and Alcohol Dependence, 39*(3), 253–261.

Thomas, A., & Chess, S. (1977). *Temperament and development.* New York: Brunner/Mazel.

Tsuang, M. T., Lyons, M. J., Eisen, S. A., Goldberg, J., True, W., Lin, N., Meyer, J. M., Toomey, R., Faraone, S. V., & Eaves, L. (1996). Genetic influences on *DSM-III-R* drug abuse and dependence: A study of 3372 twin pairs. *Journal of Medical Genetics, 67,* 473–477.

Tubman, J. G., Vicary, J. R., von Eye, A., & Lerner, J. V. (1990). Longitudinal substance use and adult adjustment. *Journal of Substance Abuse, 2*(3), 317–334.

University of Michigan. (December 18, 1998). *Drug use by American young people begins to turn downward.* Press release of the 1998 Monitoring the Future Study. Ann Arbor, MI: University of Michigan News and Information Services.

Vaillant, G. (1983). *The natural history of alcoholism: Causes, patterns, and paths to recovery.* Cambridge, MA: Harvard University Press.

Volkow, N. D., Fowler, J. S., Wolf, A. P., Schlyer, D., Shiue, C. Y., Alpert, R., Dewey, S. L., Logan, J., Bendriem, B., Christman, D., Hitzemann, R., & Henn, F. (1990). Effects of chronic cocaine abuse on postsynaptic dopamine receptors. *American Journal of Psychiatry, 147*(6), 719–724.

Volkow, N. D., Wang, G. J., Fischman, M. W., Foltin, R. W., Fowler, J. S., Abumrad, N. N., Vitkun, S., Logan, J., Gatley, S. J., Pappas, N., Hitzemann, R., & Shea, C. E. (1997). Relationship between subjective effects of cocaine and dopamine transporter occupancy. *Nature, 386,* 827–830.

Warner, L. A., Kessler, R. C., Hughes, M., Anthony, J. C., & Nelson, C. B. (1995). Prevalence and correlates of drug use and dependence in the United States. *Archives of General Psychiatry, 52,* 219–229.

White, H. R., & Labouvie, E. W. (1994). Generality vs. specificity of problem behavior: Psychological and functional differences. *Journal of Drug Issues, 24,* 55–74.

Wickelgren, I. (1997). Getting the brain's attention. *Science, 278,* 35–37.

Wilens, T., Biederman, J., Millstein, R., Wozniak, J., Hahesy, T., & Spencer, T. (1999). Risk for substance use disorders in youth with child- and adolescent bipolar disorder. *Journal of the American Academy of Child and Adolescent Psychiatry.*

Wills, T. A., McNamara, G., Vaccaro, D., & Hirky, A. E. (1996). Escalated substance use: A longitudinal grouping analysis from early to middle adolescence. *Journal of Abnormal Psychology, 105*(2), 166–180.

Wills, T. A., Vaccaro, D., & McNamara, G. (1994). Novelty seeking, risk taking, and related constructs as predictors of adolescent substance use: An application of Cloninger's theory. *Journal of Substance Abuse, 6*(1), 1–20.

Wills, T. A., Windle, M., & Cleary, S. D. (1998). Temperament and novelty seeking in adolescent substance use: Convergence of dimensions of temperament with constructs from Cloninger's theory. *Journal of Personality and Social Psychology, 74*(2), 387–406.

Windle, M. (1991). The difficult temperament in adolescence: Associations with substance use, family support, and problem behaviors. *Journal of Clinical Psychology, 47*(2), 310–315.

Windle, M. (1994). Temperamental inhibition and activation: Hormonal and psychosocial correlates and associated psychiatric disorders. *Personality and Individual Differences, 17*(1), 61–70.

Windle, M., & Windle, R. C. (1993). The continuity of behavioral expression among disinhibited and inhibited childhood subtypes. *Clinical Psychology Review, 13*(8), 741–761.

Wise, R. A., & Rompre, P. P. (1989). Brain dopamine and reward. *Annual Review of Psychology, 40,* 191–225.

Zucker, R. A., Fitzgerald, H. E., & Moses, H. D. (1995). Emergence of alcohol problems and the several alcoholisms: A developmental perspective on etiologic theory and life course trajectory. In D. Cicchetti & D. J. Cohen (Eds.), *Developmental psychopathology: Vol. 2. Risk, disorder, and adaptation* (pp. 677–711). New York: Wiley.

Zucker, R. A., & Gomberg, E. S. L. (1986). Etiology of alcoholism reconsidered: The case for a biopsychosocial process. *American Psychologist, 41*(7), 783–793.

2

FRONTLINE SURVEILLANCE: THE COMMUNITY EPIDEMIOLOGY WORK GROUP ON DRUG ABUSE

ZILI SLOBODA AND NICHOLAS J. KOZEL

In developing epidemiologic data sources that are useful in the formation of strategies to intervene against drug abuse, it is important to understand the challenge of assessing drug-abusing behaviors. The complexity of such assessments is an outgrowth of (a) the varying patterns of drug use and drug use consequences across the population of drug abusers and (b) the degree to which drug-abusing behaviors are stigmatized by society.

Drug abuse behaviors and consequences of these behaviors are sensitive to many influences, including the existing societal norms associated with tolerance of use of drugs, the availability of drugs, the ways in which drugs are marketed, the type and quality of drugs that are available, changing modes of administration of the drugs, and social and economic trends. The interaction of these factors over time results in a constantly changing kaleidoscope of drug abuse patterns: new drugs of abuse, new combination of drugs being abused, resurgence in the popularity of old drugs, changing demographic characteristics of users, new marketing techniques, and new social, economic, health, and legal consequences.

Trends in the *prevalence* (new and existing cases) and *incidence* (new cases) of drug abuse are sensitive to changes in the delicate balance between *supply* and *demand* factors, which are short-hand terms for the influences mentioned above. Our nation's history has taught us that the overall prevalence of drug use has been cyclical and is dependent on societal tolerance of drug abuse. Prevalence tends to respond to perceptions of the harmfulness of drugs to individuals and to the community. Furthermore, societal tolerance of drug-using behaviors has been specific to individual drugs (Bachman, Johnston, & O'Malley, 1988, 1990). At varying points in time, some drugs are considered very harmful and sanctions are imposed, stigmatizing drug use and making the measurement of use of the less tolerated drugs more difficult (Musto, 1987).

Measurement of drug use in the United States challenges the epidemiologist. The combined problems of the variation in the expressed societal concerns about drug use and in the users' abilities to maintain drug use behaviors impact the methods used to estimate the extent of drug use. Both of these factors, in addition to the low prevalence of the behavior in the general population and the stigma attached to the behavior, make assessments difficult through traditional epidemiologic methodologies.

For these reasons, two approaches have been taken to assess the nature and extent of drug-abusing behaviors in the United States: monitoring systems and surveillance systems. Monitoring systems, which make cross-sectional, direct-measurement studies with periodic data collection points over time, provide the best estimates of drug use behaviors and consequences among the general population of households and schoolchildren. Major national surveys of this nature include the National Household Survey on Drug Abuse[1] and the Monitoring the Future Survey[2] of a sample of 8th, 10th, and 12th graders. Surveillance systems provide ongoing, systematic, and timely collection, analysis, and interpretation of data about emerging drug abuse patterns and trends over time. Health-related surveillance systems generally include indicator data sets that capture information about groups of people most likely to be affected in various institutional settings (Last, 1995). For a problem such as drug abuse, these settings deal with the consequences of drug-using behaviors, such as hos-

[1] The National Household Survey on Drug Abuse, conducted by the National Institute on Drug Abuse from 1975 through 1991 and, since then, by the Office of Applied Studies of the Substance Abuse and Mental Health Services Administration, surveys a national probability sample of household members age 12 and older. Until 1990, the survey was administered every 2 to 3 years among a sample of approximately 8,000 household members. After 1989, the survey was administered annually with a sample of over 30,000.

[2] The Monitoring the Future Survey, supported through a grant from the National Institute on Drug Abuse since 1974, is conducted by the Institute for Survey Research of the University of Michigan. Until 1991, the survey was administered annually in the classroom among approximately 17,000 12th graders attending a national probability sample of both public and private high schools, beginning with the class of 1975. In 1991, the survey was expanded to include similar numbers of 8th- and 10th-grade students.

pital emergency rooms, offices of medical examiners or coroners, jails and prisons, drug abuse treatment programs, and public health surveillance systems (dealing with, for example, sexually transmitted diseases, AIDS, and other infectious diseases). Together, these systems offer a comprehensive, although overlapping, description of the drug abuse problem and of those who are involved in the problem.

Collectively, these data systems have the capacity to provide not only assessments of both drug-using behaviors and their consequences but also information that serves to identify points in which interventions can take place, preventing drug-using populations from continuing these behaviors. Interventions that readily are suggested from these systems include domestic-interdiction approaches that cut or impede the distribution of drugs; universal prevention strategies that saturate the communities through schools, media, and the environment with anti-drug-use messages and with the implementation of drug-free policies, to prevent the initiation of drug use; prevention strategies that target the needs of those most vulnerable and least resistant to drugs in the communities; and treatment strategies for those already involved with drugs in the community as well as in institutions.

In this chapter, we describe a surveillance system designed to capture emerging new drug problems at the community level: the Community Epidemiology Work Group (CEWG). To fully illustrate the nature, structure, function, and relevance of the CEWG for community planning, we present its history and evolution. We demonstrate the experience of the CEWG in detecting serious emergent drug trends with three examples— methaqualone, crack, and cocaine "blunts"—and we present data on recent drug abuse patterns. Finally, we discuss the expansion of the concept of the CEWG to larger geographic areas, such as states, and, in recognition of the global nature of drug abuse, to other countries and continents.

THE EVOLUTION OF THE COMMUNITY EPIDEMIOLOGY WORK GROUP

The CEWG consists of researchers from 20 metropolitan areas in the United States, representing areas with sizable drug-abusing populations who have differential patterns of drug use. The participants are predominantly members of state or local governments or are university affiliated, and all have varied research training (e.g., epidemiology, medicine, statistics, public health, psychology, or other social science). Most important, these members are researchers and, as a function of their professional position, are knowledgeable about the drug abuse problem in their community. The CEWG meets semiannually in June and December, rotating sites so that each member has an opportunity to host the meeting. The members present their reports on local drug abuse practices, on the basis of data from drug abuse treatment programs, hospital emergency rooms, medical examiners' offices, police and correction reports, school surveys, or other community-based sources of information on drug abusers. The CEWG has just celebrated its 20th anniversary and is recognized as a source for the most recent issues that are confronting researchers in the field and public health workers.

The concept of a network of community experts as a mechanism for the exchange of information is not new. It has its origins in social psychology and is based on information theory. Psychologists such as Lewin (1958) and Bavelas (1950) have demonstrated the impact of differential patterns of communication on group behavior. Over the past 40 years, a body of scientific knowledge has accumulated regarding the impact of varying network structures on function, process, and outcome (Dexter & White, 1964; McGrath 1965; Schramm, 1966). Excellent examples of networks used in public health are those that focus on monitoring infectious diseases. Under the auspices of the World Health Organization, an international program for reporting infectious diseases, is a communication linkage of physicians in public and private delivery systems, to monitor global trends in certain infectious diseases so as to ascertain potential outbreaks of an epidemic. This concept stimulated the establishment of the CEWG in 1976 by the National Institute on Drug Abue (NIDA).

The model on which the CEWG is based originated in the Narcotics Treatment Administration as a way to develop synthetic estimates of the number of heroin users in the city of Washington, DC, so as to plan treatment services. The stigma of heroin use serves as a barrier for ascertaining estimates of the number of users, but in the early 1970s, an additional barrier was the lack of a standard definition of *heroin addiction*. A variety of techniques were developed during that time to make estimations both at the local and national levels. A number of studies suggested that the gross addict population rate could be as high as 8 per 1,000 residents (DuPont & Katon, 1971; Kozel, DuPont & Brown, 1972), and estimates for Washington, DC, ranged from 18,000 to 20,000 (DuPont & Piemme, 1972).

It was clear during this period that estimates of the prevalence of heroin use would require the use of indirect indicators, such as those related to the health and social consequences of heroin use and to the availability of heroin. Because these indicators consisted of data housed under a variety of unaffiliated service-delivery systems, networks had to be developed to integrate the data and to interpret the results of such integration. Through contact with each agency director, key informants were identified, and monthly meetings were established to share existing information. Monitoring in this way showed that as expected, there was an increase in heroin availability—as reflected by an increase in street-level purity and a decline in price, accompanied by an increase in heroin-related deaths and medical emergencies resulting from overdoses, and by an increase in property crime, in treatment admissions, and in the rate of heroin-positive urinalyses among arrestees.

The approach of using indicator data was then implemented in several national, city-based studies through the 1970s, particularly under the auspices of the White House Special Action Office for Drug Abuse Prevention. These methods assured the rapid conduct of the studies, and therefore the results, provided sufficient information on the changing patterns of heroin use in the country to be used in the formulation of policy (Greene, Kozel, & Appletree, 1975; Green, Kozel, Hunt, & Appletree, 1974). The demonstrated usefulness of this approach and its cost-efficiency led the director of the newly formed NIDA to establish a national community-based surveillance program in 1976.

Limitations of such an approach were recognized. First, the indicators that were used has an undefined relationship to the incidence and prevalence of drug use. Second, no baseline data were available for assessment of subsequent information. Third, because the community contexts in which the data were collected varied greatly, it was difficult to standardize across sites. So comparing across sites proved to be a challenge.

Sixteen cities were represented at the first meeting of the CEWG on November 19, 1976: Washington, DC, Boston, New York, Miami, Atlanta, Philadelphia, Chicago, Detroit, Denver, Minneapolis, San Antonio, Dallas, Phoenix, Seattle, Los Angeles, and San Francisco. These cities were selected because they were large metropolitan areas, had large resident populations, and represented the various regions of the country. They were also the sites for the majority of heroin users in the country, the major drug problem at that time. Participant researchers were those who had involvement in drug abuse studies, were knowledgeable not only about drug abuse but also about descriptive research and indicator methods of analyses and had local government connections. At this first meeting, there was consensus regarding the invaluable potential of the surveillance system, the need to go beyond heroin to include other drugs, and the recognition that standardization for data collection and analysis would be extremely difficult because of the lack of control over agencies that collected the data. Over time, however, standardization of definitions and concepts was achieved, and routine reporting formats that would allow trend analyses were developed.

Over the course of subsequent years, efforts to improve the quality of reporting were pursued. Common data elements and reporting formats were agreed on, by means of discussions and Delphi-type interviews. The latter is a formal group interview led by a directive interviewer with structured questions about specific topics. A publication format that provided both an overview of drug patterns in the cities and specific city-by-city descriptions evolved. Presentations by NIDA-funded researchers on such methodological issues as geoprocessing of data, use of medical examiners' reports, and drug use assessments at the community level served to enhance the research skills of CEWG members. Up until late 1978, all of the CEWG meetings were held in Washington, DC; however, in December 1978, the decision was made to rotate the location of the meeting, to familiarize each group member with all the cities and the contexts in which the city-based data were collected. In addition, the rotation of meeting sites allowed other researchers to become acquainted with the CEWG and allowed members to be made aware of ongoing research in the various cities.

DETECTION OF TRENDS OF DRUG ABUSE

Obviously, key to a drug abuse surveillance system is the capacity to detect emergent drug abuse trends. The tracking of these trends for the country requires a number of epidemiologic approaches. In reconstructing what we have learned from the CEWG, in conjunction with national data systems such as the Monitoring the Future Survey and the National Household Survey on Drug Abuse, we have attempted to develop a surveillance model that will enable policymakers to be ahead of a potential epidemic. Three retrospective reviews, focusing on CEWG information, illustrate how effective the CEWG has been in detecting potential new drug abuse problems: that of methaqualone, crack, cocaine and blunts.

Methaqualone

Methaqualone (also known as *Quaalude* and, in combination with an antihistamine, *Mandrax*) is a synthetically derived sedative that is unrelated to barbiturates, glutethimide, or cloral hydrate. Large doses of methaqualone have been found to cause convulsions and coma, and continued heavy use leads to dependence. Its abuse liability, its popularity on the streets, and its associated health problems have prompted its placement by the Drug Enforcement Administration (DEA) in Schedule I under the Controlled Substance Act, stipulating that a substance has no currently accepted medical use in the United States.

Methaqualone was identified in 1979 to be a major drug problem in Miami. It had been first noted among 1.6% of 1975 drug abuse treatment admissions and among 14 emergency room episodes. By 1979, 27% of treatment admissions and 864 emergency room episodes were associated with methaqualone. Its use was most prevalent among young White groups, and it was reportedly used with alcohol. By 1980, methaqualone was reported to be a drug problem in Atlanta, where it also was used with alcohol by young high school students who were coming to the attention of emergency room staff. In 1981, Atlanta reported methaqualone as the second most often mentioned drug in the emergency room, and by 1982, these mentions increased by 50%. Similar occurrences were noted in Detroit; Hudson County, NJ; New Orleans; San Diego; Saint Louis; Washington, DC; and, by 1989, New York. In response to these increases, the state of Florida reclassified methaqualone as a Schedule I drug, banning its medical use. This action was followed by the state of Illinois in January 1984 and by the DEA, for the nation, in April 1984. These actions were associated with declines in the availability of the drug and with its decreased use, as reflected in the indicator data for Miami, St. Louis, and San Francisco in 1983; Detroit, Los Angeles, Boston, and New Orleans in 1984; and Atlanta in 1985.

Crack Cocaine

Professionals in the drug abuse field had long believed that an epidemic of cocaine use was very unlikely to occur in the United States. Despite the recognized strongly reinforcing effects of cocaine, the cost of the drug had proved to be a barrier to widespread use. This was true until the early 1980s, when CEWG reports from 1983 through 1984 indicated that something was changing in patterns of cocaine use, although it was not clear in what form the cocaine was being used. Reports between December 1983 and December 1985 were more certain that a new drug pattern was spreading across the country. By December of 1983, all cities reported increases in cocaine use. Of particular significance were the changing characteristics of users from the more middle and upper classes to lower socioeconomic levels. There was also increased evidence that more people were smoking the drug in Boston, Chicago, Newark, Miami, New York, Minneapolis, and San Francisco. By June of 1984, 11 of the 18 cities represented at that CEWG meeting were reported as experiencing significant increases in cocaine-related emergency room episodes between 1982 and 1983 (e.g., Detroit, 116%; Los Angeles, 73%; Chicago, 45%; and Miami, 39%). Increases in the proportion of clients entering drug abuse treatment who reported cocaine as their primary abused drug also were seen in Saint Louis, 266%; Dallas, 50%; and New York, 42%. Subsequent meetings of the CEWG saw further increases in reported cocaine use among persons seeking emergency room and drug abuse treatment services. Patterns of use were changing; ethnographic evidence indicated that smoking of cocaine had been increasing and that cocaine was becoming more available and cheaper (Schnoll, Kerrigan, Kitchen, Daghestani, & Hansen, 1985; Siegel, 1985). These studies discovered that cocaine was being sold in rock form, was being smoked, and predominated the drug-using scene across the country. "Crack," "rock," or "hit" houses, where crack was sold and used, were observed in the inner cities. It was not until the late 1980s that the media would pick up on the crack epidemic, identified as early as 1983 by CEWG members. Data from the National Household Survey on Drug Abuse indicated that by 1985, 20 million persons had used cocaine at least once during their lifetime, with half of these using in the prior year alone (Abelson & Miller, 1985). During the 10-year period between 1975 and 1985, the emergency room episodes that mentioned cocaine from the Drug Abuse Warning Network (a national surveillance system), showed a sevenfold increase: from 10.4 to 75.4 per 100,000 visits (Adams, Gfroerer, Rouse, & Kozel, 1987).[3]

Blunts

The last example of the ability of the CEWG to detect a drug abuse trend is that of the use of blunts. Blunts are marijuana and other drugs (e.g., crack or phencyclidine [PCP]), which are placed in outer cigar wrappers and smoked. All surveillance indicators, as well as the Monitoring the Future Survey and the National Household Survey on Drug Abuse, had shown decreases in marijuana use beginning in the early 1980s. The first indication of a change in this pattern was seen in the reports from the December 1992 meeting of the CEWG, reflecting data for 1991. The first reports of blunt smoking came from the representatives of New York, Philadelphia, and Washington, DC. By June 1993, Miami, Minneapolis, and Dallas reported the use of blunts, and by December 1993, Chicago reported their use. Reports from the Monitoring the Future Survey began to show significant increases in marijuana use by 1991–1992, and the National Household Survey showed increases, but only among adolescents, in 1994.

RECENT DRUG ABUSE PATTERNS

Current membership in the CEWG is shown in Exhibit 1 and includes representatives from cities and states across the country. The most current report for the CEWG is from the December 1998 meeting. An effort has been made to issue an advance report within 2 to 4 weeks after the meeting, which is sent to people in key public policy and health positions and posted on the NIDA world wide web site (National Institute on Drug Abuse, December 1998). Subsequent to the advance report, two other reports are issued within 6 weeks of the meeting. The first of these reports consists of a summary of the 21-city/state presentations by drug

---

[3]The Drug Abuse Warning Network was initiated by the DEA to monitor emerging drug problems. It was transferred to the National Institute on Drug Abuse in 1981. Until 1989, it consisted of reports from a panel of emergency rooms in sentinel cities; however, in 1989, the reporting system was expanded to include a national probability sample of emergency rooms across the country.

EXHIBIT 1
City and State Membership in the Community
Epidemiology Work Group

Atlanta, GA	New York, NY
Baltimore, MD	Newark, NJ
Boston, MA	Philadelphia, PA
Chicago, IL	Phoenix, AZ
Denver, CO	Saint Louis, MO
Detroit, MI	San Diego, CA
Honolulu, HI	San Francisco, CA
Los Angeles, CA	Seattle, WA
Miami, FL	Texas
Minneapolis, MN	Washington, DC
New Orleans, LA	

category. The second, and longest, report consists of a summary of the information from each of the cities and states. In addition, a select number of reports from other countries and research reports from the host city are included.

In December 1998, there was a clear indication that the two of the four major categories of abused drugs, heroin and marijuana, were on the increase either nationally or regionally (National Institute on Drug Abuse, 1998) whereas cocaine, although still remaining at the highest level of use, was beginning to stabilize in 17 cities, and increase in 4 others. The use of methamphetamines, which not only had been increasing in the usual endemic areas, the West and Southwest (DEA, 1997), but also had begun to appear as a new problem in several key cities in the South and Midwest, seemed to be decreasing.

Cocaine

As mentioned above, cocaine emerged as a drug problem in the mid-1970s and as crack cocaine in the 1980s. It remains the predominant drug of abuse in the United States—particularly in the form of crack cocaine. Cocaine has been the drug most often mentioned in association with drug-related medical emergencies nationally in all but a few of the CEWG cities, where it is second only to heroin. Furthermore, cocaine is the leading drug problem mentioned by persons seeking drug abuse treatment. Found to be on the increase through the 1980s and 1990s, cocaine use seems to be stabilizing in New York, Newark, and New Orleans; and increasing in Chicago, Detroit, Minneapolis, and Phoenix; however, not one city has reported a decline in cocaine-use indicators. There appears to be an aging cohort of long-term crack cocaine users, with some emerging evidence of new crack users in several cities, such as Miami, New Orleans, and San Francisco. This consistent observation of changing patterns of crack use has prompted hypotheses that warrant investigation: (a) Crack use has declined among the less frequent users because use of crack has taken on a more negative image, (b) the long-term, more frequent users of crack are experiencing more adverse health consequences, (c) the quality of crack that is being sold is uneven, being mixed with other drugs that may have adverse side effects, (d) in general, the health of the aging crack user is deteriorating, and (e) cocaine users are shifting to the intranasal use of heroin.

Heroin

Although not as pervasive as cocaine, heroin is becoming a major emerging problem throughout the country with increases noted in 12 cities. Surveillance indicators, particularly in the Northeast and in some of the Midwestern and Western cities, show a trend in the popularity of heroin use among younger cohorts including teenagers. In a focus group held in Chicago, young people were asked about their changing use of drugs to heroin. They indicated that heroin was their drug of choice because they believed that in contrast to crack cocaine use, they could control their use of heroin and that it was a less expensive habit than cocaine because they did not need to use it as often to get a high. This group disparaged crack users and injecting heroin users (because the quality of heroin is high at this time, it is used most often intranasally rather than by injection).

The introduction of South American white powdered heroin in the 1990s in high purity levels (average purity is 60–70%), has had a major effect on the east coast cities. As a result of the high purity levels, this type of heroin is snorted, rather than injected. This pattern of use has become more prevalent particularly among younger populations in Washington, DC, Miami, Newark and New York City. Mexican black tar and brown powdered heroin dominate the west coast cities but recently have been reported in Atlanta, Chicago, Minneapolis, and Saint Louis. The purity level of the Mexican heroin is much lower than that of the South American with an average purity of 39%. Because the purity level is lower, users tend to inject rather than snort brown powdered heroin. Black tar heroin can not be snorted. Injecting drugs leads to increased health problems including sepsis and other infections such as HIV. "Crisscrossing" (i.e., crossing over from cocaine or crack use to heroin use) is increasingly being observed in users seen in drug abuse treatment. In a number of cities, either to respond to the negative attitudes to cocaine use or to establish a more diverse drug trade, cocaine dealers have begun to sell heroin. In conjunction with reports of increasing use of heroin, there have been reports of health problems associated with "contaminated" heroin. In the Northeast (i.e., New York, Baltimore, Newark, and Philadelphia), heroin has been cut with scopolamine—a belladonna derivative used to treat motion sickness—and in San Francisco, there has been an increase in necrotizing fasciitis (dead connective tissue) and wound botulism.

Marijuana

Marijuana use has been increasing among adolescents since the spring of 1991. Rates of marijuana use among emergency room and drug abuse treatment admissions continued to increase in 1997 and have leveled off in 1998. This trend appears to be occurring across the country, primarily among young men. The association of high rates of marijuana use in emergency rooms and drug abuse treatment has never been noted before. Increased reports from research on the harmful consequences of marijuana use have been found to be associated with increased potency of the psychoactive component, tetrahydrocannabinol, which may be one factor in accounting for these new observations. In addition, the methods of marijuana use have changed over time. As previously mentioned, marijuana-filled cigars called "blunts" or "vegas" have become popular among young men. These cigars often are laced with crack or PCP or other drugs, and smoking of these cigars is usually accompanied with alcohol use.

Methamphetamine

For a long time methamphetamine use has been endemic in the Western states, particularly in rural areas, and had been produced in small, local laboratories, in small quantities for known customers. For years, methamphetamine use has been the dominant drug problem in San Diego, with Honolulu and San Francisco also reporting it as a substantial problem. Over the past few years, representatives from Denver, Los Angeles, Minneapolis, Phoenix, and Seattle have reported increases in the use of methamphetamines. Increases noted in the indicators for methamphetamines in San Diego prompted the establishment of a Methamphetamine Strike Force within the CEWG, which noted the change from small-scale domestic production and distribution markets to large-scale manufacturing by organized groups of Mexican nationals and Mexican Americans. Trafficking routes have become more structured, following those for cocaine and heroin. Domestic, local forms of methamphetamines are being replaced by those produced in Mexico. However, in many areas of the country, local laboratories continue to produce methamphetamines, particularly in rural areas. Users are primarily White, and they snort, smoke, or inject the drugs. Use in Seattle has been found to be associated with the transmission of HIV among the city's gay and bisexual male populations, as a result of needle sharing and risky sexual behaviors. Despite the increases that have been noted, both the drug and its users have negative reputations on the streets.

Other Drugs

Other drugs reported in the indicator data that are considered to be emergent problems are "roofies," flunitrazepam (Rohypnol) in Miami, Texas, and Phoenix; herbal stimulants (Cloud 9 and Herbal Ecstasy) in New York; PCP in the Baltimore–Washington, DC area and New York; Ritalin and fentanyl in Boston; prescription codeine in Detroit; opium among the Minneapolis Southeast Asian community; and tramadol hydrochloride in Saint Louis.

STATEWIDE NETWORKS

Clearly, the concept of the CEWG is not restricted to community- or local-level analysis, nor is it limited to drug-abusing behaviors. Because drug abuse patterns and trends vary not only between communities but also within communities, a network of local researchers is viewed as a cost-effective method for cities and states to monitor drug abuse trends and identify emerging drugs of abuse. Beginning in the mid-1980s, NIDA initiated a program of technical support to assist individual states in the development of State Epidemiology Work Groups. The state-based work groups are composed of selected researchers and other officials from drug abuse offices or from key geographic areas of the state, usually but not necessarily limited to the more populated regions or large cities. Similar to the CEWG, the state network meetings provide an opportunity for participants to discuss drug abuse trends in their local areas and to explore the implications of findings for local and state policy, particularly as it relates to prevention and treatment services. NIDA's involvement in the effort is to provide technical assistance to states in initiating the program, by sponsoring and arranging the first meeting. States then can decide whether the model has utility and can assume responsibility for arranging and conducting subsequent meetings. This program has had immediate use in many states. Other states have incorporated the work groups into their ongoing activities and have developed model programs around them. Still others have decided to expand the concept further and explore the development of even more locally based epidemiology work groups.

Furthermore, two networks targeting other public health problems have been established, one on diabetes, by Dr. William Wood of the University of Hawaii, and the other on violence by the Center for Substance Abuse Prevention of the Substance Abuse and Mental Health Services Administration.

REFLECTIONS OF THE GLOBAL NATURE OF DRUG ABUSE

As early as 1981, the global nature of drug abuse and the porousness of national boundaries with regard to changing patterns of drug abuse made it essential that a network of international surveillance be developed. Since 1981, the CEWG has included a component of epidemiologist and health scientists from selected countries and international organizations. CEWG members also assist international colleagues in developing applied epidemiology and ethnography research programs. As a result of this effort, regional drug abuse surveillance programs based on the CEWG model have been established in Europe; Central America, South America, and the Caribbean; and East and South Asia; and national programs have been established in Canada, Mexico, South Africa, and Spain. Similar networks are under development or are being considered in a number of countries and regions of the world (see Exhibit 2 for specifics). With the continued need to share information across countries, the International Epidemiology Work Group on Drug Abuse (IEWG) was formed in 1994.

The IEWG has as its mission the linkage of national and regional surveillance systems for the exchange and interpretation of information about drug use patterns to enhance the international monitoring of drug trends, to identify emerging public health issues and problems and to facilitate national and international research.

DISSEMINATION OF REPORTS

Being sure that the outcomes of the CEWG meetings are disseminated to policymakers and community leaders is the task of the CEWG as well as NIDA. The CEWG members are responsible for sharing their information and the reports of the meetings with their agencies as well as members of their city work groups, which include representatives of social, health, and law enforcement organizations. NIDA has developed other means for disseminating the outcomes of the meetings. Within a few days of the meetings, a 2-page summary is posted on the NIDA web page. Subsequently, an advanced report, which is an executive summary of the meeting, is made available to the heads of key federal agencies as well as to members of Congress. Finally, two volumes, one reporting the outcome of the meeting by drug category and the other by city, are published and disseminated to the above groups as well as to policymakers and program directors at the state and local levels. The availability of these documents is posted on the NIDA web page, and they are disseminated through the National Clearinghouse for Alcohol and Drug Information.

EXHIBIT 2
Countries Currently Involved in Networks

Europe	Asia	North America	Central & South America	Africa
Austria	Bangladesh	Canada	Costa Rica	South Africa
Belgium	Cambodia	Mexico	Dominican Republic	
Bulgaria	India	United States	El Salvador	
Croatia	Indonesia		Guatemala	
Cyprus	Korea		Honduras	
Czech Republic	Laos		Nicaragua	
Denmark	Malaysia		Panama	
Estonia	Myanmar			
Finland	Nepal			
France	Pakistan			
Germany	People's Republic of China			
Greece	Philippines			
Hungary	Singapore			
Ireland	Thailand			
Italy	Vietnam			
Luxembourg				
Malta				
The Netherlands				
Norway				
Poland				
Portugal				
Romania				
Russia				
Slovakia				
Slovenia				
Spain				
Sweden				
Switzerland				
Turkey				
United Kingdom				

CONCLUSION

It is evident that the CEWG serves a significant function in detecting emergent drug use patterns. The linking of the results of the reports from the CEWG to action at the local level has been dependent on city-based members, and over time, these members have become experienced in notifying key policymakers. Much needs to be developed in matching actions with CEWG observations. The consistency of reporting and the documentation of trends, as presented above, serve to reinforce the validity and credibility of the reporting network. The future work of the group will be to specify criteria for assessing emergent problems (e.g., at what point was it clear that crack would become a serious problem in the country?) and for determining a course of interventions to prevent an emergent problem from becoming a major public health tragedy.

REFERENCES

Abelson, H., & Miller, J. (1985). A decade of trends in cocaine use in the household population. In N. J. Kozel & E. H. Adams (Eds.), *Cocaine use in America: Epidemiologic and clinical perspectives* (NIDA Research Monograph No. 61, DHHS Publication No. ADM 85-1414, pp. 35–49). Rockville, MD: National Institute on Drug Abuse.

Adams, E. H., Gfroerer, J. C., Rouse, B. A., & Kozel, N. J. (1987). Trends in prevalence and consequences of cocaine use. *Advances in Alcohol and Substance Abuse, 6*(2), 49–72.

Bachman, J. G., Johnston, L. D., & O'Malley, P. M. (1988). Explaining the recent decline in marijuana use: Differentiating the effects of perceived risks, disapproval, and general lifestyle factors. *Journal of Health and Social Behavior, 29*, 92–112.

Bachman, J. G., Johnston, L. D., & O'Malley, P. M. (1990). Explaining the recent decline in cocaine use among young adults: Further evidence that perceived risks and disapproval lead to reduced drug use. *Journal of Health and Social Behavior, 31*, 173–184.

Bavelas, A. (1950). Communication patterns in task-oriented groups. *Journal of Acoustical Society of America, 22*, 725–730.

Dexter, L. A., & White, D. M. (Eds.). (1964). *People, society, and mass communications*. New York: Free Press.

Drug Enforcement Administration. (July, 1997). The NNICC report 1996: The supply of illicit drugs to the United States. DEA-97024, 45–54.

DuPont, R. L., & Katon, R. N. (1971). Development of a heroin-addiction treatment program. *Journal of the American Medical Association, 216*, 1320–1324.

DuPont, R. L., & Piemme, T. E. (1972). Estimation of the number of narcotic addicts in an urban area. *Medical Annals of the District of Columbia, 42*(7), 323–326.

Greene, M. H., Kozel, N. J., & Appletree, R. L. (1975, January). *An epidemiologic study of heroin use patterns and trends in four cities on the Mexican–American border* (Special Action Office for Drug Abuse Prevention Monograph Series A, No. 6). Washington, DC: Executive Office of the President, Special Action Office for Drug Abuse Prevention.

Greene, M. H., Kozel, N. J., Hunt, L. G., & Appletree, R. L. (1974, October). *An assessment of the diffusion of heroin abuse to medium-sized American cities.* (Special Action Office for Drug Abuse Prevention Monograph Series A, No. 5). Washington, DC: Executive Office of the President, Special Action Office for Drug Abuse Prevention.

Kozel, N. J., DuPont, R. L., & Brown, B. S. (1972). Narcotics and crime: A study of narcotic involvement in an offender population. *International Journal of the Addicitions, 7,* 443–450.

Last, J. M. (1995). *A dictionary of epidemiology.* New York: Oxford University Press.

Lewin, K. (1958). Group decision and social change. In E. Maccoby, T. M. Newcomb, & E. L. Hartley (Eds.), *Readings in social psychology* (pp. 197–211). New York: Holt.

McGrath, J. E. (1965). *Social psychology: A brief introduction.* New York: Holt, Rinehart & Winston.

Musto, D. F. (1987). *The American disease: Origins of narcotic control.* New York: Oxford University Press.

National Institute on Drug Abuse. (1998, December). *Epidemiologic trends in drug abuse: Advance report—December 1998.* Bethesda, MD: author.

Schnoll, S., Kerrigan, J., Kitchen, S., Daghestani, A., & Hansen, T. (1985). Characteristics of cocaine abusers presenting for treatment. In N. J. Kozel & E. H. Adams (Eds.), *Cocaine use in America: Epidemiologic and clinical perspectives* (NIDA Research Monograph No. 61, DHHS Publication No. ADM 85-1414, pp. 171–181). Rockville, MD: National Institute on Drug Abuse.

Schramm, W. (1966). Information theory and mass communiation. In B. Berelson & M. Janowitz (Eds.), *Reader in public opinion and communication* (pp. 712–732). New York: Free Press.

Siegel, R. (1985). New patterns of cocaine use: Changing doses and routes. In N. J. Kozel & E. H. Adams (Eds.), *Cocaine use in America: Epidemiologic and clinical perspectives* (NIDA Research Monograph No. 61, DHHS Publication No. ADM 85-1414, pp. 204–222). Rockville, MD: National Institute on Drug Abuse.

3

THE IMPACT OF PUBLIC ATTITUDES ON DRUG ABUSE RESEARCH IN THE TWENTIETH CENTURY

DAVID F. MUSTO

It is comforting to think that research on a scientific problem like, say, drug dependence is self-contained; that a problem is identified and studied experimentally and the results presented independent of bias and public pressure. We see one more brick added to the rising edifice of science. It may be comforting to think like that, but not very accurate when applied to much of twentieth-century drug abuse research.

The political and cultural character of the drug abuse issue, especially in the United States, places research in a whirlwind of emotions and dogmas. Scientific research is not sheltered from the storm; rather than being isolated, it is an integral part of the culture it inhabits. Researchers, after all, share their cultural reference points with society at large, and their research is funded through decisions made by others who are subject to the same influences. Furthermore, the results of the research are interpreted against the background of deeply held beliefs regarding human nature, the

This study was supported by the National Institute on Drug Abuse (NIDA) Grant 1 K05 DA00219-01.

appropriate means to control behavior, and—more closely connected with the drug issue—common assumptions about links between certain drugs and ethnic minorities, hostile foreign nations, and even feared locations, like the inner city.

A personal reminiscence illustrates this phenomenon. In 1973, I met Dr. Nathan Eddy, perhaps the leading American expert on drug research in mid-century, for what was meant to be the beginning of a series of discussions. Unfortunately, he suddenly died a few days later. Dr. Eddy was anxious to talk about what had been for decades a small world of drug abuse research in which he had been a central figure since the 1920s. He volunteered a vignette to indicate the constraints under which scientists had worked. It was while working on substitutes for cocaine anesthesia that he found a particularly useful one he said he had to report very carefully. He believed that if he sent in reports comparing it directly with cocaine, it would be rejected as a substitute because to a nonscientist it would seem too similar to the feared stimulant. Therefore, he omitted any cocaine comparison and just described the effects of the new drug, because otherwise he feared a useful substance would never see the light of day. This anecdote from Dr. Eddy shows how aware scientists were of the cultural context in which they worked and the limitations that context imposed.

EARLY CLASHES BETWEEN SCIENCE AND THE PUBLIC

During Dr. Eddy's career, the United States had reached a consensus on drugs, and he knew, as did almost all Americans, what that consensus was: Opioids and cocaine were so dangerous that even small doses could lead to addiction, cure of addiction was rare, and the health professions were among the most careless in handling these drugs. Except for certain specified medical uses—and even then one had to be extremely careful so as not to unintentionally produce dependence—opioids and cocaine had no legitimate uses whatsoever.

How different were American attitudes in the nineteenth century! For a while, cocaine was considered an "All-American" tonic, ideal for baseball players (Metcalf's CocaWine [Advertisement], 1889), and opium in reasonable doses seemed to expand "the whole moral and intellectual nature" (Wood, 1868, p. 712) of the user. As use of the drugs continued, fear came to replace the initial praise for the powerful, mood-altering substances. Concern reached higher and higher levels until the stimulating effects of cocaine were no longer thought productive or positive but, rather, uncontrollable and destructive. Likewise, falling into opiate addiction at the hands of an incompetent physician or as a result of youthful experimentation became a specter of misery and death that haunted the public.

The consequent condemnation of these drugs left no room for scientific doubt or moral temporizing.

Can a beginning be established for the conflict between science, which rarely speaks in absolutes, and the unqualified popular rejection of drugs? The nineteenth century is a reasonable origin for most controversies about epidemics, for it was then that science brought us the ingredients of the modern drug problem. In the first decade of the century, morphine was isolated from crude opium; in mid century, cocaine was isolated from coca leaves; and at the close of the century, heroin was commercially introduced by the Bayer Company. To these achievements of modern chemistry can be added barbiturates, amphetamines, and, more recently, LSD and a multitude of molecular modifications of stimulants and depressants. Although crude opium, coca leaves, peyote, and cannabis have caused alarm just by themselves, it is the extraction of purified active ingredients and the compulsive need to take them that have been the hallmark of the most disturbing drug use; here, scientific research has had a central role from the beginning.

One of the earliest clashes between public opinion and scientific research occurred when the fear of drug use in the United States reached great heights in the period around World War I. The antidrug position generally opposed opioid maintenance, and popular literature as well as government publications warned that drug taking was a direct incentive to criminal behavior. The federal government moved to end opioid maintenance the day the Harrison Anti-Narcotic Act came into force, March 1, 1915. Although this effort, aimed at the health professions, was blocked by a Supreme Court decision in 1916 (*U.S. v. Jin Fury Moy*), 3 years later, the Court approved severe restrictions on maintenance unless there was a practical medical reason for it, such as terminal cancer pain (Musto, 1999, pp. 131–132).

TREATMENT OF OPIATE ADDICTION

These legal restrictions on opioid maintenance led to a dramatic collision between scientific research and public opinion, as expressed in the law. Central to this conflict was Dr. Ernest Bishop of New York City. Dr. Bishop relied on research and his own clinical experience to conclude that there was a fundamental change in the physiology of those addicted to opioids. This change required the kind of maintenance that had been declared illegal.

> Any one—whether of lowered nervous, mental and moral will, or a giant of mental or physical resistance—will, if opiates are administered in continuing doses over a sufficient length of time, develop some form of this symptom-complex. [The most likely] physical mechanism of

narcotic drug addiction-disease [is] an autogenous antidotal or antitoxic substance. (Bishop, 1920, p. 39)

He expanded this thought through reference to recent research and concluded as follows:

> A hypothetical antidotal antitoxic substance, manufactured by the body as a protection against the toxic effects of continued administration of an opiate drug, will therefore explain the well-known development of tolerance and immunity in these cases, and will account for the violent physical withdrawal signs. In a word, it will explain the disease fundamentals on a definite physical basis. (Bishop, 1920, p. 42)

Dr. Bishop explained that in addiction, the antidotal toxic substance becomes the poison and "the narcotic drug itself has become simply the antidote demanded for its control" (Bishop, 1920, p. 42). This explained what he found to be the "mathematical exactness with which the minimum daily need can be estimated. . . . In exact proportion as the drug of addiction is present in the body to neutralize or oppose some antidotal poison, is the patient free from withdrawal symptoms and from physical craving for the narcotic drug" (Bishop, 1920, p. 43).

Bishop condemned specific cures for addiction, which often made use of belladonna, scopolamine, and similar substances to counteract withdrawal symptoms (Musto, 1999, pp. 111–112). Still, Bishop was quite vague as to how he would detoxify an addict, although he did hold out this end point as the desired result of treatment. In the meantime, he declared the following:

> I do not hesitate to state that, until we are prepared . . . to skillfully and competently handle the stage of final withdrawal to assured successful issue, it is much wiser to supply the addict who is not a public menace the drug of his addiction to the extent of his physical needs, and to teach him how to use the drug of addiction in such a way that he will maintain his physical and economic efficiency. (Bishop, 1920, p. 70)

Bishop wrote these views in *The Narcotic Drug Problem*, a little book published in New York in 1920. Less than a year earlier, however, the Supreme Court in *Webb et al. v. U.S.* (1919) and *U.S. v. Doremus* (1919) had ruled out simple addiction maintenance such as Bishop advocated and had declared that any prescription that purported to provide an opiate indefinitely for an addict's accustomed use was not a legal prescription. The Court concluded that to call "such an order for the use of morphine a physician's prescription would be so plain a perversion of meaning that no discussion of the subject is required" (*Webb et al. v. U.S.*, p. 96). Yet Bishop continued to discuss the subject and to argue against the form of narcotic control adopted in 1919. Bishop argued that "any law which renders it more difficult or impossible for a physician to conscientiously and rationally meet ... the indications of narcotic drug disease, should meet from the medical profession with a united and honest attempt at its modification" (Bishop, 1920, p. 101).

Perhaps by coincidence, the month after his book appeared, Bishop was indicted for violation of the federal antinarcotic laws. As the U.S. attorney in New York City explained it to the attorney general,

> after arresting a number of physicians it was found that Dr. Bishop was one of the leading narcotic practitioners in this part of the country. He had written and lectured on the subject of narcotic drug addiction and was the guiding spirit in a society for the study of drug addiction. Three former members of that society have been prosecuted. One was acquitted and two were convicted. ... It was found that Dr. Bishop was looked up to as an authority for the ambulatory method of practice by many physicians who engaged in it. An investigation of his own activities followed and the present indictment resulted. He has never had the large number of patients that many of the other narcotic practitioners had ... [but] there was no essential difference in the method. (Hayward, 1922)

Bishop was caught up in a campaign that had begun in 1919 to arrest physicians and pharmacists based on the *Webb* and *Doremus* decisions. In this effort, Bishop's prestige and views stood in the way of convictions. A chemist working for the City of New York conveniently concluded research that seemed to establish that addicted animals produced no morphine-neutralizing factor; a few years later, his research disproved the existence of a toxin allegedly produced in addicted animals (Pellini & Greenfield, 1920, 1924). Although this research seems to have been correct in its results, a far broader conclusion was drawn by the opponents of the theory of addiction disease: Opioid addiction was not in any way physical, but functional or psychological. If addiction was a disease that required indefinite maintenance to keep the addict in physiological balance, the government's strategy to bring addiction under control would be severely undercut, especially in jury trials.

Dr. Bishop believed that scientific evidence was on his side, but his treatment based on this belief had become illegal. The controversy over claims for an indefinite or permanent physiological alteration that would require maintenance seems to have exerted a constricting effect on research later conducted by the Public Health Service at the Lexington research center. In 1929, when the National Research Council established the Committee on Problems of Drug Dependence, they understandably chose to follow a safe route—the search for a nonaddictive analgesia, a research path that would not conflict with the antinarcotic laws of the nation (Eddy, 1973).

What happended to Dr. Bishop? When he was first indicted, expressions of outrage came from a scattering of leading physicians, newspapers, magazines, and public figures. In June 1923, the government dropped charges against the pharmacist who had been indicted as a conspirator with Dr. Bishop, but not those against Dr. Bishop. Friends wrote long letters to prominent people to try to get his charges dropped; these letters grew more urgent when Dr. Bishop was confined to bed with angina in February 1923 —3 years after the indictment. He was now in reduced circumstances, still maintaining he had done nothing wrong and strongly protesting that he was not a "script doctor," (a physician who freely wrote perscriptions— "scripts"—for addicts in order to make a profit) but a responsible clinician. Finally, in 1925, 5 years after his indictment (but no trial), the attorney general of the United States, Harlan Stone, soon to become a Supreme Court justice, agreed to drop the case on the grounds that Dr. Bishop was too ill to come to trial (Donovan, 1925). Dr. Bishop died in 1927 at the age of 50.

SUPPRESSING OPINIONS: THE LAGUARDIA COMMITTEE

Dr. Bishop persisted in his scientific position regarding toxins—which was eventually refuted—and paid quite a price for it. On the other hand, a position could be reasonably well grounded and still cause a lot of trouble when it conflicted with established opinion on drugs. In January 1939, Mayor LaGuardia of New York City appointed a committee to look into the question of marijuana's harmfulness. The Federal Bureau of Narcotics cooperated and provided the marijuana for study. The committee's report, *The Marihuana Problem in the City of New York*, was published in 1944, (Mayor's Committee on Marihuana, 1944). The report took a more relaxed view of marijuana than the one presented by the Narcotics Bureau. The reaction in Washington was furious. Narcotics Commissioner Harry J. Anslinger bitterly denounced the book as damaging to the nation's effort to repress marijuana use. Attacks on the LaGuardia committee included a sharply critical editorial in the *Journal of the American Medical Association*, reading suspiciously like Anslinger's prose ("Marihuana Problems," 1945). The committee's work, which would not seem very unusual today, was pretty well suppressed. Anslinger later spoke of his disappointment with the committee. He felt double-crossed because he had given the researchers the marijuana that was used in their work. "We never gave anyone any more after that," he said ruefully (H. J. Anslinger, personal communication, 1970).

Bishop and the Laguardia committee illustrate that scientific work in the drug abuse area can lead to difficulty when it is out of tune with broader, strongly held, and widely accepted views. A more common phenomenon involves pressure on scientific work to affirm widely held beliefs: harmony rather than conflict.

Broad attitudinal shifts seem to have powerfully affected cannabis research. Results of marijuana research in the 1930s, even that considered the least alarming at the time, were pretty bloodcurdling. It was hard to find a kind word. On the other hand, the 1960s research could not seem to find anything wrong with cannabis. Dr. Walter Bromberg, an active researcher on cannabis, wrote several of the least alarming studies in the 1930s and 1940s, arguing that cannabis use in itself was not a cause of crime (Bromberg, 1934, 1939; Bromberg & Rogers, 1946). Meeting accidentally at a conference in the mid-1970s, he and I chatted about cannabis, and he related something quite remarkable. He said that in the 1930s, he had regarded cannabis as a releaser of inhibition, because he regularly saw it cause impulsive actions. Forty years later, he was treating people for cannabis problems, but it seemed to him that cannabis caused the very opposite of impetuous activity: It led rather to relaxed, reflective states. He felt it was all very strange. He certainly had made a rare observation. How many researchers live through two eras of contrasting views about such a controversial topic as drugs—and how many are frank enough to admit they saw the same subject so very differently during those two times? More important, Bromberg's clinical views on marijuana changed as society became more relaxed about the drug and its dangers, even if this process apparently was not a conscious one on the part of the researcher.

ANTIALCOHOL SENTIMENT AND THE STRUGGLE FOR UNBIASED ALCOHOL RESEARCH

The interplay of popular and scientific opinion is most clear in the area of alcohol research. The alcohol problem has recurrently affected American law and social policy. The United States has had two eras marked by a peak of legal prohibition of alcohol. The first occurred in the 1850s, when about a third of Americans lived under state alcohol prohibition; the second lasted from 1920 through 1933, when the entire nation lived under federal prohibition (Musto, 1996). One might call those 13 years a form of "alcohol decriminalization," because neither drinking nor even purchasing it was illegal, but the importation, manufacture, and sale for beverage purposes were illegal. Furthermore, alcohol was available by prescription, so to be precise, it was regulated not prohibited.

However one describes these curbs on alcohol use, a large portion of the public wanted them. Neither prohibition at the state level in the nineteenth century nor national prohibition earlier this century was imposed by trickery; they came about because of intense fear of alcohol's individual and social effects. The belief in a safe threshold of alcohol use faded under an onslaught of real and pseudo science, emotional public campaigns, and single-issue politics. Even the smallest amount of alcohol was thought dangerous because it did at least a little damage and could lead to further drinking and start the experimenter down the road to alcoholism.

Ordinary science, the kind found in peer-reviewed journals, supported the concern over alcohol, especially when a fetus or young child was involved. Researchers studied animals and found that alcohol had a deleterious effect on offspring of mice, rats, and guinea pigs. This supported other studies that presented evidence that the children of drinkers had more personality troubles, less intelligence, and more problems at school (Warner & Rosett, 1975).

Although the prohibition amendment to the Constitution was ratified in January 1919—to take effect a year later—the run-up to the amendment was marked by decades of growing antialcohol agitation and shifting public sentiment. State after state restricted alcohol years before national prohibition. Canada experienced a similar powerful campaign against alcohol. A national plebiscite was held in 1898, in which the vote for prohibition was just over 52%. It was overwhelmingly supported in Ontario but even more overwhelmingly opposed in Quebec, and no government action followed the close vote. By 1907, however, Prince Edward Island had gone dry, and by 1916, Saskatchewan, Alberta, Ontario, Manitoba, and Nova Scotia were legally dry. Even Quebec, with its high percentage of Catholic population—traditionally unsympathetic to prohibition—briefly experienced alcohol restriction in 1918 (Smart & Ogborne, 1986).

In Canada, the McGill University economist and consummate humorist Stephen Leacock found himself confused as Canadians and Americans changed their image of alcohol—one of his favorite consumables. Leacock complained in 1918 that

> something is happening, I regret to find, to the world in which we used to live [. . . .] I am being left behind. Take, for example, the case of alcohol. That, at least, is what it is called now. There were days when we called it Bourbon whiskey and Tom Gin, and when the very name of it breathed romance. That time is past. The poor stuff is now called alcohol, and none so low that he has a good word for it. . . . Alcohol is doomed; it is going; it is gone. Yet when I think of a hot Scotch on a winter evening, or a Tom Collins on a summer morning, or a gin Rickey beside a tennis court, or a stein of beer on a bench beside a bowling green—I wish somehow we could prohibit the use of alcohol and merely drink beer and whiskey and gin as we used to. (Leacock, 1918, p. 200–201)

In the American and Canadian battles against alcohol, science was the authority to which temperance forces appealed. One of the most prominent sections in both the Canadian and United States' Women's Christian Temperance Unions (WCTU) was the Department of Scientific Temperance Instruction. This department gathered information, worked to require mandatory antialcohol courses in schools, and also strongly influenced the content of the temperance textbooks used in those courses. By 1901, every American state required temperance instruction. Science, as it appeared in the WCTU-approved texts, was colorful, extreme, and distorted—the overall message being that any alcohol consumption was extremely dangerous and, if continued, could be disastrous to the body. The Committee of Fifty, a group of prominent American authorities, criticized the WCTU for its distortions, but the head of the Department of Scientific Temperance Instruction, Mary Hunt, saw the purpose of temperance education as more than a simple information campaign; in fact, it should "produce trained haters of alcohol to pour a whole Niagara of ballots upon the saloon" (McClary, 1984, p. 22).

Putting aside the WCTU's extreme statements, for example, that most beer drinkers die of dropsy, one finds that a massive amount of research then concluded that drinking had bad effects not only on the drinker and his or her life, family, and friends but even on the next generation through alcohol's effect on the fetus. There were studies showing that children of drinkers had reduced mental ability. A 1905 survey of schoolchildren in New York City showed that 53% of children of drinking parents were "dullards," whereas only 10% of 13,523 children of abstainers were "dullards" (MacNicholl, 1907). A 1916 study of families showed that alcoholism in a given generation was followed in the next two to three generations by epilepsy, imbecility, stillbirth, infant death, chorea, and tremor (Gordon, 1916).

Evidence suggesting that alcohol affected the germ cells came from studies of animals. They indicated that alcohol not only could damage the developing fetus, especially in its early stages of development, but also could permanently change what we would call the DNA pattern, so that damage in one generation would be transmitted to later generations. One scientist who provided this worrisome information was Dr. Charles Stockard, Professor of Anatomy at Cornell Medical School. In 1916, he reported his conclusion, after a study of guinea pigs, that

> the experiments show the hereditary transmission through several generations of conditions resulting from an artificially induced change in the germ cells of one generation by treating them with alcohol. (Stockard, 1916, p. 403)

Stockard's research was taken up by persons dealing with humans and was quickly applied. A New York pediatrician wrote the next year on "Disease Conditions in Older Babies That Can Be Attributed to Prenatal Influences":

> This work of Stockard and other laboratory workers and the observations quoted from clinicians would lead us to believe that cases of retarded development in older children, nervous and irritable conditions, epilepsy, and the various forms of infantilism and idiocy, are in

many cases the result of alcoholism in one or both of the parents before conception or possibly of alcoholism in the grandparents or great-grandparents. (Freeman, 1917, p. 462)

A contrary position was presented, most notably by the biometrician Karl Pearson, who studied schoolchildren and their parents, among other subjects, and concluded that parental alcohol use was not linked to defects in their offspring (Elderton & Pearson, 1910). Needless to say, the vast majority of writers on the subject attacked him, and even John Maynard Keynes wrote a refutation of Pearson's methods in the *Journal of the Royal Statistical Society* (Keynes, 1910, 1911).

A second doubter was Henry H. Goddard, the renowned director of research at the Vineland Training School for Feeble-minded Boys and Girls in New Jersey. Strongly disagreeing that alcoholism was a cause of feeble-mindedness, he was surprised "that anyone could have reasoned so falsely" (Goddard, 1916, p. 442). Goddard found that the retardation observed in the families he studied could be accounted for by heredity and accidents, including disease in the child and mother (p. 445). Goddard had made a famous study of the Kallikak family, a large group of related persons who were marked by retardation, antisocial behavior, and poverty (Goddard, 1912). He had concluded that here too the cause was heredity that per-petuated feeblemindedness over several generations. His research bolstered the Supreme Court decision in 1927 that permitted sterilization of the mentally defective because, as Supreme Court Justice Oliver Wendell Holmes remarked, "three generations of imbeciles are enough" (*Buck v. Bell*, 274 US 200, 207).

The general attitude of writers on alcohol in the era just before na-tional prohibition was summed up by Dr. Alfred Gordon, Professor of Phys-iology at Jefferson Medical School, when, in 1911, he warned that alcoholism

> leads to a degeneration not only of the individual, but also of the species, to depopulation; it is dangerous to society as it produces a slow and progressive deterioration of the individual and an intellectual and physical sterility of the race. (Gordon, 1911, p. 98)

This is echoed in a social scientist's warning from 1913:

> To sociologists it is evident that the question of maternal inebriety is one of national importance, for many women fail to realize that alcohol taken in small amounts, if taken every day, may have serious results. (Irwell, 1913, p. 114)

Looking back at these claims made in the first two decades of this century, one can see that the language may differ from how people today might express the same thoughts and policies, but the content bears a strong similarity to today's concern over the recently named fetal alcohol syndrome. One can note a familiar worry over a pregnant woman's consumption of small amounts of alcohol, especially in the first trimester, when the nervous system is in the process of rapid development.

Consider some recent studies that reflect the worries of 80 years ago. One study, published in 1990, studied women whose drinking habits were considered moderate, but whose children at the age of 7 years had an IQ estimated to be 7 points lower than the control group. This suggested to the authors that even moderate drinking could cause measurable and persistent deficits (Streissguth, Barr, & Sampson, 1990). From studies like this, the *New York Times* framed a headline that read "Lasting Costs for Child Are Found From a Few Early Drinks" (1989). Another study from the *Journal of the American Medical Association* in 1991 reported on fetal alcohol syndrome (FAS) among adolescents and older persons. Their mothers were often chronic alcoholics, so this was not a question of social drinking. The cost to society for caring for these affected persons was estimated to be $1.2 million in a lifetime. The incidence of FAS ranged from 1 in 700 in Seattle to as high as 1 in 8 in a British Columbia Indian village. The authors concluded that "gestational exposure to alcohol can cause a wide spectrum of disabilities that have lifelong physical, mental, and behavioral implications" (Streissguth et al., 1991, p. 1967).

Numerous studies implicate alcohol, even in moderation, for causing enduring intellectual and social deficits, sometimes so catastrophic that a person is fated to become a ward of society. A study published in 1995 in the Archives of Pediatric and Adolescent Medicine has even revised Goddard's (1912) above-mentioned findings about the Kallikak family. It now seems that after all it was alcohol that caused the Kallikaks' terrible outcome. Armed with the knowledge of FAS, Karp, Qazi, Moller, Angelo, and Davis (1995) examined evidence (e.g., records and photographs) Goddard had collected and came to the conclusion that it "confirms the associations of parental alcoholism with mental retardation in childhood and with infant mortality" (p. 47). Even the exceptions of 80 years ago, then, are being posthumously converted into support of alcohol's effects on the fetus.

The first two decades of the 20th century and what will soon be the last two decades share a common view of the effect of alcohol on the fetus. The two eras share other characteristics, one of the most important being a confidence in the biological basis of human behavior. One aspect of this faith in the first period was called *eugenics*. The goal of eugenics was to devise ways in which the better, more productive physiologies could be promoted and the less desirable reduced. The quality individuals would be increased through, say, fertile marriages of good stock, whereas the undesirable stock would be curbed through sterilization.

Another characteristic of this century's margins is a strong condemnation of dangerous substances. The Canadian Opium and Drug Act was passed in 1911; 3 years later the American Harrison Act, aimed at opiates and cocaine, was enacted (Erickson, Adalf, Murray, & Smart 1987, p. 18). In 1919, the American prohibition amendment was adopted. Moving to this end of the century, the 1986 and 1988 U.S. anti-drug-abuse acts established severe drug penalties. We have not heard any advocates for prohibition recently, but a strong temperance spirit has led to raised drinking ages, warning labels on all alcoholic beverages, and more severe drunk-driving penalties. Although we have not gone as far as to prohibit the smoking of cigarettes, as was done about 1900 by 14 American states, the antitobacco spirit nevertheless is strong and getting stronger (Tate, 1989).

Scientific research at both the beginning and the end of the twentieth century has been, therefore, harmonious with popular antipathy toward alcohol. Even more than supporting public opinion, scientific research has intensified general concern about infants, schoolchildren, older truants, the feebleminded, and generations yet unborn, all of whom may be cursed by the use of alcohol.

Now let us turn to the time when that antialcohol attitude was rejected. When prohibition was repealed in 1933, the process was a swift one. The arguments advanced by those who wanted continued control of alcohol disintegrated under scorn and ridicule. Extreme claims about alcohol's dangers were laughed into silence. The once formidable WCTU faded (but did not vanish); the Anti-Saloon League, once the most powerful single-issue lobby in the United States, was no more.

What happened to scientific research on alcohol? It continued, not at the rate of earlier decades, but it did go on. Most telling, the research began to support the new, less anxious view of alcohol. Dr. Stockard continued his research, but his conclusions now harmonized with the new vision of alcohol. Regarding animal embryo studies, he wrote the following in 1932 as repeal of prohibition was imminent:

> What do we know of the nature of alcohol action on embryonic development? ... In sufficient concentrations we have found that it is effective, but such alcohol concentrations as are necessary to directly effect [sic] the development of lower animals are far in excess of the possible alcohol content of human blood compatible with human survival.... Results from these experiments on the embryos of lower animals justify only the conclusion—that if comparisons with human embryos are possible[—]they indicate that the content of alcohol in human blood is fortunately never sufficiently high to present a danger to the developing embryo. (Stockard, 1932, p. 111)

This was just the beginning of a new authoritative view of alcohol and the fetus that would dominate teaching and advice regarding alcohol for the next 40 years. Perhaps the leading American authority on alcohol during this period was E. M. Jellinek. In 1940, Jellinek commented on the danger of alcohol intake during pregnancy by declaring that "the idea of germ poisoning by alcohol in humans" was now "safely dismissed" by "practically unanimous opinion" (Jellinek & Jolliffe, 1940 p. 162). Two years later, Jellinek and Howard Haggard wrote in their book for the public *Alcohol Explored* that "no acceptable evidence has ever been offered to show that acute alcoholic intoxication has any effect whatsoever on the human germ, or has any influence in altering heredity, or is the cause of any abnormality in the child" (Haggard & Jellinek, 1942, p. 207).

In their 1975 review of research on alcohol and offspring, Warner and Rosett suggested that such a rejection of biological explanation for the apparent effects of alcohol was due to a broader shift toward environmental explanations for development (p. 1409). The environmental approach was more cheerful because aid could be given through psychotherapy, improvement in living conditions, reorganization of communities, and education. The idea that the central fact about someone's life was the inexorable unfolding of innate biological patterns, a view championed in the 1920s through the 1950s by Arnold Gesell, now seemed discouraging and subversive of a belief in equal opportunity (Ames, 1989).

These three eras—biological, then environmental, and once again biological—illustrate how closely research can accompany as well as validate larger, popular changes in attitude. Science is an integral part of our culture and does not exist above or outside it. Many ingenious statistical devices have been designed to increase the protection of research from bias. As researchers know, however, these same statistical devices also can be used to bring research into harmony with nonscientific pressures. Influences include ideological or political goals that are so unconditionally accepted that nudging research into alignment does not seem wrong; rather, it is just a matter of getting experts to state a little early what they will surely prove in the near future.

CONCLUSION

It is not surprising that research would strike out in directions that would affirm strongly held beliefs about a drug. It is also not strange that this kind of research would get support. Many forces in American society spur the momentum of public issues like drugs. Caught up in an energetic campaign, research can have imposed on it demands for results that cannot, either in the time allowed or because of the questions asked, be supplied. Furthermore, the interpretation of results that are obtained takes place in a political context that makes it easier to go in one direction than another. One protection against this natural, human tendency to prefer harmony to conflict is to demand extremely high levels of proof for what appear to be reasonable and commonsense conclusions. An interesting question to consider is how best to present information that runs counter to current popular convictions to the public and decision makers. It is important to introduce contrary data, if valid, to public debate—you could say it is a duty of science to do so—but actually doing so on controversial topics requires at least some political savvy.

With all the protection a current viewpoint enjoys—the case of Dr. Bishop is one extreme example—how do we ever change viewpoints? The changes that have been discussed (e.g., biology switching to environment or vice versa) are the product of events and dynamics in society, of which the scientific hardly seems the strongest. There is no adequate answer to this large question. One cause for change, however, is frustration at failing to solve deep and abiding social problems—like poverty and violence—with simple reliance on one or the other explanation. These shifts in explanation are reminiscent of shifts in therapies for a disease for which no cure has been found: If one direction does not solve the problem, the opposite is tried. Also, extreme claims that are later perceived to be exaggerations undercut public confidence in scientific authority.

The value of studying the congruity between research and arbitrary cultural assumptions is that this awareness is one of the few ways to rise above it. It would be a mistake, though, to assume that if we find research retracing a path once rejected, it is necessarily in error. The fetal alcohol syndrome cannot be discounted by an historical study. One should not assume that the view from his or her current perch is the right one. Take, for example, the 60 years since repeal of prohibition. One can look back on those years in two ways: either as a normal pattern of alcohol use and freedom from prohibitory laws or as decades of denying that alcohol causes real problems to which society is, once again, awakening. These extreme positions about drugs and alcohol are imbued with moral certainty, so it is not surprising that we reframe past episodes each time we enter a new phase. The impact of cultural attitudes on drug research is profound. One should expect that it would be so and that efforts to rise above it will be difficult.

REFERENCES

Ames, L. B. (1989). *Arnold Gesell: Themes of his work*. New York: Human Sciences Press, Inc.

Bishop, E. S. (1920). *The narcotic drug problem*. New York: Macmillan.

Bromberg, W. (1934). Marihuana intoxication: A clinical study of *cannabis sativa* intoxication. *American Journal of Psychiatry 91*, 303–330.

Bromberg, W. (1939). Marihuana: A psychiatric study. *Journal of the American Medical Association, 113*, 4–12.

Bromberg, W., & Rogers, T. C. (1946). Marihuana and aggressive crime. *American Journal of Psychiatry, 102*, 825–827.

Buck v. Bell, 274 U.S. 200 (1927).

Donovan, W. J. (1925, February 16). [Letter to William Hayward, Jr., U.S. attorney for Southern District of New York]. Record Group 60, Records of the U.S. Department of Justice, National Archives of the United States, Washington, DC.

Eddy, N. B. (1973). *The National Research Council involvement in the opiate problem: 1928–1971.* Washington, DC: National Academy of Sciences.

Elderton, E. M., & Pearson, K. (1910). *A first study of the influence of parental alcoholism on the physique and ability of the offspring* (Eugenics Laboratory Memoirs X). London: Dulan.

Erickson, P. G., Adalf, E. M., Murray, G. F., & Smart, R. G. (1987). *The steel drug: Cocaine in perspective.* Lexington, MA: Lexington Books.

Freeman, R. G. (1917). Disease conditions in older babies that can be attributed to prenatal influences. *American Journal of Obstetrics, 77,* 459–462.

Goddard, H. H. (1912). *The Kallikak family: A study in the heredity of feeble-mindedness.* New York: Macmillan.

Goddard, H. H. (1916). Alcoholism and feeble-mindedness. *Interstate Medical Journal, 23,* 442–445.

Gordon, A. (1911). Parental alcoholism as a factor in the mental deficiency of children: A statistical study of 117 families. *Journal of Inebriation, 33,* 90–99.

Gordon, A. (1916). The influence of alcohol on the progeniture. *Interstate Medical Journal, 23,* 431–436.

Haggard, H. W., & Jellinek, E. M. (1942). *Alcohol explored.* Garden City, NY: Doubleday, Doran.

Hayward, W. (1922, May 31). [Letter to attorney general from William Hayward, U.S. attorney for Southern District of New York]. Record Group 60, Records of the U.S. Department of Justice, National Archives of the United States, Washington, DC.

Irwell, L. (1913, April). Influence of parental alcoholism upon the human family. *The Medical Times,* pp. 114–115.

Jellinek, E. M., & Jolliffe, N. (1940). Effect of alcohol on the individual: Review of the literature of 1939. *Quarterly Journal of Studies on Alcohol, 1,* 110–181.

Karp, R. J., Qazi, Q. H., Moller, K. A., Angelo, W. A., & Davis, J. M. (1995). Fetal alcohol syndrome at the turn of the 20th century. *Archives of Pediatrics and Adolescent Medicine, 149,* 45–47.

Keynes, J. M. (1910). Influence of parental alcoholism [Letter to the editors]. *Journal of the Royal Statistical Society, 74,* 114–121.

Keynes, J. M. (1911). Influence of parental alcoholism [Letter to the editors]. *Journal of the Royal Statistical Society, 75,* 339–345.

Lasting costs for child are found from a few early drinks. (1989, February 16). *The New York Times,* p. B16.

Leacock, S. (1918). This strenuous age. In S. Leacock, *Frenzied fiction* (pp. 119–201). New York: Lane.

MacNicholl, T. A. (1907). Alcohol and the disabilities of school children. *Journal of the American Medical Association, 48,* 396–398.

Marihuana problems. (1945). *Journal of the American Medical Association, 127,* 1129.

Mayor's Committee on Marihuana. (1944). *The marihuana problem in the City of New York.* Lancaster, PA: Cattell Press.

McClary, A. (1984). The WCTU discovers science: The Women's Christian Temperance Union. Teachers, doctors and scientific temperance. *Michigan History, 68,* 16–22.

Metcalf's Coca Wine (Advertisement). (1889). *New York Medical Times,* April, p. xxi.

Musto, D. F. (1996). Alcohol in American history. *Scientific American, 274*(4), 78–83.

Musto, D. F. (1999). *The American disease: Origins of narcotics control* (Third rev. ed.). New York: Oxford University Press.

Pellini, E. J., & Greenfield, A. D. (1920). Narcotic drug addiction: I. The formation of protective substances against morphine. *Archives of Internal Medicine, 26,* 279–292.

Pellini, E. J., & Greenfield, A. D. (1924). Narcotic drug addiction: II. The presence of toxic substances in the serum in morphine addiction. *Archives of Internal Medicine, 33,* 547–565.

Smart, R. G., & Ogborne, A. C. (1986). *Northern spirits: Drinking in Canada then and now.* Toronto, Ontario, Canada: Addiction Research Foundation.

Stockard, C. R. (1916). The hereditary transmission of degeneracy and deformities by the descendants of alcoholized mammals. *Interstate Medical Journal, 23,* 385–403.

Stockard, C. R. (1932). The effects of alcohol in development and heredity. In H. Emerson (Ed.), *Alcohol and man* (pp. 103–119). New York: Macmillan.

Streissguth, A. P., Ase, J. M., Clarren, S. K., Randels, S. P., LaDue, R. A., & Smith, D. F. (1991). Fetal alcohol syndrome in adolescents and adults. *Journal of the American Medical Association, 265,* 1961–1967.

Streissguth, A. P., Barr, H. M., & Sampson, P. D. (1990). Moderate prenatal alcohol exposure: Effects on child IQ and learning problems at age 71/2 years. *Alcoholism: Clinical and Experimental Research, 14,* 662–669.

Tate, C. (1989, July). Anti-smoking campaigns. *Smithsonian Magazine, 20,* 106–117.

U.S. v. Doremus, 249 US, 1919.

U.S. v. Jin Fury Foy, 241 US, 1916.

Warner, R. H., & Rosett, H. L. (1975). The effects of drinking on offspring: An historical survey of the American and British literature. *Journal of Studies on Alcohol, 36,* 1395–1420.

Webb et al. v. U.S., 249 U.S. 96 (1919).

Wood, G. B. (1868). *A treatise on therapeutics and pharmacology or materia medica* (3rd ed., Vol. 1). Philadelphia: Lippincott.

4

EXPLAINING ATTITUDES ABOUT PUBLIC POLICY ON DRUG AVAILABILITY: THE ROLE OF EXPECTANCIES ABOUT DRINKING AND DRUG EFFECTS

ROBIN ROOM AND ANGELA PAGLIA

Public opinion about psychoactive drugs and drug policies has varied greatly over time in North America and varies considerably among different psychoactive drugs. Understanding of the determinants of popular sentiment on drug policies, however, is limited. Researchers know even less in a comparative sense, looking over the diverse range of drugs and opinions about them.

One fundamental aspect of drug policy is the laws and regulations about availability. Should any adult consumer be able to purchase as much of a drug as he or she can afford, as would be implied by a *doctrine of consumer sovereignty*? In this chapter, we explore this dimension in terms of the extent of approval or disapproval of the sale of three index psycho-

This chapter was written while both authors were at the Addiction Research Foundation, Toronto, Ontario, Canada.

active drugs—tobacco, alcohol, and marijuana—at a corner store or supermarket in people's neighborhood.

Our analysis examines how other attitudes and experiences relate to opinions favoring or disfavoring each drug being freely available for sale. In particular, we look at the role of *expectancies* about the effects, positive and negative, of each drug. Using alcohol as an example, we show that respondents generally have stronger expectations of effects—positive or negative—on others than on themselves, that these expectancies are particularly strong when it is daily use that is in question, and that expectations of negative effects on others are fairly strongly related to disapproval of neighborhood availability of alcoholic beverages. Using such expectancies about the effects of regular use on others, we compare the structures of expectations about the effects of the three drugs and examine the relation of these expectations to attitudes about neighborhood availability of the drugs. For each drug, we find that expecting negative effects on others is fairly strongly related to disfavoring neighborhood availability, whereas own use and friends' use of the drug are associated with favoring availability. The analysis suggests that for alcohol, tobacco, and marijuana, attitudes about restrictions on consumer access to a considerable degree reflect the degree to which each drug is expected to have negative effects.

CONSUMER SOVEREIGNTY AND DRUG-CONTROL POLICIES

We live in an era in which the doctrine of consumer sovereignty has triumphed. The break up of the Soviet system has released the ideals and demons of nationalism from their prison, but it is not so much the ideology of capitalism that has triumphed, but rather the doctrine of consumer sovereignty: the idea that the consumer's choice of purchases should be absolutely free—limited only by the cash in the consumer's pocket or his or her credit limit. When East Germans joyfully traversed the Berlin Wall at the end of 1989, it was not to invest in the stock market, but rather to buy bananas, as symbols of their freedom to consume as they chose within the limit of their means.

However, even in the most free-market environment, consumer sovereignty has its limits. No government in the world, for instance, would permit a citizen, however wealthy, to purchase atomic bombs. In most societies, a citizen's choice to pay a hit man to commit homicide would be forbidden. Governments routinely interfere in the free market in commodities or services, on behalf of a variety of goals and interests.

For some commodities, the long-term trend over the last century in Europe and North America has been toward the state allowing more sovereignty to the consumer. The degree of sexual expression allowed in books, films, and other media is much greater in most places than it was 40 years ago. Gambling, which was illegal or tightly controlled in many English-speaking countries at the turn of the century, is now not only allowed but also promoted as a source of revenue to many states.

The picture regarding psychoactive substances is more mixed. Efforts by the state to limit consumer sovereignty in purchasing them have a long history. In the modern era, a peak of efforts to restrict access to psychoactive substances came in the period from 1910 to 1935, with alcohol prohibition in several countries and the strengthening of systems to limit access to psychoactive drugs by requiring a doctor's prescription. Since the 1930s, policies on the availability of alcohol and other drugs tend to have developed in opposite directions: Alcohol gradually has become increasingly available in places where access to it had been restricted, whereas controls on the sale of most other psychoactive substances have generally become more restrictive.

Drugs have, in fact, taken on an unusual or even unique status in modern European and North American societies in the extent to which consumer choice is denied. Christie and Bruun (1985) have discussed some of the positive functions for the modern state of declaring an anathema on drugs; drugs, as their book's title states, are "suitable enemies" for the modern state. How unusual this total denial of consumer sovereignty is can be gauged by the recent history of tobacco control. Despite the argument of harm to the smoker and the more recent arguments about harm to those around the smoker, the principle that cigarettes are available for purchase by anyone over a minimum age has not been breached. This risk of harm from cigarettes has been seen as justifying warning labels providing information to the consumer, high taxes (interfering with purchases by manipulating price but not availability), and increasingly stringent controls on where a smoker can smoke. But to interfere with the right of an adult consumer with enough cash to purchase a pack of cigarettes has been seen so far as too extreme a proposal even for discussion.

Similarly, both in the United States and in Canada, assertions of consumer sovereignty concerning the purchase of firearms have conflicted with the interests of public order and injury prevention and have been a constraint on government control of the market for firearms—although much more of a constraint in the United States than in Canada. In both countries, the consumer interests of gun owners and purchasers have attained much more legitimacy in public discourse than the consumer interests of illicit drug users.

PUBLIC OPINION AND DRUG-CONTROL POLICIES

In modern industrial societies, there are three fundamental policy options for controlling the market in psychoactive drugs (Kaplan, 1970).

One is to prohibit the sale outright. This is, of course, the option that has been applied in the United States and in Canada for such drugs as marijuana and heroin. A second option is to make physicians the gatekeepers delegated by government to control availability to consumers. Benzodiazepides, methadone, and a host of other psychoactive substances are available to consumers only through a doctor's prescription. The third option is to make the psychoactive substance more or less freely available at the consumer's choice. Within this third option, there are suboptions in terms of how much the government controls and structures the market. In beverage form, caffeine, for instance, is treated in North America like any other comestible. In the 1940s and 1950s, nicotine products were treated in the same way, but in both the United States and Canada, there has been a long and slow process of imposing controls on the tobacco market, through such mechanisms as increased taxes and advertising restrictions. In Ontario, for instance, a corner store or supermarket can now lose the right to sell cigarettes for a time in case of repeated sales to minors.

Alcohol has been something of a special case in North America. Both the United States and Canada went through a period earlier in the century in which sales of alcoholic beverages were forbidden. In retreating from prohibition, both societies adopted strong and specific control systems for the legal market. In 18 American states and all the Canadian provinces, this included the direct operation of at least part of the alcohol market through a government monopoly. Although this alcohol-control system has been considerably weakened, it is still the case in many places that beer, wine, and spirits cannot be purchased in supermarkets or corner stores. Alcohol is thus legally available as an adult consumer's choice but is still quite far from being treated like any other comestible.

Government policies on the extent of consumer sovereignty thus vary widely across the spectrum of psychoactive drugs. There is also a great deal of variation in public opinion on how available the different drugs should be. In a democratic society, public opinion and government policy are, of course, related. But the relationship is complex and not simply a matter of policy following the dictates of public opinion. As the long struggle over gun control in the United States shows, a determined interest group can put in place policies that are at considerable odds with public opinion (Spitzer, 1998). Historically, prohibitions or controls on psychoactive substances have sometimes offered an attractive target for major generational reactions, with public opinion often eventually shifting against the policy (Austin, 1979; Room, 1984).

Nevertheless, the more common pattern is that a policy is considerably legitimated by the very fact of being in effect. Thus, for instance, support for random breath testing for drinking driving increased in Australian states after this policy went into effect (Beel & Stockwell, 1993; Homel, Carseldine, & Kearns, 1988). Policymaking can thus influence public opinion rather than the other way around. For one thing, to make a purchase illegal is to force those who nevertheless consume to associate with criminals and to take on some of their derogated status. For another, the fact that sale of a drug has long been prohibited may make it difficult for a respondent even to imagine an alternative reality where it would be freely available for sale.

In the present analysis, the focus is on three drugs: tobacco, alcohol, and marijuana. Setting aside caffeine and prescription medications, these are the most commonly used drugs in Canadian society (Health Canada, 1995). They also provide a representative spread on the spectrum of availability of drugs to consumers. For an adult, cigarettes are available readily in many kinds of stores; alcoholic beverages are sold in a more restrictive set of locations, as noted above; and marijuana is not legally available to consumers at all.

POTENTIAL INFLUENCES ON OPINIONS ON POLICY: EXPECTANCIES AND EXPERIENCE

As mentioned, a psychoactive drug's control status can influence public opinion, although mapping this influence would be a complex task that would require data over time. However, it may be hypothesized that a variety of other factors influence public opinion on the availability of different drugs. Many of these can be directly measured and the relationship mapped in a cross-sectional survey, although such a study cannot, of course, prove the existence and direction of any causal relationship.

Among the factors that might be hypothesized to influence attitudes on availability of alcohol, tobacco, and drugs are beliefs about the drug's effects. The perceived dangerousness of a drug is an element of public policy on availability, and expectations that a drug will have adverse effects might logically also affect individual attitudes on availability. On the other hand, perceived positive effects from the drug might be associated with favoring greater availability.

The study of expectancies for alcohol, that is, of the effects that people expect from drinking, is by now well developed (Goldman, Brown, Christenson, & Smith, 1991; Leigh, 1989a, 1989b; Leigh & Stacy, 1991), and there are a few studies of tobacco smoking and of illicit drug expectancies (Bauman, Fisher, & Koch, 1989; Schafer & Brown, 1991). The main thrust of the alcohol-expectancies literature has been on the extent to which drinking behavior can be predicted by the drinker's alcohol expectancies (Adams & McNeil, 1991). In this context, the focus has been on expectancies for one's own drinking and on expectancies that are positive and might, therefore, be expected to reinforce drinking behavior. However, a number of studies have included measures of putatively aversive expectancies (Fromme, Stroot, & Kaplan, 1993; Leigh & Stacy, 1993; Stacy, Widaman, & Marlatt, 1990). Heavier drinkers, it has been found, are more likely to expect both negative and positive consequences from drinking (Leigh, 1989a; Roizen, 1983).

Some research also has been done on expectancies about the effects of drinking on others' behavior (Gustafson, 1987; Rohsenow, 1983). Respondents in a U.S. community survey rated others as more likely than themselves to experience most behavioral effects of drinking, both positive and negative (Leigh, 1987). The difference was particularly strong for socially undesirable effects such as "aggressive," "get into fights," and "lose self-control."

Although there is some recognition in the alcohol-expectancy literature of *distal* consequences (Leigh, 1989b)—that people have expectations about the long-term consequences of a sustained pattern of drinking—the literature has been focused around *proximal* consequences, that is, expectations concerning the effects of a particular drinking occasion. Adding expectancies about the long-term consequences of patterns of drinking might well improve the predictions on which the literature has focused, those concerning individual drinking patterns. Turning to tobacco, expectancies about long-term negative effects of a pattern of smoking would seem to be important in quitting tobacco smoking.

In the present context, however, the focus was not on predicting drinking, smoking, or drug use behavior. Instead, the measurement of expectancies was used for another purpose: to predict attitudes about public policy on alcohol and drug availability. In this context, expectancies about others' drug use, particularly negative expectancies, might be more closely related to policy attitudes than expectancies about one's own drug use. However, we hypothesized that both proximate and distal expectancies about effects of a single drinking or drug use occasion and about effects of a pattern of use would be related to policy attitudes.

We expected that alcohol- and drug-policy attitudes also would be related to various aspects of the respondent's experience and self-interest: how much the respondent's convenience, lifestyle, or experience was affected by the availability of the product. Self-interest has, in fact, been shown to be significantly related to negative views of smoking restrictions (Dixon, Lowery, Levy, & Ferraro, 1991; Green & Gerkin, 1989). Although this result might not seem surprising, in fact, it pulls against the general findings in public opinion research that self-interest has a negligible influence on various other political and social attitudes. The result for smoking policy is reminiscent of the result for alcohol-policy attitudes, in earlier studies, that there was greater public support for policies that would mostly impact on others than for policies that would mostly impact on oneself (Cameron, 1981).

Drug-related experience might be related to attitudes on availability in three main ways. One would be a direct connection between convenience of supply and use: The more frequent the use, the more the respondent might be expected to have an interest in and favor the availability of a convenient supply. Another relation might be through the shared attitudes of subcultures of users: Those who have many friends who use the product frequently or heavily might be expected to favor greater availability. A third relation, in the opposite direction, might be with the respondent's adverse experiences with others' drug use: Those who have been adversely affected by the drug use of a family member or friend might favor restrictions on availability. Although there is some alcohol literature on such experiences (Eliany, Giesbrecht, Nelson, Wellman, & Wortley, 1990; Fillmore, 1985; Room, 1989), there has been no known prior attempt to connect this domain with policy attitudes.

METHOD

Participants and Procedure

A probability sample of 1,058 Ontario adults age 18 and over were interviewed in June and July 1992 (Ontario Alcohol and Other Drug Opinion Survey; Ferris, Templeton, & Wong, 1994). The sample was chosen by random-digit dialing, and the interviews were conducted by telephone by the fieldwork contractor. The questionnaire consisted of approximately 195 items (but the average respondent was asked approximately 120 questions) regarding opinions on, and experience with, alcohol, tobacco, and other drugs. Those interviewed constituted 65% of the eligible base of respondents. The data were weighted for representativeness, taking into account such factors as the number of eligible respondents and the number of telephone lines in the household. To facilitate more accurate testing for statistical significance, the sample was down weighted to a size of 887, to reflect the average design effect.

Measures

Alcohol-and-Drug-Policy Attitudes

The measures of alcohol-and-drug-policy attitudes were derived from a set of questions concerning approval of the sale of various commodities in a corner store or supermarket in one's neighborhood. The list of commodities covered can be found in Table 1. For each commodity, respondents were asked whether they "strongly approved," "somewhat approved," "somewhat disapproved," or "strongly disapproved" of sales of the commodity, with a random half of the sample being asked the questions concerning a corner

TABLE 1
Mean Approval Scores of Commodity Availability in Corner Stores and Supermarkets for the Populations of Ontario and the United States

	Population					
	Ontario				U.S.	
	Corner store[a]		Supermarket[a]		Supermarket or convenience store	
Commodity	M	SD	M	SD	M	SD
Wine	1.42	1.1	1.61	1.0	1.30	1.0
Wine coolers	1.56	1.1	1.62	1.0	1.27	1.0
Beer	1.24	1.2	1.27	1.1	1.38	1.1
Whiskey and other liquor	0.71	1.0	0.79	1.0	0.81	1.0
Nonalcoholic beer[b]	2.00	1.1	2.18	0.9	—	—
Cigarettes	1.83	1.0	1.71	1.0	1.42	1.0
Sleeping pills	0.61	0.9	0.65	0.9	0.86	1.0
Marijuana joints (cigarettes)	0.28	0.7	0.25	0.7	—	—
Condoms (prophylactics)	2.53	0.8	2.47	0.9	2.25	1.0
Lottery tickets	2.35	0.8	2.25	0.8	2.05	1.0
Design-weighted ns	449[c]		435[c]		1,626	

Note. Ontario data are from the Ontario Alcohol and Other Drug Opinion Survey, 1992 (Ferris, Templeton, & Wong, 1994). U.S. data are from a 1989 survey (Hilton & Kaskutas, 1991). The approval scores range from 0 (*strongly disapprove*) to 3 (*strongly approve*). Dashes indicate that sample was not asked.
[a]On a random basis, approximately half of the sample in Ontario was asked the questions for a supermarket and half for a corner store.
[b]Repondents were prompted if necessary: Beer with alcohol removed (e.g., Molson's EXEL).
[c]Sample sizes vary slightly because of missing responses.

store, and the other half concerning a supermarket. For statistical purposes, these response categories were assigned a value between 0 (*strongly disapprove*) and 3 (*strongly approve*). In the case of alcohol, a summation of these values for wine, wine coolers, beer, and liquor also was used.

Alcohol and Drug Expectancies

For alcohol, 10 expectancy items were asked: 5 items about the effects of having "a few drinks, enough to feel the effects" on an occasion, and 5 about the effects of drinking "enough to feel the effects" every day (see Table 2).[1] Each set of 5 items included one or two presumably positive expectancies (e.g., relaxation, sociability), with the remainder presumably negative (e.g., lose control, harm health, aggression). The same items were asked concerning the expected effects on oneself and concerning the ex-

---

[1]Elsewhere in the survey, it was established that according to 53% of the sample, three or four drinks was the amount an average person could drink before they "felt the effects," with a further 27% of the sample choosing two drinks as the amount (Ferris et al., 1994).

TABLE 2
Mean Alcohol-Expectancy Scores for Effects on Others and on Self, for Drinking on One Occasion and Drinking Every Day

Expectancy	Effects on other[a]		Effects on self[b]		t	df
	M	SD	M	SD		
Drinking enough to feel the effects on one occasion						
Make more relaxed than otherwise	2.10	0.9	2.01	0.9	2.13	709*
Make more sociable	1.96	0.8	1.65	1.0	7.78	715***
Make aggressive and possibly violent	2.14	0.8	0.55	0.9	36.93	711***
Make forget any worries or troubles	1.85	1.1	1.09	1.0	16.44	726***
Make lose self-control	2.07	0.9	0.99	1.1	22.99	731***
Drinking enough to feel the effects every day						
Get more enjoyment from life than otherwise	0.50	0.9	0.29	0.7	6.47	752***
Harm physical health	2.77	0.6	2.64	0.8	4.39	766***
Distress or annoy family	2.76	0.6	2.69	0.8	2.29	759*
Get aggressive or possibly violent	2.43	0.7	1.32	1.2	23.13	702***
Become addicted	2.76	0.6	2.27	1.1	11.76	730***

Note. Data are from the Ontario Alcohol and Other Drug Opinion Survey, 1992 (Ferris, Templeton, & Wong, 1994). Expectancy scores range from 0 (*very unlikely*) to 3 (*very likely*).
[a]Design-weighted *n*s range from 830 to 876 because of missing responses.
[b]Design-weighted *n* range from 744 to 773 because of missing responses.
*$p < .05$. ***$p < .001$.

pected effects on someone else, using the four response categories "very likely," "somewhat likely," "somewhat unlikely," and "very unlikely." For all expectancy items, responses about the likelihood of effect were assigned a value from 0 (*very unlikely*) to 3 (*very likely*) and were used in subsequent analyses.

For tobacco and marijuana, only the 5 items concerning the effects of someone else's daily use were included (i.e., someone smoking a pack of cigarettes a day and someone smoking marijuana every day; see Table 3). The 4 negative items for each drug were summed into an overall negative expectancy score for others' daily use (Cronbach's α = .77, .47, and .72, for alcohol, tobacco, and marijuana, respectively).

Dimensions of Drug-Related Experience

Three measures were used in this domain. For each drug, frequency of use during the past year (including a zero category for abstainers) served as an indicator of use relevant to the salience of convenient availability. Proportion of close friends who used marijuana, drank quite a bit, and smoked

TABLE 3
Mean Expectancy Scores for the Effects of Daily Use of Marijuana, Alcohol, and Tobacco on Others

Expectancy for others' daily use	Substance					
	Marijuana		Alcohol		Tobacco	
	M	SD	M	SD	M	SD
Get more enjoyment from life than otherwise	0.84	1.0	0.52	0.9	0.84	1.0
Harm physical health	2.65	0.7	2.76	0.6	2.78	0.6
Distress or annoy family	2.75	0.6	2.74	0.6	2.27	0.9
Get aggressive and possibly violent	2.01	1.1	2.43	0.8	0.74	1.0
Become addicted	2.70	0.7	2.75	0.6	2.84	0.6

Note. Data are from the Ontario Alcohol and Other Drug Opinion Survey, 1992 (Ferris, Templeton, & Wong, 1994). Design-weighted *n* = 886 (varies slightly because of missing responses). Expectancy scores ranged from 0 (*very unlikely*) to 3 (*very likely*). The items for marijuana began with "Suppose that someone smoked marijuana every day, how likely would he or she . . ."; the items for alcohol began with "Suppose that someone was drinking a few drinks, enough to feel the effects every day, how likely would he or she . . ."; the items for tobacco began with "Suppose that someone smoked a pack of cigarettes every day, how likely would he or she. . . ."

every day provided an indicator of immersion in a subculture of use. Furthermore, a score was constructed for each drug pertaining to the degree the respondent was affected by family members' or friends' problems with the drug, by using responses to whether the respondent had a family member or friend who ever had a problem with the drug and whether this had a major effect, a minor effect, or not much of an effect at all on the respondent.

RESULTS

Alcohol and Drug Policy Attitudes

There are only minor differences in the opinions of Ontarians about commodity availability in corner stores versus availability in supermarkets, except for wine and wine coolers, where there is somewhat greater approval of sales in supermarkets (see mean scores in Table 1). Because wine is available in separate stores within some Ontario supermarkets, the greater approval may simply be an endorsement of the status quo. Overall, the differences for corner stores and supermarkets were small enough that the subsamples were combined in further analyses.

The Ontario data presented in Table 1 generally show a considerable endorsement of the status quo on availability of commodities. The ready availability of lottery tickets, condoms, and nonalcoholic beer was endorsed, whereas corner store sale of marijuana joints, sleeping pills, and whiskey and other liquor received low approval. Ontario adults were fairly evenly split on wine and beer sales in corner stores and a little more favorable than not to the sale of cigarettes.

In Table 1, data from a probability survey of the U.S. adult population, interviewed in June and July of 1989, is presented for comparison (sample described in Hilton & Kaskutas, 1991). Note that the questions used in the U.S. sample survey pertained to a convenience store or supermarket. Column 5 of the table shows that public opinion on these issues was very much the same in the United States as in Ontario. Approval of sales of wine and wine coolers in a supermarket or convenience store in the United States was slightly less than in Ontario. In the United States, there was somewhat more approval of ready availability of sleeping pills, but somewhat less approval than in Ontario of ready availability of condoms, lottery tickets, and cigarettes. The attitudes on commodity availability of Ontario respondents thus seem to be consistent with a general ranking of preferences about availability in North America. That is, whereas lottery tickets and condoms should be readily available, the majority leans against ready access to liquor, sleeping pills, and marijuana, and views on wine, beer, and cigarettes are fairly evenly split.

Expectancies About the Effects of Drinking "Enough to Feel the Effects"

We now explore the full series of drinking expectancies and their correlates. In terms of the effects of a single drinking occasion on oneself, Table 2 (top right quadrant) shows high likelihood scores for the positive expectancies (first two items) but relatively low scores for the negative expectancies, particularly for the idea that drinking enough to feel the effects would make the respondent aggressive and possibly violent. For daily drinking, respondents felt that they would be unlikely to get enjoyment, somewhat unlikely to become aggressive, and more likely to harm their health, distress their family, or become addicted. Regarding alcohol's effects on others, respondents felt that all the effects listed in Table 2 would be moderately or highly likely to occur, with the exception of getting more enjoyment due to daily drinking.

Using repeated measures t tests, we compared the mean likelihood scores for self-expectancies to the mean scores for other expectancies, both for one drinking occasion and daily drinking (Table 2). For the effects of a single drinking occasion, the positive expectancies (i.e., relaxation, sociability) for someone else were slightly stronger than those held for oneself. But the results for the negative expectancies differed dramatically. Drinking enough to feel the effects was considered more likely to make someone else lose self-control, compared with oneself. For the aggression expectancy, the magnitude of difference was even more striking. As for the effects of drinking enough to feel the effects every day, respondents felt that most of the effects were slightly more likely to occur to others. The magnitude of difference for aggression, however, was again quite large. Thus, according to our sample, aggression is a drinking consequence more likely to happen to others.

Expectancies About the Effects of Daily Drug Use by Others

As noted earlier, for tobacco and marijuana, only the expectancies about daily use by others were asked. As we turn to a comparison across drugs of the relations of expectancies to policy attitudes, our analysis is thus confined to these expectancies. Table 3 shows that for all three drugs, the two most likely effects were harm to physical health and becoming addicted. For alcohol and marijuana, but not so much for tobacco, there was also an indication that distress or annoyance to the family would be a likely effect.

Expectancies about the three drugs were most sharply differentiated concerning the user becoming aggressive and possibly violent. Although as many as 21% of the respondents thought aggression was somewhat or very likely from smoking a pack of cigarettes a day (frequency data not shown), the aggression expectancy was lowest for tobacco and highest for alcohol. There was also some differentiation by drugs in expecting that the user would get more enjoyment from life than otherwise; more respondents thought this unlikely for alcohol than for the other drugs.

Predicting Alcohol-Control Attitudes With Alcohol Expectancies

Table 4 shows the zero-order Pearson product–moment correlations between each of the 20 alcohol-expectancy items (using mean scores) and an alcohol-availability score—an index of the extent to which the respondent approved of selling wine, wine coolers, beer, and liquor in a neighborhood supermarket or corner store. Many of the expectancy items were significantly associated with approval for alcohol availability, with positive correlations for the positive expectancies and negative correlations for negative expectancies. Expecting that a few drinks makes someone else lose self-control showed the strongest relationship with the alcohol-availability score ($r = -.25$). Thus, a high expectancy of others to lose control was related to disapproval of increased alcohol availability. For several negative effects (i.e., losing self-control, making one aggressive and possibly violent, and becoming addicted), disapproval of availability was associated more with expectancies about someone else than about oneself. At least at the level of bivariate relationships, expectancies about drinking were moderately associated with attitudes toward alcohol availability, and

TABLE 4
Pearson Correlations Between Alcohol Expectancies (for Others and Self) and the Alcohol-Availability Score, for Drinking on One Occasion and Drinking Every Day

Expectancy	Effects on other	Effects on self
Drinking "enough to feel the effects" on one occasion		
Make more relaxed than otherwise	.10**	.14***
Make more sociable	.14***	.15***
Make aggressive and possibly violent	−.14***	−.07*
Make forget any worries or troubles	−.03	.05
Make lose self-control	−.25***	−.14***
Drinking "enough to feel the effects" every day		
Get more enjoyment from life than otherwise	.11**	.10**
Harm physical health	−.12**	−.10**
Distress or annoy family	−.10**	−.11**
Get aggressive or possibly violent	−.18***	−.15***
Become addicted	−.16***	−.11**

Note. Data are from the Ontario Alcohol and Other Drug Opinion Survey, 1992 (Ferris, Templeton, & Wong, 1994). Design-weighted *ns* range from 830 to 876 because of missing responses.
*$p < .05$. **$p < .01$. ***$p < .001$.

the relation was generally strongest for expectancies about alcohol's negative effects on others.

Predicting Drug Policy Attitudes With Expectancy and Experience Measures

Table 5 shows the results of nine standard multiple regression analyses, three each on approval for the availability of alcohol, tobacco, and marijuana. Column 1 show the regression of positive and negative expectancies, and of three experience dimensions, on the alcohol-availability score. A modest proportion of the variance (11%) in the score was accounted for, with frequency of drinking making the strongest prediction. Negative expectancies of others' use and the proportion of close friends drinking "quite a bit" also made significant contributions to the prediction. The regression in column 2 under alcohol shows that approval for alcohol availability also was moderately predicted by just educational level and gender, with males and the more educated tending to support greater availability. Combining all the predictors in column 3, apart from the demographics, only frequency of use and negative expectancies made a significant contribution to prediction. The total variance accounted for rose to 16%.

Column 4 applies a regression analysis parallel to that of column 1, to approval of tobacco availability. The expectancy and experience variables accounted for a higher proportion of variance in tobacco availability

TABLE 5
Summary of Standard Multiple Regressions: Approval of Alcohol, Tobacco, or Marijuana Being Sold in a Neighborhood Store, Predicted by Expectancies, Experience Variables, and Demographics

| | Beta weights | | | | | | | | |
| | Alcohol[a] | | | Tobacco[b] | | | Marijuana[c] | | |
Variable	Exp.	Demog.	E&D	Exp.	Demog.	E&D	Exp.	Demog.	E&D
Positive expectancies of others' daily use	.06		.08*	.08*		.09**	.05		.05
Negative expectancies of others' daily use	-.13***		-.12***	-1.8***		-.17***	-.32***		-.31***
Frequency of own use	.23***		.20***	.23***		.23***	.18***		.18***
Proportion of close friends using	.09***		.05	.16***		.15***	.23***		.21***
Extent affected by families' or friends' problems	-.06		-.04	-.12***		-.12***	-.04		-.03
Educational level		.12***	.13***		-.03	.04		.04	.01
Age		-.04	-.07*		-.13***	-.09**		-.12***	-.04
Gender: male		.24***	.16***		.12***	.05		.19***	.08*
R	.34	.27	.40	.45	.18	.46	.54	.24	.54

Note. Alcohol-availability approval score based on the sale of wine, wine coolers, beer, and liquor. Age = year of age; educational level = 14-category ordinal scale. Beta weights are shown for all predictors entered simultaneously in a particular regression.
[a] ns range from 855 to 875.
[b] ns range from 830 to 866.
[c] ns range from 777 to 869.
* p < .05. ** p < .01. *** p < .001.
Exp. = Expectancies and experience variables
Demog. = Demographics
E&D = Expectancies, experiences, and demographics

(20%) than the equivalent variables did for alcohol availability. All five of the variables made significant contributions to prediction, with frequency of use and negative expectancies again showing the highest beta weights. Gender (male) was a weaker predictor of support for tobacco availability (column 5) than of support for alcohol availability, and age (younger persons) also made a significant contribution, whereas educational level did not. Adding demographics to the regression (column 6) neither significantly changed the beta weights of the expectancy and experience variables nor strongly increased the variance explained.

The last three columns show parallel regression analyses for marijuana availability. In column 7, negative expectancies made the strongest contribution to the prediction (in a negative direction), with membership in a friendship network of marijuana users and frequency of marijuana use also providing significant prediction. The expectancy and experience variables together accounted for 29% of the variance in support for marijuana availability, a stronger prediction than the analogous variables can make for alcohol and tobacco availability. As with tobacco, being younger and being male modestly predicted support for marijuana availability, with educational level not significantly related (column 8). But adding the demographics to the other predictors (column 9) did not substantially change the total variance accounted for, nor did it affect the beta weights for the expectancy and experience variables.

For all three drugs, negative expectancies significantly predicted lack of support for drug availability, controlling for other relevant predictors. Whereas frequency of own use was the strongest predictor for opinions on alcohol and tobacco availability, negative expectancies were the strongest predictors for opinions on marijuana availability.

CONCLUSION

The present study sought to explain the public's attitudes toward policies on the availability of alcohol, tobacco, and marijuana. It was shown that expectancies, particularly negative expectancies about someone else's use of the drug, and drug-related experience variables are related to attitudes about availability policies for all three of the drugs considered. The structure of relationships between the expectancy and experience variables and attitudes about availability appears rather similar for the three drugs. However, the end point, in terms of the distribution of policy attitudes, is rather different. Only one tenth of the population approve of making marijuana available in a neighborhood store, whereas two thirds show approval for cigarettes.

To explain such a difference, we must look elsewhere and with different methods. The results of the study may, however, offer us some clues.

Negative expectancies about other people's use are particularly important in predicting attitudes on the availability of marijuana. Yet actual experience in the population of the effects of the drug is much rarer for marijuana than for tobacco and alcohol: Significantly fewer respondents use regularly, and fewer have witnessed or been party to problems from the drug in the family or among friends. The negative expectancies for marijuana thus seem to be much less grounded in actual lived experience of the drug's effects on oneself or on others. This relative lack of grounding of the marijuana expectancies may help explain why two thirds of respondents think that marijuana would be likely to make someone get aggressive and possibly violent—an effect that is not objectively supported by the research literature (Hall, Solowij, & Lemon, 1994).

The lack of support for marijuana availability, in the relative absence of lived experience of the drug's effects, may thus be informed primarily by the existing legal status of marijuana. Conversely, for alcohol and tobacco, existing availability regulations and structures may help to maintain support for availability at its present level despite the wide experience in the population of problems from their own alcohol or tocacco use and from use by their family or friends.

As noted earlier, fully unraveling the puzzle of the relationship between actual policies and public attitudes on policy will require further work and other methods. In the meantime, our analysis points down several paths for further exploration. We have illustrated the potential utility of a new direction in drug-expectancy research: using expectancies to predict drug-policy attitudes. In so doing, we have used (and in some cases opened up) several dimensions across which expectancies can be systematically varied in comparative analyses: across drug types; between expectancies for a particular drug-use occasion and expectancies of longer term patterns of use; between expectancies of the self and of the other; and between positive and negative expectancies.

The approach we have adopted to measuring attitudes to drug availability might also be further developed. Our focus has been on attitudes toward various commodities being sold in local stores. We have suggested that this is a relatively direct indicator of the extent to which a respondent applies the doctrine of consumer sovereignty to a particular commodity and that it offers a comparative frame among commodities that does not depend in any formal way on the current availability status of a commodity. The present study focused on commodities whose ready availability might reasonably be questioned or considered in our particular cultural frame; the approach is probably inapplicable for the many commodities where asking about limiting availability would not seem to make cultural sense.

In the field of drugs, licit and illicit, however, our results reemphasize that the consumer is not entirely sovereign and apparently does not necessarily wish to be so. The field thus offers a rich soil for further development of research on the conditions of support for limitations on ideologies of free-market availability.

REFERENCES

Adams, S. L., & McNeil, D. W. (1991). Negative alcohol expectancies reconsidered. *Psychology of Addictive Behavior, 5,* 9–14.

Austin, G. A. (1979). *Perspectives on the history of psychoactive substance use* (DHEW Publication No. ADM 79-810). Washington, DC: U.S. Government Printing Office.

Bauman, K. E., Fisher, L. A., & Koch, G. G. (1989). External variables, subjective expected utility, and adolescent behavior with alcohol and cigarettes. *Journal of Applied Social Psychology, 19,* 789–804.

Beel, A. J., & Stockwell, T. (1993). *The introduction of 0.05 legislation in Western Australia: A preliminary research report* (Tech. Rep). Perth, Western Australia: Curtin Institute of Technology.

Cameron, T. (1981). *Alcohol and public problems: Public opinion in California, 1974–1980* (Report No. C31). Berkeley, CA: Alcohol Research Group.

Christie, N., & Bruun, J. (1985). *Den goda fienden: narkotikapolitik i Norden* [Suitable enemies: Drug policies in the Nordic countries]. Kristianstad, Norway: Boktryckeri AB.

Dixon, R. D., Lowery, R. C., Levy, D. E., & Ferraro, K. R. (1991). Self-interest and public opinion toward smoking policies: A replication and extension. *Public Opinion Quarterly, 55,* 241–254.

Eliany, M., Giesbrecht, N., Nelson, M., Wellman, B., & Wortley, S. (Eds.). (1990). *National Alcohol and Other Drugs Survey (1989): Highlights report.* Ottawa, Ontario, Canada: Health and Welfare Canada, Health Promotion Directorate.

Ferris, J., Templeton, L., & Wong, S. (1994). *Alcohol, tobacco and marijuana: Use, norms, problems and policy attitudes among Ontario adults. A report of the Ontario Alcohol and Other Drug Opinion Survey, 1992* (Document No. 118). Toronto, Ontario, Canada: Addiction Research Foundation.

Fillmore, K. M. (1985). The social victims of drinking. *British Journal of Addiction, 80,* 307–314.

Fromme, K., Stroot, E., & Kaplan, D. (1993). Comprehensive effect of alcohol: Development and psychometric assessment of a new expectancy questionnaire. *Psychological Assessment, 5,* 19–26.

Goldman, M. S., Brown, S. A., Christenson, B. A., & Smith, G. T. (1991). Alcoholism and memory: Broadening the scope of alcohol expectancy research. *Psychological Bulletin, 110,* 137–146.

Green, P., & Gerkin, A. E. (1989). Self-interest and public opinion toward smoking restrictions and cigarette taxes. *Public Opinion Quarterly, 53,* 1–16.

Gustafson, R. (1987). Lack of correspondence between alcohol-related aggressive expectancies for self and others. *Psychological Reports, 60,* 707–710.

Hall, W., Solowij, N., & Lemon, J. (1994). *The health and psychological consequences of cannabis use* (National Drug Strategy Monograph Series No. 25). Canberra: Australian Government Publishing Service.

Health Canada. (1995). *Canada's Alcohol and Other Drugs Survey factsheet.* Ottawa, Ontario, Canada: Minister of Supply and Services.

Hilton, M. E., & Kaskutas, L. (1991). Public support for warning labels on alcoholic beverage containers. *British Journal of Addiction, 86,* 1323–1333.

Homel, R., Carseldine, D., & Kearns, I. (1988). Drink-driving countermeasures in Australia. *Alcohol, Drugs and Driving, 4,* 113–144.

Kaplan, J. (1970). *Marijuana: The new prohibition.* New York: World Publishing.

Leigh, B. C. (1987). Beliefs about the effects of alcohol on self and others. *Journal of Studies on Alcohol, 48,* 467–475.

Leigh, B. C. (1989a). Attitudes and expectancies as predictors of drinking habits: A comparison of three scales. *Journal of Studies on Alcohol, 50,* 432–440.

Leigh, B. C. (1989b). In search of the seven dwarves: Issues of measurement and meaning in alcohol expectancy research. *Psychological Bulletin, 105,* 361–373.

Leigh, B. C., & Stacy, A. W. (1991). On the scope of alcohol expectancy research: Remaining issues of measurement and meaning. *Psychological Bulletin, 110,* 147–154.

Leigh, B. C., & Stacy, A. W. (1993). Alcohol outcome expectancies: Scale construction and predictive utility in higher order confirmatory models. *Psychological Assessment, 5,* 216–229.

Rohsenow, D. J. (1983). Drinking habits and expectancies about alcohol's effects for self versus others. *Journal of Consulting and Clinical Psychology, 51,* 752–756.

Roizen, R. (1983). Loosening up: General-population views of the effects of alcohol. In R. Room & G. Collins (Eds.), *Alcohol and disinhibition: Nature and meaning of the link* (NIAAA Research Monograph No. 12, pp. 236–257). Washington, DC: Government Printing Office.

Room, R. (1984). A reverence for strong drink: The lost generation and the elevation of alcohol in American culture. *Journal of Studies on Alcohol, 45,* 540–546.

Room, R. (1989). The U.S. general population's experience of responses to alcohol problems. *British Journal of Addiction, 84,* 1291–1304.

Schafer, J., & Brown, S. A. (1991). Marijuana and cocaine effect expectancies and drug use patterns. *Journal of Consulting and Clinical Psychology, 59,* 558–565.

Spitzer, R. J. (1998). *The politics of gun control* (2nd ed.). Chatham, NJ: Chatham House.

Stacy, A. W., Widaman, K. F., & Marlatt, G. A. (1990). Expectancy models of alcohol use. *Journal of Personality and Social Psychology, 58,* 918–928.

5

A DEVELOPMENTAL PSYCHOPATHOLOGY PERSPECTIVE ON DRUG ABUSE

DANTE CICCHETTI

During the course of the past several decades, important empirical advances have been made in our knowledge of the epidemiology, classification, etiology, course, consequences, prevention, and treatment of drug abuse (Institute of Medicine; IOM; 1985, 1994). Numerous theoretical conceptualizations have been invoked in an attempt to comprehend this complex societal, individual, and family problem. Such divergence in thinking indicates that the topic of drug abuse has evolved into an active and significant domain of scientific inquiry.

Although existing work within particular scientific disciplines and subdisciplines has made substantial contributions to the understanding of drug abuse, these accounts typically have not considered the broader matrix of complex and evolving biological and psychological capacities of the developing individual. Despite Kandel's (1978) assertion that "drug use and related behaviors ... cannot be properly studied apart from concurrent developmental processes" (p. 34), classic disease models of addiction have been the predominant viewpoint espoused in the drug abuse literature (Fitzgerald, Davies, Zucker, & Klinger, 1994). These classic disease models posit that drug abuse is a mental disorder characterized by an ineluctable expression of an underlying endogenous pathogen and a clearly demarcated and unchanging structure and course (cf. Sroufe, 1997; Zucker, Fitzgerald & Moses, 1995). Consequently, extant theoretical formulations are generally too narrow in focus to address the range of processes and mechanisms that will be necessary to explain how and why manifestations of drug abuse emerge, change, or remain over time and are influenced by individuals' biological and psychological developmental organization and functioning and the varying and dynamic social contexts within which they are immersed. In this chapter, a *developmental psychopathology* perspective is brought to bear on drug abuse. This approach has enormous potential not only for guiding investigations but also for helping to inform prevention and intervention initiatives.

A DEVELOPMENTAL PSYCHOPATHOLOGY PERSPECTIVE

Developmental psychopathology, an emerging multidisciplinary perspective, proffers a developmental, life span perspective that has the potential to unify the various conceptual approaches to drug abuse that have emanated from multiple fields of inquiry (Cicchetti, 1984, 1990). Developmental psychopathology represents a movement toward understanding drug abuse and its determinants, pathways, sequelae, prevention, and treatment by integrating knowledge from disciplines such as epidemiology, genetics, neuroscience, psychology, sociology, psychiatry, and criminology, within a process-oriented developmental framework (Cicchetti, 1993). The undergirding developmental orientation compels theoreticians and scientists to introduce new questions about the phenomena they investigate. For example, drug abuse does not emerge in full-blown form but rather unfolds throughout various periods of the life span (e.g., Block, Block, & Keyes, 1988; Glantz, 1992; Kandel, 1978). Accordingly, it becomes essential for researchers to move beyond merely identifying the incidence and prevalence of drug abuse to an articulation of how and why the behavior pattern of engaging in drug use and abuse evolves in some persons and not others over the developmental life course (Luthar, Cushing, & McMahon, 1997).

The developmental perspective also focuses attention on specific evolving capacities and limitations that are characteristic of individuals at varying developmental stages across the life span (Sroufe & Rutter, 1984). This requires formulating questions about phenomena in terms of capacities that are inherent within an individual during particular developmental periods and how given processes or mechanisms become manifested in view of those developmental capacities and attainments and the social contexts within which the individual is embedded (Richters & Cicchetti, 1993).

For example, the cognitive, representational, interpersonal, and social–cognitive capacities of preschoolers, fourth graders, and adolescents are progressively more advanced. These developmental progressions, in turn, have implications for the meanings attributed to events and for the cognitive capacities available to children and adolescents at different developmental levels for dealing with new experiences. Thus, to understand drug abuse, it is necessary to consider developmental variations in cognitive, representational, interpersonal, and social–cognitive capacities, in addition to other psychological and biological domains of functioning, to ascertain how individual differences in these domains may impact on the developing individual's conceptualization of drug abuse and how particular outcomes (e.g., abstinence, initiation, experimentation, cessation, maintenance, and abuse) are manifested during different developmental periods.

Additionally, developmental analyses seek to ascertain how prior sequences of adaptation in development contribute to outcomes in current developmental periods (Kandel, 1978). This requires that the present status of an individual's functioning be examined within the broader context of how that status was attained across the earlier course of development. Consequently, the life span perspective strives to move beyond the proximal causes of current outcomes to examining the developmental progression of distal sources of influence that have eventuated in present functioning (Cicchetti & Tucker, 1994; Sroufe, Egeland, & Kreutzer, 1990). For example, the social, biological, and psychological factors that are connected with initiating a pattern of drug use are not necessarily isomorphic with those factors that influence the persistence of the pattern and subsequent abuse. Individuals exhibit variability in neuronal circuitry and neurochemistry that affect their likelihood of becoming compulsive drug users (Wise & Bozarth, 1987). Likewise, drugs alter numerous biological processes, including neurotransmitter formation, reuptake, and receptor function and brain neuroregulators (Bloom, 1993; Hyman & Nestler, 1996; IOM, 1985). Furthermore, individual differences exist in how persons react to the pharmacological effects of drugs, including their differential sensitivity to the reinforcing effects of drugs, the varying expectancies associated with drug use, and variability in the likelihood of developing sensitization, tolerance, and addiction to drugs (Sher, 1994; Wise & Bozarth, 1987). Finally, there is heterogeneity in the motivational processes underlying individuals' inclinations to engage in drug use, including factors such as varying predispositions to experiencing negative affect and, therefore, to seek out altered states of consciousness; heightened life stress; and adequacy of coping skills (Sher, 1994). Thus, given that a confluence of different influences contribute to the use and abuse of drugs at different developmental periods and that entry into or out of a problem drug-consumption pathway may occur at any point in the life course, it is critical that researchers not view the initiation, cessation, or maintenance of drug use as the sole or primary phenomenon of interest (cf. Block et al., 1988; Zucker et al., 1995).

Researchers who investigate the causes and consequences of drug abuse must now begin to answer the developmental questions of how individual differences in the functioning characteristics of persons who engage in drug abuse have evolved and about the specific interactive roles they play in the context of drug-abusing behavior (Shedler & Block, 1990). The conceptualization of these questions within a developmental perspective provides a richer, more in-depth understanding of processes that both engender and maintain drug abuse. The resulting analysis would include an examination of why some individuals who abuse drugs persist on drug-abusing trajectories whereas others do not, as well as why some people do not cease their addictive behavior even if they have the opportunity and support to do so. The implications of such investigations also are important for determining how best to provide interventions for the prevention and treatment of drug abuse. To examine the value of a developmental psychopathology perspective to drug abuse research and intervention, I next explicate some of the principles that define the discipline. In so doing, I also address ways in which these principles can inform intervention efforts.

PRINCIPLES OF DEVELOPMENTAL PSYCHOPATHOLOGY

A focus on the boundary between normal and abnormal development is central to the developmental psychopathology perspective (Cicchetti & Toth, 1991). This viewpoint emphasizes not only how knowledge from the study of normal development can inform the study of high-risk conditions and psychopathology but also how the study of risk and psychopathology can contribute to an understanding of normal development (Cicchetti, 1993). Thus, the application of knowledge concerning normal biological, emotional, cognitive, representational, social–cognitive, and interpersonal development to an understanding of drug abuse results in a clarification of how components of individual functioning in persons who use and abuse drugs contribute to their symptomatic presentation.

For example, many of the internal processes implicated in causal models of drug abuse tend not to occur in isolation. Deficits in social learning; social cognition; neurobiological, neuropsychological, and psychophysiological functioning; processing inhibitory cues; impulse control; emotion regulation; child–parent attachment; peer relations; and other systems tend to covary significantly. This covariance, in turn, often renders difficult the important task of disentangling causal influences. In some instances, suspected causal processes actually may be the products of other covarying systems and only spuriously related to drug-abusing behavior. In other instances, a process may indeed influence drug use or abuse, but the nature and extent of its causal influence may be masked or clouded by the influence of other interacting systems. Disentangling the relative contributions of interrelated influences can provide valuable insights on how best to prioritize the targeted areas for intervention.

Moreover, the study of atypicalities in the biological and psychological functioning and organization of individuals who abuse drugs may assist in providing a more complete understanding of how these same processes function in the course of normal ontogenesis. Thus, the study of abnormal and normal processes are intimately intertwined, and it is through this dialectic that knowledge advances in both domains can be attained.

In addition to their interest in the extremes of the distribution (e.g., individuals with disorders), developmental psychopathologists are interested in examining variations along the continuum between the mean and both positive and negative extremes. Variations such as these may represent individuals who are currently not divergent enough to be considered disordered but who may progress to further maladaptive extremes as development continues. They may be individuals who are vulnerable to developing future disorder. Or, viewed within Wakefield's (1992) concept of harmful dysfunction, developmental deviations may, for some individuals, reflect either the earliest signs of an emerging dysfunction or an already-existing dysfunction that is partially compensated for by other processes within or outside the individual. Therefore, tracking the developmental course of these individuals is likely to broaden the complexity and richness of psychopathologic understanding of developmental processes. Such an understanding also can be used in the development of prevention strategies for individuals considered to be at risk for the emergence of a drug abuse problem.

Diversity in both process and outcome is the hallmark of the developmental psychopathology perspective. It is expected that there are multiple contributors to drug abuse outcomes within any individual, that the relevant causal processes vary among individuals who abuse drugs, that there is heterogeneity in the expression of their behavior disturbances and (in some instances) underlying dysfunctions, and that there are a myriad of pathways to any particular manifestation of drug-abusing behavior (Cadoret, Yates, Troughton, Woodworth, & Stewart, 1995; Fitzgerald et al., 1994; Glantz, 1992). For example, drug abusers represent a heterogeneous group of individuals (Tarter & Vanyukov, 1994). Likewise, there are numerous reasons for engaging in drug abuse, and there are multiple patterns of drug abuse, each of which possess numerous potential etiologies (Glantz, 1992). Furthermore, different classes of drugs vary in their abuse-inducing liability, and some drugs appear to be compatible with specific neurotransmitter receptor sites in the brain, which allows the drugs to be positively reinforcing and to become addictive (Bloom, 1993; Koob & Bloom, 1988; Wise & Bozarth, 1987). In a related vein, individuals possess differential susceptibility to various psychoactive substances (Glantz, 1992; Korenman & Barchas, 1993). In accordance with these expectations, the principles of equifinality and multifinality, derived from general systems theory, are germane (Cicchetti & Rogosch, 1996; von Bertalanffy, 1968).

Equifinality refers to the observation that in any open system, a diversity of pathways may lead to same outcome. More specifically, in an open system, the same end state may be reached from a variety of different initial conditions and through different processes. This alerts us to the possibility that a variety of developmental progressions may eventuate in drug abuse rather than assuming a singular primary pathway. Thus, it should not be surprising that no biological or psychological characteristic has been identified that antedates initiation into drug abuse in all individuals or that there is no common predisposing factor, other than drug use, that is shared by all individuals who develop into drug abusers (Tarter & Vanyukov, 1994). In contrast, in a closed system, the outcome is inextricably linked to and determined by the initial conditions: If either the conditions change or the processes are modified, then the end state also will be modified (von Bertalanffy, 1968). Equifinality is a particularly salient concept for the study of drug abuse because most efforts to identify or to classify subtypes of individuals who abuse drugs are based on overt patterns of drug use, not on the presumed or postulated underlying causal processes of ultimate interest to developmentalists (cf. Cicchetti & Rogosch, 1996).

The principle of *multifinality* (Wilden, 1980) suggests that any one component may function differently depending on the organization of the system in which it operates. The concept of multifinality specifies that the effect on functioning of any one component's value may vary in different systems. Thus, diverse outcomes are likely to result from any one source of influence. Actual effects will depend on the conditions set by the values of additional components with which the source of influence is structurally linked.

Consequently, the health or pathology of a system must be identified in terms of how adequately its essential functions are maintained. Accordingly, a particular adverse event would not necessarily contribute to the same outcome in every person. Likewise, individuals may begin on the same major pathway and, as a function of their subsequent choices, exhibit very different patterns of adaptation or maladaptation. For example, although a significant life stressor or trauma may be identified as a factor that has initiated a given person into a pattern of drug abuse, a similar life event may occur with no linkage with drug abuse in another person. Similarly, the trajectories followed by drug abusers of similar substances may be very different, depending on how these individuals respond to their drug abuse.

Because of the diversity in processes and outcomes evident in development, not surprisingly, a developmental psychopathology approach to drug abuse does not advocate a unitary etiologic explanation. Although commonalities in pathways among different relatively homogeneous clusters of individuals diagnosed as drug abusers may be delineated, it also is conceivable that drug abuse is not the only outcome associated with those pathways. Thus, there are likely to be generic pathways that contribute to a range of dysfunctions and disorders, of which drug abuse may be only one (cf. Kessler et al., 1994; Regier et al., 1994; Sroufe, 1997). As such, the scientific study of drug abuse must be conceived within the larger body of investigations on the developmental patterns promoting adjustment problems and mental disorders. Consequently, those individuals interested in studying drug abuse or developing prevention and intervention strategies grounded in a developmental psychopathology perspective need to be knowledgeable about pathways of normal development, identify deviations from these pathways, articulate the developmental transformations that take place as individuals progress through these deviant developmental courses, and discover the processes that may deflect an individual off a particular trajectory and onto a more or less adaptive course (Sroufe, 1989). Toward this end, efforts to understand individual differences among similar groups of drug abusers are critical. Reliance on group data may preclude the elucidation and subsequent understanding of the myriad factors, both intrinsic and extrinsic to the individual drug user, that result in the continuation of drug abuse or abstinence.

This attention to diversity in origin, processes, and outcomes in understanding developmental pathways does not suggest that prediction is futile as a result of the many potential individual patterns of adaptation. There are constraints on how much diversity is possible, and not all outcomes are equally likely (Cicchetti & Tucker, 1994; Sroufe et al., 1990). The existence of equifinality and multifinality in development requires that drug abuse researchers increasingly should strive to demonstrate the multiplicity of processes and outcomes that may be articulated at the individual, person-oriented level as opposed to the prevailing variable-oriented strategies that dominate the field (cf. Bergman & Magnusson, 1997). Future endeavors in the field of drug abuse that are guided by a developmental psychopathology approach must conceptualize and design empirical research and intervention strategies at the outset, with these differential pathways concepts as a foundation. Doing so will help researchers in the field of drug abuse in achieving the unique goals of developmental psychopathology: the explanation of individual patterns of adaptation and maladaptation.

Investigators interested in applying a developmental psychopathology perspective to drug abuse also could benefit from recognizing that individuals may move between pathological and nonpathological forms of functioning. Moreover, even in the midst of pathology, adaptive coping mechanisms may be displayed (Cicchetti & Schneider-Rosen, 1986; Zigler & Glick, 1986). Some drug abusers may be extremely adept at generating income to support their drug dependence. Similarly, they may be very attuned to their own behavioral presentations and be able to assess how best to modify their presentations so as to connect extremely well with diverse individuals. Such skills, although most likely used to support the drug abuse habit, could be channeled in more productive ways. Thus, it is only through the joint consideration of adaptive and maladaptive processes within individuals that it becomes possible to speak in meaningful terms about the existence, nature, and boundaries of the underlying psychopathology.

Relatedly, drug abuse researchers, as well as clinicians, who wish to apply a developmental psychopathology perspective to their work need to emphasize the importance of comprehending the functioning of individuals who, after having diverged onto deviant developmental pathways, recover positive function and resume more adequate adaptation, in addition to the functioning of those who do not succumb to the stresses that eventuate in developmental deviation in others. Future research on drug abuse would do well to focus on the processes and mechanisms contributing to resilient adaptations. Moreover, such knowledge on the processes by which drug-abusing individuals attain adaptive outcomes could be factored into the implementation of intervention designs.

The course of adaptation once drug abuse has remitted also warrants investigation from a developmental perspective. It would be very revealing, for example, to study the characteristics of individuals formerly diagnosed (or diagnosable) as drug abusers who have successfully reentered the mainstream. In keeping with the concept of multifinality discussed earlier, it may be possible to identify core characteristics, such as impulsivity, sensation seeking, or executive functioning deficits, that remain stable but no longer culminate in drug abuse because of protective or buffering factors in the environmental context or within the person. Research such as this might reveal that certain characteristics that once were causally relevant to drug-abusing behavior in an earlier environment have become positively adaptive in a new environment. They may actually facilitate adaptive and successful functioning. For example, a person who has used manipulation to attain drugs may be able to channel this attribute into a career involving persuasive abilities, such as sales. Again, just as it is unwise to assume that drug-abusing behavior is always caused by an underlying dysfunction, it also may be misdirected to assume that normalized behavior necessarily reflects improvements in processes that were once causal to drug-abusing behavior. Thus, a developmental psychopathology perspective would encourage one to remain open to the possibility that many of the characteristics that are typically viewed as functioning deficits (e.g., impulsivity, sensation seeking, or insecurity) in fact may be neutral. That is, they may translate into deficits or assets depending on other characteristics of the individual or the environmental context.

AN ORGANIZATIONAL PERSPECTIVE ON DEVELOPMENT

Over the course of the past several decades, a number of developmental psychopathologists have adopted the *organizational* perspective on development as a guiding theoretical orientation for their research (Cicchetti, 1993; Sroufe, 1997). This approach offers developmental psychopathology a powerful framework for conceptualizing the intricacies of a life span viewpoint on the evolution of drug abuse.

The organizational perspective depicts development as probabilistic in nature (cf. Zucker et al., 1995; Zucker & Gomberg, 1986). Development is portrayed as a series of qualitative reorganizations among and within biological, psychological, and social systems as growth of the individual proceeds (Cicchetti & Schneider-Rosen, 1986; Sroufe & Rutter, 1984; see also Werner & Kaplan 1963). The analysis of this organization involves components at many levels, including the genetic, biological, behavioral, psychological, environmental, and sociological. Processes within these domains are viewed as being in dynamic transaction across the course of development, and the person plays an increasingly active role in his or her own development over time. Through differentiation and hierarchic integration, continuity of functioning may be maintained over time, as prior patterns of adaptation (i.e., developmental history) are incorporated into successive reorganizations at subsequent periods of development.

Across the developmental course, the evolving capacities of the person and his or her active choices allow for new aspects of experience, both internal (e.g., genes turning on and off or biological changes) and external, to be coordinated in increasingly complex ways (Cicchetti & Tucker, 1994; Sroufe et al., 1990). Because change in developmental course is always possible as a result of new experiences and reorganizations and the individual's active biological and psychological self-organizing strivings for adaptation, organizational theorists do not subscribe to the notion that individuals are either immutably controlled or unaffected by their early experiences (cf. Kagan, 1996). The self-promulgating properties of the individual can lead to the development of new structures that actively influence the future developmental course (Cicchetti & Tucker, 1994; Tarter & Vanyukov, 1994).

For example, inadequate resolution of developmental challenges may result in a lag or delay in one of the biological or psychological (e.g., cognition, emotion, or representation) systems. As a result, less than adequate integration within that domain will occur, and that poor within-domain integration will compromise adaptive integration across domains as hierarchical integration proceeds (cf. Tarter & Vanyukov, 1994). Thus, incompetent or maladaptive development may be viewed as a problematic integration of pathological structures. Over time, difficulty in the organization of one biological or psychological system may tend to promote difficulty with the way in which other systems are organized as hierarchical integration between separate systems occurs (cf. Fitzgerald et al., 1994; Hinde, 1992). The person's organization may then appear to consist of poorly integrated component systems. Such a conceptualization suggests that a psychopathological organization may become more entrenched over time; therefore, the importance of intervention early in development when incipient psychopathology is identified is highlighted.

Although early incompetence (i.e., maladaptive organization) tends to promote later incompetence because the person arrives at successive developmental stages or transitions with less than optimal resources available for responding to the challenges of that period, this progression is not inevitable, but probabilistic. Changes in the internal and external environment may lead to improvements in the ability of the individual to grapple with developmental challenges, resulting in a redirection in the developmental course. Thus, although historical factors canalize and constrain the adaptive process to some degree, because biological factors can exert impact on psychological processes and because psychological experiences can modify brain structure, functioning, and organization, developmental plasticity is possible as a result of adaptive biological and psychological self-organization (Cicchetti & Tucker, 1994). A probabilistic model of development allows for the occurrence of mediator variation, wherein processes may be substantially influenced by experiences during earlier developmental periods yet also influenced and capable of being transformed by the impact of more recent context-dependent learning or triggering experiences (Baron & Kenny, 1986; Cicchetti & Tucker, 1994; Sher, 1991; Sroufe et al., 1990; Zucker et al., 1995).

During the course of development, there may be prototypic organizations of biological and psychological systems that have the potential for transformation into a spectrum of drug-abusing presentations. The relation among components of each system rather than the individual components of each system per se generates patterns or levels of drug-abusing organization (cf. Zucker et al., 1995). Aberrations in the organization of the cognitive, emotional, interpersonal, representational, and biological domains most likely exist to different degrees among drug-abusing individuals and their offspring. Notably, these varied developmental systems do not exist in isolation. Rather, they are complexly interrelated and mutually interdependent. In adaptively functioning individuals, there is a coherent organization among these psychological and biological domains (Cicchetti & Schneider-Rosen, 1986; Sroufe, 1979). In contrast, in drug-abusing individuals, there is likely to be an incoherent organization among these systems or an organization of pathological structures, that is, a prototypic drug-abusing organization. Such problematic organizations evolve developmentally and may eventuate in substance abuse disorders at different points in the life span. Consequently, comprehending the interrelations among these psychological and biological domains is vital for delineating the nature and course of these drug-abusing disorders, as well as for elucidating how these domains also promote adaptive functioning.

There may be numerous forms of such incoherent organizations that, depending on the nature of subsequent experiences in development, may eventuate in drug abuse or other psychopathological outcomes. For example, in a longitudinal investigation of drug abuse and other problem behaviors, Jessor and Jessor (1977) examined three classes of variables: personality, perceived environment, and behavior. These investigators theorized that each system comprised structures of variables that were organized and interrelated so as to generate a resultant dynamic state, which they designated a "problem behavior proneness" (Jessor & Jessor, 1977, p. 26) that had implications for a greater or lesser likelihood of engaging in problematic behaviors, including drug abuse.

Early forms of maladaptive prototypic organizations of biological and psychological systems may not resemble later drug abuse phenotypically, even though coherence in molar organization between a prior prototype and later drug abuse may be discerned. For example, difficulties modulating emotional impulses may be an early prototypic feature with linkages to later drug abuse (Block et al., 1988; Glantz, 1992) and perhaps to subsequent conduct disorder and antisocial personality disorder (Kessler et al., 1994). These difficulties with emotion regulation throughout development also may become integrated with other changes in psychological (e.g., cognitive, interpersonal, social–cognitive, and representational) and biological development that eventually may result in a drug-abusing presentation. Alternatively, difficulties modulating and regulating emotion, given disparate developmental experiences, including social, biological, and psychological, might eventuate in different forms of disorder or comorbidity of disorders (Kessler et al., 1994; Sroufe, 1997). For some individuals, however, there may be continuity between early difficulties in emotion regulation and later drug abuse, although the phenotypic presentation in later life might appear discontinuous with its early-life predecessor.

In summary, the possibility of a prototypic drug-abusing organization suggests an integration of maladaptive features across the different psychological and biological systems. Difficulties may arise in one component system and subsequently, through hierarchic integration, affect other psychological or biological systems. Such a prototypic drug-abusing organization might have high potential for transforming into later drug abuse, depending on subsequent biological, social, and psychological transactions in development (cf. Luthar, Burack, Cicchetti, & Weisz, 1997). The recognition of prototypic organizations that predate actual clinical levels of drug abuse can be factored into prevention programs, to deflect a person from a maladaptive pathway.

TRANSACTIONAL INFLUENCE ON DRUG ABUSE

Up until this point, I have focused on the organization of psychological and biological processes occurring within developing individuals, as influenced by their embeddedness in the social contextual matrix within which they unfold, which may contribute to drug abuse. I now examine the means by which individual differences in developmental outcomes among drug abusers may be conceptualized. A *transactional* model of development (Sameroff & Chandler, 1975) offers a framework for a perspective on how internal and external sources of influence are coordinated to shape the organizational structure of individuals along alternate pathways throughout the life course. Transactional theorists decry reductionism and argue that except in extreme cases, it is unlikely that a unitary cause in the biological, psychological, or social environmental sphere will be found for drug abuse (cf. Fitzgerald et al., 1994; Zucker et al., 1995; Zucker & Gomberg, 1986).

The transactional model specifies that the interrelations between the organization of the developmental domains of the individual (e.g., biological, socioemotional, cognitive, social–cognitive, representational) and the environment (e.g., culture, society, community, family) are in a continuous, progressive exchange of mutual influence (Cicchetti & Lynch, 1993). Not only is the individual influenced by environmental input, resulting in transformations and reorganization, but also the environment is influenced by and responds to characteristics of the developing individual. At successive points in development, the organizational structures of both the individual and the environment are in a state of bidirectional influence. These transactions of bidirectional influence will generate variations in the quality of the organization of the individual, competent versus incompetent, and will alter the manner in which the individual is able to respond to new experiences—be they biological, social, or psychological and positive or negative—and the pathways toward adaptation or maladaptation that unfold. Thus, for a drug-abusing individual, the transactions occurring between the individual and his or her environment will affect how subsequent challenges or opportunities are met and whether the drug abuse will continue, accelerate, decrease, or be eliminated.

The study of the dynamic balance between potentiating risk and compensatory protective factors, as they relate to the development of psychopathology, has been an area of active inquiry consistent with transactional concepts of development (Haggerty, Sherrod, Garmezy, & Rutter, 1994;

Richters & Weintraub, 1990; Rolf, Masten, Cicchetti, Nuechterlein, & Weintraub, 1990). In keeping with a developmental formulation, it is likely that a multitude of rather general factors (i.e., nonspecific drug abuse potentiating and compensatory factors) from the biological, social, and psychological systems will be at least indirectly related to drug-abusing outcomes because the nature of the organization of these systems represents the range of potential determinants of individual adaptation more generally. A comprehensive articulation of the processes and mechanisms that have promoted or inhibited development and, in particular, have resulted in disorders such as drug abuse may be more important than specific predictors of the immediate or proximal onset of drug abuse (cf. Tarter & Vanyukov, 1994; Zucker et al., 1995). This is an important distinction because numerous individual characteristics related to drug abuse, such as interpersonal relationship difficulties, problems regulating impulses and emotions, and low self-esteem, inevitably are arrived at developmentally and may function as vulnerability factors for or predispositions to drug abuse in and of themselves (Block et al., 1988; Jessor, Donovan, & Costa, 1991; Kandel, 1978; Kellam, Brown, Rubin, & Ensminger, 1983; Shedler & Block, 1990; Tarter & Mezzich, 1992).

Vulnerability factors are typically regarded as enduring or long-standing life circumstances or conditions within the person that promote maladaptation (Cicchetti & Rizley, 1981). Major domains of influence on the individual, including external (e.g., intrafamilial, social environmental) and internal (e.g., biological, psychological) factors, may serve as sources of vulnerability because they detract from the achievement of successful adaptation and competence. These vulnerability factors then may transact with the evolving organization of biological and psychological systems within the individual to potentiate the attainment of incompetence and maladaptation. Furthermore, these vulnerability factors may promote a prototypic drug abuse organization across the cognitive, emotional, social–cognitive, interpersonal, representational, and biological domains. For other individuals, however, these factors instead may represent the sequelae of earlier coping failures. Although we know a considerable amount about the biological correlates of drug abuse behavior (Hyman & Nestler, 1996; Koob & Bloom, 1988; Korenman & Barchas, 1993), the tendency has been to assume that these factors always reflect underlying vulnerabilities or causes of such behavior. Far less attention has been paid to the possibility that individual differences in the functioning or organization of biological systems or processes may reflect, for some individuals, reactions or adaptations to particular patterns of behavior or environmental circumstance (Cicchetti & Tucker, 1994; Eisenberg, 1995). There are also enduring protective factors that may promote competent adaptation. Many of these, within the psychological, social environmental, and biological systems, are viewed as the polar opposites of vulnerability factors. These features are likely to enhance rather than hinder development (Cicchetti & Garmezy, 1993; Luthar, Burack, Cicchetti, & Weisz, 1997).

In addition to these enduring competence-detracting and competence-promoting vulnerability and protective factors, *transient* influences also exist. Although temporary in duration, these transient factors may have a critical positive (i.e., buffering) or negative (i.e., challenging) impact, depending on the timing of such events or transitions in circumstances and the pertinent developmental issues of the individual at the time. Furthermore, the potency of specific buffering and challenging transient factors in influencing development will vary as a result of the developmental period in which they occur; a specific factor may be more influential in one developmental period than another. For example, Johnson (1994) has conjectured that during infancy, biological factors may have the most influential impact on a child's development, whereas in early childhood, later childhood, and adolescence, respectively, the child's family, community, and peer groups exert the most potent impact. Moreover, identical factors may function differently depending on the context in which they occur. Thus, it is critical that the effects of risk and protective processes be based on both the developmental and social environmental context in which they occur. For any individual, the specific enduring features encountered, both vulnerability and protective, will vary and must be assessed within a dynamic balance. A greater likelihood for the development of incompetence and a prototypic drug-abusing organization would be expected to occur among those for whom vulnerability and challenging factors outweigh the protective and buffering influences (cf. Cicchetti & Lynch, 1993). Drug abuse has the greater potential to emerge in those individuals for whom such a prototypic organization has evolved transactionally through development and whose coping capacities and protective resources are no longer effective in counteracting long-standing vulnerabilities and current stressors or acute challenging factors.

These *potentiating* (i.e., enduring vulnerability factors and transient challengers) and *compensatory* (i.e., enduring protective factors and transient buffers) factors are indicators of more complex processes and mechanisms that impact on individual adaptation (Cicchetti & Rogosch, in press; Rutter, 1990). Hence, it is essential to specify the processes or mechanisms involved. They are expected to operate chiefly by the significance they have in promoting or detracting from the development of competence at progressive stages of development and the consequent likelihood of an emerging drug abuse disorder. But in some persons these factors may contribute to a sequence of negative transformations in the various psychological and biological systems over the course of development. These changes, in turn, may result in the emergence of a prototypic drug-abusing organization and strong potential for drug-abuse-disordered outcomes.

RESEARCH DIRECTIONS FROM A DEVELOPMENTAL PSYCHOPATHOLOGY PERSPECTIVE

A developmental psychopathology approach to understanding drug abuse represents a comprehensive framework for unifying, clarifying, and conceptualizing into an integrated whole the contributions of multiple fields of inquiry (Cicchetti & Luthar, in press; Cicchetti & Rogosch, in press). Because current adaptation at any point is viewed as the product of extant circumstances and conditions as well as earlier experiences and adaptations, drug abuse is best understood in terms of current vulnerability, challenging, protective, and buffering factors within the context of prior developmental experiences that have been hierarchically integrated into the individual's organization of biological, social, and psychological systems. Understanding the developmental pathways between successive prior adaptations and current functioning is central to the developmental psychopathology approach. The developmental perspective holds considerable promise for expanding and integrating various theoretical models of drug abuse within a developmental psychopathology framework, as well as for informing prevention and treatment efforts. To attain these goals, however, future research on drug abuse must be conceived within a developmental framework. The developmental psychopathology approach allows for new questions to be addressed, moving beyond a description of differences inherent among drug-abusing individuals to exploring how such differences have evolved.

Because developmental psychopathology is a newly emerging discipline, there is much to be accomplished in advancing a developmental understanding of drug abuse. For example, the neuroscientist Bloom (1993) has emphasized the criticality of examining two temporal phases in the ontogenesis of drug addiction. Specifically, Bloom has underscored the importance of investigating the neuronal and behavioral changes that occur with multiple drug exposures over extended time periods and how these contribute to the development of the altered drug sensitivities of tolerance and sensitization. Furthermore, he has stressed the need to study the residual changes that persist even after prolonged periods of drug abstinence and contribute to the phenomenon of drug craving. Congruent with an organizational developmental psychopathology perspective, which posits that biological and psychological systems are hierarchically integrated and organized and that biological and psychological variables need to be examined concurrently within individuals, Bloom has advocated the combination of research at the molecular, cellular, and behavioral levels as the most effective strategy for addressing the questions he has posed.

The burgeoning literature emanating from attachment theory on internal representational processes also is likely to prove fruitful in providing increased depth to our understanding of how organizations of biological, emotional, cognitive, social–cognitive, and interpersonal domains are represented and carried forward developmentally and affect the course of adaptation and the evolution of drug abuse (cf. Cummings & Cicchetti, 1990). Future research also will benefit from an increased integration of the psychological and biological systems, studied in context. How, for example, might insecure representational models of attachment figures and of the self in relation to others develop and affect brain functioning, neurophysiological reactivity and information processing (cf. Pollak, Cicchetti, Klorman, & Brumaghim, 1997), and how might genetic heritage alter tendencies for certain forms of representational processes to occur, in individuals who develop problems with drug abuse?

Research also is needed to provide more detail concerning the differential strength of various potentiating and compensatory factors and how they vary during different developmental periods. For example, might there be more experience-dependent "sensitive periods" (cf. Cicchetti & Tucker, 1994) during which a confluence of factors is more likely to result in the emergence of drug use and abuse? Greater attention to the types and variety of precursor prototypic drug-abusing organizations and how potentiating and compensatory factors influence these organizations also will be important.

Additionally, increased attention to the pathways and trajectories followed by individuals who avoid developing drug abuse despite the presence of significant enduring vulnerability and transient challenging factors may be helpful in informing prevention and intervention efforts. For example, what mechanisms protect a child who lives in an environment permeated by intrafamilial, community, and sociocultural risk factors from becoming involved in drug-abusing behavior? In high-risk environmental contexts, a child may be placed at risk for drug abuse through the presence of factors such as family history (e.g., the presence of drug abuse or antisocial personality disorder in one or both parents), learning (e.g., modeling drug-using behaviors), and the pursuit of concrete needs (e.g., food, clothing) because of pervasive poverty conditions. Despite this aggregation of risk factors, however, many children experiencing these circumstances avoid developing drug abuse. To address questions such as these, prospective longitudinal investigations of individuals at risk for the development of disorders of drug abuse must be initiated.

Moreover, the identification and detailed examination of children, adolescents, and adults who evidence drug abuse but subsequently alter their developmental trajectories in a more adaptive direction (e.g., by ceasing to associate with antisocial peers) may elucidate efforts to treat drug-abusing individuals effectively. Similarly, research on the developmental characteristics of individuals who cease to engage in drug-abusing behavior may be informative for prevention and intervention efforts.

Finally, the developmental psychopathology framework directs attention not only to new ways of conceptualizing and framing questions about drug abuse but also to the kinds of research strategies that will be required to pursue those questions in a manner commensurate with their true complexity. Most of what is known about the predictors, correlates, and consequences of drug-abusing behavior has been gleaned from investigations that have focused on relatively narrow domains of variables. For example, neurobiological studies tend not to measure attachment organization, neuropsychology studies tend not to assess parental disciplinary practices, attachment studies tend to be devoid of assessments of neurobiological functioning and organization, and studies of social cognition tend not to address genetics. Yet it is apparent from the developmental considerations addressed herein that progress toward a process-level understanding of drug-abusing behavior will require research designs and strategies that call for the simultaneous assessment of multiple domains of variables within and outside the developing person. In some instances, reference to variables measured in other domains is essential to clarify the role(s) of variables of interest; for other questions, variables from other domains are necessary to consider as competing explanations for postulated causal paths. Clearly, many of the most pressing and exciting research questions are those that can be answered only in the broader context of other variables within and outside the drug-abusing person, particularly as these variables change and influence one another over developmental time.

An unusual level of interest, excitement, and research productivity has been accorded to the study of normal and abnormal processes related to drug abuse. To maximize the potential application of these scientific advances to questions of clinical importance, it is critical that researchers engage the inherently challenging and complex issues concerning drug abuse that remain to be solved and do so in coordinated, interdisciplinary ways within a developmental psychopathology framework. It is my hope that this chapter will serve as an impetus to encourage the talented people working in the area of drug abuse to incorporate a developmental psychopathology perspective into their theoretical, research, prevention, and treatment initiatives.

REFERENCES

Baron, R. M., & Kenny, D. A. (1986). The mediator–moderator variable distinction in social psychological research: Conceptual, strategic, and statistical considerations. *Journal of Personality and Social Psychology, 51*, 1173–1182.

Bergman, L., & Magnusson, D. (1997). A person-oriented approach in research on developmental psychopathology. *Development and Psychopathology, 9*, 291–319.

Block, J., Block, J. H., & Keyes, S. (1988). Longitudinally foretelling drug usage in adolescence: Early childhood personality and environmental precursors. *Child Development, 59,* 336–355.

Bloom, F. (1993). The neurobiology of addiction: An integrative view. In S. Korenman & J. Barchas (Eds.), *Biological basis of substance abuse* (pp. 3–16). New York: Oxford University Press.

Cadoret, R., Yates, W., Troughton, E., Woodworth, G., & Stewart, M. (1995). Adoption study demonstrating two genetic pathways to drug abuse. *Archives of General Psychiatry, 52,* 42–52.

Cicchetti, D. (1984). The emergence of developmental psychopathology. *Child Development, 55,* 1–7.

Cicchetti, D. (1990). A historical perspective on the discipline of developmental psychopathology. In J. Rolf, A. Masten, D. Cicchetti, K. Nuechterlein, & S. Weintraub (Eds.), *Risk and protective factors in the development of psychopathology* (pp. 2–28). New York: Cambridge University Press.

Cicchetti, D. (1993). Developmental psychopathology: Reactions, reflections, projections. *Developmental Review, 13,* 471–502.

Cicchetti, D., & Garmezy, N. (Eds.). (1993). Milestones in the development of resilience [Special issue]. *Development and Psychopathology, 5*(4).

Cicchetti, D., & Luthar, S. (Eds.). (in press). Developmental approaches to substance use and abuse. *Developmental Psychopathology, 11*(4).

Cicchetti, D., & Lynch, M. (1993). Toward an ecological/transactional model of community violence and child maltreatment: Consequences for children's development. *Psychiatry, 56,* 96–118.

Cicchetti, D., & Rizley, R. (1981). Developmental perspectives on the etiology, intergenerational transmission and sequelae of child maltreatment. *New Directions for Child Development, 11,* 32–59.

Cicchetti, D., & Rogosch, F. (1996). Equifinality and multifinality in developmental psychopathology. *Development and Psychopathology, 8,* 597–600.

Cicchetti, D., & Rogosch, F. A. (in press). Psychopathology as risk for adolescent substance use disorders: A developmental psychopathology perspective. *Journal of Clinical Child Psychology.*

Cicchetti, D., & Schneider-Rosen, K. (1986). An organizational approach to childhood depression. In M. Rutter, C. Izard, & P. Read (Eds.), *Depression in young people: Clinical and developmental perspectives* (pp. 71–134). New York: Guilford Press.

Cicchetti, D., & Toth, S. L. (1991). The making of a developmental psychopathologist. In J. Cantor, C. Spiker, & L. Lipsitt (Eds.), *Child behavior and development: Training for diversity* (pp. 34–72). Norwood, NJ: Ablex.

Cicchetti, D., & Tucker, D. (1994). Development and self-regulatory structures of the mind. *Development and Psychopathology, 6,* 533–549.

Cummings, E. M., & Cicchetti, D. (1990). Attachment, depression, and the transmission of depression. In M. T. Greenberg, D. Cicchetti, & E. M. Cummings (Eds.), *Attachment in the preschool years* (pp. 339–372). Chicago: University of Chicago Press.

Eisenberg, L. (1995). The social construction of the human brain. *American Journal of Psychiatry, 152,* 1563–1575.

Fitzgerald, H., Davies, W. H., Zucker, R., & Klinger, M. (1994). Developmental systems theory and subtance abuse: A conceptual and methodological framework for analyzing patterns of variation in families. In L. L'Abate (Ed.), *Handbook of developmental family psychology and psychopathology* (pp. 350–372). New York: Wiley.

Glantz, M. (1992). A developmental psychopathology model of drug abuse vulnerability. In M. Glantz & R. Pickens (Eds.), *Vulnerability to drug abuse* (pp. 389–418). Washington, DC: American Psychological Association.

Haggerty, R., Sherrod, L., Garmezy, N., & Rutter, M. (Eds.). (1994). *Stress, risk, and resilience in children and adolescents.* New York: Cambridge University Press.

Hinde, R. (1992). Developmental psychology in the context of other behavioral sciences. *Developmental Psychology, 28,* 1018–1029.

Hyman, S. E., & Nestler, E. J. (1996). Initiation and adaptation: A paradigm for understanding psychotropic drug action. *American Journal of Psychiatry, 153,* 151–162.

Institute of Medicine. (1985). Research on mental illness and addictive disorders: Progress and prospects. *American Journal of Psychiatry, 142,* 1–41.

Institute of Medicine. (1994). *Reducing risks for mental disorders.* Washington, DC: National Academy Press.

Jessor, R., Donovan, J., & Costa, F. (1991). *Beyond adolescence: Problem behavior and young adult development.* New York: Cambridge University Press.

Jessor, R., & Jessor, S. L. (1977). *Problem behavior and psychosocial development: A longitudinal study of youth.* New York: Academic Press.

Johnson, J. L. (1994). Developmental theory and alcohol-related phenomena: A discussion of Robert Zucker's paper "Pathways to alcohol problems and alcoholism." In R. Zucker, J. Howard, & G. Boyd (Eds.), *The development of alcohol problems: Exploring the biopsychosocial matrix of risk* (pp. 291–301). Rockville, MD: National Institute on Alcohol Abuse and Alcoholism.

Kagan, J. (1996). Three pleasing ideas. *American Psychologist, 51,* 901–908.

Kandel, D. (1978). Convergences in prospective longitudinal surveys of drug use in normal populations. In D. Kandel (Ed.), *Longitudinal research on drug use* (pp. 3–38). Washington, DC: Hemisphere.

Kellam, S., Brown, C. H., Rubin, B., & Ensminger, M. (1983). Paths leading to teenage psychiatric symptoms and substance use: Developmental epidemiological studies in Woodlawn. In S. Guze, F. Earls, & J. Barrett (Eds.), *Childhood psychopathology and development* (pp. 17–51). New York: Raven Press.

Kessler, R. C., McGonagle, K. A., Zhao, S., Nelson, C. B., Hughes, M., Eshleman, S., Wittchen, H., & Kendler, K. S. (1994). Lifetime and 12-month prevalence of *DSM–III–R* psychiatric disorders in the US: Results from the National Comorbidity Survey. *Archives of General Psychiatry, 51,* 8–19.

Koob, G., & Bloom, F. (1988). Cellular and molecular mechanisms of drug dependence. *Science, 242,* 715–723.

Korenman, S., & Barchas, J. (Eds.). (1993). *Biological basis of substance abuse*. New York: Oxford University Press.

Luthar, S., Burack, J., Cicchetti, D., & Weisz, J. (Eds.). (1997). *Developmental psychopathology: Perspectives on adjustment, risk, and disorder*. New York: Cambridge University Press.

Luthar, S., Cushing, G., & McMahon, T. (1997). Substance abusers and their families: Developmental perspectives. In S. Luthar, J. Burack, D. Cicchetti, & J. Weisz (Eds.), *Developmental psychopathology: Perspectives on adjustment, risk, and disorder* (pp. 437–456). New York: Cambridge University Press.

Pollak, S., Cicchetti, D., Klorman, R., & Brumaghim, J. (1997). Cognitive brain event-related potentials and emotion processing in maltreated children. *Child Development, 68*, 773–787.

Regier, D. A., Narrow, W. E., Rae, D. S., Manderscheid, R. W., Locke, B. Z., & Goodwin, F. K. (1994). The de-facto US mental and addictive disorders service system: Epidemiologic Catchment Area prospective 1-year prevalence rate of disorders and services. *Archives of General Psychiatry, 50*, 85–94.

Richters, J. E., & Cicchetti, D. (1993). Mark Twain meets *DSM–III–R*: Conduct disorder, development, and the concept of harmful dysfunction. *Development and Psychopathology, 5*, 5–29.

Richters, J. E., & Weintraub, S. (1990). Beyond diathesis: Toward an understanding of high-risk environments. In J. Rolf, A. S. Masten, D. Cicchetti, K. G. Nuechterlein, & S. Weintraub (Eds.), *Risk and protective factors in the development of psychopathology* (pp. 67–96). New York: Cambridge University Press.

Rolf, J., Masten, A., Cicchetti, D., Nuechterlein, K., & Weintraub, S. (Eds.). (1990). *Risk and protective factors in the development of psychopathology*. New York: Cambridge University Press.

Rutter, M. (1990). Psychosocial resilience and protective mechanisms. In J. Rolf, A. S. Masten, D. Cicchetti, K. H. Nuechterlein, & S. Weintraub (Eds.), *Risk and protective factors in the development of psychopathology* (pp. 181–214). New York: Cambridge University Press.

Sameroff, A. J., & Chandler, M. J. (1975). Reproductive risk and the continuum of caretaking casualty. In F. D. Horowitz (Ed.), *Review of child development research* (Vol. 4, pp. 187–244). Chicago: University of Chicago Press.

Shedler, J., & Block, J. (1990). Adolescent drug use and psychological health: A longitudinal inquiry. *American Psychologist, 45*, 612–630.

Sher, K. (1991). *Children of alcoholics: A critical appraisal of theory and research*. Chicago: University of Chicago Press.

Sher, K. (1994). Individual-level risk factors. In R. Zucker, J. Howard, & G. Boyd (Eds.), *The development of alcohol problems: Exploring the biopsychosocial matrix of risk* (pp. 77–108). Rockville, MD: National Institute of Alcohol Abuse and Alcoholism.

Sroufe, L. A. (1979). The coherence of individual development: Early care, attachment, and subsequent developmental issues. *American Psychologist, 34*, 834–841.

Sroufe, L. A. (1989). Pathways to adaptation and maladaptation: Psychopathology as developmental deviation. In D. Cicchetti (Ed.), *The emergence of a discipline: Rochester Symposium on Developmental Psychopathology* (Vol. 1, pp. 13–40). Hillsdale, NJ: Erlbaum.

Sroufe, L. A. (1997). Psychopathology as an outcome of development. *Development and Psychopathology, 9,* 251–268.

Sroufe, L. A., Egeland, B., & Kreutzer, T. (1990). The fate of early experience following developmental change: Longitudinal approaches to individual adaptation in childhood. *Child Development, 61,* 1363–1373.

Sroufe, L. A., & Rutter, M. (1984). The domain of developmental psychopathology. *Child Development, 55,* 17–29.

Tarter, R., & Mezzich, A. (1992). Ontogeny of substance abuse: Perspectives and findings. In M. Glantz & R. Pickens (Eds.), *Vulnerability to drug abuse* (pp. 149–177). Washington, DC: American Psychological Association.

Tarter, R., & Vanyukov, M. (1994). Stepwise developmental model of alcoholism etiology. In R. Zucker, J. Howard, & G. Boyd (Eds.), *The development of alcohol problems: Exploring the biopsychosocial matrix of risk* (pp. 303–330). Rockville, MD: National Institute on Alcohol Abuse and Alcoholism.

von Bertalanffy, L. (1968). *General system theory.* New York: Braziller.

Wakefield, J. (1992). Disorder as harmful dysfunction: A conceptual critique of DSM–III–R's definition of mental disorder. *Psychological Review, 99,* 232–247.

Werner, H., & Kaplan, B. (1963). *Symbol formation: An organismic–developmental approach to language and the expression of thought.* New York: Wiley.

Wilden, A. (Ed.). (1980). *System and structure.* London: Tavistock.

Wise, R., & Bozarth, M. (1987). A psychomotor stimulant theory of addiction. *Psychological Review, 94,* 469–492.

Zigler, E., & Glick, M. (1986). *A developmental approach to adult psychopathology.* New York: Wiley.

Zucker, R. A., Fitzgerald, H. E., & Moses, H. D. (1995). Emergence of alcohol problems and the several alcoholisms: A developmental perspective on etiologic theory and life course trajectory. In D. Cicchetti & D. Cohen (Eds.), *Developmental psychopathology: Vol. 2. Risk, disorder, and adaptation* (pp. 677–711). New York: Wiley.

Zucker, R. A., & Gomberg, E. (1986). Etiology of alcoholism reconsidered: The case for a biopsychological process. *American Psychologist, 41,* 783–793.

6

WHY PEOPLE USE, ABUSE, AND BECOME DEPENDENT ON DRUGS: PROGRESS TOWARD A HEURISTIC MODEL

ROBERT J. PANDINA AND VALERIE L. JOHNSON

The question most frequently asked of scientists conducting drug abuse research or practitioners providing direct services, who venture forth to speak in public forums, is, Why do people use drugs? A variety of audiences seem to focus in on this question irrespective of the speaker's stated topic or discipline. Biologists, psychologists, and sociologists are subjected to the same line of questioning. Listeners may be clients, students, community groups, educators, legislators, media, policymakers, law enforcement officials, judges, attorneys, or health care providers. These diverse audiences focus on this question because they hope that the answer will provide clues as to what to do about the problem as they see and experience it.

In this sense, the *why* question—the question of origins—is the gateway question in the study of drug abuse. Unfortunately, the question is disturbing to scientist and practitioner alike because no satisfying answer, let alone consensus, has been articulated; certainly not one that has led to the development of a universally effective set of prevention or treatment interventions.

A FIVE-TIER TAXONOMY OF *WHY* QUESTIONS

The question that forms the central focus of this chapter, Why do people use, abuse, and become dependent on drugs? is a root question that gives rise to a family of questions branching off into quite diverse areas of inquiry. Each one has yielded an important body of research. Taken together, the questions flowing from the branching process form a rough taxonomy of key lines of research that shed light on the origins of drug use, abuse, and dependence. In this chapter, we identify five major related families of questions. Some of these questions may seem obvious, perhaps even trivial, to professionals in the field. However, examination of formal theories, control or intervention policies and strategies, and public opinions and attitudes suggests strongly that these basic questions are not considered fully in forming adequate conceptual or practical responses to the drug problem.

A wide range of theories have been offered over the past two decades (e.g., Glantz & Pickens, 1992; Lettieri, Sayers, & Pearson, 1980) to address these basic questions. Typically, each of these formulations has focused on a limited number of questions drawn from a single family. For the most part, models emphasize *either* neurobiological *or* psychobehavioral *or* socioenvironmental factors and dynamics, often reflecting the orientation of the theorist. Few comprehensive theories, addressing a wide range of questions from multiple families, have been articulated. In general, theories are strong in description of relationships among constructs but lack explanatory power when put to the test empirically. Further, the more comprehensive a theory becomes, the less likely it is to maintain empirical support. (For an interesting discussion of weak and strong theory development in science, see Turkheimer, 1998.) These limitations may reflect more the complexities of developing a comprehensive model that addresses the full range of key questions than the inadequacies of theory builders. Exhibit 1 outlines the five families of questions forming the basis of the proposed taxonomy. Also listed are key subquestions for each family.

Family 1: Properties of Drugs

The first family of questions highlights the nature or special properties of a drug that form the basis of concern. The root question is: What is the nature of a drug that contributes to the development of dependency? Ancillary questions in this family include: What kinds of drugs ought we be

EXHIBIT 1
Taxonomy of Root Questions

Family 1: Properties of drugs
   Root question: What is the nature of a drug that contributes to the
      development of dependency?
   Ancillary question: Do all drugs possess the same properties or cause
      similar problems?
Family 2: Outcome characteristics
   Root question: What outcomes, statuses, or conditions associated with use
      are of concern?
   Ancillary question: Do all drugs represent the same type and level of risk or
      hazard potential?
Family 3: Dynamics of use behavior
   Root question: Is there a common, identifiable sequence in and process of
      the transition to dependency?
   Ancillary question: Is there a unitary process of addiction applicable to all
      drugs?
Family 4: Individual differences in vulnerabilities
   Root question: What are the individual characteristics leading to initiation
      and progression?
   Ancillary questions: Does the process apply to individuals in an equivalent
      manner?
      Why do some high-risk individuals appear immune?
Family 5: Life space structure and dynamics
   Root question: In what ways can the environment influence the decision to
      use?
   Ancillary questions: Are some environments more conducive to use?
      Can the environment be modified to change the use behavior of
      individuals, groups, or institutions?

---

concerned about? Do all drugs possess the same properties or cause similar problems? Is there one common property that causes problems?

Exhibit 2 contains a summary of principal drugs (or drug classes) commonly considered as potentially hazardous. Common descriptives often used to characterize properties of interest also are listed. These include chemical composition, biological targets, potency, toxicity, mechanism of action, and estimates of harm potential. Various methods have been used to quantify these terms.

Family 2: Outcomes of Drug Use

The second family of questions is characterized by the root question: What kinds of outcomes, statuses, or conditions associated with use should we be concerned about? Exhibit 3 contains descriptors used to capture qualitative conditions associated with hazardous drug use. Note that these are listed (approximately) in order of presumed increased magnitude of severity and, to some extent, presumed developmental sequence of appearance. Recovery is listed last on the basis of the supposition that a

EXHIBIT 2
Common Drugs and Delineators of Interest

Common Drug Varieties	Delineators of Interest
Alcohol	Chemical composition
Tobacco	Biological targets
Marijuana	Action mechanisms
Stimulants	Potency
Sedative–hypnotics	Toxicity
Hallucinogens	Harm potential
Prescribed and over-the-counter medications	

person achieving this status would have probably experienced many, if not all, of the earlier and less severe statuses.

Cross-listing terms found in Exhibit 3 with those in Exhibit 2 illustrates the increasing order of complexity introduced when one asks such questions as Do all drugs represent the same type and level of risks? or Are there common properties that can be used to characterize dependence generically or to classify hazard potential? The degree of complexity that this type of matrixing introduces to the *why* question is important to recognize.

An example of the potential complexity involved in characterizing even a portion of the matrix is instructive. In an attempt to develop a prototype model for comparing relative hazards (i.e., harm potential) associated with the use of 20 drugs representing six major drug classes, using only two criteria (quantitative estimates of dependence potential and toxicity), Gable (1993) identified about 1,000 relevant articles covering a period of about 25 years, which he used to construct an interesting two-factor model of harm potential (see Figure 1). Gable's exercise points out

EXHIBIT 3
Drug Use Outcomes, Conditions, and Statuses

Nonuse
Use
Misuse
Abuse–Abuser
Problem use–user
Dependence–dependent user
Addiction–addict
First- and second-degree diseases
Recovery–recovering addict
Estimates of aggregated consequences–outcomes impacting
    Individuals (or groups)
    Short- or long-term behavior (e.g., skills, competence, personality)
    Organ systems
    Interpersonal interactions
    Systemic relationships

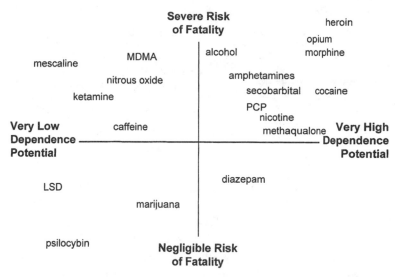

Figure 1. Harm Potential Matrix
MDMA = methylenedioxymeth-amphetamine, PCP = phencyclidine. LSD = lysergic acid diethylamide.
Note. After Gable, (1993).

the enormity, complexity, yet possibility of developing methods for better characterizing key parameters (e.g., harm potential) in substance abuse research.

Family 3: Dynamics of Use Behavior

The third family of questions highlights the importance of the dynamics of use behavior. The root question is: Is there a common, identifiable sequence in and process of the transition to dependency? Ancillary questions include: Is there a unitary process of addiction that can be applied to all drugs? Alternatively, are there different processes (qualitatively and quantitatively distinct) for each drug? If there is a process, what are its essential features?

Exhibit 4 contains a composite prototype (Pandina, 1998), incorporating and summarizing features of several models that attempt to capture generic stages in the progression from use initiation to full-blown dependency, as well as dynamics operational in movement toward use cessation. This overview illustrates the importance of viewing use as a dynamic construct within a developmental context and of highlighting some of the key features of use development that must be accounted for by etiological theories. In the model, outlined below, development of use patterns is partitioned into three developmental stages, and a series of developmental phases is embedded in each stage. Hence, a number of stage–phase se-

EXHIBIT 4
Developmental Stages in Drug Use

Acquisition
   Priming
   Initiation
   Experimentation
Maintenance
   Habit formation
   Dependence
   Obsessive–compulsive use
Control
   Problem awareness
   Interruption–suspension
   Cessation

quences can be identified that have both quantitative and qualitative properties.

The *acquisition* stage marks the part of use trajectory before the actual onset of use, through engagement in experimental ingestion. The *priming* phase represents a developmental period in which individuals are oriented to the formal and informal rules and guidelines about drugs and their use. Individuals learn that a variety of drugs exist, are available under certain conditions, and can be and are used by a wide range of individuals with a range of effects and consequences. Beliefs and attitudes about specific drugs and use practices also are communicated. These instructions can be quite complex even when delivered to relatively young children. For example, some drugs may be viewed as bad (e.g., cigarettes), whereas others may be viewed as beneficial (e.g., prescription medications properly dispensed and administered). Others may be given mixed reviews; for example, social alcohol use may be modeled by parents, but drinking and driving may be viewed negatively. During priming, the person learns about the response capacity of biological tissue to drugs, about individual differences and preferences, and about the customs of use practices in the local life space. All of these events occur before *initiation* and *experimentation*. During these two phases, the person begins to engage in applying the rules and guidelines for herself or himself. During the acquisition stage, use behavior is marked as a unique or foreground event. Many individuals never progress to initiation from the priming phase for most drugs (e.g., heroin). For other drugs (e.g., alcohol), the majority of our society progresses to experimentation, with a significant proportion moving on to the *maintenance* stage. For still other drugs (e.g., marijuana), many individuals may not move beyond experimentation.

The maintenance stage of use trajectory begins with the *habit-formation* phase. During this period, unique use behaviors are integrated into the general response repertoire. Thus, use responses become routinized or habitualized. Use is often paired with a variety of other behaviors and becomes part of the background rather than foreground of the individual response repertoire. In this phase, use is under the behavioral control of the individual and does not dominate the response repertoire. Use behavior can be engaged in selectively with few consequences. In the *dependence* phase, the person comes to rely on use and the states it induces (i.e., intoxication) to maintain homeostatic stability. Interestingly, in the dependence phase, use reacquires its centrality in the life of the individual and dominates the response repertoire. Often, use behavior results in significant and frequent negative consequences. The *obsessive–compulsive* phase is marked by increased use in the absence of, or significant decrease in, apparent efficacy of a drug to maintain the homeostasis of the organism. It could be argued that this phase is an end-state pathological condition of dependence and not itself a unique phase. For some drugs (e.g., alcohol), most individuals who enter the maintenance phase do not progress beyond habit formation, although some do become dependent. For other drugs (e.g., heroin), most individuals who enter the maintenance phase progress to dependence.

The *control–extinction* stage marks that part of the use trajectory extending from identification of a potential or real cost (i.e., negative, damaging consequence) of a particular form of drug use behavior through attempts to interrupt (i.e., prevent onset, halt progression, block expression), to elimination from the response pool (i.e., cessation or relative abstinence). Note that control can occur at any phase of acquisition or maintenance. In fact, for some drugs (e.g., heroin, marijuana, or cigarettes) control–extinction occurs during the priming phase.

The complexity of each of the first three families of questions is heightened further when consideration is given to the often observed phenomena that individuals may exhibit variable patterns of concurrent, sequential, or intermittent use of different drugs. Hence, a given person may find himself or herself in a variety of stage–phase sequences for a number of substances. For example, a person may simultaneously exhibit alcohol maintenance–habit formation, marijuana acquisition–experimentation, heroin acquisition–priming stage–phase sequences. Of course, a variety of sequences are possible. Kandel and colleagues (Kandel, 1975; Kandel, Yamaguchi, & Chen, 1992) were among the first to describe a simple sequence pattern of drug use initiation, including for tobacco and alcohol. Figure 2 contains a typical pattern of initiation sequencing that has been replicated across samples and historical epochs.

Results from other studies suggest the importance of including richer measures of use intensity, to understand transitions across use stages beyond initiation as well as other aspects of the complex nature of developmental stages (Labouvie, Pandina, & Johnson, 1991). More recently, the availability of use-stage data from a broader range of the life span suggests that

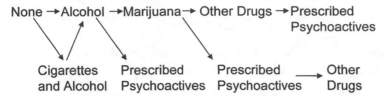

Figure 2. A typical pattern of the sequential stages of drug involvement. *Note.* After Kandel, Yamaguchi, and Chen, (1992).

staging is not necessarily unidirectional (Labouvie, Bates, & Pandina, 1997). Individuals may move backward in the sequence, in qualitative (type of drug) and quantitative (quantity and frequency of use) terms, to what appears to be more controlled forms of use behavior. Hence, control-extinction staging can be superimposed on acquisition and maintenance staging.

Thus, adequate consideration of the dynamic and developmental nature of the process raises a number of challenges for etiological theories. Individuals may be in a variety of stage–phase sequences for different drugs. The boundary between sequences may be fluid across time for some, although not all, individuals. It is also likely that different drugs exhibit quite different properties regarding probability and rate of movement (both forward and backward) among stages and phases. These properties may be more or less stable across individuals. In fact, individual variability may be an important consideration in assessing harm potential. For example, variability in progression in alcohol and marijuana use appears to be greater than that of heroin and tobacco progression.

Family 4: Individual Differences in Vulnerabilities

The fourth family of questions emphasizes the importance of individual differences in determining vulnerability to drug use and its sequelae. Understanding individual differences and incorporating them into etiological models may be the most difficult of challenges. These questions highlight the fact that broad behavioral capacities lie within the human organism. Drugs may modify these capacities, but drugs do not themselves possess the capacity to behave. A key issue is recognizing that individuals can and do regulate drug intake. Drug use can be viewed as purposeful and goal-directed behavior. Significant attention has focused on the instrumental value of use and the states use induces, to understand user motivation. Biological (e.g., genetic predisposition and neural adaptation), psychological (e.g., personality profile and emotional regulation), and socioenvironmental (e.g., peer-group membership and geopolitical climate) dynamics all have been cited as motivational substrata. It is likely that no single motivational factor can account for all forms of use. Particularly important is the characterization of motivational states that are significantly related to transitions in stage–phase sequences, for example, transitions from acquisition–priming to acquisition–initiation or acquisition–experimentation to maintenance–habit formation or from maintenance–dependence to control–problem awareness. Different stage–phase sequences may be differentially sensitive to various motivational dynamics. For example, shifts from priming to initiation may be heavily influenced by socioenvironmental factors (e.g., peer group or drug availability), but the transition from experimentation to habit formation may be more under the control of psychobehavioral factors, such as the need for affect regulation (Pandina, Johnson & Labouvie, 1992).

The root question is, What are the characteristics of individuals (singly and in aggregate) that lead some to select and participate in drug use behavior? Ancillary questions are, What causes movement or progression (and possibly regression) through use stages to dependence by only a fraction of those who initiate use? Does the process (or processes) of addiction apply to all individuals in an equivalent manner? What are the important parameters of individual (or group) differences that influence the course of progression? Why is relapse a common occurrence among many formerly dependent users, even after prolonged abstinence periods? Why do some people seem immune or resistant even when they may appear to be at high risk? In what ways do drug use, abuse, and dependence relate to other dysfunctional states, including so-called internalized disorders (e.g., depression or anxiety) or externalized disorders (e.g., aggression or antisocial personality) that seem to frequently aggregate with drug use?

Family 5: Life Space Structure and Dynamics

The fifth family of questions recognizes the importance of environmental or ecological determinants of drug use behavior, including physical and social environments. Environmental conditions may even affect physiological reactivity to drug ingestion (e.g., Siegel & Allan, 1998; Siegel, Hinson, Krank, & McCully, 1982). These questions also suggest that individuals shape their environments, at least in part, to meet their real and perceived needs. Note that person–environment influences are bidirectional, that is, whereas environments impose themselves, individuals may both select and shape their environments to accommodate their needs. Thus, relatively static considerations, such as social institutions (e.g., school, work place, banks, governmental agencies) and their role-specific relationships (e.g., student, worker, customer, subject, or client), and more fluid considerations, such as peer-group membership and personal status (e.g., teenager, computer nerd, athlete, child of an alcoholic), are viewed as potentially powerful determinants of use.

Questions in this domain parallel those of the individual-differences family. The root question is: In what ways can the physical and social environment influence the decision to use drugs and the forms the behavior might take? Ancillary questions include: How are the environmental messages transmitted? Are some environments more conducive of or inductive to use? Are inclined individuals more likely to choose or, perhaps, even create supportive environments? Can the environment modify the use experience of an individual, groups of individuals, or institutions? Can the environment be modified to change its ability, if any, to shape drug use behavior?

The taxonomy of questions, while helpful in identifying and organizing seminal questions by primary domains, serves to illustrate further the diversity and complexity of the nature of drug use phenomena that must be accounted for by any complete theory of etiology. This complexity seems to preclude the development of a single, parsimonious theory that could even integrate the data generated to date aimed at addressing questions in a given domain, let alone across the domains of this rough taxonomy.

The ability of any theory, heuristic model, or answer to address adequately the generic and seminal *why* question can be judged, in part, by assessing its ability to address adequately issues raised by each and all families. Hence, the tentative answer that is offered below is guided by considering its adequacy to meet this satisfaction standard. We format an answer by examining it through the lenses provided by the family of questions. Thus, analysis of the degree to which the answer's features meet criteria as necessary or sufficient explanations to each family of questions serves as a method to develop the answer and offers an approach to assess its adequacy.

A GUIDING FRAMEWORK: THE BIOPSYCHOSOCIAL PARADIGM

The research community has come to adopt the position that drug use results from a complex interaction of biological, psychological, and sociological factors (e.g., Institute of Medicine, 1996). This paradigm is typified by the work of Ford (1987). Figure 3 (derived from Ford, 1987) summarizes the basic characteristics of living-systems models that seek to integrate neurobiological, psychobehavioral, and socioenvironmental factors in explaining behavior in general. Such models also have been used as heuristic aids to account for a wide range of dysfunctional behaviors (Miller, 1978; Shapiro, Schwartz, & Astin, 1996). Implicit in such formulations is that a significant portion of a person's behavioral repertoire is goal directed, purposeful, and aimed at gaining control over a constantly changing, hence, demanding, environment (Heckhausen & Schulz, 1995; Shapiro et al., 1996). Individuals may not always be fully aware of the full

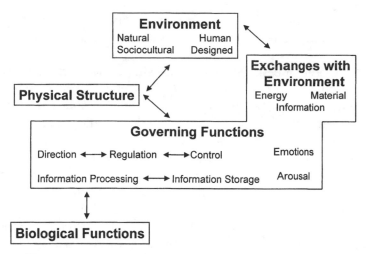

Figure 3. The person as a living control system. Adapted from Ford (1987).

range of consequences of a given behavior. And many behavior patterns, including drug use, may develop an automatic quality through complex conditioning processes (see e.g., Ramsay & Woods, 1997; Siegel & Allan, 1998). Of course, these considerations do not preclude the possibility that some behavior is spontaneous or random. Likewise, there is room for behaviors that are life sustaining and under autonomic control.

Also implicit is the notion that the organism develops, through experience, relatively permanent, or at least stable but malleable, complex psychobehavioral responses congruent with the tissue capacities of the body (particularly those of the central nervous system: CNS). In other words, individuals have the ability to develop rather elaborate general behavioral programs to produce more specific behavior patterns (including drug use). This process is regulated, shaped, and limited by the capacity of underlying brain circuits to change and adapt to the outside environment. Brain circuits have the capacity to control behavior, yet these circuits are responsive and can be shaped by experience.

The relative efficacy (both short and long term) of such learned brain responses in regulating environmental transactions is monitored through cognitive and emotional mechanisms that rise from neural circuits. Thus, what we experience as thinking and feeling states are products of our brain's capacity, and at the same time, these abilities serve to provide feedback as to how responsive our actions are in shaping or controlling our environment. Presumably, these neural assemblies that give rise to the experience of feeling and thinking have evolved as adaptive mechanisms designed to respond to naturally occurring and biologically significant rewarding and punishing stimuli (for application to drug abuse, see Jaffe, 1992; Nestler, Hope, & Widnell, 1993; Piazza & LeMoal, 1996; Wise, 1996). In this regard, evolutionary pressure and opportunity have provided the organism with the capacity to reflect and map inwardly the external environment's demands, to select, organize, and execute responses, and to appraise the effects and determine the state of well-being or satisfaction that may or may not accrue. One key role of affective appraisal is to attach valence-loaded and arousal-laden charges to behavior–outcome networks. Thus, the significance of what we do (i.e., our behavior) is constantly being judged by feedback about how we feel emotionally. Storage or memory capabilities of neural nets also are implicit in this model.

Such models view motivational processes as complex, organized patterns composed of directive, regulatory, and arousal functions (see Figure 4). Presumably, these patterns arise from the cooperation and coordination of neural circuits and manifest themselves as overt behavior. Hence, motivational processes have a prewired (perhaps "wet-wired" is a more appropriate description) feature that because of their nature plays a central role in requiring the organism to act in and on the environment. In other words, the capacity to act results in the predisposition to act. These processes (and their underlying *wetware*) provide the substrata for what might be termed the *need* or *drive for self-efficacy* in behavioral regulation. The dynamics of motivational processes are central to and essential for an understanding of drug use (e.g., Cox & Klinger, 1988; Poulos & Cappell, 1991; Solomon, 1980).

Although use of such models has become popular in describing drug use, abuse, and dependence, the full import of this position has yet to be explored. During the past three decades, drug abuse researchers have characterized a myriad of constructs from each domain (neurobiological, psy-

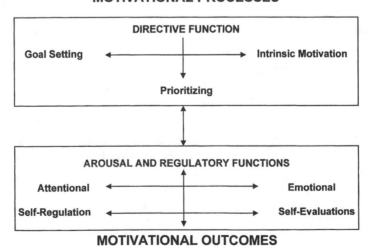

Figure 4. Motivation as a complex, regulatory function. Adapted from Ford (1987).

chobehavioral, socioenvironmental) that play a significant role in the acquisition, maintenance, and control of a broad range of drug use behaviors, outcomes, and related phenomena. These include selection of the behavior, progression from initiation to dependence, development of highly energized drive states characteristic of obsessive–compulsive drug use, efficacy of drugs in producing states of well-being, resistance to use, and relapse. However, to date, no single domain, let alone a single factor, has generated satisfactory answers to core questions in any of the families discussed above. Neither have we determined the relative contribution or interplay of factors to predict key aspects of drug use, drug use outcomes, or related phenomena. In fact, most of the success of our models lies in *post hoc* descriptive analysis.

Dozens of major reviews have been published focusing on one or another perspective (e.g., Glantz & Pickens, 1992; Hawkins, Catalano, & Miller, 1992; Jaffe, 1992; Petraitis, Flay, & Miller, 1995; Ramsay & Woods, 1997; Scheier & Newcomb, 1991; Stitzer & Cox, 1996; Wise, 1996; see also Kandel, 1980; Lettieri, Sayers, & Pearson 1980). These have cited literally thousands of empirical studies. Not included in the direct count are reviews that include drug use as a cofactor in their subject area.

At least a dozen of these reviews focus on drug use behaviors of adolescents (chiefly, use initiation and experimentation). Putative risk factors have been identified although no particular factor (or combination) appears determining (Glantz & Pickens, 1992; Hawkins et al., 1992; Pandina, 1998; Petraitis et al., 1995). Etiological literature reflecting middle- and late-stage uses and a broader range of adult populations (i.e., broader than adults in treatment) is emerging from longitudinal studies begun in the early to mid 1970s (e.g., Bachman, Wadsworth, O'Malley, Johnston & Schulenberg, 1997; Brook, Whiteman, Cohen, & Tanaka, 1992; Chen & Kandel, 1995; Jessor, Van Den Bos, Vanderryn, Costa, & Turbin, 1995; Kaplan, 1995; Newcomb & Bentler, 1988; Pandina, Labouvie, & White, 1984), as are studies focusing on alcohol use and dependence through the life span (e.g., Fillmore et al., 1994; Vaillant, 1983).

In fact, a quick count of apparently salient constructs yields between 40 and 60 qualitatively distinct factors (e.g., Pandina, 1998). Equally problematic is the fact that the universe of factors is distributed across the set of even more carefully documented pathways and appears to be coincident with many factors accounting for other apparently dysfunctional behaviors or disturbing outcomes, such as delinquency, violence, and mental illnesses (Coie et al., 1993; Jessor et al., 1995; Johnson, 1995). Of course, drug use of varying degrees has been viewed as both cause and effect of many such outcomes (Compas, Hinden, & Gerhardt, 1995; McGee & Newcomb, 1992).

The general degree of overlap in these models has led to the development of several common-factors theories (e.g., problem-behavior theory,

Jessor, 1987; self-derogation theory, Kaplan, 1980) that have been useful and productive in stimulating theoretical thinking across several fields. However, multiple pathways, risk and protective factors, and other such vulnerability models (including what have been characterized as common-factors theories) pose major theoretical problems and challenges for etiological research that extend to the applied arena of drug abuse policy and intervention programs. Overly specific formulations limit applications to narrow ranges within the drug use–outcome matrix or within limited samples. Overly general formulations appear to yield diluted effects. Multiple-pathway approaches appear to require many approaches and require that they be applied to appropriately aggregated individuals or to other targets (e.g., communities). Identification of underlying common principles could provide a unifying framework that would guide theory and applications.

Hence, although the biopsychosocial concept has provided a broad context for viewing the vast array of salient research literature, a basic understanding of how the pieces function in concert to produce the panoply of use-related phenomena has not been achieved. At this point in time, to assume that the biopsychosocial model is an adequate theory of drug abuse would place serious limitations on advancement in the understanding of the origins of drug abuse.

How then to approach organizing an answer or at least a heuristic model that could assist in forming an answer? It seems wise to step back from the literature, take a deep breath, and take a small, although necessary, leap of speculation. The following discussion offers some of the major aspects of this small leap toward a model.

STRUCTURING AN ANSWER:
DIMENSIONS AND CRITICAL ELEMENTS

During the discussion of taxonomy, it was suggested that organizing the apparent diversity within and between families of questions along key dimensions or vectors would be a useful first step in structuring an answer. The dimensions need to hold their strength and lend utility to answering the root questions in each of the families, when tested against the existing theoretical and empirical literature. A further consideration is that using these dimensions to form answers should reduce (or at least organize) the confusion implicit and embedded in existing multiple-pathway models.

By first extracting and then recombining what appears to be dominant features of related questions from each root family, two major dimensions can be identified that embrace a satisfying number of questions for all five families. The first dimension revolves around the topography of the drug use response itself. The second dimension revolves around the dynamic interaction between the respondent (particularly, selective tissue and psychobehavioral capacities of individuals) and responding or operating environment (particularly, the conditional status of the life space or operating environment).

Dimension 1: Generalized Drug Use Environment

The first dimension seems to be suited to addressing the question, What does drug use space look like? The boundaries of the first proposed dimension are defined by the matrix produced when one crosses the generic developmental use-stage matrix and the drug-typology matrix. In defining this dimension, we make three principal assumptions: (a) Drug use is a developmental phenomenon both within individuals and across drug types; (b) stages and processes exist along the lines specified in the generic stage–phase model and can be reasonably defined or marked; and (c) all drugs share, at least qualitatively, the same features and can be characterized (and compared, at least qualitatively), and these features lend themselves to quantification along key dimensions.

As was discussed in relationship to Exhibit 4, which outlines a generic model of use stages, reasonable definitions of and markers for use stages can be identified. These stages represent qualitative and quantitative changes in use status. The definitions share features derived from many different perspectives. Likewise, methods of characterizing and comparing different drugs along key dimensions are readily available, as in the methods proposed by Gable (1993).

This exercise produces a kind of generalized drug use space or environment. Virtually all use behaviors and use-related processes, no matter how they are defined or delineated, can be identified in this space. Likewise, the use-behavior status of any individual or group of individuals can be identified and located in the space. By adding time as a dynamic variable, the history or use trajectory of an individual (or, in a more complex algorithm, an aggregation of individuals) can be charted and specified along a number of key factors currently used to define and assess associated qualitative states. Specification can involve as many or as few drug-typology features as are available.

The use of such a matrix combines quantitative and qualitative descriptions of use with dynamic-process descriptions. Hence, this space and the structure it provides can be used to address questions about the topography of any and all use behaviors, as well as the dynamics of the process through which various use behaviors are acquired, maintained, and controlled. This matrix provides a way of conceptualizing and synthesizing, in a metatheoretical sense, the nature of drug use space and the relative place and profile of any user in that space.

These considerations stress the importance of placing an understanding of the dynamics of drug use behaviors in the foreground of our research agenda. The discussion of Family 3 questions regarding developmental processes highlights the difficulties in, and advantages of, qualitatively and quantitatively characterizing a parsimonious set of stage—phase sequences that captures key features for all drug types. Certain parametric values associated with stage—phase sequences for specific drugs may change (e.g., mode of ingestion, pharmacological nature, typical doses and frequency, age of onset, rate of use escalation, degree of harm, disease outcomes, even popularity of a particular drug in a given population), but the underlying processes are common. Fluctuation in expression (phenotype) of behavior may be more driven by dynamic or process-related mechanisms. Much of the apparent or phenotypic variability may be obscuring more fundamental commonality. Hence, the common processes may also be fundamentally stable, although certain local features of a particular drug may change. Looking for more fundamental commonalities also can help in identifying processes that may make a unique contribution for a specific drug type. Without a parsimonious set of common processes, it is necessary to examine separately etiological factors for each stage—phase sequence for each drug.

If drug use trajectories could be described by the fundamental developmental processes and transforming features, irrespective of type of substance, then it would be possible to determine if origins of apparently very different drug use behaviors were quite similar, if not identical. Even if some drug types displayed unique features, a systematic assessment of stage—phase commonalities would facilitate identification of these special rules.

These observations point out the advantages of characterizing carefully the dynamics of drug use processes. In addition, a better understanding of structure of use dynamics could have a major impact on the manner in which etiological model development proceeds. Having a better drug use template would permit a more careful and finer grained analysis of the manner in which specific etiological factors drawn from each domain of the biopsychosocial paradigm might operate to influence stage—phase sequencing and transitions. A finer grained assessment would permit the decomposition of bio-psycho-social factors in relationship to qualitatively and quantitatively distinct processes that are well characterized empirically and theoretically. In a sense, we are suggesting the need to take a step back to better understand the complex nature of what we are attempting to predict. In this way, one could construct a simultaneous equation with the drug use environment on one side and some dynamic formulation of the biopsychosocial model on the other.

Dimension 2: Dynamics of the Respondent-Operating Environment

To construct a generalized drug use environment, as illustrated in Dimension 1, we began with a relatively large but reasonably identifiable universe of use events and related phenomena. This universe was structured into a generic stage model, capturing many central facets of drug-using behavior by making a few basic assumptions about its developmental nature and organization. Construction of Dimension 2, that is, the person–environment side of the equation, is considerably more demanding. The first problem is defining a reasonable universe of person–environment phenomena.

The broadest set of person (respondent) processes, as outlined in a general biopsychosocial paradigm, could be chosen (e.g., Ford, 1987). Or one could start with the 40–60 putative risk factors for drug abuse (e.g., Hawkins et al., 1992; Pandina, 1998; Petraitis et al., 1995). Certainly these are inclusive, but far from parsimonious, sets. On the other hand, the question could be posed in a different way: What are the minimum qualities or characteristics resident in the organism (the person or respondent) and the life space (the responding–operating environment) that can account for the broadest range of phenomena in the drug use space? Beginning with this more parsimonious set, an attempt can be made to identify the dynamic processes that link these characteristics with those of the drug use environment. Furthermore, if this set can be linked to a significant portion of the drug use dimension, then this will lend support to the view that these generic etiologic factors represent a reasonable distillation of the putative universe of risk and protective factors. This is where the small speculative leap is required. In some sense, this is not unlike the selection of start values in developing a structural equation model.

Exhibit 5 contains a simplified listing of generic properties of the person-operating environment that are required to permit the emergence of the range of drug use phenomena. This set was chosen because it seems to encompass the majority of putative etiological factors consistently identified in the drug abuse literature. Furthermore, these factors are consistent with major constructs in general life system models that form the basis of

EXHIBIT 5
Minimum Biopsychosocial Criteria
Yielding Drug Use Behavior

Tissue capacity
  Sensitive
  Controlling of critical circuits
  Conditionally responsive
Organismic status
  Response ready
  Performance capable
  Motivated
Life space conditions
  Supportive
  Opportunistic
  Sustaining

the biopsychosocial paradigm. Hence, these properties (the functional tiers represented as tissue capacity, organismic status, and life space conditions in Exhibit 5) and relationships among them can be viewed in the context of the general operating rules of a living systems perspective. Note also that the distinctions made by separating these components (that is, bio-psycho-social) for separate analysis are somewhat artificial in that all systems are mutually immersed. In the case of the tissue–organism tiers, it is easier to recognize the artificiality of the separation because the organism is composed of tissue systems and, it could be argued, organismic processes are the wetware (i.e., arising from tissue-bound systems). This is true even though tissue systems (and subcompartments within systems—e.g., cell nuclei, mitochondria, hippocampi, reticular activating system) can be viewed as independent components. However, living systems theory would view the interactions between the life space and the organism (including its quasi-independent wetware systems) as equally important and interdependent determinants of individual behavior. Interdependence is recognized as bidirectional, that is, the organism's behavior is shaped by the demands of the environment and, at the same time, the organism shapes its environment. Included within the framework of environmental shaping is the notion that organisms may select their environments to meet needs.

In what ways, then, do these biopsychosocial components contribute to various forms of drug-using behavior? In its simplest form, the answer is that the tissue is sensitive and critical for functioning, the person is needy and driven, the life space is conducive and inductive, and the timing is right. The following three sections provide an outline of the key features of each component as well as a discussion of their relative contributions to the development of use, abuse, and dependence.

Tissue Capacity

For the purposes of this overview, the focus is on central nervous system tissue and circuits. However, other body system tissues (e.g., the liver) merit attention and are pertinent for understanding relevant aspects of drug use behavior. First and foremost, tissue needs to be sensitive, that is, responsive to the drug substance or substances. The gains in knowledge in the field of tissue responsivity made in the past decade are truly remarkable. Understanding of receptor sites and systems, mechanisms of action (both short and long), and complex circuitry and circuit control clearly demonstrates that drugs selected by humans have an important capacity to regulate neural tissue and circuits both acutely and chronically (Nestler et al., 1993; Poulos & Cappell, 1991). This has contributed somewhat to the "chaos factor" of our field as well. So much is now known about so many substances that it is becoming difficult to focus on the commonality among the detail and diversity. However, several reviews (e.g., Piazza & LeMoal, 1996; Wise, 1996) have identified potential common pathways, hence mechanisms, through which a variety of substances may exert their influence both acutely and chronically over an organism.

What seems particularly salient is the common ability of drugs of abuse to regulate and modulate circuits that govern appreciation of biologically significant and naturally occurring rewarding and punishing stimuli. The tissue targeted by drugs selected by organisms regulates arguably the most fundamental processes required for survival. The wetware circuits evolve to be responsive to objects and events that occur in nature and have significant physical consequences. Successful individuals must be able to appraise accurately objects and events that signal the likelihood of pleasure and harm. Signals of pleasure and harm shape the basic response tendencies of approach and avoidance. The appraisal process is cognitive and emotive in nature. The emotive aspects of the circuitry appear particularly sensitive to drug effects.

Hence, the tissue is generally sensitive and important. Through complex circuitry, it has the capacity to regulate the transcription and proliferation of a salient message about potential and likely efficacy of a behavioral response. These events, transcription and proliferation, are probably expressed through positive- and negative-reinforcement-feedback circuits. The transcription carries, among other things, a message about the affective well-being of the organism that results from the response. The message can be spread throughout a variety of neural networks that regulate other important functions.

Furthermore, the tissue is responsive to and can be driven by a wide range of exogenous analogues of endogenous materials that drive key effector neural regulatory systems. The neural circuits served by the target tissue are vital for the recognition and registration of positive- and negative-reinforcement messages and the transcription of those messages to other neural systems that alert and arouse the organism as to the quality and magnitude of the reinforcement. Because drugs are, in a sense, summative, their actions can supplement, complement, or substitute for the actions of behavioral responses that naturally drive the system.

One other property of the drug-sensitive wetware is critical. These primary circuits are subject to conditioning. Responses are not hardwired; only the capacity to make responses exists within the neural networks. Thus, responses are quite malleable, and no one response is wired as correct. Some responses may appear to be preferred, but the manner in which preference is determined is complex. Circuits necessary for transcription and proliferation of a particular response can, in a very real sense, learn, retain, recall, and reinstate their message. In addition, these drug-sensitive circuits are critically positioned within the central nervous system to influence other operating circuits that build, execute, and retain psychobehavioral responses (i.e., specific behavior routines and programs) for future use.

Hence, these primary drug-sensitive circuits can guide the building of relatively elaborate segments of an organism's instrumental response repertoire (e.g., Baker & Tiffany, 1985). It is becoming increasingly clear that such conditioning and learning processes occurring at the neural circuit level can play an important role for many key dynamic processes at work in dependence, including stimulus recognition and generalization, anticipatory and compensatory sensitization, tolerance, withdrawal, and relapse (Ramsay & Woods, 1997; Siegel & Allan, 1998). Thus, the influence that drug action can have on critical drug-sensitive circuits can long outlast the period of time during which a drug may directly alter the function of a particular cell or cellular circuit.

There is an interesting and critical consequence for neural regulation through drug ingestion, however. The potential for feedback distortion is quite high. In other words, augmenting feedback about the efficacy of a response alters the evaluation of efficacy. One possibility is that a response is given more credit than it deserves: positive augmentation. Another possibility is that the drug use response itself substitutes for, and may displace, the more natural and ecologically valid response (i.e., a response that more accurately portrays the individual's response capacity). Remember that any drug use behavior is by its nature instrumental: an action that produces results. Hence, when drug action augments a response (e.g., by enhancing an emotional state), the individuals can be led to believe that the response is more effective or salient in that particular situation. In this case, the drug-enhanced response may gain a preference in the response repertoire of the individual: "Things go better . . . with coke, . . . when I'm drinking . . . when I'm smoking . . . when I'm high." The new, more complex response (engaging in a given behavior, X, while taking or being under the influence of drugs) may substitute for a response that may have greater ecological validity but is less emotionally satisfying.

Thus, drug use behavior can not only augment but also potentially supplant, or substitute for, a natural ecologically valid response given certain conditions. Absence of an adequate or effective ecologically valid response when such a response is called for, or high-frequency engagement in the use behavior that overwhelms the natural response repertoire, may result in substitution of the drug use response for a more appropriate and ecologically relevant behavior. There are other important, relevant features of drug use that build from these few properties. Because drug use can be superimposed on the general response repertoire, it is transferable across circumstances and venues. Hence, it can happen that a generic, drug-sensitized utility program that enhances perceived efficacy can be automatically evoked on a general need basis.

There are a number of other ways one can imagine that such tissue can contribute to one or more of the processes outlined in drug use space. Given that it is biologically determined, it might not be merely sensitive, but also differentially sensitive, both for varying drugs within an individual or for different individuals. Likewise, the tissue itself has a history—both developmental and genetic. Thus, tissue apparently can "cause" drug use because tissue, particularly drug-sensitive CNS tissue, that is vital for key psychological and behavioral processes can be altered (i.e., conditioned) by drug use behavior and can be rendered both overly capable (inappropriately enhanced) and incapable of valid self-regulation (Ramsay & Woods, 1997; Siegel & Allan, 1998).

Organismic Status

How does the tissue know what drugs can do to it? How does it find drugs? How does it learn the use rules? Here again, it is instructive to turn briefly to the general life systems models for guidance. A key characteristic of the person is readiness to respond to environmental change. In fact, the person as an individual is under general tension to respond to a changing environment, even to the point where no change may be painful, as occurs in sensory deprivation. A key aspect of being response ready is the individual's general sensitization to the salience of feedback messages about efficacy. Like its tissue, the whole organism evaluates its response in terms of its own efficacy and well-being.

The person, of course, can respond in a manner unavailable to tissue systems. He or she can appreciate a much wider variety of stimuli and form very complex maps of the external and internal environment, including maps about drug use. He or she can form complex psychobehavioral programs to perform a multitude of responses, including many forms of drug use. He or she can accomplish these tasks by summing, coordinating, and reintegrating functions or processes drawn from tissue capabilities to meet his or her real and perceived needs.

Hence, the whole organism has the ability to comprehend and build a complex response array; that is, to be response ready for action in and on the environment. The whole organism can mobilize all of its critical circuits and apply them as needed. In a sense, the whole organism can act as a virtual master, able to access, cross-access, and intermix its own Internet of potential responses. In this way, the organism can create and display very diverse abilities beyond those that would be predicted by examination of individual circuits.

The organism can reach out to interact with the environment. In fact, it is under pressure to reach out, because the environment is imposed on the organism. Unlike individual CNS systems, the whole individual is directly connected to the operating environment. This is actually a vulnerability, in that the organism can and must be influenced by the external operating environment. The relationship between the organism and the environment is bidirectional and highly interactive. Because of these attributes, the organism is performance capable. In fact, the individual must be performance capable to be successful. It has the flexibility to learn about behaviors and to learn to perform those necessary to meet its needs. Its performance capacity is governed by the general rules of behavior. Thus, it has the capacity to learn and execute the necessary behaviors, including drug use behaviors. Like tissue, it can be influenced by the reinforcing value of the drug intoxication accompanying use. Note that the organism can and does learn that abstinence from drug use is a form of drug-using behavior. This fact is sometimes overlooked by etiologic theorists.

Repetitious interactions of the response-ready, performance-capable organism with the same or similar environmental pressures and scenarios have other important consequences. As Neiss (1988) has observed, a central guiding purpose of an organism's response readiness and performance capability is the regulation of transient and more permanent psychobiological states that arise from these constructs and the dynamic forces that appear to generate and regulate them. Globally, positively valued states are pleasing, indicative of successful responding, and induce approach, whereas negatively valued states signal failure, are dysphoric, and induce avoidance. Thus, responses that signal satisfying psychobiological states are considered successful and are likely to be repeated. From the living systems perspective, it can be argued that many of the relatively permanent constructs (e.g., self-identity, cognitive and affective processing, personality, and coping style) as well as more labile or transient states (e.g., thoughts, speech, action, emotions, and moods) arise from a combination of structural control of tissue composition and the dynamic capacity of the organism to mobilize and perform its functions with purpose. Construction of functions also represents an efficient means for the organism to respond quickly and consistently to a changing environment.

Of particular relevance for understanding the origins of drug use is that the very domains that arise from organismic capacities are those most frequently nominated as producing mechanisms to control psychobiological states. A common feature of vulnerability to various forms of drug use, particularly more intensive use, is the lack of successful regulation of psychobiological states. In the vulnerability literature, it is postulated that regulation of these states through drug use is likely to be manifested by individuals who are unable to mobilize other effective responses, whose response efficacy is blocked in some way, or who come to view drug use as advantageous (e.g., by supplementing or enhancing performance capacity and response readiness or by directly producing satisfying states; Labouvie, 1986).

Hence, the person is guided, pressured, incited, and motivated to develop effective methods of regulating psychobiologic states. These states arise from the structures, functions, and capacities of identifiable tissues of the CNS (e.g., dopaminergic neurons, ventral tegmentum, and autoregulation). Separate tissue circuits recombined by anatomical location and functional interaction result in useful, malleable functions and capacities, some of which have apparent or virtual structures (e.g., coping strategies, self-efficacy, personal identity). These physical and apparently virtual mechanisms are available to the person as he or she negotiates the pressured waters of the physical, psychological, and social environment.

In the same way that drugs can stimulate and satisfy critical drug-sensitive CNS circuits, they may satisfy more complex need states. In this regard, the advantage of having the flexibility to use all of one's CNS tissue resources escalates the risks as well as rewards. All of the contributions of tissue to drug use are magnified by the degree of complexity that is afforded the whole organism. In addition, CNS tissue or circuits are not capable of seeking and taking drugs. It is the motivated, performance-capable, and response-ready person who must balance his or her psychobiological states when under the pressure to perform in a demanding and competitive operating environment. The person is capable of learning new ways of managing these states. And, like vital tissue, the person can be rendered first capable, then incapable, of self-regulation. Therefore, it seems, individual characteristics can cause drug use.

Life Space Conditions

How does the organism come to know about drugs? Learn the rules of use? How does it find them? What makes drug use an attractive alternative? Let's turn to the life space, the operating environment of the individual.

In keeping with a living systems analysis of drug-use-related phenomena, the life space or operating environment can be parceled into levels or milieus: physical, social systems (formal and informal), and interpersonal. Each of these may be characterized by a number of parameters. The potential for the development of use, abuse, and dependence appears to increase dramatically as a function of the magnitude that each milieu displays and the properties identified in minimal conditions outlined, thus creating a favorable, disposing, and essential operating environment.

The life space carries and transduces messages about the potential efficacy, desirability, availability, and topography of drug use behaviors of all kinds. Messages for any and all substances carry positively and negatively valenced material, accurate and inaccurate. Messages are often competing and conflicting. They also contain information regarding use, both prescriptive and proscriptive in nature. The sources of information are varied in nature and credibility. Parents, peers, and social institutions represent media of all types. The messages are reasonably densely packed. To some extent, the message is generic, hence transferable, and is conducive to rules transmissions. How to get it, how to use, what it can and cannot, will and will not do. Who should or could use or not. And what risks and benefits might be.

Consider just a few examples. Prescription and nonprescription medications (including those for managing psychological distress) and the so-called licit, available although controlled, substances (i.e., alcohol and tobacco) have formal and informal prescription and proscription. In addition, certain forms of "softer" drug use (e.g., occasional marijuana smoking, a line or two of "recreational cocaine") are tolerated, if not promoted, by social attitudes in certain sectors. (Note that these characterizations do not reflect the opinions of the authors. Rather, they reflect the mixture of attitudes, lifestyles, and social norms of the times.) In a similar vein, even generally positively valued behaviors such as alcohol use are known to produce significant negative effects.

Thus, the socially carried message is a complex mix about recreation and remediation, efficacy and risk, prescription and proscription. There are even messages about what to do if rules violations are committed (e.g., the availability of treatment). There are elaborate and effective means of transmitting the message. Thus, the operating environment supports and transcribes the message to a variety of targets whether or not the target intends to listen.

An opportunistic environment also provides the means of use. These include indirect (e.g., action modeling) and direct instructive opportunity to practice and engage in one or more forms of the behavior (including informal and formal, prescriptive and proscriptive structure), in other words, the transcription of rules and guidelines. Supportive environments also may provide help for those who violate the rules or randomly experience dysfunction. Opportunistic environments make available the actual materials to be used in the proper forms, doses, or prices. Equally important, opportunistic environments create and provide venues for use. Finally, the operating environments most likely to induce use are those in which support and opportunity are sustained across time and across the three milieus: physical, socioenvironmental, and interpersonal.

Thus, the operating environment can cause drug use in its many forms. It can establish the forms of the behavior, train to the forms, provide the drugs, and transcript the behaviors to a wide variety of consumers. But the environment could not remain sustaining if the consumer did not choose from the menu or were not satisfied in some important ways by outcomes from the behavior. This, of course, brings us back to the organism, the individual, and that drug-sensitive CNS tissue.

IMPLICATIONS FOR UNDERSTANDING THE ORIGINS OF DRUG USE PHENOMENA

A central thesis of this chapter is that any useful explanation of the origins of drug use and related phenomena must address not only the core question of why people use, abuse, and become dependent on drugs, but also the myriad of questions that spring from this root issue. We suggest that these questions can be organized meaningfully into five interrelated families of questions. Two factors appear to characterize major dimensions that cut across the family domains. One dimension is specified by phenomena related to the generalized drug use environment, and a second dimension delineates the dynamics of the person-operating environment. Taken together, these families and their two cross-cutting dimensions form a rough taxonomy that can be used to frame, structure, and guide approaches that seek to synthesize the volumes of empirical research that has been generated over the past several decades. Such a guiding framework is especially needed at this time in the history of drug abuse research inasmuch as the etiologic literature spans subject matter that seeks to identify the unique and relative contributions of neurobiological, psychobehavioral, and socioenvironmental factors to an increasingly wide range of use-related phenomena within the context of life systems theory. This task is complicated further in that factors from these domains (taken either singly or in combinations) vary in salience, depending on which drug use phenomenon or set of phenomena is being explained.

We believe that using this or similar frameworks can facilitate the development of a wide variety of relevant schema, such as those developed in this chapter, that can be used in identifying basic contributions (and limitations) of each component of the biopsychosocial model to various drug use phenomena. Awareness of, if not adherence to, such frameworks also forces consideration of questions often remote to the immediate interests of investigators who, out of technical necessity, may be overly focused on a given compartment of the model. For example, the issue of how the CNS comes to know what drug will work under which set of rules and what circumstances may yield important insights as to how tissue becomes primed for various drug effects (e.g., Ramsay & Woods, 1997; Siegel & Allan, 1998; Siegel et al., 1982).

Limited application of the framework in this chapter yields the identification of an appealing (although admittedly simplified) set of minimal conditions of tissue, organism, and life space necessary and sufficient to produce a wide range of conditions and outcomes specified in a generalized drug use environment. The exercise also suggests the nature of the dynamic processes that link these minimal conditions. Thus, challenging the minimal conditions to address major aspects of the five families of questions yields an answer, of sorts, to the core *why* question. Furthermore, the answer is couched in terms of a generic living systems model of behavior.

In its simplest form, the answer yielded in this application is that the tissue is sensitive to, capable of being driven by, and inclined to respond to a wide variety of pharmacological agents. These drugs, if prescriptively applied, share a common capacity to stimulate and satisfy neural circuits, whose role it is to convince the organism that it can and has gained control over circumstances. The tissue accomplishes this feat by producing an extreme and clear sense of satisfaction. These circuits are most susceptible when they are in a needy and motivated organism, especially in circumstances when other, more natural responses are not available. Both the tissue and the organism acting as a whole are bounded by laws of conditioning and more complex learning. Drugs can exert their influence over the behavior of both the tissue and the individual by capitalizing on the flexible nature of conditioning and learning principles. Use behaviors are most likely to occur and persist in life spaces that support such behavior by providing learning opportunities about the utility of the behavior, by providing multiple opportunities for performing the behavior, and by providing continuity in support and occasions for use in its many forms. The sample application and simplified answer presented here are, of course, only a few of those that could be developed from the heuristic approach outlined in this chapter.

Needless to say, the synthesis attempted here has not yielded any startling definitive answers and leaves many questions open. The effort also may raise new challenges. However, these endeavors have emphasized the need for, and possibility of, deriving general principles from data collected over the past 30 years aimed at understanding the origins of drug use, abuse, and dependence. The drug abuse field is in need of such organizing attempts at this point of its development. The principles articulated here, or ones quite similar, will be useful heuristics in the search for meaningful and fruitful synthesis of past researching and theorizing. Just as important, such efforts will open new and exciting avenues for research from the many subspecialties of biology, psychology, and sociology.

REFERENCES

Bachman, J. G., Wadsworth, K. N., O'Malley, P. M., Johnston, L. D., & Schulenberg, J. E. (1997). *Smoking, drinking, and drug use in young adulthood: The impacts of new freedoms and new responsibilities.* Hillsdale, NJ: Erlbaum.

Baker, T. B., & Tiffany, S. T. (1985). Morphine tolerance as habituation. *Psychological Review, 92,* 78–108.

Brook, J. S., Whiteman, M., Cohen, P., & Tanaka, J. S. (1992). Childhood precursors of adolescent drug use: A longitudinal analysis. *Genetic, Social, and General Psychology Monographs, 118,* 195–213.

Chen, K., & Kandel, D. B. (1995). The natural history of drug use from adolescence to the mid-thirties in a general population sample. *American Journal of Public Health, 85,* 41–47.

Coie, J. D., Watt, N. F., West, S. G., Hawkins, J. D., Asarnow, J. R., Markman, H. J., Ramey, S. L., Shure, M. B., & Long, B. (1993). The science of prevention: A conceptual framework and some directions for a national research program. *American Psychologist, 48,* 1013–1022.

Compas, B. E., Hinden, B. R., & Gerhardt, C. A. (1995). Adolescent development: Pathways and processes of risk and resilience. In J. T. Spence, J. M. Darley, & D. J. Foss (Eds.), *Annual review of psychology* (Vol. 46, pp. 265–293). Palo Alto, CA: Annual Reviews.

Cox, W. M., & Klinger, E. (1988). A motivational model of alcohol use. *Journal of Abnormal Psychology, 97,* 168–180.

Fillmore, K. M., Golding, J. M., Leino, E. V., Motoyoshi, M., Ager, C. R., & Ferrer, H. P. (1994). Relationships of measures of alcohol consumption with alcohol-related problems in multiple studies: A research synthesis from the collaborative alcohol-related longitudinal project. *Addiction, 89,* 1143–1156.

Ford, D. H. (1987). *Humans as self-constructing living systems: A developmental perspective on behavior and personality.* Hillsdale, NJ: Erlbaum.

Gable, R. S. (1993). Toward a comparative overview of dependence potential and acute toxicity of psychoactive substances used nonmedically. *American Journal of Drug and Alcohol Abuse, 19,* 263–281.

Glantz, M., & Pickens, R. (Eds.). (1992). *Vulnerability to drug abuse.* Washington, DC: American Psychological Association.

Hawkins, J. D., Catalano, R. F., & Miller, J. Y. (1992). Risk and protective factors for alcohol and other drug problems in adolescence and early adulthood: Implications for substance abuse prevention. *Psychological Bulletin, 112,* 64–105.

Heckhausen, J., & Schulz, R. (1995). A life-span theory of control. *Psychological Review, 102,* 284–304.

Institute of Medicine. (1996). *Pathways of addiction: Opportunities in drug abuse research.* Washington, DC: National Academy Press.

Jaffe, J. H. (1992). Current concepts of addiction. In C. P. O'Brien & J. H. Jaffe (Eds.), *Addictive states* (pp. 1–21). New York: Raven Press.

Jessor, R. (1987). Problem-behavior theory, psychosocial development, and adolescent problem drinking. *British Journal of Addiction, 82,* 331–342.

Jessor, R., Van Den Bos, J., Vanderryn, J., Costa, F. M., & Turbin, M. S. (1995). Protective factors in adolescent problem behavior: Moderator effects and developmental change. *Developmental Psychology, 31,* 923–933.

Johnson, V. (1995). The relationship between parent and offspring comorbid disorders. *Journal of Substance Abuse, 7,* 267–280.

Kandel, D. (1975). Stages in adolescent involvement in drug use. *Science, 190,* 912–914.

Kandel, D. B. (1980). Drug and drinking behavior among youth. *Annual Review of Sociology, 6,* 235–285.

Kandel, D. B., Yamaguchi, K., & Chen, K. (1992). Stages of progression in drug involvement from adolescence to adulthood: Further evidence for the gateway theory. *Journal of Studies on Alcohol, 53,* 447–457.

Kaplan, H. B. (1980). *Deviant behavior in defense of self.* New York: Academic Press.

Kaplan, H. (Ed.). (1995). *Drugs, crime, and other deviant adaptations: Longitudinal studies.* New York: Plenum.

Labouvie, E. W. (1986). The coping function of adolescent alcohol and drug use. In R. K. Silbereisen, K. Eyferth, & G. Rudinger (Eds.), *Development as action in context* (pp. 229–240). New York: Springer.

Labouvie, E., Bates, M. E., & Pandina, R. J. (1997). Age of first use: Its reliability and predictive utility. *Journal of Studies on Alcohol, 58,* 638–643.

Labouvie, E. W., Pandina, R. J., & Johnson, V. (1991). Developmental trajectories of substance use in adolescence: Differences and predictors. *International Journal of Behavioral Development, 14,* 305–328.

Lettieri, D. J., Sayers, M., & Pearson, H. W. (Eds.). (1980). Theories on drug abuse: Selected contemporary perspectives. *NIDA Research Monograph, No. 30.* DHHS Publication No. 30 (ADM) 80–967. Washington, DC: National Institute on Drug Abuse.

McGee, L., & Newcomb, M. (1992). General deviance syndrome: Expanded hierarchical evaluations at four ages from early adolescence to adulthood. *Journal of Consulting and Clinical Psychology, 60,* 766–776.

Miller, J. G. (1978). *Living systems.* New York: McGraw-Hill.

Neiss, R. (1988). Reconceptualizing arousal: Psychobiological states in motor performance. *Psychological Bulletin, 103,* 345–366.

Nestler, E. J., Hope, B. T., & Widnell, K. L. (1993). Drug addiction: A model for the molecular basis of neural plasticity. *Neuron, 11,* 995–1006.

Newcomb, M. D., & Bentler, P. M. (1988). *Consequences of adolescent drug use: Impact on the lives of young adults.* Beverly Hills, CA: Sage.

Pandina, R. J. (1998). Risk and protective factor models on adolescent drug use: Putting them to work for prevention. In *National Conference on Drug Abuse Prevention Research: Presentations, papers, and recommendations* (pp. 17–26). Washington, DC: National Institutes of Health.

Pandina, R. J., Johnson, V., & Labouvie, E. W. (1992). Affectivity: A central mechanism in the development of drug dependence. In M. Glantz & R. Pickens (Eds.), *Vulnerability to drug abuse* (pp. 179–209). Washington, DC: American Psychological Association.

Pandina, R. J., Labouvie, E. W., & White, H. R. (1984). Potential contributions of the life span developmental approach to the study of adolescent alcohol and drug use: The Rutgers Health and Human Development Project, a working model. *Journal of Drug Issues, 14,* 253–268.

Petraitis, J., Flay, B. R., & Miller, T. Q. (1995). Reviewing theories of adolescent substance use: Organizing pieces in the puzzle. *Psychological Bulletin, 117,* 67–86.

Piazza, P. V., & Le Moal, M. (1996). Pathophysiological basis of vulnerability to drug abuse: Role of an interaction between stress, glucocorticoids, and dopaminergic neurons. *Annual Review of Pharmacology and Toxicology, 36,* 359–378.

Poulos, C. X., & Cappell, H. (1991). Homeostatic theory of drug tolerance: A general model of physiological adaptation. *Psychological Review, 98,* 390–408.

Ramsay, D. S., & Woods, S. C. (1997). Biological consequences of drug administration: Implications for acute and chronic tolerance. *Psychological Review, 104,* 170–193.

Scheier, L. M., & Newcomb, M. D. (1991). Psychosocial predictors of drug use initiation and escalation: An expansion of the multiple risk factors hypothesis using longitudinal data. *Contemporary Drug Problems, 18,* 31–73.

Shapiro, D. H., Schwartz, C. E., & Astin, J. A. (1996). Controlling ourselves, controlling our world: Psychology's role in understanding positive and negative consequences of seeking and gaining control. *American Psychologist, 51,* 1213–1230.

Siegel, S., & Allan, L. G. (1998). Learning and homeostasis: Drug addiction and the McCollough effect. *Psychological Bulletin, 124,* 230–239.

Siegel, S., Hinson, R. E., Krank, M. D., & McCully, J. (1982). Heroin "overdose" death: Contribution of drug-associated environmental cues. *Science, 216,* 436–437.

Soloman, R. L. (1980). The opponent-process theory of acquired motivation: The costs of pleasure and the benefits of pain. *American Psychologist, 35,* 691–712.

Stitzer, M. L., & Cox, W. M. (1996). Introduction to special section: Relapse to substance abuse. Recent findings from basic and clinical research. *Experimental and Clinical Psychopharmacology, 4,* 3–4.

Turkheimer, E. (1998). Heritability and biological explanation. *Psychological Review, 105,* 782–791.

Vaillant, G. E. (1983). *The natural history of alcoholism.* Cambridge, MA: Harvard University Press.

Wise, R. A. (1996). Addictive drugs and brain stimulation reward. *Annual Review of Neuroscience, 19,* 319–340.

7

PREVENTION AND TREATMENT OF DRUG ABUSE: USE OF ANIMAL MODELS TO FIND SOLUTIONS

MARILYN E. CARROLL

Animal models have been developed to study many aspects of drug abuse. For example, the phases of drug abuse (i.e., acquisition, maintenance, withdrawal, craving, and relapse) have been studied with animal models. Behavioral and psychiatric disorders associated with drug abuse, such as aggression, depression, and anhedonia, also have been modeled in animals. These animal models are valuable because some aspects of drug abuse, such as acquisition, withdrawal, relapse, and aggression, are ethically difficult to produce and study in depth in the laboratory with humans. The findings from animal models of drug abuse agree closely with the results of laboratory studies with humans (Foltin, 1992; Griffiths, Bigelow, & Henningfield, 1980). There is also generality of the results across several other species (i.e., mice, rats, monkeys, baboons, and dogs), different pharmacological classes of drugs, routes of drug self-administration, and a variety of experimental procedures.

Although there is considerable generality from animals to humans, considering the factors responsible for the initiation, maintenance, termination, and reinstatement of drug abuse, there are notable exceptions that warrant further study. The most striking lack of generality from animals to humans is in the prevalence of those that self-administer drugs of abuse. In the laboratory, nearly 100% of the animals exposed to psychomotor stimulants, such as cocaine, or opioids, such as heroin, acquire drug-reinforced behavior. In contrast, the percentage of the human population that abuses illicit drugs is in the single digits.

ENVIRONMENTAL FACTORS

The difference in the rates of initiation of drug use between laboratory animals and the human population is predominantly determined by environmental factors. Laboratory animals have limited access to alternative activities and rewards, whereas for humans, these alternatives are abundant in the environment. However, in human situations where nondrug activities and rewards are extremely limited, such as in war zones, prisons, homeless camps, and low-income, inner-city life, the rate of drug abuse is quite high. The manipulation of nondrug-alternative events and rewards has been systematically studied as a means of preventing and treating drug abuse. This review focuses on this manipulation, and parallels among animal laboratory, human laboratory, and clinical findings are drawn.

NONDRUG-ALTERNATIVE REWARDS PREVENT DRUG TAKING

Studies in animals and humans have been designed to test the hypothesis that alternative nondrug reinforcers or activities prevent the acquisition of drug-reinforced behavior. In an initial study, four groups of 12 drug-naive rats were given different experiences with a sweetened liquid, glucose and saccharin (G+S; alternative reinforcer), before, during, or before and during acquisition of intravenous cocaine self-administration (Carroll & Lac, 1993). Group 1 had access to the alternative reinforcer 3 weeks before and during cocaine exposure. Groups 2 and 3 had G+S either before or during cocaine exposure, respectively, and Group 4 had no exposure to G+S. Each rat was given 60 randomly spaced infusions during a 6-hour period and then was allowed to self-administer cocaine infusions contingent on lever-press responses for another 6 hours. The criterion for acquisition was 5 consecutive days with a mean of at least 100 self-administered infusions, and the time to acquire was limited to 30 days. The group that had the most exposure to G+S (Group 1) was the slowest to acquire cocaine self-administration, and only 50% of the rats met the criterion. In contrast, 100% of the group with no G+S exposure (Group 4) acquired rapidly. The group with G+S before cocaine exposure (Group 2) acquired rapidly also, and 100% of the rats met the criterion; however, the group with G+S access only during cocaine acquisition (Group 3) showed slower acquisition, and only 75% of the group met the criterion. These results indicated that current access, but not prior access, to an alternative nondrug reinforcer prevented the acquisition of intravenous cocaine self-administration in half of the rats tested. A fifth group of rats which had unlimited access to food as an alternative nondrug reward, was added. The preceding four groups were limited to 20 g of food per day, only slightly less than the amount that is consumed when access is unlimited (23 g). This free-fed group also showed a slower rate of acquisition, and only 75% reached the criterion within 30 days. This study was the first among several analyses of acquisition in rats, to identify factors that slowed or prevented the initiation of drug-reinforced behavior. A subsequent study indicated that combining the amount of food (unlimited food) with increased palatability (adding saccharin 2.2% wt/wt) resulted in even fewer rats per group (40%) meeting the acquisition criterion (Carroll & Lac, 1998). Other studies have identified factors that accelerate acquisition, such as preexposure to drugs (Horger, Shelton, & Schenk, 1990; Piazza, Deminiere, Le Moal, & Simon, 1989; Valadez & Schenk, 1994); prenatal exposure (Keller, LeFevre, Raucci, Carlson & Glick, 1996; Ramsey, 1991); stress (Goeders & Guerin, 1994; Haney, Maccari, Le Moal, Simon, & Piazza, 1995; Piazza, Deminiere, Le Moal, & Simon, 1990; Ramsey & van Ree, 1993; Schenk, Lacelle, Gorman & Amit, 1987), and exposure to higher doses of drug during acquisition (Carroll & Lac, 1997; DeVry, Donselaar & van Ree, 1989).

The study of the effect of nondrug alternative reinforcers has been extended to Rhesus monkeys. An earlier study compared the acquisition of orally delivered phencyclidine (PCP) in food-restricted versus food-satiated monkeys (Carroll, 1982). Although all monkeys in both groups acquired PCP as a reinforcer within about 50 days, the group with free access to food consumed less (106.9 ml/day) than the food-restricted group (169.3 ml/day). Restricting feeding to meals is a normal animal-care practice, because long-term exposure to unlimited food results in obesity and other health problems. In a recent study (Campbell, Thompson, & Carroll, 1998), a noncaloric alternative reinforcer, saccharin (0.03% wt/vol), was examined in drug-naive monkeys acquiring self-administration of orally delivered PCP, and results were compared with those of a group receiving only water. A food-induced drinking procedure was used to establish oral contact with the drug. The reinforcement schedule was increased from a fixed ratio of 1 (FR 1) to FR 8 (deliveries were contingent upon 1 to 8 responses on a lip-operated drinking spout), and then concurrent access to the vehicle was added. Drug reinforcement occurred if drug intake exceeded that of the vehicle. The results showed that only 50% of the monkeys with saccharin access acquired PCP-reinforced responding, whereas 80% of the water-exposed control group acquired the responding. Another group that had a lower PCP dose and only water to drink also was studied, and only 50% of this group acquired as well. These data concur with the rat data and suggest that factors that reduce vulnerability to drug abuse are a low dose of drug and access to an alternative nondrug reinforcers.

Results of prevention studies in humans agree with the findings of animal studies. For example, Project Northland, a 3-year alcohol use prevention program for 6th to 8th graders in northeastern Minnesota, systematically used a component that involved nondrug-alternative reinforcers (Perry et al., 1996). The Amazing Alternatives program was used in addition to other components involving education, peer leadership, and parental involvement. It consisted of social activities that were created and organized by the participants. Although it is not possible to analyze the results of the Amazing Alternatives component separately, the overall outcomes of the program were significantly less "last week" and "last month" alcohol use and less combined use of alcohol and cigarettes in the intervention groups versus matched school district controls. It appears, therefore, that the systematic programming of nondrug substances or events into the environment is an effective strategy for preventing the initiation of drug abuse. Even if these methods served to slow the escalation of dose and frequency of use, they are secondarily beneficial because lower dose exposure enhances prevention.

NONDRUG-ALTERNATIVE REWARDS REDUCE ONGOING DRUG TAKING

The question of whether nondrug-alternative reinforcers can reduce the level of drug use in those that have already established steady patterns of use also has been examined experimentally with animals, and initial human clinical trials with similar methods agree with the laboratory findings. A study was conducted with rats and intravenous cocaine self-administration (Carroll, Lac, & Nygaard, 1989). One group's cocaine infusions had stabilized at high rates (800/day) while food and water were the only other substances available. When the nondrug-alternative reinforcer, G+S, was added to the environment, the number of infusions was reduced to approximately 175/day. Infusions returned to nearly 800/day as soon as the G+S was removed. Another group was trained to self-administer cocaine intravenously with G+S also available, and their mean infusion rate was approximately 260/day. When G+S was removed, the infusions rapidly increased to almost 800/day. However, when G+S was reintroduced, infusions decreased to only about 600/day. These findings indicate that even a simple addition of a single alternative reinforcer can have a dramatic effect on drug-maintained responding, but the increase in drug-maintained responding results from a restricted environment may be only partially irreversible.

BEHAVIORAL ECONOMICS

In monkeys whose oral-ethanol- or PCP-reinforced behavior has been well established, the addition of saccharin to the environment also has been effective at reducing drug intake (Carroll, Carmona & May, 1991; Carroll & Rodefer, 1993). The effort required to obtain the drug is an important factor in the magnitude of the effect of an alternative reinforcer. When the FR for PCP or ethanol was increased from 4 to 8, 16, 32, 64, and 128, the number of drug deliveries decreased. The addition of saccharin reduced drug taking at all prices (FRs), but greatest percentage reductions occurred when the price of the drug (FR) was high. A similar relationship occurred when unlimited food was used as the nondrug-alternative reinforcer. These results were replicated in monkeys smoking cocaine base; however, the effect of saccharin or unlimited food on this form of drug abuse was much weaker than on behavior maintained by orally delivered PCP or ethanol.

Laboratory studies in human participants have reported similar findings. Cocaine smoking is reduced when money is provided as an alternative reinforcer (Hatsukami, Thompson, Pentel, Flyaare & Carroll, 1994). Zacny, Divane, and deWitt (1992) reported decreased beer consumption when pizza was served as an alternative reinforcer. In a study in which the response requirement was varied, Bickel and DeGrandpre (1995) showed that when money could be earned as an alternative to cigarette smoking, cigarette consumption was reduced across a wide range of response requirements. Overall, it appears that the effect of nondrug alternatives is higher when the unit price of the drug is high. Unit price (responses/mg) can be increased either by lowering the dose per delivery or by increasing the response requirement. In fact, as the concentration of PCP decreases, the effect of nondrug-alternative reinforcers, such as saccharin or unlimited food, increases (Carroll, Stitzer, Strain, & Meisch, 1990). One limitation of nondrug alternatives is that at high drug concentrations, they are ineffective (Carroll et al., 1990).

The magnitude of the nondrug-alternative reinforcer has received less experimental attention, although studies in monkeys and humans indicate that there is a dose effect. For example, in an experiment by Nader and Woolverton (1991), monkeys were given an exclusive choice between food pellets and cocaine. Percentage of cocaine choices increased as cocaine dose increased; however, at a given cocaine dose, percentage of cocaine choices decreased as the number of food pellets per trial increased from 1 to 4 to 16. Higgins et al. (1994) offered human participants a choice between cocaine (10 mg) and money. As the amount of money increased from 0 to $2.00, participants changed their behavior from the maximum of 10 cocaine choices to 0. When the monetary reinforcer was $0.50 or $1.00 versus 10 mg cocaine, they chose a mean of approximately 6 out of 10 cocaine choices.

In summary, laboratory studies have identified several factors that determine the magnitude of effect a nondrug-alternative reinforcer has on drug-reinforced behavior. The type of drug and route of administration must be considered. For instance, drugs like ethanol or PCP, when taken orally, are markedly suppressed by saccharin or unlimited food, whereas cocaine smoking in monkeys is only slightly affected by these manipulations. The higher the unit price of the drug, the more effective the alternative reinforcer. Unit price can be increased either by increasing the response requirement or by decreasing the dose. Finally, the greater the magnitude of the alternative reinforcer, the more effective it will be at suppressing drug intake.

USE OF NONDRUG-ALTERNATIVE REWARDS IN THE CLINICAL SETTING

The ultimate test of the alternative-reinforcer hypothesis is whether it can effectively reduce drug abuse or prevent relapse in a clinical setting. The use of a nondrug-alternative reinforcer would seem to be implicit in drug abuse treatment programs. The social rewards of group therapy and the ability to function at a higher level at school or in an occupation would function as nondrug rewards. This method, termed the *community-reinforcement* approach, has been used successfully in the treatment of alcohol abuse (Sisson & Azrin, 1989), and it has been applied to cocaine and opioid abuse (Higgins et al., 1993; Silverman et al., 1996). The alternative-reinforcement approach was tested clinically by Higgins et al. (1994) in an outpatient program for cocaine-dependent patients. Patients could earn vouchers, that could be traded for desired retail items or events, by providing drug-free urine samples when they were called in on a random time schedule. The points earned increased with successive negative urine samples. The mean number of weeks of continuous abstinence during the first 24 weeks was approximately 12 in the voucher group and only about 6 in a control group that received counseling only. Also, the percentage of clients completing treatment at 24 weeks was approximately 75% in the voucher group and about 40% in the control group. In a 1996 study, Silverman et al. used a similar alternative reinforcement approach to decrease opioid use in heroin-dependent patients receiving methadone-maintenance treatment. They used a within-subject design in which they compared 5 weeks without vouchers, 12 weeks with vouchers, and 8 weeks without.

The percentage of participants with opioid-positive urine samples decreased from almost 80% to approximately 25% during the voucher period, and it rose to about 40% when vouchers were no longer available. A major difference in the design of the human clinical studies and most of the animal studies is that in the human studies there is a contingency between not using the drug and obtaining the alternative reinforcer. In the animal studies, both drug and nondrug reinforcers are concurrently available or a choice between them must be made on any given trial (e.g., Nader & Woolverton, 1991), but both drug and nondrug reinforcer can be obtained, and there is no punishment for drug use. Further animal work is needed to compare the effect of alternative reinforcers on drug intake under concurrent-access conditions, discrete-trial choice conditions, and conditions under which the alternative is contingent on not using the drug.

COMBINING NONDRUG-ALTERNATIVE REINFORCERS WITH MEDICATION FOR DRUG ABUSE

These behavioral methods for treating cocaine and opioid abuse are as or more effective than existing medications for drug abuse. However, a final question to be considered is whether the effectiveness of nondrug-alternative reinforcers is enhanced when used in combination with drug therapy. Buprenorphine, a partial agonist at the *mu* receptor, is a medication that reduces behavior reinforced by cocaine, ethanol, opioids, and PCP in animals, and it helps maintain abstinence from cocaine and opioids in humans. The effectiveness of buprenorphine treatment and that of the use of nondrug-alternative reinforcers was tested separately and in combination in several animal studies, and the results indicated that the effects of each form of treatment added to each other to produce a dramatic reduction in drug intake. In these experiments, buprenorphine was injected intramuscularly (in monkeys) or intraperitoneally (in rats) 30 minutes before drug self-administration sessions for 3 to 5 days. Drug treatment was studied with and without access to the nondrug alternative, saccharin (for monkeys) and G+S (for rats). The animals always had access to water, and food was available after daily 3-hour (for monkeys) or 12-hour (for rats) sessions. In the rat studies, the FR schedules ranged from 2 to 32 (Comer, Lac, Wyvell & Carroll, 1996). Buprenorphine or G+S reduced cocaine infusions by 37% or 21%, respectively, but the combination of treatments reduced responding by 70%. In a group of 5 monkeys trained to smoke cocaine base the FR values ranged from 64 to 1,024 (Rodefer, Mattox, Thompson, & Carroll, 1997). Buprenorphine and saccharin reduced smoking by 3% or 21%, respectively, but the combined treatments reduced smoking by 36%. Finally, when buprenorphine and concurrent saccharin were tested on monkeys self-administering orally delivered PCP under FRs ranging from 4 to 128, the PCP intake was reduced by 36% or 44% percent, respectively, and the combined treatments reduced PCP intake by 70% (Rawleigh, Rodefer, Hansen, & Carroll, 1996). Each of these studies also showed that the behavioral and pharmacological treatments alone or combined were generally more effective at higher FR values (lower unit prices). The results from these animal studies predict that clinical application of nondrug-alternative reinforcers combined with traditional medications (e.g., buprenorphine) will produce a greater outcome than either treatment alone. Similar studies have been conducted in the human behavioral laboratory with money and cigarette smoking (Bickel, Madden, & De-Grandpre, 1997) and in a clinical setting with buprenorphine and vouchers for clean urine samples in opioid abusers (Bickel, Amass, Higgins, Badger, & Esch, 1997), and results concur with the animal studies. Combined treatments are more effective than either one alone, and there is a greater suppression of drug choice when the price of drug (FR) increases. A review of the smoking-cessation literature (Hughes, 1995) and the opioid abuse treatment literature (McLellan, Arndt, Woody, & Metzger, 1993) also indicate that combined behavioral and pharmacological therapy substantially increases smoking cessation over either therapy alone (Hughes, 1995).

CONCLUSION

This review illustrates that nondrug-alternative reinforcers prevent the acquisition and reduce the maintenance of drug-reinforced behavior. The results of community alcohol abuse prevention programs have produced similar findings. Laboratory studies with human participants agree with animal studies that combined medication and alternative-reinforcer interventions reduce drug taking more than either treatment alone, and the effect is enhanced when FR requirements for drug are increased. Finally, the clinical treatment results indicate that nondrug incentives increase treatment retention and decrease drug use for extended periods of time.

REFERENCES

Bickel, W. K., Amass, L., Higgins, S. T., Badger, G. J., & Esch, R. A. (1997). Effects of adding behavioral treatment to opioid detoxification with buprenorphine. *Journal of Clinical and Consulting Psychology, 6*, 803–810.

Bickel, W. K., & DeGrandpre, R. J. (1995). Modeling drug abuse policy in the behavioral economics laboratory. In L. Green & J. Kagel (Eds.), *Advances in behavioral economics* (3rd ed., pp. 69–95). New York: Ablex.

Bickel, W. K., Madden, G. J., & DeGrandpre, R. J. (1997). Modeling effects of combined behavioral and pharmacological treatment on cigarette smoking:

Behavioral-economic analysis. *Experimental and Clinical Psychopharmacology, 5,* 334–343.

Campbell, U. C., Thompson, S. S., & Carroll, M. E. (1998). Acquisition of oral phencyclidine (PCP) self-administration in rhesus monkeys: Effects of dose and an alternative nondrug reinforcer. *Psychopharmacology, 6,* 22–31.

Carroll, M. E. (1982). Rapid acquisition of oral phencyclidine self-administration in food-deprived and food-satiated rhesus monkeys. *Pharmacology Biochemistry and Behavior, 17,* 341–346.

Carroll, M. E., Carmona, G. N., & May, S. (1991). Modifying drug-reinforced behavior by altering the economic conditions of the drug and a nondrug reinforcer. *Journal of the Experimental Analysis of Behavior, 56,* 361–376.

Carroll, M. E., & Lac, S. T. (1993). Autoshaping i.v. cocaine self-administration in rats: Effects of nondrug alternative reinforcers on acquisition. *Psychopharmacology, 110,* 5–12.

Carroll, M. E., & Lac, S. T. (1997). Acquisition of i.v. amphetamine and cocaine self-administration in rats as a function of dose. *Psychopharmacology, 129,* 206–214.

Carroll, M. E., & Lac, S. T. (1998). Dietary additives and the acquisition of cocaine self-administration in rats. *Psychopharmacology, 137,* 132–138.

Carroll, M. E., Lac, S. T., & Nygaard, S. L. (1989). A concurrently available nondrug reinforcer prevents the acquisition or decreases the maintenance of cocaine-reinforced behavior. *Psychopharmacology, 97,* 23–39.

Carroll, M. E., & Rodefer, J. S. (1993). Income alters choice between drug and alternative nondrug reinforcer in monkeys. *Experimental and Clinical Psychopharmacology, 1,* 110–120.

Carroll, M. E., Stitzer, M. L., Strain, E., & Meisch, R. A. (1990). Behavioral pharmacology of ethanol and other drugs: Emerging issues. In M. Galanter (Ed.), *Recent developments in alcoholism* (Vol. 8, pp. 5–46). New York: Plenum.

Comer, S. D., Lac, S. T., Wyvell, C. L., & Carroll, M. E. (1996). Combined effects of buprenorphine and a nondrug alternative reinforcer on i.v. cocaine self-administration in rats maintained under FR schedules. *Psychopharmacology, 125,* 355–360.

DeVry, J., Donselaar, I., & van Ree, J. M. (1989). Food deprivation and acquisition of intravenous cocaine self-administration in rats: Effects of naltretone and haloperidol. *Journal of Pharmacology and Experimental Therapeutics, 251,* 735–740.

Foltin, R. W. (1992). The importance of drug self-administration studies in the analysis of abuse liability. *The American Journal of the Addictions, 1,* 139–149.

Goeders, N. E., & Guerin, G. F. (1994). Non-contingent electrical footshock facilitates the acquisition of intravenous cocaine self-administration in rats. *Psychopharmacology, 114,* 63–70.

Griffiths, R. R., Bigelow, G. E., & Henningfield, J. E. (1980). Similarities in animal and human drug-taking behavior. In N. K. Mello (Ed.), *Advances in substance abuse* (Vol. 1, pp. 1–90). Greenwich, CT: JAI Press.

Haney, M., Maccari, S., Le Moal, M., Simon, H., & Piazza, P. V. (1995). Social stress increases the acquisition of cocaine self-administration in male and female rats. *Brain Research, 698,* 46–52.

Hatsukami, D. K., Thompson, T., Pentel, P. R., Flygaare, B., & Carroll, M. E. (1994). Self-administration of smoked cocaine. *Experimental and Clinical Psychopharmacology, 2,* 115–125.

Higgins, S. T., Budney, A. J., Bickel, W. K., Foerg, F., Donham, R., & Badger, G. J. (1994). Incentives improve outcome in outpatient behavioral treatment of cocaine dependence. *Archives of General Psychiatry, 51,* 568–576.

Higgins, S. T., Budney, A. J., Bickel, W. K., Hughes, J. R., Foerg, F., & Badger, G. (1993). Achieving cocaine abstinence with a behavioral approach. *American Journal of Psychiatry, 150,* 763–769.

Horger, B. A., Shelton, K., & Schenk, S. (1990). Preexposure sensitizes rats to the rewarding effects of cocaine. *Pharmacology Biochemistry and Behavior, 37,* 707–711.

Hughes, J. R. (1995). Combining behavioral therapy and pharmacotherapy for smoking cessation: An update. In L. S. Onken, J. D. Blaine, & J. J. Boren (Eds.), *Integrating behavior therapies with medication in the treatment of drug dependence,* pp. 92–109. Washington, DC: US National Institute on Drug Abuse.

Keller, R. W., LeFevre, R., Raucci, J., Carlson, J. N., & Glick, S. D. (1996). Enhanced cocaine self-administration in adult rats prenatally exposed to cocaine. *Neuroscience Letters, 205,* 153–156.

McLellan, A. T., Arndt, I. D., Woody, G. E., & Metzger, D. (1993). Psychosocial services in substance abuse treatment? A dose-ranging study of psychosocial services. *Journal of the American Medical Association, 269,* 1953–1959.

Nader, M. A., & Woolverton, W. L. (1991). Effects of increasing the magnitude of an alternative reinforcer on drug choice in a discrete-trials choice procedure. *Psychopharmacology, 105,* 69–74.

Perry, C. L., Williams, C. L., Veblen-Mortenson, S., Toomey, T. L., Komro, K. A., Anstine, P. S., McGovern, P. G., Finnegan, J. R., Forster, J. L., Wagenaar, A. C., & Wolfson, M. (1996). Project Northland: Outcomes of a community wide alcohol use prevention program during early adolescence. *American Journal of Public Health, 86,* 956–965.

Piazza, P. V., Deminiere, J. M., Le Moal, M., & Simon, H. (1989). Factors that predict individual vulnerability to amphetamine self-administration. *Science, 245,* 1511–1513.

Piazza, P. V., Deminiere, J. M., Le Moal, M., & Simon, H. (1990). Stress- and pharmacologically-induced behavioral sensitization increases vulnerability to acquisition of amphetamine self-administration. *Brain Research, 514,* 22–26.

Ramsey, N. F. (1991). *Cocaine dependence: Factors in the initiation of self-administration in rats* (pp. 125–136). Doctoral dissertation, Rudolf Magnus Institute, University of Utrecht, Netherlands.

Ramsey, N. F., & van Ree, M. (1993). Emotional but not physical stress enhances intravenous cocaine self-administration in drug naive rats. *Brain Research, 608,* 216–222.

Rawleigh, J. M., Rodefer, J. S., Hansen, J. J., & Carroll, M. E. (1996). Combined effects of buprenorphine and an alternative nondrug reinforcer on phency-clidine self-administration in rhesus monkeys. *Experimental and Clinical Psychopharmacology, 4,* 68–76.

Rodefer, J. S., Mattox, A. J., Thompson, S., & Carroll, M. E. (1997). Effects of buprenorphine and an alternative nondrug reinforcer, alone and in combination on smoked cocaine self-administration in monkeys. *Drug and Alcohol Dependence, 45,* 21–29.

Schenk, S., Lacelle, G., Gorman, K., & Amit, Z. (1987). Cocaine self-administration in rats influenced by environmental conditions: Implications for the etiology of drug abuse. *Neuroscience Letters, 81,* 227–231.

Silverman, K., Higgins, S. T., Brooner, R. K., Montoya, I. D., Cone, E. J., Schuster, C. R., & Preston, K. L. (1996). Sustained cocaine abstinence in methadone maintenance patients through voucher-based reinforcement therapy. *Archives of General Psychiatry, 53,* 409–415.

Sisson, R. W., & Azrin, N. H. (1989). The community reinforcement approach. In R. K. Hesler & W. R. Miller (Eds.), *Handbook of alcoholism treatment approaches: Effective alternatives* (pp. 242–258). New York, Pergamon Press.

Valadez, A., & Schenk, S. (1994). Persistence of amphetamine preexposure to facilitate acquisition of cocaine self-administration. *Pharmacology Biochemistry and Behavior, 47,* 203–205.

Zacny, J. P., Divane, W. T., & deWitt, H. (1992). Assessment of magnitude and availability of a non-drug reinforcer on preference for a drug reinforcer. *Human Psychopharmacology, 7,* 281–286.

8

NEUROBIOLOGY OF DRUG ADDICTION

GEORGE F. KOOB, S. BARAK CAINE, PETRI HYYTIA,
ATIIINA MARKOU, LOREN H. PARSONS, AMANDA J. ROBERTS,
GERY SCHULTEIS, AND FRIEDBERT WEISS

Substance dependence is a chronic relapsing disorder that is characterized by many different behavioral manifestations but several common elements. Two characteristics that are common to definitions of substance dependence and addiction are a compulsion to take the drug, with a narrowing of the behavioral repertoire toward excessive drug intake and a loss of control in limiting intake, and a withdrawal syndrome that results in physical as well as motivational signs of discomfort when the drug is removed (American Psychiatric Association, 1994; World Health Organization, 1992). However, as stated by Wikler (1973),

> In terms of the pain–pleasure principle, is the speed-freak impelled
> to self-inject methamphetamine in closely spaced doses and to relapse
> in the Haight-Ashbury environment after crashing there because

Support for this chapter was provided by Public Health Service Research Grants DA04043, DA04398 (both from the National Institute on Drug Abuse), and AA08459 (from the National Institute on Alcohol Abuse and Alcoholism). The authors would like to thank Mike Arends for his assistance with manuscript preparation.

of the memories of the highs produced by the first dose or of the lows that followed? Similar questions may be asked about cocaine self-administration and marihuana smoking. However, answers to these questions in terms of the pain–pleasure principle will not be meaningful; rather, the answers should be sought in terms of the biochemical–neurophysiological mechanisms that are involved in the development of successive counter adaptations to the initial receptor actions of such drugs and in reinforcement. (p. 614)

There are multiple sources of reinforcement or motivation within the framework of the substance-dependence syndrome (see Table 1). For the purposes of this review, a *reinforcer* is defined operationally as any event that increases the probability of a response. This definition can also be used as definition for *reward*, and the two words are often used interchangeably. However, *reward* often connotes some additional emotional value, such as pleasure. On the basis of Wikler's extensive work with opiate drugs and his innovative conceptualizations about dependence (Wikler, 1973), the primary pharmacological effect of a drug was hypothesized to produce a direct effect through positive reinforcement or negative reinforcement as a process (e.g., self-medication) and possibly an indirect motivational effect through drug-engendered dependence (relief from aversive abstinence signs). The secondary pharmacological effects of the drug also were hypothesized to have motivating properties. Again, direct effects can be obtained through conditioned reinforcement (e.g., pairing of previously neutral stimuli with acute reinforcing effects of drugs), or indirect effects can be obtained through removal of the conditioned negative-reinforcing effects of conditioned abstinence.

Thus, most definitions of substance dependence also involve a major source of negative reinforcement, in addition to positive reinforcement, that can be associated with alleviation of withdrawal or conditioned withdrawal symptoms (American Psychiatric Association, 1994; Wikler, 1973). Note, however, that the emotional aspects of withdrawal provide the motivational component, not the physical signs of withdrawal (Koob, Markou,

TABLE 1
Relationship of Addiction Components, Behavior Constructs, and Treatment Focus

Addiction component	Operational construct	Treatment focus
Pleasure	Positive reinforcement	Motivational
Self-medication	Negative reinforcement	Alcoholics Anonymous and motivational
Habit	Conditioned positive reinforcement	Cognitive–behavioral
	Conditioned negative reinforcement	Cognitive–behaviorial

Weiss, & Schulteis, 1993; Schulteis & Koob, 1996). The development of an abstinence syndrome with motivational consequences is an integral part of the hypothesis that adaptive processes are initiated to counter the acute positive-reinforcing effects of a drug. These processes persist long after the drug has cleared from the brain, thus leaving opposing adaptive processes unopposed during abstinence, which may contribute to a negative affective state. Such conceptualizations have been explored at all levels of drug-dependence research, from the behavioral to the molecular (Koob & Bloom, 1988; Wikler, 1973), and provide the framework for identifying the neurobiological bases for drug dependence. The present review first focuses on the neurobiological substrates for the acute reinforcing effects of the major classes of drugs of abuse, follows with a discussion of how these neurobiological systems change with the development of dependence, and then discusses the limited research to date on the neurobiology of protracted abstinence and relapse.

NEUROBIOLOGICAL SUBSTRATES FOR THE POSITIVE-REINFORCING EFFECTS OF DRUGS OF ABUSE

In recent conceptualizations of drug reinforcement, the positive-reinforcing properties of drugs have been thought to play an important role in drug dependence (Wikler, 1973; Wise, 1988). Animals and humans will readily self-administer drugs in the nondependent state, and it is clear that drugs have powerful reinforcing properties in that animals will perform many different tasks to obtain drugs. The drugs that have positive-reinforcing effects correspond very well with the drugs that have high abuse potential in humans (Carr, Fibiger, & Phillips, 1989; Collins, Weeks, Cooper, Good, & Russell, 1984; Johanson & Balster, 1978; Kornetsky & Esposito, 1979; Schuster & Johanson, 1988; Schuster & Thompson, 1969). Indeed, this relationship is so strong that intravenous drug self-administration is considered an animal model that is predictive of abuse potential (Collins et al., 1984) and has been suggested to be used as part of a battery for the preclinical assessment of the abuse liability of new agents (Johanson & Balster, 1978). Whereas much of the earlier work focused on operant paradigms in primates, studies in the past few years have illustrated that many of these same paradigms can be used in rodent models, and continued work in rodent models has provided great impetus to studies focusing on the neurobiology of addiction (Koob & Bloom, 1988; Koob & Goeders, 1989).

Psychomotor Stimulants

Neuropharmacological studies have established an important role for central nervous system dopamine in the acute reinforcing effects of cocaine.

Low doses of dopamine receptor antagonists, when injected systemically, reliably block cocaine and amphetamine self-administration in the rat (Bergman, Kamien, & Spealman, 1990; Davis & Smith, 1975; deWit & Wise, 1977). This is reflected in an actual increase in amphetamine and cocaine infusions or a decrease in the interinjection interval, a pattern consistent with a shift to the right of the inverted-U-shaped function characterizing the dose–effect function for cocaine or amphetamine in the absence of pharmacological blockade.

The midbrain dopamine system is composed of two major projections: the nigrostriatal system, which projects from the substantia nigra to the corpus striatum, and the mesocorticolimbic dopamine system, which project from the ventral tegmental area to the nucleus accumbens, olfactory tubercle, frontal cortex, and amygdala (see Figure 1). A role for mesocorticolimbic dopamine in the reinforcing properties of cocaine was provided by the observation that 6-hydroxydopamine (6-OHDA) lesions of the basal forebrain terminal projections of this pathway in the region of the nucleus accumbens produced extinction-like responding in cocaine self-administration, as reflected in a significant and long-lasting reduction in responding over days (Lyness, Friedle, & Moore, 1979; Roberts, Koob, Klonoff, & Fibiger, 1980). Similar decreases in the reinforcing effects of cocaine have been observed following 6-OHDA lesions of the nucleus accumbens using a progressive ratio schedule (Koob, Vaccarino, Amalric, & Bloom, 1987). Moreover, identical selective decreases in cocaine self-administration were observed following mesolimbic dopamine lesions in rats responding under a multiple schedule for cocaine or food (Caine & Koob, 1994). Neurochemical evidence using in vivo microdialysis has confirmed increases in nucleus accumbens dopamine release during intravenous cocaine self-administration (Hurd, Weiss, Koob, Anden, & Ungerstedt, 1989; Pettit & Justice, 1989, 1991; Weiss, Hurd, et al., 1992). When saline is replaced by cocaine, the rats rapidly extinguish self-administration, and dopamine levels in the nucleus accumbens rapidly decline (Weiss, Markou, Lorang, & Koob, 1992; see Figure 2).

Multiple receptor subtypes exist for translation of the increase in extracellular dopamine induced by psychomotor stimulants into behavioral action, and experiments investigating the effects of antagonists selective for dopamine receptor subtypes reveal that antagonists for the D_1 (Bergman et al., 1990; Koob, Le, & Creese, 1987), D_2 (Bergman et al., 1990; Woolverton & Virus, 1989), and D_3 receptors decrease the reinforcing properties of cocaine (Caine & Koob, 1993; see Table 2). In addition, microinjection of the D_1 antagonist SCH 23390 directly into the brain has shown that the shell region of the nucleus accumbens and the central nucleus of the amygdala are particularly sensitive sites (Caine, Heinrichs, Coffin, & Koob, 1995; see Figure 3). Here, rats trained to self-administer cocaine intravenously and implanted with bilateral cannulas aimed at the shell of the

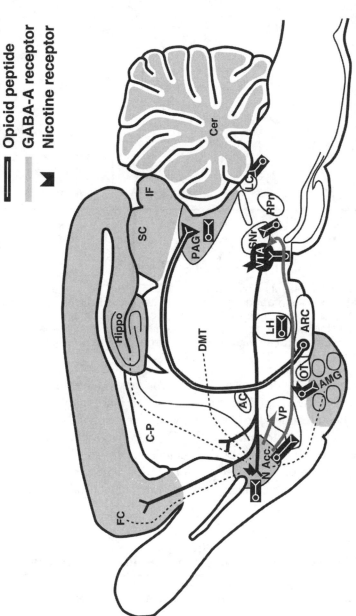

Figure 1. Sagittal rat brain section illustrating a drug (e.g., cocaine, amphetamine, opiate, nicotine, or alcohol) neural reward circuit that includes a limbic–extrapyramidal motor interface. FC = frontal cortex; Hippo = hippocampus; SC = superior colliculus; IF = inferior colliculus; PAG = periaqueductal gray; DMT = dorsomedial thalamus; Cer = cerebellum; AC = anterior commissure; LC = locus coeruleus; SNr = substantia nigra pars reticulata; RPn = rostral pontine nucleus; LH = lateral hypothalamus; VP = ventral pallidum; OT = olfactory tract; ARC = arcuate nucleus; AMG = amygdala. Modified with permission from Koob, 1992b.

NEUROBIOLOGY OF DRUG ADDICTION   *165*

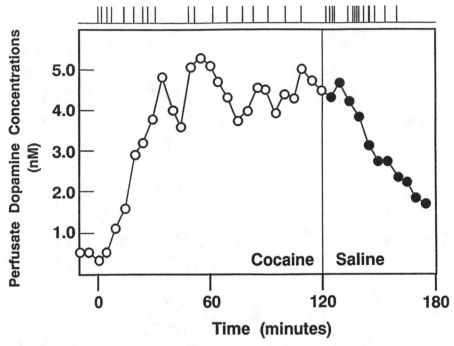

Figure 2. Extracellular levels of dopamine in the nucleus accumbens during cocaine self-administration as measured by in vivo microdialysis. Response record at the top shows a regular pattern of cocaine self-administration during the first 2 hours, followed by an extinction-like pattern when saline is substituted for cocaine. Taken with permission from Weiss, Hurd, et al., 1992.

nucleus accumbens, the central nucleus of the amygdala, and the caudate nucleus showed a site-related increase in cocaine self-administration or a decrease in the interinjection interval during the first 20 minutes after injection of microgram amounts of the D_1 antagonist SCH 23390. The most sensitive site was the shell of the nucleus accumbens. Microinjections in the caudate nucleus had no effect during this time period. There was also a moderate effect from microinjections into the central nucleus of the amygdala (Caine et al., 1995).

TABLE 2
Functional Classification of Dopamine Receptor Subtypes

Subtype	Adenylate cyclase linkage	Brain localization	Cocaine's reinforcing effects
D_1	Stimulatory	Nucleus accumbens Corpus striatum	Possible agonist
D_2	Unlinked or inhibitory	Nucleus accumbens Corpus striatum	Agonist
D_3	Unlinked	Shell of nucleus accumbens	Agonist Possible antagonist

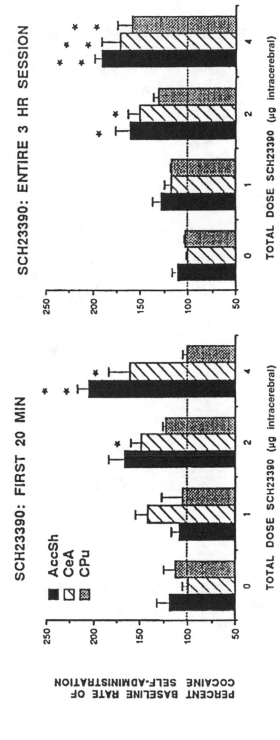

Figure 3. Effects of the dopamine D$_1$ selective antagonist on cocaine self-administration when directly injected into the shell of the nucleus accumbens, the amygdala, and the caudate nucleus in the rat. Doses of 0, 0.5, 1.0, 2.0, and 4.0 μg total dose were microinjected into the accumbens shell (AccSh), central amygdala (CeA), and dorsal striatum (CPu) in separate groups of rats. Values are group means and standard errors (n = 6/brain region). Data represent the first 230 minutes after injections. Three-hours totals showed no significant differences among the groups but an overall main effect of injection. (*p < .05. **p < .01. Taken with permission from Caine et al., 1995.

NEUROBIOLOGY OF DRUG ADDICTION   167

Opiates

Heroin and other opiate drugs, much like psychostimulants, are readily self-administered intravenously by rats. If opiates are provided in limited-access situations, rats and primates (Deneau, Yanagita, & Seever, 1969) will maintain stable levels of intake on a daily basis without any major signs of physical dependence (Koob, Pettit, Ettenberg, & Bloom, 1984). Similar to cocaine, the function relating dose of heroin to the amount self-administered is an inverted-U-shaped function, and decreases in the dose of heroin available to a nondependent animal will change the pattern of self-administration so that the interinjection interval decreases and the number of injections increases (Koob et al., 1987). Both systemic and central administration of competitive opiate antagonists produce similar increases in the number of self-administered infusions (Ettenberg, Pettit, Bloom, & Koob, 1982; Goldberg, Woods, & Schuster, 1971; Koob et al., 1984; Vaccarino, Pettit, Bloom, & Koob, 1985; Weeks & Collins, 1976), suggesting that the animal attempts to compensate for the opiate antagonism by increasing the amount of drug injected and that there is a competitive interaction between antagonist and agonist at the receptor.

The opiate receptor subtype important for the reinforcing actions of opiates appears to be the mu receptor. Mu opioid agonists produce dose-dependent decreases in heroin self-administration, and irreversible mu-selective antagonists dose-dependently increase heroin self-administration (Negus et al., 1993). Mice bearing mu receptor knockouts fail to show a conditioned place preference to morphine (Matthes et al., 1996).

The location of opioid receptors in the central nervous system important for the reinforcing properties of heroin appears to involve the same circuitry implicated in the actions of psychomotor stimulants, but engaging both a dopamine-dependent and dopamine-independent component (Britt & Wise, 1983; Vaccarino, Bloom, & Koob, 1985; see Figure 1). Intracerebroventricular administration of quaternary derivatives of opiate antagonists, charged hydrophilic compounds that do not readily spread from the sites in the brain at which they are injected (Schroeder, Weinger, Vakassian, & Koob, 1991), dose-dependently blocked heroin self-administration in nondependent rats (Vaccarino, Bloom, & Koob, 1985; Vaccarino, Pettit, et al., 1985). A similar blockade was observed when these antagonists were injected into the ventral tegmental area (VTA; Britt & Wise, 1983) and the nucleus accumbens (Vaccarino, Bloom, et al., 1985; Vaccarino, Pettit, et al., 1985). Rats also will self-administer opioid peptides in the region of the nucleus accumbens (Goeders, Lane, & Smith, 1984). In addition, opioid peptides injected into either nucleus accumbens or the VTA produce dose-related increases in locomotor activity (West, 1991).

Opioids also are self-administered directly into the region containing the cell bodies of origin of the mesocorticolimbic dopamine system, the

VTA, and microinjections into the VTA produce robust conditioned place preferences (DiChiara & North, 1992). Opiates, like other drugs of abuse, can increase dopamine release in the nucleus accumbens as measured by in vivo microdialysis in awake, freely moving animals (DiChiara & Imperato, 1988a, 1988b). However, significant evidence exists to suggest that the reinforcing effect of opiates in the nucleus accumbens can be independent of dopamine release (Pettit, Ettenberg, Bloom, & Koob, 1984; Stinus et al., 1989). Thus, the reinforcing actions of opiates may involve both a dopamine-dependent (VTA) and a dopamine-independent (nucleus accumbens) mechanism.

Sedative–Hypnotics

Ethanol, barbiturates, and benzodiazepines all are considered sedative–hypnotics and produce behavioral effects such as euphoria, disinhibition, anxiety reduction, sedation, and sleep induction. These disinhibitory and antianxiety effects are reflected in animal models in a reversal of behavior suppressed by punishment in conflict situations. These anticonflict effects correlate well with the ability of sedative–hypnotics to act as anxiolytics in the clinic (Sepinwall & Cook, 1978) and may be a major component of the reinforcing actions of these drugs.

Sedative–hypnotics, including ethanol, have long been hypothesized to modulate receptors for the major inhibitory neurotransmitter in the brain gamma-aminobutyric acid (GABA) receptors (Richards, Schoch, & Haefely, 1991). At the electrophysiological level, GABA acts to produce postsynaptic inhibition, and at the molecular level, GABA increases chloride ion flux in synaptic neurosomal preparations. This increase in ion flux produced by GABA is potentiated by benzodiazepines, barbiturates, and ethanol (Suzdak et al., 1986).

GABAergic antagonists reverse many of the behavioral effects of ethanol, which has provided some of the first clues to their reinforcing properties and their abuse potential (Frye & Breese, 1982; Koob & Britton, 1996; Liljequist & Engel, 1982). The partial inverse benzodiazepine agonist, RO 15-4513, which has been shown to reverse some of the behavioral effects of ethanol (Suzdak et al., 1986), produces a dose-dependent reduction of oral ethanol (10%) self-administration in rats (Rassnick et al., 1992; Samson, Tolliver, Pfeffer, Sadeghi, & Mills, 1987). Similar effects have been observed with potent GABA antagonists microinjected into the brain, with one of the most effective sites to date being the central nucleus of the amygdala (Hyytia & Koob, 1995; see Figure 4).

Reinforcing doses of ethanol also appear to activate brain dopamine systems. Dopamine receptor antagonists reduce lever pressing for ethanol in nondeprived rats (Pfeffer & Samson, 1988), and extracellular dopamine levels are increased in rats orally self-administering low doses of ethanol

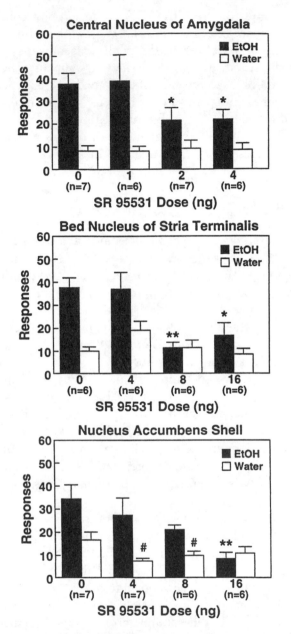

Figure 4. The effect of SR 95531 injections into the central nucleus of the amygdala, the bed nucleus of the stria terminalis, and the shell of the nucleus accumbens on responding for ethanol (EtOH) and water. Data are expressed as the mean ($\pm$ *SEM*) number of responses for EtOH and water during 30-minute sessions for each injection site. Note the change in the abscissa scale for injections into the bed nucleus of the stria terminalis and the nucleus accumbens shell. Significance of differences from the corresponding saline control values: $*p < .05$. $**p < .01$ for EtOH responses. $\#p < .05$ for water responses (adjusted = means test). Taken with permission from Hyytia & Koob, 1995.

(Weiss, Hurd, et al., 1992). However, virtually complete 6-hydroxydopa-mine denervation of the nucleus accumbens fails to alter voluntary responding for alcohol (Rassnick, Stinus, & Koob, 1993). Thus, as with opiates, these results suggest that although mesocorticolimbic dopamine transmission may be associated with important aspects of ethanol reinforcement, it is not critical in this regard, and other dopamine-independent neurochemical systems may participate in the mediation of ethanol's reinforcing actions. In fact, the view is emerging that multiple neurotransmitters combine to orchestrate the reward profile of alcohol (Engel et al., 1992).

For example, low doses of ethanol in the intoxicating range can antagonize the actions of glutamate, suggesting a role for glutamate systems in the actions of ethanol (Hoffman, Rabe, Moses, & Tabakoff, 1989; Lovinger, White, & Weight, 1989). Also, modulation of various aspects of brain serotonin systems, including increases in the synaptic availability of serotonin with precursor loading, blockade of serotonin reuptake, or blockade of certain serotonin receptor subtypes, can decrease ethanol intake (Eckardt et al., 1998; Grant, 1995; Sellers, Higgins, & Sobell, 1992). Consistent with a serotonergic role in ethanol abuse, in several double-blind, placebo-controlled clinical studies, serotonin reuptake inhibitors have produced mild-to-moderate decreases in alcohol consumption in humans (Naranjo, Kadlec, Sanhueza, Woodley-Remus, & Sellers, 1990).

The opiate antagonists naloxone and naltrexone reduce alcohol self-administration in several animal models, implicating opioid peptide systems in alcohol reinforcement (Hubbell et al., 1991). Both mu and delta opiate receptor subtypes may be important for these effects (Froehlich, Zweifel, Harts, Lumeng, & Li, 1991; Hyytia, 1993), and recent data suggest that the central nucleus of the amygdala is a particularly sensitive site for opioid antagonism of oral ethanol self-administration (Heyser, Roberts, Schulteis, Hyytia, & Koob, 1995). Consistent with a role for opioid peptides in alcohol reinforcement, two double-blind, placebo-controlled clinical trials have shown that naltrexone significantly reduces alcohol consumption, frequency of relapse, and craving for alcohol in humans (Volpicelli, Alterman, Hayashida, & O'Brien, 1992). Thus, alcohol interactions with opioid neurotransmission may contribute to certain aspects of alcohol reinforcement that may be of particular importance to the motivation associated with relapse.

Nicotine

The initial molecular site of action for the reinforcing actions of nicotine has been hypothesized to be the nicotinic acetylcholine receptors specifically in the brain mesolimbic dopamine system (Dani & Heinemann, 1996). Self-administration of nicotine is blocked by dopamine and opioid peptide antagonists (Malin et al., 1994; Malin, Lake, Carter, Cunningham, & Wilson, 1993). Nicotine thus may activate both dopamine system and opioid peptide elements in the same neural circuitry associated with other drugs of abuse (Corrigall, Franklin, Coen, & Clarke, 1992; see Figure 1).

MOTIVATIONAL VIEW OF DRUG DEPENDENCE

Initial drug use probably can be linked to the positive affective state produced by a drug. Certainly, the positive-reinforcing effects of drugs are critical for establishing self-administration behavior (Stewart, deWit, & Eikelboom, 1984; Wise & Bozarth, 1987), and this has led to the hypothesis that positive reinforcement is the key to drug dependence. However, this position clouds the distinction among drug use, drug abuse, and drug dependence (Institute of Medicine, 1996). The transition from drug use to drug dependence has historically invoked a recruitment of another source of reinforcement. Continued use leads to neuroadaptation in the brain reinforcement circuits to the presence of drug and to the negative reinforcement associated with relieving negative affective consequences of drug termination. Indeed, the defining feature of drug dependence has been argued to be the establishment of a negative affective state (Russell, 1976). In keeping with this position, all major drugs of abuse produce some form of negative affective state in humans during acute abstinence (see Exhibit 1).

Thus, although alleviation of withdrawal symptoms is not likely to be a major motivating factor in the initiation of drug use, neuroadaptation theories, such as opponent-process theory, postulate that the processes of affective habituation (hedonic tolerance) and affective withdrawal may be the driving force of addiction. Hypothetically, this construct would play an important role in the maintenance of drug use after the development of dependence.

The construct of a negative affective state is difficult to measure in animals; however, there is evidence of a compromised brain reward system during drug withdrawal in chronically drug-exposed animals. Intracranial self-stimulation (ICSS) behavior has proven to be particularly sensitive to changes in the brain reward systems during the course of drug dependence. Acute administration of drugs increases the reward value of ICSS (for a review, see Kornetsky & Esposito, 1979), and drug withdrawal decreases the reward value of ICSS (Koob, Markou, et al., 1993; Schulteis, Markou, Cole, & Koob, 1995; Schulteis, Markou, Gold, Stinus, & Koob, 1994). These increases or decreases in reward have been observed after the withdrawal of psychomotor stimulants, opiates, ethanol, and nicotine and ap-

EXHIBIT 1
Diagnostic Criteria for Drug Withdrawal

Opioid	Alcohol	Cocaine	Nicotine
Dysphoric mood	Autonomic hyperactivity	Dysphoric mood	Dysphoric or depressed mood
Nausea or vomiting	Hand tremor	Fatigue	Insomnia
Muscle aches	Insomnia	Unpleasant dreams	Irritability
Lacrimation	Nausea or vomiting	Insomnia or hypersomnia	Anxiety
Rhinorrhea	Hallucinations	Increased appetite	Difficulty concentrating
Pupillary dilation	Illusions	Psychomotor retardation or agitation	Restlessness
Piloerection	Psychomotor agitation		Decreased heart rate
Sweating	Anxiety		Increased appetite
Diarrhea	Seizures		Weight gain
Yawning			
Fever			
Insomnia			

Note. Data are from the *Diagnostic and Statistical Manual of Mental Disorders* (4th ed.); American Psychiatric Association, 1994.

pear to be dose related in that the more drug that is administered, the larger the withdrawal response (see Table 3).

Within-System and Between-System Neuroadaptations

The neurobiological basis for these changes in the reward system presumably involves the same neural elements that have been hypothesized to mediate the acute reinforcing actions of these drugs, but a distinction is made at the cellular, molecular, and system levels of analysis between adaptations occurring within the drug-sensitive reinforcement system and adaptations that occur between interacting systems (Koob & Bloom, 1988). In a within-system adaptation, repeated drug administration elicits an opposing reaction within the same system that mediates the primary reinforcing actions of the drug. For example, if the synaptic availability of the neurotransmitter dopamine is responsible for the acute reinforcing actions of cocaine, then the within-system neuroadaptation is a decrease in synaptic availability of dopamine. In a *between-system* adaptation, repeated drug administration recruits a different neurochemical system, one not involved in the acute reinforcing effects of the drug, but one that acts in opposition to the primary reinforcing effects of the drug. For example, the neuropeptide dynorphin acting on kappa receptors may be engaged by

TABLE 3
Drug Effects on Thresholds for Rewarding Brain Stimulation

Drug class	Acute administration	Withdrawal from chronic treatment	Study
Psychostimulants (e.g., cocaine, amphetamines)	Increase	Decrease	Esposito, Motola, & Kornetsky (1978); Kokkinidis, Zacharko, & Predy (1980); Kokkinidis, Zacharko, & Anisman (1986); Markou & Koob (1991); Frank, Martz, & Pommering (1988)
Opiates (e.g., morphine, heroin)	Increase	Decrease	Schaefer & Michael (1986); Schulteis, Heyser, & Koob (1995); Hubner & Kornetsky (1992); Schulteis et al., (1994)
Nicotine	Increase	Decrease	Huston-Lyons & Kornetsky (1992); Bauco & Wise (1994); Legault & Wise (1994)
Sedative–hypnotics	Increase	Decrease	Kornetsky, Moolten, & Bain (1991); Schulteis, Markou, Cole, & Koob (1995)

chronic cocaine administration, and dynorphin produces dysphoric-like effects that are opposite to those of dopamine (Shippenberg, LeFevour, & Heidbreder, 1996).

Molecular, Cellular, and System Adaptations Associated With Brain Motivational Systems

There are multiple examples of within-system and between-system adaptations that are relevant to the reinforcing actions of drugs (Koob, 1996). Some of these neuroadaptations may be specific to each drug class, and some may be common to all drugs of abuse. Even more intriguing is the possibility that within the dimension of neurobiological circuitry, the reward system may represent a common substrate not only for the reinforcing actions of drugs but also for the neuroadaptations known as *substance dependence* or *addiction*.

Opiates

Although there is little evidence of changes in opioid peptide activity or changes in the number of opioid receptors associated with chronic opiate administration, there is ample evidence that a dramatic change in sensitivity to the action of opioid antagonists can occur in brain areas implicated in the acute reinforcing effects of opiates (Nestler, 1992). Opiate receptors in the region of the nucleus accumbens are much more sensitive to the aversive effects of opiate antagonists in dependent rats (Stinus, Le Moal, & Koob, 1990). The molecular basis for this effect may be at the signal-transduction level. Acute morphine decreases adenylate cyclase activity, whereas chronic morphine treatment has long been associated with increases in adenylate cyclase activity, an action opposite to that of acute administration effects observed in the nucleus accumbens (Nestler, 1996).

Psychomotor Stimulants

Neurochemical measures to assess extracellular dopamine levels in the nucleus accumbens before, during, and after a cocaine self-administration bout by means of in vivo microdialysis have shown that extracellular dopamine levels in the nucleus accumbens are decreased 30% to 40% during cocaine withdrawal compared with presession levels (Weiss, Markou, et al., 1992). This dopamine decrease is correlated with the amount of cocaine consumed during the preceding binge and is maximal at the time points when maximal elevation in ICSS thresholds is observed (Markou & Koob, 1991). Similar decreases in basal extracellular dopamine levels in the accumbens also have been observed during withdrawal from experimenter-administered cocaine injections, although the time course of the effect is different (Parsons, Smith, & Justice, 1991; Rossetti, Hamaidan, & Gessa, 1992). Perhaps even more interesting is that extracellular serotonin levels decrease even more dramatically than dopamine levels during cocaine withdrawal (see Figure 5). The duration of the serotonin decrease and the time course of recovery are not known at this time.

There are several molecular actions that also could represent motivationally important neuroadaptations to chronic cocaine or amphetamine administration. Activation of D_1 receptors stimulates a cascade of events that ultimately lead to cyclic adenosine monophosphate response element binding protein (CREB) phosphorylation and intermediate gene expression (Hyman, 1996). These within-system adaptations not only could change the function of the dopamine system itself but also may trigger a second major neurobiological action, the stimulation of expression of protachykinin and prodynorphin messenger RNA (mRNA). The subsequent activation of dynorphin systems could contribute to the dysphoric syndrome associated with cocaine dependence and also feedback to decrease dopamine release. Enhanced dynorphin actions could be considered a between-system adaptation. The significance of the D_1 receptor–cyclic adenosine monophosphate response element binding protein (cAMP)–CREB pathway is supported by the recent evidence of anticocaine priming effects of D_1 agonists (Self, Barnhart, Lehman, & Nestler, 1996).

Extracellular DA and 5-HT in the Nucleus Accumbens During Cocaine Self-Administration and Withdrawal

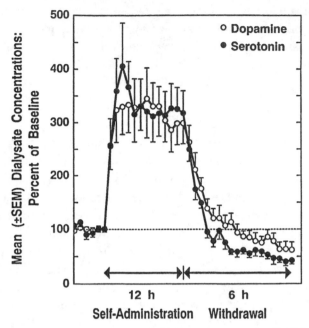

Figure 5. Extracellular dopamine (DA) and serotonin (5-HT) levels in the nucleus accumbens during and after a 12-hour (h) binge of cocaine self-administration in the rat. The mean ($\pm SEM$) presession baseline dialysate concentrations of 5-HT and DA were 0.98 $\pm$ 0.1 nM and 5.3 $\pm$ 0.5 nM, respectively ($n = 7$). All rats self-administered cocaine with regular interinfusion intervals; 6 out of 7 rats self-administered cocaine for the entire 12-hour session. The average cocaine intake was 28.8 $\pm$ 2.1 mg/12 hours. Taken with permission from Parsons, Koob, and Weiss, 1995.

Nicotine

Nicotinic acetylcholine receptors located in the brain mesolimbic dopamine system are a likely site for the initial molecular actions of nicotine, and the capability of these receptors to exist in many different functional states has led to a combined within-system–between-system adaptation hypothesis to explain tolerance and dependence (Dani & Heinemann, 1996). According to this hypothesis, acute nicotine briefly stimulates receptors that are normally in a closed resting state, but then they return to a desensitized inactive state where they are unresponsive to the agonist. Possibly as a result, long-term nicotine exposure causes an increase in the actual number of nicotinic acetylcholine receptors (Collins, Bhat, Pauly, & Marks, 1990).

Thus, nicotine has been hypothesized by Dani and Heinemann (1996) to stimulate the mesolimbic dopamine system through activation of nicotinic acetylcholine receptors to produce the reinforcing effects of nicotine, and the inactivation of the receptors by desensitization leads to acute tolerance, which is compensated for by an increase in nicotinic receptors. During abstinence, nicotine levels fall, and the increased nicotinic acetylcholine receptors begin to recover to a responsive state. However, this heightened nicotinic receptor responsivity is not restricted just to the nicotinic receptors on the dopamine system but may engage other nicotinic receptors in non-reward-related pathways that can contribute to the negative affective state associated with nicotine withdrawal. According to this hypothesis, smokers would be, in effect, ultimately medicating themselves with nicotine to regulate the number of functional nicotinic acetylcholine receptors (Dani & Heinemann, 1996).

Ethanol

Dopamine, opioid peptide, and GABAergic systems that are linked to the motivational effects of acute ethanol also have been implicated in within-systems adaptations to chronic ethanol exposure. Extracellular dopamine levels in the nucleus accumbens are decreased during ethanol withdrawal, and this decrease is reversed by ethanol self-administration during withdrawal (Diana, Pistis, Carboni, Gessa, & Rossetti, 1993; Weiss et al., 1996). A role for opioid peptides in ethanol dependence derives from the preclinical observation of a decrease in ethanol self-administration with opioid antagonists (Reid & Hunter, 1984) and from the clinical observation that opioid antagonist administration can help prevent relapse in detoxified alcoholics (O'Malley et al., 1992; Volpicelli et al., 1992). All of these changes are considered within-system changes, where the neurotransmitter system responsible for part of the acute reinforcing actions of ethanol is altered by chronic exposure to ethanol.

One example of a potential between-system neuroadaptation with chronic ethanol is the activation of corticotropin-releasing factor (CRF), a neuropeptide implicated in behavioral responses to stressors (Koob, Heinrichs, Menzaghi, Pich, & Britton, 1994). CRF antagonists injected into the amygdala reverse the anxiogenic-like effects of ethanol withdrawal (Rassnick, Heinrichs, Britton, & Koob, 1993), and ethanol withdrawal is characterized by increased release of CRF into the amygdala (Pich et al., 1995).

COMMON NEUROPHARMACOLOGICAL ELEMENTS IN ADDICTION

The changes in the brain associated with the development of drug dependence have several common elements that may define a circuitry for drug addiction and may involve both within-system and between-system neuroadaptations (Koob, 1992b). The mesolimbic dopamine system appears to be common to the acute and chronic actions of all drugs of abuse. Activation of this system is critical for the reinforcing actions of stimulants, possibly including nicotine. The mesolimbic dopamine system also participates in opiate and alcohol reinforcement, although it is not critical (Koob, 1992a, 1992b). In addition, drug withdrawal is accompanied by a decrease in dopamine function, and elements of protracted abstinence may involve long-term changes in the dopamine system (Nestler, 1996). Another neurotransmitter system in which the development of dependence may involve a within-system neuroadaptation is the opioid peptide system. Evidence is strong for changes in signal transduction associated with chronic opiates, but indirect evidence exists for similar changes with cocaine and even chronic ethanol (Nestler, 1992).

Evidence for between-systems adaptations following chronic administration of drugs of abuse can be found in studies exploring the role of several neuropeptides, notably dynorphin, neuropeptide FF (NPFF), and CRF. Dynorphin peptides in the nucleus accumbens may regulate the dopamine system through a presynaptic action on kappa opioid receptors, and kappa agonists produce aversive effects in rodents and humans (Hyman, 1996). Thus, chronic administration of cocaine or amphetamine induces prodynorphin gene expression in the nucleus accumbens, which has the opposite effects on reward than cocaine does.

Antiopiate activities have been hypothesized for NPFF, previously called F8Fa, on the basis of effects of intracerebroventricular injection of NPFF-related peptides. NPFF attenuates morphine- and stress-induced analgesia (Kavaliers, 1990) and precipitates morphine withdrawal (Malin et al., 1990). An NPFF antagonist can increase both morphine- and stress-induced analgesia, reverse morphine tolerance (Lake et al., 1992), and attenuate naloxone-precipitated withdrawal syndrome in morphine-dependent rats. An NPFF antagonist also blocks some aspects of nicotine withdrawal (Malin et al., 1996). Similar antiopiate-like effects have recently been observed with administration of the orphan receptor binding peptide orphanin (Mogil, Grisel, Zhangs, Belknap, & Grady, 1996). It remains to be determined whether these antiopiate peptides have motivational significance and contribute to the negative affective state produced during drug abstinence.

Another neuropeptide that may be involved in the motivational aspects of drug dependence is CRF. Rats treated repeatedly with cocaine and ethanol show significant anxiogenic-like responses after cessation of chronic drug administration, which are reversed with intracerebroventricular administration of a CRF antagonist (Rassnick, Heinrichs, et al., 1993; Sarnyai et al., 1995). Similar effects have been observed with ethanol and similar doses of the CRF antagonist injected into the amygdala were active in reversing the aversive effects of opiate withdrawal (Heinrichs,

Menzaghi, Schulteis, Koob, & Stinus, 1995). In vivo microdialysis studies have confirmed an increase in extracellular CRF during ethanol withdrawal (Pich et al., 1995). Thus, CRF activation may be a common element associated with the development of drug dependence and may be associated with motivational effects involving such subjective symptoms as increased stress and negative affect.

EXTENDED AMYGDALA

Recent neuroanatomical studies may have provided a key link among the substrates for brain reward, as measured by intracranial self-stimulation, natural reward, and drug reward. The shell of the nucleus accumbens—the bed nucleus of the stria terminalis, and the central nucleus of the amygdala share certain cyto-architectural similarities. This has led to the concept of the *extended amygdala*, a brain system in the basal forebrain that may be involved in emotional behavior and motivation (Heimer & Alheid, 1991; Koob, Robledo, Markou, & Caine, 1993). Particularly striking is that the extended amygdala has significant afferents from limbic structures such as the basolateral amygdala and send not only efferents to the medial part of the ventral pallidum but also a large projection to the lateral hypothalamus, further defining the specific brain areas that interface classical limbic (emotional) structures with the extrapyramidal motor system.

Evidence is now accumulating that suggests that the extended amygdala mediates not only the acute reinforcing actions of drugs of abuse but also the neuroadaptations associated with drug dependence. Acute administration of all the major drugs of abuse produces increases in extracellular levels of dopamine in the shell of the nucleus accumbens (Pontieri, Tanda, & DiChiara, 1995). The ventromedial shell of the nucleus also expresses high levels of the D_3 dopamine receptor mRNA (Diaz et al., 1995), and the shell of the nucleus accumbens is particularly sensitive to the cocaine antagonist activity of a D_1 antagonist (Caine et al., 1995). Evidence for a role for the central nucleus of the amygdala in ethanol reinforcement comes from studies showing that microinjection of GABA antagonists or opioid peptide antagonists into the central nucleus can attenuate lever pressing for oral ethanol (Heyser et al., 1995; Hyytia & Koob, 1995).

Perhaps more intriguing is the recent observation that microinjections of previously ineffective doses of a GABA agonist into the amygdala, without effects in nondependent rats, decrease ethanol self-administration in dependent rats (Roberts, Cole, & Koob, 1996). These results suggest that the GABAergic system has been altered significantly during the course of dependence. Also, the CRF interaction with ethanol in dependent animals appears to involve the central nucleus of the amygdala (Koob, Heinrichs, et al., 1994; Koob, Rassnick, Heinrichs, & Weiss, 1994). Thus, one may speculate that the same neurochemical components that constitute the neurocircuitry of the extended amygdala that is involved in acute drug actions may be the substrates for the within-system and between-system changes that represent the motivational aspects of dependence, namely, a compromised reward system (Koob & Bloom, 1988).

CRAVING AND RELAPSE

The nature of drug addiction as a chronic relapsing disorder makes compelling the study of vulnerability to relapse, which is associated with states of craving and protracted abstinence that are difficult to define. Presumably such states reflect some prolonged post-acute-withdrawal perturbation or vulnerability to reinstatement of drug-taking behavior and ultimately compulsive use. A residual deficit state in the reward system or a sensitization of the reward system to stimuli that predict drug effects, or both, could be responsible for this vulnerability. One could speculate that the combination would be particularly powerful as a motivator for reinstatement of drug use.

Animal models of drug craving and relapse continue to be developed and refined and usually reflect secondary sources of reinforcement (Koob, 1994; Markou et al., 1993; Stewart, 1992). The neural substrates for conditioned positive reinforcement may involve elements of afferent input of the extended amygdala, such as the afferents from the basolateral amygdala (Everitt, Morris, O'Brien, & Robbins, 1991) and the dopaminergic afferents that form the mesolimbic dopamine system. The neural substrates for conditioned negative reinforcement are largely unknown. The challenge for future studies in the neurobiology of substance dependence will be to elucidate the neuroadaptive changes produced by chronic drug use in animal models that convey protracted abstinence and vulnerability to relapse. Presumably, the answers will be found in the same molecular and cellular elements of the neurochemical systems and neurocircuitry responsible for the positive and negative reinforcement associated with chronic drug use.

REFERENCES

American Psychiatric Association. (1994). *Diagnostic and statistical manual of mental disorders* (4th ed.). Washington, DC: American Psychiatric Press.

Bauco, P., & Wise, R. A. (1994). Potentiation of lateral hypothalamic and midline mesencephalic brain stimulation reinforcement by nicotine: Examination of repeated treatment. *Journal of Pharmacology and Experimental Therapeutics, 271*, 294–301.

Bergman, J., Kamien, J. B., & Spealman, R. D. (1990). Antagonism of cocaine self-administration by selective dopamine D1 and D2 antagonist. *Behavioural Pharmacology, 1,* 355–363.

Britt, M. D., & Wise, R. A. (1983). Ventral tegmental site of opiate reward: Antagonism by a hydrophilic opiate receptor blocker. *Brain Research, 258,* 105–108.

Caine, S. B., Heinrichs, S. C., Coffin, V. L., & Koob, G. F. (1995). Effects of the dopamine D-1 antagonist SCH 23390 microinjected into the accumbens, amygdala or striatum on cocaine self-administration in the rat. *Brain Research, 692,* 47–56.

Caine, S. B, & Koob, G. F. (1993). Modulation of cocaine self-administration in the rat through D-3 dopamine receptors. *Science, 260,* 1814–1816.

Caine, S. B., & Koob, G. F. (1994). Effects of mesolimbic dopamine depletion on responding maintained by cocaine and food. *Journal of Experimental Analysis of Behavior, 61,* 213–221.

Carr, G. D., Fibiger, H. C., & Phillips, A. G. (1989). Conditioned place preference as a measure of drug reward. In J. M. Liebman, S. J. Cooper (Eds.), *The neuropharmacological basis of reward: Topics in experimental psychopharmacology, 1,* (pp. 264–319. Oxford: Oxford University Press.

Collins, A. C., Bhat, R. V., Pauly, J. R., & Marks, M. J. (1990). Modulation of nicotine receptors by chronic exposure to nicotinic agonists and antagonists. In G. Bock & J. Marsh (Eds.), *The biology of nicotine dependence* (pp. 87–105). New York: Wiley.

Collins, R. J., Weeks, J. R., Cooper, M. M., Good, P. I., & Russell, R. R. (1984). Prediction of abuse liability of drugs using IV self-administration by rats. *Psychopharmacology, 82,* 6–13.

Corrigall, W. A., Franklin, K. B. J., Coen, K. M., & Clarke, P. B. S. (1992). The mesolimbic dopamine system is implicated in the reinforcing effects of nicotine. *Psychopharmacology* (Berlin), *107,* 285–289.

Dani, J. A., & Heinemann, S. (1996). Molecular and cellular aspects of nicotine abuse. *Neuron, 16,* 905–908.

Davis, W. M., & Smith, S. G. (1975). Effect of haloperidol on (+)-amphetamine self-administration. *Journal of Pharmacy and Pharmacology, 27,* 540–542.

Deneau, G., Yanagita, T., & Seever, M. H. (1969). Self-administration of psychoactive substances by the monkey. *Psychopharmacology, 16,* 30–48.

deWit, H., & Wise, R. A. (1977). Blockade of cocaine reinforcement in rats with the dopamine receptor blocker pimozide, but not with the noradrenergic blockers phentolamine and phenoxybenzamine. *Canadian Journal of Psychology, 31,* 195–203.

Diana, M., Pistis, M., Carboni, S., Gessa, G. L., & Rossetti, Z. L. (1993). Profound decrement of mesolimbic dopaminergic neuronal activity during ethanol withdrawal syndrome in rats: Electrophysiological and biochemical evidence. *Proceedings of the National Academy of Sciences, USA, 90,* 7966–7969.

Diaz, J., Lévesque, D., Lammers, C. H., Griffon, N., Martes, M.-P., Schwartz, J.-C., & Sokoloff, P. (1995). Phenotypical characterization of neurons expressing the dopamine D3 receptor in the rat brain. *Neuroscience, 65,* 731–745.

DiChiara, G., & Imperato, A. (1988a). Drugs abused by humans preferentially increase synaptic dopamine concentrations in the mesolimbic system of freely moving rats. *Proceedings of the National Academy of Sciences, USA, 85,* 5274–5278.

DiChiara, G., & Imperato, A. (1988b). Opposite effects of mu and kappa opiate agonists on dopamine release in the nucleus accumbens and in the dorsal caudate of freely moving rats. *Journal of Pharmacology and Experimental Therapeutics, 244,* 1067–1080.

DiChiara, G., & North, R. A. (1992). Neurobiology of opiate abuse. *Trends in Pharmaceutical Sciences, 13,* 185–193.

Eckardt, M. J., File, S. E., Gessa, G. L., Grant, K. A., Guerri, C., Hoffman, P. L., Kalant, H., Koob, G. F., Li, T.-K., & Tabakoff, B. (1998). The effects of moderate alcohol consumption on the central nervous system. *Alcoholism: Clinical and Experimental Research, 22,* 998–1040.

Engel, J. A., Enerback, C., Fahlke, C., Hulthe, P., Hard, E., Johannessen, K., Svensson, L., & Soderpalm, B. (1992). Serotonergic and dopaminergic involvement in ethanol intake. In C. A. Naranjo & E. M. Sellers (Eds.), *Novel pharmacological interventions for alcoholism* (pp. 68–82). New York: Springer.

Esposito, R. U., Motola, A. H. D., & Kornetsky, C. (1978). Cocaine: Acute effects on reinforcement thresholds for self-stimulation behavior to the medial forebrain bundle. *Pharmacology Biochemistry and Behavior, 8,* 437–439.

Ettenberg, A., Pettit, H. O., Bloom, F. E., & Koob, G. F. (1982). Heroin and cocaine intravenous self-administration in rats: Mediation by separate neural systems. *Psychopharmacology, 78,* 204–209.

Everitt, B. J., Morris, K. A., O'Brien, A., & Robbins, T. W. (1991). The basolateral amygdala–ventral striatal system and conditioned place preference: Further evidence of limbic–striatal interactions underlying reward-related processes. *Neuroscience, 42,* 1–18.

Frank, R. A., Martz, S., & Pommering, T. (1988). The effect of chronic cocaine on self-stimulation train-duration thresholds. *Pharmacology Biochemistry and Behavior, 29,* 755–758.

Froehlich, J. C., Zweifel, M., Harts, J. Lumeng, L., & Li, T.-K. (1991). Importance of delta opioid receptors in maintaining high alcohol drinking. *Psychopharmacology, 103,* 467–472.

Frye, G. D., & Breese, G. R. (1982). GABAergic modulation of ethanol-induced motor impairment. *Journal of Pharmacology and Experimental Therapeutics, 223,* 750–756.

Goeders, N. E., Lane, J. D., & Smith, J. E. (1984). Self-administration of methionine enkephalin into the nucleus accumbens. *Pharmacology Biochemistry and Behavior, 20,* 451–455.

Goldberg, S. R., Woods, J. H., & Schuster, C. R. (1971). Nalorphine-induced changes in morphine self-administration in rhesus monkeys. *Journal of Pharmacology and Experimental Therapeutics, 176,* 464–471.

Grant, K. A. (1995). The role of 5-HT3 receptors in drug dependence. *Drug and Alcohol Dependence, 38,* 155–171.

Heimer, L., & Alheid, G. (1991). Piecing together the puzzle of basal forebrain anatomy. In T. C. Napier, P. Kalivas, & I. Hanin (Eds.), *The basal forebrain: Anatomy to function* (pp. 1–42). New York: Plenum.

Heinrichs, S. C., Menzaghi, F., Schulteis, G., Koob, G. F., & Stinus, L. (1995). Suppression of corticotropin-releasing factor in the amygdala attenuates aversive consequences of morphine withdrawal. *Behavioural Pharmacology, 6,* 74–80.

Heyser, C. J., Roberts, A. J., Schulteis, G., Hyytia, P., & Koob, G. F. (1995). Central administration of an opiate antagonist decreases oral ethanol self-administration in rats. *Society for Neuroscience Abstracts, 21,* 1698.

Hoffman, P. L., Rabe, C., Moses, F., & Tabakoff, B. (1989). N-methyl-D-aspartate receptors and ethanol: Inhibition of calcium flux and cyclic GMP production. *Journal of Neurochemistry, 52,* 1937–1940.

Hubbell, C. L., Marglin, S. H., Spitalnic, S. J., Abelson, M. L., Wild, K. D., & Reid, L. D. (1991). Opioidergic, serotonergic and dopaminergic manipulations and rats' intake of a sweetened alcoholic beverage. *Alcohol, 8,* 355–367.

Hubner, C. B., & Kornetsky, C. (1992). Heroin, 6-acetylmorphine, and morphine effects on threshold for rewarding and aversive brain stimulation. *Journal of Pharmacology and Experimental Therapeutics, 260,* 562–567.

Hurd, Y. L., Weiss, F., Koob, G. F., Anden, N.-E., & Ungerstedt, U. (1989). Cocaine reinforcement and extracellular dopamine overflow in rat nucleus accumbens: An in vivo microdialysis study. *Brain Research, 498,* 199–203.

Huston-Lyons, D., & Kornetsky, C. (1992). Effects of nicotine on the threshold for rewarding brain stimulation in rats. *Pharmacology Biochemistry and Behavior, 41,* 755–759.

Hyman, S. E. (1996). Addiction to cocaine and amphetamine. *Neuron, 16,* 901–904.

Hyytia, P. (1993). Involvement of μ-opioid receptors in alcohol drinking by alcohol-preferring AA rats. *Pharmacology Biochemistry and Behavior, 45,* 697–701.

Hyytia, P., & Koob, G. F. (1995). $GABA_A$ receptor antagonism in the extended amygdala decreases ethanol self-administration in rats. *European Journal of Pharmacology, 283,* 151–159.

Institute of Medicine. (1996). *Pathways of addiction.* Washington, DC: National Academy Press.

Johanson, C. E., & Balster, R. L. (1978). A summary of the results of a drug self-administration study using substitution procedures in rhesus monkeys. *Bulletin on Narcotics, 30,* 43–54.

Kavaliers, M. (1990). Inhibitory influences of mammalian FMRFamide (Phe-Met-

Arg-Phe-amide)-related peptides on nociception and morphine- and stress-induced analgesia in mice. *Neuroscience Letters, 115,* 307–312.

Kokkinidis, L., Zacharko, R. M., & Anisman, H. (1986). Amphetamine withdrawal: A behavioral evaluation. *Life Sciences, 38,* 1617–1623.

Kokkinidis, L., Zacharko, R. M., & Predy, P. A. (1980). Post-amphetamine depression of self-stimulation responding from the substantia nigra: Reversal by tricyclic antidepressants. *Pharmacology Biochemistry and Behavior, 13,* 379–383.

Koob, G. F. (1992a). Dopamine, addiction and reward. *Seminars in the Neurosciences, 4,* 139–148.

Koob, G. F. (1992b). Drugs of abuse: Anatomy, pharmacology, and function of reward pathways. *Trends in Pharmacological Sciences, 13,* 177–184.

Koob, G. F. (1994). Animal models of drug addiction. In F. E. Bloom, & D. J. Kupfer, (Eds.), *Psychopharmacology: The fourth generation of progress* (pp. 759–772). New York: Raven Press.

Koob, G. F. (1996). Drug addiction: The yin and yang of hedonic homeostasis. *Neuron, 16,* 893–896.

Koob, G. F., & Bloom, F. E. (1988). Cellular and molecular mechanisms of drug dependence. *Science, 242,* 715–723.

Koob, G. F., & Britton, K. T. (1996). Neurobiological substrates for the anti-anxiety effects of ethanol. In H. Begleiter & B. Kissin (Eds.), *The pharmacology of alcohol and alcohol dependence* (pp. 477–506). New York: Oxford University Press.

Koob, G. F., & Goeders, N. E. (1989). Neuroanatomical substrates of drug self-administration. In J. M. Liebman & S. J. Cooper (Eds.), *The neuropharmacological basis of reward,* (pp. 214–263). New York: Oxford University.

Koob, G. F., Heinrichs, S. C., Menzaghi, F., Pich, E. M., & Britton, K. T. (1994). Corticotropin-releasing factor, stress and behavior. *Seminars in the Neurosciences, 6,* 221–229.

Koob, G. F., Le, H. T., & Creese, I. (1987). The D-1 receptor antagonist SCH 23390 increases cocaine self-administration in the rat. *Neuroscience Letters, 79,* 315–320.

Koob, G. F., Markou, A., Weiss, F., & Schulteis, G. (1993). Opponent process and drug dependence: Neurobiological mechanisms. *Seminars in the Neurosciences, 5,* 351–358.

Koob, G. F., Pettit, H. O., Ettenberg, A., & Bloom, F. E. (1984). Effects of opiate antagonists and their quaternary derivatives on heroin self-administration in the rat. *Journal of Pharmacology and Experimental Therapeutics, 229,* 481–486.

Koob, G. F., Rassnick, S., Heinrichs, S., & Weiss, F. (1994). Alcohol: The reward system and dependence. In B. Janson, H. Jornvall, U. Rydberg, L. Terenius, & B. L. Vallee (Eds.), *Toward a molecular basis of alcohol use and abuse* (pp. 103–114). Proceedings of Nobel Symposium on Alcohol.

Koob, G. F., Robledo, P., Markou, A., & Caine, S. B. (1993). The mesocortico-limibic circuit in drug dependence and reward: A role for the extended amygdala? In P. W. Kalivas & C. D. Barnes (Eds.), *Limbic motor circuits and neuropsychiatry* (pp. 289–309). Boca Raton, FL: CRC Press.

Koob, G. F., Vaccarino, F. J., Amalric, M., & Bloom, F. E. (1987). Positive reinforcement properties of drugs: Search for neural substrates. In J. Engel, L. Oreland, D. H. Inguar, B. Pernow, S. Rossner, & L. A. Pellborn (Eds.), *Brain reward systems and abuse* (pp. 35–50). New York: Raven Press.

Kornetsky, C., & Esposito, R. U. (1979). Euphorigenic drugs: Effects on the reward pathways of the brain. *Federation Proceedings, 38,* 2473–2476.

Kornetsky, C., Moolten, M., & Bain, G. (1991). Ethanol and rewarding brain stimulation. In R. E. Meyer, G. F. Koob, M. J. Lewis, & S. M. Paul (Eds.), *Neuropharmacology of ethanol: New approaches* (pp. 179–199). Boston: Birkhauser.

Lake, J. R., Hebert, K. M., Payza, K., Deshotel, K. D., Hausam, D. D., Witherspoon, W. E., Arcangeli, K. A., & Malin, D. H. (1992). Analog of neuropeptide FF attenuates morphine tolerance. *Neuroscience Letters, 146,* 203–206.

Legault, M., & Wise, R. A. (1994). Effects of withdrawal from nicotine on intracranial self-stimulation. *Society for Neuroscience Abstracts, 20,* 1032.

Liljequist, S., & Engel, J. (1982). Effects of GABAergic agonists and antagonists on various ethanol-induced behavioral changes. *Psychopharmacology, 78,* 71–75.

Lovinger, D. M., White, G., & Weight, F. F. (1989). Ethanol inhibits NMDA-activated ion current in hippocampal neurons. *Science, 243,* 1721–1724.

Lyness, W. H., Friedle, N. M., & Moore, K. E. (1979). Destruction of dopaminergic nerve terminals in nucleus accumbens: Effect of *d*-amphetamine self-administration. *Pharmacology Biochemistry and Behavior, 11,* 553–556.

Malin, D. H., Lake, J. R., Carter, V. A., Cunningham, J. S., Hebert, K. M., Conrad, D. L., & Wilson, O. B. (1994). The nicotinic antagonist mecamylamine precipitates nicotine abstinence syndrome in the rat. *Psychopharmacology, 115,* 180–184.

Malin, D. H., Lake, J. R., Carter, V. A., Cunningham, J. S., & Wilson, O. B. (1993). Naloxone precipitates nicotine abstinence syndrome in the rat. *Psychopharmacology, 112,* 339–342.

Malin, D. H., Lake, J. R., Hammond, M. V., Fowler, D. E., Rogillio, R. B., Brown, S. L., Sims, J. L., Leecraft, B. M., & Yang, H-Y. T. (1990). FMRF-NH2-like mammalian octapeptide: Possible role in opiate dependence and abstinence. *Peptides, 11,* 969–972.

Malin, D. H., Lake, J. R., Short, P. E., Blossman, J. B., Lawless, B. A., Schopen, C. K., Sailer, E. E., Burgess, K., & Wilson, O. B. (1996). Nicotine abstinence syndrome precipitated by an analog of neuropeptide FF. *Pharmacology Biochemistry and Behavior, 54,* 581–585.

Markou, A., & Koob, G. F. (1991). Post-cocaine anhedonia: An animal model of cocaine withdrawal. *Neuropharmacology, 4,* 17–26.

Markou, A., Weiss, F., Gold, L. H., Caine, S. B., Schulteis, G., & Koob, G. F. (1993). Animal models of drug craving. *Psychopharmacology, 112,* 163–182.

Matthes, H. W. D., Maldonado, R., Simonin, F., Valverde, O., Slowe, S., Kitchen, I., Befort, K., Dierich, A., Le Meur, M., Dolle, P., Tzavara, E., Hanoune, J., Roques, B. P., & Kieffer, B. L. (1996). Loss of morphine-induced analgesia, reward effect and withdrawal symptoms in mice lacking the mu-opioid-receptor gene. *Nature* (London), *383*, 819–823.

Mogil, J. S., Grisel, J. E., Zhangs, G., Belknap, J. K., & Grady, D. K. (1996). Functional antagonism of mu-, delta- and kappa-opioid antinociception by orphanin FQ. *Neuroscience Letters, 214*, 131–134.

Naranjo, C., Kadlec, K., Sanhueza, P., Woodley-Remus, D., & Sellers, E. M. (1990). Fluoxetine differentially alters alcohol intake and other consummatory behaviors in problem drinkers. *Clinical Pharmacology and Therapeutics, 47*, 490–498.

Negus, S. S., Henriksen, S. J., Mattox, A., Pasternak, G. W., Portoghese, P. S., Takemori, A. E., Weinger, M. B., & Koob, G. F. (1993). Effect of antagonists selective for mu, delta, and kappa opioid receptors on the reinforcing effects of heroin in rats. *Journal of Pharmacology and Experimental Therapeutics, 265*, 1245–1252.

Nestler, E. J. (1992). Molecular mechanisms of drug addiction. *Journal of Neuroscience, 12*, 2439–2450.

Nestler, E. J. (1996). Under siege: The brain on opiates. *Neuron, 16*, 897–900.

O'Malley, S. S., Jaffe, A. J., Chang, G., Schottenfeld, R. S., Meyer, R. E., & Rounsaville, B. (1992). Naltrexone and coping skills therapy for alcohol dependence: A controlled study. *Archives of General Psychiatry, 49*, 881–887.

Parsons, L. H., Koob, G. F., & Weiss, F. (1995). Serotonin dysfunction in the nucleus accumbens of rats during withdrawal after unlimited access to intravenous cocaine. *Journal of Pharmacology and Experimental Therapeutics, 274*, 1182–1191.

Parsons, L. H., Smith, A. D., & Justice, J. B., Jr. (1991). Basal extracellular dopamine is decreased in the rat nucleus accumbens during abstinence from chronic cocaine. *Synapse, 9*, 60–65.

Pettit, H.-O., Ettenberg, A., Bloom, F. E., & Koob, G. F. (1984). Destruction of dopamine in the nucleus accumbens selectively attenuates cocaine but not heroin self-administration in rats. *Psychopharmacology, 84*, 167–173.

Pettit, H.-O. & Justice, J. B., Jr. (1989). Dopamine in the nucleus accumbens during cocaine self-administration as studied by *in vivo* microdialysis. *Pharmacology Biochemistry and Behavior, 34*, 899–904.

Pettit, H.-O. & Justice, J. B., Jr. (1991). Effect of dose on cocaine self-administration behavior and dopamine levels in the nucleus accumbens. *Brain Research, 539*, 94–102.

Pfeffer, A. O., & Samson, H. H. (1988). Haloperidol and apomorphine effects on ethanol reinforcement in free-feeding rats. *Pharmacology Biochemistry and Behavior, 29*, 343–350.

Pich, E. M., Lorang, M., Yaganeh, M., Rodriguez de Fonseca, F., Raber, J., Koob, G. F., & Weiss, F. (1995). Increase of extracellular corticotropin-releasing factor-like immunoreactivity levels in the amygdala of awake rats during restraint stress and ethanol withdrawal as measured by microdialysis. *Journal of Neuroscience, 15,* 5439–5447.

Pontieri, F. E., Tanda, G., & DiChiara, G. (1995). Intravenous cocaine, morphine, and amphetamine preferentially increase extracellular dopamine in the "shell" as compared with the "core" of the rat nucleus accumbens. *Proceedings of the National Academy of Sciences, USA, 92,* 12304–12308.

Rassnick, S., D'Amico, E., Riley, E., Pulvirenti, L., Zieglgansberger, W., & Koob, G. F. (1992). GABA and nucleus accumbens glutamate neurotransmission modulate ethanol self-administration in rats. In P. W. Kalivas & H. H. Samson (Eds.), *Annals of the New York Academy of Sciences: The neurobiology of drug and alcohol addiction* (pp. 502–505). New York: New York Academy of Sciences.

Rassnick, S., Heinrichs, S. C., Britton, K. T., & Koob, G. F. (1993). Microinjection of a corticotropin-releasing factor antagonist into the central nucleus of the amygdala reverses anxiogenic-like effects of ethanol withdrawal. *Brain Research, 605,* 25–32.

Rassnick, S., Stinus, L., & Koob, G. F. (1993). The effects of 6-hydroxydopamine lesions of the nucleus accumbens and the mesolimbic dopamine system on oral self-administration of ethanol in the rat. *Brain Research, 623,* 16–24.

Reid, L. D., & Hunter, G. A. (1984). Morphine and naloxone modulate intake of ethanol. *Alcohol, 1,* 33–37.

Richards, G., Schoch, P., & Haefely, W. (1991). Benzodiazepine receptors: New vistas. *Seminars in Neuroscience, 3,* 191–203.

Roberts, A. J., Cole, M., & Koob, G. F. (1996). Intra-amygdala muscimol decreases operant ethanol self-administration in dependent rats. *Alcoholism: Clinical and Experimental Research, 20,* 1289–1298.

Roberts, D. C. S., Koob, G. F., Klonoff, P., & Fibiger, H. C. (1980). Extinction and recovery of cocaine self-administration following 6-hydroxydopamine lesions of the nucleus accumbens. *Pharmacology Biochemistry and Behavior, 12,* 781–787.

Rossetti, Z. L., Hamaidan, Y., & Gessa, G. L. (1992). Marked inhibition of mesolimbic dopamine release: A common feature of ethanol, morphine, cocaine and amphetamine abstinence in rats. *European Journal of Pharmacology, 221,* 227–234.

Russell, M. A. H. (1976). What is dependence? In G. Edwards, M. A. H. Russell, D. Hawks, & M. MacCafferty (Eds.), *Drugs and drug dependence* (pp. 182–187). Lexington, MA: Lexington Books.

Samson, H. H., Tolliver, G. A., Pfeffer, A. O., Sadeghi, K. G., & Mills, F. G. (1987). Oral ethanol reinforcement in the rat: Effect of the partial inverse benzodiazepine agonist RO15-4513. *Pharmacology Biochemistry and Behavior, 27,* 517–519.

Sarnyai, Z., Biro, E., Gardi, J., Vecsernyes, M., Julesz, J., & Telegdy, G. (1995). Brain corticotropin-releasing factor mediates "anxiety-like" behavior induced by cocaine withdrawal in rats. *Brain Research, 675,* 89–97.

Schaefer, G. J., & Michael, R. P. (1986). Changes in response rates and reinforcement thresholds for intracranial self-stimulation during morphine withdrawal. *Pharmacology Biochemistry and Behavior, 25,* 1263–1269.

Schroeder, R. L., Weinger, M. B., Vakassian, L., & Koob, G. F. (1991). Methylnaloxonium diffuses out of the brain more slowly than naloxone after direct intracerebral injection. *Neuroscience Letters, 121,* 173–177.

Schulteis, G., Heyser, C. J., & Koob, G. F. (1995). Acute dependence on opiates: Progressive increase in severity with long intervals between successive morphine treatments. *Society for Neuroscience Abstracts, 21,* 723.

Schulteis, G., & Koob, G. F. (1996). Reinforcement processes in opiate addiction: A homeostatic model. *Neurochemical Research, 21,* 1437–1454.

Schulteis, G., Markou, A., Cole, M., & Koob, G. F. (1995). Decreased brain reward produced by ethanol withdrawal. *Proceedings of the National Academy of Sciences, USA, 92,* 5880–5884.

Schulteis, G., Markou, A., Gold, L., Stinus, L., & Koob, G. F. (1994). Relative sensitivity to naloxone of multiple indices of opiate withdrawal: A quantitative dose–response analysis. *Journal of Pharmacology and Experimental Therapeutics, 271,* 1391–1398.

Schuster, C. R., & Johanson, C. E. (1988). Relationship between the discriminative stimulus properties and subjective effects of drugs. In F. C. Colpaert & R. L. Balster (Eds.), *Transduction mechanisms of drug stimuli* (Psychopharmacology Series, Vol. 4, pp. 161–175). Berlin: Springer-Verlag.

Schuster, C. R., & Thompson, T. (1969). Self-administration and behavioral dependence on drugs. *Annual Review of Pharmacology and Toxicology, 9,* 483–502.

Self, D. W., Barnhart, W. J., Lehman, D. A., & Nestler, E. J. (1996). Opposite modulation of cocaine-seeking behavior by D_1- and D_2-like dopamine receptor agonists. *Science, 271,* 1586–1589.

Sellers, E. M., Higgins, G. A., & Sobell, M. B. (1992). 5-HT and alcohol abuse. *Trends in Pharmacological Sciences, 13,* 69–75.

Sepinwall, J., & Cook, L. (1978). Behavioral pharmacology of anti-anxiety drugs. In L. L. Iversen, S. D. Iversen, & S. H. Snyder (Eds.), *Biology of mood and antianxiety drugs: Handbook of psychopharmacology* (Vol. 13, pp. 345–393). London: Plenum.

Shippenberg, T. S., LeFevour, A., & Heidbreder, C. (1996). Kappa-opioid receptor agonists prevent sensitization to the conditioned rewarding effects of cocaine. *Journal of Pharmacology and Experimental Therapeutics, 276,* 545–554.

Stewart, J. (1992). Conditioned stimulus control of the expression of sensitization of the behavioral activating effects of opiate and stimulant drugs. In I. Gormezano & E. A. Wasserman (Eds.), *Learning and memory: The behavioral and biological substrates* (pp. 129–151). Hillsdale, NJ: Erlbaum.

Stewart, J., deWitt, H., & Eikelboom, R. (1984). Role of unconditioned and conditioned drug effects in the self-administration of opiates and stimulants. *Psychological Review, 91,* 251–268.

Stinus, L., Le Moal, M., & Koob, G. F. (1990). Nucleus accumbens and amygdala are possible substrates for the aversive stimulus effects of opiate withdrawal. *Neuroscience, 37*, 767–773.

Stinus, L., Nadaud, D., Deminiere, J. M., Jauregui, J., Hand, T. T., & Le Moal, M. (1989). Chronic flupentixol treatment potentiates the reinforcing properties of systemic heroin administration. *Biological Psychiatry, 26*, 363–371.

Suzdak, P. D., Glowa, J. R., Crawley, J. N., Schwartz, R. D., Skolnick, P., & Paul, S. M. (1986). A selective imidazobenzodiazepine antagonist of ethanol in the rat. *Science, 234*, 1243–1247.

Vaccarino, F. J., Bloom, F. E., & Koob, G. F. (1985). Blockade of nucleus accumbens opiate receptors attenuates intravenous heroin reward in the rat. *Psychopharmacology* (Berlin), *86*, 37–42.

Vaccarino, F. J., Pettit, H. O., Bloom, F. E., & Koob, G. F. (1985). Effects of intracerebroventricular administration of methylnaloxonium chloride on heroin self-administration in the rat. *Pharmacology Biochemistry and Behavior, 23*, 495–498.

Volpicelli, J. R., Alterman, A. I., Hayashida, M., & O'Brien, C. P. (1992). Naltrexone in the treatment of alcohol dependence. *Archives of General Psychiatry, 49*, 876–880.

Weeks, J. R., & Collins, R. J. (1976). Changes in morphine self-administration in rats induced by prostaglandin E1 and naloxone. *Prostaglandins, 12*, 11–19.

Weiss, F., Hurd, Y., Ungerstedt, U., Markou, A., Plotsky, P. M., & Koob, G. F. (1992). Neurochemical correlates of cocaine and ethanol self-administration. In P. W. Kalivas & H. H. Samson (Eds.), *Annals of the New York Academy of Sciences: Vol. 654. The neurobiology of drug and alcohol addiction* (pp. 220–241). New York: New York Academy of Sciences.

Weiss, F., Markou, A., Lorang, M. T., & Koob, G. F. (1992). Basal extracellular dopamine levels in the nucleus accumbens are decreased during cocaine withdrawal after unlimited-access self-administration. *Brain Research, 593*, 314–318.

Weiss, F., Parsons, L. H., Schulteis, G., Hyytia, P., Lorang, M. T., Bloom, F. E., & Koob, G. F. (1996). Ethanol self-administration restores withdrawal-associated deficiencies in accumbal dopamine and serotonin release in dependent rats. *Journal of Neuroscience, 16*, 3474–3485.

West, T. E. (1991). *The effects of nucleus accumbens injections of receptor-selective opiate agonists on brain stimulation reward.* Unpublished doctoral dissertation, Concordia University, Montreal, Quebec, Canada.

Wikler, A. (1973). Dynamics of drug dependence: Implications of a conditioning theory of research and treatment. *Archives of General Psychiatry, 28*, 611–616.

Wise, R. (1988). The neurobiology of craving: Implications for the understanding and treatment of addiction. *Journal of Abnormal Psychology, 97*, 118–132.

Wise, R. A., & Bozarth, M. A. (1987). A psychomotor stimulant theory of addiction. *Psychological Review, 94,* 469–492.

Woolverton, W. L., & Virus, R. M. (1989). The effects of a D1 and a D2 dopamine antagonist on behavior maintained by cocaine or food. *Pharmacology Biochemistry and Behavior, 32,* 691–697.

World Health Organization. (1992). *International statistical classification of diseases and related health problems* (10th revision). Geneva, Switzerland: Author.

9

ETHNIC MINORITY WOMEN, HEALTH BEHAVIORS, AND DRUG ABUSE: A CONTINUUM OF PSYCHOSOCIAL RISKS

KATHY SANDERS-PHILLIPS

For far too long, the differences in drug use by men and women were noted only in national surveys, which showed that more men than women used illegal drugs and that men were apt to use them more frequently and more heavily than women. More recently, however, evidence has accumulated that indicates that the differences in men's and women's drug use may reflect differences in both causes and effects. Drug use results in different health effects for women, and women require different approaches to treatment than those needed by men. Researchers also have learned that among women, ethnic minority women suffer disproportionately from the effects of illegal drug use.

During the same period, a great deal has been learned about factors that influence women's general health decisions and behaviors, as well as factors that are barriers to healthy behaviors (Baum & Grunberg, 1991; Brown-Bryant, 1985; Calnan & Johnson, 1985; Makuc, Fried, & Kleinman, 1989). There is also growing awareness of factors influencing health behaviors in ethnic minority women (Cope & Hall, 1985; Leigh, 1994; Sanders-Phillips, 1994a, 1994b, 1996a). Strategies for promoting healthier behaviors in the general population of women and in ethnic minority women have been identified (Eng, 1993; Eng, Hatch, & Callan, 1985; Levine, Becker, & Bone, 1992; Schaefer, Falciglia, & Collins, 1990).

Despite these findings, drug abuse by women has rarely been examined in the larger context of a woman's health decisions and behaviors. Relationships between women's drug use and other health and risk behaviors (see Exhibit 1) are poorly understood. In addition, programs developed for drug-abusing women often fail to acknowledge and incorporate previous findings regarding successful health-promotion interventions for women.

Both the magnitude of drug abuse and the repercussions of women's drug abuse for their health as well as that of their children, reinforced that drug abuse among women is a significant public health problem (Carr, 1975; National Institute on Drug Abuse, 1996). More than 4.5 million women currently use illicit drugs, and women constitute more than 36% of the illicit-drug-using population in the United States (Substance Abuse and Mental Health Services Administration, 1997). Women who abuse drugs also engage in other risk behaviors and tend to have other health problems (Curtiss, Lenz, & Frei, 1993). Thus, women's drug use is often associated with other unhealthy behaviors and may reflect a broader spectrum of unhealthy lifestyle behaviors.

Currently available data and approaches from the field of public health and results from previous studies of women's health behaviors offer insights regarding the factors influencing risk behaviors in women and potential strategies for prevention and intervention for drug-using women. Data from this literature indicate that health behaviors occur on a continuum from healthy to unhealthy behaviors (Berkanovic, 1981–1982; McLeroy, Steckler, Goodman, & Burdine, 1992; Weinstein, 1993) and there is consistency in personal-health habits over time (Rakowski, 1987). In addition, health behaviors are multiply determined and must be understood in terms of how they are created and maintained in individuals in a

EXHIBIT 1

Health Behaviors[1]	Risk Behaviors
Eating breakfast	Failure to eat breakfast
Sleeping 7–8 hours per night	Failure to sleep 7–8 hours per night
Abstaining from tobacco use	Smoking
Moderate use of alcohol	Excessive alcohol use
Avoiding drug abuse	Drug abuse
Exercising at least three times per week	Failure to exercise
Eating a high-fiber, low-fat diet	Eating a high-fat, low-fiber diet

[1]Baum & Grunberg, 1991; Cohen et al., 1982; Cohen et al., 1991; Gottlieb & Green 1984, 1987; Rakowski, 1988; Rodin & Ickovics, 1990.

specific society. The social processes through which health behaviors are produced, potential points of intervention, and types of interventions that are successful with specific populations and social conditions must be assessed (McLeroy et al., 1992). Once these factors and processes are understood, programs of intervention can be developed.

Within this context, drug abuse can be viewed as a risk behavior that represents an end point in a series of risk behaviors. To effect change in the health behaviors of drug-abusing women, health care professionals must begin to identify and examine factors that promote risk behaviors as well as those that encourage healthier behaviors. Public health theory and research have identified many of the factors and mechanisms by which health and risk behaviors are initiated and maintained (Berkanovic, 1981–1982, DiClemente et al., 1991, Weinstein, 1993).

Placing drug abuse on a continuum of women's health decisions, health behaviors, and risk behaviors allows for examination of relationships between drug abuse and other health and risk behaviors, identification of the barriers and correlates of each, and determination of common etiologies. For example, by examining drug use in the context of other health behaviors, one can begin to identify successive factors that may place a woman at risk for abuse of alcohol or tobacco and, subsequently, illegal drugs.

Finally, examining drug abuse in the context of other health decisions and behaviors also focuses attention on the psychosocial and cultural variables that influence risk behaviors for women as a whole and for ethnic minority subgroups. Although variables related to health and risk behaviors and specific to drug abuse in women have not been fully examined, there is increasing evidence that psychosocial factors such as levels of perceived stress, experiences of racism, and exposure to community violence significantly influence women's health behaviors, especially for ethnic minority women. Closer examination of these factors may reveal ethnic differences in severity and types of drug abuse, as well as social and cultural influences on women's drug abuse. This knowledge will enhance the development of intervention programs targeted to all women, particularly ethnic minority women.

This chapter is divided into four major parts. First, factors that influence general health and risk behaviors in women, particularly ethnic minority women, are examined, with emphasis on the social, psychological, and cultural factors influencing these behaviors. Because previous research indicates that Black and Latino low-income women may be at high risk for poor health status and outcomes (Brown-Bryant, 1985; Cope & Hall, 1985; Rodin & Ickovics, 1990), findings specific to these two groups of women are reviewed. For the purposes of this chapter, *health behaviors* refer primarily to behaviors known to be associated with decreased mortality and morbidity, whereas *risk behaviors* are those that are associated with increased mortality and morbidity.

Second, factors specifically related to alcohol and tobacco use in women are identified. Third, similarities in the factors associated with risk behaviors in women and the use of illegal drugs are discussed. Finally, approaches to health-promotion intervention for women that may be applicable to drug abuse prevention and intervention programs for women, specifically Black and Latino women, are reviewed.

FACTORS INFLUENCING HEALTH AND RISK BEHAVIORS IN WOMEN

There is considerable evidence that factors related to health and risk behaviors may be gender specific (Auerbach & Figert, 1995; Baum & Grunberg, 1991; Calnan & Johnson, 1985; Cohen et al., 1982; Cohen, Schwartz, Bromet, & Parkinson, 1991; Gottlieb & Green, 1984, 1987; Rakowski, 1988; Rodin & Ickovics, 1990). A wide range of factors has been associated with health and risk behaviors in women. In general, the factors listed in Exhibit 2 are related to more healthy behaviors—such as eating breakfast, getting adequate sleep, not smoking, exercising moderately, using alcohol moderately—and fewer risk behaviors.

Both psychological and social variables are significant correlates of health and risk behaviors in women, as summarized in Exhibits 2 and 3. For example, higher levels of social support are associated with healthier lifestyle behaviors. Fewer stressful life events, such as marital conflict, are

EXHIBIT 2
Factors Associated With Healthy Behaviors

Demographic
  High education level
  High income
  Employment
  Positive marital status[3]
Psychosocial
  High level of social support[2]
    Emotional support
    Information sharing
    Provision of tangible goods and services
  Church participation
Individual
  Internal locus of control
  Greater self-efficacy regarding the prevention of disease
  Positive perceptions of health status
  Greater knowledge and positive attitudes about health-promoting behaviors

[2]Gottlieb & Green, 1984; Neighbors & Jackson, 1984; Shumaker & Hill, 1991
[3]Cohen et al., 1991; Gottlieb & Green, 1984; Rakowski, 1988

EXHIBIT 3
Factors Associated With Risk Behaviors

Demographic
  Less education
  Low income
  Unemployment
Psychosocial
  High level of stressful life events
  Poor social support[4]
  Poor ethnic identity[5]
Ecological
  Exposure to community and interpersonal violence[6]
  Poor interactions with health care workers[7]
Individual
  Psychological status (e.g., alienation,[8] powerlessness, depression,[9] or post-
    traumatic stress disorder)
  Perceptions of levels of stress
  Experiences of racism

[4]Neighbors & Jackson, 1984; Gombeski et al., 1982
[5]Bullough, 1967; Abrams, Allen, & Gray, 1993; Carter, 1991; Munford, 1994
[6]Sanders-Phillips, 1994a, 1994b, 1996a; Cohen et al., 1991
[7]Freimuth & Mettzger, 1990; Harrison & Harrison, 1971; James et al., 1984; Perez-Stable, 1987;
Webb, 1984; Makuc, Fried, & Kleinman, 1989; Sanders-Phillips, 1996a; Balsheim, 1991; Farris &
Glenn, 1976
[8]Bullough, 1972; Cohen et al., 1982; Hibbard, 1985; Morris, Hatch, & Chipman, 1966; Seeman &
Evans, 1962; Seeman & Seeman, 1983
[9]Cohen et al., 1991; Leftwich & Collins, 1994

related to healthier behavior, especially in low-income groups. Conversely, both lack of social support and higher levels of stressful life events are associated with risk behaviors. Because levels of social support and stressful life events also are related to age and income, these factors may mediate relationships among age, income, and risk behaviors in women (Gottlieb & Green, 1984). Psychological status, which is related to levels of stressful life events and social support (Cohen et al., 1991; Shumaker & Hill, 1991), also influences risk behaviors in women. Poorer health behaviors are more common in women with symptoms of depression.

Relationships between stressful life events and risk behaviors may be intensified in low-income, ethnic minority groups. Gottlieb and Green (1984) reported that poor women reported more stressful life events than higher income women and practiced fewer health-promoting behaviors, both of which were related to decreased involvement in social networks. Family and friends are primary sources of health information for low-income, ethnic minority women, and lack of family or social support for healthy behaviors is a deterrent to healthy behaviors. Social and ecological factors, such as community and interpersonal violence, also are related to fewer health-promoting behaviors and poorer perceptions of health. Women who have had a family member murdered and those who have experienced domestic violence engage in fewer healthy behaviors than women not exposed to violence (Sanders-Phillips, 1994a; 1996a). Psychological factors, such as alienation and powerlessness, which are related to exposure to violence and racial discrimination, also are correlates of poor health behaviors in Black women and Latinas.

Krieger and Sidney (1996) have reported that experiences of racial discrimination among Black women may be a risk factor for high blood pressure. Black women who reported higher levels of racial discrimination had higher levels of systolic blood pressure. These findings suggest that stressful life events, such as experiences of racial discrimination, may directly influence health outcomes for ethnic minority women.

Similarly, ethnic identity, which may be related to experiences of racism, also influences health and risk behaviors in Black and Latino groups. *Ethnic identity* is defined as that part of an individual's self-concept that derives from his or her knowledge of membership in a particular group and value ascribed to that membership (Phinney, 1992). Lower levels of ethnic identity are related to poor health behaviors, poor eating habits, and depression in Black women and Latinas.

In Black women and Latinas, lack of trust in the health care system and perceptions that they are disrespected by it are associated with poorer health behaviors, fewer health-promoting behaviors, and delay of treatment. Quality of interactions with health care workers, coupled with high levels of fatalism and low levels of self-efficacy, also influences health behaviors in these groups.

The above findings suggest that psychosocial variables—such as stressful life events, psychological status, social support, ethnic identity, and quality of interactions with the health care system—may significantly influence health behaviors and decisions in women. Although the mechanisms by which these factors modify health decisions and behaviors have not been fully explored, they may play a more critical role in determining the health decisions and behaviors of women than men.

Causal relationships among these variables have not been established; however, stressful life events and lack of social support may be specifically related to the initiation and maintenance of risk behaviors in women. Stressful life events, such as exposure to violence, may result in feelings of powerlessness and alienation that are related to perceptions of poor health status and fewer health-promoting behaviors (Sanders-Phillips, 1996b). Perceptions of the health care system and quality of interactions with health care staff appear to modify the level of healthy behaviors and compliance with treatment. Thus, ecological variables, such as a woman's exposure to violence and the nature of interactions with health facilities—as well as individual variables, such as psychological status, perceptions of stress, and experiences of racism—should be considered when assessing women's health behavior and decisions.

FACTORS RELATED TO ALCOHOL AND TOBACCO
USE IN WOMEN

Research on factors related to alcohol and tobacco use among women provides additional support for the concept that there are gender differences in risk and health behaviors. The research also suggests that factors influencing the use of alcohol and tobacco among women are similar to those influencing other health and risk behaviors. For example, there is a well-documented relationship between stressful life events and women's use of tobacco and alcohol. Stressful life events are related to smoking initiation and cessation and alcohol use for women (Gottlieb & Green, 1984). Gottlieb and Green (1984) have concluded that relationships among stress, alcohol consumption, and smoking in women may be strong enough to justify sex-specific norms for smoking and drinking as coping mechanisms for stress.

Social support, as measured by church attendance and marital status, is related to lower levels of smoking and consumption of alcohol in women. Social network influences, including the availability of substances, modeling of their use, and attitudes toward their use, are correlates of substance abuse in women (Ferguson, Lennox, & Lettieri, 1976; Gottlieb, 1982). Women's substance use, particularly alcohol use, is related to parental substance abuse and the quality of family relationships (Beckman, 1975; Ensminger, Brown, & Kellam, 1982; Swinson, 1980). Demographic characteristics, such as older age and full-time employment, are related to higher alcohol consumption in women, but unlike men, older age in women is not related to smoking cessation (Gottlieb & Green, 1984). Definitions of gender roles also influence alcohol consumption in women. Problem drinking is highest among women with untraditional gender role identities (Wilsnak, Klassen, & Wright, 1985).

Mental health status also is a predictor of women's smoking and drinking behavior. A history of marital conflict and depression is associated with higher levels of drinking and smoking (Cohen et al., 1991; Lex, 1991). Among women with depression, the odds of smoking are 90% greater and the odds of moderate or heavy drinking are 120% greater than for women without a history of depression (Cohen et al., 1991). Marital conflict is related to an increased probability of smoking only among women who are not working full-time. This supports the conclusion that relationships between stress and risk behaviors may be more significant for women of lower income. The findings also confirm that mental health factors may be better predictors of health behaviors for women than for men, particularly for substance abuse (Lex, 1991).

Although relationships among stressful life events, depression, smoking, and drinking have also been found for ethnic minority women, the sources of stress related to substance use and factors related to depression in these women may differ. Social norms and support for smoking vary within groups of ethnic minority women, and factors such as acculturation and racial discrimination may be significantly related to depression, as well as to smoking and drinking behaviors.

Among Black women, education is negatively related to age of smoking onset, amount smoked, and perceived difficulties in quitting (Manfredi, Lacey, Warnecke, & Buis, 1992). It is positively related to plans to quit, beliefs that smoking is related to lung cancer and serious health problems, and knowledge of where to go for help. Black women with more education also are more likely to live in environments that support smoking cessation and have fewer smokers.

Education and level of American acculturation are important predictors of smoking behavior in Latinas in the United States, but the nature of the relationships differs. More acculturated Latinas tend to smoke in greater numbers than women with lower levels of acculturation and those with less education (Marin, Marin, & Perez-Stable, 1989), and Mexican American women have been found to smoke at higher levels than Mexican immigrant women in the United States (Zambrana, Hernandez, Dunkel-Schetter, & Scrimshaw, 1991). Level of acculturation also has been shown to influence attitudes, norms, and expectancies about smoking in Latino groups (Marin, Marin, Otero-Sabogal, Sabogal, & Perez-Stable, 1989).

Higher levels of acculturation and education in Latinas are positively related to alcohol consumption, as are older age and employment; however, drinking patterns among Latinas are not related to length of residence in the United States (Black & Markides, 1993; Caetano & Mora, 1988). These findings support prior reports that risk behaviors such as smoking and alcohol consumption tend to increase as Latinos become more acculturated (Marcus & Crane, 1985; Marcus, Herman-Shipley, Crane, & Enstrom, 1986), although these reports are not unanimous (Zambrana et al., 1991). Low income in Latinas also is an important predictor of alcohol consumption, with poor Latinas consuming more drinks per occasion and more likely to be heavy drinkers than higher income Latinas (Black & Markides, 1993).

In a study of factors related to alcohol consumption in Black women, Taylor, Henderson, and Jackson (1991) have found that stressful life events, such as exposure to violence and internalized racism, account for a significant proportion of variance in alcohol consumption. They have defined *internalized racism* as the degree to which Black women internalized negative racial stereotypes from the dominant society. Higher levels of internalized racism are associated with higher consumption of alcohol. Greater involvement in religious activities is related to higher alcohol consumption, depression, and internalized racism. These findings are consistent with previous reports that increased religious involvement is associated with higher depression among Blacks experiencing chronic economic strain (Brown, Gary, Greene, & Milburn, 1992).

Singleton, Harrell, and Kelly (1986) also have reported that smoking among Black women is related to psychosocial stress and experiences of racism. They have noted that smoking in Black women may be related to gender role difficulties, including problems of assertion, independence, rebellion, or identification in relationships with men. This conclusion is supported by findings that women who quit smoking are more likely to be married, to have spousal support, and to be employed (U.S. Public Health Service, 1980). Conversely, Black women, who are more likely to be single and live in environments of high stress, are less likely to quit smoking than White women (Singleton et al., 1986).

Studies of depression in Black and Latino women indicate that negative life events, internalized racism, and lack of social support are significant predictors of depression. In Black women, negative life events, including exposure to violence, internalized racism, and absence of social support, predict depression, but stressful life events have a greater effect than lack of social support (Taylor et al., 1991). Several investigators have shown that the stress of acculturation is related to depression in Latinos (Golding & Burnam, 1990; Ring & Marquis, 1991; Salgado de Snyder, 1987; Vega, Kolody, Valle, & Hough, 1986; Williams & Berry, 1991). As with Black women, Latinas who experience racial discrimination exhibit higher rates of stress from acculturation and of depression (Salgado de Snyder, 1987). Among Latino professional women, marital conflict and racial discrimination are significant predictors of depression (Amaro, Russo, & Johnson, 1987).

The above studies document relationships between stressful life events with rates of depression, alcohol consumption, and tobacco use in women. They also suggest that racial discrimination, exposure to violence, and lack of social support may precipitate both stress from acculturation and depression, particularly in Black women and Latinas. These findings are consistent with Ferrence's (1988) observation that women's risk behaviors are related to social status and interactions outside the home and that experiences of racism affect health outcomes (Kreiger, 1990).

These results also underscore the importance of psychological and social variables to the use and abuse of tobacco and alcohol in women. They support previous findings that psychological and social factors are significant predictors of risk behaviors among women in general and among ethnic minority women in particular. It is clear that ethnic differences exist in the sources of stress related to health behaviors and in the factors that precipitate stress and depression.

FACTORS RELATED TO RISK BEHAVIORS, INCLUDING DRUG USE, BY WOMEN

Most previous research on factors related to drug abuse has been conducted with men, so there are little data available on drug use by women (Hser, Anglin, & Booth, 1987). It has been reported that more White women (35%) and Black women (33%) report using illicit drugs at some point in their lives than do Latinas (25%). Current use of any illicit drug (i.e., drug use within the last 30 days) is higher among Black women than White women or Latinas (Leigh, 1994).

Patterns of drug use and factors related to drug use differ for men and women (Lex, 1991). Women who use illegal drugs tend to be multiple drug users, that is, they use a number of drugs concurrently. They report somewhat higher levels of drug use but spend less money on drugs than do men. Women drug users are more likely to be living with a drug-dependent partner; they also are likely to show symptoms of depression and isolation. They report more family and job pressures (Carr, 1975; Frank et al., 1988; Lex, 1991; Singer, Arendt, & Minnes, 1993; Singer, Farkas, & Kleigman, 1992; Streissguth et al., 1991). Girls are more likely than boys to become polydrug users or to self-medicate for depression (Booth, Castro, & Anglin, 1991). Women's initiation into drug use and their progression through the addiction cycle are significantly influenced by their male partners (Hser et al., 1987).

In comparison with women who do not use illegal drugs, drug-using women are more likely to be single, separated, or divorced; to have less than a high school education; to use alcohol and tobacco in addition to illegal drugs; and to have fewer sources of social support (Beckwith, 1986; Singer et al., 1993; Streissguth et al., 1991). Risk factors for drug use by women are summarized in Exhibit 4. Trauma, especially exposure to violence, may be a particularly important predictor of women's illegal drug

EXHIBIT 4
Risk Factors for Drug Abuse by Women

Poor maternal–child relationships
Other poor family relationships
Parental substance abuse
Child abuse and neglect
Sexual abuse
Partner violence
Posttraumatic stress disorder
Depression
Poverty
Being a single parent: Excessive stress and social isolation
Level of acculturation
Low educational level

use. Pregnant victims of abuse are more likely than other women to use alcohol, marijuana, and cocaine. Women who have experienced maternal battering admit more alcohol and cocaine use than do nonbattered women (Singer et al., 1993). In addition to having histories of childhood physical and sexual abuse, women drug abusers are more likely to be physically and sexually abused during the time of their drug use and to be exposed to stigmatization from the public and peers (Fullilove, Lown, & Fullilove, 1992).

In a study of personality characteristics of male and female cocaine abusers, Johnson, Tobin, and Cellucci (1992) discovered that female cocaine abusers were more likely than male cocaine abusers to have a clinically defined psychopathology (Axis I, *Diagnostic and Statistical Manual of Mental Disorders*; American Psychiatric Association, 1987). Depression was the most common disorder in women, whereas only men reported antisocial personality characteristics. Gender differences in depression persisted over time, and women showed slower recovery from depression than men regardless of sociodemographic characteristics (Griffin, Weiss, Mirin, & Lange, 1989). These findings suggest that previous reports of high rates of antisocial behaviors by female cocaine users may have been confounded by collapsing data from male and female samples.

Women who abuse illegal drugs also experience a wide range of health problems, and they engage in other risk behaviors as well. Marijuana, alcohol, and cigarette use are almost three times higher in other-drug-abusing women as compared with non-drug-abusing women from similar racial and social class groups (Frank et al., 1988; Singer, Song, Warshawsky, & Kliegman, 1991). In addition, poor prenatal care is common among drug-using pregnant women. Women who use cocaine during pregnancy tend to weigh less during pregnancy and at delivery, which may be related to anorexia and poor nutrition (Frank et al., 1988; Singer et al., 1991).

Drug-using women are more likely to have a high prevalence of health problems, including sexually transmitted diseases, anemia, and dental disease. Medical problems such as heart disease, surgical conditions, and breast disease are higher (Curtiss et al., 1993). Use of illegal drugs, and possible involvement in prostitution, increases risk for HIV exposure and AIDS (Fullilove, Fullilove, Bowser, & Gross, 1990). Current statistics indicate that approximately 64% of AIDS cases among women are drug related (Centers for Disease Control and Prevention, 1996).

Many studies of women using illegal drugs have used samples from public, urban hospitals serving predominantly low-income, ethnic minority populations, so relatively few comparative studies of drug use among ethnic and economic subgroups of women have been conducted. The tendency to report ethnic minority drug-abusing women more often than other groups to public health and social service agencies has skewed and biased previous samples (Chasnoff, Landress, & Barrett, 1990). Thus, the number of studies of ethnic differences among women drug abusers is quite limited.

Zambrana et al. (1991) have examined ethnic differences in alcohol, cigarette, and illegal drug use in Mexican American, Mexican immigrant, and Black women in the United States. Consumption of alcohol and use of marijuana, cocaine, phencyclidine, heroin, and over-the-counter medications were highest in Black women. Use of illegal drugs was low in the Mexican American and immigrant groups. However, Mexican immigrant women were slightly more likely to report using illegal drugs. There was also a trend for Black women to be smokers; Mexican American women were more likely to be smokers than Mexican immigrant women. Women who used alcohol, illegal drugs, or cigarettes during pregnancy tended to be older; more likely to report negative life events; less likely to be living with the baby's father; and less likely to have planned the pregnancy.

In this study, the relationship between a planned pregnancy and drug use is interesting, particularly in the light of previous data that a planned pregnancy is highly correlated with healthier behaviors, more positive health attitudes, greater involvement in prenatal care, and higher levels of self-care practices to protect the health of the baby (Cramer, 1987). Conversely, failure to plan pregnancy is associated with depression, alienation, and powerlessness (Groat & Neal, 1967), which, as indicated above, are related to poorer health behaviors in women.

De La Rosa, Khalsa, and Rouse (1990) have reported that prevalence of drug use differs among Latino subgroups; degree of acculturation influences rates of drug use in Hispanic populations. Puerto Ricans and Mexican Americans who were born in the United States and whose primary language is English are most likely to use illegal drugs. Greater drug use in these groups may be related to higher rates of poverty, limited school and employment opportunities, and racial discrimination (De La Rosa et al., 1990). Drug use among younger Hispanics is associated with the stress of acculturation, particularly the loss of identification with Hispanic culture. Lower levels of ethnic identity also are related to an increased risk of illegal drug use among Blacks (Ringwalt & Paschall, 1995).

Several studies have documented gender and ethnic differences in the initiation, addiction, and treatment phases of narcotic drug use. Male–female differences in drug use behavior are more pronounced among Latinos than for other ethnic or cultural groups. For example, shorter times from drug initiation to addiction have been noted for Latinas; they also are more likely than other groups to use heroin (Anglin, Hser, & McGlothlin, 1987). Both illegal and prescription drug use may serve as forms of self-medication to cope with the stresses of acculturation in Latinas (Booth et al., 1991). Latina drug abusers also have lower self-esteem and self-efficacy and more risk behaviors than Black women drug users (Grella, Annon, & Anglin, 1995).

Compared with White female narcotics users, Latinas are less likely to be employed and more likely to receive welfare or disability payments. Latina narcotic users also are more likely to come from single-parent, low-income households and to report family dysfunction. These circumstances, combined with lower education and a cultural milieu that disapproves both of drug use in women and of women working outside of the home, encourage greater dependence on an addicted partner or on welfare and disability payments (Anglin, Booth, Ryan, & Hser, 1988). They also suggest that Latinas who use drugs are significantly influenced by cultural gender norms (Booth et al., 1991). Cultural differences in expectations regarding women and their roles may also contribute to drug-dependent Latinas becoming *marginal* persons: marginal to the larger White society and marginal within the Latino community as well (Anglin et al., 1988). Anglin, Hser, and Booth (1987) have concluded that sex role conflicts, restricted job opportunities, and other marginal attributes influence all women addicts, but their impact may be more severe on Latinas.

Response to drug treatment also differs by gender and ethnicity. Perceived need for treatment is higher among women drug abusers than among men, but women are more likely to seek treatment based on crisis events rather than degree of drug dependence (Longshore, Hsieh, & Anglin, 1993). Black and Latino drug users are less likely to report having been in drug treatment than White drug users. Latino drug users are most likely to report that they do not seek treatment because they do not need it, and Blacks are most likely to hold unfavorable views of treatment (Longshore, Hsieh, Anglin, & Annon, 1992). Both Blacks and Latinos may refuse treatment because they may view it as a form of oppression that is associated with racism (Longshore et al., 1993). Latinas may cite pregnancy as a reason for seeking drug treatment, but they also report that treatment programs do not help (Anglin et al., 1987).

Finally, social and environmental risk factors occurring at the community level appear to be important correlates of patterns of drug use. Community norms regarding alcohol and drug use influence perceptions of the prevalence of drug use and acceptance of drug use (Fitzpatrick & Gerard, 1993). In a study conducted by Lillie-Blanton, Anthony, and Schuster (1993), the availability of drugs, community contacts with police, premature death rates, mechanisms for coping with life stressors, distribution of wealth, and access to social resources were related to residents' drug use patterns. Ethnic differences in illegal drug use did not persist after accounting for differences in these factors.

The findings on risk factors related to drug use for women and ethnic minority subgroups (summarized in Exhibit 4) are important for several reasons:

1. There is consistency in the factors related to unhealthy lifestyle behaviors, alcohol and tobacco use, and illegal substance

abuse among women. Psychological, ecological, and interpersonal variables are salient factors related to risk behaviors in women, and relationships between these variables and drug abuse in ethnic minority women, particularly Latinas, are pronounced.

2. Drug use is associated with involvement in other unhealthy behaviors, although it is not clear whether other unhealthy behaviors precede, accompany, or succeed drug addiction. Physical disability and poor health are cited as primary reasons for discontinuing drug use for many women (Longshore et al., 1993).

3. In some drug-abusing women, pregnancy is a time of greater motivation to engage in healthier behaviors, decreased drug use, and improved self-care practices.

4. For ethnic minority women, factors related to drug use are complex. It appears that ethnic minority women are exposed more often to the factors related to unhealthy lifestyle behaviors and to alcohol, tobacco, and illegal drug use. Psychological status and functioning may be more marginal in these groups, and issues related to ethnic identity and acculturation may influence drug abuse behavior.

5. Trauma and depression have been identified as etiologic factors in women's drug abuse. It has been suggested that women drug users experience a cycle of initiating drug use to relieve symptoms of depression or trauma, experiencing trauma in their efforts to secure drugs, and relieving the new trauma by continuing drug use (Fullilove et al., 1992).

HEALTH PROMOTION PROGRAMS FOR WOMEN: IMPLICATIONS FOR PREVENTION OF DRUG ABUSE AND INTERVENTION WITH DRUG-USING WOMEN

The review of factors related to unhealthy behaviors and use of alcohol, tobacco, and illegal drugs suggests that involvement in risk behaviors is associated with a complex array of individual, psychosocial, and environmental factors that may influence a woman's health decisions and behaviors. Therefore, intervention and prevention programs to promote healthier behaviors in women should acknowledge and address the multiple determinants of health and risk behaviors.

The Ecological Approach

The findings regarding women's health behaviors are consistent with the ecological conceptualization of health behaviors and suggest an ecological approach to intervention. The ecological approach focuses on the environmental, cultural, and social correlates of health behaviors, acknowledges the individual factors that contribute to health behaviors, and uses social networks to effect behavior change. In an ecological framework, effective health-promotion programs must identify and address the social, cultural, psychological, and economic factors that influence health behaviors in women, as well as the cultural and community factors that maintain health behaviors (Stokols, 1992).

Much is known about successful health intervention programs for women that have used an ecological approach. For example, in the absence of attention to psychological, social, and cultural determinants of health behaviors, cognitive approaches to health-behavior change may be ineffective (Israel, 1982, 1985; Lacey, 1992; Lacey, Manfredi, & Warnecke, 1991; Schorr, 1990; Thomas, 1990). Self-efficacy is an important predictor of health-behavior change in women, cooperative learning methods may be most effective in promoting behavior change, and knowledge is a relatively poor predictor of behavior change (Amezucua, McAlister, Ramirez, & Espinoza, 1990; Hargreaves, Baquet, & Gamshadzahi, 1989; Schaefer et al., 1990; Vega et al., 1988).

Successful interventions should be based in the community and should use naturally occurring social networks. Low-income, socially isolated women may profit most from health intervention programs that address their immediate needs for companionship and mutual support and provide them with methods of self-improvement (Lacey, 1992). In the light of relationships between exposure to violence and health behaviors in women (Sanders-Phillips, 1994a, 1996b) and the knowledge that low-income ethnic minority women are more likely to experience traumatic events, such as violence (Bell & Jenkins, 1991), health-promotion programs for women must acknowledge the impact of trauma or exposure to violence on risk behaviors.

Lay Health Advisors

Lay health advisors have been used successfully to promote health-behavior change in women, especially ethnic minority women, and to address the social and cultural barriers to healthy behaviors (Amezucua et al., 1990; Hargreaves et al., 1989). The effectiveness of lay health advisors in overcoming the cultural and social barriers to healthy behaviors, in recruiting women to health-promotion interventions, and in increasing health-promoting behaviors in women has been well documented (Brownstein, Cheal, Ackerman, Bassford, & Campos-Outcalt, 1992; Levine et al., 1992; Salber, 1979; Warnecke, Graham, Mosher, & Montgomery, 1976; Warnecke, Graham, Mosher, Montgomery, & Schotz, 1975). The effectiveness of using lay health advisors who are similar to the target population and who conduct interventions in programs where there is a shared sense of identity also has been stressed (Israel, 1982, 1985; Warnecke et al., 1975). The success of health intervention programs for women that focus on increasing ethnic identity and pride as a mechanism for changing health behaviors (DiClemente & Wingood, 1995) also supports the use of indigenous community workers and underscores the importance of addressing issues related to ethnicity.

Indigenous, lay health advisors operating in close-knit social networks may exert a greater social influence than those functioning in loosely knit programs that lack a common identity or purpose (Gottlieb, 1981; Israel, 1985). The use of lay health advisers in health-promotion or intervention programs also is consistent with findings that women tend to turn to informal support systems and other women for health advice and information (Leutz, 1976; Neighbors & Jackson, 1984; Schaefer et al., 1990; Warnecke et al., 1976). Among low-income, Black women, the use of lay health advisers is related to lower levels of depression and healthier behaviors (Cohen et al., 1991; Gottlieb & Green, 1987; Rhodes, Ebert, & Fisher, 1992; Taylor et al., 1991). Lay health advisers also may provide social support for women that is necessary for health-behavior change to occur (Israel, 1985). Social support offered by lay health advisers may reduce stress, increase coping skills (Gottlieb, 1981; Hirsch, 1981; Salber, 1979), and increase self-efficacy and perceived control over health (Hibbard, 1985).

Combining Approaches to Intervention

In keeping with these findings, an ecological approach to intervention and treatment of drug-abusing women has been recommended by other investigators. For example, Longshore et al. (1993) have concluded that special efforts may be needed to engage women, particularly ethnic minority women, into treatment. Special efforts may be especially important for clients who seek treatment because of family pressure, legal coercion, or other external motivators. Engagement of clients can be facilitated by designing intake and referral services that are culturally specific and appropriate and by providing staff who are ethnically compatible with the targeted group. Staff–client interactions may improve if staff are bilingual and trained to adopt interaction styles that are consistent with the cultural group being served. Closer ties also should be established between treatment providers and community caregivers in neighborhood health clinics, school programs, and churches. Lay counselors may be recruited, and community-based resources should be used as adjuncts or alternatives to formal treatment.

The development of trauma-treatment services also may be an integral component of drug treatment for women. Fullilove et al. (1992) have suggested that peer support to address experiences of trauma may be a critical element in recovery for women addicts. A focus on self-affirmation and self-efficacy in overcoming drug abuse problems may need to be incorporated into drug treatment. In addition, given the unique influence of a male partner on drug use patterns among women, intervention programs may need to provide treatment for or solicit the support of male partners in the treatment of women (Anglin et al., 1987). Finally, treatment programs for women drug addicts may need to capitalize on the motivation of pregnant addicts to improve their health for the well-being of the baby. This may be a critical point of intervention for health-behavior change in drug-abusing women.

Increased rates of disease and disability in drug-abusing women suggest that programs of intervention should provide comprehensive medical care and must address other risk behaviors in this population. A more comprehensive approach to health that does not focus exclusively on drug abuse behavior but addresses the factors that promote unhealthy lifestyle behaviors including drug abuse may result in better overall health outcomes and changes in drug abuse behavior.

Finally, drug abuse behaviors in women, particularly those of ethnic minority groups, must be understood and addressed in terms of both the personal characteristics that promote drug use and the community characteristics that contribute to drug use, regardless of individual characteristics (Lillie-Blanton et al., 1993). An ecological approach suggests that interventions designed to promote healthier behavior and prevent or change drug abuse behaviors may have to be implemented at the macrosystem, mesosystem, and microsystem levels (Taylor et al., 1991).

At the microsystem level, the effects of life events, social support, depressive symptoms, and poor health on risk behaviors in women suggest the need for programs to enhance coping skills, to improve social management skills, and to encourage health promotion. At the mesosystem level, the roles of religious orientation, internalized racism, and socioeconomic status in promoting risk behaviors suggest the need for church-based support and intervention, cultural programs to replace negative racial stereotypes, and social vocational programs to improve educational and economic status. Macrosystem approaches should include public and cultural policies that support the microsystem and mesosystem interventions (e.g., public policies supporting job development, technical training, and employment). As McLeroy et al. (1992) has concluded, the goals of health education for all women should not only include changes in health-related behaviors and health status but also changes in the capacity of individuals, networks, organizations, communities, and political structures to address health problems.

SUMMARY, CONCLUSIONS, AND FUTURE RESEARCH

Efforts to understand drug abuse in women, particularly in ethnic minority subgroups, and to develop successful programs of intervention should be guided by previous findings regarding women's health and risk behaviors, as well as knowledge of factors related to substance use in women. Programs of intervention for drug-abusing women also should be based on findings from previously developed health-promotion programs that have been effective in modifying health behaviors in women.

Baum and Grunberg (1991) have argued that cigarette smoking, alcohol abuse, and illegal drug use are coping behaviors for women. Gender differences in the use of these substances may be related to gender differences in perceptions of stress or in motivations to regulate mood through substance use. Thus, women may be at greater risk for coping with stress by altering behaviors that affect health. Increased understanding of relationships between stress and unhealthy behaviors may be critical to the understanding of the development of risk behaviors and to the consequences of high levels of stress for women.

The similarities in factors related to women's risk behaviors highlight the common experiences and events that may precipitate risk behaviors in women. Much of the previous research on drug abuse in women appears to have been based on the implicit assumptions that women who use illegal drugs differ considerably from other groups of women and the factors that influence drug use differ from factors that influence other risk behaviors. The findings described in this chapter contradict these assumptions and support the conclusion that women's risk behaviors have common etiologies and are greatly influenced by psychosocial factors. This view is consistent with increasing evidence that psychosocial factors may be more important than demographic or biomedical factors in determining health outcomes, especially in low-income, ethnic minority groups (Pincus & Callahan, 1995; Rodin & Ickovics, 1990).

On the basis of the literature cited in this chapter, it is possible that drug-abusing women differ from women who engage in risk behaviors other than drug abuse primarily in their level of exposure to critical psychosocial experiences rather than in the types of experiences to which they are exposed. For example, degree or nature of exposure to events such as violence, trauma, stress, or racism may distinguish women who use illegal drugs from women who do not. Time of exposure to specific events may contribute to a woman's decision to use illegal drugs or may encourage a transition from other risk behaviors to drug abuse. Future research is needed to clarify relationships between these factors and women's risk behaviors.

It does appear that unhealthy behaviors in women may be precipitated by similar factors and that women's drug abuse may be associated with a pattern of unhealthy behaviors that is established before the onset of drug abuse. Gender-specific models of health behavior are needed that include, rather than exclude, drug abuse and that conceptualize drug abuse as a risk behavior that is related to other risk behaviors. Future research also should focus on protective factors that may insulate against progression along a continuum from unhealthy behaviors to drug abuse.

The findings presented in this chapter reaffirm the conclusion that health behaviors, particularly for women, do not develop and occur in a vacuum. Health and risk behaviors are significantly affected by the social and cultural environment and by the context in which they occur. Efforts to address more global lifestyle behaviors, as well as drug abuse, and to foster health-behavior change must focus on these determinants of women's health and risk behaviors and incorporate them into planning. An ecological approach to drug abuse prevention and intervention acknowledges the importance of effecting change in individual health behaviors but also emphasizes the need to create health-promoting environments as adjuncts to behaviorally oriented health-promotion programs (Stokols, 1992). This approach assumes that both health and risk behaviors are influenced by the social environment. Efforts to promote well-being should be based on an understanding of the interplay between environmental and individual factors.

Last, as patterns and profiles of risk factors and illness by gender change in the coming decades and as rates of substance use among women increase, research on psychosocial factors related to women's health will be urgently needed (Rodin & Ickovics, 1990). Increasing rates of mortality and morbidity for women, as well as increased substance use, appear to be related to psychosocial factors such as changes in definitions of gender roles, experiences of life roles, ethnic identity and experiences of racial discrimination, abilities to adapt and cope with stress, and perceptions of control that directly influence health outcomes (Auerbach & Figert, 1995; Krieger, 1990; Rodin & Ickovics, 1990). As awareness of relationships between psychosocial variables and women's health outcomes increases, it will be important to examine the extent to which psychosocial factors may affect health outcomes in women by influencing health and risk behaviors (Rodin, 1986).

Understanding successive relationships between psychosocial factors, health and risk behaviors, and health outcomes in women may greatly improve our ability to develop effective health-promotion programs. Greater attention to psychosocial factors, such as experiences of racial discrimination and ethnic identity, may specifically influence health behaviors and outcomes for minority women. They also may enhance theoretical understanding of health and risk behaviors, particularly illegal drug use, in these populations.

REFERENCES

Abrams, K., Allen, L., & Gray, J. (1993). Disordered eating attitudes and behaviors, psychological adjustment, and ethnic identity: A comparison of Black and White female college students. *International Journal of Eating Disorders*, *14*, 49–57.

Amaro, H., Russo, N. F., & Johnson, J. (1987). Family and work predictors of psychological well-being among Hispanic women professionals. *Psychology of Women Quarterly*, *11*, 505–521.

American Psychiatric Association. (1987). *Diagnostic and statistical manual of mental disorders* (3rd ed., rev.). Washington, DC: Author.

Amezucua, C., McAlister, A., Ramirez, A., & Espinoza, R. (1990). A su salud: Health promotion in a Mexican-American border community. In N. Bracht (Ed.), *Health promotion at the community level* (pp. 257–276). Newbury Park, CA: Sage.

Anglin, M. D., Booth, M. W., Ryan, T. M., & Hser, Y. I. (1988). Ethnic differences in narcotics addiction: II. Chicano and Anglo addiction career patterns. *The International Journal of the Addictions*, *23*, 1011–1027.

Anglin, M. D., Hser, Y. I., & Booth, M. W. (1987). Sex differences in addict careers: 4. Treatment. *American Journal of Drug and Alcohol Abuse*, *13*, 253–280.

Anglin, M. D., Hser, Y. I., & McGlothlin, W. H. (1987). Sex differences in addict careers: 2. Becoming addicted. *American Journal of Alcohol Abuse*, *13*, 59–71.

Auerbach, J. D., & Figert, A. E. (1995). Women's health research: Public policy and sociology. *Journal of Health and Social Behavior*, *36*, 115–131.

Balshiem, M. (1991). Cancer control and causality: Talking about cancer in a working class community. *American Ethnologist*, *18*, 152–172.

Baum, A., & Grunberg, N. (1991). Gender, stress, and health. *Health Psychology*, *10*, 80–85.

Beckman, L. J. (1975). Women alcoholics: A review of social and psychological studies. *Journal of Studies on Alcohol*, *36*, 797–824.

Beckwith, J. B. (1986). Eating, drinking, and smoking and their relationship in adult women. *Psychological Reports*, *59*, 1075–1089.

Bell, C., & Jenkins, E. (1991). Traumatic stress and children. *Journal of Health Care for the Poor and Underserved*, *2*, 175–188.

Berkanovic, E. (1981–1982). Who engages in health protective behaviors? *International Quarterly of Community Health Education*, *2*, 225–237.

Black, S. A., & Markides, K. S. (1993). Acculturation and alcohol consumption in Puerto Rican, Cuban-American, and Mexican-American women in the United States. *American Journal of Public Health*, *83*, 890–893.

Booth, M. W., Castro, F. G., & Anglin, M. D. (1991). What do we know about Hispanic substance abuse? A review of the literature. In R. Click & J. Moore (Eds.), *Drugs in Hispanic communities* (pp. 21–43). New Brunswick, NJ: Rutgers University Press.

Brown, D. R., Gary, L. E., Greene, A. D., & Milburn, N. G. (1992). Patterns of social affiliation as predictors of depressive symptoms among urban Blacks. *Journal of Health and Social Behavior, 33,* 242–253.

Brown-Bryant, R. (1985). The issue of women's health: A matter of record. *Family and Community Health, 7,* 53–65.

Brownstein, J. N., Cheal, N., Ackerman, S. P., Bassford, T. L., & Campos-Outcalt, D. (1992). Breast and cervical cancer screening in minority populations: A model for using lay health educators. *Journal of Cancer Education, 7,* 321–326.

Bullough, B. (1967). Alienation in the ghetto. *Journal of Sociology, 72,* 469–478.

Bullough, B. (1972). Poverty, ethnic identity and preventive health care. *Journal of Health and Social Behavior, 13,* 347–359.

Caetano, R., & Mora, E. M. (1988). Acculturation and drinking among people of Mexican descent in Mexico and the United States. *Journal of Studies on Alcohol, 49,* 462–471.

Calnan, M., & Johnson, B. (1985). Health, health risks and inequalities: An exploratory study of women's perceptions. *Sociology of Health and Illness, 7,* 55–75.

Carr, J. N. (1975). Drug patterns among drug-addicted mothers. *Pediatric Annals, 4,* 65–77.

Carter, R. (1991). Racial attitudes and psychological functioning. *Journal of Multicultural Counseling and Development, 19,* 105–114.

Centers for Disease Control and Prevention. (1996, June). *HIV/AIDS surveillance report, 8*(1).

Chasnoff, I. J., Landress, H. J., & Barrett, M. E. (1990). The prevalence of illicit-drug use during pregnancy and discrepancies in mandatory reporting in Pinellas County, Florida. *The New England Journal of Medicine, 322,* 1202–1206.

Cohen, P., Struening, E., Muhlin, G., Genevie, L., Kaplan, S., & Peck, H. (1982). Community stressors, mediating conditions and well-being in urban neighborhoods. *Journal of Community Psychology, 10,* 377–391.

Cohen, S., Schwartz, J., Bromet, E., & Parkinson, D. (1991). Mental health, stress, and poor health behaviors in two community samples. *Preventive Medicine, 20,* 306–315.

Cope, N., & Hall, H. (1985). The health status of Black women in the U.S.: Implications for health psychology and behavioral medicine. *Sage, 2,* 20–24.

Cramer, J. C. (1987). Social factors and infant mortality: Identifying high risk groups and proximate causes. *Demography, 24,* 299–322.

Curtiss, M. A., Lenz, K. M., & Frei, N. R. (1993). Medical evaluation of African American women entering drug treatment. *Journal of Addictive Diseases, 12,* 29–44.

De La Rosa, M. R., Khalsa, J. H., & Rouse, B. A. (1990). Hispanics and illicit drug use: A review of recent findings. *The International Journal of the Addictions, 25,* 665–691.

DiClemente, C. C., Prochaska, J. O., Fairhurst, S. K., Velicer, W. F., Velasquez, M. M., & Rossi, J. S. (1991). The process of smoking cessation: An analysis of precontemplation, contemplation, and preparation stages of change. *Journal of Consulting and Clinical Psychology, 59,* 295–304.

DiClemente, R., & Wingood, G. (1995). A randomized controlled trial of an HIV sexual risk-reduction intervention for young African-American women. *Journal of the American Medical Association, 274,* 1271–1276.

Eng, E. (1993). The Save Our Sisters project: A social network strategy for reaching rural Black women. *Cancer, 72,* 1071–1077.

Eng, E., Hatch, J., & Callan, A. (1985). Institutionalizing social support through the church and into the community. *Health Education Quarterly, 12,* 81–92.

Ensminger, M. E., Brown, C. H., & Kellam, S. G. (1982). Sex differences in antecedents of substance use among adolescents. *Journal of Social Issues, 38,* 25–42.

Farris, B., & Glenn, N. (1976). Fatalism and familism among Anglos and Mexican-Americans in San Antonio. *Sociology and Social Research, 60,* 393–402.

Ferguson, P., Lennox, T., & Lettieri, D. (Eds.). (1976). *Drugs and family/peer influence: Research issues* (NIDA Research Issues Series, No. 4, DHEW Publication No. ADM 4, 77–186). Rockville, MD: National Institute on Drug Abuse.

Ferrence, R. G. (1988). Sex differences in cigarette smoking in Canada, 1900–1978: A reconstructed cohort study. *Canadian Journal of Public Health, 79,* 160–165.

Fitzpatrick, M. L., & Gerard, K. (1993). Community attitudes toward drug use: The need to assess community norms. *The International Journal of the Addictions, 28,* 947–957.

Frank, D. A., Zuckerman, B. S., Amaro, H., Aboagye, K., Baucher, H., Cabral, H., Fried, L., Hinson, R., Kayne, H., Levenson, S., Parker, S., Reece, H., & Vinci, R. (1988). Cocaine use during pregnancy: Prevalence and correlates. *Pediatrics, 82,* 888–895.

Freimuth, V., & Mettzger, W. (1990). Is there a hard-to-reach audience? *Public Health Reports, 105,* 232–238.

Fullilove, M. T., Lown, E. A., & Fullilove, R. E. (1992). Crack "hos and skeezers": Traumatic experiences of women crack users. *The Journal of Sex Research, 29,* 275–287.

Fullilove, R. E., Fullilove, M. T., Bowser, B., & Gross, S. (1990). Crack users: The new AIDS risk group. *Cancer Detection and Prevention, 14,* 363–368.

Golding, J., & Burnam, A. (1990). Immigration, stress, and depressive symptoms in a Mexican-American community. *The Journal of Nervous and Mental Disease, 178,* 161–171.

Gombeski, W., Ramirez, A., Kautz, J., Farge, E., Moore, T., & Weaver, F. (1982). Communicating health information to urban Mexican Americans: Sources of health information. *Health Education Quarterly, 9,* 293–309.

Gottlieb, B. H. (1981). Preventive interventions involving social networks and social support. In B. H. Gottlieb (Ed.), *Social networks and social support*. Beverly Hills, CA: Sage.

Gottlieb, N. H. (1982). The effects of peer and parental smoking and age on the smoking careers of college women: A sex-related phenomena. *Social Science and Medicine, 16*, 595–600.

Gottlieb, N. H., & Green, L. (1984). Life events, social network, life-style, and health: An analysis of the 1979 National Survey of Personal Health Practices and Consequences. *Health Education Quarterly, 11*, 91–105.

Gottlieb, N. H., & Green, L. (1987). Ethnicity and lifestyle health risk: Some possible mechanisms. *American Journal of Health Promotion, 2*, 37–51.

Grella, C. E., Annon, J. J., & Anglin, M. D. (1995). Ethnic differences in HIV risk behaviors, self-perceptions, and treatment outcomes among women in methadone maintenance treatment. *Journal of Psychoactive Drugs, 27*, 421–433.

Griffin, M. L., Weiss, R. D., Mirin, S. M., & Lange, U. (1989). A comparison of male and female cocaine abusers. *Archives of General Psychiatry, 34*, 122–126.

Groat, H., & Neal, A. (1967). Social psychological correlates of urban fertility. *American Sociological Review, 32*, 945–949.

Hargreaves, M. K., Baquet, C., & Gamshadzahi, A. (1989). Diet, nutritional status and cancer risk in American Blacks. *Nutrition and Cancer, 12*, 1–28.

Harrison, I., & Harrison, D. (1971). The Black family experience and health behavior. In C. Crawford (Ed.), *Health and the family: A medical–sociological analysis* (pp. 175–199). New York: Macmillan.

Hibbard, J. (1985). Social ties and health status: An examination of moderating factors. *Health Education Quarterly, 12*, 23–34.

Hirsch, B. J. (1981). Social networks and the coping process: Creating personal communities. In B. H. Gottlieb (Ed.), *Social networks and social support*. Beverly Hills, CA: Sage.

Hser, Y. I., Anglin, M. D., & Booth, M. W. (1987). Sex differences in addict careers: 3. Addiction. *American Journal of Drug and Alcohol Abuse, 13*, 231–251.

Israel, B. A. (1982). Social networks and health status: Linking theory, roles and practice. *Patient Counseling and Health Education, 4*, 65–77.

Israel, B. A. (1985). Social networks and social support: Implications for natural helper and community level interventions. *Health Education Quarterly, 12*, 65–80.

James, S., Wagner, E., Strogatz, D., Bresford, S., Kleinbaum, D., Williams, C., Vutchin, L., & Ibraham, M. (1984). The Edgecombe County (NC) high blood pressure control program: II. Barriers to the use of medical care among hypertensives. *American Journal of Public Health, 74*, 468–472.

Johnson, R. S., Tobin, J. W., & Cellucci, T. (1992). Personality characteristics of cocaine and alcohol abusers: More alike than different. *Addictive Behaviors, 17*, 159–166.

Krieger, N. (1990). Racial and gender discrimination: Risk factors for high blood pressure. *Social Science and Medicine, 30,* 1273–1281.

Krieger, N., & Sidney, S. (1996). Racial discrimination and blood pressure: The CARDIA study of young Black and White adults. *American Journal of Public Health, 86,* 1370–1378.

Lacey, L. (1992). Helping low-income minority women reduce cancer risk. *Oncology, 7,* 22.

Lacey, L., Manfredi, C., & Warnecke, R. B. (1991). Use of lay health educators for smoking cessation in a hard-to-reach urban community. *Journal of Community Health, 16,* 269–282.

Leftwich, M. J. T., & Collins, F. L. (1994). Parental smoking, depression, and child development: Persistent and unanswered questions. *Journal of Pediatric Psychology, 19,* 557–570.

Leigh, W. A. (1994). *The health status of women of color: A women's health report of the Women's Research and Education Institute.* Washington, DC: The Women's Research and Education Institute.

Leutz, W. (1976). The informal community caregiver: A link between the health care system and local residents. *American Journal of Orthopsychiatry, 44,* 678–683.

Levine, D. M., Becker, D. M., & Bone, L. R. (1992). Narrowing the gap in health status of minority populations: A community–academic medical center partnership. *American Journal of Preventive Medicine, 8,* 319–323.

Lex, B. W. (1991). Some gender differences in alcohol and polysubstance users. *Health Psychology, 10,* 121–132.

Lillie-Blanton, M., Anthony, J., & Schuster, C. (1993). Probing the meaning of racial/ethnic group comparisons in crack cocaine smoking. *Journal of the American Medical Association, 269,* 993–997.

Longshore, D., Hsieh, S., & Anglin, M. D. (1993). Ethnic differences in drug user's perceived need for treatment. *The International Journal of the Addictions, 28,* 539–558.

Longshore, D., Hsieh, S., Anglin, M. D., & Annon, T. A. (1992). Ethnic patterns in drug abuse treatment utilization. *Journal of Mental Health Administration, 19,* 268–277.

Makuc, D. M., Fried, V. M., & Kleinman, J. (1989). National trends in the use of preventive health care by women. *American Journal of Public Health, 79,* 21–26.

Manfredi, C., Lacey, L., Warnecke, R., & Buis, M. (1992). Smoking-related behavior, beliefs, and social environment of young Black women in subsidized public housing in Chicago. *American Journal of Public Health, 82,* 267–272.

Marcus, A., & Crane, L. (1985). Smoking behavior among US Latinos: An emerging challenge for public health. *American Journal of Public Health, 75,* 169–172.

Marcus, A., Herman-Shipley, N., Crane, L., & Enstrom, J. (1986). *Recent trends in cancer incidence among U.S. Latinos.* Proceedings of the meeting of the American Public Health Association, Las Vegas, NV.

Marin, G., Marin, B. V. O., Otero-Sabogal, R., Sabogal, F., & Perez-Stable, E. (1989). The role of acculturation in the attitudes, norms, and expectancies of Hispanic smokers. *Journal of Cross-Cultural Psychology, 20,* 399–415.

Marin, G., Marin, B. V., & Perez-Stable, E. (1989). Cigarette smoking among San Francisco Hispanics. *American Journal of Public Health, 79,* 196–199.

McLeroy, K. R., Steckler, A. B., Goodman, R. M., & Burdine, J. N. (1992). Health education research: Theory and practice—Future directions. *Health Education Research, Theory and Practice, 7,* 1–8.

Morris, N., Hatch, M., & Chipman, S. (1996). Alienation as a deterrent to well-child supervision. *American Journal of Public Health, 56,* 1874–1882.

Munford, M. (1994). Relationship of gender, self-esteem, social class, and racial identity to depression in Blacks. *Journal of Black Psychology, 20,* 157–174.

National Institute on Drug Abuse. (1996). *Drug abuse among women delivering livebirths: 1992* (NIH Publication No. 96-3819). Washington, DC: U.S. Government Printing Office.

Neighbors, H. W., & Jackson, J. S. (1984). The use of informal and formal help: Four patterns of illness behavior in the Black community. *American Journal of Community Psychology, 12,* 629–644.

Perez-Stable, E. (1987). Issues in Latino health care—Medical staff conference. *The Western Journal of Medicine, 146,* 213–218.

Phinney, J. (1992). The Multigroup Ethnic Identity Measure: A new scale for use with diverse groups. *Journal of Adolescent Research, 7,* 156–176.

Pincus, T., & Callahan, L. (1995). What explains the association between socio-economic status and health: Primarily access to medical care or mind–body variables. *Advances: The Journal of Mind–Body Health, 11,* 4–36.

Rakowski, W. (1987). The persistence of personal health practices over a one year period. *Public Health Reports, 102,* 483–493.

Rakowski, W. (1988). Predictors of health practices within age–sex groups: National Survey of Personal Health Practices and Consequences, 1979. *Public Health Reports, 103,* 376–386.

Rhodes, J. E., Ebert, L., & Fisher, K. (1992). Natural mentors: An overlooked resource in the social networks of young, African American mothers. *American Journal of Community Psychology, 20,* 445–461.

Ring, J., & Marquis, P. (1991). Depression in a Latino immigrant medical population: An exploratory screening and diagnosis. *American Journal of Orthopsychiatry, 61,* 298–302.

Ringwalt, C., & Paschall, M. (1995). *Ethnic identity, drug use, and violence among African-American male adolescents.* Paper presented at the meeting of the American Public Health Association, San Diego, CA.

Rodin, J. (1986). Aging and health: Effects of the sense of control. *Science, 233,* 1271–1276.

Rodin, J., & Ickovics, J. (1990). Women's health: Review and research agenda as we approach the 21st century. *American Psychologist, 45*, 1018–1034.

Salber, E. (1979). The lay advisor as a community health resource. *Journal of Health Politics, Policy and Law, 3*, 469–478.

Salgado de Snyder, V. N. (1987). Factors associated with acculturative stress and depressive symptomatology among married Mexican immigrant women. *Psychology of Women Quarterly, 11*, 475–488.

Sanders-Phillips, K. (1994a). Correlates of healthy eating habits in low-income Black women and Latinas. *Preventive Medicine, 23*, 781–787.

Sanders-Phillips, K. (1994b). Health promotion behavior in low-income Black and Latino women. *Women & Health, 21*, 71–83.

Sanders-Phillips, K. (1996a). Correlates of health promotion behaviors in low-income Black women and Latinas. *American Journal of Preventive Medicine, 12*, 450–458.

Sanders-Phillips, K. (1996b). The ecology of urban violence: Its relationship to health promotion behaviors in Black and Latino communities. *American Journal of Health Promotion, 10*, 88–97.

Schaefer, N., Falciglia, G., & Collins, R. (1990). Adult African-American females learn cooperatively. *Journal of Nutrition Education, 22*, 240D.

Schorr, L. B. (1990). Successful health programs for the poor and underserved. *Journal of Health Care for the Poor and Underserved, 1*, 271–277.

Seeman, M., & Evans, J. (1962). Alienation and learning in a hospital setting. *American Sociological Review, 27*, 772–782.

Seeman, M., & Seeman, T. (1983). Health behavior and personal autonomy: A longitudinal study of the sense of control in illness. *Journal of Health and Social Behavior, 24*, 144–160.

Shumaker, S. A., & Hill, D. R. (1991). Gender differences in social support and physical health. *Health Psychology, 10*, 102–111.

Singer, L., Arendt, R., & Minnes, S. (1993). Neurodevelopmental effects of cocaine. *Clinics in Perinatology, 20*, 245–262.

Singer, L., Farkas, K., & Kleigman, R. (1992). Childhood medical and behavioral consequences of maternal cocaine use. *Journal of Pediatric Psychology, 17*, 389–406.

Singer, L. T., Song, L., Warshawsky, L., & Kleigman, R. (1991). Maternal gravidity predicts prematurity in cocaine-exposed infants. *Pediatric Research, 26*, 266A.

Singleton, E. G., Harrell, J. P., & Kelly, L. M. (1986). Racial differentials in the impact of maternal cigarette smoking during pregnancy on fetal development and mortality: Concerns for Black psychologists. *Journal of Black Psychology, 12*, 71–83.

Stokols, D. (1992). Establishing and maintaining healthy environments. *American Psychologist, 47*, 6–22.

Streissguth, A. P., Grant, T. M., Barr, H. M., Brown, Z. A., Martin, J. C., Mayrock, D. E., Ramey, S. L., & Moore, L. (1991). Cocaine and the use of alcohol and other drugs during pregnancy. *American Journal of Obstetrics and Gynecology, 164*, 1239–1243.

Substance Abuse and Mental Health Services Administration. (1997). *National Household Survey on Drug Abuse*. Washington, DC: U.S. Government Printing Office.

Swinson, R. P. (1980). Sex differences in the inheritance of alcoholism. In O. J. Kalant (Ed.), *Alcohol and drug problems in women: Research advances in alcohol and drug problems*. New York: Plenum.

Taylor, J., Henderson, D., & Jackson, B. B. (1991). A holistic model for understanding and predicting depressive symptoms in African-American women. *Journal of Community Psychology, 19*, 306–320.

Thomas, S. B. (1990). Community health advocacy for racial and ethnic minorities in the United States: Issues and challenges for health education. *Health Education Quarterly, 17*, 13–19.

U.S. Public Health Service. (1980). *The health consequences of smoking for women* (DHEW Publication No. 0-326-003). Washington, DC: U.S. Government Printing Office.

Vega, W., Kolody, B., Valle, R., & Hough, R. (1986). Depressive symptoms and their correlates among immigrant Mexican women in the United States. *Social Science and Medicine, 22*, 645–652.

Vega, W. A., Sallis, J. F., Patterson, T. L., Rupp, J. W., Morris, J. A., & Nader, P. R. (1988). Predictors of dietary change in Mexican American families participating in a health behavior change program. *American Journal of Preventive Medicine, 4*, 194–199.

Warnecke, R. B., Graham, S., Mosher, W., & Montgomery, E. (1976). Health guides as influentials in Central Buffalo. *Journal of Health and Social Behavior, 17*, 22–34.

Warnecke, R. B., Graham, S., Mosher, W., Montgomery, E., & Schotz, W. E. (1975). Contact with health guides and use of health services among Blacks in Buffalo. *Public Health Reports, 90*, 213–222.

Webb, H. (1984). Community health centers: Providing care for urban Blacks. *Journal of the National Medical Association, 76*, 1063–1067.

Weinstein, N. D. (1993). Testing four competing theories of health-protective behavior. *Health Psychology, 12*, 324–333.

Williams, C. L., & Berry, J. W. (1991). Primary prevention of acculturative stress among refugees: Application of psychological theory and practice. *American Psychologist, 46*, 632–641.

Wilsnak, R. W., Klassen, A. D., & Wright, S. I. (1985). Gender-role orientations and drinking among women in a U.S. national survey. In S. C. Wilsnak (Ed.), *Women and alcohol: Health-related issues*. Rockville, MD: National Institute on Alcohol Abuse and Alcoholism, Division of Extramural Research.

Zambrana, R. E., Hernandez, M., Dunkel-Schetter, C., & Scrimshaw, S. C. M. (1991). Ethnic differences in the substance use patterns of low-income pregnant women. *Family and Community Health, 13*, 1–11.

II

INTERVENTIONS

The preceding chapters have described an extremely complex array of factors that are involved in the development and maintenance of drug abuse. Some theories that attempt to unify these underlying factors have also been explicated, and their ramifications presented. In an ideal world, we could create prevention and treatment interventions based on the etiological factors and underlying concepts and then evaluate the success of our interventions.

But, in our real world, some approaches to drug abuse prevention and treatment were developed and found to be at least partly effective before consistent and coherent etiological explanations could be devised. In fact, treatment successes frequently revealed unexpected information about etiological factors, especially regarding the biological bases of drug abuse and the reinforcing effects of drugs. So studying the origins of drug abuse and developing interventions to prevent and treat it are not really independent processes, but like all research and practice, they continually inform and shape each other.

Chapters 10 and 11 are overviews of the prevention and treatment interventions that have been developed and used during the last 70 years or so, as the societal impact of drug abuse has become more and more apparent. In the chapters following, we present some forward looking speculations about the future of the prevention and treatment fields, as well as some new theoretical formulations that might drive additional research or new prevention or treatment protocols. The last chapter describes one of the best documented instances of the effects that basic and applied research on a drug (nicotine) has had on social policy, a policy which will itself further the prevention of smoking, the most common form of drug abuse in the United States.

10

THE PREVENTION OF DRUG ABUSE: INTERRUPTING THE PATHS

ZILI SLOBODA

THE HISTORY OF PREVENTION RESEARCH IN THE UNITED STATES

Continuous research has caused the prevention of drug abuse in the United States to develop and change rapidly over the past 50 years. The scope of this research is broad but shares one principle: Research should be applicable to creating more effective prevention programs. In this chapter I will provide an overview of prevention research and then go over some broad principles of prevention.

During World War II, the United States Army used scare techniques and other approaches to discourage negative health behaviors and reinforce positive behaviors. These approaches and the associated research influenced the development of a number of theories about health and health-related behaviors (Hovland, Janis, & Kelley, 1953). It was this theoretical base, in conjunction with empirical data and informed observations, that served to shape drug abuse prevention approaches of the 1950s and 1960s.

Botvin pointed out in a recent paper (Botvin, 1998, p. 43), "The goal of identifying effective prevention approaches has been elusive. While many approaches have increased knowledge of the adverse consequences of using drugs and some have increased anti-drug attitudes, very few programs have demonstrated an impact on drug use behavior." Indeed, the field of prevention research has progressed since the 1960s from strategies that emphasized information dissemination and affective education to strategies that focus on social influence and skills building.

Information-dissemination-based programs presumed rational decision making. The belief was that once children are provided the facts about the negative consequences of drug use, they would choose not to initiate their use. Some investigators used fear-arousal techniques in providing information to emphasize the dangers of drug use. The evaluations of such studies failed to demonstrate any positive effects on behaviors but have shown increased knowledge about the negative aspects of drugs and, in some cases, increased anti-drug-use attitudes (Dorn & Thompson, 1976; Schaps, Bartolo, Moskowitz, Palley, & Churgin, 1981).

Early research suggested that the initiation of drug use was associated with ambiguous beliefs about the negative value associated with drug abuse. On the basis of this perspective, programs that focused on affect that included values clarification, increased self-understanding and self-worth, and effective communication were developed. Again, evaluation studies did not demonstrate that such programs were effective against drug use, although many did show an impact on factors that were correlates of drug use, such as feelings of self-worth (Kearney & Hines, 1980; Kim, 1988).

ESTABLISHING A RESEARCH BASE FOR PREVENTION

Like the other sciences, prevention research relative to drug abuse evolved through a series of empirical and observational studies yielding findings that resulted in theory development to be further tested and refined. It is this ongoing interactive feedback system that has served to better inform the design of effective interventions.

During the late 1970s, primarily through support from the National Institute on Drug Abuse, a national research program was initiated consisting of prospective studies of children and adolescents to determine the origins and pathways to drug abuse. In addition, it was at this time that the Institute also designed a monitoring and surveillance system to include population surveys of households and of high school students, to derive an informed estimate of the nature and extent of the use of drugs and other substances.

Perhaps one of the most important outcomes of the research of that period was the ability to pinpoint the periods when youngsters were most at risk to initiate drugs. For example, the results of long-term epidemiologic studies of drug abuse suggest that the age of initiation of drug use in the majority of cases is between 12 and 17. Tobacco use and alcohol use, which have been associated with the use of marijuana and other drugs, generally have earlier ages of onset (Substance Abuse and Mental Health Services Administration, 1998). The sequencing from tobacco and alcohol use to marijuana use and then to the use of other drugs has been a consistent finding in most of the longitudinal studies of young people (Kandel & Davies, 1992; Newcomb & Bentler, 1986). There are no research findings that explain the mechanisms underlying these connections. Sequencing does not imply inevitability; for example, it does not follow that because one smokes cigarettes or drinks alcohol that one will use marijuana or move onto use other drugs. Rather, it shows that there is a common but not invariant sequence and that one's risk to move on to marijuana is much higher than if one never smokes or drinks (an estimated 65 times higher); and, the risk of moving on to cocaine is also much higher for someone who ever used marijuana than if one never did (an estimated 104 times higher; National Institute on Drug Abuse, 1998). These findings suggest that interventions need to focus on children at early ages and must address the prevention or delayed use of tobacco and alcohol. They also suggest that prevention interventions must be designed to be developmentally appropriate.

Trend analyses of data on drug-using behaviors among school children, such as the United States national survey, the Monitoring the Future Study of 8th, 10th, and 12th graders, have shown the prevalence of drug use over time. These surveys show two types of patterns. First, they show that use of illicit substances increases across grades, with lower prevalence among 8th graders, increasing in 10th graders, and highest among the 12th graders (National Institute on Drug Abuse, 1998). Second, the trend analyses show that marijuana use, which had been declining during the 1980s, began to rise in 1991 across all three grades, with continued increases each year, with particularly rising steep slopes for the youngest students (Johnston, O'Malley & Bachman, 1996). The challenge to the prevention practitioner is to reverse, or at least slow, this upward trajectory, and the challenge to the epidemiologist is to understand why these new increases are occurring.

Several hypotheses have been posited, but studies addressing this issue are too preliminary at this point. We do know that these trends have been preceded by changes in perceptions held by these students of the harmful effects of marijuana and cocaine and of the social acceptability for their use. Increased negative perceptions were associated in earlier time periods with decreases in use, and as these negative perceptions eroded, use increased (Bachman, Johnston, & O'Malley, 1990; Bachman, Johnston, O'Malley, & Humphrey, 1988; Bachman, Johnston, & O'Malley 1998).

These findings indicate that prevention programs must be more effective in reaching youngsters with accurate information about health risk and consequences of using drugs in order to influence their attitudes.

Furthermore, studies that follow youngsters over time clearly show that the process of initiating or continuing drug use is complex and that multiple factors are involved. Domains in which factors have been found to be associated with drug use range from genetics and biology to personality, emotion, and psychological factors; family, school, experiences, and peer and other relationships; and environmental and community influences (Hawkins, Catalano & Miller, 1992; Pandina, 1998). The strongest influences on initiating drug use, however, are interpersonal relationships—the family and peers. Family variables such as parental neglect, family disruption, failure in setting rules and monitoring behaviors, and lack of family bonding have been found to be associated with involvement with drugs (Brook, Whitman, Nomura, Gordon, & Cohen, 1988; Dishion & McMahon, 1998).

Peer influences that include modeling behaviors, making drugs accessible, and encouraging and reinforcing drug use also have strong associations with the initiation of drug use and its progression (Bauman & Ennett, 1996; Brook, Whiteman & Gordon, 1982; Dinges & Oetting, 1993; Kandel & Yamaguchi, 1985; Oetting, Donnermeyer, & Deffenbacher, 1998; Steinberg, Fletcher, & Darling, 1994). Other social factors, such as poor school performance, lack of internalization of educational norms, and lack of identification with school rules and mores have also been found to be related to drug use and abuse (Kandel & Davies, 1992; Newcomb, 1992).

Individual factors found to be associated with drug abuse are low self-esteem, poor self-control, difficult temperament, interpersonal incompetencies, and poor social coping skills; attitudinal factors such as tolerance for deviant attitudes and behaviors; emotional factors such as sensation seeking; and psychopathological factors such as stressful life events, depression, and anxiety (Botvin, Malgady, Griffin, Scheier & Epstein, 1998; Dawes, Tarter & Kirisci, 1997; Tarter, Blackson, Brigham, Moss & Caprara, 1995). In addition, it has been found that the greater number of all of these factors influencing an individual, the greater likelihood of drug use and abuse (Bry, McKeon & Pandina, 1982). This research suggests that prevention interventions should address risk factors and enhance protective factors in both general and more vulnerable populations.

Much of the research on risk factors conducted during the 1970s and the 1980s focused on factors associated with the initiation of drug use. By the late 1980s, epidemiologists began to differentiate those who initiate drug use and discontinue use from those who initiated use and maintained use over time, in many cases progressing to abuse and dependence using criteria such as those from *DSM-III-R* and *DSM-IV* systems (Glantz &

Pickens, 1992). Glantz and Pickens (p. 9) wrote "In general, drug use appears to be more a function of social and peer factors, whereas abuse appears to be more a function of biological and psychological processes."

For most children who are vulnerable to drug abuse, research suggests that the periods when they are most at risk are the times when they make transitions from one developmental stage to another. The first major transition for children is when they leave the security of the family and enter school. When they advance from elementary school to middle school or junior high school, they often face social challenges, such as learning to get along with a wider group of peers. It is at this stage, early adolescence, that children are likely to encounter drug use for the first time. Later on, when they enter high school, young people face social, psychological, and educational hurdles as they prepare for the future, and these challenges can lead to use and abuse of alcohol, tobacco, and other drugs. Even when young adults go on to college or get married or enter the workforce, they again face new risks from alcohol and other drugs in their new adult environments (Bachman, Wadsworth, O'Malley, Johnston, & Schulenberg, 1997). Although there is a dearth of evidence about the relationship between transitions in middle and older adult years and drug abuse, these periods also represent stressful times with both role and lifestyle changes that are associated with emotional and physical disorders (Glantz & Sloboda, 1995). Because risks are present at every transition from infancy through young, middle, and late adulthood, prevention planners need to develop programs that provide support at each developmental stage, particularly for those most at risk. These research findings suggest that prevention must occur across the life cycle, particularly during periods of transitions.

Basic laboratory research is critical to prevention, because the findings provide credible information that can be readily communicated. For example, the new brain imaging technologies, such as magnetic resonance imaging (MRI), position emission tomography (PET), and single photon emission computed tomography (SPECT) scans, have allowed us to actually view the living brain in humans to learn about the basic brain mechanisms involved in drug abuse and addiction and the specific areas in the brain where these effects occur (Altman, 1996; Childress et al., 1995; Volkow et al., 1991). We also have been able to observe changes in the brain associated with craving and other physiological processes that are significantly altered in the drug dependent state. This information can be used in prevention programs to demonstrate the negative physiological impact of drugs of abuse. For example, visual cues associated with cocaine use activate blood flow to the amygdala, but neutral cues do not (Childress et al., 1995). These research findings and imaging also provide demonstrations and educational tools to illustrate drug mechanisms to youngsters.

APPLICATION OF EPIDEMIOLOGIC, ETIOLOGIC, AND BASIC RESEARCH FINDINGS FOR EFFECTIVE PREVENTION INTERVENTIONS

Evans and his colleagues (Evans, 1976; Evans et al., 1978) were among the first investigators to build on these etiologic findings and to develop a novel prevention approach, social inoculation, influenced directly by the work of McGuire (1964) in persuasive communication, referred to as "psychological inoculation." Evans' approach was to counter pro-cigarette-use messages from peers, family, and the media by arming children with the skills to discern the sources of pressures to smoke and to resist them. Other important components of the program were designed to demonstrate to children that smoking was not a normative behavior. The findings from this research were positive; this was the first instance in which a theoretical basis was used to develop an effective intervention that could be used in the prevention of the use of illicit drugs. Over the next two decades, variations on the social influence model were widely tested. Importantly, the combination of social norm development, with the correction of misperceptions of the normative nature of drug use, and training in drug resistance skills, as well as coping and decision-making skills, have been demonstrated to have a positive effect in preventing drug using behaviors (Botvin, Baker, Dusenbury, Botvin & Diaz, 1995; Hansen & Graham, 1991; Pentz et al., 1989).

An excellent example of a successful program emerging from this perspective is Life Skills Training, developed by Gilbert Botvin, incorporating both social learning theory (Bandura, 1977) and problem behavior theory (Jessor & Jessor, 1977). In this context, drug abuse is viewed as a learned and functional behavior that emerges from social influences that promote the behavior. This program combines training in the skills and knowledge to resist social pressure to use drugs and in basic interpersonal skills with information about the risks and prevalence of drug abuse, to increase competence to deal with drug abuse as well as with other everyday problems. In a recent study involving junior high students (ages 12–14 years) from 56 schools in New York State, Life Skills Training sessions consisting of 15 classes were given to 7th graders (around age 13 years), with 10 booster sessions given in 8th grade and 5 booster sessions given in 9th grade. By the end of the 12th grade, students who received the full program reported significantly reduced use of tobacco, alcohol, and marijuana compared to those who did not receive the training (44% reduction; Botvin, 1998).

More recent studies have focused on factors that have been found to decrease potential for use of drugs. These protective factors include school achievement and strong bonds with prosocial institutions such as the family, school, and religious organizations. Given the key roles and functions of the family in any society, it is not surprising to find that this domain is one of the most powerful in both etiological and consequence studies of drug abusing behaviors and serves as the target and mechanism for drug abuse prevention interventions.

The family functions as the primary socialization channel in society, passing societal values, norms, and mores to the next generation. The family unit also serves to mold the genetic and phenotypic personality of offspring and influences greatly the future "person" of its members. The influence of the family on the development of offspring probably has been the most widely studied aspect of family life. However, the interactions among family members, particularly among adult family members and among siblings, has recently come under scientific investigation using complex, multidimensional paradigms (Clayton, 1991; Needle, Su, & Doherty, 1990). These paradigms must show not only the relationship of these independent components to the full range of drug using behaviors, but also the interrelationships and interactions among these components and drug using behaviors (Brook, Brook, Gordon & Whiteman, 1990; Dembo et al., 1991; Gfroerer, 1987).

There is much more information available regarding family process variables and their relationship to the initiation of drug using behaviors. These factors include quality of the parent–child relationship and of parent–child attachment; quality of parenting in setting rules and limitations with consistent enforcement and in establishing a supportive environment, clarification of norms against the use of drugs, modeling behavior, and family identification and bonding (Brook et al., 1990; Cadoret, 1992; Cadoret, Troughton, O'Gorman & Heywood, 1986; Cohen, Brook, Cohen, Velez & Garcia, 1990; Demarsh & Kumpfer, 1986; Hirschi, 1969; Jessor & Jessor, 1977; Kandel, Kessler, & Margulies, 1978; Kaplan, 1985; McCord & McCord, 1959; Pandina & Johnson, 1989; Patterson, Reid & Dishion, 1992; Shedler & Block, 1990).

More recently, these same researchers have been attempting to tease out protective factors. Dishion and McMahon (1998) have determined that parental monitoring is key to positive family management. Encouragement of positive parental monitoring requires experiences with positive behaviors on the part of children at all phases of their development, particularly during the teenage years. Research is available that shows that interventions that have as their objectives improving parenting practices have reduced the initiation of drug use even when these interventions target adolescents. Studies of interventions targeting early childhood have not followed children long enough to observe impact on drug use (Webster-Stratton, 1984, 1990); however, these studies have found significant impacts on improvements in child–parent relationships and school behaviors. More information is available for middle childhood and adolescence. Early in the 1970s, Patterson found that parent training of preadolescents reduced problem behaviors in the home as well as in school (1974), and other studies targeting adolescents showed reductions of substance abuse (Bry and Canby, 1986; Friedman, 1989, Lewis, Piercy, Sprendle & Trepper, 1990; Schmidt, Liddle, & Dakof, 1996). For certain populations who are more at risk for problem behaviors and drug abuse, it has been found that not including the family in the intervention could lead to deterioration of family functioning and increased risk for the index individual, as well as other family members (Dishion & Andrews, 1995; Dishion, Andrews, Kavanagh & Soberman, 1996; Szapocznik & Kurtines, 1989).

An example of a program that focuses on parenting practices that is delivered in the school setting is the Adolescent Transitions Program, developed by Thomas Dishion and his associates. This program targets young adolescents in middle and junior high school. It includes a family resource room with a video, *Parenting in the Teenage Years* (Dishion, 1995), and other materials designed to help parents identify observable risk factors. The program teaches effective family management skills, including positive reinforcement, monitoring, limit setting, and skills to build a strong relationship with children. In addition, the program offers the Family Check-Up, which allows the family to assess their problems. Those with problems engage with professional support in a parent focus curriculum and a teen focus curriculum. Studies of the effectiveness of these interventions indicate that parent interventions are needed for youth at high risk for problem behaviors and that repeated booster sessions are needed throughout the period of risk (Dishion & McMahon, 1998).

Other researchers have focused on those risk factors found in the school setting. Such risk factors as academic failure, antisocial behaviors, and failure to identify or bond (i.e., feel successful and confident in the school setting) have been targets of effective interventions. For example, Hawkins and his fellow researchers (O'Donnell, Hawkins, Catalano, Abbott & Day, 1995) tested the efficacy of a comprehensive family, school, and peer focused prevention program with students in grades 4 to 6. The experimental program is designed to promote social bonding, and students are exposed to instructional methods to enhance effective learning, cooperation among peers, and positive attitudes toward school. Children are also taught peer refusal skills to resist social pressure to use drugs. Parents are trained to increase their children's involvement in the family through productive roles and activities, clarify and communicate family expectations about drug use by family members, and teach their children to resist peer pressure to use drugs. Preliminary results indicate positive outcomes for experimental students on five factors: reductions of antisocial behavior, improved academic skills, increased commitment to school, reduced levels of alienation and poor bonding to prosocial others, and reduced school misbehavior. In addition, reduced incidents of getting high on drugs at school are also reported. The children in the study are only now entering adolescence and a period of increased risk for substance abuse. The program has demonstrated some positive effects on the function of the families (Kosterman, Hawkins, Spoth, Haggerty & Zhu, 1997), but it is too soon to determine what effects the program will have on the children's avoidance of substance use.

Focus on an integrated comprehensive approach to drug abuse prevention has grown out of community, multiple-level interventions designed to reduce heart disease in the United States (Farquhar et al., 1990). This approach was based on observations by Sechrest (1985) and others (Cassel, 1976) that interventions to change people's lifestyles and behaviors such as use of tobacco, involvement in exercise, and diet had to flow from the clinical environment into the community. Despite the mixed results of these early studies that targeted blood pressure and early heart disease through the media, educational programs, and health promotion campaigns that encompassed restaurants and other businesses, recent findings show that for many people most at risk for cardiovascular morbidity and mortality, the comprehensive nature of the programs supported change (Winkleby, Flora & Kraemer, 1994).

In programs designed to have an impact on the community prevalence level of drug abuse, components were designed to have parallel messages for the target group, children in their preteen years. The most successful of these programs was designed by Mary Ann Pentz (Pentz et al., 1989) and her colleagues and is called the Midwestern Prevention Program or Project STAR. In this program, five interventions are being tested using controlled experimental conditions in the two cities, Kansas City and Indianapolis. The central core of this program is a school-based peer resistance program called STAR (Students Taught Awareness and Resistance) that consists of a social influence curriculum that is incorporated into 10 classroom and homework sessions focused on the psychosocial consequences of drug abuse; correction of misconceptions concerning the prevalence of drug use by teens; social resistance training to offset and counter adult, media, peer and community influences to use drugs; assertiveness and problem solving training; and a statement of public commitment to avoid using drugs. The other components include parent organization and drug abuse education encouraging better communications between parents and children; community organization through task groups that promote anti-drug-abuse activities; and health policy implementation focusing on eliminating the use of drugs in the schools and in the community, for example, creation of drug-free zones and no smoking areas. All of these components are supported by a mass media campaign that heightens community awareness of the drug abuse problem and introduces the interventions being implemented by the program.

Research results have shown positive long-term effects: Students who began the program in junior high school, and whose results were measured in their senior year of high school, showed significantly less use of marijuana (30% less), cigarettes (25% less), and alcohol (20% less) than children in schools that did not receive the program (Pentz et al., 1989). Further analyses of these data by MacKinnon and his colleagues (1991) show that the program had an impact on children's perceptions of the negative effects of the use of these drugs, that their friends were more intolerant of the use of drugs, and that they were better able to communicate with their friends about drug as well as other problems. The most powerful mediator found to reduce drug use was the increased perception of friends' intolerance of the use of drugs.

In addition to prevention researchers focusing on risk factors and behaviors, many have developed programs for children who, by virtue of their family or their own behaviors, are at most risk for drug abuse, such as the children of substance abusers or children who have behavioral problems. Such interventions target these problems directly. Examples of effective programs of this nature include: Strengthening Families, designed by Karol Kumpfer and colleagues (Kumpfer, Molraad, & Spoth, 1996), and Reconnecting Youth by Leona Eggert (Eggert, Thompson, Herting, Nicholas, & Dicker, 1994).

The Strengthening Families program is a multicomponent, family-focused program that provides prevention programming for 6- to 10-year old children of substance abusers. The program helps these parents improve their parenting skills and consists of three elements: a parent training program, a children's skills-training program, and a family skills-training program. In each of the 14 two-hour weekly sessions, the parents and children are trained separately in the first hour. During the second hour, the parents and children come together in the family-skills training. The parent component improves parenting skills and reduces substance abuse by parents. The child component decreases negative behaviors and increases socially acceptable behaviors. Finally, the family component improves the family environment by allowing parents and children to learn and practice their new behaviors and skills. The program has undergone multiple assessments and has demonstrated reductions in family conflict, improvement in family communication and organization, and reductions in youth conduct disorders, aggressiveness, and substance abuse (Kumpfer et al., 1996).

In the Reconnecting Youth program, young people in grades 9 through 12 with multiple risk factors for substance abuse and signs of multiple problem behaviors such as substance abuse, depression, and suicidal ideation are taught skills to build resiliency with respect to risk factors and to moderate the early signs of substance abuse. The three components of the program, Personal Growth Class, Social Activities and School Bonding, and School System Crisis Response Plan, are designed to provide social support and life skills training. Research has shown that the program improves school performance; reduces drug involvement; decreases deviant peer bonding; increases self-esteem, personal control, school bonding, and social support; and decreases depression, anger and aggression, feelings of hopelessness, stress, and suicidal behaviors (Eggert et al., 1994).

PRINCIPLES OR LAWS OF DRUG ABUSE PREVENTION

A great deal of progress has been made in the area of drug abuse prevention over the past two decades. This progress has been the result of evolving theory, the availability of epidemiologic and biological information that has helped to unfold the complexity of drug abuse to better focus interventions, and the improved statistical techniques that have allowed better analyses of data to determine effectiveness and to understand the processes of the interventions themselves. It is from this extensive and comprehensive research base that we begin to elucidate principles or laws of drug abuse prevention. The following preliminary principles address the content, structure, and delivery of prevention services. (These principles have previously been published in Sloboda & David, 1997.)

Prevention Principles for Children and Adolescents

- Prevention programs should be designed to enhance protective factors and move toward reversing or reducing known risk factors.
- Prevention programs should target all forms of drug abuse, including the use of tobacco, alcohol, marijuana, and inhalants.
- Prevention programs should include skills to resist drugs when offered, strengthen personal commitments against drug use, and increase social competency (e.g., in communications, peer relationships, self-efficacy, and assertiveness), in conjunction with reinforcement of attitudes against drug use.
- Prevention programs for adolescents should include interactive methods, such as peer discussion groups, rather than didactic teaching techniques alone.
- Prevention programs should include a parent's or caregiver's component that reinforces what the children are learning—such as facts about drugs and their harmful effects—and that opens opportunities for family discussions about use of legal and illegal substances and family policies about their use.
- Prevention programs should be long-term, over the school career with repeat interventions to reinforce the original prevention goals. For example, school-based efforts directed at elementary and middle school students should include

booster sessions to help with critical transitions from middle to high school.

- Family-focused prevention efforts have a greater impact than strategies that focus on parents only or children only.
- Community programs that include media campaigns and policy changes, such as new regulations that restrict access to alcohol, tobacco, or other drugs, are more effective when they are accompanied by school and family interventions.
- Community programs need to strengthen norms against drug use in all drug abuse prevention settings, including the family, school, and the community.
- Schools offer opportunities to reach all populations and also serve as important settings for specific subpopulations at risk for drug abuse, such as children with behavior problems or learning disabilities and those who are potential dropouts.
- Prevention programming should be adapted to address the specific nature of the drug abuse problem in the local community.
- The higher the level of risk for the target population, the more intensive the prevention effort must be and the earlier it must begin.
- Prevention programs should be age-specific, developmentally appropriate, and culturally sensitive.

These principles should be seen as preliminary and perhaps not sufficient to inform those who wish to establish effective prevention strategies. Key to the principles at this time, however, is the notion that there are underlying constructs or elements that guide effective prevention programming. It is clear that barriers exist in communities to delivering full-blown prevention intervention programs that have been tested under controlled conditions. These barriers are limited not only to the scarcity of resources, but also to conflicting attitudes and values as well as the special nature of the community setting, and the ways in which each community defines its drug abuse problem. Other building blocks are needed in addition to these principles to serve communities in need. These may include quantifying the relative impact of each intervention component so that communities may opt to use one or more components to achieve an effect that would be less than if the program as a whole were delivered, but would maximize the effect under the circumstances. Much more work needs to be done in this area.

SUMMARY AND FUTURE DIRECTIONS

Despite the tremendous achievements, as mentioned above, there are significant gaps in our knowledge about the prevention process. For instance, although much attention has been given to the efficacy of information, education, and other interventions for school-aged children, there is still much to be learned about the influence of the school environment on prevention outcomes. Even today little is known about how the classroom and school composition influence the effectiveness of interventions. Very little is known about school policies on drug use, how they vary, and how they are implemented. For example, in some schools children found to be involved with drugs may be expelled, but in others children may be referred for counseling. How do these decisions affect the impact of school-based curriculum about drugs? There is also a general belief that drug prevention must occur earlier in the school career, but there is a dearth of research findings as to the effectiveness of earlier exposure to prevention efforts.

Another critical gap includes the use of early markers for later problems. Research suggests that initial markers of later problem behavior can be identified as early as elementary school. Some of these markers are inconsistent and inadequate parenting practices, physical or sexual abuse, low degree of social bonding to family and school, positive beliefs and attitudes toward drug use, aggressivity and shyness, high levels of sensation seeking, rebelliousness, and early age at onset of use of drugs. Significantly more work is needed to understand the relationship of these markers to each other and on the biological (including genetic) factors that predispose individuals to drug use. Special attention should be given to children of alcoholics and children of substance abusers. This is one area in which epidemiologists can work more closely with the prevention intervention researchers to develop reliable profiles of risk and protective factor configurations that predict drug use, as well as diagnostic techniques and checklists to assess early on which youth may be at highest risk for drug abuse and associated problems.

Other areas that are of importance relate to the use of persuasive communication techniques for prevention and the diffusion of this cumulative knowledge from research to practice. As communications research has become more sophisticated, the recognition that it is necessary for prevention practitioners to use the channels of communications that reach particular audiences with specific messages has become more essential. But not enough research has been conducted to determine the efficiency and effectiveness of these channels. Also, the newly emerging information highway challenges the prevention field to recognize the advantages of new, multiple opportunities to reach audiences, and we must recognize that competitive, negative uses of those same channels can undermine preventive efforts. Just as television can serve both a positive and negative role, so does this new technology present challenges both to the researchers and practitioners.

It is telling about the growing sophistication of the prevention field that, given the myriad risk factors, a new classification system for interventions needed to be developed. This system recognized that (a) people are at varying levels of risk and (b) different types and intensities of interventions are needed to address this variation. The new system, adapted from mental health concepts, consists of three approaches: *universal* strategies that reach the general population, *selective* strategies that target subsets of the general population at elevated risk, and *indicated* strategies that target people who are already experimenting with drugs or who exhibit other risk-related behaviors (Mrazek & Haggerty, pp. 20–21, 1994). This is but one dimension of a classification scheme for prevention interventions. Other dimensions that reflect target group (individual, family, school, community), developmental age groups, and risk levels and intensities also need to be entered into the classification system. An analysis of prevention interventions that have published positive findings would reveal a number of gaps. For example there are few interventions available that target post-high-school young adults in colleges and in the workplace, infants of drug abusing parents including fathers, communities and the environment, especially for youth at high risk for drug abuse, and people over 55 who because of transition out of the workplace and into retirement and reduced family roles may be at risk for drug abuse. Furthermore, prevention models are needed that include chronically ill families, those who are disabled, or families and individuals that manifest predisposing psychopathologies, such as clinical depression and anxiety, as well as conduct disorders and post-traumatic stress disorder. It is yet unclear how both pharmacotherapeutic and behavioral treatment of these groups intervenes to prevent drug abuse.

Finally, although the prevention research field has made much progress in developing and testing new models for family, school, and community-based programs, we have few replication studies that validate these programs, and even fewer to test various diffusion methods to put them into practice. This is a serious gap and one that prevention researchers are seeking to address in the United States.

REFERENCES

Altman, J. (1996, June). A biological view of drug abuse. *Molecular Medicine Today, 2*(6), 237–241.

Bachman, J. G., Johnston, L. D., & O'Malley, P. M. (1990). Explaining the recent decline in cocaine use among young adults: Further evidence that perceived risks and disapproval lead to reduced drug use. *Journal of Health and Social Behavior, 31*(2), 173–184.

Bachman, J. G., Johnston, L. D., & O'Malley, P. M. (1998). Explaining recent increases in students' marijuana use: Impacts of perceived risks and disapproval, 1976 through 1996. *American Journal of Public Health*, 88(6), 887–892.

Bachman, J. G., Johnston, L. D., O'Malley, P. M., & Humphrey, R. H. (1988). Explaining recent decline in marijuana use: Differentiating the effects of perceived risks, disapproval, and general lifestyle factors. *Journal of Health and Social Behavior*, 29, 92–112.

Bachman, J. G., Wadsworth, K. N., O'Malley, P. M., Johnston, L. D., & Schulenberg, J. E. (1997). *Smoking, drinking, and drug use in young adulthood*. Hillside, NJ: Erlbaum.

Bandura, A. (1977). *Social learning theory*. Englewood Cliffs, NJ: Prentice-Hall.

Bauman, K. E., & Ennett, S. T. (1996). On the importance of peer influence for adolescent drug use: Commonly neglected considerations. *Addiction*, 91(2), 185–198.

Botvin, Gilbert J. (1998). Preventing drug abuse through the schools: Intervention programs that work. In *National Conference on Drug Abuse Prevention Research: Presentations, Papers, and Recommendations* (NIH Publication No. 98-4293). Rockville, MD: Department of Health and Human Services, National Institutes of Health, National Institute on Drug Abuse.

Botvin, G. J., Baker, E., Dusenbury, L., Botvin, E. M., & Diaz, T. (1995). Long-term followup results of a randomized drug abuse prevention trial in a white middle-class population. *Journal of the American Medical Association*, 273, 1106–1112.

Botvin, G. J., Malgady, R. G., Griffin, K. W., Scheier, L. M., & Epstein, J. A. (1998). Alcohol and marijuana use among rural youth: Interaction of social and intrapersonal influences. *Addictive Behaviors*, 23(3), 379–387.

Brook, J. S., Brook, D. W., Gordon, A. S., & Whiteman, M. (1990). The psychological etiology of adolescent drug use: A family interactional approach. *Genetic, Social & General Psychology Monographs*, 116(2), 111–267.

Brook, J. S., Whiteman, M., & Gordon, A. S. (1982). Qualitative and quantitative aspects of adolescent drug use: Interplay of personality, family, and peer correlates. *Psychological Reports*, 51, 1151–1163.

Brook, J. S., Whiteman, M., Nomura, C., Gordon, A. S., & Cohen, P. (1988). Personality, family, and ecological influences on adolescent drug use: A developmental analysis. In R. H. Coombs (Ed.), *The family context of adolescent drug use*. New York: Haworth.

Bry, B. H., & Canby, C. (1986). Decreasing adolescent drug use and school failure: Long-term effects of targeted family problem-solving training. *Child and Family Behavior Therapy*, 8, 43–59.

Bry, B. H., McKeon, P., & Pandina, R. J. (1982). Extent of drug use as a function of number of risk factors. *Journal of Abnormal Psychology*, 91(4), 273–279.

Cadoret, R. J. (1992). Genetic and environmental factors in initiation of drug use and the transition to abuse. In M. D. Glantz & R. W. Pickens (Eds.), *Vulnerability to drug abuse* (pp. 99–114). Washington, DC: American Psychological Association.

Cadoret, R. J., Troughton, E., O'Gorman, T. W., & Heywood, E. (1986). An adoption study of genetic and environmental factors in drug abuse. *Archives of General Psychiatry, 43,* 1131–1136.

Cassel, J. (1976). The contribution of the social environment to host resistance. *American Journal of Epidemiology, 104,* 107–123.

Childress, A. R., Mozley, D., Fitzgerald, J., Reivich, M., Jaggi, J., & O'Brien, C. P. (1995). Limbic activation during cue-induced cocaine craving. *Society for Neuroscience Abstracts, 21*(3), 1956.

Clayton, R. (1991). Transitions in drug use: Risk and protective factors. In M. D. Glantz & R. W. Pickens (Eds.), *Vulnerability to drug abuse* (pp. 15–52). Washington, DC: American Psychological Association.

Cohen, P., Brook, J. S., Cohen, J., Velez, C. N., & Garcia, M. (1990). Common and uncommon pathways to adolescent psychopathology and problem behavior. In L. Robins & M. Rutter (Eds.), *Straight and devious pathways from childhood to adulthood,* (pp. 242–258). London: Cambridge University Press.

Dawes, M. A., Tarter, R. E., & Kirisci, L. (1997). Behavioral self-regulation: Correlates and 2 year follow-ups for boys at risk for substance abuse. *Drug and Alcohol Dependence, 45*(3), 165–176.

Demarsh, J., & Kumpfer, K. L. (1986). Family oriented interventions for the prevention of chemical dependency in children and adolescents. In S. Griswold, S. Ezekoye, K. L. Kumpfer, & W. J. Bukoski. (Eds.), *Childhood and chemical abuse: Prevention and intervention* (pp. 117–151). New York: Haworth.

Dembo, R., Williams, L., Getreu, A., Genung, L., Schmeidler, J., Berry, E., Wish, E. D., & LaVoie, L. (1991). A longitudinal study of the relationships among marijuana/hashish use, cocaine use and delinquency in a cohort of high risk youths. *Journal of Drug Issues, 21,* 271–312.

Dinges, M. M., & Oetting, E. R. (1993). Similarity in drug use patterns between adolescents and their friends. *Adolescence, 28*(110), 253–266.

Dishion, T. J. (Producer, 1995). *Parenting in the teenage years.* [video]. (Available from Independent Video Services, 401 East 10th Ave., Suite 160, Eugene, OR 97401.)

Dishion, T. J., & Andrews, D. W. (1995). Preventing escalation in problem behaviors with high-risk young adolescents: Immediate and 1-year outcomes. *Journal of Consulting and Clinical Psychology, 63,* 538–548.

Dishion, T. J., Andrews, D. W., Kavanagh, K., & Soberman, L. H. (1996). Preventive interventions for high-risk youth: The adolescent transitions program. In R. Peters & R. J. McMahon (Eds.), *Preventing childhood disorders, substance abuse and delinquency* (pp. 184–214). Thousand Oaks, CA: Sage.

Dishion, T. J., & McMahon, R. J. (1998). Parental monitoring and the prevention of problem behavior: A conceptual and empirical reformulation. *Clinical Child and Family Psychological Review, 7,* 154–161.

Dorn, N., & Thompson, A. (1976). Evaluation of drug education in the longer term is not an optional extra. *Community Health, 7,* 154–161.

Eggert, L. L., Thompson, E. A., Herting, J. R., Nicholas, L. J., & Dicker, B. G.

(1994). Preventing adolescent drug abuse and high school dropout through an intensive school-based social network development program. *American Journal of Health Promotion, 8*(3), 202–215.

Evans, R. I. (1976). Smoking in children: Developing a social psychological strategy of deterrence. *Preventive Medicine, 5*, 122–127.

Evans, R. I., Rozelle, R. M., Mittlemark, M. B., Hansen, W. B., Bane, A. L., & Havis, J. (1978). Deterring the onset of smoking in children: Knowledge of immediate physiological effects and coping with peer pressure, media pressure, and parent modeling. *Journal of Applied Social Psychology, 8*, 126–135.

Farquhar, J. W., Fortmann, S. P., Flora, J. A., Taylor, C. B., Haskell, W. L., Williams, P. T., Maccoby, N., & Wood, P. D. (1990). Effects of community wide education on cardiovascular disease risk factors: The Stanford five-city project. *Journal of the American Medical Association, 264*, 359–365.

Friedman, A. S. (1989). Family therapy versus parent groups: Effects on adolescent drug abusers. *American Journal of Family Therapy, 17*, 335–347.

Gfroerer, J. (1987). Correlation between drug use by teenagers and drug use by older family members. *American Journal of Drug and Alcohol Abuse, 13*(1, 2), 95–108.

Glantz, M. D., & Pickens, R. W. (1992). Vulnerability to drug abuse: Introduction and overview. In M. D. Glantz & R. W. Pickens (Eds.), *Vulnerability to drug abuse* (pp. 1–14). Washington, DC: American Psychological Association.

Glantz, M. D., & Sloboda, Z. (1995). The prevention of drug abuse among the elderly. In R. Coombs & D. Zeidonis (Eds.), *Handbook on drug abuse prevention: A comprehensive strategy to prevent abuse of alcohol and other drugs* (pp. 429–444). Needham Heights, MA: Allyn Bacon.

Hansen, W. B., & Graham, J. W. (1991). Preventing alcohol, marijuana, and cigarette use among adolescents: Peer pressure resistance training versus establishing conservative norms. *Preventive Medicine, 20*, 414–430.

Hawkins, J. D., Catalano, R. F., & Miller, J. Y. (1992). Risk and protective factors for alcohol and other drug problems in adolescence and early adulthood: Implications for substance abuse prevention. *Psychological Bulletin, 112*, 64–105.

Hirschi, T. (1969). *Causes of delinquency*. Berkeley, CA: University of California Press.

Hovland, C. I., Janis, I. L., & Kelley, H. H. (1953). *Communication and persuasion*. New Haven, CT: Yale University Press.

Jessor, R., & Jessor, S. L. (1977). *Problem behavior and psychosocial development: A longitudinal study of youth*. New York: Academic Press.

Johnston, L. D., O'Malley, P. M., & Bachman, J. G. (1996). *National survey results on drug use from the monitoring the future study, 1975–1995* (National Institute on Drug Abuse, NIH Publication No. 96-4139). Rockville, MD: National Institute on Drug Abuse.

Kandel, D. B., & Davies, M. (1992). Progression to regular marijuana involvement: Phenomenology and risk factors for near-daily use. In M. D. Glantz & R. W.

Pickens (Eds.), *Vulnerability to drug abuse* (pp. 211–254). Washington, DC: American Psychological Association.

Kandel, D. B., Kessler, R. C., & Margulies, R. Z. (1978). Antecedents of adolescent initiation into stages of drug use: A developmental analysis. *Journal of Youth and Adolescence, 7*(1), 13–40.

Kandel, D. B., & Yamaguchi, K. (1985). Developmental patterns of the use of legal, illegal, and medically prescribed psychotropic drugs from adolescence to young adulthood. In C. L. Jones & R. Battjes (Eds.), *Etiology of drug abuse: Implications for prevention Monograph No. 56* (pp. 193–235). Rockville, MD: National Institute on Drug Abuse.

Kaplan, H. B. (1985). Testing a general theory of drug abuse and other deviant adaptations. *Journal of Drug Issues, 15,* 477–492.

Kearney, A. L., & Hines, M. H. (1980). Evaluation of the effectiveness of a drug prevention education program. *Journal of Drug Education, 10,* 127–134.

Kim, S. (1988). A short- and long-term evaluation of "Here's Looking at You." II. *Journal of Drug Education, 18,* 235–242.

Kosterman, R., Hawkins, J. D., Spoth, R., Haggerty, K. P., & Zhu, K. (1997). Effects of "Preparing for the Drug Free Years" on parenting behavior and family interactions. *Journal of Community Psychology, 25*(4), 337–352.

Kumpfer, K. L., Molraard, V., & Spoth, R. (1996). The Strengthening Families Program for the prevention of delinquency and drug use. In R. Peters & R. J. McMahon. (Eds.), *Preventing childhood disorders, substance abuse, and delinquency* (pp. 241–267). Thousand Oaks, CA: Sage.

Lewis, R. A., Piercy, F. P., Sprendle, D. H., & Trepper, T. J. (1990). Family-based interventions for helping drug-using adolescents. *Journal of Adolescent Research, 5,* 82–95.

MacKinnon, D. P., Johnson, C. A., Pentz, M. A., Dwyer, J. H., Hansen, W. B., Flay, B. R., & Wang, E. Y. I. (1991). How school-based drug education works: One year effects of the midwestern prevention project. *Health Psychology, 10,* 164–172.

McCord, W., & McCord, J. (1959). *Origins of crime: a new evaluation of the Cambridge-Somerville study.* New York: Columbia University Press.

McGuire, W. J. (1964). Inducing resistance to persuasion: Some contemporary approaches. In L. Berkowiz (Ed.), *Advances in experimental social psychology* (pp. 192–227). New York: Academic Press.

Mrazek, P., & Haggerty, R. J. (Eds.). (1994). *Reducing risks for mental disorders: Frontiers for preventive intervention research.* Washington, DC: National Academy Press.

National Institute on Drug Abuse. (1996). Calculations derived from the 1994 National Household Survey on Drug Abuse by staff of the Division of Epidemiology and Prevention Research. Bethesda, MD: Author.

National Institute on Drug Abuse. (1998). National survey results in drug use from *The Monitoring the Future Study, 1975–1997.* Volume 1: Secondary Students National Institutes of Health (Publication No. 98-4345), 49–60, Bethesda, MD: Author.

Needle, R. H., Su, S., & Doherty, W. J. (1990). Divorce, remarriage, and adolescent substance abuse: A prospective longitudinal study. *Journal of Marriage and the Family, 52,* 157–169.

Newcomb, M. D. (1992). Understanding the multidimensional nature of drug use and abuse: The role of consumption, risk factors, and protective factors. In M. D. Glantz & R. W. Pickens, (Eds.), *Vulnerability to drug abuse* (pp. 255–289). Washington, DC: American Psychological Association.

Newcomb, M. D., & Bentler, P. M. (1986). Frequency and sequence of drug use: A longitudinal study from early adolescence to young adulthood. *Journal of Drug Education, 16,* 101–120.

O'Donnell, J., Hawkins, J. D., Catalano, R. F., Abbott, R. D., & Day, L. E. (1995). Preventing school failure, drug use, and delinquency among low-income children: Long-term intervention in elementary schools. *American Journal of Orthopsychiatry, 65*(1), 87–100.

Oetting, E. R., Donnermeyer, J. F., & Deffenbacher, J. L. (1998). Primary socialization theory. The influences of the community on drug use and deviance. III. *Substance Use and Misuse, 33*(8), 1629–1665.

Pandina, R. J. (1998). Risk and protective factors in adolescent drug use: Putting them to work for prevention. In *national conference on drug abuse prevention research: Presentations, papers, and recommendations* (NIH Publication No. 98-4293). Rockville, MD: Department of Health and Human Services, National Institutes of Health, National Institute on Drug Abuse.

Pandina, R. J., & Johnson, V. (1989). Familial history as a predictor of alcohol and drug consumption among adolescent children. *Journal of Studies on Alcohol, 50,* 245–253.

Patterson, G. R. (1974). Interventions for boys with conduct problems: Multiple setting, treatments, and criteria. *Journal of Consulting and Clinical Psychology, 42,* 471–481.

Patterson, G. R., Reid, J. B., & Dishion, T. J. (1992). *Antisocial boys.* Eugene, OR: Castalia.

Pentz, M. A., Dwyer, J. H., MacKinnon, D. P., Flay, B. R., Hansen, W. B., Wang, E. Y., & Johnson, C. A. (1989). A multi-community trial for primary prevention of adolescent drug abuse: Effects of drug use prevalence. *Journal of the American Medical Association, 261,* 3259–3266.

Schaps, E., Bartolo, R. D., Moskowitz, J., Palley, C. S., & Churgin, S. (1981). A review of 127 drug abuse prevention program evaluations. *Journal of Drug Issues, 11,* 17–43.

Schmidt, S. E., Liddle, H. A., & Dakof, G. A. (1996). Changes in parenting practices and adolescent drug abuse during multidimensional family therapy. *Journal of Family Psychology. 10,* 12–27.

Sechrest, L. (1985). Experiments and demonstrations in health services research. *Medical Care, 23*(5), 677–695.

Shedler, J., & Block, J. (1990). Adolescent drug use and psychological health: A longitudinal study. *American Psychologist, 45,* 612–630.

Sloboda, Z., & David, S. L. (1997). *Preventing drug use among children and adolescents: A research base guide.* Rockville, MD: National Institute on Drug Abuse.

Steinberg, L., Fletcher, A., & Darling, N. (1994). Parental monitoring and peer influences on adolescent substance use. *Pediatrics, 93*(6, Pt. 2), 060–1064.

Substance Abuse and Mental Health Services Administration. (1998). Preliminary results from the 1997 *National Household Survey on Drug Abuse.* DHHS Publication No. (SMA) 98–3251, Tables 38–45. Rockville, MD: Author.

Szapocznik, J., & Kurtines, W. M. (1989). *Breakthroughs in family therapy with drug-abusing and problem youth.* New York: Springer.

Tarter, R. E., Blackson, T., Brigham, J., Moss, H., & Caprara, G. V. (1995). The association between childhood irritability and liability to substance use in early adolescence: A 2-year follow-up study of boys at risk for substance abuse. *Drug and Alcohol Dependence, 39*(3), 253–261.

Volkow, N. D., Fowler, J. S., Wolf, A. P., Hitzemann, R., Dewey, S., Bendriem, B., Alpert, R., & Hoff, A. (1991). Changes in brain glucose metabolism in cocaine dependence and withdrawal. *American Journal of Psychology, 148,* 621–626.

Webster-Stratton, C. (1984). Randomized trial of two parent training programs for families with conduct disordered children. *Journal of Consulting and Clinical Psychology, 52,* 666–678.

Webster-Stratton, C. (1990). Enhancing the effectiveness of self-administered videotape parent training for families with conduct problem children. *Journal of Abnormal Child Psychology, 18,* 479–492.

Winkleby, M. A., Flora, J. A., & Kraemer, H. C. (1994). A community-based heart disease intervention: Predictors of change. *American Journal of Public Health, 84*(5), 767–772.

11

THE TREATMENT OF DRUG ABUSE: CHANGING THE PATHS

CHRISTINE R. HARTEL AND MEYER D. GLANTZ

WHAT DOES DRUG ABUSE TREATMENT DO FOR SOCIETY?

Drug abuse treatment is preordained to fail if the notion of treatment implies a permanent cure. If drug addiction is a chronic and relapsing disorder, as it certainly seems to be, then treatment becomes an ongoing process rather than an endpoint, and it becomes possible to measure the outcomes of treatment and to weigh its cost against its benefits.

The United States has tried various methods to reduce drug consumption in this country: source-country control, which attacks drug production abroad; interdiction, which keeps drugs out of the country by stopping it at our borders or in transit; domestic law enforcement, which targets drug sellers, buyers, and users; and finally, drug treatment. In 1994, Rydell and Everingham compared the effectiveness of these drug control programs by calculating what it would cost to use each method to reduce national cocaine consumption by an additional 1%. Source-country control would cost $783 million more than we are currently spending on all four methods

The authors thank Jack S. Blaine, MD and Lisa S. Onken, PhD for their helpful comments on an earlier draft of this chapter.

together; interdiction $366 million more; domestic law enforcement $246 million; and drug treatment only $34 million more. These startling differences in costs for the same amount of benefit (a 1% reduction in drug consumption) make it puzzling indeed why drug treatment is not universally and immediately available.

One answer is distressingly simple: There are just not enough treatment facilities available to treat all the people who need and want to engage in treatment programs. Estimates vary, but it is probable that as many as 2,603,000 treatment slots are needed in addition to the 950,000 that already exist.

What else does treatment do for the drug user—and society—besides reducing the use of drugs? The Office of National Drug Control Policy (ONDCP, 1996) concludes that it:

- Reduces crime
- Reduces drug use
- Reduces domestic violence
- Reduces risk for HIV infection
- Increases days of employment
- Brings positive changes in social values and networks

The Services Research Outcomes Study by the Substance Abuse and Mental Health Services Administration (SAMHSA, 1998) added the following benefits for the treated individuals:

- Regaining and retaining child custody
- Securing more reliable housing

The Services Research Outcomes Study was sufficiently large that it was possible for the researchers to extrapolate what was happening in the overall U.S. population of treatment clients (976,012 people) five years after their 1990 discharge from treatment. The researchers estimated that as a result of the treatment of these people in 1990, five years later there were an estimated:

- 156,000 fewer illicit drug users
- 187,000 fewer cocaine users
- 152,000 fewer marijuana users
- 101,000 fewer drug sales
- 165,000 fewer driving while intoxicated and 131,000 fewer driving under the influence cases

These remarkable figures validate the findings of numerous other studies that drug treatment brings significant benefits and cost savings to society as well as to the drug users themselves.

TREATMENT MODALITIES: PSYCHOPHARMACOLOGICAL AND PSYCHOSOCIAL THERAPIES

Having established that many benefits to society are realized by spending money on drug abuse treatment, what are reasonable treatment goals for the individual client? Frequently, the outcomes of very different types of approaches to drug abuse treatment are very similar for the client; they may include reduced drug use, decreased criminality, increased productivity, fewer medical problems, improved psychological functioning, and improved social functioning. Outpatient treatment programs specifically for women drug users also focus on improved perinatal outcomes and parenting skills. Inpatient treatment programs, which have been shortened significantly with the advent of managed health care programs, often have as their primary objective the achievement and maintenance of a drug-free life. They share with other treatment modalities the outcomes of decreased involvement in illegal activities; increased productivity in work, school, or home; improved social, family, and psychological functioning; and improved physical health.

If all these goals are reasonable for many forms of treatment, what are the differences among treatment modalities? Do some work better than others, and why? That is the topic of this chapter; we will examine more closely each of the primary types of drug abuse treatment programs and describe their current status. These include both psychopharmacological and psychosocial approaches.

Psychopharmacological Approaches

Many people are surprised to learn that medication is frequently a starting point and a necessity for most drug abuse treatment, especially for alcohol, tobacco, opiate, and cocaine abuse. Some people are even more surprised that treatment beyond pharmacological detoxification is available, effective, and necessary; these kinds of treatment are generally known as behavioral–psychosocial approaches. The most successful treatment programs tie psychopharmacological and behavioral–psychosocial treatment together, to ensure that the client is detoxified and physically comfortable, so that he or she can focus on and make a firm commitment to achieve personal success in treatment. For most clients that means learning new skills in order to maintain total abstinence from drugs. In the first section of this chapter, we will look at the types of medications that form one part of the multifaceted approach to drug abuse treatment.

History

The use of an alternate drug to treat drug addiction is not new. Sigmund Freud described giving cocaine to ease the addiction of his friend,

Fleischl, an opiate addict (Jones, 1953). This was one of his treatment failures that caused Freud great anguish, for Fleischl became addicted to cocaine and eventually died.

In the 1960s, Vincent Dole and Marie Nyswander (1965) made the first modern attempts to treat heroin addition with "medicine": They gave their patients methadone. Methadone is a longer acting opioid that gives a lower high than heroin, but also satisfies the overwhelming craving that heroin dependence induces. Unlike heroin, methadone need only be taken once a day, allowing patients to concentrate on holding a job or learning basic skills. For many addicts, methadone makes psychosocial therapy for addiction possible—and more often successful.

Rapid developments in opiate pharmacology and in our understanding of the neurobiology of addiction more generally have opened the way to the development of medications for addiction to other types of drugs of abuse, as well: nicotine, alcohol, and possibly even stimulants like cocaine and methamphetamine. Elsewhere in this volume (chap. 8), Koob has discussed the neurobiology of addiction. He points out that drugs of abuse affect the major neurotransmitter systems in the brain. Narcotics like heroin and morphine hijack the brain's natural opioid receptor system, using it beyond its normal functional limits and sometimes changing it permanently. Stimulants like cocaine and amphetamine similarly disrupt the brain's reward pathways where dopamine plays a major role. Nicotine increases dopamine in certain brain regions through effects on the neurotransmitter gamma-aminobutyric acid (GABA), but nicotine affects the endogenous opioid and glucocorticoid systems as well. Alcohol also has broad neurotransmitter effects, increasing concentrations of dopamine and serotonin (5-HT) in critical brain regions.

Primary Concept

The medications used to treat drug abuse have been reviewed extensively elsewhere (Altman et al., 1996; O'Brien, 1997). Like drugs of abuse themselves, drug abuse medications act in a variety of ways in the brain. They stimulate some neurotransmitter systems and inhibit the activity of others. Some medications, like methadone and LAAM (levo-alpha-acetyl methadol), substitute for drugs of abuse, but without many of their damaging effects. These drugs are called agonists. Others are antagonists, blocking the ability of abused drugs to exert their usual effects. Some are only partial agonists and others are mixed agonist–antagonists having properties of both types; others suppress the craving for a drug, or cause an aversion to the drug to develop. Pharmacologically reversing or altering the effects of abused drugs by administering treatment medications is very useful and often necessary in treating drug addiction, but medications can be only part of the treatment regimen. To be most effective, drug abuse treatment must also address behavioral and social aspects of the problem for the individual patient. This is especially true if the patient has a mental disorder, like depression or bulimia, as is so often the case. (See the section on comorbidity that follows.)

Description

Drug antagonists. Some treatment medications directly counteract the effects of other drugs by occupying the nerve cell receptors that can be occupied by drugs of abuse. Such medications are pharmacological antagonists. In the case of the opioid antagonist naltrexone and its shorter acting analog naloxone, they are sometimes called "Lazarus" drugs because of their dramatic effects in reversing heroin overdose, rapidly and visibly bringing people back from the edge of death. They are used in emergency rooms because they reverse all the toxic effects of heroin overdose.

Unfortunately, even though naltrexone and naloxone are used successfully in emergency treatment, they are not usually suitable for long-term treatment of opiate addiction. Many people simply will not take them on a regular basis, because naltrexone and naloxone completely block the reinforcing "rush" of morphine and heroin. This neutral state sometimes leaves the addict feeling slightly depressed or dysphoric, although the antagonists themselves do not induce this feeling. Also, naltrexone and naloxone do nothing to satisfy the intense craving for more opiates. There is a small group of highly motivated patients for whom naltrexone can be used to inhibit heroin use; frequently, these are physicians or nurses who have ready access to morphine and have become addicted. Interestingly, it turns out that naltrexone may be useful in treating alcohol abuse, because it seems to decrease the craving for alcohol but does not cause an alcohol withdrawal syndrome. This use of naltrexone in alcohol abuse treatment is discussed later.

Another example of a drug antagonist is mecamylamine, which directly blocks the effects of nicotine. Like using naltrexone to treat heroin or morphine addiction, mecamylamine alone has not proven very useful in smoking cessation treatment, because smokers either increase their nicotine intake to compensate for the blocked effects or simply do not take the medication at all. Again, the craving for the effects of the drug of abuse, nicotine, proves to be the driver for relapse. Simply blocking the reinforcing effects of the drug of choice is usually not sufficient for stopping addiction. Mecamylamine has been used with some success when given in combination with nicotine patches and behavioral treatment programs (Rose et al., 1994).

The use of drug antagonists to block the effects of drugs of abuse provides only a temporary cessation of drug use. Once the client stops using the medication because he or she believes that the blockade is no longer necessary to stay drug-free, the client typically relapses to drug use because the antagonist has not met the craving the client feels for more drugs.

Drug agonists, replacement or substitution therapy. As mentioned above, Dole and Nyswander (1965) gave their heroin addicted patients methadone, a long-lasting opioid that substitutes for heroin or morphine and reduces the necessity for seeking multiple doses of heroin or morphine daily. Instead, one dose of methadone given at a treatment clinic lasts all day, preventing opiate withdrawal from occurring as the client ceases drug-use. This allows the addict to engage in more productive and therapeutic behaviors. LAAM is another long-lasting opioid agonist that provides stability for the addict. It was approved in 1993 as a pharmacotherapy for opiate addiction. However, it is not as well accepted by heroin addicts as methadone, because methadone at times produces a slight high, that some addicts say makes them feel normal. LAAM produces a more level state with no boost after the dose is taken. Doses of LAAM are needed only three times a week, releasing the patient from dependence on the clinic, which is very important for someone trying to hold down a job or go to school. However, in some cases, especially early in treatment, the daily clinic contact for receiving methadone actually provides a therapeutic benefit to opiate addicts, bringing them on-site for additional psychosocial therapy and rehabilitation training.

Both methadone and LAAM stabilize the addicts physiologically, and let them concentrate on things other than getting the next dose of heroin. But the treatment regimen can take several weeks to establish successfully, and there are other issues as well. The use of opioid agonists has been steeped in controversy because of concerns about diversion of methadone for illegal purposes and the possibility of overdose, and because methadone continues instead of curing the addiction. Nevertheless, the efficacy of substitution pharmacotherapy for opiate abuse in conjunction with psychosocial therapy was recently reaffirmed at a National Institutes of Health Consensus Development Program (1998). This form of treatment for opiate dependence confers other public health benefits, as well: Rates of HIV and drug resistant tuberculosis infection are lower in methadone-maintained addicts than in the heroin-dependent population. Babies born to mothers maintained on methadone are healthier than those born to their heroin-using counterparts.

The nicotine patch, nicotine chewing gum, and nicotine nasal sprays are familiar forms of replacement therapy for cigarette addiction. Use of these methods of nicotine self-administration makes it possible for smokers to avoid nicotine withdrawal symptoms as they lower their doses of nicotine gradually, and learn to substitute other behaviors for those associated with smoking. Package inserts with these products state that they work best when used in conjunction with a behavioral treatment program— another instance of the necessity of combining therapies for the most effective results. This is especially true for women, who are generally less sensitive to the effects of nicotine than men, and are much more sensitive to the social and contextual cues of the act of smoking (Perkins, DiMarco, Grobe, Scierka, & Stiller, 1994; Perkins, Sanders, DiAmico, & Wilson, 1997). They are therefore in particular need of psychosocial therapy to increase the likelihood that they will stop smoking.

Currently, there are no medications approved for use in substitution treatment of stimulant (cocaine, methamphetamine) abuse, marijuana abuse, hallucinogen abuse (LSD), or inhalant abuse, although there are some medications that can treat the immediate consequences of acute intoxication with these drugs. Advances in drug development methods hold great promise in this area of addiction treatment research. Meanwhile, behavioral treatment of these addictions can be effective. As we learn more about how these various drugs of abuse affect the brain, we will undoubtedly find additional pharmacotherapies that will complement behavioral and psychosocial treatments.

Agonist–antagonist combinations. There is some evidence that combinations of agonist and antagonist drugs in careful doses may be useful in treating addiction, especially to nicotine. A combination of nicotine and mecamylamine has shown some promise in treating nicotine addiction (Rose et al., 1994), but further studies are needed before this type of drug treatment is considered effective. There are even some individual drugs that have both agonist and antagonist properties in the opiate system; buprenorphine is one of these. It has shown efficacy as a medication for heroin treatment, because of its overall antagonist-like effects, and its use is likely to be approved soon. It is always useful to have a selection of medications available for treatment, because people respond so differently to different drugs.

Alternative appetite (craving) suppressants. No one doubts that among addicts craving for drugs of abuse is a serious problem that must be overcome if treatment is to be successful, but craving is a very difficult concept to define in a way that can be measured reliably. There is no accurate scale for measuring craving or comparing craving for one drug with craving for another, yet many patients report that their craving for certain drugs of abuse is suppressed by specific medications. The mechanisms of action in the brain for craving are not at all clear, and the drugs that people say block their craving often have very different mechanisms of action.

Both naltrexone and acamprosate decrease craving for alcohol, but apparently through different mechanisms of action. Evidently, alcohol stimulates the endogenous opioid system (among others) and naltrexone blocks these effects, as it does for those of morphine. However, acamprosate seems to reduce craving by blocking the ability of glutamate to stimulate electrical activity in cortical neurons (Spanagel & Zieglgansberger, 1997).

There is a strong correlation between smoking and depression (Anda et al., 1990). Depression is four times more common in women than in men, and smoking rates among women are rising, making this public health issue particularly important for women. Fortunately, there is considerable evidence that the use of antidepressants in conjunction with the nicotine patch may be effective in smoking cessation. For example, bupropion (Zyban) is an antidepressant drug that also decreases craving for nicotine, even in people who are not depressed, perhaps because of its effects on the dopamine system.

Other medications that are regularly used to treat mental disorders have been found to be useful in reducing craving for drugs of abuse, reminding us once again that all these drugs have broad and multiple effects on a variety of neurotransmitter systems. For example, buspirone is an effective agent in treating anxiety disorders in alcoholics and may also reduce craving for alcohol, presumably by increasing brain serotonin (5-HT) levels (Kranzler et al., 1994). Tiapride also reduces craving for alcohol, and has antipsychotic effects as well, through effects on brain dopamine levels (Shaw et al., 1994). Desipramine is another antidepressant that has had limited effectiveness in reducing craving for cocaine in nondepressed addicts by raising brain dopamine levels (Gawin et al., 1989).

Research into medications to control drug craving is expanding rapidly, as we learn more and more about the way drugs affect the brain. For example, Dewey et al. (1998) recently found that in animals, an epilepsy drug called gamma vinyl-GABA (GVG) blocks the rise in levels of the neurotransmitter dopamine in certain areas of the brain. Using GVG to modulate dopamine levels is a novel approach to treating cocaine and nicotine craving: Dewey and his colleagues are now developing trials with GVG to assess its effectiveness in treating human addiction.

Aversion or avoidance. It is possible to treat drug addiction by pairing ingestion of the drug with an aversive event, like an electric shock or the administration of another drug that induces vomiting. When this has been done repeatedly, the patient finds that even thinking about the drug of choice induces fear or nausea. This sort of pharmacotherapy has been used most successfully in treating alcohol abuse, but the method fell into disfavor and was abandoned—prematurely, say some authorities (Altman et al., 1996).

It is also possible to give the patient a drug that interferes with the metabolism of the drug of choice, again resulting in aversive effects. For example, disulfiram (Antabuse) and calcium carbamide (Abstem) block the metabolism of alcohol, increasing the amount of acetylaldehyde present in the blood stream. This makes anyone who has taken disulfiram and then drinks an alcoholic beverage very sick. In fact, the results of taking disulfiram and then drinking alcohol are so aversive that most patients simply stop taking the disulfiram and keep on drinking. This failure to comply with the medication regimen can sometimes be changed with behavioral contracts (see Psychotherapy and Related Approaches, following), but usually, other drugs and methods are tried first.

Vaccines. The concept of using the immune system to produce antibodies to the presence of cocaine or other drugs of abuse is not new. However, the major problem with a vaccine is that the drug user can choose to overwhelm the vaccine's effects by taking a massive dose of the drug of choice. This does overwhelm the body's vaccine-induced immune response, but it also puts the user at grave risk of death or other toxic effects of drug overdose. Or, the user could simply substitute a similar drug (say, methamphetamine) for the drug against which he or she had been inoculated (cocaine). The immunity to cocaine would not confer immunity to methamphetamine's effects, and the user would get the desired high anyway. In addition, the effects of such vaccines are short-lived and frequent revaccination would be required; the continuing effectiveness of repeated vaccinations is unknown. Clearly, patient compliance would be a serious issue with this form of pharmacological treatment.

Targeting comorbidity–underlying states. As described in detail in chapter 1 of this volume, many, perhaps most, drug abusers also have from other psychiatric disorders, such as depression, antisocial personality disorder, or anxiety disorders. This condition of having more than one disorder is called comorbidity, and it sometimes happens that treating the patient for the underlying mental disorder significantly alters the drug abuse behavior. Occasionally, the reverse happens and treating a patient for drug abuse unmasks a comorbid mental disorder. The causes of comorbidity are not at all clear (see chap. 1), and research in this area is extremely difficult, so proper treatment in these cases can be very challenging.

Medications commonly used to treat conditions like depression in nonaddicts can sometimes be useful in treating depression in addicts. Desipramine, for example, has been used successfully to treat depression in cocaine addicts, and it appears to decrease craving for cocaine as well. However, many therapists have found that treatment of a mental disorder with abusable medications like benzodiazepines (Librium, Valium) can frequently lead to relapse to drug abuse, although other medications can be useful. Unfortunately, for the most part, the prognosis is usually poorer for drug abuse patients with comorbid severe psychiatric conditions.

Current Status

Psychopharmacological approaches to drug abuse treatment form an essential part of the therapist's treatment inventory. It has been demonstrated repeatedly, however, that medication alone is not enough to cure drug abuse. Medication can make it possible for the patient to be physically comfortable enough to initiate and to continue to participate in behavioral and psychosocial programs that will teach him or her the skills and behaviors needed to build a life without drugs. Because drug abuse is a chronic, relapsing disorder, medication may be needed continuously or intermittently for many years to break the cycle of addiction.

Psychosocial Approaches

12 Step Programs

History. Fellowship/self-help 12 step programs are probably the most available and commonly used intervention for substance abuse. The original and still most widely used of these programs is Alcoholics Anonymous (AA), which was developed in relation to and primarily targets alcohol problems. However, many drug abusers and polysubstance abusers attend or at least try AA or its counterpart organization, Narcotics Anonymous (NA), which has the same structure and guiding principles. Many other modalities of drug abuse intervention either include a 12 step program component or refer their patients to one. AA groups are available in most cities in the United States and can be found in over 150 countries around the world. Other related groups include Al-Anon, which helps the families and friends of alcoholics; Alateen, which helps teenagers who have family or friends who are alcoholics; and Adult Children of Alcoholics to help those who grew up with alcoholic parents.

Derived from the teachings of the Oxford Group and begun in 1935 by "Bill W." Wilson and "Dr. Bob" Smith, two men attempting to cope with their own alcohol dependence, the program has continued to be a grassroots lay organization eschewing psychiatric and behavioral science research, intervention techniques, and concepts. In fact, AA is not technically psychotherapy or treatment, although it is certainly an often helpful intervention. Basically, 12 step programs are support groups whose benefits are achieved through participation in a strong and active fellowship that provides clear coping directives and interpersonal resources. (A description of AA can be found in Alcoholics Anonymous, 1976.)

NA was first developed in 1947 at the U.S. Public Health Service Hospital in Lexington, Kentucky but expanded and disseminated in subsequent years in the AA tradition, independent of specific institutional affiliation, by individuals coping with drug abuse problems. Cocaine Anonymous (CA) also follows the AA model. Whereas AA focuses on alcohol and alcoholism as the target problems, the members of NA and CA generally are abusers of heroin and cocaine, respectively. The three programs are largely the same and can be described together under the general category of 12 step substance abuse programs.

Primary concept. Substance-abuse-focused 12 step programs consider abuse–addiction–dependence to be a disease whose remedy must be an essentially spiritual one. Participants are encouraged to admit their powerlessness over their disease (step 1), to turn their lives over to a higher power (steps 2 and 3, also related to steps 6, 7, and 11), and to focus on the present; taking one day at a time, avoiding drinking or drug use one day at a time. The disease is assumed to be a biologically based vulnerability to loss of control over any use of the alcohol or drug. The metaphor is recovery from an illness. Alcoholism (or drug addiction) is viewed as a progressive illness that can never be cured. Therefore, abstinence is a necessary goal and the problem that alcoholics and addicts must conquer is alcohol or drugs. Abstinence permits correction of the problems that substance abuse caused. Other steps involve making a "searching and fearless inventory" of one's self (steps 4 and 10), admitting past wrongs (steps 5 and 10), making amends (steps 8 and 9), and practicing and propagating the spiritual message to others (step 12).

Description. Participants attend group meetings that are the primary activity of the program. When first coming to AA or NA, new members are strongly encouraged to attend 90 meetings in 90 days. This facilitates an intense immersion and provides a great deal of support for abstinence, as well as alternative structured activities. Research has shown that the first 90 days after the discontinuance of drug or alcohol abuse is the period of highest risk for relapse (Marlatt and Gordon, 1985). Reactions to 12 step programs vary, and many who attend do not continue; according to data collected by AA in its triennial surveys conducted since 1968, there is a 50% dropout rate within the first 3 months (Chappel, 1993).

Although meetings vary in constituency, tone, format, and leadership, there are three primary types. The first type is a speaker meeting during which participants tell their story including their history, insights, current challenges, and attempts to overcome their problems. Speaker presentations often facilitate insights in the listeners, provide coping models, enhance the sense of a fellowship facing a common adversary, offer instruction in dealing with problems, and, despite the anonymity of the meetings, foster a sense of personal involvement and intimacy with other AA members. The second type of meeting is an open discussion in which issues, problems, and experiences are raised and discussed in a group format. A third type of meeting is a step meeting in which different steps are a theme for discussion and members talk about the relationship of the step to their past or present experience.

An important component of 12 step substance abuse programs is the system of sponsorship. A sponsor is a program member who has preceded the newer member and has an experience-based understanding of both the problems of the substance abuser and the 12 step path. The sponsor becomes a mentor, a guide, often a confidante, and a person to turn to when help is needed, including during a crisis of temptation. Sponsors often play a critical role, particularly for the newly sober member. Although not every

12 step member has a sponsor, many do, and many attribute their success in the 12 step programs to the sponsorship system. It is not an uncommon observation that sponsorship helps the sponsor as much as it does the member.

Current status. Research on self-help groups is difficult in general and particularly so for groups that emphasize anonymity and independence from the institutional research and clinical communities. There are only a few outcome studies of the effectiveness of 12 step substance abuse programs, and the subjects of these studies were alcohol abusers. Research is limited and somewhat equivocal on the effectiveness of these programs for alcoholics, and research is not available on their effectiveness with drug addicts. However, as part of Project MATCH (1998), a program for facilitating 12 step interventions for alcoholics was developed. The program has been published in a manual (Nowinski, Baker, & Carroll, 1994) and shows promise for use with drug users. Although 12 step programs may have diverse benefits for participants with varying degrees of involvement, there is some indication that benefit is associated with a high level of involvement; Vaillant (1983) reported that AA members who achieved a "stable sobriety" were more likely to have attended at least 300 meetings.

Despite the absence of empirical support for the 12 step programs, they are widely believed to be helpful for at least some substance abusers. Even those who question the effectiveness of these programs as a primary intervention often consider them to be useful adjuncts to other interventions either as supplements during therapy or as aftercare. In addition, 12 step programs are not the only drug abuse self-help programs. Smart Recovery, Women for Sobriety, Save Our Selves, and Overcomers Outreach are examples of other groups and it is likely that new models and organizations will continue to emerge.

Therapeutic Communities

History. Therapeutic communities arose from the popular culture of the 1960s during which like-minded people banded into communes to support and live with each other. Charles Dederich and a group of recovering drug addicts and alcoholics founded a self-help community of heroin addicts, basing their treatment on their own experiences and mutual encouragement (Deitch, 1973). Since that era, distrust of the services of mental health professionals has faded somewhat, and professional treatment services have been added to the therapeutic community milieu. Therapeutic communities now treat diverse populations with a wide range of addictions and combine what they believe are the most useful aspects of self-help programs and professional treatment services in the therapeutic community setting.

Primary concept. Therapeutic communities are based on the concept that addiction is a disorder of the whole person, both psychologically and socially. The therapeutic community is essentially a massive and broad spectrum developmental effort to rebuild the person through a long-term, residential drug-free treatment program. The community actually becomes the treatment agent: All the members and activities of the community are involved in and devoted to producing therapeutic changes in each individual. Therapeutic communities differ from other treatment approaches by "the purposive use of the peer community to facilitate social and psychological change in individuals" (De Leon, chap. 15, this volume). The addict is expected to learn "right living" from the other members of the community.

Description. There are three stages of treatment in a therapeutic community. The initial orientation–induction phase lasts up to 8 weeks and has the highest dropout rate. During this period, the addict is isolated from his home community and ties while trying to adjust to the mores and customs of the therapeutic community. During the second stage of treatment, which can last from 15 to 24 months, clients participate in group therapy sessions, jobs within the community, and constant feedback by peers and staff on performance. The group therapy and feedback sessions are often very confrontational and may resemble encounter group sessions. This is quite different from some forms of group therapy (see Group Therapy Approaches that follow), which usually emphasize empathy with the client. In the final stage of treatment, called "re-entry," the client gradually moves out to the "real world," but maintains many ties with the therapeutic community.

Current status. In the era of managed care, therapeutic communities, like so many other drug abuse treatment services, have come to realize that their funding depends on their ability to prove their efficacy and cost-effectiveness. This is especially true because of the very long-term nature of treatment in a therapeutic community. It can be difficult to do evaluative research on therapeutic communities, but there are limited demonstrations of their effectiveness. De Leon (chap. 15, this volume) describes in detail the many different structures of today's therapeutic communities and current research on their effectiveness.

Psychodynamic Approaches

History. The earliest psychoanalytic concepts of substance abuse were developed by Freud and described in the late 1880s in his *Cocaine Papers* (Byck, 1974). His theory of addiction stressed the "id dynamic," the gratification of instinctual needs, oral cravings, and regression toward infantile fixations (see Freud, 1905/1949, 1930/1964). Although Freud hypothesized that masturbation was the "primal addiction" for which all later addictions are substituted, most early psychoanalytic views of addiction saw alcohol and drug abuse as "oral phenomena."

Numerous alternative psychodynamic theories have been proposed, and the approaches to substance abuse have evolved along with the psychodynamic perspective. In addition to the need gratification approaches described above, some approaches following the "ego psychology" tradition have focused on substance abuse in relation to the defensive structures, particularly defense against dysphoric self-judgments (e.g., guilt, shame, denial of homosexuality), against unacceptable drives (e.g., aggression), or the defense against and management of intolerable or overwhelming affects (i.e., the self-medication hypothesis). Other approaches have focused on the loss of control associated with substance abuse and the inadequacy or deterioration of underlying states and structures. These theories emphasize psychic trauma, neurotic conflict, and psychotic disintegration. Still other dynamic theories of substance abuse are based on object relations approaches, whereas others emphasize interpersonal relationships. Although there has been considerable psychodynamic theorizing about substance abuse, this has not resulted in widespread efforts to provide psychodynamically oriented treatment.

Primary concept. Although there is enormous variability among psychodynamic approaches to understanding drug and alcohol abuse, it is generally characteristic of these approaches to view alcohol and drug abuse as symptoms of underlying dynamics and not the cause of the primary problems. Psychodynamic "insight oriented" treatment of drug abuse focuses on the underlying causes and processes, with relatively little attention focused on the concrete aspects and manifest behaviors of drug abuse as primary targets of treatment.

Description. Although historically there have continued to be psychodynamically oriented psychotherapists who have theorized about and developed treatments for alcoholics and drug abusers, many dynamically oriented psychotherapists have viewed substance abusers as unsuitable for psychoanalysis. As a result, it was not uncommon for substance abusers to be referred by psychodynamically oriented psychotherapists to programs such as Alcoholics Anonymous. More recently, many psychodynamically based psychotherapists have taken a more optimistic perspective and have offered treatment and developed specific approaches to treatment for substance abusers. For both older and contemporary dynamic therapies for substance abuse, techniques of treatment are drawn from the standard psychodynamic repertoire being selected or modified in accordance with the specific theoretical orientation of the therapist and the presentation of the patient.

Current status. There is little empirical support for psychodynamic therapies for substance abuse, and for the most part, they are not a primary intervention modality used with drug abusers. Several recent psychodynamically oriented approaches have been developed that have attracted some attention and present interesting possibilities. One of these approaches has been developed by Khantzian (1997) and is based on a self-medication hypothesis of drug abuse. Another uses an interpersonal therapy approach (Klerman, Weissman, Rounsaville, & Chevron, 1984) and emphasizes interpersonal relationships (Carroll, Rounsaville, & Gawin, 1991), and a third emphasizes a supportive–expressive psychotherapy approach (Crits-Christoph et al., 1999; Woody et al., 1983; Woody, McLellan, Luborsky, & O'Brien, 1987, 1995).

Behavioral Approaches

History. Behavioral approaches to drug abuse treatment have their theoretical roots in the work of Pavlov and Skinner on classical and operant conditioning. Their roots in clinical applications go back to the use of behavioral principles in the treatment and training of mentally ill and mentally handicapped patients in the 1950s and 1960s (e.g., Ayllon & Azrin, 1965; Ayllon & Haughton, 1962). In addition, the powerful pharmacological reinforcing characteristics of abused drugs encouraged behaviorally oriented theorists and clinicians to apply behavioral concepts to the understanding and treatment of drug abuse. The first drug abuse treatment programs using behavioral and social learning principles were developed by Azrin and his colleagues (Azrin, Sisson, Meyers, & Godley, 1982), Martlatt (1978), Sobell and Sobell (1978), and Bandura (1977) in the 1960s and 1970s. The first programs were developed for treating alcoholics and then later adapted for use with other substance abusers.

Today, virtually every type of drug abuse therapy incorporates at least some aspect of behavioral and social learning theory in its treatment program. For example, many psychopharmacological treatments could be said to be compatible with the behavioral principle of reducing the occurrence of a behavior by reducing the positive reinforcement associated with that behavior, that is, by using a medication that blocks the high of drugs like heroin or cocaine. Similarly, many other approaches, such as therapeutic communities, could be said to be compatible with the behavioral principle of reducing the occurrence of an undesirable behavior like drug use by controlling or reducing the discriminative stimuli associated with drug use in the environment. However, the most direct applications of behavioral principles to the treatment of drug addiction involve contingency management.

Primary concept. The main principle of operant behavior theory is that behavior is controlled by (or is contingent on) its consequences. A variety of environmental stimuli (both external and internal) become signals (or cues) that elicit a behavioral response. In turn, the response is reinforced (made more likely to occur again) positively (by a reinforcer or reward) or negatively. Negative reinforcement (making a behavior *more* likely to occur) is frequently confused with punishment, which reduces or extinguishes responding (making it *less* likely to occur). For a complete discussion of the major principles of behavior modification, see Bandura (1969).

Social learning theory (see Bandura, 1977) is part of behavior theory that describes and explains the many ways people learn from each other. This may be by direct instruction or teaching, by example (modeling, or imitating behavior observed in someone else), or by role playing (rehearsing ahead of time a behavior or response one expects to have to make in a certain situation).

Description. Behavioral approaches have used the principles of both classical and operant conditioning and of social learning theory to treat recovering addicts. The principles are applied to increase the occurrence of desirable behaviors like improved exercise and sleeping habits, and to decrease the occurrence of undesirable behaviors like drug use and associating with other drug users.

The principles of classical (Pavlovian) conditioning have been applied during research on drug abuse treatment by the use of aversive conditioning and cue extinction techniques. Although there have been many attempts to apply aversive conditioning (pairing electric shocks or emetics with drug use [see Aversion or Avoidance earlier in this chapter]) to the treatment of alcohol and nicotine dependence, this approach has not generally been applied to illicit drug abuse. The few reported efforts have mostly been case studies or studies with small numbers of subjects, and they have been only moderately successful.

Cue extinction techniques involve repeatedly exposing the client to triggers or cues associated with drug use, like injection equipment, but without the rewarding rush or high of drug use. By repeated exposure to the cue, disassociated from the usual reward, the cue can lose its power to elicit drug cravings. Sometimes the clients are also taught relaxation and resistance techniques to use when faced with drug-associated stimuli. Because these procedures work in the laboratory but have been only moderately successful clinically, they have generally not been incorporated into treatment programs, except for cocaine treatment programs that have reported some success. When cue extinction procedures have been used, it is generally as part of managing the client's environment in a larger therapy program (Childress, Hole, Ehrman, & Robbins, 1993).

On the other hand, the use of operant conditioning techniques has been so successful in treating drug abuse that many types of treatment programs incorporate some of them into some aspects of therapy. The consequences may be rewarding or aversive, but they are tied directly to the patient's behavior. In practice, the approach frequently uses behavioral contracting or some other form of contingency management. For example, a mutually agreed on contract is established with the patient in which behaviors under his or her control related to the use of drugs (or other therapeutic goals) are described. By accomplishing one or more of these behaviors, the patient earns predetermined rewards or positive reinforcement. When a patient satisfies a behaviorally defined criterion, for example, having a drug screening urinalysis show that he or she has not used prohibited drugs in the last month, he or she gets a reward.

A variety of incentives have been used in the treatment milieu: money, vouchers to obtain retail goods, food, or access to recreational or social opportunities in the community. For many opiate-addicted patients, the privilege of taking their methadone doses at home for two weeks, rather than having to come daily to a clinic to take the doses under supervision, is a very desirable incentive. In the community reinforcement approach (CRA), clients are rewarded for submitting drug-free urine samples with vouchers that can be exchanged for needed items or services in the general community. The items must be deemed by the counselor to be therapeutically beneficial, that is, used to develop prosocial behaviors and activities.

Contingent punishments, sometimes identified as "limit setting" approaches, are also sometimes incorporated into behavioral contracts. They are based on the principle that a violation of a behaviorally defined criterion results in a punishment, like a fine, the loss of take-home methadone privileges, or being required to do specific chores around the treatment facility. In some contracts, the punishment can be quite severe, like the loss of probation, or the loss of a medical or legal license. Behavioral contracts involving such punitive consequences must be entered into by client and therapist alike with serious consideration and commitment.

Structured behavioral therapy programs can be used for inpatient or outpatient settings; they are frequently found in methadone-maintenance clinics and in private therapy sessions. In the clinic, the contingency contract is usually quite simple, for example, provide six consecutive drug-free urine samples and receive a take-home dose of methadone. As the client proves himself or herself capable of submitting more and more drug-free urine samples, the greater the number of take-home doses of methadone he or she receives. In private therapy sessions, the approach is individualized and the behavioral contracts are frequently very elaborate, spelling out a wide range of behaviors and contingencies.

Another application of behavioral principles, social learning techniques, is used in most therapeutic milieus. By use of direct instruction, role playing, or watching someone else act as a model or example, clients can be taught a variety of skills that will be useful to them as they strive to achieve drug-free lives. Training sessions are usually selected to fit the client's particular needs, and might include:

- social skills training (refusal skills, assertiveness training)
- coping and problem solving skills

- relaxation and other affect management skills
- relapse prevention
- behavioral self-control
- stress management

For a thorough discussion of behavioral approaches to drug abuse therapy, see Rotgers (1996).

Current status. The use of these principles in drug abuse treatment has had considerable success, especially those based on positive reinforcement. The most effective incentives have been money (Stitzer, Bigelow, & Liebson, 1980), or money-based vouchers (Higgins, Budney, Bickel, Foerg et al., 1994), and take-home doses of methadone (Stitzer, Iguchi, & Felch, 1992). The techniques work well with both heroin users (Hall, Bass, Hargreaves, & Loeb, 1979; Milby, Garrett, English, Fritschi, & Clarke, 1978; Kidorf, Hollander, King, & Brooner, 1998) and cocaine users (Higgins, Budney, Bickel, Foerg et al., 1994; Silverman et al., 1996). In their recent book, Higgins and Silverman (1999) present a complete and critical review of research on contingency management interventions.

There are, of course, some practical difficulties in the application of behavioral techniques to substance abuse treatment. For example, the reinforcers and the frequent analysis of urine specimens can be quite costly. By basing the contingent behavior on drug-free urines, the therapists may fail to take advantage of the usefulness of drug abuse counseling (McLellan, Woody, Luborsky, & Goehl, 1988). Furthermore, as many as 50% of clients fail to earn even one reinforcer, which suggests that the desired behavior (producing a drug-free urine sample) is too hard for those clients or that the reinforcer simply is not reinforcing enough (Stitzer et al., 1992). Much higher rates of success have been achieved when this approach is combined with others (see community-based approaches following).

Iguchi and his colleagues (Iguchi, Belding, Morral, Lamb, & Husband, 1997) have recently described a more sophisticated behavioral treatment approach based on the use of positive reinforcement that obviates some of these problems. Instead of reinforcing behavior directly related to treatment (drug-free urine samples, attending therapy sessions), they found that by reinforcing behavior incompatible with drug use, they could gradually shape the desired drug-free behaviors. For example, the counselor and client might determine that the client needed a job, and they would agree that the client would earn a certain number of vouchers for bringing job-related literature to the next counseling session. If the client did that and received his or her vouchers, then he or she and the counselor would agree on a new goal for the next week, for example, signing up for a training or refresher class—again earning more vouchers. This would give the client the skills he or she needed to do something usually incompatible with drug use: holding a job.

If a client found attending necessary counseling sessions difficult, the client and counselor might work out a plan whereby he or she could earn vouchers for phoning in for a brief counseling session. Once that behavior was established, he or she could earn vouchers simply for showing up for an in-clinic session and even more for staying for a certain period of time. Eventually, the client and counselor would work on establishing other drug-free behaviors as well. Clearly, this approach of using differential reinforcement of alternative behavior works best with individualized treatment plans that have specific treatment-related tasks defined for each client. Iguchi and his colleagues reported that the clients in this program demonstrated significant abstinence rates over time, and that these gains were maintained after the intervention period.

Cognitive and Cognitive–Behavioral Approaches

History. Contemporary cognitive and cognitive–behavior therapies originated during the 1960s and 1970s. Primarily focusing on affective disorders, Beck, Ellis, Meichenbaum, Goldfried, and others developed short-term, focused, skills-based, cognitively oriented and structured protocols that quickly become recognized and increasingly adopted as effective therapies for depression and anxiety disorders. With the rapidly expanding interest in cognitively oriented therapies, applications were developed for the treatment of other psychopathologies.

Based on these approaches, several cognitive therapy protocols were developed for the treatment of alcoholism. Sanchez-Craig (1974, 1980) described the effective use of a cognitively oriented therapy with alcoholics. Glantz (Glantz, 1987; Glantz & McCourt, 1983; McCourt & Glantz, 1980) proposed a multidimensional cognitive model of alcoholism and described a successful modification of cognitive therapies combined with behavioral techniques for use with alcoholics. Abrahms (1979) reported the effective use of an adaptation of cognitive therapy with drug abusers. Marlatt (1978, 1979) developed a cognitive–behavioral model of alcoholism that focused on craving and relapse and recommended a treatment approach that is a combination of existing skills training techniques. Beck and Ellis, two of the originators of cognitively oriented therapies, subsequently developed modifications of their approaches specifically for substance abusers (Beck, Wright, Newman, & Liese, 1993; Ellis, McInerney, DiGiuseppe, & Yaeger, 1988). Marlatt's model and his approach (see Marlatt & Gordon, 1985) have become the foundation of substance abuse relapse prevention in many treatment protocols; this approach will be discussed separately. There are numerous variations of cognitively oriented therapy with substance abusers developed by various practitioners. Some are more cognitively based (e.g., the cognitive therapy developed by Beck). Some integrate cognitive techniques with behavioral and skills based techniques; these are usually referred to as cognitive behavioral approaches (such as those therapies based on Marlatt's models and relapse prevention techniques). There are significant differences between these various therapies and there is some empirical indication that they may vary in their effectiveness. For the purposes of this overview, the general modality of cognitively oriented therapies with substance abusers will be discussed under the general rubric of cognitive therapy.

Primary concept. Although cognitive therapies draw heavily on social learning theories and most use adjunct behavioral techniques, the defining characteristic of the modality is that it is built on the premise of the cognitive mediation of behavior. Cognitive therapies focus on altering the thoughts, beliefs, and cognitive patterns and processes that lead to maladaptive behaviors including substance abuse. For example, in Beck's approach (Beck et al., 1993), substance abuse is viewed as a maladaptive coping response reinforced by dysfunctional beliefs and automatic negative thoughts, soon becoming a vicious cycle of using and maladaptive coping with the consequences. Ellis and colleagues (1988) postulate that irrational beliefs lead to low frustration tolerance, particularly in people with impulse control problems; as a result, individuals following this pattern are unable to resist the feeling of deprivation they associate with abstaining from their desired abusable substance. Glantz (1995) proposes a multidimensional maladaptive coping model of alcoholism in which the maladaptive cognitive determinants are more complex and individualized and frequently intertwined with comorbid psychiatric conditions.

Cognitive therapy focuses on changing cognitive patterns and the information processing problems that help to reinforce them, for example, dichotomous (i.e., black–white) thinking. General coping skills are taught, but there is a great emphasis on skills that are specifically related to anticipating and coping with thoughts, feelings, and circumstances related to substance use, craving, and relapse. Alternative adaptive patterns of thought and behavior, as well as alternative reinforcers, are developed. Although structured, cognitive therapy is individualized in the sense that it focuses on the specific needs and circumstances of the particular patient. Cognitive therapy for substance abuse always includes a strong emphasis on relapse prevention.

Description. Cognitive therapy approaches for drug abusers are very similar in concept and methods to those designed for use with alcoholics. The approach is relatively short term and fairly structured and is readily described step by step in a treatment manual, even though the treatment plan is individualized for each patient. It is used in both individual and group formats. There are basic components common to most versions of the approach:

- teaching of the cognitive mediation model
- individual case formulation, that is, identification of the in-

dividual patient's maladaptive conceptualizations, patterns, and responses, particularly those related to substance abuse

- identification of the individual's high risk situations for craving and drug use
- development of alternative conceptualizations and responses including training for specific drug-abuse-related avoidance skills
- lifestyle changes including setting and working toward realistic goals
- teaching general coping skills, including the management of practical life problems, affect management, and others
- relapse prevention
- treatment of comorbid psychiatric conditions as appropriate

Several detailed manuals are available describing particular cognitive therapy protocols with alcoholics (Glantz & McCourt, 1983; Kadden et al., 1995) and drug abusers (Carroll, 1998).

Current status. Empirical evidence supports the efficacy of cognitive therapy adaptations for the treatment of drug abuse (e.g., Carroll, 1998; Carroll et al., 1991; Carroll, Nich, Ball, McCance, & Rounsaville, 1998; Carroll, Rounsaville, Gordon, et al., 1994; Carroll, Rounsaville, Nich, et al., 1994; Maude-Griffin et al., 1998; McKay, Alterman, Cacciola, Rutherford, & O'Brien, 1997; Woody et al., 1983; Woody et al., 1987), as well as for alcoholism (e.g., Project MATCH Research Group, 1998). However, not all studies have demonstrated the comparative effectiveness of cognitive therapy (Crits-Christoph et al., 1999) which may be related to a number of factors including the variation of cognitive therapy that is used. The effectiveness of the cognitive-therapy-based relapse prevention as proposed by Marlatt (1979) is also clearly supported and is an integral part of many diverse treatment programs. Cognitive therapy for drug abuse is gaining increasing acceptance and use, and further development and research investigation of the modality are likely to continue.

Relapse Prevention

History. In the mid-1970s, Marlatt (1978, 1979) developed a structured approach to preventing relapse to alcohol use. Relapse prevention is a cognitive behavioral approach that draws on many principles of social learning theory to teach the addict how to maintain abstinence. The approach was not conceptualized as a stand-alone theory, but as an adjunctive strategy for therapy. Marlatt observed that two thirds of relapses occur within the first 90 days of treatment and that 80% of clients relapse by the end of the first year. It was clear that clients did not have the skills to maintain abstinence and that this deficiency must be addressed directly during treatment. These observations have been key in shaping our contemporary understanding of drug abuse as a chronic, relapsing disorder and in shaping our attempts to deal with it.

Primary concept. Relapse prevention strategies recognize that lapses are virtually inevitable. The therapist and client must prepare for, and even rehearse responses to, lapses from a drug- or alcohol-free life. In this model, substance abuse is construed to be a learned behavior. To prevent relapse or to recover again after a lapse, the therapist helps the client to identify personal, specific, high-risk situations for relapse and to develop anticipatory coping strategies for dealing with them.

Description. Marlatt and Gordon (1985) observed that once a client lapsed to drug use, even after many weeks or months of abstinence, the client was very likely to relapse completely. It was as if the client felt that because he or she had failed and was abusing drugs or alcohol again, he or she might as well give up trying not to. This is called the *abstinence violation effect:* the return to increased drug use because of the client's cognitive and emotional reaction to an initial lapse. The lapse violates the client's self-image as a recovering person, one who has vowed to be and was being abstinent. Furthermore, the client attributes the lapse to critical and enduring faults in himself or herself.

In addition, lapses are more likely to occur if the individual does not believe he or she has effective coping responses to deal with situations of potential use, and he or she expected beneficial effects from substance use in the particular situation, like peer approval or a better mood. Clearly, it is necessary to train the patient to realize that a lapse is only one choice point, not ultimate failure. The patient must be prepared in advance to re-attempt abstinence and must believe that he or she can do it. An important aspect of the relapse prevention approach is to increase the clients' sense of self-efficacy. They must believe they have the skills to cope with lapses, because relapse is more likely when the client attributes the lapse to internal, stable, and global causes: that he or she is weak and lacks moral fiber or willpower, and thus it is futile to even try to be abstinent. They must be taught techniques to avoid high-risk situations and how to avoid treating a lapse as a trigger for further drug use. In accomplishing this, relapse prevention uses many of the techniques of cognitive–behavioral therapy, described previously, to achieve its goals.

First, the client and therapist must learn to identify high-risk situations specific to the individual. Participants in Marlatt's research reported that three types of situations accounted for three quarters of their relapses: negative emotional states (35%), social pressure to use alcohol or drugs (20%), and interpersonal conflict (16%). Other clinicians (Annis & Graham, 1995; Gorski, 1988a, 1988b) have developed concrete methods for helping the therapist and the client to identify specific triggers (internal or environmental cues) or patterns of triggers for drug use.

Then, the therapist and client must develop strategies for avoiding these situations or dealing with them appropriately when they are un-avoidable. These techniques focus on maintenance of behavior change and may involve cue extinction, the development of new skills, the use of drug screening, the adoption of behaviors incompatible with drug use (see above), and so on. Cue extinction refers to the process by which triggers (cues) for drug use (like associating a specific street corner with buying drugs) are made less salient for drug use and are made neutral or even cues for some other incompatible behavior. New skills might involve learning how to make new friends who are not involved with drugs, or assertiveness training that will enable the client to avoid being put into situations in which drug use is likely to occur. They might also include positive, healthy behaviors, like daily exercise or relaxation techniques, that are incompat-ible with drug use. Drug screening may be used to help the client and therapist to determine whether the client is meeting his or her goals. Clearly, relapse prevention techniques do not stand alone; they are typi-cally adjunctive to or combined with many other therapeutic strategies, particularly the many forms of cognitive and behavioral therapies.

Current status. Relapse prevention approaches have been adapted to a variety of different uses; the techniques were quickly extended to treat-ment strategies for drugs of abuse other than alcohol. The effectiveness of these approaches has been supported by considerable empirical research on established therapies with or without a relapse prevention component in-cluded (Allsop, Saunders, Phillips, & Carr, 1997; O'Farrell, Choquette, & Cutter, 1998). Relapse prevention has also been incorporated into treat-ment effectiveness studies that compare two different therapy formats, both of which incorporate relapse prevention techniques—for example, group versus individual therapy in Schmitz et al. (1997) and Graham, Annis, Brett, and Venesoen (1996). In these two cases at least, format apparently does not alter the efficacy of the relapse prevention training.

Not all of Marlatt's original theoretical contributions regarding the abstinence violation effect have proved completely correct when subjected to further research. However, the general approach has been shown re-peatedly to be supported empirically, and effective in reducing relapse to drug use. The techniques and strategies of relapse prevention have provided therapists and clients alike with necessary tools in the treatment of drug addiction.

Community-Based Approaches

History. In its original form, community-based treatment was envi-sioned as a comprehensive, multimodal, and labor intensive type of ther-apy. Ideally, it would reach all levels in the community, tying together a broad range of social services, vocational training, health and mental health care, child care, and education. Local ordinances, laws, and policies would be modified to contribute to treatment goals. Local businesses and schools would provide easy access to treatment for employees and students. Drop-in clinics would be available, and treatment groups would be meeting at a variety of times and places to accommodate the schedules of addicts, families, or employees involved in treatment. Unfortunately, this vision remained only a vision because competing interests made the establishment of such a system both impractical and very expensive.

As visions of this comprehensive approach faded, Azrin and his colleagues (Azrin et al., 1982; Sisson & Azrin, 1989) originated the use of the community reinforcement approach (CRA) for the treatment of alcoholism. Stitzer and colleagues (1980) adapted contingency management procedures for use with opiate addicts, proving their usefulness. Building on both kinds of research, Higgins and his colleagues have developed a program of treating cocaine addiction through the community reinforcement plus vouchers approach (CRA+Vouchers). The CRA+Vouchers approach has achieved significant success and is described in its entirety in a recent therapy manual (Budney & Higgins, 1998).

Primary concept. The approach is built on structured counseling sessions that use behavioral techniques to help the client get involved in new social and recreational activities, begin new employment or educational opportunities, and obtain more satisfaction from relationships with family and friends. This is done through behavioral contracting for drug abstinence; the incentives used in this program are vouchers that the client earns by staying in treatment and having drug-free urine specimens. The vouchers are redeemable for activities available in the community that promote healthy behaviors, like dues for a hiking club, tickets to movies, or clothes to wear for a job interview. The therapist approves the requested items and then obtains them for the client once the client has earned enough points. Over a 12-week period, the vouchers can reach a total value of nearly $1,000.

Description. The CRA+Vouchers approach uses many techniques of contingency management, as described previously. These include the following:

- behavioral contracting
- effective goal setting
- modeling (or imitation) and role playing
- shaping successive approximations
- self-monitoring
- therapist prompting and monitoring
- the Premack principle (using a more frequently occurring preferred and socially acceptable behavior as reinforcement for a less frequently occurring nonpreferred and socially unacceptable one)

- skills training (e.g., social skills, problem solving, task analysis, relaxation, time management)

Structured counseling sessions are designed as modules to be incorporated as needed into individual treatment plans. These sessions are designed to teach clients the skills they will need to replace drugs in their lives. They are focused on topics like goal setting, sleep hygiene, HIV–AIDS prevention, social skills training, drug refusal and avoidance training, and counseling on relationships, employment, and developing social and recreational activities. The client is encouraged to develop these skills by the use of social reinforcement, not by the use of vouchers. The vouchers are used to reinforce the drug abstinence contract, which is an essential part of this form of therapy. The contract may include the use of medications to assist the client in achieving abstinence. In particular, because 60% of clients are alcohol as well as drug dependent, disulfiram (Antabuse) therapy (see Psychopharmacology pp. 245–252) is included as part of the abstinence contract.

Current status. Higgins and his colleagues have conducted five controlled clinical trials to test the effectiveness of the CRA+Vouchers program. In two of these (Higgins et al., 1991, 1993), CRA+Vouchers proved more effective than standard counseling in retaining clients in treatment and in obtaining significant periods of cocaine abstinence. A third trial (Higgins, Budney, Bickel, Foerg et al., 1994) proved that the vouchers component of the program was critical to keeping patients in treatment and achieving longer periods of cocaine abstinence. Use of the vouchers in outpatient treatment was supported by a fourth trial as well (Budney & Higgins, 1998). The fifth trial, which was initially thought to be successful, tested whether social reinforcement provided by the clients' significant others was also effective in sustaining abstinence from cocaine use (Higgins, Budney, Bickel, Badger et al., 1994), but this later proved not to be the case.

The effectiveness of the CRA+Vouchers program has also been tested by other researchers. Silverman et al. (1996) and Tusel et al. (1995) examined the efficacy of the voucher aspect of the program in their clinical trials. They found that use of the vouchers increased abstinence significantly in cocaine abusers. Most recently, Abbott, Weller, Delaney, and Moore (1998) compared the contingency management aspect of the program with standard treatment at a methadone maintenance clinic by requiring weekly urinalysis drug screens. They found that CRA was significantly more effective than the standard treatment group in the number of consecutive opiate-negative drug screens and on the clients' self-assessment of the severity of their addiction.

Family Approaches

History. During the last 25 years, family approaches to drug abuse treatment and therapy have been increasingly recognized as more than just adjuncts to standard drug abuse treatment, which was frequently aimed at the young, single male, who was usually thought not to be in touch with his family. Study after study has shown that 85% to 90% of drug abusers are in touch with their families at least once a week and frequently even more often. Clinicians have found not only that do family dynamics sometimes explain how drug abuse became a problem for the family, but that changing these dynamics often provides the most effective type of treatment.

Primary concept. Family therapists often come from differing theoretical viewpoints, but most believe that abstinence must be achieved before treatment of the dysfunctional family can begin. Once abstinence has been achieved—no matter how fragile or temporary that state might be—the work of changing the destructive and repetitive patterns of family interactions must begin. This is a complex and long-term task for the family, the patient, and the therapist. Szapocznik and Kurtines (1989, 1993) emphasize that this is the defining characteristic of all family therapy approaches to drug abuse treatment: the transformation of maladaptive, repetitive patterns of family interactions.

There are a number of different theoretical orientations among family therapists.

- The disease model perceives not only the identified client as needing treatment, but also family members who are codependent parts of the addiction disorder.
- In the family behavior model, the interaction of all the family members is seen as a trigger or cue for the drug abuse behavior of one member. That behavior in turn triggers more maladaptive responses on the part of other family members. These behaviors reinforce even more drug use.
- In the family system model, each family member is perceived as having a role in the family system that he or she plays during interactions with other family members, including the identified client. These roles are frequently maladaptive attempts to handle the many problems associated with addiction. The object of therapy is to restore the family to homeostasis, with each member playing the appropriate role in the family system.

Despite these differences in theoretical orientation, the main task for the therapist and the family is the same: to recognize and alter as necessary each individual family member's contribution to the problem and the solution.

Description. Margolis and Zweben (1998) define the tasks faced by the family therapist, no matter what his or her theoretical orientation, as joining, stabilization, education, analysis of the family system or structures, teaching alternative coping strategies, and relapse prevention. All of these tasks are difficult and may use techniques and theoretical constructs from several different forms of therapy.

Joining refers to careful listening the therapist must do for each member of the family in order to affiliate with them and address their concerns. This can be very difficult when the family believes that "everything would be ok if only he'd stop using drugs," or, possibly even more difficult, the opposite, "He's definitely not using drugs, but we have these other issues we need to deal with." The therapist's task at this point is not to confirm or deny either viewpoint, but to support all the family members so that they know their contributions to each session will be valued and attended to.

Stabilization "refers to a set of intervention strategies that are designed to assist the patient in either abstaining from mood altering chemicals completely, or, when appropriate, reducing alcohol or other drug use to the point at which the patient's functioning is not impaired" (Margolis & Zweben, p. 211, 1998). The patient's loss of control must be the chief issue during this period, not the reasons why, which the family may think are all important. This makes it possible for the therapist to set up a behavioral contract with the patient (see Behavioral Approaches, previous) and to observe the effects of abstinence on all the members of the family. If abstinence is not a plausible immediate goal, alternative behaviors (attending classes, attending more to the children) may be established first, making abstinence possible later. There may also be other therapeutic tasks assigned to the drug user such as taking a therapeutic medication like methadone or Antabuse, or making the entire household drug- and alcohol-free.

As the patient's drug use decreases, he or she begins to discover that drug use had become the preferred method for coping with stress. Without drugs, the patient feels helpless and may become irritable or depressed or may even turn to violence or rage as outlets. This naturally disturbs the other family members. It is during this, the education phase of therapy, that the therapist reassures the family through his or her knowledge of dynamics of addiction and the usual sequence of events that occur during the passage from addiction to recovery. This is particularly important as the family sees the patient spending more time recovering than he or she does with them. It is also the appropriate time for the family members to begin to seek help from recovery programs themselves. This can reduce anxiety for both the patient and the family members.

The next stage of family therapy for addiction is the analysis of the family's systems and structures to determine which are dysfunctional and contributing to the addiction problem. It is a period of destabilization, as family members learn about the habits of interaction that continue to contribute to the family's main problems, and begin to build their own programs of recovery.

Obviously, now the therapist must begin to teach the family alternative coping strategies, to deal with the anxiety that will accompany these changes in behavior, many of which will reveal painful emotions of anger, depression, and distrust. New skills in communication and in handling family conflict are desperately needed by the family to continue to move forward.

The final and ongoing stage of family therapy is relapse prevention. Because drug addiction is a chronic, relapsing disorder, the family must be prepared not only to try to prevent relapse, but also to know what to do when it occurs. This includes recognizing the signs of relapse to drug use and recognizing relapse to dysfunctional behaviors by other family members. The family and the therapist must identify behaviors that trigger relapse for the patient; these may be feelings (anger or sadness) or pressure from peers, or major life stressors such as moving to a new city, starting a new job, or the serious illness or death of a family member. Then they must plan how to cope with these, so that relapse to drug use is prevented. Relapse prevention is discussed at length on page 263.

Current status. In 1997, Stanton and Shadish conducted a meta-analysis of 15 controlled studies that compared various forms of therapy for drug abuse with family therapy. Over 3,500 individuals participated in these 15 studies. Stanton and Shadish (p. 187) found that "studies that compared family—couple therapy with non-family modalities, such as individual counseling-therapy and peer group therapy, showed superior results for family therapy." This was true for families in which either an adolescent or an adult was the identified drug abuse client. Stanton and Shadish also point out the family therapies have high rates of engagement and retention, making them cost effective in today's managed care environment.

Group Therapy Approaches

History. Group therapy shares some of its history with 12 step programs and other self-help groups, but group therapy differs in that a therapist uses his or her knowledge of the addiction and recovery process to guide therapy sessions, and the group provides support, education, and understanding for its members, as well as expectations for success. There are many variations on the group approach, but usually they include therapist-led sessions.

Primary concept. Unlike the 12 step program and self-help groups, group therapy relies on the guidance and direction of the therapist, as well as the power of the group to effect change in its members. The group provides an empathetic milieu that promotes recovery by example, by some teaching based on experience, and by providing a mirror for new members of their own actions and motives. Recovery from addiction requires a long-term commitment, and group therapy can provide the venue the addict needs, which sometimes the individual therapist cannot.

Description. Groups led by professional therapists may be quite different in their nature and purposes. Some groups do not actually offer treatment, but are intended to motivate the addict to enter treatment, by allowing them to "see what it's all about," before making a commitment (Washton & Stone-Washton, 1991). Once the addict is motivated to begin treatment, he or she may join a recovery group. Most recovery groups are abstinence-based, but recently harm-reduction groups have begun to offer education and training to addicts who either cannot or will not abstain from drug use, but who do want to try to minimize the harm to themselves and others caused by their addiction.

Abstinence-based recovery groups may be part of large or small treatment programs. Larger programs may have enough clients to sort them into groups depending on their stage of recovery. Margolis and Zweben (pp. 240–241, 1998) define these as transition groups, for those who "are on a waiting list for treatment; Phase I groups for those in the process of establishing abstinence; Phase II groups for those in later stages of recovery." Thus, the client moves from group to group after meeting certain criteria, say, a particular length of continuous abstinence. The advantages here are that all the people in one group are facing similar problems, and movement from one group to the next allows the patient to mark progress. The disadvantage is that clients frequently do not want to leave a group with whom they shared so much.

Smaller programs or private practitioners usually find that their groups must include clients in various stages of recovery; this too has advantages and disadvantages. Clients can stay in such a group as long as they are making progress and have before them role models for better and for worse. No matter which model is used, it is the therapist's job to screen potential group members for appropriateness to the group with respect to the individual's treatment plan, and to ascertain their commitment to the rules and requirements of the group. Most clients who are going to drop out of treatment do so within 30 days; this can be very disruptive to the group's functioning.

The rules for group therapy are not the same as those for 12 step programs or other self-help groups. The group leader and the other members of the group provide feedback to each speaker, unlike 12 step programs, where commentary by others is discouraged. In ongoing therapy groups, members are expected to attend regularly and to participate actively, which is not the case in most 12 step or self-help programs. Both types of programs do emphasize total abstinence as the goal of group members; resistance, ambivalence, and denial about this goal are subjects for discussion.

Historically, therapy groups have been confrontational, although this is gradually changing. The therapist's skills are brought into play by making the confrontation of issues healing, not harsh. The emphasis is on empathy and sympathy, not on negative criticism. For a more complete description of the goals and techniques of group therapy, see Margolis and Zweben (1998).

Current status. In its many forms, group therapy is probably the most common type of treatment in use today. But, because of its many variations, it is difficult to measure the effectiveness of group therapy in treating drug abuse. There is no single concept, set of concepts, or protocols that guide the delivery of group therapy, so there is relatively little supporting evidence for its efficacy. Group therapy is often used in combination with individual therapy to extend the impact and length of treatment in outpatient settings. However, it should be mentioned that several investigators have achieved some success by using cognitive behavioral techniques in a group therapy setting (Maude-Griffin et al., 1998) Also, a 12-step oriented drug counseling group proved very effective in the collaborative cocaine treatment study, especially when combined with individual drug counseling (Crits-Christoph et al., 1999).

Other Promising Approaches

There are a number of other approaches to drug abuse treatment that are currently being developed and evaluated by the treatment community. Some of the most promising of these are described briefly here and include motivational interviewing, multisystemic therapy, and network therapy. For complete descriptions, the reader is referred to the cited articles.

Motivational interviewing. William Miller (1983, 1995; Miller & Rollnick, 1991) developed a technique called motivational interviewing, which empathetically attempts to identify, guide, and enhance a patient's motivation to change, continually responding to the patient's current stage of change. The model was developed for alcohol abusers and has not yet been widely tested in drug abuse treatment. The technique is based heavily on Prochaska and DiClemente's (1986) comprehensive model of change.

Motivational interviewing is based on principles of experimental social psychology, using the processes of attribution, cognitive dissonance, and self-efficacy. The model emphasizes individual responsibility and internal attribution of change. The therapist helps the client create cognitive dissonance by contrasting the client's behavior with his or her awareness of the behavior's negative consequences, and then channeling this dissonance toward behavior change, using a variety of behavioral and cognitive–behavioral techniques. Clearly, the technique requires a very empathetic approach on the part of the therapist.

Miller and Tonigan (1996) have developed an instrument to assess motivation for change in problem drinkers. Called SOCRATES (Stages of Change Readiness and Treatment Eagerness Scale), it has been tested successfully for reliability in a multisite clinical sample. Budney and Higgins (1998) also use this instrument during the initial stages of their CRA+Vouchers program (see p. 266) to provide information on clients' perceptions of the severity of their cocaine, alcohol, and other drug abuse problems, and their readiness to engage in behaviors that reduce use. Motivational interviewing was evaluated and found to be one of the effective treatments in Project MATCH (1998). In fact, one of the treatment manuals developed and used for Project MATCH is based on motivational interviewing (Miller, Zweben, DiClemente, & Rychtarik, 1992).

Multisystemic therapy. Based on the fact that substance abuse has multiple determinants (see Glantz, Weinberg, Miner, & Colliver, chap. 1, this volume), Henggeler, Borduin, Melton, and Mann (1991) have developed a treatment model known as multisystemic therapy (MST). MST is a social and ecological approach that intervenes in all the systems involved in establishing drug use and dependence, particularly in adolescent criminal offenders. Like many other approaches, MST also relies on behavioral, cognitive, and social techniques for achieving reductions in substance use and incarceration (Pickrel & Henggeler, 1996). MST can be home based, and it lowered the treatment dropout rate to 2% in at least one study (Henggeler, Pickrel, Brondino, & Crouch, 1996). The approach has been useful in decreasing hospitalization–residential treatment days and incarceration costs for this population (Schoenwald, Ward, Henggeler, & Pickrel, 1996).

Network therapy. Galanter's strategy of network therapy reaches out to individuals who are part of the client's social network, but who are not themselves the subjects of treatment (Galanter, 1993a). They are enlisted to act as a team to promote the client's recovery, and are taught appropriate techniques for helping the client achieve and maintain abstinence, and to develop alternative behaviors to drug use. The network may consist of family members and long time friends and business associates, but these must be selected carefully to avoid active drug users and to exclude those with whom the client has conflicts. The network members are encouraged to contact the therapist if they see potential for relapse, and the therapist may call on them if he or she sees an unhealthy pattern emerging. The main task of the network is to focus on treatment goals that may include compliance with medications, attendance at therapy meetings, developing an exercise program, and so on. The techniques used by the network members may be taken from a variety of approaches (behavioral, cognitive, etc.). The idea is to develop a healthy continuing network of support for the client. The approach has been tested in a clinical trial and found effective (Galanter, 1993b).

Treatment Effectiveness

Despite many complexities, it is possible to evaluate the effectiveness of different forms of drug abuse treatment. In fact, evaluation of treatment effectiveness is an essential component of intervention. In the previous descriptions of different types of treatment, there are citations of studies confirming that each particular treatment approach has demonstrated that it is more effective than no treatment at all, or more effective than some other type of treatment. The criteria for effectiveness are generally straightforward, although not necessarily easy to measure. As mentioned at the beginning of this chapter, the Office of National Drug Control Policy (1996) cites the following indicators of treatment effectiveness as the most important:

- reduced crime
- reduced drug use
- reduced domestic violence
- reduced behavior at risk for HIV infection
- increased days of employment
- positive changes in social values and networks

From study to study, measures of such outcomes may vary widely. The same ONDCP paper points out, for example, that measures of criminality may be expressed as number of arrests, time spent in jail, number of days involved in crime, percentage of income derived from crime, or dollar amount of income derived from crime. In research articles comparing the effectiveness of one type of therapy with another, the measures of outcome are sometimes reduced to the lowest common denominator, like time in treatment or length of abstinence, sometimes measured only 8 or 12 weeks after treatment.

Beyond these measures and the treatment protocols, there are other aspects of treatment that also must be evaluated, especially in terms of the needs of the particular individual client. In addition to the psychological services provided, the effective treatment program will probably include a variety of social and medical services for its clients. The clients may require assistance in their legal, medical, family, financial, vocational, and educational affairs. Many treatment programs fall short in integrating these services for their clients, or even in detecting what services the client actually needs. Other areas that frequently do not meet the standards of good care for addicts include client retention, intensity of services, cultural sensitivity in treatment programs, staff training and retention, data collection and management services, and stable sources of funding (ONDCP, 1996).

At the beginning of this chapter, we discussed the enormous costs that drug abuse has imposed on our society. It was stated that the costs of treatment were by far the least expensive way to reduce this burden. But what is the really convincing evidence that treatment works, both for individuals and for our society?

Because of the expense, time, and amount of data coordination required, the ONDCP (1996) reports that there have been only three national studies of treatment effectiveness: the Drug Abuse Reporting Program (DARP), the Treatment Outcome Prospective Study (TOPS), and the Drug Abuse Treatment Outcome Study (DATOS). There has been one statewide study: the California Drug and Alcohol Treatment Assessment (CALDATA). These four studies compared the effectiveness of four types of programs, broadly defined: pharmacotherapies, therapeutic communities, inpatient treatment, and outpatient treatment. They collected data from very large populations over long periods, and the results are encouraging.

The earliest of these studies, DARP, concluded that treatment in outpatient drug-free programs, methadone maintenance, and therapeutic communities produced positive outcomes, but that detoxification alone or treatment of less than three months—usually because of client dropout—was not effective. The TOPS study was even more definitive: more than one third of clients in all programs reported abstinence from their drugs of choice during the 3- to 5-year follow up period after treatment. In addition, measures of criminality showed significant reduction, whereas productive behavior (employment and education) increased. Data from DATOS presented an even more encouraging picture of the effectiveness of treatment modalities in general, but also documented a dramatic decline in the availability of support services such as medical, legal, financial, psychological, employment, and family services since the TOPS study was completed in 1981.

The CALDATA study was particularly interesting because, in addition to documenting treatment-induced reductions in drug use, crime, and illness, it also assessed the economic costs of those problems and compared them with the costs of drug abuse treatment. The findings were dramatic: In 1992, the cost of treatment was $209 million, and the benefits to society derived from treatment during that time and in the follow-up year was over $1.5 billion, more than seven times the amount spent on treatment. For a more detailed description of these treatment effectiveness studies, the reader is referred to the ONDCP Treatment Protocol Effectiveness Study (1996). Even from the brief description given here, it can be seen that drug abuse treatment does work for society and for individuals and that it is higly cost effective.

Special Issues and Special Populations

Abstinence or Controlled Use?

There is debate among alcohol treatment specialists about the controlled use of alcohol being an appropriate treatment goal, rather than complete abstinence. However, until recently, there has been virtually no such debate among drug abuse treatment specialists, who generally believe that complete abstinence is the only feasible treatment goal. As described in the section on relapse prevention (p. 263), a single use is often the precipitating factor for a return to uncontrolled drug use.

However, both therapists and patients recognize that the nature of drug abuse as a chronic, relapsing disease means that total abstinence is sometimes a goal that can be achieved only for a period of time. It is so difficult for some to achieve abstinence that recently harm reduction approaches have been developed to attempt to minimize the damage caused by drug use, not only to the addict, but to society in general. For example, as public health measures, needle exchange programs have been shown to decrease the spread of HIV/AIDS and hepatitis. Harm reduction uses educational and other methods that offer practical benefits to drug users and society. In addition, the approach may well act as a gateway to treatment for some addicts. They may find that as they act to reduce harm to themselves, abstinence looks more attainable, and enter into full treatment. Until drug abuse treatment programs can offer the best possible treatment for every person who needs it, harm reduction approaches should not be dismissed or ignored.

Targeting Interventions for Special Populations

It is beyond the scope of this overview to describe the many attempts to elucidate the prevention and treatment needs of special populations of drug users. These populations include women, pregnant women, single parents, adolescents, the elderly, and racial and ethnic minorities (see Sanders-Phillips, chap. 9, this volume). Unfortunately, although the accounts of their needs are often quite clear, how to go about providing for them is not always so evident. Frequently, this is because the added costs of these needs make intervention seem particularly expensive. For example, many single parents who are drug users need good and reliable child care for them to be able to attend treatment sessions, but providing child care in a drug treatment program is both expensive and administratively complex. Nevertheless, the costs of not taking effective measures to prevent or treat drug abuse in given populations are so enormous that there is no doubt that more specialized and targeted programs must be developed in the future.

CONCLUSION

It is often the perception that drug abuse prevention and treatment programs are too expensive, too impractical, and, worst of all, unlikely to succeed. But these are not futile endeavors. The evidence presented here makes it clear that prevention and treatment are successful, useful, and almost unbelievably cost effective. They deserve the support of the public and the best efforts of the most talented people in the addictions field.

REFERENCES

Abbott, P. J., Weller, S. B., Delaney, H. D., & Moore, B. A. (1998). Community reinforcement approach in the treatment of opiate addicts. *American Journal of Drug and Alcohol Abuse, 24*(1), 17–30.

Abrahms, J. L. (1979). A cognitive–behavioral versus nondirective group treatment program for opioid-addicted persons: An adjunct to methadone maintenance. *International Journal of the Addictions, 14*(4), 503–511.

Alcoholics Anonymous. (1976). *Alcoholics anonymous: The story of how many thousands of men and women have recovered from alcoholism* (3rd ed.). New York: Alcoholics Anonymous World Services.

Allsop, S., Saunders, B., Phillips, M., & Carr, A. (1997). A trial of relapse prevention with severely dependent male problem drinkers. *Addiction, 92*(1), 61–73.

Altman, J., Everitt, B. J., Glautier, S., Markou, A., Nutt, D., & Oretti, R. (1996). The biological, social and clinical bases of drug addiction: Commentary and debate. *Psychopharmacology, 125*, 285–345.

Anda, R. F., Williamson, D. F., Escobedo, L. G., Mast, E. E., Giovino, G. A., & Remington, P. L. (1990). Depression and the dynamics of smoking: A national perspective. *Journal of the American Medical Association, 264*, 1541–1545.

Annis, H. M., & Graham, J. M. (1995). Profile types on the Inventory of Drinking Situations: Implications for relapse prevention counseling. *Psychology of Addictive Behaviors, 9*, 176–182.

Ayllon, T. & Azrin, N. H. (1965). The measurement and reinforcement of behavior of psychotics. *Journal of the Experimental Analysis of Behavior, 8*, 357–383.

Ayllon, T. & Haughton, E. (1962). Control of the behavior of schizophrenic patients by food. *Journal of the Experimental Analysis of Behavior, 5*, 343–352.

Azrin, N. H., Sisson, R. W., Meyers, R., & Godley, M. (1982). Alcoholism treatment by disulfiram and community reinforcement therapy. *Journal of Behavior Therapy and Experimental Psychiatry, 13*, 105–112.

Bandura, A. (1969). *Principles of behavior modification.* New York: Holt, Rinehart & Winston.

Bandura, A. (1977). *Social learning theory.* Englewood Cliffs, NJ: Prentice Hall.

Beck, A. T., Wright, F. D., Newman, C. F., & Liese, B. S. (1993). *Cognitive therapy of substance abuse.* New York: Guilford Press.

Budney, A. J., & Higgins, S. T. (1998). *A community reinforcement plus vouchers approach: Treating cocaine addiction* (NIH Publication No. 98-4309). Rockville, MD: National Institute on Drug Abuse.

Byck, R. (Ed.). (1974). *Cocaine papers: Sigmund Freud.* New York: Stonehill. (Original work written 1884–1887.)

Carroll, K. M. (1998). *A cognitive behavorial approach: Treating cocaine addiction* (NIH Publication No. 98-4308). Rockville, MD: National Institute on Drug Abuse.

Carroll, K. M., Nich, C., Ball, S. A., McCance, E., & Rounsaville, B. J. (1998). Treatment of cocaine and alcohol dependence with psychotherapy and disulfiram. *Addiction, 93*(5), 713–727.

Carroll, K. M., Rounsaville, B. J., & Gawin, F. H. (1991). A comparative trial of psychotherapies for ambulatory cocaine abusers: Relapse prevention and interpersonal psychotherapy. *American Journal of Drug and Alcohol Abuse, 17*(3), 229–247.

Carroll, K. M., Rounsaville, B. J., Gordon, L. T., Nich, C., Jatlow, P., Bisighini, R. M., & Gawin, F. H. (1994). Psychotherapy and pharmacotherapy for ambulatory cocaine abusers. *Archives of General Psychiatry, 51,* 177–187.

Carroll, K. M., Rounsaville, B. J., Nich, C., Gordon, L. T., Wirtz, P. W., & Gawin, F. (1994). One-year follow-up of psychotherapy and pharmacotherapy for cocaine dependence: Delayed emergence of psychotherapy effects. *Archives of General Psychiatry, 51,* 989–997.

Chappel, J. N. (1993). Long term recovery from alcoholism. *Psychiatric Clinics of North America, 16*(1), 177–187.

Childress, A. R., Hole, A. V., Ehrman, R. N., & Robbins, S. J. (1993). Cue reactivity and cue reactivity interventions. In L. S. Onken, J. D. Blaine, & J. J. Boren (Eds.), *Behavioral treatments for drug abuse and dependence* (NIDA Research Monograph Series No. 137, pp. 73–96). Rockville, MD: National Institute on Drug Abuse.

Crits-Christoph, P., Siqueland, L., Blaine, J., Frank, A., Luborsky, L., Onken, L. S., Muenz, L. R., Thase, M. E., Weiss, R. D., Gastfriend, D. R., Woody, G. E., Barber, J. P., Butler, S. F., Daley, D., Salloum, I., Bishop, S., Najavits, L. M., Lis, J., Mercer, D., Griffin, M. L., Moras, K., & Beck, A. T. (1999). Psychosocial treatments for cocaine dependence: National Institute on Drug Abuse Collaborative Cocaine Treatment Study. *Archives of General Psychiatry, 56,* 493–502.

Deitch, D. (1973). The treatment of drug abuse in the therapeutic community: Historical influences, current considerations, future outlook. *Drug Abuse in America: Volume IV.* Rockville, MD: National Commission on Marijuana and Drug Abuse.

Dewey, S. L., Morgan, A. E., Ashby, C. R., Jr., Horan, B., Kushner, S. A., & Logan, J. (1998). A novel strategy for the treatment of cocaine addiction. *Synapse, 30,* 119–129.

Dole, V. P., & Nyswander, M. (1965). A medical treatment for diacetylmorphine (heroin) addiction. *Journal of the American Medical Association, 193,* 646–650.

Ellis, A., McInerney, J. F., DiGiuseppe, R., & Yeager, R. J. (1988). *Rational–emotive therapy with alcoholics and substance abusers*. New York: Pergamon Press.

Freud, S. (1949). Three essays on the theory of sexuality. In J. Strachey (Ed. and Trans.), *The standard edition of the complete psychological works of Sigmund Freud* (Vol. 7, pp. 125–245). London: Hogarth Press. (Original work published 1905)

Freud, S. (1964). *Civilization and its discontents*. New York: Norton. (Original work published 1930)

Galanter, M. (1993a). *Network therapy for alcohol and drug abuse: A new approach in practice*. New York: Basic Books.

Galanter, M. (1993b). Network therapy for substance abuse: A clinical trial. *Psychotherapy, 30*(2), 251–258.

Gawin, F. H., Kleber, H. D., Byck, R., Rounsaville, B. J., Kosten, T. R., Jatlow, P. I., & Morgan, C. (1989). Desipramine facilitation of initial cocaine abuse. *Archives of General Psychiatry, 46*, 117–121.

Glantz, M. (1987). Day hospital treatment of alcoholics. In A. Freeman & V. Greenwood (Eds.), *Cognitive therapy: Applications in psychiatric and medical settings* (pp. 51–68). New York: Human Sciences Press.

Glantz, M. (1995). Cognitive therapy with elderly alcoholics. In T. P. Beresford & E. Gomberg (Eds.), *Alcohol and aging* (pp. 211–229). New York: Oxford University Press.

Glantz, M., & McCourt, W. (1983). Cognitive therapy in groups with alcoholics. In A. Freeman (Ed.), *Cognitive therapy with couples and groups* (pp. 157–182). New York: Plenum Press.

Gorski, T. T. (1988a). *The staying sober workbook: Exercise manual*. Independence, MO: Independence Press.

Gorski, T. T. (1988b). *The staying sober workbook: Instruction manual*. Independence, MO: Independence Press.

Graham, K., Annis, H. M., Brett, P. J., & Venesoen, P. (1996). A controlled field trial of group versus individual cognitive–behavioural training for relapse prevention. *Addiction, 91*(8), 1127–1139.

Hall, S. M., Bass, A., Hargreaves, W. A., & Loeb, P. (1979). Contingency management and information feedback in outpatient heroin detoxification. *Behavior Therapy, 10*, 443–451.

Henggeler, S. W., Borduin, C. M., Melton, G. B., & Mann, B. J. (1991). Effects of multisystemic therapy on drug use and abuse in serious juvenile offenders: A progress report from two outcome studies. *Family Dynamics of Addiction Quarterly, 1*(3), 40–51.

Henggeler, S. W., Pickerl, S. G., Brondino, M. F., & Crouch, J. L. (1996). Eliminating (almost) treatment dropout of substance abusing or dependent delinquents through home-based multisystemic therapy. *American Journal of Psychiatry, 153*(3), 427–428.

Higgins, S. T., Budney, A. J., Bickel, W. K., & Badger, G. J. (1994). Participation of significant others in outpatient behavioral treatment predicts greater co-caine abstinence. *American Journal of Drug and Alcohol Abuse, 20*(1), 47–56.

Higgins, S. T., Budney, A. J., Bickel, W. K., Foerg, F., Donham, R., & Badger, G. J. (1994). Incentives improve outcome in outpatient behavioral treatment of cocaine dependence. *Archives of General Psychiatry, 54*, 568–576.

Higgins, S. T., Budney, A. J., Bickel, W. K., Hughes, J. R., Foerg, F., & Badger, G. J. (1993). Achieving abstinence with a behavioral approach. *American Journal of Psychiatry, 150*(5), 763–769.

Higgins, S. T., Delaney, D. D., Budney, A. J., Bickel, W. K., Hughes, J. R., Foerg, F., & Fenwick, J. W. (1991). A behavioral approach to achieving initial co-caine abstinence. *American Journal of Psychiatry, 148*(9), 1218–1224.

Higgins, S. T., & Silverman, K. (Eds.). (1999). *Motivating behavior change among illicit-drug abusers: Research on contingency management interventions.* Washing-ton, DC: American Psychological Association.

Iguchi, M. Y., Belding, M. A., Morral, A. R., Lamb, R. J., & Husband, S. D. (1997). Reinforcing operants other than abstinence in drug abuse treatment: An effective alternative for reducing drug use. *Journal of Consulting and Clinical Psychology, 65*, 421–428.

Jones, E. (1953). *The life and work of Sigmund Freud*, Vol. 1, pp. 78–97. New York: Basic Books.

Kadden, R. K., Carroll, K., Donovan, D., Cooney, N., Monti, P., Abrams, D., Litt, M., & Hester, R. (1995). *Cognitive behavioral coping skills therapy manual: A clinical research guide for therapists treating individuals with alcohol abuse and de-pendence* (NIH Publication No. 94-3724). Rockville, MD: National Institute on Alcohol Abuse and Alcoholism.

Khantzian, E. J. (1997). The self-medication hypothesis of substance use disorders: A reconsideration and recent applications. *Harvard Review of Psychiatry, 45*(5), 231–244.

Kidorf, M., Hollander, J. R., King, V. L., & Brooner, R. K. (1998). Increasing employment of opioid dependent outpatients: An intensive behavioral inter-vention. *Drug and Alcohol Dependence, 50*(1), 73–80.

Klerman, G. L., Weissman, M. M., Rounsaville, B. H., & Chevron, E. (1984). *The theory and practice of interpersonal psychotherapy for depression.* New York: Basic Books.

Kranzler, H. R., Burleson, J. A., DelBoca, F. K., Babor, T. F., Korner, P., Brown, J., & Bohn, M. J. (1994). Buspirone treatment of anxious alcoholics. *Archives of General Psychiatry, 51*, 720–731.

Margolis, R. D., & Zweben, J. E. (1998). *Treating patients with alcohol and other drug problems: An integrated approach.* Washington, DC: American Psychological Association.

Marlatt, G. A. (1978). Craving for alcohol, loss of control, and relapse: A cognitive–behavioral analysis. In P. E. Nathan, G. A. Marlatt, & T. Leberg (Eds.), *Alcoholism: New directions in behavioral research and treatment* (pp. 271–314). New York: Plenum Press.

Marlatt, G. A. (1979). Alcohol use and problem drinking: A cognitive–behavioral analysis. In P. C. Kendall & S. P. Hollon (Eds.), *Cognitive–behavioral interventions: Theory, research and procedures* (pp. 319–355). New York: Academic Press.

Marlatt, G. A., & Gordon, J. R. (Eds). (1985). *Relapse prevention: Maintenance strategies in the treatment of addictive behaviors.* New York: Guilford Press.

Maude-Griffin, P. M., Hohenstein, J. M., Humfleet, G. L., Reilly, P. M., Tusel, D. J., & Hall, S. M. (1998). Superior efficacy of cognitive-behavioral therapy for urban crack cocaine abusers: Main and matching effects. *Journal of Consulting and Clinical Psychology, 66,* 832–837.

McCourt, W., & Glantz, M. (1980). Cognitive behavior therapy in groups for alcoholics. *Journal of Studies on Alcohol, 41,* 338–346.

McKay, J. R., Alterman, A. I., Cacciola, J. S., Rutherford, M. J., & O'Brien, C. P. (1997). Group counseling versus individualized relapse prevention aftercare following intensive outpatient treatment for cocaine dependence: Initial results. *Journal of Consulting and Clinical Psychology, 65,* 778–788.

McLellan, A. T., Woody, G. E., Luborsky, L., & Goehl, L. (1988). Is the counselor an "active ingredient" in substance abuse rehabilitation? *Journal of Nervous and Mental Disease, 176,* 423–430.

Milby, J. B., Garrett, C., English, C., Fritschi, O., & Clarke, C. (1978). Take-home methadone: Continguency effects on drug seeking and productivity of narcotics addicts. *Addictive Behaviors, 3,* 215–220.

Miller, W. R. (1983). Motivational interviewing with problem drinkers. *Behavioural Psychotherapy, 11*(2), 147–172.

Miller, W. R. (1995). Increasing motivation for change. In R. K. Hester & W. R. Miller (Eds.), *Handbook of alcoholism treatment approaches: Effective alternatives* (2nd ed., pp. 89–104). Needam Heights, MA: Allyn & Bacon.

Miller, W. R., & Rollnick, S. (1991). *Motivational interviewing: Preparing people to change addictive behavior.* New York: Guilford Press.

Miller, W. R., & Tonigan, J. S. (1996). Assessing drinkers' motivations for change: The Stages of Change Readiness and Treatment Eagerness Scale (SOCRATES). *Psychology of Addictive Behaviors, 10*(2), 981–989.

Miller, W. R., Zweben, A., DiClemente, C. C., & Rychtarik, R. G. (1992). *Guided Motivational Enhancement Therapy Manual: A clinical tool for therapists treating individuals with alcohol abuse and dependence* (Project MATCH Monograph Series, Vol. 2). Rockville, MD: National Institute on Alcoholism and Alcohol Abuse.

National Institutes of Health Consensus Development Program. (1998). Effective medical treatment of opiate addiction. Heroin Consensus Conference. *Journal of the American Medical Association, 280,* 1936–1943.

Nowinski, J., Baker, S., & Carroll, K. M. (1994). *12-step facilitation therapy manual: A clinical research guide for therapist treating individuals with alcohol abuse and dependence* (Project MATCH Monograph Series, Vol. 1). Rockville, MD: National Institute on Alcoholism and Alcohol Abuse.

O'Brien, C. P. (1997). A range of research-based pharmacotherapies for addiction. *Science*, *278*, 66–70.

O'Farrell, T. J., Choquette, K. A., & Cutter, H. S. (1998). Couples relapse prevention sessions after behavioral marital therapy for male alcoholics: Outcomes during the three years after starting treatment. *Journal of Studies on Alcohol*, *59*(4), 357–370.

Office of National Drug Control Policy. (1996). Treatment protocol effectiveness study. *Journal of Substance Abuse Treatment*, *13*(4), 295–319.

Perkins, K. A., DiMarco, A., Grobe, J. E., Scierka, A., & Stiller, R. L. (1994). Nicotine discrimination in male and female smokers. *Psychopharmacology*, *116*, 407–413.

Perkins, K. A., Sanders, M., D'Amico, D., & Wilson, A. (1997). Nicotine discrimination and self-administration in humans as a function of smoking status. *Psychopharmacology*, *131*, 361–370.

Pickrel, S. G., & Henggeler, S. W. (1996). Multisystemic therapy for adolescent substance abuse and dependence. *Child and Adolescent Psychiatric Clinics of North America*, *5*(1), 201–211.

Prochaska, J. O., & DiClemente, C. C. (1986). Toward a comprehensive model of change. In W. R. Miller & N. Heather (Eds.), *Treating addictive behaviors: Processes of change* (pp. 3–27). New York: Plenum Press.

Project MATCH Research Group. (1998). Matching alcoholism treatments to client heterogeneity: Project MATCH three-year drinking outcomes. *Alcoholism, Clinical and Experimental Research*, *22*(6), 1300–1311.

Rose, J. E., Behm, F. M., Westman, E. C., Levin, E. D., Stein, R. M., & Ripka, G. V. (1994). Mecamylamine combined with nicotine skin patch facilitates smoking cessation beyond nicotine patch treatment alone. *Clinical Pharmacology and Therapeutics*, *56*, 86–99.

Rotgers, F. (1996). Behavior theory of substance abuse treatment: Bringing science to bear on practice. In F. Rotgers, D. S. Keller, & J. Morganstern (Eds.), *Treating substance abuse: Theory and technique* (pp. 174–201). New York: Guilford Press.

Rydell, C. P., & Everingham, S. M. S. (1994). *Controlling cocaine: Supply versus demand programs* (RAND Doc. No. MR-331-ONDCP/A/DPRC). Santa Monica, CA: RAND Corporation.

Sanchez-Craig, M. (1974). A self-control strategy for drinking tendencies. *Ontario Psychologist*, *7*, 25–29.

Sanchez-Craig, M. (1980). Random assignment to abstinence or controlled drinking in a cognitive behavioral program: Short term effects on drinking behavior. *Addictive Behaviors*, *5*, 35–39.

Schmitz, J. M., Oswald, L. M., Jacks, S. D., Rustin, T., Rhoades, H. M., & Grabowski, J. (1997). Relapse prevention treatment for cocaine dependence: Group vs. individual format. *Addictive Behavior*, *22*(3), 405–418.

Schoenwald, S. K., Ward, D. M., Henggeler, S. W., & Pickerl, S. G. (1996). Multisystemic therapy treatment of substance abusing or dependent adolescent offenders: Costs of reducing incarceration, inpatient, and residential placement. *Journal of Child and Family Studies, 5*(4), 431–444.

Shaw, G. K., Waller, S., Majumdar, S. K., Alberts, J. L., Latham, C. J., & Dunn, G. (1994). Tiapride in the prevention of relapse in recently detoxified alcoholics. *British Journal of Psychiatry, 165,* 515–523.

Silverman, K., Higgins, S. T., Brooner, R. K., Montoya, I. D., Cone, E. J., Schuster, C. R., & Preston, K. L. (1996). Sustained cocaine abstinence in methadone maintenance patients through voucher-based reinforcement theory. *Archives of General Psychiatry, 53*(5), 409–415.

Sisson, R., & Azrin, N. H. (1989). The community reinforcement approach. In R. K. Hester & W. R. Miller (Eds.), *Handbook of alcoholism treatment approaches: Effective alternatives* (pp. 242–258). New York: Pergamon Press.

Sobell, M. B., & Sobell, L. C. (1978). *Behavioral treatment of alcohol problems.* New York: Plenum.

Spanagel, R., & Zieglgansberger, W. (1997). Anti-craving compounds for ethanol: New pharmacological tools to study addictive processes. *Trends in Pharmacological Sciences, 18,* 54.

Stanton, M. D., & Shadish, W. R. (1997). Outcome, attrition, and family-couples treatment for drug abuse: A meta-analysis and review of the controlled, comparative studies. *Psychological Bulletin, 122,* 170–191.

Stitzer, M. L., Bigelow, G. E., & Liebson, I. (1980). Reducing drug use among methadone maintenance clients: Contingent reinforcement for morphine-free urines. *Addictive Behaviors, 5,* 333–340.

Stitzer, M. L., Iguchi, M. Y., & Felch, L. J. (1992). Contingent take-home incentive: Effects on drug use of methadone maintenance patients. *Journal of Consulting and Clinical Psychology, 60,* 927–934.

Substance Abuse and Mental Health Services Administration. (1998). *Service research outcomes study* (DHHS Publication No. [SMA] 98-3177). Washington, DC: U.S. Government Printing Office.

Szapocznik, J. H., & Kurtines, W. M. (1989). *Breakthroughs in family therapy with drug abusing problem youth.* New York: Springer.

Szapocznik, J. H., & Kurtines, W. M. (1993). Family psychology and cultural diversity: Opportunities for theory, research and application. *American Psychologist, 48,* 400–407.

Tusel, D. J., Piotrowski, N. A., Sees, K., Reilly, P. M., Banys, P., Meek, P., & Hall, S. M. (1995). Contingency contracting for illicit drug use with opioid addicts in methadone treatment. In L. S. Harris (Ed.), *Problems of drug dependence, 1994: Proceedings of the 56th annual scientific meeting* (NIDA Research Monograph Series No. 153, pp. 155–160). Rockville, MD: National Institute on Drug Abuse.

Vaillant, G. E. (1983). *The natural history of alcoholism.* Cambridge, MA: Harvard University Press.

Washton, A. M., & Stone-Washton, N. (1991). *Step zero: Getting to recovery.* Center City, MN: Hazelden.

Woody, G. E., Luborsky, L., McLellan, A. T., O'Brien, C. P., Beck, A. T., Blaine, J., Herman, I., & Hole, A. (1983). Psychotherapy for opiate addicts: Does it help? *Archives of General Psychiatry, 40*, 639–645.

Woody, G. E., McLellan, A. T., Luborsky, L., & O'Brien, C. P. (1987). Twelve-month follow-up of psychotherapy for opiate dependence. *American Journal of Psychiatry, 144*, 590–596.

Woody, G. E., McLellan, A. T., Luborsky, L., & O'Brien, C. P. (1995). Psychotherapy in community methadone programs: A validation study. *American Journal of Psychiatry, 152*(9), 1302–1308.

12

ADOLESCENT DRUG ABUSE PREVENTION: CURRENT FINDINGS AND FUTURE DIRECTIONS

GILBERT J. BOTVIN

Considerable research has been conducted over the past 20 years concerning the etiology and prevention of drug abuse. This research has increased understanding of the antecedents of drug use among children and adolescents, the onset and developmental progression of drug use–abuse, and the role and relative importance of specific etiologic factors. It also has provided a firm foundation for the development and testing of promising approaches to drug abuse prevention.

However, despite these advances, there is a great divide between what research recommends to prevent drug abuse and the approaches currently being used by prevention practitioners. The purpose of this chapter is to summarize what has been learned during the past two decades, to help consolidate findings from the ever-growing drug abuse prevention literature into more general principles that can help guide program developers, practitioners, and policymakers as well as to stimulate additional research in this critically important area.

RENEWED INTEREST IN AN OLD PROBLEM

Although the problem of drug abuse has been one we have struggled with since well before the psychedelic sixties, public interest has ebbed and flowed over the years. Interest in the problem of drug abuse was so keen during the 1970s that policymakers declared "war on drugs," and in the 1980s, it culminated in the passage of important federal legislation on drug control. Billions of dollars have been expended trying to solve the drug problem in this country. Most of this money has been spent on interdiction efforts, with the remainder being spent on treatment and prevention. However, because drug abuse is but one of many serious problems, the attention of the media, the general public, and the policymakers has shifted from drug abuse to AIDS to violence to cigarette smoking and most recently back to drug abuse again.

One of the factors responsible for the renewed interest in drug abuse is the fact that drug use among U.S. youth is once again on the rise. Results of national survey data indicate that drug use has increased consistently from the early 1990s to the present (Johnston, O'Malley, & Bachman, 1998). These increases have been observed for adolescents from different regions of the country, from different social classes, and for different age groups. These trend data show a sharp rise in marijuana use among 8th, 10th, and 12th graders, as well as an increase for all three grade levels in the use of cigarettes, stimulants, LSD, and inhalants. Recognition of the ineffectiveness of supply-reduction efforts, which attempt to stem the flow of drugs across and within U.S. borders, and the limited effectiveness of demand-reduction efforts, which focus on treatment and prevention, has led to a new sense of urgency regarding the identification of effective prevention approaches.

A powerful dual impetus for developing new prevention approaches concerns both the magnitude of the drug problem in the United States and the disappointing results of past treatment and prevention approaches. Considerable drug research has been conducted over the past decade—half of it in this important area. Yet identifying effective prevention approaches has been extremely difficult. Still, progress has been made, and evidence of effective prevention approaches derived from sound empirical studies has gradually emerged over the past decade. These efforts have been chronicled in numerous review articles (e.g., Botvin & Botvin, 1992; Goodstadt, 1986; Schinke, Botvin, & Orlandi, 1991).

The most fruitful research has been conducted in school settings and has tested the impact of approaches to drug abuse prevention designed to target the psychosocial factors associated with the initiation and early stages of drug use. Studies have run the gamut from small-scale quasi-experimental studies to large-scale randomized prevention trials. Early studies focused almost exclusively on cigarette smoking. More recent studies not only have been larger and better designed but also have focused on the impact of preventive interventions on the use of multiple substances. Thus, there is mounting empirical evidence from a growing number of carefully designed and methodologically sophisticated studies clearly indicating that drug abuse prevention can work. Although considerably more research is needed in this important area, the increasing rates of drug use in recent years and the corresponding need for further refining of the prevention approaches used by schools and communities around the country warrant dissemination of information concerning the state of the art in drug abuse prevention.

CONVENTIONAL DRUG EDUCATION APPROACHES

Prior to 1980, school-based efforts to prevent drug abuse took the form of tobacco, alcohol, and drug education curricula. Of these, perhaps the most ubiquitous form of drug education involved efforts to provide students with factual information about drugs, drug use, pharmacological effects, and the adverse consequences of drug abuse. This approach to drug abuse prevention rested on the underlying assumption that the problem of drug abuse was caused by a cognitive deficit (inadequate knowledge of the dangers of using drugs). A corresponding assumption was that drug abuse could be prevented by remediating this deficit through educational approaches designed to increase students' awareness of the requisite facts. It was assumed that once armed with these facts, adolescents would make a logical, rational, and well-informed decision to avoid drug use. Many health education approaches to drug abuse prevention also used fear-arousal techniques designed to scare students into not using drugs by dramatizing the dangers of using drugs.

Evaluation studies of informational approaches to prevention have tended to show some impact on drug knowledge and anti-drug attitudes, but consistently have failed to show an impact on tobacco, alcohol, or drug use behavior or intentions to use drugs (Dorn & Thompson, 1976; Goodstadt, 1974; Kinder, Pape, & Walfish, 1980; Richards, 1969; Schaps, Bartolo, Moskowitz, Palley, & Churgin, 1981; Swisher & Hoffman, 1975). Although these approaches had little impact on drug use or intentions to use drugs, several studies indicated that they were effective in increasing knowledge and were able to demonstrate increases in antidrug attitudes. Findings from some studies suggested that this approach might lead to counterproductive results by actually increasing drug use, possibly because it could serve to stimulate curiosity (Swisher, Crawford, Goldstein, & Yura, 1971). Notwithstanding the results of studies testing the effectiveness of prevention approaches that relied either solely or primarily on teaching facts about drugs, it should not be concluded that knowledge is unimportant or irrelevant to drug abuse prevention efforts. As I argued elsewhere, it is likely that developmentally appropriate and personally relevant health information may indeed have a place in drug abuse prevention programs (Botvin, 1994). However, it is important to recognize that it is but one of many variables that play a role in the etiology of drug abuse.

Some school-based prevention programs focused primarily on the affective domain. These approaches, referred to as *affective education*, attempted to prevent drug abuse by promoting affective development. These approaches were designed to increase self-understanding and acceptance through activities such as values clarification and responsible decision making, improving interpersonal relations by promoting effective communication and assertiveness, and providing students with the opportunity to fulfill their basic needs through existing social institutions (Swisher, 1979). Despite the popularity of affective education during the 1960s and early 1970s, evaluation studies testing these approaches found little to support their effectiveness. In fact, the results of these studies were as discouraging as evaluations of knowledged-based approaches. Although there were some evidence that affective-education approaches, in certain circumstances, might be able to produce an impact on one or more correlates of drug use, they were not able to produce a measurable impact on drug use behavior (Kearney & Hines, 1980; Kim, 1988).

A PARADIGM SHIFT TO PSYCHOSOCIAL APPROACHES

Starting with a seminal study by Evans (1976), prevention research found its footing, and a host of studies reporting effects on cigarette smoking using variations on the social influence approach initially developed by Evans appeared in the literature. To a large extent, this led to a major paradigm shift in the emerging field of drug abuse prevention—away from prevention efforts based on intuition and toward efforts grounded in theory and the findings of etiological research. The hallmark of these prevention research efforts was an emphasis on scientific rigor. Although these studies used prevention approaches grounded in social psychological theories and were considerably stronger than earlier evaluation efforts, many suffered from one or more methodological weaknesses, which were appropriately identified in subsequent literature reviews (e.g., Flay, 1985).

Most of the 1980s was spent attempting to design more rigorous studies, to produce scientifically defensible evidence that prevention worked. During this time, researchers tested different intervention configurations, different types of intervention providers, different intervention components, and the impact of these interventions on substances other than tobacco. As the field of prevention matured, studies progressed from small-scale, quasi-experimental studies involving a few hundred individuals from one or two schools to large-scale, randomized field trials involving thousands of students from 40 or 50 schools (Botvin, Baker, Dusenbury, Tortu, & Botvin, 1990).

Social Influence Approach

The recognition that social factors play a major role in the initiation and early stages of drug use led to the development of a new set of prevention approaches. Social influences to use drugs come from family, the media, and peers. Of these, the most powerful and important social influence to use drugs comes from one's peers. Research by Evans (1976; Evans et al., 1978) set the stage for a flurry of prevention research studies. These studies focused initially on cigarette studies and were a major departure from health education approaches to tobacco, alcohol, and drug abuse prevention. Clearly, the most important aspects of this research were that it used reasonably strong research methods and that it became the first prevention model to produce a measurable impact on behavior. Another salient feature of the work done by Evans was that it contained several of the core components that other researchers have incorporated into their own intervention approaches. Many of these components are still used in the most recent studies of drug abuse prevention. Each of these components are briefly summarized below.

Psychological Inoculation

A central feature of the prevention approach developed and tested by Evans (1976; Evans et al., 1978) was the notion of psychological inoculation, which was derived from McGuire's (1964, 1968) persuasive communications theory. In keeping with this, the prevention approach designed by Evans was intended to expose adolescents initially to a weak form of the social influences promoting cigarette smoking followed later by progressively stronger social influences to smoke. Through this gradual exposure to stronger prosmoking persuasive messages, it was hoped that the exposed adolescents would build up resistance to the more virulent forms of these prosmoking messages that they would be likely to encounter as they progressed through junior high school.

Despite the prominence of psychological inoculation in the initial formulation of the social influence prevention model, it has received considerably less emphasis in more recent formulations of the social influence model. Other aspects of the original model developed by Evans have assumed greater emphasis in recent years in the work of other researchers. Two of the most important features of the contemporary social influence model include correcting normative expectations and teaching skills for resisting offers to use drugs. The prevalence of smoking, drinking, and illicit drug use is usually overestimated by adolescents (Fishbein, 1977). This overestimate leads to the formation of inaccurate normative expectations —the forming of a set of normative beliefs that support drug use. To reduce pressure to use drugs, social influence approaches to drug abuse prevention include a component designed to correct the misperception that many adults and most adolescents use drugs. Hansen (1996) has referred to this component as *normative education*. Two different strategies have been used to modify or correct normative expectations. The first is straightforward and simply involves providing adolescents with information from national or local survey data concerning the prevalence of drug use among adolescence and adults. A second method requires that adolescents conduct their own local surveys of drug use within their school or community.

Social Resistance Skills

The prevention research conducted by Evans (1976; Evans et al., 1978) at the end of the 1970s not only provided the first tangible evidence that prevention could work but also sparked a flurry of research activity by other researchers (e.g., Arkin, Roemhild, Johnson, Luepker, & Murray, 1981; Donaldson, Graham, & Hansen, 1994; Ellickson & Bell, 1990; Hurd et al., 1980; Luepker, Johnson, Murray, & Pechacek, 1983; McAlister, Perry, & Maccoby, 1979; Perry, Killen, Slinkard, & McAlister, 1983; Snow, Tebes, Arthur, & Tapasak, 1992; Sussman, Dent, Stacy, & Sun, 1993; Telch, Killen, McAlister, Perry, & Maccoby, 1982).

Although resistance skills training was included in the prevention model developed and tested by Evans and his colleagues, it has come to be featured more prominently in the interventions tested by other researchers during the past decade and a half. Indeed, for many, this has become the hallmark of contemporary approaches to drug abuse prevention. The primary focus of these prevention approaches has been on teaching adolescents a set of skills or tactics for resisting influences to smoke, drink, or use drugs—particularly influences coming from the media and peers. With respect to the media, adolescents are taught how to identify and respond to prodrug messages in advertisements, movies, rock videos, and so on. Special attention is generally afforded the persuasive appeals used by advertisers to promote the sale of tobacco and alcohol products. Students are taught how to identify specific advertising techniques, to analyze ads and their messages, and to formulate counterarguments to common advertising appeals. Teaching these skills is designed to provide adolescents with the tools for actively resisting advertisements promoting cigarette smoking and alcoholic beverages, particularly given the growing recognition that advertisers have developed rather sophisticated ad campaigns explicitly designed to target the youth market.

Perhaps the best known aspect of resistance skills training involves teaching adolescents a set of skills that they can use to resist offers from their peers to smoke, drink, or use drugs. Prevention programs that include resistance skills training emphasize verbal and nonverbal skills for resisting these offers to use drugs. That is to say, they teach adolescents what to say when they are offered or pressured to engage in some form of drug use as well as how to say it in the most effective way possible. Related to this, adolescents are taught how to identify high-risk situations in which they are likely to experience peer pressure to use drugs, to avoid those situations whenever possible, and to develop action plans for those situations, so that they are prepared to handle peer pressure to use drugs should it arise.

To be optimally effective, resistance skills training must provide adolescents with a general repertoire of verbal and nonverbal skills that individuals can call on when confronted by peer pressure to use drugs in a variety of situations. Adolescents must develop not only these skills but also the confidence that they can apply them when necessary. To accomplish this, in addition to teaching students these skills and their applications, training programs provide opportunities to practice the use of these skills both in and out of class. Extended practice outside of the classroom is regarded as being an important requisite to promoting the integration of these skills into adolescents' general repertoire of skills that they can call on whenever necessary in real-life situations. Therefore, extended practice is generally programmed into these prevention approaches in the form of behavioral homework assignments.

Competence-Enhancement Approach

A prevention approach also has been developed and tested during the past two decades that is designed to target a broader array of risk and protective factors than those addressed by the social influence approach. This includes research conducted by our group at Cornell (e.g., Botvin, Baker, Botvin, Filazzola, & Millman, 1984; Botvin et al., 1990; Botvin & Eng, 1982; Botvin, Renick, & Baker, 1983) and by Schinke and his colleagues (Gilchrist & Schinke, 1983; Schinke & Gilchrist, 1983, 1984). Although this approach typically has included elements of the social influence model, a distinguishing feature of this prevention approach has been its emphasis on teaching a variety of personal self-management skills and general social skills to adolescents to promote general competence and thereby reduce vulnerability to prodrug social influences, as well as to reduce intrapsychic motivations to smoke, drink, or use illicit drugs. This approach has included the teaching of generic skills, such as general problem-solving and decision-making skills, cognitive skills for resisting interpersonal and media influences, skills for increasing self-control and self-esteem, skills for coping effectively with anxiety or stress, general social skills, and general assertive skills. In our own work with a prevention approach called *life skills training* (LST), three types of self-management skills have been taught: (a) self-appraisal, goal-setting, and self-directed behavior change; (b) decision making and independent thinking; and (c) anxiety management skills. Adolescents also are taught a set of general social skills, including communications skills, conversational skills, skills for asking someone out for a date, complimenting skills, and both verbal and non-verbal assertive skills. All of these skills are taught using a combination of instruction and demonstration, behavioral rehearsal (practice during class), feedback, reinforcement, and extended practice (outside of class) through behavioral homework assignments.

EVIDENCE OF EFFECTIVENESS

Over the past two decades there has been a gradual accumulation of empirical evidence supporting the effectiveness of school-based approaches to drug abuse prevention. Together, this evidence provides strong empirical support for the short-term effectiveness of drug abuse prevention, with evidence from a few studies concerning long-term effectiveness. Although evidence exists concerning the effectiveness of these prevention approaches on alcohol and marijuana use, the largest number of studies have focused on cigarette smoking. Because most research has been conducted with White populations, less is known about the effectiveness of these approaches with minority populations. Finally, because the focus of this research has been on primary (universal) prevention, the evaluation of these prevention approaches has been determined largely with respect to the ability of these prevention approaches to decrease relatively low levels of drug involvement (e.g., occasional drug use or 30-day prevalence) rather than in terms of their impact on more serious levels of drug involvement. Still, the growing body of evidence in support of drug abuse prevention is impressive.

Short-Term Effects

The results of studies testing the effectiveness of the social influence approach to cigarette smoking generally have shown that they are able to reduce the rate of smoking by 30% to 50% after the initial intervention (Arkin et al., 1981; Donaldson et al., 1994; Ellickson & Bell, 1990; Hurd et al., 1980; Luepker et al., 1983; McAlister et al., 1979; Perry et al., 1983; Snow et al., 1992; Sussman et al., 1993; Telch et al., 1982). One study also has demonstrated that the social influence approach can reduce the use of smokeless tobacco (Sussman et al., 1993). Studies testing a blend of the social influence approach and the broader competence-enhancement approach have demonstrated that they can cut cigarette smoking by 40%

to 75% (Botvin, Baker, Botvin, et al., 1984; Botvin, Baker, Renick, Filaz-zola, & Botvin, 1984; Botvin & Eng, 1980; Botvin, Eng, & Williams, 1980; Botvin et al., 1983; Gilchrist & Schinke, 1983; Pentz, 1983; Schinke, 1984; Schinke & Gilchrist, 1983, 1984).

Effects of roughly the same magnitude have been found for the social influences approach with regard to its initial impact on alcohol and marijuana (Ellickson & Bell, 1990; McAlister, Perry, Killen, Slinkard, & Maccoby, 1980; Shope, Dielman, Butchart, & Campanelli, 1992). Similarly, evidence also exists for the efficacy of the competence-enhancement approach on the use of alcoholic beverages (Botvin, Baker, Botvin, et al., 1984; Botvin et al., 1990; Botvin, Baker, Renick, et al., 1984; Epstein, Botvin, Diaz, & Schinke, 1995; Pentz, 1983) as well as on the use of marijuana (Botvin, Baker, Botvin, et al., 1984; Botvin et al., 1990; Epstein, Botvin, Diaz, Toth, & Schinke, 1995). Examination of the impact of the competence-enhancement approach on tobacco, alcohol, and marijuana use indicates that the strongest effects have been found for cigarette smoking and marijuana use, whereas weaker and somewhat more inconsistent effects have been found for the use of alcoholic beverages.

Note that the social influence approach and the competence-enhancement approach both include program components designed to increase drug-resistance skills and promote antidrug norms. Thus, even the broader competence-enhancement approach includes problem-specific material along with the generic personal and social skills training content. The results from one study (Caplan et al., 1992) suggest that the generic competence-enhancement approach to drug abuse prevention may not be effective unless it also includes social resistance skills training content. This may be necessary because such material includes a focus on antidrug norms and helps students apply generic skills to situations related specifically to the prevention of drug abuse. Although approaches that combine the key elements of the problem-specific social influences model and the broader competence-enhancement approach appear to be the most effective on the basis of current evidence, additional research is necessary to better understand how and why effective prevention programs work.

Long-Term Effects

The results of longer term follow-up studies have gradually emerged in recent years. Although they present a mixed picture, evidence from several studies indicates that current prevention approaches have a reasonable degree of durability. For example, some studies have indicated that the social influence approach has produced reductions in cigarette smoking that last for up to 4 years (Luepker et al., 1983; McAlister et al., 1980; Sussman et al., 1993; Telch et al., 1982). The results of one multicomponent study conducted by Perry and Kelder found evidence of long-term prevention effects for cigarette smoking lasting up to 7 years (Perry & Kelder, 1992). The results of other studies, however, indicate that the prevention effects produced by the social influence approach frequently erode over time, with effects being maintained for only 1 or 2 years (Bell, Ellickson, & Harrison, 1993; Ellickson, Bell, & McGuigan, 1993; Flay et al., 1989; Murray, Davis-Hearn, Goldman, Pirie, & Luepker, 1988).

Although it has been suggested that school-based prevention approaches may not be powerful enough to produce lasting prevention effects (Dryfoos, 1993), it would seem unreasonable to expect that prevention programs targeting a limited subset of etiologic factors, with a relatively modest initial prevention dosage (typically between five and eight class sessions) and no booster sessions in subsequent years, would have the ability to produce lasting results. Indeed, it has been argued that these and other deficiencies are responsible for the erosion of prevention effects observed in several long-term follow-up studies (Resnicow & Botvin, 1993). For example, long-term prevention effects may not have been observed in some studies because (a) the length of the initial intervention may have been too short, (b) booster sessions were either inadequate or not included at all, (c) the intervention was not implemented with sufficient fidelity to be effective, or (d) the intervention was based on faulty assumptions, was incomplete, or was deficient in some other way, rendering the prevention approach ineffective.

The results of our own work suggest that the issues discussed above may indeed be legitimate concerns capable of undermining the long-term effectiveness of school-based prevention approaches. On the other hand, where these issues are addressed, prevention effects have been found to be relatively long-lasting. Results from a large-scale, randomized field trial involving nearly 6,000 7th graders from 56 public schools in New York State found long-term reductions in smoking, alcohol, and marijuana use at the end of the 12th grade (Botvin, Schinke, Epstein, Diaz, & Botvin, 1995). In this study, schools were randomly assigned to prevention and control conditions. Participating students in the prevention condition received the LST program during the 7th grade (15 sessions), with booster sessions in the 8th grade (10 sessions) and 9th grade (5 sessions). No intervention was provided during Grades 10 through 12. According to the results, the prevalence of cigarette smoking, alcohol use, and marijuana use for the students in the prevention condition was as much as 44% lower than for controls. Significant reductions also were found with respect to the percentage of students who were using multiple substances one or more times per week. These results suggest that to be effective, school-based prevention programs need to be more comprehensive and have a stronger initial dosage than most studies using the social influence approach. Another implication is that prevention programs need to include at least 2 additional years of interventions (booster sessions) and must be implemented in a manner that is consistent with the underlying prevention model.

Effectiveness With Minority Populations

A conspicuous gap in the drug abuse prevention field over the years has been the lack of high-quality research with racial-ethnic minority populations (Collins 1995; Kim, Coletti, Williams, & Hepler, 1995; Trimble, 1995). Although several national, state, and local surveys have found that the prevalence of drug use is either the same or lower for ethnic minority youth than for White youth (Oetting & Beauvais, 1987; Wallace, Bachman, O'Malley, & Johnston, 1995), ethnic minority youth have generally been found to be at disproportionately higher risk for a number of drug-related problems (Barnes & Welte, 1986; Maddahian, Newcomb, & Bentler, 1988; Newcomb, Maddahian, Skager, & Bentler, 1987).

Although some studies (e.g., Ellickson & Bell, 1990) have included at least a subsample of minority youth in their populations, few studies have been conducted with a predominantly minority sample. At the same time, demonstration projects funded by the Center for Substance Abuse Prevention have included many projects designed to target minority populations. Overall, two strategies have been followed. One strategy, common to many local prevention efforts, assumes that the etiology of drug abuse is different for different populations. Thus, many prevention providers have developed interventions designed to be population specific (e.g., projects for Black youth with an Afrocentric cultural focus). A second strategy assumes that the etiology of drug abuse is more similar than different across populations. This approach involves the development of preventive interventions designed to be generalizable to a broad range of individuals from different populations. Although relatively little is known about the etiology of drug use among minority youth, several studies indicate that there is substantial overlap in the factors promoting and maintaining drug use among different populations (Bettes, Dusenbury, Kerner, James-Ortiz, & Botvin, 1990; Botvin, Baker, et al., 1993; Botvin, Epstein, Schinke, & Diaz, 1994; Botvin, Goldberg, Botvin, & Dusenbury, 1993; Epstein, Dusenbury, Botvin, & Diaz, 1994). The results of these studies suggest that prevention approaches may have application to a broad range of individuals from different populations.

Beyond the commonality of etiologic factors for different populations, there is a very simple practical reason for pursuing this course: Most urban schools in the United States contain individuals from multiple racial-ethnic groups because schools are mandated by law to be integrated. Therefore, the reality is that even if differences across populations warranting different interventions were found, it would be extremely difficult on a logistical and political level to implement separate interventions for different racial–ethnic groups. This raises serious questions about the feasibility and acceptability of prevention approaches designed to be specific to a particular racial–ethnic population.

The work that we have conducted in recent years at Cornell has largely followed the course of testing the same underlying prevention strategy with different populations, to determine its potential effectiveness and generalizability. During the course of this work, some modifications were made, where warranted, to maximize generalizability, cultural sensitivity, relevance, and acceptability to predominantly Black and Hispanic inner-city youth. The initial focus of this research was on cigarette smoking, followed more recently by a focus on alcohol and marijuana use. This research has been conducted systematically through several different stages, including (a) exploratory (qualitative) research consisting of focus-group testing and key informant interviews, (b) expert review of prevention methods and materials, (c) consumer-based reviews of intervention materials and methods, (d) small-scale pilot studies, and (e) large-scale randomized field trials. Throughout this process, modifications in the prevention materials and methods were made as necessary. Still, none of the modifications in prevention materials and methods involved any fundamental changes to the underlying prevention strategy. Instead, these changes included such things as the reading level of the prevention materials, the inclusion of the appropriate graphics (e.g., illustrations or pictures of minority youth), language, role-play scenarios, and examples appropriate for the target population.

The results of these studies have consistently shown that the LST approach reduces cigarette smoking (relative to controls) for inner-city Hispanic youth (Botvin, Dusenbury, et al., 1992; Botvin, Dusenbury, Baker, James-Ortiz, & Kerner, 1989) and Black youth (Botvin, Batson, et al., 1989; Botvin & Cardwell, 1992). Lower levels of cigarette smoking also have been found in at least one follow-up study involving a cohort of 7th graders who were followed up to the end of 10th grade (Botvin, Schinke, Epstein, & Diaz, 1994). In addition, more recent studies have shown that this prevention approach can reduce alcohol and marijuana use in minority populations (Botvin, Schinke, et al., 1994; Botvin, et al., 1995; Botvin, Epstein, Baker, Diaz, & Ifill-Williams, 1996) and is also able to produce reductions in more serious levels of drug involvement, such as the use of multiple drugs (Botvin et al., 1996). Finally, one study indicated that tailoring the intervention to the culture of the target population can enhance its effectiveness (Botvin et al., 1995). Taken as a whole, these studies provide evidence that the same prevention approach with relatively modest modifications is effective with White, Black, and Hispanic youth. However, it also seems evident that for schools with a more homogeneous population than most inner-city schools, prevention effects may be increased by tailoring the intervention to the target population.

THE NEED FOR PREVENTION RESEARCH ON
MEDIATING MECHANISMS

The prevention literature of the early to late 1970s was replete with poorly designed studies of largely atheoretical interventions that failed to produce any measurable impact on drug use. Consequently, the primary challenge to the emerging field of drug abuse prevention was to identify and test approaches with the demonstrated potential for reducing drug use. The focus of prevention research throughout the 1980s was on behavioral outcomes rather than underlying processes, to prove that prevention worked. Given the contribution of drug use to annual mortality and morbidity, the fact that prevention research has focused almost exclusively on drug use outcomes is both natural and appropriate. However, to advance the field of prevention science and obtain the feedback needed to design more effective prevention interventions, it is now vitally important that researchers attempt to understand the mediating mechanisms of promising prevention approaches.

Although several published studies have begun to examine the impact of effective prevention approaches on hypothesized mediating variables (e.g., Botvin et al., 1990; Hansen et al., 1988), relatively few studies have attempted to examine the extent to which intervention effects are actually mediated through these variables. Still, some studies assessing mediation have been published for prevention approaches based on both the social influence model (e.g., MacKinnon et al., 1991) and broader based skills training models (e.g., Botvin et al., 1992, 1995). These studies are important initial steps, but the results produced are inconsistent. Considerably more work is needed with better measures and with the inclusion of ethnic minority youth. This is particularly true with respect to interventions hypothesized to impact on cognitive–behavioral skills, which have been criticized for failing to adequately assess the skills targeted by the interventions.

A Conceptual Framework for Studying Mediating Mechanisms

It is now clear that there is no single factor or single pathway that serves as a necessary and sufficient condition leading to drug abuse. Drug abuse is the result of a multivariate mix of factors (Hawkins, Catalano, & Miller, 1992; Newcomb & Bentler, 1989). Some of these factors (risk factors) increase risk for drug involvement, whereas other (protective) factors decrease the potential for becoming involved with drugs. Figure 1 contains

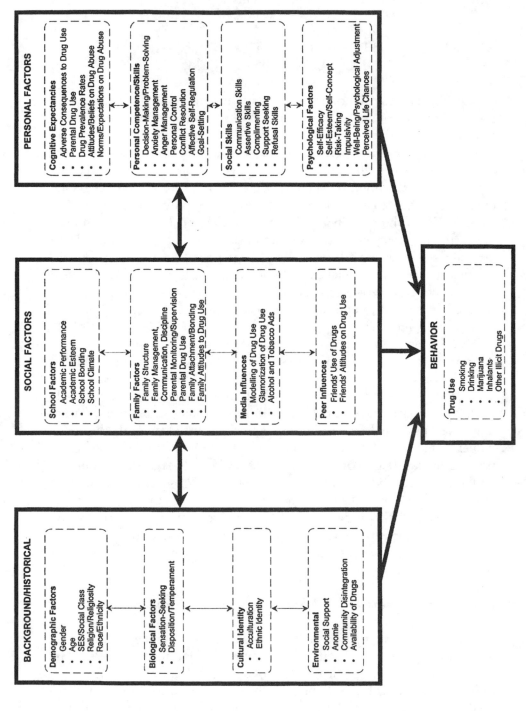

Figure 1. Integrated-domain model of drug use behavior (SES = socioeconomic status).

a general domain model of the factors that have been identified as the most important ones leading to drug-taking behavior. These factors can be grouped into broad categories or domains. The background–historical domain consists of demographic factors (e.g., age, gender, and social class), biological factors (e.g., temperament and sensation seeking), cultural factors (e.g., ethnic identity and acculturation), and environmental factors (e.g., community disintegration and drug availability). The social factors domain includes school factors (e.g., school bonding and school climate), family factors (e.g., family management practices, communication, discipline, monitoring, parental drug use, and parental attitudes toward drug use), media influences promoting attitudes and norms conducive to drug use (e.g., TV shows, movies, rock videos, and tobacco and alcohol advertising), and peer influences (e.g., friends' drug use and prodrug attitudes). These factors both shape and interact with the adolescent's cognitive expectancies (e.g., attitudes, beliefs, normative expectations, drug-related health knowledge), general competencies (e.g., personal self-management skills and social skills), and a set of skills specific to resisting social influences from both the media and peers to use drugs. Vulnerability to prodrug-use factors can be affected by psychological factors such as self-efficacy, self-esteem, personal control, psychological adjustment, and perceived life chances.

Figure 2 contains a general model of drug use initiation. This model incorporates key elements from the most prominent theories of drug use

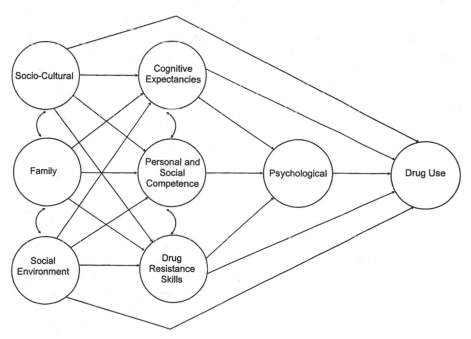

Figure 2. Hypothetical model of drug use initiation.

initiation, including social learning theory (Bandura, 1977), problem-behavior theory (Jessor & Jessor, 1977), self-derogation (Kaplan, 1980), persuasive communications (McGuire, 1968), peer-cluster theory (Oetting & Beauvais, 1987), and sensation seeking (Zuckerman, 1979). The variable domains presented in Figure 1 are organized in the model contained in Figure 2 into a causal framework in which these domains are conceptualized as superordinate constructs having specific relationships to one another. Although this model is designed to organize key factors associated with the onset of drug involvement into a coherent framework, it is done so from the perspective of how a preventive intervention may impact on these factors and prevent drug use–abuse. Although reasonably comprehensive, this model does not contain an exhaustive list of etiologic factors, nor does it posit all possible interrelationships. But it does provide a valuable heuristic for organizing and understanding the etiology of drug abuse and formulating a prevention strategy. Like other types of human behavior, drug abuse is conceptualized as being the result of a dynamic interaction of an individual and his or her environment. Social influences to use drugs (along with the availability of drugs) interact with individual vulnerability. Some individuals may be influenced to use drugs by the media (e.g., TV shows and movies glamorizing drug use or suggesting that drug use is normal or socially acceptable, as well as advertising efforts promoting the sale of alcohol and tobacco products), by family members who either use drugs or express pro-drug-use attitudes, or by friends and acquaintances who use drugs or hold attitudes and beliefs supportive of drug use. Still others may succumb to peer pressure to use drugs because of intrapersonal factors such as low self-esteem, high anxiety, hopelessness, low personal control, or the need for excitement (sensation seeking). The greater the number of risk factors that a person has, the more likely it is that she or he will become a drug user and eventually a drug abuser, because the presence of multiple risk factors is associated with both initial drug use and the severity of later drug involvement (Newcomb & Felix-Ortiz, 1992; Scheier & Newcomb, 1991).

Implications for Prevention

Inspection of the model contained in Figure 2 suggest several potential points of intervention for either preventing drug abuse or reducing drug abuse risk. Interventions can (and should) be developed to target individual, family, and community determinants of drug abuse. However, most prevention research has focused on testing the effectiveness of school-based interventions targeting individual-level factors. A school-based intervention is likely to effectively prevent drug abuse if it impacts on drug-related expectancies (e.g., knowledge, attitudes, and norms), drug-related resistance skills, and general competence (e.g., personal self-management skills and social skills). Increasing prevention-related drug knowledge and resistance skills can provide adolescents with the information and skills needed to develop antidrug attitudes and norms, as well as to resist peer and media pressure to use drugs. Teaching effective self-management skills and social skills offers the potential of reducing intrapersonal motivations to use drugs, as well as reducing vulnerability to prodrug social influences.

ADDITIONAL RESEARCH NEEDS

Beyond the need for more research concerning the mediating mechanisms of effective prevention approaches, considerably more research is needed in several different areas:

- To increase understanding of the limits of current school-based prevention approaches and to determine the long-term effectiveness of current prevention approaches. This not only means examining the effectiveness of prevention approaches that were implemented during middle–junior high school, in terms of their ability to sustain lower rates of drug use until the end of high school, but also involves conducting follow-up studies to determine the effectiveness of these prevention approaches as individuals progress through college and into young adulthood.
- With understudied racial–ethnic minority populations, to increase understanding of the etiology of drug use in these populations, to determine the extent to which current prevention approaches work with different populations, and to identify factors that may help to optimize the effectiveness of drug abuse prevention approaches with minority populations.
- As new information concerning the etiology of drug abuse becomes available, to integrate that information into efforts to further refine existing prevention approaches, as well as to identify new prevention approaches for both White and minority populations.
- To understand the etiology of drug abuse and to identify effective prevention methods with rural youth. Most prevention research has been conducted with suburban populations and, to a lesser extent, urban populations.
- To bridge the gap between research and practice. Research is needed concerning the dissemination, adoption, and institutionalization of effective prevention approaches by schools and communities.
- To determine the impact of both current and future preven-

tion approaches on other related health problems, such as violence, teenage pregnancy, and AIDS.

- To further develop and test selective and indicated prevention approaches, to increase the ability to help high-risk individuals as well as those who already have become involved with drugs.
- To identify prevention approaches suitable for both younger and older populations. Virtually all drug abuse prevention research conducted in recent years has focused on middle–junior high school populations.
- To develop additional (non-school-based) modalities for preventing drug abuse and different delivery channels, such as family-based and community-based approaches or preventive interventions conducted at community centers or as part of after-school programs.
- To develop more comprehensive approaches to drug abuse prevention that combine the best features of existing prevention methods.

CONCLUSION

Substantial progress has been made over the past 20 years in the area of drug abuse prevention. Much has been learned concerning the etiology of drug abuse and how to prevent it. The field of drug abuse prevention has matured over the years. A growing literature and a cadre of dedicated and highly competent researchers, many of whom were trained as psychologists, are responsible for the growing stature of the field, its dynamism, and its emergence as a respected area of scientific inquiry.

The accumulation of knowledge about effective approaches to drug abuse prevention provides a solid empirical foundation supporting claims that prevention can work—when using the right intervention model, an adequate initial dosage, and ongoing intervention or booster sessions and when implemented with reasonable fidelity and completeness. Largely because of the seriousness of the problem of drug abuse as well as the quality of the prevention research literature, prevention researchers increasingly find themselves asked to serve on federal, state, and local advisory panels and to respond to the sporadic queries of the media.

However, despite the progress made in drug abuse prevention research, much additional research is needed. Moreover, a considerable divide exists between research and practice. Too many prevention providers are using approaches that are based on intuition rather than on science. Therefore, researchers must do a better job of communicating their findings—not just to the scientific community (they do a reasonably good job of that) but also to policymakers, educators, parents, and community leaders. As teen drug use continues to rise, it is crucial that researchers actively disseminate the results of the best prevention research, to help take what has been learned over the years and translate that into action.

REFERENCES

Arkin, R. M., Roemhild, H. J., Johnson, C. A., Luepker, R. V., & Murray, D. M. (1981). The Minnesota Smoking Prevention Program: A seventh grade health curriculum supplement. *Journal of School Health, 51,* 616–661.

Bandura, A. (1977). *Social learning theory.* Englewood Cliffs, NJ: Prentice Hall.

Barnes, G. M., & Welte, J. W. (1986). Patterns and predictors of alcohol use among 7–12th grade students in New York State. *Journal of Studies on Alcohol, 47,* 53–62.

Bell, R. M., Ellickson, P. L., & Harrison, E. R. (1993). Do drug prevention effects persist into high school? *Preventive Medicine, 22,* 463–483.

Bettes, B. A., Dusenbury, L., Kerner, J., James-Ortiz, S., & Botvin, G. J. (1990). Ethnicity and psychosocial factors in alcohol and tobacco use in adolescence. *Child Development, 61,* 557–565.

Botvin, G. J. (1994). Principles of prevention. In R. H. Coombs & D. M. Ziedonis (Eds.), *Handbook on Drug Abuse Prevention* (pp. 19–44). Needham Heights, MA: Allyn & Bacon.

Botvin, G. J., Baker, E., Botvin, E. M., Dusenbury, L., Cardwell, J., & Diaz, T. (1993). Factors promoting cigarette smoking among Black youth: A causal modeling approach. *Addictive Behaviors, 18,* 397–405.

Botvin, G. J., Baker, E., Botvin, E. M., Filazzola, A. D., & Millman, R. B. (1984). Alcohol abuse prevention through the development of personal and social competence: A pilot study. *Journal of Studies on Alcohol, 45,* 550–552.

Botvin, G. J., Baker, E., Dusenbury, L., Tortu, S., & Botvin, E. M. (1990). Preventing adolescent drug abuse through a multimodal cognitive–behavioral approach: Results of a 3-year study. *Journal of Consulting and Clinical Psychology, 58,* 437–446.

Botvin, G. J., Baker, E., Renick, N. L., Filazzola, A. D., & Botvin, E. M. (1984). A cognitive–behavioral approach to substance abuse prevention. *Addictive Behaviors, 9,* 137–147.

Botvin, G. J., Batson, H. W., Witts-Vitale, S., Bess, V., Baker, E., & Dusenbury, L. (1989). A psychosocial approach to smoking prevention for urban Black youth. *Public Health Reports, 104,* 573–582.

Botvin, G. J., & Botvin, E. M. (1992). Adolescent tobacco, alcohol, and drug abuse: Prevention strategies, empirical findings, and assessment issues. *Journal of Developmental and Behavioral Pediatrics, 13,* 290–301.

Botvin, G. J., & Cardwell, J. (1992). *Primary prevention (smoking) of cancer in Black populations* (Final report to National Cancer Institute). New York: Cornell University Medical College.

Botvin, G. J., Dusenbury, L., Baker, E., James-Ortiz, S., Botvin, E. M., & Kerner, J. (1992). Smoking prevention among urban minority youth: Assessing effects on outcome and mediating variables. *Health Psychology, 11,* 290–299.

Botvin, G. J., Dusenbury, L., Baker, E., James-Ortiz, S., & Kerner, J. (1989). A skills training approach to smoking prevention among Hispanic youth. *Journal of Behavioral Medicine, 12,* 279–296.

Botvin, G. J., & Eng, A. (1980). A comprehensive school-based smoking prevention program. *Journal of School Health, 50,* 209–213.

Botvin, G. J., & Eng, A. (1982). The efficacy of a multicomponent approach to the prevention of cigarette smoking. *Preventive Medicine, 11,* 199–211.

Botvin, G. J., Eng, A., & Williams, C. L. (1980). Preventing the onset of cigarette smoking through life skills training. *Preventive Medicine, 9,* 135–143.

Botvin, G. J., Epstein, J. A., Baker, E., Diaz, T., & Ifill-Williams, M. (1996). School-based drug abuse prevention with inner-city minority youth. *Journal of Child and Adolescent Substance Abuse, 6,* 5–19.

Botvin, G. J., Epstein, J. A., Schinke, S. P., & Diaz, T. (1994). Predictors of cigarette smoking among inner-city minority youth. *Journal of Developmental and Behavioral Pediatrics, 15,* 67–73.

Botvin, G. J., Goldberg, C. J., Botvin, E. M., & Dusenbury, L. (1993). Smoking behavior of adolescents exposed to cigarette advertising. *Public Health Reports, 108,* 217–224.

Botvin, G. J., Renick, N., & Baker, E. (1983). The effects of scheduling format and booster sessions on a broad-spectrum psychosocial approach to smoking prevention. *Journal of Behavioral Medicine, 6,* 359–379.

Botvin, G. J., Schinke, S. P., Epstein, J. A., & Diaz, T. (1994). The effectiveness of culturally-focused and generic skills training approaches to alcohol and drug abuse prevention among minority youth. *Psychology of Addictive Behaviors, 8,* 116–127.

Botvin, G. J., Schinke, S. P., Epstein, J. A., Diaz, T., & Botvin, E. M. (1995). Effectiveness of culturally focused and generic skills training approaches to alcohol and drug abuse prevention among minority adolescents: Two-year follow-up results. *Psychology of Addictive Behaviors, 9,* 183–194.

Caplan, M., Weissberg, R. P., Grober, J. S., Sivo, P., Grady, K., & Jacoby, C. (1992). Social competence promotion with inner-city and suburban young adolescents: Effects of social adjustment and alcohol use. *Journal of Consulting and Clinical Psychology, 60,* 56–63.

Collins, R. L. (1995). Issues of ethnicity in research on the prevention of substance abuse. In G. J. Botvin, S. Schinke, & M. Orlandi (Eds.), *Drug abuse prevention with multi-ethnic youth* (pp. 28–45). Thousand Oaks, CA: Sage.

Donaldson, S. I., Graham, J. W., & Hansen, W. B. (1994). Testing the generalizability of intervening mechanism theories: Understanding the effects of adolescent drug use prevention interventions. *Journal of Behavioral Medicine, 17,* 195–216.

Dorn, N., & Thompson, A. (1976). Evaluation of drug education in the longer term is not an optional extra. *Community Health, 7,* 154–161.

Dryfoos, J. G. (1993). Common components of successful interventions with high-risk youth. In N. J. Bell & R. W. Bell (Eds.), *Adolescent risk taking* (pp. 131–147). Newbury Park, CA: Sage.

Ellickson, P. L., & Bell, R. M. (1990). Drug prevention in junior high: A multi-site longitudinal test. *Science, 247*, 1299–1305.

Ellickson, P. L., Bell, R. M., & McGuigan, K. (1993). Preventing adolescent drug use: Long term results of a junior high program. *American Journal of Public Health, 83*, 856–861.

Epstein, J. A., Botvin, G. J., Diaz, T., & Schinke, S. P. (1995). The role of social factors and individual characteristics in promoting alcohol among inner-city minority youth. *Journal of Studies on Alcohol, 56*, 39–46.

Epstein, J. A., Botvin, G. J., Diaz, T., Toth, V., & Schinke, S. P. (1995). Social and personal factors in marijuana use and intentions to use drugs among inner city minority youth. *Journal of Developmental and Behavioral Pediatrics, 16*, 14–20.

Epstein, J. A., Dusenbury, L., Botvin, G. J., & Diaz, T. (1994). Determinants of intentions of junior high school students to become sexually active and use condoms: Implications for reduction and prevention of AIDS risk. *Psychological Reports, 75*, 1043–1053.

Evans, R. I. (1976). Smoking in children: Developing a social psychological strategy of deterrence. *Preventive Medicine, 5*, 122–127.

Evans, R. I., Rozelle, R. M., Mittlemark, M. B., Hansen, W. B., Bane, A. L., & Havis, J. (1978). Deterring the onset of smoking in children: Knowledge of immediate physiological effects and coping with peer pressure, media pressure, and parent modeling. *Journal of Applied Social Psychology, 8*, 126–135.

Fishbein, M. (1977). Consumer beliefs and behavior with respect to cigarette smoking: A critical analysis of the public literature. In *Federal Trade Commission report to Congress: Pursuant to the Public Health Cigarette Smoking Act of 1976* (p. 113). Washington, DC: U.S. Government Printing Office.

Flay, B. R. (1985). Psychosocial approaches to smoking prevention: A review of findings. *Health Psychology, 4*, 449–488.

Flay, B. R., Keopke, D., Thomson, S. J., Santi, S., Best, J. A., & Brown, K. S. (1989). Long-term follow-up of the first Waterloo smoking prevention trial. *American Journal of Public Health, 79*, 1371–1376.

Gilchrist, L. D., & Schinke, S. P. (1983). Self-control skills for smoking prevention. In P. F. Engstrom, P. Anderson, & L. E. Mortenson (Eds.), *Advances in cancer control* (pp. 125–130). New York: Alan R. Liss.

Goodstadt, M. S. (1974). Myths and methodology in drug education: A critical review of the research evidence. In M. Goodstadt (Ed.), *Research on methods and programs of drug education*. Washington, DC: U.S. Government Printing Office.

Goodstadt, M. S. (1986). Drug education: The prevention issues. *Journal of Drug Education, 19*, 197–208.

Hansen, W. B. (1996). Pilot test results comparing the All Stars Program with seventh grade D.A.R.E.: Program integrity and mediating variable analysis. *Substance Use and Misuse, 31,* 1359–1377.

Hansen, W. B., Graham, J. W., Wolkenstein, B. H., Lundy, B. Z., Pearson, J., Flay, B. R., & Johnson, C. A. (1988). Differential impact of three alcohol prevention curricula on hypothesized mediating variables. *Journal of Drug Education, 18,* 143–153.

Hawkins, J. D., Catalano, R. F., & Miller, J. Y. (1992). Risk and protective factors for alcohol and other drug problems in adolescence and early adulthood: Implications for substance abuse prevention. *Psychological Bulletin, 112(1),* 64–105.

Hurd, P., Johnson, C. A., Pechacek, T., Bast, C. P., Jacobs, D., & Luepker, R. (1980). Prevention of cigarette smoking in 7th grade students. *Journal of Behavioral Medicine, 3,* 15–28.

Jessor, R., & Jessor, S. L. (1977). *Problem behavior and psychosocial development: A longitudinal study of youth.* New York: Academic Press.

Johnston, L. D., O'Malley, P. M., & Bachman, J. G. (1998). *National survey results on drug use from the Monitoring the Future Study, 1975-1997, Vol. I Secondary school students.* (NIH Publication No. 98-4346). Rockville, MD: National Institute on Drug Abuse.

Kaplan, H. B. (1980). *Deviant behavior in defense of self.* New York: Academic Press.

Kearney, A. L., & Hines, M. H. (1980). Evaluation of the effectiveness of a drug prevention education program. *Journal of Drug Education, 10,* 127–134.

Kim, S. (1988). A short- and long-term evaluation of "Here's Looking at You": II. *Journal of Drug Education, 18,* 235–242.

Kim, S., Coletti, D., Williams, C., and Hepler, N. A. (1995). Substance abuse prevention involving Asian/Pacific Islander American communities. In G. J. Botvin, S. Schinke, M. Orlandi (Eds.), *Drug abuse prevention with multi-ethnic youth* (pp. 295–326). Thousand Oaks, CA: Sage.

Kinder, B. N., Pape, N. E., & Walfish, S. (1980). Drug and alcohol education programs: A review of outcome studies. *International Journal of the Addictions, 15,* 1035–1054.

Luepker, R. V., Johnson, C. A., Murray, D. M., & Pechacek, T. F. (1983). Prevention of cigarette smoking: Three year follow-up of educational programs for youth. *Journal of Behavioral Medicine, 6,* 53–61.

MacKinnon, D. P., Johnson, C. A., Pentz, M. A., Dwyer, J. H., Hansen, W. B., Flay, B. R., & Wang, E. (1991). Mediating mechanisms in a school-based drug prevention program: First year effects of the Midwestern Prevention Project. *Health Psychology, 10,* 164–172.

Maddahian, E., Newcomb, M. D., & Bentler, P. M. (1988). Adolescent drug use and intention to use drugs: Concurrent and longitudinal analyses of four ethnic groups. *Addictive Behaviors, 13,* 191–195.

McAlister, A., Perry, C. L., Killen, J., Slinkard, L. A., & Maccoby, N. (1980). Pilot study of smoking, alcohol, and drug abuse prevention. *American Journal of Public Health, 70,* 719–721.

McAlister, A., Perry, C., & Maccoby, N. (1979). Adolescent smoking: Onset and prevention. *Pediatrics, 63,* 650–658.

McGuire, W. J. (1964). Inducing resistance to persuasion: Some contemporary approaches. In L. Berkowitz (Ed.), *Advances in experimental social psychology* (pp. 192–227). New York: Academic Press.

McGuire, W. J. (1968). The nature of attitudes and attitude change. In G. Lindzey & E. Aronson (Eds.), *Handbook of social psychology* (pp. 136–314). Reading, MA: Addison-Wesley.

Murray, D. M., Davis-Hearn, M., Goldman, A. I., Pirie, P., & Luepker, R. V. (1988). Four and five year follow-up results from four seventh-grade smoking prevention strategies. *Journal of Behavioral Medicine, 11,* 395–405.

Newcomb, M. D., & Bentler, P. M. (1989). Substance use and abuse among children and teenagers. *American Psychologist, 44,* 242–248.

Newcomb, M. D., & Felix-Ortiz, M. (1992). Multiple protective and risk factors for drug use and abuse: Cross-sectional and prospective findings. *Journal of Consulting and Clinical Psychology, 63,* 280–296.

Newcomb, M. D., Maddahian, E., Skager, R., & Bentler, P. M. (1987). Substance abuse and psychosocial risk factors among teenagers: Associations with sex, age, ethnicity, and type of school. *American Journal of Drug & Alcohol Abuse, 13,* 413–433.

Oetting, E. R., & Beauvais, F. (1987). Peer cluster theory, socialization characteristics, and adolescent drug use: A path analysis. *Journal of Consulting & Clinical Psychology, 34,* 205–213.

Pentz, M. A. (1983). Prevention of adolescent substance abuse through social skill development. In T. J. Glynn, C. G. Leukefeld, & J. B. Ludford (Eds.), *Preventing adolescent drug abuse: Intervention strategies* (NIDA Research Monograph No. 47, pp. 195–232). Washington, DC: U.S. Government Printing Office.

Perry, C. L., & Kelder, S. H. (1992). Models for effective prevention. *Journal of Adolescent Health, 13,* 355–363.

Perry, C., Killen, J., Slinkard, L. A., & McAlister, A. L. (1983). Peer teaching and smoking prevention among junior high students. *Adolescence, 9,* 277–281.

Resnicow, K., & Botvin, G. J. (1993). School-based substance use prevention programs: Why do effects decay? *Preventive Medicine, 22,* 484–490.

Richards, L. G. (1969, August–September). *Government programs and psychological principles in drug abuse prevention.* Paper presented at the 77th Annual Convention of the American Psychological Association, Washington, DC.

Schaps, E., Bartolo, R. D., Moskowitz, J., Palley, C. S., & Churgin, S. (1981). A review of 127 drug abuse prevention program evaluations. *Journal of Drug Issues, 11,* 17–43.

Scheier, L. M., & Newcomb, M. D. (1991). Psychosocial predictors of drug use initiation and escalation: An expansion of the multiple risk factors hypothesis using longitudinal data. *Contemporary Drug Problems, Spr,* 31–73.

Schinke, S. P. (1984). Preventing teenage pregnancy. In M. Hersen, R. M. Eisler,

& P. M. Miller (Eds.), *Progress in behavior modification* (16th ed., pp. 31–63). New York: Academic Press.

Schinke, S. P., Botvin, G. J., & Orlandi, M. (1991). *Substance abuse in children and adolescents.* Newbury Park, CA: Sage.

Schinke, S. P., & Gilchrist, L. D. (1983). Primary prevention of tobacco smoking. *Journal of School Health, 53,* 416–419.

Schinke, S. P., & Gilchrist, L. D. (1984). Preventing cigarette smoking with youth. *Journal of Primary Prevention, 5,* 48–56.

Shope, J. T., Dielman, T. E., Butchart, A. T., & Campanelli, P. C. (1992). An elementary school-based alcohol misuse prevention program: A follow-up evaluation. *Journal of Studies on Alcohol, 53,* 106–121.

Snow, D. L., Tebes, J. K., Arthur, M. W., & Tapasak, R. C. (1992). Two-year follow-up of a social–cognitive intervention to prevent substance use. *Journal of Drug Education, 22,* 101–114.

Sussman, S., Dent, C. W., Stacy, A. W., & Sun, P. (1993). Project Towards No Tobacco Use: 1-year behavior outcomes. *American Journal of Public Health, 83,* 1245–1250.

Swisher, J. D. (1979). Prevention issues. In R. I. Dupont, A. Goldstein, & J. O'Donnell (Eds.), *Handbook on drug abuse* (pp. 49–62). Washington, DC: National Institute on Drug Abuse.

Swisher, J. D., Crawford, J. L., Goldstein, R., & Yura, M. (1971). Drug education: Pushing or preventing? *Peabody Journal of Education, 49,* 68–75.

Swisher, J. D., & Hoffman, A. (1975). Information: The irrelevant variable in drug education. In B. W. Corder, R. A. Smith, & J. D. Swisher (Eds.), *Drug abuse prevention: Perspectives and approaches for educators* (pp. 49–62). Dubuque, IA: William C. Brown.

Telch, M. J., Killen, J. D., McAlister, A. L., Perry, C. L., & Maccoby, N. (1982). Long-term follow-up of a pilot project on smoking prevention with adolescents. *Journal of Behavioral Medicine, 5,* 1–8.

Trimble, J. E. (1995). Toward an understanding of ethnicity and ethnic identity, and their relationship with drug use research. In G. J. Botvin, S. Schinke, & M. Orlandi (Eds.), *Drug abuse prevention with multi-ethnic youth* (pp. 3–27). Thousand Oaks, CA: Sage.

Wallace, J. M., Jr., Bachman, J. G., O'Malley, P. M., & Johnston, L. D. (1995). Racial/ethnic differences in adolescent drug use: Exploring possible explanations. In G. J. Botvin, S. Schinke, & M. Orlandi (Eds.), *Drug abuse prevention with multi-ethnic youth* (pp. 59–80). Thousand Oaks, CA: Sage.

Zuckerman, M. (1979). *Sensation seeking: Beyond the optimal level of arousal.* Hillsdale, NJ: Lawrence Erlbaum Associates.

13

HIV PREVENTION: WE DON'T NEED TO WAIT FOR A VACCINE

THOMAS J. COATES AND CHRIS COLLINS

Trends in the spread of HIV/AIDS reveal something most people don't know about the disease: The largest number of new cases are occurring in intravenous drug users (IDUs) and their sex partners, not among gay men. Drug use is largely responsible for the spread of HIV/AIDS into the heterosexual population. Another startling fact is that HIV/AIDS is preventable. Why then does it continue to spread?

Simply put, strategies proven to be effective in preventing HIV/AIDS have not been implemented because of political opposition and because the resources dedicated to prevention efforts have been inadequate to address the problem sufficiently. Everyone is waiting for the "magic bullet:" a vaccine. An effective vaccine will save many lives. But the entire developed world spends only $600 million annually on HIV prevention in the developing world, as much as we spend in the United States alone. Increasing the resources spent on HIV/AIDS prevention around the world

Preparation of this chapter was supported in part by National Institute of Mental Health Grant No. MH42459 (Center for AIDS Prevention Studies), by a grant from the Henry J. Kaiser, Jr., Family Foundation, titled HIV Prevention: Looking Back, Looking Ahead, and by a grant from SmithKline Beecham Pharmaceuticals.

309

would save innumerable lives. HIV prevention science is at a highly advanced stage. We need to use it, and we need to use it now.

HIV IN THE UNITED STATES: AN UNNECESSARY EPIDEMIC

It is estimated that between 40,000 and 80,000 new HIV infections occur annually in the United States (National Institutes of Health, 1997). Evaluations from developed and developing countries have demonstrated unequivocally that epidemics of HIV can be avoided and also can be turned around once they appear to be out of control, so most of the new HIV infections in the United States are avoidable. The United States has lacked the political will to implement strategies known to be effective in managing the epidemic (see Coates, Aggleton, et al., 1996). Australia and New Zealand contained the spread of HIV through quick implementation of sound prevention practices. Neither Australia nor New Zealand experienced an HIV epidemic among IDUs. The strategies for accomplishing this were not complicated but relied on close and continuing collaboration between affected communities and public health officials, treatment for drug and alcohol abuse on demand, and pragmatic harm-reduction strategies to ensure that HIV would spread as little as possible.

Des Jarlais et al. (1995) have demonstrated that HIV prevention can work among IDUs when strategies to control the spread of HIV are implemented early. Several cities around the world have maintained HIV prevalence among IDUs at less than 5%, including Glasgow, Scotland; Lund, Sweden; Sydney, New South Wales, Australia; Toronto, Ontario, Canada; and Tacoma, Washington. These cities began HIV prevention programs early, made clean needles and syringes available, and developed outreach programs to reach out-of-treatment IDUs. Evidence from San Francisco (Coates, 1990), Uganda (Konde-Lule, 1995), and Thailand (Nelson et al., 1996) demonstrates that epidemics once thought to be out of control can be stabilized.

TARGETING OF RESOURCES

To be cost-effective, intervention efforts (both services and research) need to be targeted both to where HIV is now and to where it is heading (Kahn, 1996). The Centers for Disease Control and Prevention (CDC; 1997) estimate that 650,000–900,000 persons with HIV are living in the United States. About 50% of these are gay or bisexual men, about 25%–30% are IDUs, and about 20% are women. Of course, there is overlap among these categories. Most new HIV infections could be prevented by intensive efforts aimed at the populations in which HIV is spreading

(Kahn, 1996). The CDC estimates that 35%–50% of new infections are occurring among injection drug users, that 25%–40% are occurring among gay men, and that 25% are occurring among women (primarily from male IDUs to their heterosexual female partners; Holmberg, 1996).

However, these statistics vary by region of the country. Mills, Stall, Catania, and Coates (1997) have noted that national data can obscure locally important characteristics. The AIDS epidemic varies enormously across the nation, particularly with regard to risk-group composition. In the western United States, for example, the primary mode of HIV transmission is male–male sexual contact, whereas in other parts of the country, the primary mode of transmission may be heterosexual contact or injection drug use. These facts underscore the wisdom of community planning for HIV prevention and the necessity of collaboration by social and behavioral scientists in its execution (Valdiserri, Aultman, & Curran, 1995).

MULTIPLE LEVELS OF INTERVENTION AMONG AT-RISK POPULATIONS

HIV transmission is caused, as with most health problems, by processes at the individual and societal levels. We conceptualize HIV prevention at six levels of influence (see Tables 1 and 2) and present examples of effective strategies at every level.

Interventions at the *individual* level help people to change by providing knowledge or altering beliefs, attitudes, perceived norms, motivations, skills, or biological states related to high-risk activities. Such interventions attempt to change intrapsychic factors such as knowledge, skills, and motivation to use both. They also assist individuals in reducing use of drugs related to high-risk activities. Examples abound of individual and small-group strategies aimed at modifying individual-level variables to modify sexual and injection behaviors to reduce HIV transmission (DiClemente & Wingood, 1995; Jemmott, Jemmott, & Fong, 1992; Kelly et al., 1992; Rotheram-Borus, Koopman, Haignere, & Davies, 1991). These studies have demonstrated the impact of such interventions on self-reported behavior, but evaluations demonstrating reductions in incident infections are few and far between.

Project RESPECT (see Kamb et al., 1998) was a multicenter, randomized, controlled trial evaluating HIV prevention counseling in increasing condom use and reducing sexually transmitted disease (STD; including HIV) incidence conducted at 5 STD clinics. HIV-negative (HIV−) heterosexual participants were randomly assigned to one of three face-to-face interventions: HIV education (two sessions with brief HIV–STD prevention messages); HIV prevention counseling (two sessions aimed at increasing risk perception using specific, achievable steps toward behavior

TABLE 1
Levels of Causation and Change Determinants of HIV Transmission

Level	Definition	Examples
Individual	How environment is experienced and acted on by individuals; individual biological states	Knowledge, risk-perceptions self-efficacy, levels of intoxication, biological determinants of sexual behavior
Dyadic–familial	How couples interact and negotiate sexual and needle-sharing behavior; how families communicate regarding sexual behavior	Implicit and explicit rules governing power and sexual relations
Institutional–community	Social norms, resources, and opportunities; disease prevalence	Access to condoms and needles, health care behavior, and norms of peers
Policy–legal	Laws and policies	Paraphernalia laws, discriminatory practices, inheritance laws, laws and policies regarding confidentiality
Superstructural	Social and economic structures; widely held and pervasive societal customs and attitudes	Social and economic restraints on women
Medical–technological	Medical treatment	Drug, STD, mental illness, prenatal, and HIV treatment; testing of blood donations; virucides and spermicides

Note: STD = sexually transmitted disease. Adapted from Sweat and Dennison (1995).

TABLE 2
Levels of Causation and Change Mechanisms of HIV Transmission

Level	Definition	Examples
Individual	Educational, motivational appeals, skills building, counseling	Individual or small-group strategies, drug and alcohol treatment
Dyadic–familial	Skills building, couples counseling with or without testing	Couples counseling and testing, family skills training
Institutional–community	Community organization and mobilization, condom marketing and distribution, syringe distribution, access to care	Peer outreach, community mobilization, condom marketing and distribution, syringe exchange, drug and alcohol treatment on demand
Policy–legal	Legislation and policy reform	Legislating syringe exchange and antidiscrimination, anonymous testing, movements and laws
Superstructural	Social movements, revolution	Antipoverty programs, antidiscrimination programs, education opportunity programs
Medical–technological	Treatment to reduce the likelihood of engaging in high-risk behavior	Drug treatment, STD treatment, prenatal care, virucides and microbicides

Note: STD = sexually transmitted disease. Adapted from Sweat and Dennison (1995).

change); and enhanced counseling (four sessions based on theoretical constructs of behavior change also using small steps). A total of 5,872 patients were enrolled: 3,340 men and 2,532 women. Follow-up was 70% at 3 and 6 months and 65% at 9 and 12 months. Through the 6-month follow-up, participants in both counseling arms had a reduced risk of a new STD (enhanced counseling vs. control, = 0.80, p = .003; HIV prevention counseling vs. control, = .84, p = .02). The two counseling conditions did not differ from each other. Reported condom use increased in all intervention arms, although the enhanced counseling had the highest condom use at each follow-up.

An intervention study conducted recently among commercial sex workers in India demonstrates both the potential and the limits of individual-level interventions. Bhave et al. (1995) developed an innovative intervention to reduce new infections among commercial sex workers in the red light areas of Bombay. The brothels contain 100–150 women, and the women are virtually captive once they are sold into prostitution. Their access to medical care is limited. Two relatively comparable houses were chosen in which to conduct an evaluation of the intervention. A quasi-experimental design was chosen because a design using randomization of individuals would have been subject to contamination across treatment conditions. The intervention consisted of a 6-month program using educational videos, small-group discussions, and pictorial educational methods to address variables related to high-risk behavior. Three hundred thirty-four commercial sex workers received the experimental intervention, and 207 commercial sex workers participated as controls. The 1-year seroconversion rates for the intervention versus the control group were 6% versus 15% for HIV, 8% versus 21% for syphilis, and 4% versus 11% for hepatitis B surface antigen (all ps < .01). Certainly, the seroconversion rates in the intervention group were dramatically below that of the control group, but no one could be satisfied as long as 6% of any group was still seroconverting to HIV.

The *Dyadic–Familial* Level refers to interpersonal processes occurring between two individuals likely to have sexual intercourse or to share injection equipment. This level also refers to familial interactions likely to affect the course of HIV transmission. An example would be parent–child communication about sexuality. Interventions at this level attempt to influence the couple or the family.

The need for interventions focused on couples comes from a variety of findings. Catania et al. (1992) and Catania, Binson, and Dolcini (1995), in the National AIDS Behavioral Surveys, found that women were more likely than men to have risky sexual partners, especially if both the women and the men were in the same income strata. Women, relative to men, were more likely to be in risky partnerships (i.e., where the partner injected drugs or had other male or female sex partners) where condoms were not being used. Sixty-four percent of women with risky partners were in cities where the prevalence of HIV is high. Women in these relationships may feel powerless to influence the risk behavior of their partner or to insist on protective actions that prevent HIV transmission. Clearly, it is essential to focus on risk reduction in intimate relationships, and dyadic approaches may be essential for this process.

We are aware of few attempts to intervene at the dyadic level. One study carried out in Rwanda among a cohort of childbearing women showed that whereas the prevalence of HIV infection was 32%, it was 25% among the majority of women who reported only one lifetime partner. Women exposed to HIV counseling and testing showed increases in reported condom use (Allen et al., 1992). Only 7% of the women had used condoms before the study, but after 1 year of follow-up, 16% of HIV− and 35% of HIV-positive (HIV+) women reported using condoms. Among a subsample of women whose partners volunteered to be tested, condom use rates were even higher (23% and 55% among HIV− and HIV+ women, respectively). HIV seroconversion rates decreased to 1.8 per 100/person year of observation in HIV− women whose partners were tested but remained at 3.4 per 100/person year among women whose partners were not tested. In another analysis of this study, marked increases in reported condom use were noted among discordant couples. Fifty-seven percent of discordant couples were using condoms at the 1-year follow-up. Intensive and repeated counseling also led to large increases in reported condom use (from less than 5% ever use to 71% regular use) and abstinence (from 0 to 28%) among couples found to be discordant in a research project in Zaire. This research was confirmed by similar findings in a multicenter, randomized, controlled study in three developing countries (De Zoysa et al., 1995).

Interventions at the *institutional–community* level attempt to modify social norms; influence social networks, resources, and opportunities, and reduce barriers to preventive practices in the community. Examples of change strategies include peer outreach, diffusion of innovation, community mobilization, television, condom marketing, and syringe exchange. Outreach and community mobilization strategies have been used effectively to reduce HIV risk among gay and bisexual men. Kelly et al. (1992) demonstrated the impact of social influence intervention in small communities in the United States. Surveys were conducted of all men patronizing gay clubs in each city, to establish risk behavior base rates. After a small cadre of popular "trendsetters" were identified by their peers, they received training in approaches for peer education and then contracted to communicate risk-reduction recommendations and endorsements to friends. Surveys were repeated at regular intervals in all cities, with the same intervention introduced in all cities in a lagged fashion. The interventions consistently produced systematic reductions in the population's high-risk behavior (unprotected anal intercourse reductions of 15% to 29% from baseline levels), with the same pattern of effects sequentially replicated in all three cities.

Kegeles, Hays, and Coates (1996) developed and implemented a community-level HIV prevention program in midsize communities. The peer-led program had three components: outreach, small groups, and a publicity campaign. Independent from the prevention program, a cohort of young gay men were surveyed in this and in a similar comparison community pre- and postintervention. After the intervention, the proportion of men engaging in any unprotected anal intercourse decreased from 41% to 30%, from 20% to 11% with nonprimary partners, and from 59% to 45% with primary partners. No significant changes occurred in the comparison community over the same period. These data demonstrate the efficacy of a community-based prevention approach that is embedded into social activities and community life.

Interventions at the *policy–legal* level attempt to influence laws and policies. Examples from other fields of disease prevention have documented the potency of changes at this level. Taxing cigarettes to reduce consumption, outlawing smoking in workplaces, requiring helmets for motorcycle riders, fluoridating water to reduce cavities, and increasing penalties for driving while under the influence of alcohol all have had documented and important impacts on risk behaviors and disease prevention.

Examples of changes at this level include widespread advertisement of condoms, laws allowing syringe and needle acquisitions, laws regulating commercial sex work, laws and policies regarding HIV testing and counseling, and laws outlawing discrimination on the basis of HIV disease. Change strategies include positive policies regarding condom advertisements, over-the-counter sale of syringes, and medical care for persons with HIV. Evaluations of syringe exchanges in the United States and abroad provide an example of an environmental strategy dependent on structural level changes. Syringe exchange is a strategy to increase access to sterile needles and syringes and thereby reduce the need for individuals to reuse or share contaminated needles and syringes (Lurie et al., 1993). Unfortunately, syringe exchanges in the United States have run afoul of political issues: Their implementation has not been endorsed by the federal government and has often been blocked in the courts. The cost in lives lost is enormous (Lurie & Drucker, 1997). This is in stark contrast to the governments of Europe and Australia, where harm-reduction approaches were embraced with predictable beneficial effects.

Connecticut recently changed its laws regarding syringe sales and possession, with dramatic effect (Groseclose et al., 1995; Valleroy et al., 1995). In July 1992, pharmacists were permitted to sell and individuals were permitted to possess up to 10 syringes without medical prescriptions. Groseclose conducted two serial cross-sectional surveys with IDUs recruited in drug-treatment centers, correctional facilities, and health department settings before and after the enactment of these laws. Among IDUs who reported ever sharing a syringe, syringe sharing decreased after the new laws (52% before vs. 31% after; $p = .02$). Fewer IDUs reported purchasing syringes on the street after the new laws (74% before vs. 28% after; $p < .0001$), and more IDUs reported purchasing syringes from a pharmacy after the new laws (19% before vs. 78% after; $p < .0001$). Among Hartford police officers, needle-stick injury rates after the new laws were lower after the new laws (6 per 1,007 drug-related arrests before vs. 2 per 1,032 arrests after).

Diaz, Chu, Winstein, Mokotoff, and Jones (1998) analyzed data from an interview survey of 11,757 patients 18 years of age or older with HIV or AIDS between June 1990 and August 1995 in 12 state or city health departments in the United States (Arizona; Delaware; New Mexico; Washington; South Carolina; Connecticut; Florida; Los Angeles, CA; Atlanta, GA; Denver, CO; Detroit, MI; and Jersey City, NJ). A total of 1,525 persons had ever shared syringes and reported injection drug use in the past 5 years, and 784 (51%) had injected in the year before the interview, and of these, 389 (49%) had shared during that year. The only statistically significant time trend was that the proportion of IDUs who shared decreased from 71% in 1992 to 15% in 1995. This trend appeared to be related to the 1992 changes in Connecticut laws that allowed purchase and possession of syringes without a prescription.

Interventions at the *superstructural* level attempt to identify and change a society's deep and pervasive attitudes and structures that facilitate HIV transmission. Examples include sex phobia, homophobia, racism, acceptance of social and economic inequality, and sexism (see Lurie, Hintzen, & Lowe, 1995; O'Reilly & Piot, 1996). Change strategies at the superstructural level include social movements, changes in constitutions governing countries (e.g., the fact that the Constitution of South Africa outlaws discrimination based on sexual orientation is important), legislative changes, and revolutions. Such changes take a long time, and their modification is not easy; nonetheless, consideration of possibilities should be undertaken in a comprehensive HIV prevention strategy. Clearly, HIV prevention for women will require considerable effort at this level to ensure better educational and occupational opportunities for women and to ensure legal protections and power in society.[1]

---

[1]An example identified recently is a manual detailing the rights of Islamic women, titled "Claiming Our Rights: A Manual for Women's Human Rights Education in Muslim Societies" (1996). The manual contains instructions for conducting grassroots discussions and interpretations of the Koran, along with texts of major international agreements on human rights, particularly women's rights, which many Muslim nations have signed. The objective is to stimulate a women's movement and gradual cultural change.

HIV prevention also can be accomplished through *medical–technological* interventions (see Tables 1 and 2, and Exhibit 1). New technological and medical advances provide both hope for victims and challenges for the behavioral and social sciences. Advances in medicine and technology offer promise only if they are used fully by the people who need them. For that to happen, behavioral and social scientists will have to provide innovative research on the topics of decision making and use of medical services. Some of the important research questions are displayed in Exhibit 2.

Treatment of HIV disease

It has been observed recently that triple combination therapy for HIV (with nucleoside analogs and protease inhibitors) can reduce circulating HIV in the blood to nondetectable levels (Carpenter et al., 1996). These findings offer great hope to HIV-infected individuals; both length and quality of life should be increased as a result (Feinberg, 1996). How this will affect HIV prevention is unknown. Certainly, people with HIV infection will be living longer; programs must be created to attend to their special needs to maintain low-risk behaviors over a long period of time. It is also possible that effective treatment of HIV might reduce the potential for transmission through sharing of injecting equipment or through sexual intercourse.

Counseling and testing

Counseling and testing have been important mainstays of HIV prevention and are essential for getting infected individuals into care (Coates, 1990; Higgins et al., 1991). An important means of reducing HIV transmission in this country has been through routine HIV screening and testing of blood donations; only 12 to 14 infectious donations are detected annually from a total of 12 million donations (Schreiber, Busch, Kleinman,

EXHIBIT 1
Technologies and Treatment to Reduce HIV Transmission

Routine HIV testing of the blood supply
More accessible HIV counseling and testing
Treatment of HIV using triple combination therapy
Treatment of sexually transmitted diseases
Antiviral treatment pre- and postpartum to reduce vertical transmission
Treatment of drug and alcohol abuse
Treatment of mental illness

EXHIBIT 2
Important Research Questions Concerning HIV Prevention

Vertical Parental Transmission

What are the optimal ways to offer counseling and testing to women of child-bearing age?

What decision-making strategies are used by women of childbearing age to determine contraceptive strategies?

What decision-making strategies are used by pregnant HIV positive women to determine whether to use antiretroviral therapy to reduce vertical transmission?

What are the barriers and facilitators of medical care during pregnancy?

HIV Treatment

What decision-making strategies are used by HIV-infected individuals in determining choices among antiretroviral therapies?

What are the facilitators and barriers to medical care?

What are the determinants of adherence to antiretroviral therapy?

What is the impact of triple combination therapy on behaviors capable of transmitting HIV?

Does sero-incidence rise when triple combination therapy becomes widespread in an area of high HIV prevalence? Are resistant strains transmitted?

Sexually Transmitted Diseases

What strategies are useful in primary and secondary prevention of sexually transmitted diseases?

Vaccines

What are the determinants of participation in HIV vaccine trials?

What is the impact of vaccine trials, and ultimately vaccines, on behaviors capable of transmitting HIV?

Does sero-incidence rise when vaccine trials or vaccines are introduced into areas of high prevalence of HIV?

& Korelitz, 1996). Although there has been much discussion of the potential psychological consequences of HIV, most studies document the fact that most individuals cope with the results and do not experience long-term psychological consequences (Phillips & Coates, 1995). The social consequences, however, can be devastating and merit more discussion and strategies to protect HIV-infected individuals, especially women, against abuse and other negative effects (Van der Stratten, Vittinghoff, Glass, Quan, & Padian, 1996).

STDs

STDs have long been implicated as a cofactor for HIV transmission (Adler, 1996). Such diseases are a major public health problem in most developing countries and are endemic in certain parts of the United States.

In fact, the United States has the highest rates of STDs of any developed country (Eng & Butler, 1996). A recent randomized clinical trial demonstrated the efficacy of aggressive syndromic treatment of STDs in reducing HIV transmission by 40% in rural Tanzania (Grosskurth et al., 1995). Strategies are needed both for primary prevention of STDs (e.g., Project RESPECT, see Kamb et al., 1998) and for early diagnosis and treatment of STDs to reduce HIV transmission.

Vertical transmission

Over 1.5 million children worldwide have been infected with HIV through maternal–child transmission. The Pediatric AIDS Clinical Trials Group (Protocol 076) demonstrated that treatment with zidovudine before, during, and after delivery (to mother and infant) reduced vertical transmission by over 60% (Connor et al., 1994). After the release of these results, the CDC in collaboration with the National Institutes of Health (NIH) and the Health Research and Services Administration in Bethesda, Maryland drafted guidelines to promote routine and universal HIV counseling and voluntary testing for all pregnant women and AZT therapy for HIV-infected pregnant women and their babies.

These efforts have dramatically reduced AIDS cases in children. The incidence of perinatally acquired AIDS peaked in the United States in 1992; cases began to decline in 1993 and dropped dramatically in 1994 (by 8% from 1993) and 1995 (by 17% from 1994). Thus, the number of perinatally acquired AIDS peaked at 905 during 1992 and was 663 in 1995 (CDC, 1996a). Studies are now under way to determine if triple combination therapy reduces chances of infection even further and if other regimens that are simpler to administer and perhaps carry less danger to the fetus might be just as effective. Other strategies for reducing maternal–child transmission can involve effective family planning and contraceptive counseling for HIV-infected mothers (Allen et al., 1993; King et al., 1995), reduction of unprotected intercourse (presumably from an HIV-infected partner) before, during, and after pregnancy (Bulterys et al., 1993; Matheson et al., 1996), and cesarean delivery (Kuhn et al., 1996).

Vaccines

The NIH has declared development of an effective vaccine against HIV-1 to be one of its highest priorities (Cohen, 1996); certainly control of infectious disease epidemics usually do not occur until an inexpensive, effective, and easily administered vaccine is available. HIV offers special challenges, not the least of which is its ability to mutate rapidly, leading to high genetic diversity (Hu et al., 1996). The scientific challenges in vaccine development are considerable, but the social and behavioral challenges may be more so. It is unlikely that vaccines will be able to eradicate HIV in high-prevalence areas unless they are combined with considerable risk behavior reduction (Blower & McLean, 1994). If risk behavior increases as a result of a vaccination campaign, then vaccination could have a perverse outcome by increasing the severity of the epidemic.

STARTING RESEARCH ON U.S. DRUG POLICY

Because 50% to 75% of new HIV infections in the United States can be attributed to injection drug use (Holmberg, 1996), developing and implementing strategies to reduce this route of new infections is a major national priority. Added to this is the role that alcohol and noninjected drugs play in facilitating HIV transmission. Research to date has identified several important and useful strategies for reducing drug-related HIV transmission. These include enhanced access to drug treatment (Ball, Lange, Myers, & Friedman, 1996; Hubbard, Marsden, Cavanaugh, Rachal, & Ginzburg, 1988; National Commission on AIDS, 1991), psychoeducational interventions (Baker, Heather, Wodak, Dixon, & Holt, 1993; Platt, Husband, Iguchi, & Baxter, 1993; Sorensen, London, & Morales, 1991), syringe exchanges (CDC, 1995; Lurie, & Reingold, 1994), syringe availability through increased access at pharmacies (Diaz et al., 1998; Groseclose et al., 1995), outreach programs (Booth & Wiebel, 1992; Colon, Sahai, Robles, & Matos, 1995; Wiebel, 1988; Wiebel et al., 1996), and counseling and testing (Mandel et al., 1994).

It is clear that these strategies, when actually applied, can reduce HIV transmission (see Coates, Aggleton, et al., 1996). It is also clear that failure to apply these strategies (e.g., needle exchange) has resulted in unnecessary loss of life (Lurie & Drucker, 1997) and financial expenditures (Kaplan, 1995). The United States needs to move from intolerance and an interdiction approach to a harm-reduction and medicalization approach to HIV prevention, as in other countries (e.g., Australia, Nepal, Thailand, and Great Britain) that have effectively prevented HIV transmission in IDUs. There are examples of countries (e.g., Sweden) where intolerance may have worked, through a combination of education, aggressive interdiction, and prosecution (Gruenwald, 1996). Drucker (1996), however, maintained that prohibition policies and practices increase individual and public health risk by stigmatizing and marginalizing the drug user, isolating the individual from AIDS prevention and treatment services. Furthermore, zero-tolerance policies inhibit the development and use of alternative drug control strategies based on public health principles.

Nowhere is the rift between research and policy more evident than in this arena. The difficulty in controlling the spread of HIV through injection drug use lies less in the strategies and more in their implementation.

Research is needed that focuses on barriers to adoption of harm-reduction strategies and the government's resistance to offering effective treatment in reasonable periods of time.

HIV PREVENTION AMONG WOMEN: ONE OF THE HIGHEST PRIORITIES

Women are especially vulnerable to HIV and yet at the same time are neglected in treatment and prevention programs. AIDS incidence among women has increased steadily since 1983; women now account for 19% of AIDS cases (CDC, 1996b). Although women do not constitute a majority of AIDS cases in the United States, they do in developing countries (Cohen & Trussell, 1996). Women are exposed to HIV because they are IDUs themselves, are sex partners of IDUs, exchange sex for drugs, or have sex with an infected partner. Women need all the prevention strategies described earlier in this chapter, and more (see also Ehrhardt, Exner, & Seal, 1995):

- Women need interventions that are targeted to their special needs and that take into account their multiple roles;
- Interventions at all levels need to be developed including those at the individual level (to increase knowledge, skills, and motivation), the dyadic level (to provide strategies for developing safety within relationships), the community level, the policy–legal level (to develop laws and legal systems that protect the rights of women and also increase women's equality in society), and the superstructural level (to overcome economic and social barriers to women's rights);
- Medical and technological strategies need to assist women in treating their own HIV disease (apart from the need to prevent vertical transmission), to provide women-controlled HIV prevention technologies, to ensure diagnosis and treatment of STDs, and to assist women in making decisions about counseling and testing, family planning, and treatment for HIV;
- Strategies for reaching young women are essential, because the age of infection among women tends to be lower than the age of infection among men (Cohen & Trussell, 1996);
- Reform of drug policy, especially as it relates to access to treatment and harm minimization, is essential, because the vast majority of heterosexual transmission in the United States occurs from IDUs to their sexual partners;
- Strategies targeted at communities of color in the United States and developing countries are essential, because this is

where the majority of new HIV infections among women are occurring;

- Social movements to increase educational and occupational equality and opportunities and to reduce legal discrimination and provide equal protection for women are needed.

CONCLUSION

HIV will continue to spread, but not because we don't know how to prevent it. Prevention science and practice have yielded strategies that can, if applied, decrease new HIV infections (see Coates, Chesney, et al., 1996; Stryker et al., 1995). The challenges of HIV prevention have been enormous. HIV prevention research began in an extremely unfriendly era. Social and behavioral science research was deemed of little value and received few resources in the 1980s. Sexual behavior research had all but been stopped; note that early estimates of the potential for the spread of HIV had to rely on Kinsey's statistics from the 1940s and 1950s. Drug abuse research was dominated by treatment and interdiction; harm-reduction approaches took a long time to gain credence and to receive funding support.

But now, HIV prevention research has provided proven strategies for reducing high-risk behaviors and HIV transmission. The following are recommendations for future HIV prevention research by behavioral and social scientists:

- Research must identify impediments to implementation of HIV prevention strategies and collect empirical data to repudiate or support those impediments.
- Research must be targeted to populations, geographic areas, and behaviors most associated with prevalence and incidence of HIV infection.
- Government agencies must support HIV prevention research at all six levels of influence. Research to date has been conducted primarily at the individual level. Research is especially needed at the community, policy–legal, and superstructural levels.
- Prevention research must become integrated with treatment research. It is essential to determine the ways in which anti-retroviral therapy might lead to reductions in HIV transmission.
- Science and philosophy of science must be developed further to provide a comprehensive framework for determining when and under what circumstances various design options are ap-

propriate and considered definitive in HIV prevention research.

- Radically new approaches to HIV prevention among adolescents are essential.
- Research to determine the proper balance of zero-tolerance and harm-reduction approaches is needed.
- Concerted efforts are needed to reduce HIV transmission among Black and Hispanic populations.
- The U.S. government and research institutions need to make a long-lasting and useful commitment to HIV prevention research in developing countries.
- A comprehensive women's HIV prevention research and action agenda needs to become a top priority for funding and service agencies.

- All HIV prevention research should be evaluated for its importance by asking whether findings have useful impact in moving theory, practice, or policy.

Major advances have been made in the first 19 years of the HIV epidemic in identifying pathogenic mechanisms, in diagnosing and treating opportunistic infections, in developing therapies that have extended the length and increased the quality of life of infected individuals, and in developing effective prevention strategies. Although some, especially in the popular media, have heralded the recent advances as the end of the epidemic, others have acknowledged that the advances are important and useful but perhaps only signal the end of the beginning of the epidemic. Current scientific progress only points the way to the possible; the remaining tasks are numerous and daunting.

REFERENCES

Adler, M. W. (1996). Sexually transmitted disease control in developing countries. *Genitourinary Medicine, 72,* 83–88.

Allen, S., Serufilira, A., Bogaerts, J., Van de Perre, P., Nsengumuremyi, F., & Lindan, C. (1992). Confidential HIV testing and condom promotion in Africa. *Journal of the American Medical Association, 268,* 3338–3343.

Allen, S., Serufilira, A., Gruber, V., Kegeles, S., Van de Perre, P., & Carael, M. (1993). Pregnancy and contraception use among urban Rwandan women after HIV testing and counseling. *American Journal of Public Health, 83,* 705–709.

Baker, A., Heather, N., Wodak, A., Dixon, J., & Holt, P. (1993). Evaluation of a cognitive–behavioural intervention for HIV prevention among injecting drug users. *AIDS, 7,* 247–256.

Ball, J. C., Lange, W. R., Myers, C. P., & Friedman, S. R. (1996). Reducing the risk of AIDS through methadone maintenance treatment. *Journal of Health and Social Behavior, 29*, 214–226.

Bhave, G., Lindan, C. P., Hudes, E. S., Desai, S., Wagle, U., & Tripathi, S. P. (1995). Impact of an intervention on HIV, sexually transmitted diseases, and condom use among commercial sex workers in Bombay, India. *AIDS, 9*(Suppl. 1), S21–S30.

Blower, S. M., & McLean, A. R. (1994). Prophylactic vaccines, risk behavior change, and the probability of eradicating HIV in San Francisco. *Science, 265*, 1451–1454.

Booth, R., & Wiebel, W. W. (1992). Effectiveness of reducing needle-related risks for HIV through indigenous outreach to injection drug users. *American Journal on Addictions, 1*, 277–287.

Bulterys, M., Chao, A., Dushimimana, A., Habimana, P., Nawrocki, P., & Kurawige, J. B. (1993). Multiple sexual partners and mother-to-child transmission of HIV-1. *AIDS, 7*, 1639–1645.

Carpenter, C. C. J., Fischl, M. A., Hammer S. M., Hirsch, M. S., Jacobsen, D. M., & Katzenstein, D. A. (1996). Antiretroviral therapy for HIV infection in 1996: Recommendations of an international panel. *Journal of the American Medical Association, 276*, 146–154.

Catania, J. A., Binson, D., & Dolcini, M. M. (1995). Risk factors for HIV and other sexually transmitted diseases and prevention practices among US heterosexual adults: Changes from 1990 to 1992. *American Journal of Public Health, 85*, 1492–1495.

Catania, J. A., Coates, T. J., Stall, R., Turner, H., Peterson, J., & Hearst, N. (1992). Prevalence of AIDS-related risk factors and condom use in the United States. *Science, 258*, 1101–1106.

Centers for Disease Control and Prevention. (1995). Syringe exchange programs —United States, 1994–1995. *Morbidity and Mortality Weekly Report, 44*, 684–685, 691.

Centers for Disease Control and Prevention. (1996a). AIDS among children—U.S. *Morbidity and Mortality Weekly Report, 45*, 1005–1009.

Centers for Disease Control and Prevention. (1996b). HIV testing among women aged 18–44 years. *Morbidity and Mortality Weekly Report, 45*, 733–736.

Centers for Disease Control and Prevention. (1997). *HIV/AIDS Surveillance Report, 9*(2), 10.

Claiming our rights: A manual for women's human rights education in Muslim societies. (1996, December 29). *New York Times*, p. 5.

Coates, T. J. (1990). Strategies for modifying sexual behavior for primary and secondary prevention of HIV disease. *Journal of Consulting and Clinical Psychology, 58*, 57–69.

Coates, T. J., Aggleton, P., Gutzwiller, F., Des Jarlais, D., Kihara, M., & Kippax, S. (1996). HIV prevention in developed countries. *Lancet, 348*, 1143–1148.

Coates, T. J., Chesney, M., Folkman, S., Hulley, S. B., Haynes-Sanstad, K., & Lurie, P. (1996). Designing behavioural and social science to impact practice and policy in HIV prevention and care. *International Journal of STD and AIDS*, 7(Suppl. 2), 2–12.

Cohen, B., & Trussell, J. (1996). *Preventing and mitigating AIDS in Sub-Saharan Africa*. Washington, DC: National Academy Press.

Cohen, J. (1996). Baltimore to head new vaccine panel. *Science, 274*, 2005.

Colon, H. M., Sahai, H., Robles, R. R., & Matos, T. D. (1995). Effects of a community outreach program in HIV risk behaviors among injection drug users in San Juan, Puerto Rico. *AIDS Education and Prevention, 7*, 195–209.

Connor, E. M., Sperling, R. S., Gelber, R., Kiseler, P., Scott, G., & O'Sullivan, M. J. (1994). Reduction of maternal–infant transmission of human immunodeficiency virus type 1 with zidovudine treatment. *New England Journal of Medicine, 331*, 1173–1180.

Des Jarlais, D. C., Hagan, H., Friedman, S. R., Friedman, P., Goldberg, D., & Frisher, M. (1995). Maintaining low HIV seroprevalence in populations of injecting drug users. *Journal of the American Medical Association, 274*, 1226–1231.

De Zoysa, I., Phillips, K. A., Kamenga, M. C., O'Reilly, K. R., Sweat, M. D., & White, R. A. (1995). Role of HIV counseling and testing in changing risk behaviors in developing countries, *AIDS, 9*(Suppl. A), S95–S101.

Diaz, T., Chu, S. Y., Winstein, B., Mokotoff, E., & Jones, T. S. (1998). Injection and syringe sharing among HIV-infected injection drug users: Implications for prevention of HIV transmission. *Journal of Acquired Immune Deficiency Syndrome and Human Retrovirology, 18*(Suppl. 1), S76–S81.

DiClemente, R. J., & Wingood, G. M. (1995). A randomized controlled trial of an HIV sexual risk-reduction intervention for young African-American women. *Journal of the American Medical Association, 274*, 1271–1276.

Drucker, E. (1996, June). *The failure of prohibition as a drug control strategy: The case of AIDS*. Debate presented at the XI International Conference on AIDS, Vancouver, British Columbia, Canada.

Ehrhardt, A. A., Exner, T. M., & Seal, D. W. (1995). *A review of HIV interventions for at-risk women*. Washington, DC: Office of Technology Assessment.

Eng, T. R., & Butler, W. T. (1996). *The hidden epidemic: Confronting sexually transmitted diseases*. Washington, DC: National Academy Press.

Feinberg, M. B. (1996). Changing the natural history of HIV disease. *Lancet, 348*, 239–246.

Groseclose, S. L., Weinstein, B., Jones, T. S., Valleroy, L. A., Fehrs, L. T., & Kassler, W. J. (1995). Impact of increased legal access to needles and syringes on practices of injecting drug users and police officers—Connecticut, 1992–1993. *Journal of Acquired Immune Deficiency Syndrome, 10*, 82–89.

Grosskurth, H., Mosha, F., Todd, J., Mwijarubi, E., Klokke, A., & Senkoro, K. (1995). Impact of improved treatment of sexually transmitted diseases on HIV infection in rural Tanzania: Randomised control trial. *Lancet, 346*, 530–536.

Gruenwald, A. B. (1996, June). *Narcotic drug abuse: The Swedish experience*. Debate presented at the XI International Conference on AIDS, Vancouver, British Columbia, Canada.

Higgins, D. L., Galavotti, C., O'Reilly, K. R., Schnell, D. J., Moore, M., & Rugg, D. L. (1991). Evidence for the effects of HIV antibody counseling and testing on risk behaviors. *Journal of the American Medical Association*, 266, 2419–2429.

Holmberg, S. D. (1996). The estimated prevalence and incidence of HIV in 96 large US metropolitan areas. *American Journal of Public Health*, 86, 642–654.

Hu, D. J., Dondero, T. J., Rayfield, M. A., George, J. R., Schochetman, G., Jaffe, H., Luo, C.-C., Kalish, M. L., Weniger, B. G., Pau, C.-P., Schable, C., & Curran, J. W. (1996). The emerging genetic diversity of HIV: The importance of global surveillance for diagnostics, research, and prevention. *Journal of the American Medical Association*, 275, 210–216.

Hubbard, R. L., Marsden, M. E., Cavanaugh, E., Rachal, J. V., & Ginzburg, H. M. (1988). Role of drug abuse treatment in limiting the spread of AIDS. *Review of Infectious Diseases*, 10, 377–384.

Jemmott, J. B., Jemmott, L. S., & Fong, G. T. (1992). Reductions in HIV risk-associated sexual behaviors among Black male adolescents: Effects of an AIDS prevention intervention. *American Journal of Public Health*, 82, 372–377.

Kahn, J. G. (1996). The cost-effectiveness of HIV prevention targeting: How much more bang for the buck? *American Journal of Public Health*, 86, 1–4.

Kamb, M. L., Fishbein, M., Douglas, J. M., Rhodes, F., Rogers, J., & Bolan, G. (1998). Efficacy of risk-reduction counseling to prevent human immunodeficiency virus and sexually transmitted diseases: A randomized controlled trial. Project RESPECT Study Group. *Journal of the American Medical Association*, 280, 1161–7.

Kaplan, E. H. (1995). Economic analysis of needle exchange. *AIDS*, 9, 1113–1119.

Kegeles, S. M., Hays, R., & Coates, T. J. (1996). The Mpowerment project: A community-level HIV prevention intervention for young gay men. *American Journal of Public Health*, 86, 1129–1136.

Kelly, J. A., St. Lawrence, J. S., Stevenson, L. Y., Hauth, A. C., Kalichman, S. C., & Diaz, Y. E. (1992). Community AIDS/HIV risk reduction: The results of endorsements by popular people in three cities. *American Journal of Public Health*, 82, 1483–1489.

King, R., Estey, J., Allen, S., Kegeles, S., Wolf, W., & Valentine, C. (1995). A family planning intervention to reduce vertical transmission of HIV in Rwanda. *AIDS*, 9(Suppl. 1), S45–S51.

Konde-Lule, J. K. (1995). The declining HIV seroprevalence in Uganda: What evidence? *Health Transition Review*, 5(Suppl.), 27–33.

Kuhn, L., Bobat, R., Coutsoudis, A., Moodley, D., Coovadia, H. M., & Tsai, W.-Y. (1996). Cesarean deliveries and maternal–infant HIV transmission: Results from a prospective study in South Africa. *Journal of Acquired Immune Deficiency Syndrome and Human Retrovirology*, 11, 478–483.

Lurie, P., & Drucker, E. (1997). An opportunity lost: Estimating the number of HIV infections associated with lack of a national needle exchange programme in the USA. *Lancet, 349,* 604–608.

Lurie, P., Hintzen, P., & Lowe, R. A. (1995). Socioeconomic obstacles to HIV prevention and treatment in developing countries: The roles of the International Monetary Fund and the World Bank. *AIDS, 9,* 539–546.

Lurie, P., & Reingold, A. L. (Eds.). (1994). *The public health impact of needle exchange programs in the United States and abroad* (Vol. 1). San Francisco: University of California Press.

Lurie, P., Reingold, A. L., Bowser, B., Chen, D., Foley, J., & Guydish, J. (1993). *The public health impact of needle exchange programs in the United States and abroad.* Rockville, MD: CDC National AIDS Clearinghouse.

Mandel, W., Vlahov, D., Latkin, C. A., Carran, D., Oziemkowska, M. J., & Reedt, L. (1994). Changes in HIV risk behaviors among counseled injecting drug users. *Journal of Drug Issues, 24,* 555–567.

Matheson, P. B., Thomas, P. A., Abrams, E. J., Pliner, V., Lambert, G., Bamji, M., & the New York City Perinatal HIV Transmission Collaborative Study Group. (1996). Heterosexual behavior during pregnancy and perinatal transmission of HIV-1. *AIDS, 10,* 1249–1256.

Mills, T., Stall, R., Catania, J. A., & Coates, T. J. (1997). Interpreting HIV prevalence and incidence among Americans: Bridging data and public policy. *American Journal of Public Health, 87,* 864–866.

National Commission on AIDS. (1991). *The twin epidemics of substance use and HIV.* Washington, DC: National Commission on AIDS.

National Institutes of Health. (1997, February 11). Interventions to prevent HIV risk behaviors. *NIH Consensus Statement Online* [on-line serial], *15*(104), 1–41.

Nelson, K. E., Celentano, D. D., Eiumtrakol, S., Hoover, D. R., Beyrer, C., & Suprasert, S. (1996). Changes in sexual behavior and a decline in HIV infection among young men in Thailand. *New England Journal of Medicine, 335,* 297–303.

O'Reilly, K. R., & Piot, P. (1996). International perspectives on individual and community approaches to the prevention of sexually transmitted disease and human immunodeficiency virus infection. *Journal of Infectious Diseases, 174*(Suppl. 2), S214–S222.

Phillips, K., & Coates, T. J. (1995). HIV counseling and testing: Policy and research issues. *AIDS Care, 7,* 115–124.

Platt, J. J., Husband, S. D., Iguchi, M. Y., & Baxter, R. (1993). Problem-solving skills training: Addressing high-risk behaviors in Newark and Jersey City. In B. S. Brown & G. M. Beschner (Eds.), *Handbook on risk of AIDS* (pp. 483–498). Westport, CT: Greenwood Press.

Rotheram-Borus, M. J., Koopman, C., Haignere, C., & Davies, M. (1991). Reducing HIV sexual risk behaviors among runaway adolescents. *Journal of the American Medical Association, 266,* 1237–1241.

Schreiber, G. B., Busch, M. P., Kleinman, S. H., & Korelitz, J. J. (1996). The risk of transfusion-transmitted viral infections. The Retrovirus Epidemiology Donor Study. *New England Journal of Medicine, 334,* 1685–1690.

Sorenson, J. L., London, J., & Morales, E. S. (1991). Group counseling to prevent AIDS. In J. L. Sorenson, L. A. Wermuth, D. R. Gibson, K.-H. Choi, J. R. Guydish, & S. L. Batki (Eds.), *Preventing AIDS in drug users and their sexual partners* (pp. 99–115). New York: Guilford Press.

Stryker, J., Coates, T. J., DeCarlo, P., Haynes-Sanstad, K., Shriver, M., & Makadon, H. J. (1995). Prevention of HIV infection: Looking back, looking ahead. *Journal of the American Medical Association, 273,* 1143–1148.

Sweat, M. & Dennison, J. (1995). Reducing HIV incidence in developing countries with structural and environmental interventions. *AIDS, 9,* [Supplement A] S251–257.

Valdiserri, R. O., Aultman, T. V., & Curran, J. W. (1995). Community planning: A national strategy to improve HIV prevention programs. *Journal of Community Health, 20,* 87–100.

Valleroy, L. A., Weinstein, B., Jones, T. S., Groseclose, S., Rolfs, R., & Kassler, S. W. (1995). Impact of increased legal access to needles and syringes on community pharmacies' needle and syringe sales—Connecticut, 1992–1993. *Journal of Acquired Immune Deficiency Syndrome, 10,* 73–81.

Van der Stratten, A., Vittinghoff, E., Glass, S., Quan, J., & Padian, N. (1996, November). *Sexual risk behavior with primary and non-primary partners among heterosexuals in HIV-discordant couples.* Poster presented at the XI International Conference on AIDS, Vancouver, British Columbia, Canada.

Wiebel, W. W. (1988). Combining ethnographic and epidemiologic methods in targeted AIDS interventions: The Chicago model. In R. J. Battjes & R. W. Pickens (Eds.), *Needle sharing among intravenous drug users: National and international perspectives,* NIDA Research Monograph No. 80 (pp. 137–150). Bethesda, MD: National Institute on Drug Abuse.

Wiebel, W. W., Jimenez, A., Johnson, W., Ouellet, L., Jovanovic, B., & Lampinen, T. (1996). Risk behavior and HIV serocoincidence among out-of-treatment infection drug users: A four-year prospective study. *Journal of Acquired Immune Deficiency Syndrome and Human Retrovirology, 12,* 282–289.

14

AN ECODEVELOPMENTAL FRAMEWORK FOR ORGANIZING THE INFLUENCES ON DRUG ABUSE: A DEVELOPMENTAL MODEL OF RISK AND PROTECTION

JOSÉ SZAPOCZNIK AND J. DOUGLAS COATSWORTH

The purpose of this chapter is to present a parsimonious explanatory framework for the complex body of knowledge on risk and protective factors for adolescent drug abuse. This explanatory framework is described as *Structural Ecosystems Theory* (SET; Szapocznik & Williams, 1999). SET organizes the information on social and behavioral risk and protective factors in terms of complex developmental processes that occur within and across various domains in a child's social ecology. SET highlights the interrelatedness and connectedness of different risk and protective factors across social domains and over time. The framework is broadly inclusive, but in this article, we do not attempt to integrate the important and sub-

This work was supported in part by Center for Substance Abuse Prevention Grants 1 HD1 SPO 7446, 1 HD1 SPO 7117, H86 SPO 4927, and H86 SPO 2350 and National Institute on Drug Abuse Grant 1 R01 DA10574.

stantial literature on genetic, biological, and intrapersonal factors predisposing to behavior problems and drug abuse. Instead, we focus our discussion on the literature that highlights the social and interpersonal factors that accentuate or diminish the probability of adolescent deviancy that includes drug abuse.

The major research paradigm guiding the development of preventive intervention research is the *risk and protective factors model* (Hawkins, Catalano, & Miller, 1992; Institute of Medicine, 1994). This research strategy attempts to identify the conditions that increase or decrease the probability of children and adolescents manifesting psychopathology or behavioral problems. Risk and protective factors research evolved out of the fields of epidemiology and experimental psychopathology (Garmezy, 1985), but its applicability and promise are reflected in its position as a cornerstone of developmental psychopathology (e.g., Cicchetti & Cohen, 1995; Rutter & Garmezy, 1983; Sroufe & Rutter, 1984). The concepts of risk and protection and malleable risk and protective factors are pivotal to prevention science (Coie et al., 1993; Reiss & Price, 1996).

More than 20 years of research have yielded a complex set of findings on the risk and protective factors associated with child and adolescent psychopathology, including behavior problems and substance use. Generally, the search for risk and protective factors has proceeded in a linear but somewhat fragmented fashion, with researchers attempting to identify new variables or factors that alter the probability of a group of children or adolescents manifesting behavior problems. This search has been successful in identifying numerous factors that demonstrate a statistical association with the disorder of interest. In the drug abuse area, for example, Alan Leshner, Director of the National Institute on Drug Abuse, has suggested that there may be as many as 72 risk and protective factors for drug abuse (Leshner, 1996). Such large numbers of apparently disparate factors create a daunting task if a systematic attempt is made to consider all of these factors when designing preventive interventions. It is for this reason that we propose the need for a new model for organizing and understanding risk and protective factors that will guide the construction of science-based interventions for the prevention of drug abuse and other associated problem behaviors.

This chapter is organized into three sections. First, we describe general trends and qualitative reorganizations in the risk and protective factors literature. Risk and protective factors have been identified for many psychological and behavioral outcomes in childhood, adolescence, and adulthood. Despite a great deal of overlap among the listings of risk and protective factors for the different disorders, we use, as our exemplar, risk and protective factors for adolescent drug abuse. Second, we offer SET as a framework for organizing the literature on risk and protective factors for adolescent drug abuse. SET has evolved from our 20-year history of integrating theory, research, and application (Coatsworth, Szapocznik, Kurtines, & Santisteban, 1997; Szapocznik, Kurtines, & Santisteban, 1994; Szapocznik et al., 1996) in working with families of drug-abusing and behavior-problem youth. It derives from theoretical tenets that have guided our systematic research program over the years, including focusing on the family from an interactional and systemic approach and attending to the multiple ecological domains in which families interact (Szapocznik & Kurtines, 1989, 1993). The theory is influenced strongly by Urie Bronfenbrenner's work on the social ecology of human development (Bronfenbrenner, 1979, 1986) but also derives uniqueness from our own structural (social interactional) roots (see also Kurtines & Szapocznik, 1996; Minuchin, 1974; Minuchin & Fishman, 1981; Minuchin, Rosman, & Baker, 1978; Szapocznik & Kurtines, 1989). Third utility of the framework in organizing the existing body of empirical findings is illustrated with examples from various research programs examining risk and protective factors in the development of adolescent substance use and other behavior problems. Fourth, we discuss the implications of the SET framework for formulating theory-driven preventive interventions that encompass the complexity of findings of risk and protective processes across social domains and life span development and the usefulness of the SET framework in avoiding iatrogenic effects.

GENERAL TRENDS AND QUALITATIVE REORGANIZATIONS IN RISK AND PROTECTIVE FACTORS RESEARCH

The literature on risk and protective factors for the development of psychopathology is diverse and has undergone a series of important developmental steps, each of which has served as a building block for new ideas. As this body of research has grown, the complexities inherent in this line of inquiry have emerged, and like human development itself, the risk and protective factor literature has required periods of reorganization.

Over the past three decades, a considerable amount of empirical and theoretical attention has been given to identifying the antecedent conditions to psychopathology and behavioral disturbances, including adolescent drug abuse. The high-risk research strategy was a natural outgrowth of the basic experimental psychopathology approach for studying the etiology of psychopathology (Garmezy, 1974). *Risk* research provided the promise of studying a group of children vulnerable to disorder to isolate the genetic, individual, and environmental factors implicated in the causes of psychopathology. However, risk researchers confronted several primary methodological problems, including how to identify children who were at risk for developing disorder. In response, risk research blossomed, with substantial intellectual efforts directed at identifying the individual, social, and situational conditions that predicted manifest disorder. On the heels of risk research came the search for *protective* factors (Garmezy, 1985), those factors that pulled children who were at risk for developing manifest behavior problems toward a nonproblematic developmental outcome. As with risk factors, the search for protective factors was originally focused on the identification of the correlates or predictors of a specific behavioral outcome.

Identification of Risk and Protective Factors

The excitement and promise of the risk and protective factors paradigm led to proliferation in studies designed to identify factors related to maladaptive outcomes in children and adolescents. Initially, the search was defined by attempts to understand what all the pieces were. The guiding assumption was that once all the influential variables were chronicled, then we could predict and ultimately manipulate the developmental trajectories of children and adolescents toward healthy and adaptive outcomes. Over the years, the list of risk and protective factors predicting to one of the many psychological or behavioral disorders of interest has grown almost exponentially. Traditionally, risk and protective factors were conceptualized in static terms. These factors were identified because children who experienced the event or possessed the characteristic were as a group more likely to result in a negative developmental outcome. The early search had three distinct forms (Masten & Garmezy, 1985): (a) a focus on a relatively discrete factor or event (e.g., divorce); (b) a focus on a specific disorder (e.g., adolescent drug abuse), or (c) focus on general factors that relate to a range of subsequent outcomes (e.g., family conflict). Although initial investigations were guided by a mechanistic, reductionistic model, much was learned about the identification of risk.

As the number of identified risk and protective factors grew, a reorganization was required, and investigators attempted to classify risk and protective factors according to broad categories. A classic example of this reorganization is the seminal piece by Hawkins et al. (1992) on risk and protective factors for alcohol and other drug problems in adolescence. These authors reviewed the existing evidence for risk and protective factors and categorized them into 17 domains, which in turn were grouped into two higher order categories: *contextual* factors and *individual and interpersonal* factors. SET is primarily concerned with those factors categorized by Hawkins and his colleagues as contextual factors. Recently, the literature on risk and protection has taken a decidedly more contextual flavor, with attention being given to risk and protective factors within the various developmental domains for children and adolescents: *family, peer, school,* and *neighborhood.* A long list of factors associated with negative developmental outcomes can be generated across individual and contextual developmental domains. Individual factors associated with maladaptive developmental outcomes, including drug abuse and misuse, in children and adolescents include variables such as attitudes favorable toward drug use (Kandel, Kessler, & Margulies, 1978; Smith & Fogg, 1978); low levels of social or cognitive competencies, such as decision-making and problem-solving skills, conflict-resolution skills, and peer-resistance skills, (Caplan, Jacoby, Weissberg, & Grady, 1988; Dodge & Crick, 1990; Guerra & Slaby, 1990; Pentz et al., 1989). Within the family domain, parenting style, harsh and inconsistent discipline techniques, high parent–youth conflict with poor resolution, and communication skills all have been identified as risks (Dishion, French, & Patterson, 1995; Hawkins et al., 1992; Patterson & Stouthamer-Loeber, 1984; Steinberg, Mounts, Lamborn, & Dornbusch, 1991). The school domain contains risk and protective factors such as academic achievement or failure and low school bonding (Gottfredson, 1988; Johnson, O'Malley, & Bachman, 1992).

This kind of organizational structure has provided a framework to identify classes of factors common across research studies. Yet, the theoretical orientation and the organization of the list tend to focus almost exclusively on the interactions of the person within a singular domain, neglecting the potentially powerful effects of interactions among domains (Szapocznik & Pantin, 1996a, 1996b; Szapocznik, Pantin, & Scopetta, 1996). Thus, the risk and protective factors model effectively organizes our knowledge into the various systems within a child's social ecology but fails to explain adequately the embeddedness and interconnectedness of the child's social ecosystem.

Multiple Risk

The use of multiple-risk indexes represents another reorganization in the search for risk and protective factors. Multiple-risk indexes that sum factors into a single index of risk exposure help researchers cope with the large number of possible risk factors in their studies. With the main objective of much risk research being the prediction of psychopathology, combining many factors into a singular index of multiple risk increases predictive power (Bry, McKeon, & Pandina, 1982; Bry, Pedraza, & Pandina, 1988; Newcomb, Maddahian, & Bentler, 1986; Sameroff, Seifer, Barocas, Zax, & Greenspan, 1987).

A primary assumption of multiple-risk models is that risk or protective factors have an independent and separate effect that can be summed (or subtracted) to produce a single index that is linearly related to the outcome of interest. Although they increase predictive power, multiple-risk indexes do not inform us about the mechanisms by which risk factors exert their influence. Distinguishing between risk and protective factors and the processes, or mechanisms, of risk and protection, has served as another important point of reorganization in the field (Reiss & Price, 1996; Rutter,

1987). Moving beyond factor identification, more effort should have been directed toward understanding how risk and protective mechanisms operate (Rutter, 1987).

Risk and Protective Processes

The study of processes, and the mechanisms by which these processes influence development, shifts the emphasis of study from factor to developmental process. We agree with Rutter (1987, 1990) that the effects of interest, movement toward or away from psychopathology, cannot lie in the factor alone, rather, they must be evident in the process. Discerning the mechanisms that connect multiple risk and protective factors with outcomes over time is very complex. The processes of risk and protection may be characterized by the way a constellation of risk and protective factors gives rise to other risks (Reiss & Price, 1996; Rutter, 1987; Rutter, Champion, Quinton, Maughan, & Pickles, 1995). Over time, risk and protection are most likely to be evident in the patterning of operating risk and protective factors within the child's social ecology. That is, the relation is less likely to be linear and direct. Rather, risk and protection will be apparent in the patterning of relations among seemingly disconnected variables in a child's social ecology and in the manner in which a certain patterning gives rise to increased probability of other risks becoming operative. Viewed in terms of processes that comprise patterns of variables across domain and over time, it becomes clear that the role of any single indicator (i.e., factor) in a developmental process is likely to be overstated if studied in isolation from other operating factors (Magnusson, 1995; Magnusson, Andersson, & Torestad, 1993).

The challenge to understanding risk and protection is to step back from viewing all the fragmentary components (factors) in isolation or summed into a composite index of risk and instead to view the coherence of the whole. In vivo, the variables are quite interdependent, and new models are needed to help represent the interrelatedness of systemic functions (Bronfenbrenner, 1979). Understanding risk and protection in the social ecology of human development and how it relates to adaptive and maladaptive developmental trajectories requires complex integrative theories that link component pieces. Contemporary intervention science demands a new generation of theoretical models that represent a reorganization to a new level of understanding.

STRUCTURAL ECOSYSTEMS THEORY: AN ECODEVELOPMENTAL ORGANIZING FRAMEWORK

SET, a next generation theoretical framework, emerged from a context of applied theoretical and empirical studies conducted over 20 years at the University of Miami Center for Family Studies (Coatsworth et al., 1997; Szapocznik et al., 1994; Szapocznik, et al., 1996). SET represents an integration of 20 years of empirical studies in the areas of structural family therapy and family-based interventions focused on the identification and alteration of interactions (Szapocznik & Kurtines, 1989; Szapocznik et al., 1996; see also Minuchin, 1974; Minuchin & Fishman, 1981; Minuchin et al., 1978); the social ecology model of human development popularized by Urie Bronfenbrenner (Bronfenbrenner, 1979, 1986); the multisystemic interventions of Henggeler (Henggeler & Borduin, 1990; Henggeler, Melton, & Smith, 1992); and a life span developmental approach (e.g., Baltes, Reese, & Nesselroade, 1977). Standing on the shoulders of structural family theory, social ecological theory, and multisystemic therapy, SET, like its predecessors, places the family at the center of the child's social ecology, working under the assumption that the family is, or can be, the most fundamental system in a child's social ecology, the bedrock of child development. Moreover, SET is built on a philosophy that is concerned not only with children's social ecology but also with the social and cultural context that sustains families and supports their preventive functions (cf. Szapocznik & Mancilla, 1995). As an organizing framework for risk and protection, three important features of SET are emphasized: (a) attention to the multiple domains in a child or adolescent's *social ecology*, (b) an *ecodevelopmental* perspective, and (c) an *interactional* perspective.

The Social Ecology Paradigm

The social ecology theory of Urie Bronfenbrenner (1979, 1986) proposes that the social domains for human development can be represented by a "set of nested structures, each inside the next, like a set of Russian dolls" (Bronfenbrenner, 1979, p. 22). In his pioneering work, Bronfenbrenner organized the structures into four primary systems: *microsystems*, *mesosystems*, *exosystems*, and *macrosystems* (see Figure 1). In naming and describing these environmental structures, Bronfenbrenner offered a language to guide the organization of the child's social ecology and to organize the scientific study of the influence of various social ecological factors on human development.

Central to social ecology theory (e.g., Bronfenbrenner, 1979, 1986; Bronfenbrenner & Ceci, 1994), is the child as a living organism with an active genetic, biologic, and psychologic organization. SET acknowledges the importance of genetic susceptibilities (e.g., Bohman, Cloninger, Sigvardsson, & von Knorring, 1987; Devor, 1993; McGue, Pickens, & Svikis, 1992) and physiologic and neurochemical–biochemical influences (e.g., Kranzler & Anton, 1994) in the development of drug abuse. In this chapter, however, we focus on organizing the complex social interactional

SZAPOCZNIK AND COATSWORTH

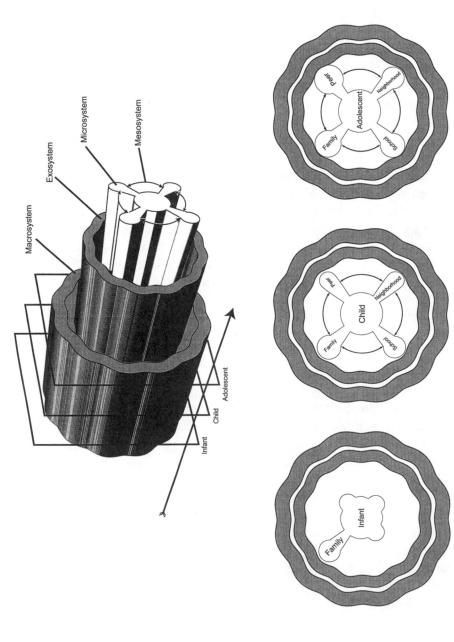

Figure 1. A life span ecodevelopmental trajectory. The top portion of the figure represents the entire ecosystem developing over time and space. The lower section demonstrates changes in the organization and structure of the social ecology, as represented in three cross sections of the life span trajectory at infancy, childhood, and adolescence. Changes in the microsystemic organization are depicted by the increasing size of the ecological domains (family, school, peer, and neighborhood) over time. Changes in mesosystemic functioning are depicted by the boldening of the arrows between microsystems. Not all mesosystemic interactions are depicted because of the two-dimensional space (e.g., the family–neighborhood or school–peer mesosystems). Changes in the social ecosystemic domains and in the processes of risk and protection are depicted by changes in the shape and linkages within and between ecosystems and are fully integrated parts of the developmental pathway.

processes in the child's social ecology that contribute to the development of drug abuse.

Of the four social systems–domains for development suggested by Bronfenbrenner, the microsystems are the most proximal for the developing child. These are the settings in which the child participates directly. The most prominent microsystems for a developing child include the family, school, peer group, and neighborhood–community. An important characterizing feature of microsystems are within-system reciprocal relationships that become increasingly greater in number and complexity with development. These qualities of the microsystems provide social contexts of developmental risk or opportunity. An increase in number and complexity of relations, as long as they are reciprocal in nature, provides richer contexts (protection) for enhanced development (Bronfenbrenner, 1979). The increased complexity of these contexts progresses in a developmental fashion, with the multistrandedness of each domain changing at different rates and at different points in time. For example, as depicted in the leftmost cross section of Figure 1, the family is the primary domain for infant social development, and relations in this domain will increase in intricacy and complexity earlier than relations in other domains. Similarly, the reciprocal relationships in the school microsystem are likely to increase before the multistrandedness of reciprocal peer relationships becomes a prominent influence on development.

Mesosystems are relations between microsystems. These relationships do not include the child directly but are considered to indirectly influence development. As with microsystems, the richness of mesosystems are evidenced by the number and quality of the connections among the microsystems that they comprise. A main principle of mesosystemic functioning is that the stronger and more complementary the linkages between systems, the more positive the influence of this mesosystem on a child's development (Garbarino & Abramowitz, 1992). Mesosystems that contain few linkages or comprise relationships that are antagonistic increase a child's risk for maladaptive development. In contrast, when mesosystem linkages are strong and the members of both microsystems work together synchronously, the effect fosters a positive developmental trajectory. For example, a family–school mesosystem in which parents and teachers hold similar values for the child's social and academic development, where parents communicate a positive orientation toward school by encouraging school activities (e.g., checking homework), and where parents and teachers maintain a relationship that values and is supportive of the missions of both school and family is likely to have a positive influence on a child's academic and social development, both predictors of later drug abuse.

Exosystems are systems that are entirely independent of the child. These systems influence the child indirectly through their influence on mesosystemic relationships and through their influence on the functioning of individuals within the child's microsystems. Given our emphasis on the family in SET, the theory suggests that one of the most important exosystems for a child is the social support network of the parent. Parents who have a broad social support network on which they can rely for assistance with daily tasks and for emotional and instrumental support in stressful times are more likely to parent the child in a positive nurturing manner (e.g., Taylor, 1996). The climate of a parent's workplace also can have important influences on a child's developmental opportunities (e.g., Mason, Cauce, Gonzales, Hiraga, & Grove, 1994). Stressful working experiences, long hours, travel, and other elements of today's demanding workplace may result in impoverished developmental opportunities for the child.

Macrosystems are society's broad ideological and cultural patterns. They are the cultural "blueprints" that influence the development of the ecosystems. The political, social, and cultural ideologies shape individual development by enriching or impoverishing a child's microsystems, mesosystems and exosystems. Examples of recent macrosystemic interventions that affect families and family–child relationships include the Family and Medical Leave Act, which permits adults to take leave from work to care for a sick relative (e.g., child) and the Newborn and Mother's Health Protection Act of 1996, which compels health care providers to grant new mothers 2-day stays in the hospital postdelivery. Both acts support families in their efforts to provide healthy social ecologies for their child's development. Social norms, including norms about drug use and parenting styles, are considered macrosystemic influences. Culture also represents an important macrosystemic influence. Examples of traditional macrosystem influences are culturally determined parenting styles and culturally defined gender roles. In our work on acculturation (e.g., Szapocznik & Kurtines, 1979, 1993; Szapocznik, Kurtines, & Fernandez, 1980; Szapocznik, Santisteban, Kurtines, Perez-Vidal, & Hervis, 1984; Szapocznik et al., 1986; Szapocznik, Scopetta, & King, 1978), we have investigated the impact of cultural context on intergenerational family gaps and family intergenerational, intercultural conflict and their implications for risk for later drug abuse in Hispanic adolescents.

Risk and Protection Across Domains

One of the most important challenges inherent to the analysis of risk and protection is to ensure that the interrelatedness of risk and protective factors is considered within its full social ecological context. By that, we mean the operation of social risk and protective processes occurs across domains within the child's social ecology. For this reason, it is critical to encourage investigators to look beyond the primary social ecological domain of interest and across to the other social systems that may be involved in risk and protective processes (Garbarino & Abramowitz, 1992). For example, parenting behaviors and parenting style have been identified as critical risk and protective factors for the development of drug abuse (cf. Brook, Brook, Gordon, Whiteman, & Cohen, 1990; Bry, 1993). However, the risk or protective processes involved in good or poor parenting are always couched in the broader contexts of the social ecology. Parenting processes may be influenced by macrosystemic forces (e.g., governmental policies or social and cultural norms and values), by exosystemic factors (e.g., the degree to which a single mother has a strong social support network), or by mesosytemic relations (e.g., the relationship between parents and the child's peers or the level of shared parenting within the neighborhood). Models investigating risk and protection must account for the contextual nature of social influences.

Yet, another critical aspect of considering risk and protective processes across domains is the potential for iatrogenic effects in interventions that narrowly target a single domain without adequate consideration of the potentially deleterious impact of that intervention on risk and protective processes in other parts of the child's social ecology. More about this substantive consideration is discussed below under SET applications.

A Developmental Focus

Risk and protective factors provide snapshots of risk and protection, failing to foster an understanding of the developmental processes that unfold over time and ultimately lead to the behavioral outcome of drug abuse. Without a developmental perspective guiding the organization of risk and protective indicators, factors may appear to be separate and discrete when instead they are sequential elements of a risk process. For example, aggression in early childhood has been identified as an important risk factor for many poor developmental outcomes, including drug abuse (Kellam, Brown, Rubin, & Ensminger, 1983). Likewise, researchers have identified other factors, such as learning problems and low academic achievement (Jessor, 1976; Robins, 1980; Smith & Fogg, 1978), impulsivity, and rebelliousness (Brook et al., 1990), as separate risk factors predicting future drug abuse. However, if studied developmentally, it is possible that these factors are time-sequenced markers of a single developmental process (see Brook & Newcomb, 1995). Separating and labeling these three as if they were independent of each other prevent a fuller understanding of risky developmental pathways.

When tracing developmental trajectories, researchers frequently focus almost exclusively on the growth of a single characteristic or behavior (e.g., conduct problems) and attempt to identify predictors (risk and protective factors) of the degree of change in behavior over time. Although this strategy is a substantial improvement over attempting to use a single risk and protective indicator at one point in time to predict outcome at a later point in time, it does not accurately reflect the dynamic change over time in the nature of the risk process. Examining the trajectories and sequences of risk and protection and how these are dynamically related to the behavioral developmental trajectory is one of the major challenges to the investigation of risk and protective processes and requires an integrative ecodevelopmental theory.

Our conception of development has been influenced by the transactional developmental model (Sameroff, 1983; Sameroff & Chandler, 1975) and developmental systems theory (Ford & Lerner, 1992). The term *development* usually refers to changes in the structures, organization, and functioning of the child's intrapersonal processes, including biological, emotional, psychological, behavioral, or cognitive systems. *Development* in these aspects of a child's functioning usually refers to increasing complexity and integration within and across intrapersonal domains (e.g., Cicchetti & Sroufe, 1978; Werner, 1957). In our conception of ecodevelopment, we are concerned with both the emerging nature and changes in these child-focused intrapersonal dimensions of functioning across time, as well as in the emerging developmental nature of the child's social ecosystems as they evolve over time. Thus, an important element of our ecodevelopmental perspective is the structure, organization, integration, and functioning of the child's social ecology over time (cf. Cairns, Elder, & Costello, 1996).

Ecodevelopment, then, refers to the complex set of features that emerge over time within the child and in the child's social ecosystems and the nature of the interactions within and among these systems as they change and influence each other reciprocally over time. *Ecodevelopment* refers to the evolving processes that occur inside of the envelope of the social ecosystems that contain and include the child, as depicted in Figure 1.

In this conceptualization, it is not possible to separate the child's individual development from the influences of an evolving ecosystem that contains the child; nor can we separate the development of any single system, such as the family, from the changing reciprocal interactions in the ecosystem of the family. For example, the child and the family develop as the child transitions from staying at home to going to school. This evolution is influenced by the family's internal processes (e.g., parent–child attachment), the nature of their interactions with school (e.g., parent–teacher alliances or conflicts), and exosystems (e.g., parent support systems and parents' place of work), as well as by the larger societal blueprints and rules that influence each of these. We cannot understand the child's development through this important transition without understanding the family's development at this point, and in turn, we cannot understand the family's development outside of the broader social ecological context in which it occurs.

Therefore, within SET, a child's ecodevelopmental trajectory is represented by the full ecosystem moving through time and space. Figure 1 depicts the complex nature of the social ecosystem and organism developing as an integrated, interacting whole. Changes in the social ecosystemic domains and in the processes of risk and protection are depicted by changes in the shapes of and linkages among ecosystems and are fully integrated parts of the ecodevelopmental pathway. The cross-sectional slices in Figure 1 show the emerging complexity of relations within and between systems at three different time points in the ecodevelopmental life course. For example, the ecodevelopmental context of an infant lies almost exclusively within the family microsystem. Mesosystems are minimally operative. However, the exosystem (e.g., parental social support network) can be a critical element of the social ecology of a family with an infant. Support for new parents at the time of transition helps them provide an environment conducive to long-term adjustment in the child (Olds, Henderson, Tatelbaum, & Chamberlin, 1986). A few years later in childhood, depicted in the middle cross section of Figure 1, the school domain attains greater significance, and the complexity of interactions of the child within the school domain and between the school and the family (mesosystem relations) grows. These changes are delineated in the figure by the changing size of the "node" representing the school and the boldness of the arrow between the school and family, indicating more complex and important relationships. In comparison, adolescence, in the right cross section of Figure 1, brings with it a growing peer-system influence and an increase in the importance and complexity of family–peer interactions as risk and protective processes.[1] As the child matures into adolescence, the neighborhood also gains importance as a microsystem and in its mesosystemic relations with the family.

It is difficult to depict the ever-changing nature of the ecosystem in two dimensions and without real time. Changes in risk and protection may happen quickly or slowly. For example, faster changes with respect to a life course trajectory may be represented by changes at the school microsystem level: A classroom in the spring near the end of the school year is not the same developmental domain as it was in the fall. Likewise, the child is not the same child as he or she was when he or she first entered the classroom in the fall.

The complexity of relations among cumulative risk, vulnerability, and protection at a single point in time is increased exponentially with the addition of the context of ecodevelopment. As we have depicted in Figure 1, how these factors coalesce, change, and transact may be very different at different points in time. Within our theory of ecodevelopment, we are attuned to how changes in individual attributes are likely to influence how the person–environment system operates and vice versa. Just as a devel-

---

[1]Our depiction of an increase in influence of the parent–peer mesosystem (cf. Patterson & Dishion, 1985) is somewhat at odds with the popular belief that parents view adolescence as a time to step back from involvement in the youth's world.

opmental perspective on psychopathology requires an understanding of the changing nature of behavioral organization across the life span (e.g., Cicchetti, 1984, 1990, 1993), understanding risk and protective processes requires that we examine these processes within the broader ecodevelopmental context evolving over time. Risks and protection unfold across domains over the course of development with the impact and salience of a specific aspect of a given process (i.e., including the snapshots referred to as *risk* and *protective* factors), changing at different points in the child's ecodevelopment.

Here, the notion of transactional risk is critical (Rutter, 1987) and finds a parallel to organismic developmental theory (Cicchetti & Sroufe, 1978; Werner, 1957). Organismic developmental theory posits an organizational coherence to the course of development in which functioning at one point in development will influence functioning in the next. Similarly, the idea behind transactional risk is that the effect of cumulative risk, that is, risk over time, may lie in how risks at one point in development in one domain (e.g., family coercive behaviors) increase the probability of a qualitatively different risk at another point in time in another domain (antisocial peer relations in childhood through adolescence). Hence, the term *ecodevelopment* to describe the organismic coherence of the evolution of processes across domains and time.

In SET, we view risk and protective processes as a function of how distal risk and protective factors among domains bring about proximal risk and protective factors in other domains. As such, we may think of identifying risk trajectories, or cascading risk sequences. Our ecodevelopmental perspective suggests a continuity or coherence to the organization of risk and protection within the social ecology. The nature of the social ecological patterns at any one point in time will influence the nature of the social ecology at a later point in time. A social ecological organization that is risky for behavioral development at one point in development has greater likelihood of giving rise to an organization that is also risky at a later point in development (cf. Cairns et al., 1996). When viewed as an unfolding developmental process, the coherence becomes apparent.

Emphasis on Social Interactions

The theory of social ecology generally emphasizes the spatial dimensions among systems as a way of differentiating among them. These social domains differ from one another to the extent that they occupy different spatial dimensions, as well as the degree to which they are proximal or distal to the child. Indeed, at times, this emphasis on spatial dimensions has led to an accent on the boundaries between systems rather than the linkages (i.e., interactions and transactions) between and among them. In

SET, although we acknowledge the spatial differences among social ecological domains, we emphasize the interactions within and among systems.

An analogy from biology may be helpful. Initially, a cell membrane was viewed as a wall that helped contain the contents of the cell, to separate the inside of the cell from the outside of the cell. This view provided the membrane with a certain concreteness. A more contemporary view of a cell membrane, however, reveals that the wall is built from the continuous interactions among particles. According to quantum mechanics, molecules, atoms, and their component parts, which are both particles and energy, are created by moving, interacting parts that are in a constant process of transformation. Moreover, the cell membrane is constantly negotiating transfer of bio-components from inside to outside and vice versa. A cell membrane can be viewed as a wall or as a systematic mechanism for transactions among membrane particles and between the membrane and its environment. The latter view of the cell membrane is illustrative of our model for social ecological domains.

Our focus on interactions is consistent with a holistic view of development in which individual functioning and development are proposed to be a reciprocal process of continuous interaction between person and environment (Bronfenbrenner, 1979, 1986; Magnusson, 1995). The contention of an interactionist perspective is that the organization of the entire person–environment system and thus its development and functioning can be characterized parsimoniously as a function of the interactions within and among parts of the system and of the transformations that these interactions effect.

By *interactions*, we mean the patterns of relationships and direct transactions among individuals within and across the different domains and levels of the social ecology. Through these transactions, the nature of the ecosystems and the individuals within the systems are transformed in ways that reflect the malleability of the processes that influence ecodevelopmental trajectories. In focusing on transactions within the social environment, the SET framework is necessarily process oriented. This view is consistent with Bronfenbrenner's description of proximal processes, the enduring reciprocal interactions in the environment that serve as mechanisms for development (Bronfenbrenner, 1995; Bronfenbrenner & Ceci, 1994). SET proposes that these interactions represent a heuristic explanation of the mechanisms by which risk and protection operate. SET focuses on interactional processes that are associated with adaptive or maladaptive developmental trajectories. For example, SET attends to the characteristic patterns of interaction between parent and child, between child and peer, and between child and teacher, parents, and their support systems, among other systems. Because SET views family as the bedrock of child development, greatest saliency is given to the family's role in the child's ecodevelopment.

One area that deserves additional explanation is the distinction between cross-domain and mesosystemic influences, a distinction that has not been sufficiently articulated in the literature. SET operationalizes mesosystemic functioning in terms of direct interactions between participants of different microsystems. In contrast, mesosystem functioning typically has been examined as an indirect relationship between two domains, that is, how functioning in one domain modifies functioning in another. The SET framework proposes questions to examine cross-domain linkages, for example, how patterns of parent–child relations may influence patterns of child–peer interactions developmentally over time, as well as to understand direct mesosystem interactions.

It is our view that the direct mesosystem interactions are an understudied phenomenon. Greater attention to these interactions will help inform us about the process of risk and protection in the child's ecodevelopment. For example, SET proposes that parents are linked with the school domain and their children's academic achievement indirectly through the way they parent and structure a home environment, but also more directly through their transactions with the school environment. Because the risk associated with a mesosystem is derived from the number, the strength, the quality, and the diversity of the connections within it (Garbarino & Abramowitz, 1992), how well these two microsystems work together in face-to-face interactions is likely to have a strong influence on child development (cf. Comer, 1980). Home–school relationships that are nonexistent or are characterized by hostility and by conflict over values, styles, and interests will have very different influences on a child's development than will home–school relationships that work in concert to support each other.

In articulating the theoretical origins of SET we have relied on describing three main perspectives: social ecological, developmental, and interactional. The origin of SET was an effort to account for the seemingly disparate findings within the literature on risk and protection for drug abuse. For this reason, the development of SET has relied as strongly on research findings as on theory. Below, we describe some of the empirical data that have contributed to the formulation of SET. The body of literature is too vast to summarize succinctly in this chapter. Thus, we have elected to highlight representative studies to describe the nature of the data points that guided the development of SET.

EVIDENCE SUPPORTING THE STRUCTURAL
ECOSYSTEMS FRAMEWORK

The effort to use SET to organize disparate data points from the literature on risk and protection for drug abuse into a coherent whole is a difficult one. Although many data points are available, with some providing strong support for the SET model, others remain wanting or absent. In these cases, we have done our best to provide the most complete picture available. Where data points are absent, we propose that SET can be used to generate hypotheses about what the nature of those data will look like. This portion of the article is organized into two main sections: (a) discussion of the data points illustrative of the social ecology perspective and (b) presentation of some data illuminating the blending of the social ecology, developmental, and interactional perspectives.

Evidence Consistent With the Social Ecology Model

Some of the evidence from the risk and protection literature that is consistent with the social ecology model was presented above. Those data illustrated the importance of organizing risks according to individual domains as well as to the multiple microsystem domains of a child's social ecology. Typically considered in the investigation of risk and protection for adolescent drug abuse are individual and intrapersonal factors (e.g. Shedler & Block, 1990) and factors within the social domains of family (e.g., Brook et al., 1990; Bry, 1993), school (e.g. Gottfredson, 1988; Jessor, 1976; Smith & Fogg, 1978), and peer (Elliot, Huizinga, & Ageton, 1985; Newcomb & Bentler, 1986). Less common in the literature are results from empirical studies illustrating risk and protection in the mesosystemic and exosystemic domains. Some of these data are highlighted in this section, with special attention given to the family–school mesosystem and the family–peer mesosystem, two mesosystems central to a family-focused theory of ecodevelopment.

The Influence of the Family–School Mesosystem

Increasing empirical support is being gathered for the notion that the patterns of interactions characteristic of the family–school mesosystem have a strong relationship to healthy developmental outcomes. The work of Epstein (e.g., Epstein, 1983, 1986, 1987, 1991; see also Epstein & Lee, 1995), Comer (1980), Stevenson and Baker (1987), and Slaughter-Defoe (1995) illustrates the power of this mesosystem to shape a developmental course of the child. As noted above, we wish to distinguish mesosystemic effects from cross-domain effects. However, we review these together under the same heading.

The parent–school–community partnership movement, which has grown in numbers and strength in recent years, is predicated on the notion that changing the patterns of interaction between parents, community and school will alter the academic and social development of the child.

Results from numerous studies indicate that direct parental involvement in schools at a variety of levels, from volunteering in the classroom to participation in school governance, is associated with higher academic achievement and social development (e.g., Baker & Stevenson, 1986; Epstein, 1983, 1986, 1987, 1991; Paulson, 1994; Singh et al., 1995; Stevenson & Baker, 1987). Interventions also have successfully demonstrated the effects of altering the mesosystemic interactions on children's social and academic development. Comer's School Development Program was one of the first efforts at restructuring schools to actively involve parents in their child's schooling (Comer, 1980, 1988). In Comer's model, the richness and influence of the mesosystem are seen in the process of joining students, parents, and school staff together in collaborative projects that create a sense of community and the conditions conducive for healthy child development. Reorganizing the pattern of parent–school interactions increased child attendance and academic achievement while decreasing behavior problems (Cauce, Comer, & Schwartz, 1987; Comer, 1988).

Cross-domain influences have been studied extensively. For example, family-level variables like parenting style or values can influence school-domain outcomes like child and adolescent achievement. Slaughter-Defoe (1995) found that maternal caretaking characteristics (e.g., warm and caring or able to exercise discipline and control) and parental beliefs and values about their children's academic worth were correlated over time with African American children and adolescents' school performance and achievement aspirations. Parenting style also appears to have a cross-domain (indirect) effect on school performance in children and adolescents, that is, an authoritative parenting style is more strongly associated with academic achievement than a nonauthoritative parenting style (Steinberg, Darling, Fletcher, Brown, & Dornbusch, 1995; Steinberg et al., 1991). However, this relationship appears to be moderated by ethnicity and by peer-group membership (further evidence of cross-domain influence). European and Hispanic American adolescents benefit more from authoritative parenting than African or Asian American adolescents (Steinberg et al., 1991; see also Florscheim, Tolan, & Gorman-Smith, 1996). In part, this appears to be due to the nature of the peer groups with whom they affiliate. Although, adolescents from authoritative homes tend to associate with competent peers, in some ethnic groups, it appears that the choice of which peer group one can associate with is restricted. Steinberg, Dornbusch, and Brown (1992) found that Asian Americans tended to associate with peers who supported academic achievement, whereas the opposite was true for African American adolescents. Thus, the nature of the peer group may constrain the relationship between parenting style and academic achievement.

The Influence of the Family–Peer Mesosystem

Families and peers are increasingly recognized as mutually interdependent and influential ecological domains (Parke & Ladd, 1992). However, data on the direct mesosystemic interactions of parents and peers are limited. Results do suggest that both fathers and mothers can be effective facilitators of their children's play with peers and that parental supervision may enhance the play of younger children more than older children (Bhavnagri & Parke, 1985). Developmental trajectories also may be influenced by the quality of direct advice and consultation parents provide around issues of peer relationships (Ladd, Le Sieur, & Profilet, 1994) and the amount of parental supervision or monitoring of their children (e.g. Patterson, Reid, & Dishion, 1992; Steinberg, 1986). The evidence for the importance of parental monitoring of peer relationships as a protective process for antisocial behavior and drug abuse is striking (e.g., Dishion, Capaldi, Spracklin, & Li, 1995; Patterson & Stouthamer-Loeber, 1984). We propose that in addition to distal parental monitoring, active, direct parental involvement in peer activities across the developmental spectrum is protective. Here we assume that parents will have direct contact with their child's peers, will supervise peer-based activities, and may actually orchestrate social opportunities for their children and peers. Understanding the processes by which parents involve themselves directly in their child's peer selection and interactions requires considerably more study.

Evidence for the importance of cross-domain linkages between parents and peer domain is more available. The quality of parenting and specific parenting behaviors has been associated with the quality of child–peer relations for young children (Booth, Rose-Krasnor, McKinnon, & Rubin, 1994; Kahen, Fainsilber-Katz, & Gottman, 1994) and adolescents (Brown, Mounts, Lamborn, & Steinberg, 1993). As noted above, Steinberg and his colleagues found that adolescents of authoritative parents were more likely to belong to a peer group that supported both adolescent and adult norms, whereas adolescents of uninvolved or indulgent parents were likely to associate with peers who did not support adult values or were oriented to having fun (e.g., "partyers"; Durbin, Darling, Steinberg, & Brown, 1993). Additional work that contributes evidence to this area of cross-domain influence by the Oregon Social Learning Center is described in a subsequent section.

Exosystem Influences

Exosystem processes, such as parent support network or quality of workplace environment, have a significant influence on the developmental trajectory of children. Perhaps the most outstanding experiment in this regard has been conducted by Olds and colleagues, involving prenatal and early home visitation for preventing long-term maladaptation in children (cf. Olds et al.; 1986, Olds, Henderson, Kitzman, & Cole, 1995; Olds, Kitzman, Cole, & Robinson, 1997). The effects were dramatic. First, the exosystemic interventions had significant effects on mothers' behaviors, thereby reducing risk within several domains of the social ecology of the child. The risk trajectory was altered by first altering the mother's life course trajectory. Fifteen years postintervention, the children of the experimental condition manifested significantly lower rates of delinquency, a correlate of adolescent drug abuse.

Several other studies support the contention that parental exosystemic relations affect other domains of a child's social ecology. Taylor (1996; Taylor & Roberts, 1995) examined the relations among kinship support, parenting practices, and adolescent well-being in disadvantaged African American families. He found that kinship social support to mothers was positively related to better parental management practices, which was positively related to adolescent well-being. Similarly, Mason et al. (1994) examined the linkages among parental job satisfaction and social support (exosystem variables), parental control, parental warmth, and family conflict (family microsystem variables) and externalizing behaviors in African American seventh and eighth graders. Using structural equation modeling, Mason et al. found that including exosystem-level variables in their model showed the best fit to the data. Two specific pathways were particularly relevant. First, dissatisfaction with one's workplace and one's social support affects family conflict, which in turn influences levels of adolescent externalizing behavior. Second, parental feelings of being overcontrolled at work influence their own use of controlling behaviors as parents, which then leads to increased adolescent externalizing behavior.

Integrating Three Perspectives: Social Ecology, Development, and Interactions

Two models consistent with the SET framework in their efforts to integrate the social ecological, developmental, and interactional perspectives are: (a) a conceptual model described by Dodge (1996) and (b) the body of theoretical and empirical work conducted by Patterson, Reid, Dishion, and colleagues at the Oregon Social Learning Center (cf. Patterson, 1982; Patterson et al., 1992).

Dodge's (1996) conceptual model integrates the social ecological cross-domain perspective with a strongly developmental focus for the development of conduct disorder (which in turn is considered a risk for drug abuse). In this model, he has demonstrated how risk factors from different domains of a child's ecosystem that are correlated with each other and may even cause each other to unfold over time direct and redirect a developmental course. He has proposed that experiential factors (processes) may mediate, at least partially, early biological predispositions and sociocultural contexts. For example, a process that links different risks to conduct disorder may unfold as follows: A child with a difficult temperament (biological predisposition; e.g., Lerner & Vicary, 1984), may elicit less than optimal parenting behaviors (e.g., harsh discipline; e.g., Bry, 1993; Peters & McMahon, 1996), which contributes to a cycle of coercive behavioral interactions between parent and child in which the child's negative–antisocial behaviors are reinforced (Patterson, 1982). The child fails to learn critical skills such as behavioral control and self-regulation (Brook, Gordon, Whiteman, & Cohen, 1986), and when placed in new developmental domains, such as school, she or he does poorly academically (Gottfredson, 1988; Kandel et al., 1978; Kellam, Branch, Agrawal, & Ensminger, 1975), and she or he is unable to interact effectively and is rejected by peers (Asher & Coie, 1990). Both poor academic performance and rejection by peers are likely to lead to involvement with deviant peers (Elliott et al., 1985). This hypothetical example describes a process by which distal factors are linked to proximal factors and coalesce into an ecodevelopmental process that influences the child's development toward conduct disorders, which are considered a risk for drug abuse.

The work of Patterson and colleagues at the Oregon Social Learning Center is exemplary in its integration of the social ecological, developmental, and interactional perspectives. This model is the closest to fitting SET, although this excellent program of research has included microsystem interactions and cross-domain influences, but not mesosystem or exosystem interactional patterns.

Founded in a behavioral tradition, the research of Patterson and colleagues has a decidedly interactional focus. In addition, although they have focused on the family as a central agent in the development of antisocial behavior and drug abuse, they also have investigated the role of other social ecological domains, specifically, the peer and teacher domains. All this has been investigated within a developmental perspective, so the studies are attuned to the age-salient domains and processes that intertwine in a developmental trajectory. In their models, Patterson and colleagues focus on social interactional patterns as the causal mechanisms leading to antisocial behavior and drug abuse. Patterson's (1982) coercion model describes the initiation of a developmental trajectory to antisocial behavior. Beginning in the family domain, the model focuses on the parent–child interactions as the primary contributor to establishing the evolution of antisocial behavior. Patterson articulates a process of coercive interactions in which children learn to avoid parents' attempts at discipline through negative reinforcement. Central to this process is the parents' inability to set and carry out consistent and clear limits with their children. Through this process, the child develops an aversive behavioral pattern that can generalize to other settings of the social ecology. Over time, parents may diminish in their attempts to control their child's behavior. This can be especially problematic in adolescence, when parental monitoring becomes increasingly important as a parenting practice (Patterson & Dishion, 1985).

Patterson and colleagues extended their work across domains to investigate the influence of peers in the developmental course toward antisocial behavior and drug abuse. Their data points to the importance of looking across social ecological domains, viewing the processes developmentally, and examining the interactional patterns that emerge within and across domains. For example, Dishion, Patterson, Stoolmiller, and Skinner (1991) found that low parental monitoring (family domain), poor academic skills (school domain), and peer rejection in middle childhood (peer domain) predicted association with deviant peers by early adolescence even after controlling for prior levels of antisocial behavior. This in turn predicted antisocial behavior. These same patterns of relationships are evident in predicting drug abuse in adolescence (Dishion, Capaldi, et al., 1995). Results from this study suggested that the effects of parental monitoring and earlier antisocial behavior on drug abuse in adolescence were mediated by an association with deviant peers. These analyses provided a global level description of the relationships across domains. Yet even more compelling, the investigators provided evidence of the nature of early deviant peer relations that might eventuate in drug abuse. They examined the direct face-to-face interactional patterns among peers as predictors of later behavior. Discussions of rule breaking and normative topics and peers' responses (reinforcing versus nonreinforcing) were coded from videotapes of an interactional task between peers. In general, peer interactions that reinforced antisocial views and substance use predicted later levels of drug abuse 1 to 2 years later. In addition, the investigators classified the peer dyads into three groups that either disproportionately reinforced rule-breaking talk, disproportionately reinforced normative talk, or reinforced neither. The probability of escalating in use over a 2-year window was greatly increased in the group that reinforced rule-breaking talk.

These examples of work conducted by the scientists at the Oregon Social Learning Center demonstrate the importance of integrating social ecological, developmental, and interactional perspective elements into a single explanatory model. Integration of these elements into frameworks such as SET provides a new way to reorganize the broad literature on risk and protective factors, so that the coherence between seemingly disparate elements is evident. Building on a foundation with such a coherent view of risk and protective processes, we now prepare to illustrate implications for the design of preventive interventions.

STRUCTURAL ECOSYSTEMS THEORY: A GUIDE TO INTERVENTION DESIGN

SET is a useful heuristic for designing preventive interventions. In this section, the implications of SET for prevention intervention are illustrated by a specific application from our program of research.

The primary goals of an SET-informed preventive intervention is to modify risky ecodevelopmental trajectories (see also Tolan, Guerra, & Kendall, 1995). Risky ecodevelopmental trajectories are defined by the reciprocal interactional processes that evolve over time inside the envelope of the social ecosystems that contain and include the child (see Figure 1). Consequently, SET-informed interventions target interactional processes, that occur inside of the envelope of the child's social ecology and evolve over time to create risk or protective factors for adolescent drug abuse.

Structural Ecodevelopmental Preventive Interventions

In our program of research, we have developed an SET-informed preventive application that we refer to as *structural ecodevelopmental preventive intervention* (SEPI; Pantin & Szapocznik, 1996). In addition to the SET-informed principles focusing on interactions that are inside the envelope of the child's social ecology that evolve over time, there are other important features of the SEPI application that deserve mention. Perhaps the most important additional aspect is the strong emphasis on the family as the bedrock of child development. Consequently, in our construction of SEPI, all interventions are organized around a conception of strengthening parenting functions and other social ecosystemic functions that can support family functioning.

Because SET emphasizes the family as the most proximal and influential of the social ecological domains, it follows that we view family functioning, particularly parenting as a critical element of the ecodevelopmental risk and protective process (Tolan & Gorman-Smith, 1997). Thus, in SEPI, our emphasis is on the family as the major determinant of the actual impact of social and individual influences on development and risk. Note that such an emphasis on the family is consistent with most minority culturally defined values that give family a pivotal role in human development (Boyd-Franklin, 1989; McAdoo, 1997; Szapocznik, 1994).

Which reciprocal interactions should be selected for intervention? Those that are linked over time to risk and protection of adolescent drug abuse. In fact, changing certain patterns of interactions may, through cascading effects across the social ecological domains, have an impact on other ecosystemic areas of functioning. The cascading impact across domains suggests that particular areas can be strategically selected for intervention because of their potential impact on ecodevelopment. For example, SEPI interventions are family oriented and may place a greater emphasis on the interactions within a family and between the family and its social ecological context. However, we realize that changes in one aspect of the social ecological system will have cross-domain effects. Changing how parents interact with their children may lead to changes in how their children interact with peers. Directly modifying the patterns of peer interactions that reinforce deviant behavior (Dishion, Capaldi, et al., 1995), changing parental monitoring of peer relations (Patterson & Dishion, 1985), or establishing a mechanism for direct parental leadership in organizing and supervising prosocial peer activities change parent-child interactions. They also alter the interpersonal variables of attitudes toward drug use and perceptions of peer substance use. Thus, modifying interactions also changes intrapersonal processes that contribute to risk or protection for drug abuse.

Targeting Intervention to the Developmental Moment

One ecodevelopmental sequence described above begins with the infant's temperament and coercive behaviors, which may encourage a certain parenting response that fails to set the kinds of limits that shape self-regulation and control in the child, which in turn causes that child to be rejected by teachers and peers, which in turn causes the child to fail to bond to school and to achieve poorly in school, and to affiliate with deviant peers in school. Both of these latter outcomes place the child at risk for adolescent drug abuse.

A SEPI intervention targeting this ecodevelopmental risk process would be tailored to the developmental moment to which the intervention would be applied. Thus, at the earliest stage, the intervention might target the infant–parent interaction, to transform parental responses toward parenting behaviors that do shape self-regulation and control. This means that parental responses to the infant's coercive behaviors would need to be modified and that effective parental support systems would be required to support parents through this difficult parenting phase. On the other hand, if the SEPI intervention is initiated several years later, when the child is entering middle school, there may be a number of deficit component areas that may require a coherent multipronged intervention. Such an intervention might include (a) components to restore parents to positions of parenting leadership within the family, (b) support systems for parents who have a long history of failing with their child, (c) parent–teacher interventions to correct the lack of teamwork that occurs between parents and teachers of these problem children, both of whom are likely to be discouraged about the likelihood of correcting a lifelong history of problems with this youth, and (d) interventions to create new, prosocial peer groups.

The Coherence of the Intervention

SET defines risk and protective processes in terms of the interactions that occur within and across social ecological domains (e.g., parental non-involvement in a child's academic achievement) as they evolve over time. Consequently, SEPI interventions target interactional processes that occur within this social ecological envelope (e.g., parental roles in organizing activities, such as tutoring to enhance the child's academic achievement). This emphasis on targeting interactions within and among social ecological domains is in marked contrast to interventions that directly target risk or protective factors (e.g., programs that provide tutoring directly for the youth).

There are two interrelated aspects of coherence that are important for the construction of the intervention. First is the vision of the eco-developmental process, as depicted in Figure 1, with its wholeness, (i.e., an understanding of the interrelatedness of the parts across space–domains and time). Second is the vision of the intervention as entering the social context of the child in a way that strategically influences ecodevelopment. This means, influencing key relationships that have the potential for cascading effects (e.g., changes in parent–child relationships that can change child–peer relationships from antisocial to prosocial) and ensuring that interventions in one area do not have undesirable effects in another area (e.g., direct child services might weaken child bonding to parents). It is this dual vision of the wholeness of the social ecological process as it evolves over time and of wholeness of the impact of the intervention throughout the entire social ecology and over time that gives the intervention its sense of coherence.

From such an SET-informed perspective, SEPI models have been designed to attend to the coherent interdependence of the interactions between and across ecosystems as they evolve over time. Hence, in SEPI, a component intervention can do a lot more than target a specific risk or protective factor. Component interventions are designed to influence several simultaneously occurring elements of a single risk process—thereby attending to the interdependent nature of the elements of the risk process across the wholeness of the ecodevelopmental spectrum. Beyond the economy of using single components of an SEPI intervention to attend to multiple aspects of the risk process, such an approach to the conceptualization of SEPI provides considerable coherence to the intervention as a whole.

A specific example of how we use a single-component activity to influence multiple elements of ecodevelopmental risk is found in the implementation of a tutoring program (Pantin & Szapocznik, 1996). Tutoring is a common intervention in drug abuse prevention programs, which is typically used to target low academic achievement, an empirically demonstrated risk factor for drug abuse (Gottfredson, 1986). The challenge in

SEPI is to use tutoring as a content around which to organize a coherent intervention in which multiple elements of risk and protective processes are influenced simultaneously. In SEPI (Pantin & Szapocznik, 1996), for example, tutoring influences (a) the parental exosystem, by giving the parent support network the task of managing the tutoring program and thereby increasing the cohesiveness of the parent support group; (b) the family microsystem, by using schoolwork as the content around which parents and children transform their interactions, enhancing parental involvement with the child, and enhancing parental leadership and guidance skills, particularly around issues relevant to academic achievement; (c) the parent–school mesosystem, by increasing direct parental involvement with school and teachers, and (d) the parent–peer mesosystem, by increasing parental participation with and direct monitoring of their child's peers (who are also participating) and by parental participation in organizing prosocial activities in addition to tutoring for their child's peer group. Thus, tutoring, like each of the component elements in an SEPI application, is designed with an understanding of the coherence of the ecodevelopmental process, to influence the interlocking processes of risk and protection across domains of the child's social ecology.

Specific Concerns About Iatrogenic Effects

Because of our view that the ecodevelopmental process has considerable coherence, any consideration of an intervention must be concerned with the impact of each element of the intervention on all aspects of the ecodevelopmental process. Although in the medical field it is customary to investigate both efficacy and safety of interventions, in psychosocial interventions the emphasis has tended to be on efficacy, with a relative neglect of iatrogenic effects and safety considerations (Szapocznik et al., 1989). In SET-informed interventions, because of our interest in the impact of component elements on multiple aspects of the social ecology, we are particularly alert to the beneficial as well as deleterious effects of a particular intervention in every aspect of the social ecology.

In our prior research, given our central concern with families, we have investigated the impact of nonfamily interventions on family functioning. We have now replicated, in two separate treatment trials, findings that reveal that nonfamily interventions can have iatrogenic effects on family functioning (see also Dishion & Andrews, 1995). In one randomized study, we compared the relative efficacy of structural family therapy and child-focused psychodynamics (Szapocznik et al., 1989) in the treatment of Hispanic boys with behavioral or emotional problems. Both interventions had a positive effect on reducing symptoms in the child and improving the child's psychodynamic functioning, but families in the child-focused, psychodynamic intervention condition also demonstrated the unexpected effect of deteriorated family functioning postintervention (compared with improvements in family functioning in the family intervention condition). Thus, the child-focused intervention had detrimental effects in one of the most important ecological domains for the child, the family. A second study with Hispanic problem-behavior adolescents demonstrated a similar effect (Santisteban et al., 1999, unpublished manuscript). In this randomized study, structural family therapy was compared with an adolescent-only group intervention. Although both interventions reduced behavior problems in the adolescents, the families of adolescents in the group-format condition demonstrated a deterioration in family functioning.

Given these findings and our theoretical concern for the coherence of the ecodevelopmental processes of risk and protection, we strongly encourage investigators and practitioners to evaluate each intervention component in terms of its beneficial or undesirable impact on the entire social ecology and not on just a particular targeted factor or process. This kind of holistic perspective is common in general clinical practice, in which studies of efficacy of medical interventions are always accompanied by studies of safety because there is a clear understanding of the body as a whole system in which interventions may have their desirable target effects, as well as undesirable nontargeted effects in other organ systems.

It would appear that the family may be particularly vulnerable to interventions that build on a service-delivery philosophy that values individualism (Szapocznik, 1994; Szapocznik et al., 1996). This is of particular concern for a model such as SET that considers the family as the bedrock of human development. When the well-being of the entire social ecology is considered, it is possible to conclude that some well-meaning child-oriented interventions may represent threats to prevention because although they may achieve their desired effects with the child, family or parental functioning may be undermined. Given this perspective, it appears that it is just as critical to encourage development and testing of well-informed preventive interventions as it is to encourage more complete assessment of the safety and efficacy of existing interventions.

REFERENCES

Asher, S. R., & Coie, J. D. (1990). *Peer rejection in childhood*. Cambridge, England: Cambridge University Press.

Baker, D., & Stevenson, D. (1986). Mothers' strategies for school achievement: Managing the transition to high school. *Sociology of Education, 59,* 157–167.

Baltes, P. B., Reese, H. W., & Nesselroade, J. R. (1977). *Life-span developmental psychology: Introduction to research methods*. Monterey, CA: Brooks/Cole.

Bhavnagri, N., & Parke, R. D. (1985). *Parents as facilitators of preschool peer–peer interaction*. Paper presented at the biennial meeting of the Society for Research in Child Development, Toronto, Ontario, Canada.

Bohman, M., Cloninger, C. R., Sigvardsson, S., & von Knorring, A.-L. (1987). The genetics of alcoholism and related disorders. *Journal of Psychiatric Research, 21*, 447–452.

Booth, C. L., Rose-Krasnor, L., McKinnon, J. A., & Rubin, K. H. (1994). Predicting social adjustment in middle childhood: The role of preschool attachment security and maternal style. *Social Development 3*, 189–204.

Boyd-Franklin, N. (1989). *Black families in therapy: A multisystems approach*. New York: Guilford Press.

Bronfenbrenner, U. (1979). *The ecology of human development: Experiments by nature and design*. Cambridge, MA: Harvard University Press.

Bronfenbrenner, U. (1986). Ecology of the family as a context for human development. *American Psychologist, 32*. 513–531.

Bronfenbrenner, U. (1995). Developmental ecology through space and time: A future perspective. In P. Moen, G. H. Elder, & K. Luscher (Eds.), *Examining lives in context: Perspectives on the ecology of human development* (pp. 619–647). Washington, DC: American Psychological Association.

Bronfenbrenner, U., & Ceci, S. J. (1994). Nature–nurture reconceptualized: A bioecological model. *Psychological Review, 101*, 568–586.

Brook, J. S., Brook, D. W., Gordon, A. S., Whiteman, M., & Cohen, P. (1990). The psychological etiology of adolescent drug use: A family interactional approach. *Genetic, Social, and General Psychology Monographs, Vol. 116(2)*, 111–267.

Brook, J. S., Gordon, A. S., Whiteman, M., & Cohen, P. (1986). Some models and mechanisms for explaining the impact of maternal and adolescent characteristics on adolescent stage of drug use. *Developmental Psychology, 22*, 460–467.

Brook, J. S., & Newcomb, M. D. (1995). Childhood aggression and unconventionality: Impact on later academic achievement, drug use and workforce involvement. *Journal of Genetic Psychology, 156*, 393–410.

Brown, B. B., Mounts, N., Lamborn, S. D., & Steinberg, L. (1993). Parenting practices and peer group affiliation in adolescence. *Child Development, 64*, 467–482.

Bry, B. H. (1993). *Research on family setting's role in substance abuse*. Piscataway, NJ: Rutgers—The State University of New Jersey Press.

Bry, B. H., McKeon, P., & Pandina, R. J. (1982). Extent of drug use as a function of number of risk factors. *Journal of Abnormal Psychology, 91*, 273–279.

Bry, B. H., Pedraza, M., & Pandina, R. J. (1988). Number of risk factors predicts three-year probabilities of heavy drug and alcohol use in adolescents. In L. S. Harris (Ed.), *Problems of drug dependence* (NIDA Research Monograph No. 81, p. 301). Rockville, MD: National Institute on Drug Abuse.

Cairns, R. B., Elder, G. H., & Costello, E. J. (1996). *Developmental science*. New York: Cambridge University Press.

Caplan, M. Z., Jacoby, C., Weissberg, R. P., & Grady, K. (1988). *The positive youth development program: A substance abuse prevention program for young adolescents*. New Haven, CT: Yale University Press.

Cauce, A. M., Comer, J. P., & Schwartz, D. (1987). Long-term effects of a systems-oriented school prevention program. *American Journal of Orthopsychiatry, 57,* 208–217.

Cicchetti, D. (1984). The emergence of developmental psychopathology. *Child Development, 55,* 1–7.

Cicchetti, D. (1990). A historical perspective on the discipline of developmental psychopathology. In J. Rolf, A. S. Masten, D. Cicchetti, K. H. Nuechterlein, & S. Weintraub (Eds.), *Risk and protective factors in the development of psychopathology* (pp. 2–28). New York: Cambridge University Press.

Cicchetti, D. (1993). Developmental psychopathology: Reactions, reflections, projections. *Developmental Review, 13,* 471–502.

Cicchetti, D., & Cohen, D. J. (Eds.) (1995). *Developmental psychopathology: Vol. 1. Theory and methods.* New York: Wiley.

Cicchetti, D., & Sroufe, L. A. (1978). An organizational view of affect: Illustration from the study of Down's syndrome infants. In M. Lewis & L. Rosenblum (Eds.), *The development of affect.* New York: Plenum.

Coatsworth, J. D., Szapocznik, J., Kurtines, W., & Santisteban, D. A. (1997). Culturally competent psychosocial interventions with antisocial problem behavior in Hispanic youth. In D. M. Stoff, J. Breiling, & J. D. Maser (Eds.), *Handbook of antisocial behavior* (pp. 395–404). New York: Wiley.

Coie, J. D., Watt, N. F., West, S. G., Hawkins, J. D., Asarnow, J. R., Markman, H. J., Ramey, S. L., Shure, M. B., & Long, B. (1993). The science of prevention. A conceptual framework and some directions for a national research program. *American Psychologist, 48,* 1013–1022.

Comer, J. P. (1980). *School power: Implications of an intervention project.* New York: Free Press.

Comer, J. P. (1988). Educating poor minority children. *Scientific American, 259*(5), 42–48.

Devor, E. J. (1993). Why is there no gene for alcoholism. *Behavior Genetics, 23,* 145–151.

Dishion, T. J., & Andrews, D. W. (1995). Preventing escalation in problem behaviors with high-risk young adolescents: Immediate and 1-year outcomes. *Journal of Consulting and Clinical Psychology, 63,* 538–548.

Dishion, T. J., Capaldi, D., Spracklin, K. M., & Li, F. (1995). Peer ecology of male adolescent drug use. *Development and Psychopathology, 7,* 803–824.

Dishion, T. J., French, D. C., & Patterson, G. R. (1995). The development and ecology of antisocial behavior. In D. Cicchetti & D. J. Cohen (Eds.), *Developmental psychopathology: Vol. 4.* (pp. 509–527). New York: Wiley.

Dishion, T. J., Patterson, G. R., Stoolmiller, M., & Skinner, M. (1991). Family, school, and behavioral antecedents to early adolescent involvement with antisocial peers. *Developmental Psychology, 27,* 172–180.

Dodge, K. A. (1996, May). *Biopsychosocial perspectives on the development of conduct disorders*. Poster presented at the Fifth National Conference on Prevention Research, Washington, DC.

Dodge, K. A., & Crick, N. R. (1990). Social information-processing bases of aggressive behavior in children. *Personality and Social Psychology Bulletin, 16*, 8–22.

Durbin, D., Darling, N., Steinberg, L., & Brown, B. B. (1993). Parenting style and peer group membership among European-American adolescents. *Journal of Research on Adolescents, 3*, 87–100.

Elliot, D. S., Huizinga, D., & Ageton, S. S. (1985). *Explaining delinquency and drug use*. Beverly Hills, CA: Sage.

Epstein, J. L. (1983). Longitudinal effects of family–school–person interactions on student outcomes. In A. Kerckhoff (Ed.), *Research in sociology of education and socialization* (Volume 4, pp. 42–68). Greenwich, CT: JAI Press.

Epstein, J. L. (1986). Parents' reactions to teacher practices of parent involvement. *Elementary School Journal, 86*, 277–294.

Epstein, J. L. (1987). Toward a theory of family–school connections: Teacher practices and parent involvement. In K. Hurrelmann, F. Kaufmann, & F. Losel (Eds.), *Social intervention: Potential and constraints*. New York: Aldine de Gruyter.

Epstein, J. L. (1991). Effects on student achievement of teacher practices of parent involvement. In S. Silvern (Ed.), *Advances in reading/language research: A research annual, Vol. 5. Literacy through family, community, and school interaction* (pp. 261–276). Greenwich, CT: JAI Press.

Epstein, J. L., & Lee, S. (1995). National patterns of school and family connections in the middle grades. In B. A. Ryan, G. R. Adams, T. P. Gullotta, R. P. Weissberg, & R. L. Hampton (Eds.) *The family–school connection: Theory, research and practice. Vol. 2: Issues in children's and families' lives*. Thousand Oaks, CA: Sage.

Florscheim, P., Tolan, P. H., & Gorman-Smith, D. (1996). Family processes and risk for externalizing behavior problems among African American and Hispanic boys. *Journal of Consulting and Clinical Psychology, 64*(6), 1–9.

Ford, D. H., & Lerner, R. M. (1992). *Developmental systems theory: An integrative approach*. Newbury Park, CA: Sage.

Garbarino, J., & Abramowitz, R. H. (1992). The ecology of human development. In J. Garbarino (Ed.), *Children and families in the social environment* (pp. 11–33). New York: Aldine de Gruyter.

Garmezy, N. (1974). Children at risk: The search for the antecedents of schizophrenia. *Schizophrenia Bulletin, 8*, 14–90.

Garmezy, N. (1985). Stress-resistant children: The search for protective factors. In J. E. Stevenson (Ed.), *Recent research in developmental psychopathology* (pp. 213–234). Oxford, England: Pergamon Press.

Gottfredson, D. (1986). An empirical test of school-based environmental and individual interventions to reduce the risk of deliquent behavior. *Criminology, 24*, 705–731.

Gottfredson, D. (1988). An evaluation of an organization development approach to reducing school disorder. *Evaluation Review, 11*, 739–763.

Guerra, N. G., & Slaby, R. G. (1990). Cognitive mediators of aggression in adolescent offenders: 2. Intervention. *Developmental Psychology, 26*, 269–277.

Hawkins, J. D., Catalano, R. F., & Miller, J. Y. (1992). Risk and protective factors for alcohol and other drug problems in adolescence and early childhood: Implications for substance abuse prevention. *Psychological Bulletin, 112*, 64–105.

Henggeler, S. W., & Borduin, C. M. (1990). *Family therapy and beyond: A multisystemic approach to treating the behavior problems of children and adolescents.* Pacific Grove, CA: Brooks/Cole.

Henggeler, S. W., Melton, G. B., & Smith, L. A. (1992). Family preservation using multisystemic therapy: An effective alternative to incarcerating serious juvenile offenders. *Journal of Consulting and Clinical Psychology, 60*, 953–961.

Institute of Medicine. (1994). *Reducing risks for mental disorders: Frontiers for preventive intervention research.* Washington, DC: National Academy Press.

Jessor, R. (1976). Predicting time of onset of marijuana use: A developmental study of high school youth. *Journal of Consulting and Clinical Psychology, 44*, 125–134.

Johnson, L. D., O'Malley, P. M., & Bachman, J. G. (1992). *National survey results on drug use from the Monitoring the Future Study, 1975–1992: Vol. 1. Secondary school students.* Rockville, MD: National Institute on Drug Abuse.

Kahen, V., Fainsilber-Katz, L., & Gottman, J. M. (1994). Linkages between parent–child interaction and conversations of friends. *Social Development, 3*, 238–254.

Kandel, D. B., Kessler, R. C., & Margulies, R. Z. (1978). Antecedents of adolescent initiation into stages of drug use: A developmental analysis. *Journal of Youth and Adolescence, 7*, 13–40.

Kellam, S. G., Branch, J. D., Agrawal, K. C., & Ensminger, M. (1975). *Mental health and going to school: The Woodland program of assessment, early intervention, and evaluation.* Chicago: University of Chicago Press.

Kellam, S. G., Brown, C. H., Rubin, B. R., & Ensminger, M. (1983). Paths leading to teenage psychiatric symptoms and substance use: Developmental epidemiological studies in Woodlawn. In S. B. Guze, F. J. Earls, & J. E. Barrett (Eds.), *Childhood psychopathology and development* (pp. 17–51). New York: Raven Press.

Kranzler, H. R., & Anton, R. F. (1994). Implications of recent neuropsychopharmacologic research for understanding the etiology and development of alcoholism. *Journal of Consulting and Clinical Psychology, 62*, 1116–1126.

Kurtines, W. M., & Szapocznik, J. (1996). Structural family therapy in contexts of cultural diversity. In E. Hibbs & R. Jensen (Eds.), *Psychosocial treatment research with children* (pp. 671–697). Washington, DC: American Psychological Association.

Ladd, G. W., Le Sieur, K., & Profilet, S. M. (1994). Direct parental influences on young children's peer relations. In S. Duck (Ed.), *Learning about relationships (Vol. 2)*. London: Sage.

Lerner, J. V., & Vicary, J. R. (1984). Difficult temperament and drug use: Analyses from the New York longitudinal study. *Journal of Drug Education, 14*, 1–8.

Leshner, A. I. (1996, August). *Behavioral science and drug abuse: A half century of productive partnership*. Presentation at the annual convention of the American Psychological Association, Toronto, Ontario, Canada.

Magnusson, D. (1995). Individual development: A holistic, integrated model. In P. Moen, G. H. Elder, & K. Luscher (Eds.), *Examining lives in context: Perspectives on the ecology of human development* (pp. 19–60). Washington, DC: American Psychological Association.

Magnusson, D., Andersson, T., & Torestad, B. (1993). Methodological implications of a peephole perspective on personality. In D. C. Funder, R. D. Parke, C. Tomlinson-Keasey, & K. Widaman (Eds.), *Studying lives through time: Personality and development*. Washington, DC: American Psychological Association.

Mason, C. A., Cauce, A. M., Gonzales, N., Hiraga, Y., & Grove, K. (1994). An ecological model of externalizing behaviors in African American adolescents: No family is an island. *Journal of Research on Adolescence, 4*, 639–655.

Masten, A. S., & Garmezy, N. (1985). Risk, vulnerability, and protective factors in developmental psychopathology. In B. B. Lahey, & A. E. Kazdin (Eds.), *Advances in clinical child psychology* (Vol. 8, pp. 1–52). New York: Plenum.

McAdoo, H. P. (1997). *Black families*. Thousand Oaks, CA: Sage.

McGue, M., Pickens, R. W., & Svikis, D. S. (1992). Sex and age effects on the inheritance of alcohol problems: A twin study. *Journal of Abnormal Psychology, 101*, 3–17.

Minuchin, S. (1974). *Families and family therapy*. Cambridge, MA: Harvard University Press.

Minuchin, S., & Fishman, H. C. (1981). *Family therapy techniques*. Cambridge, MA: Harvard University Press.

Minuchin, S., Rosman, B. L., & Baker, L. (1978). *Psychosomatic families: Anorexia nervosa in context*. Cambridge, MA: Harvard University Press.

Newcomb, M. D., & Bentler, P. (1986). Substance use and ethnicity: Differential impact of peer and adult models. *Journal of Psychology, 120*, 83–95.

Newcomb, M. D., Maddahian, E., & Bentler, P. M. (1986). Risk factors for drug use among adolescents: Concurrent and longitudinal analyses. *American Journal of Public Health, 76*, 525–531.

Olds, D. L., Henderson, C. R., Kitzman, H., & Cole, R. (1995). Effects of prenatal and infancy nurse home visitation on surveillance of child maltreatment. *Pediatrics, 93*, 221–227.

Olds, D. L., Henderson, C. R., Tatelbaum, R., & Chamberlin, R. (1986). Improving the delivery of prenatal care and outcomes of pregnancy: A randomized trial of nurse home visitations. *Pediatrics, 77*, 16–28.

Olds, D. L., Kitzman, H., Cole, R., & Robinson, J. (1997). Theoretical foundations of a program of home visitation for pregnant women and parents of young children. *The Journal of Community Psychology, 25*(1), 9–25.

Pantin, H., & Szapocznik, J. (1996). *Manual for structural ecosystems prevention interventions (SEPI) for application with minority families and their 12 year-old adolescents*. Unpublished manuscript, University of Miami, FL.

Parke, R. D., & Ladd, G. W. (1992). *Family–peer relationships: Modes of linkage*. Hillsdale, NJ: Erlbaum.

Patterson, G. R. (1982). *Coercive family process*. Eugene, OR: Castalia.

Patterson, G. R., & Dishion, T. J. (1985). Contributions of families and peers to delinquency. *Criminology, 23*, 63–79.

Patterson, G. R., Reid, J. B., & Dishion, T. J. (1992). *Antisocial boys*. Eugene, OR: Castalia.

Patterson, G. R., & Stouthamer-Loeber, M. (1984). The correlation of family management practices and delinquency. *Child Development, 55*, 1299–1307.

Paulson, S. E. (1994). Relations of parenting style and parental involvement with ninth-grade students' achievement. *Journal of Early Adolescence, 14*, 250–267.

Pentz, M. A., Dweyer, J. H., MacKinnon, D. P., Flay, B. R., Hansen, W. B., Wang, E. Y. I., & Johnson, C. A. (1989). A multicommunity trial for primary prevention of adolescent drug abuse: Effects on drug use prevalence. *Journal of the American Medical Association, 261*, 3259–3266.

Peters, R., & McMahon, R. J. (1996). *Preventing childhood disorders, substance abuse and delinquency*. Thousand Oaks, CA: Sage.

Reiss, D., & Price, R. H. (1996). National research agenda for prevention: The National Institute of Mental Health report. *American Psychologist, 51*, 1109–1115.

Robins, L. N. (1980). The natural history of drug abuse. *Acta Psychiatrica Scandinavia, 62*, 7–20.

Rutter, M. (1987). Psychosocial resilience and protective mechanisms. *American Journal of Orthopsychiatry 57*, 316–331.

Rutter, M. (1990). Psychosocial resilience and protective mechanisms. In J. Rolf, A. S. Masten, D. Cicchetti, K. H. Nuechterlein, & S. Weintraub (Eds.), *Risk and protective factors in the development of psychopathology* (pp. 181–124). Cambridge, England: Cambridge University Press.

Rutter, M., Champion, L., Quinton, D., Maughan, B., & Pickles, A. (1995). Understanding individual differences in environmental-risk exposure. In P. Moen, G. H. Elder, & K. Luscher (Eds.), *Examining lives in context: Perspectives on the ecology of human development* (pp. 61–93). Washington, DC: American Psychological Association.

Rutter, M., & Garmezy, N. (1983). Developmental psychopathology. In P. Mussen (Ed.), *Handbook of child psychology*. New York: Wiley.

Sameroff, A. J. (1983). Developmental systems: Context and evolution. In P. H. Mussen (Ed.) *Handbook of child psychology. Vol. 1.* (pp. 237–284). New York: Wiley.

Sameroff, A. J., & Chandler, M. J. (1975). Reproductive risk and the continuum of caretaking causality. In F. D. Horowitz, M. Hetherington, S. Scarr-Salapatek, & G. Siegal (Eds.), *Review of child development research Vol. 4* (pp. 187–244). Chicago: University of Chicago Press.

Sameroff, A. J., Seifer, R., Barocas, R., Zax, M., & Greenspan, S. (1987). IQ scores of 4-year-old children: Social environmental risk factors. *Pediatrics, 79*, 343–350.

Santisteban, D. A., Szapocznik, J., Perez-Vidal, A., Kurtines, W. M., Coatsworth, D., & LaPerriere, A. (1999). *The efficacy of brief strategic/structural family therapy in modifying behavior problems and an exploration of the mediating role that family functioning plays in behavior change.* Unpublished manuscript.

Shedler, J., & Block, J. (1990). Adolescent drug use and psychological health: A longitudinal inquiry. *American Psychologist, 58*, 1220–1234.

Singh, K., Bickley, P. G., Trivette, P., Keith, T. Z., Keith, P. B., & Anderson, E. (1995). The effects of four components of parental involvement on eighth grade student achievement: Structural analysis of NELS–88 data. *School Psychology Review, 24*, 299–317.

Slaughter-Defoe, D. T. (1995). Revisiting the concept of socialization: Caregiving and teaching in the 90s—a personal perspective. *American Psychologist, 50*, 276–280.

Smith, G. M., & Fogg, C. P. (1978). Psychological predictors of early use, late use, and non-use of marijuana among teenage students. In D. B. Kandel (Ed.), *Longitudinal research on drug use: Empirical findings and methodological issues* (pp. 101–113). Washington, DC: Hemisphere–Wiley.

Sroufe, L. A., & Rutter, M. (1984). The domain of developmental psychopathology. *Child Development, 55*, 17–29.

Steinberg, L. (1986). Latchkey children and susceptibility to peer pressure: An ecological analysis. *Developmental Psychology, 22*, 433–439.

Steinberg, L., Darling, N., Fletcher, A. C., Brown, B. B., & Dornbusch, S. M. (1995). Authoritative parenting and adolescent adjustment: An ecological journey. In P. Moen, G. H. Elder, & K. Luscher (Eds.), *Examining lives in context: Perspectives on the ecology of human development* (pp. 423–466). Washington, DC: American Psychological Association.

Steinberg, L., Dornbusch, S., & Brown, B. (1992). Ethnic differences in adolescent achievement: An ecological perspective. *American Psychologist, 47*, 723–729.

Steinberg, L., Mounts, N., Lamborn, S., & Dornbusch, S. (1991). Authoritative parenting and adolescent adjustment across varied ecological niches. *Journal of Research on Adolescence, 1*, 19–36.

Stevenson, D. L., & Baker, D. P. (1987). The family–school relation and the child's school performance. *Child Development, 58*, 1348–1357.

Szapocznik, J. (Ed.) (1994). *A Hispanic/Latino family approach to substance abuse prevention.* Rockville, MD: Center for Substance Abuse Prevention.

Szapocznik, J., & Kurtines, W. (1979). Acculturation, biculturism and adjustment among Cuban Americans. In A. Padilla (Ed.), *Psychological dimensions on the* acculturation process: Theory, models, and some new findings. Boulder, CO: Westview Press.

Szapocznik, J., & Kurtines, W. (1989). *Breakthroughs in family therapy with drug abusing problem youth*. New York: Springer.

Szapocznik, J., & Kurtines, W. M. (1993). Family psychology and cultural diversity: Opportuities for theory, research and application. *American Psychologist, 48*, 400–407.

Szapocznik, J., Kurtines, W. M., & Fernandez, T. (1980). Bicultural involvement and adjustment in Hispanic American youths. *International Journal of Intercultural Relations, 4*, 353–366.

Szapocznik, J., Kurtines, W. M., & Santisteban, D. A. (1994). The interplay of advances among theory, research and application in family interventions for Hispanic behavior problem youth. In R. G. Malgady & O. Rodriguez (Eds.), *Theoretical and conceptual issues in Hispanic mental health* (pp. 156–180). Malabar, FL: Krieger.

Szapocznik, J., Kurtines, W. M., Santisteban, D. A., Pantin, H., Scopetta, M., Mancilla, Y., Aisenberg, S., McIntosh, S., Perez-Vidal, A., & Coatsworth, J. D. (1996). The evolution of structural ecosystemic theory working with Latino families. In J. G. Garcia & M. C. Zea (Eds.), *Psychological interventions and research with Latino populations* (pp. 166–190). Boston, MA: Allyn & Bacon.

Szapocznik, J., & Mancilla, Y. (1995). Rainforests, families and communities: Ecological perspectives on exile, return and reconstruction. In W. J. O'Neill (Ed.), *Family: The First Imperative. A Symposium in Search of Root Causes of Family Strength and Family Disintegration* (pp. 279–294). Cleveland, OH: The William J. and Dorothy K. O'Neill Foundation.

Szapocznik, J., & Pantin, H. M. (1996a). *UJIMA: A randomized study investigating the efficacy and mechanisms of change in structural ecosystems prevention intervention for reducing risk and enhancing prevention for drug use in a universal sample of African American 4th graders*. Unpublished report. Rockville, MD: Center for Substance Abuse Prevention Grant No. 1 HD1 SPO 7117, 1995–1998.

Szapocznik, J., & Pantin, H. M. (1996b). *Structural ecosystems preventive intervention: A randomized study investigating the efficacy and mechanisms of change in structural ecosystems prevention intervention for reducing risk and enhancing prevention for drug use in a universal sample of 12–14-year-old inner-city African American and Hispanic adolescents*. Unpublished report. Rockville, MD: Center for Substance Abuse Prevention.

Szapocznik, J., Pantin, H., & Scopetta, M. (1996). *Latinas: A randomized study investigating the efficacy and mechanisms of change in structural ecosystems prevention intervention in reducing risk and enhancing prevention for drug use in a selected sample of high-risk 12-year-old Hispanic inner-city female adolescents*. Unpublished manuscript. Rockville, MD: Center for Substance Abuse Prevention. Grant No. 1 HD1 SPO7446-01, 1995–1998.

Szapocznik, J., Rio, A., Murray, E., Cohen, R., Scopetta, M. A., Rivas-Vasquez, A., Hervis, O. E., & Posada, V. (1989). Structural family versus psychodynamic child therapy for problematic Hispanic boys. *Journal of Consulting and Clinical Psychology, 57,* 571–578.

Szapocznik, J., Santisteban, D., Kurtines, W. M., Perez-Vidal, A., & Hervis, O. E. (1984). Bicultural effectiveness training: A treatment intervention for enhancing intercultural adjustment. *Hispanic Journal of Behavioral Sciences, 6,* 317–344.

Szapocznik, J., Santisteban, D., Rio, A., Perez-Vidal, A., Kurtines, W. M., & Hervis, O. E. (1986). Bicultural effectiveness training (BET): An intervention modality for families experiencing intergenerational/intercultural conflict. *Hispanic Journal of Behavioral Sciences, 6,* 303–330.

Szapocznik, J., Scopetta, M. A., & King, O. E. (1978). The effect and degree of treatment comprehensiveness with a Latino drug abusing population. In D. E. Smith, S. M. Anderson, M. Burton, N. Gotlieb, W. Harvey, & T. Chung (Eds.), *A multicultural view of drug abuse.* Cambridge, MA: G. K. Hall.

Szapocznik, J., & Williams, R. A. (1999). *Brief strategic family therapy: Twenty-five years of interplay among theory, research and practice.* Unpublished manuscript.

Taylor, R. D. (1996). Adolescents' perceptions of kinship support and family management practices: Association with adolescent adjustment in African American families. *Developmental Psychology, 32,* 687–695.

Taylor, R. D., & Roberts, D. (1995). Kinship support and maternal and adolescent well-being in economically disadvantaged African American families. *Child Development, 66,* 1585–1597.

Tolan, P. H., & Gorman-Smith, D. (1997). Families and development of urban children. In H. J. Walburg, O. Reyes, & R. P. Weissburg (Eds.), *Urban children and youth: Interdisciplinary perspective on policies and programs* (pp. 67–91). Thousand Oaks, CA: Sage.

Tolan, P. H., Guerra, N. G., & Kendall, P. C. (1995). Introduction to special section: Prediction and prevention of antisocial behavior in children and adolescents. *Journal of Consulting and Clinical Psychology, 63,* 515–517.

Werner, H. (1957). The concept of development from a comparative and organismic point of view. In D. B. Harris (Ed.), *The concept of development* (pp. 125–148). Minneapolis: University of Minnesota Press.

15

DEVELOPMENT, EVALUATION, AND DISSEMINATION OF EFFECTIVE PSYCHOSOCIAL TREATMENTS: LEVELS OF DISORDER, STAGES OF CARE, AND STAGES OF TREATMENT RESEARCH

MARSHA M. LINEHAN

Mental health professionals and researchers are at a crossroads right now in the development, validation, and dissemination of effective psychosocial interventions for emotional and behavioral disorders, including substance use disorders. Although there has been much progress over the last 30 or 40 years in our understanding of and ability to treat various mental disorders and behavioral problems, our current treatments, biologic and psychosocial alike, are still woefully inadequate for the task at hand. What we have is often more effective than nothing, but it's not effective enough for the problems that we face. Although costs of health care have

Writing of this chapter was partially supported by National Institute of Mental Health Grant MH34486 and National Institute on Drug Abuse Grant DA08674. I thank Kelly Koerner for her editorial assistance.

been rising for many years, the more recent involvement of business in the provision of health care, particularly that of for-profit managed care, has increased our awareness and sensitivity to issues of costs and effectiveness of treatments that we offer. Our ability to develop effective treatment interventions and the effectiveness of the treatments that we already offer are open to question. Health care providers are increasingly required to defend what they are doing not only to the recipient of the care but to business and government agencies that pay for the care.

I have been in the field of treatment development, evaluation, and dissemination for the past 20 years. What follows are observations about some of the problems that we are facing now and some thoughts about how we might proceed. The spark for these is my emerging belief that discussions about what mental health treatments should be given by whom to what population are often fraught with terminological and theoretical obfuscation. Researcher, treatment provider, administrator, payer, and consumer, alike, often are like blind people each touching some different part of the proverbial elephant; heated arguments ensue about whether an elephant is a trunk or a tail. We each give answers, but often we give answers to very different questions. Although there are any number of ways to structure a discussion of treatment development, evaluation, and dissemination, I have structured it around three different themes. The themes have to do with what I see as the impediments in treatment research as we're carrying it on today, and they have to do with the relationship of treatment development to (a) level of disorder treated, (b) level of patient care addressed by the treatment, and (c) the stage of treatment development where a specific therapeutic intervention is. Although examples of each of these themes could be drawn from any area of treatment research, with few exceptions, I have drawn all of my examples from treatment development in the field of drug abuse.

LEVELS OF DISORDER AND STAGES OF TREATMENT

Arguments about what works for whom are often confounded by lack of clarity regarding the stage of disorder the treatment is intended to address. Level of disorder refers to both severity of dysfunction as well as pervasiveness, complexity, and comorbidity of individual disorder. Relative advantages of various treatments cannot be considered without clarity on the level of disorder the treatment is designed for (Beutler & Clarkin, 1990; Chambless et al., 1996; Garfield, 1994). The appropriate focus and outcomes of clinical interventions are intimately related to the level of disorder that a person has when entering treatment. For example, there are very good treatment protocols for heroin addiction, major depression, panic disorder, and posttraumatic stress disorder (PTSD). But what do you do if you are treating a person with all four disorders plus a number of other major problems of potentially crises proportion, such as young children to care for, homelessness, no job or job skills, and an abusive, harassing spouse? Does one simply sequence the four protocols in order? How does one integrate these interventions with attention to other problem behaviors and events? Does one apply the same treatment for depression to this individual as to the high-powered career individual who is drinking a bit too much and believes life has lost much of its meaning following the last child leaving for college? The complex problems of the first individual are likely to be more than the sum of a sequence of simple problems. While complex treatments will undoubtedly combine elements of simpler, more focused treatments, the very rules for combining elements must be worked out empirically. In discussion of what works for whom in what context, level of disorder is critical in determining the goals of treatment. Goals, in turn, are essential in determining treatment effectiveness.

Comprehensive treatments, especially those for severely disordered individuals, must also be flexible so that they can change over time to address different, but progressively more functional, goals. In developing treatments for severely dysfunctional and suicidal or drug-addicted women meeting criteria for borderline personality disorder, I was faced with just this task and proposed three levels of disorder (Linehan, 1993). I have recently added a fourth level (Linehan, 1997). These levels of disorder are, in turn, linked to stages of treatment, each with a corresponding set of goals and problems to be solved. Although individuals may enter therapy at very different levels, may not go through all levels, and once at a level may go back and forth between that level and previous levels, the idea of a level of disorder, nonetheless, can structure the tasks of therapy in such a way as to clarify which treatments already known to be efficacious should be tried at which time in which context. Goals of treatment organized by stage of treatment and corresponding level of disorder are outlined in Exhibit 1.

Level 1 Disorder, From Behavior Dyscontrol to Stage 1 Goal, Behavior Control

Level 1 is the most severe level of disorder. Individuals at Level 1 have complex multiple problems, meet criteria for severe and/or multiple *Diagnostic and Statistical Manual for Mental Disorders* (American Psychiatric Association, 1994) Axis I and/or Axis IV disorders, and may meet criteria for severe Axis II disorders, such as borderline personality disorder. At this level, the immediate problem is that of behavioral dyscontrol, and the major treatment goal of the corresponding stage 1 of treatment is simply to get these individuals in control of their own behavior and their lives. Four goals take priority. First, when life-threatening behaviors (e.g., suicidal

EXHIBIT 1

Levels of Disorder	Goals of Treatment Stages
1. Severe behavioral dyscontrol	1. Behavior control ■ Reasonable (immediate) life expectancy ■ Connection to help giver(s) ■ Stability and control of action ■ Basic capabilities
2. Quiet desperation	2. Emotional experiencing ■ Nontraumatizing emotional experiencing ■ Connection to the environment

3. Problems in living	3. Ordinary happiness and unhappiness
	■ Self-respect
	    Mastery
	    Self-efficacy
	    Sense of morality
	■ Tolerable problems in living

4. Incompleteness	4. Capacity for sustained joy
	■ Expanded awareness
	    Self
	    Past to present
	    Self to other
	■ Spiritual fulfillment
	■ Experiences of flow; peak experiencing

or homicidal behaviors, severe anorexia, accidental drug overdoses, or immediate and very high-risk, unsafe sex or other practices) are occurring, a reasonable immediate life expectancy is the primary goal. If you can't keep the patient alive, it doesn't make much difference how effective the treatment is. Second, when necessary, treatment must focus on keeping the individual in the therapy. Behaviors of therapist and of patient that interfere with continued therapy or compliance with necessary treatment protocols are the targets here. This focus is especially important in treatments of drug abusers and other individuals who frequently drop out of treatment, are aversive to treatment providers, are noncompliant with treatment prescriptions, and/or elicit countertherapeutic behaviors from therapists. Treatments don't work with people who are not in treatment. When the expectancies for life and for continued treatment are reasonable, the next goal must be to get at least minimal stability and control of action. If you can't get behavior under some control, you really can't get anything else under control. Finally, treatment at this stage must also pay attention to helping the individual acquire at least the basic capabilities needed to meet other goals. Highly structured, highly controlled, multisystemic, multimodal, and multicomponent treatments developed by systems and behavioral therapists might be most effective here. Intensity of treatment may range from one or more weekly outpatient visits plus as-needed crisis intervention and comprehensive case management programs to day treatment, day hospital, and/or brief inpatient stays.

Depending on the variables controlling out-of-control actions in the specific case, once action is under control and adequate functioning is restored, the individual may progress to Level 2, may jump over Level 2 and go to Level 3 or 4, or may not be disordered at all. An example of the latter would be a person who is out of control due to an extreme, but temporary, environmental stress or biological anomaly. The schizophrenic patient who has gone off his or her medications or is subjected to temporary environmental stress and criticism may be the person who will jump back and forth between Level 1 and 3. The out-of-control PTSD and the borderline personality disorder patients are examples of patients who are likely to be at Level 2 once action is under control.

Level 2 Disorder, From Quiet Desperation to Stage 2 Goal, Emotional Experiencing

At Level 2, the person has action under reasonable control but is out of control of emotional experiencing, most importantly, emotional pain. At this level, the experience of emotion itself is a traumatic experience, and avoidance of emotions and associated cues is a key problem. Extreme emotional pain in the presence of control of action, including emotion-linked action, can be thought of as the level of quiet desperation. (Although it trivializes it somewhat, Level 1 can be thought of as the level of loud desperation.) PTSD is the prototypic example of Level 2 disorder, as are other severe anxiety disorders, complicated grieving, and severe depression. PTSD plus severe suicidal behavior and risk would be an example of Level 1 disorder, as would the PTSD individual who consistently drops out of treatment due to drug use. At this level, the corresponding Stage 2 of treatment is to enhance the ability of the individual to experience emotions without trauma. When the painful emotions are due to exposure to trauma-associated cues (whether of childhood, adulthood, or the often neglected trauma of disorder itself), an important treatment task in this stage is to provide new experiences that provide corrective information and permit learning of new responses to trauma-associated cues.

Treatment tasks here are different from those in Stage 1 and will generally include interventions that focus on emotional processing. For example, behavior therapists might do response prevention–exposure-based treatments (e.g., Foa, Hearst-Ikeda, & Perry, 1995), psychodynamic therapists might do uncovering (e.g., Herman, 1992), and experiential therapists might do experiential emotional processing work (e.g., Greenberg, Rice, & Elliott, 1993). Each of these interventions will focus on identification of emotions and emotional cues, exposure to emotional cues in the presence of corrective information, and learning new opposite-to-the-emotion responses to these cues. In uncomplicated cases, treatment at this stage may be brief. For example, 9 to 15 sessions may be sufficient (Foa,

Jaycox, Meadows, Hembree, & Dancu, 1996). For individuals with more than one trauma or with pervasive emotional avoidance, successive or integrative treatments covering each area may be necessary.

An individual can enter treatment at Level 2 disorder (never having the behavioral dyscontrol of Level 1) or can vacillate back and forth between Level 2 and higher levels. What often occurs, however, is that individuals at Level 1 (serious behavior dyscontrol), such as the drug addicts whose behavior is dysfunctional across many domains, are treated long enough to get behavior under control but not long enough to treat the traumatic and/or unendurable emotional experiencing that precipitates the behavior dyscontrol in the first place. Once the behavior is under control, the individual at this point has Level 2 disorder, and Stage 2 treatment goals are appropriate. However, individuals without adequate finances may not meet levels of care criteria for continued treatment. Although some seem able to lead lives of quiet desperation without coming to the attention of mental health professionals, many cannot. Those who cannot tolerate Level 2 disorder and who cannot get treatment are, it seems, likely to eventually deteriorate to Level 1 and be seen again in the hospital emergency rooms, inpatient units, and crisis care services. Stage 1 of treatment may need to be repeated.

Level 3 Disorder, From Problems in Living to Stage 3 Goal, Ordinary Happiness and Unhappiness

In Stage 3 of treatment, the person either has done the work necessary in earlier stages of treatment or was never severely disordered enough to need it. The disorder at Level 3 consists of problems in living and unacceptable unhappiness or both. Although the problems may be very serious, as in the case of uncomplicated or mild depression or a very troubled marriage, they are not themselves disabling, and the individual does not have other comorbid, severe, and disabling disorders. Uncomplicated, hidden, drug addiction that does not seriously interfere with daily living is an example. The individual is functional in major domains of living. The goal of the corresponding Stage 3 of treatment is to achieve a state of "acceptable" problems in living, that is, ordinary happiness and unhappiness as well as a stable sense of self-respect. By *self-respect*, I mean a sense of mastery or self-efficacy as well as a sense that one is living according to one's own sense of morality and personal values.

Protocol-based treatments may be effective for some Level 3 problems (e.g., interpersonal or cognitive therapy for depression; cognitive–behavioral treatments for obesity and eating disorders; contingency management or other behavioral and/or cognitive treatments for problems of self-management; assertiveness training, interpersonal therapy, or other interpersonally focused treatments for relationship problems; and various marital therapy protocols for unhappy marriages). For others, the availability of a wise person with whom to process current concerns may be sufficient. For still others, treatments aimed at insight and restructuring one's understanding of one's self and one's past may be useful.

Level 4 Disorder, From Incompleteness to Stage 4 Goal, Capacity for Sustained Joy

Many, if not most, individuals are content with Level 3 functioning. Some, however, have a residual sense of incompleteness, and its resolution and achieving a capacity of sustained joy are the goals of Stage 4 treatment. The highly functioning drug abuser is often at Level 4. For example, this would be the case when drugs are an escape from a sense of meaninglessness or when the person, while highly functioning, craves the "high" that drugs can give. Drugs can mask incompleteness and mimic the joy of intense spiritual experiences. For the drug abuser at Level 4, treatment might look very different from treatment for a person abusing the same drug but at a lower level of disorder. Here, the goals are expanded awareness, spiritual fulfillment, and the movement into experiencing flow. For individuals with Level 4 disorder, long-term, insight-oriented psychotherapy, spiritual direction or practices, or other organized experiential treatments and life experiences may be of most benefit.

Pretreatment Stage of Therapy

No matter the level of disorder, all treatments must begin with a stage of negotiation between therapist and patient about goals, methods of treatment, fees and requirements, session timing and length, and so on. If one assumes that therapy does not actually start until a formal agreement or contract is entered into between therapist and patient (and sometimes, also, with the insuring agency), then the initial interchanges between patient and therapist can be considered pretreatment. Although this is not a level of disorder, it is a stage of treatment. Regardless of the level of disorder, the tasks of pretreatment are to assess the needs of the patient and obtain agreement between patient and therapist on goals of the treatment and a commitment from both to the treatment program selected and/ or offered. This is a particularly special problem in treating substance abusers given their very high dropout rates and failure to follow through with treatment. A number of innovative interventions have been developed, such as motivational interviewing (Miller & Rollnick, 1991), and much more work is needed.

LEVEL OF PATIENT CARE: FIVE FUNCTIONS OF TREATMENT

Another way to look at goals of treatment is to consider them in the light of the level of care that the treatment aims to provide. A given treatment program may be aimed at providing total care, whereas another may be aimed at partial and very narrowly focused goals. The former is a comprehensive package, and the latter usually consists of protocols in addition to standard care. When the level of care provided by treatments is confused or unclear, comparison of outcomes within studies or across treatment studies may be like comparing apples and oranges; the discourse itself doesn't get us very far. An example of comprehensive care would be a drug abuse treatment that provides replacement-drug maintenance (e.g., methadone maintenance), standard pharmacotherapy, case management, behavioral skills training, relapse prevention, AIDS counseling, vocational guidance and training, support groups, and frequent urinalyses testing. Any component (e.g., skills training or relapse prevention) might be an add-on component to the care the individual is getting in the basic treatment-as-usual. Although it is frequently assumed that there is no interaction between a new add-on treatment and the standard or comprehensive treatment, this remains an open question. The merits of various treatment options may well be dependent on level of care within which the treatment is offered and evaluated.

A comprehensive intervention program must attend to at least five major functions of treatment. Treatments can be compared on the basis of how well they attend to each of the functions: (a) capability enhancement, (b) motivational enhancement, (c) generalization of gains, (d) structuring of the environment to support clinical progress, and (e) enhancement of capabilities and motivation of therapists. A given treatment may be very effective for some functions and not for others. For a particular disorder, such as drug abuse, we may have an array of treatments that when put together accomplish some or all functions. Indeed, one way to evaluate progress in treating particular disorders might be to examine the domain of treatments for that disorder in the light of which of these functions are met by the sum total of interventions available. To the extent that one or more functions are not addressed, then new treatment approaches are needed. In what follows, I describe in more detail the five functions and provide examples from the domain of drug abuse treatments.

Capability Enhancement

The first function of a mental health treatment is to enhance the capabilities of the patient. Behavioral performance, in its broadest sense, depends on the presence of the requisite behaviors in the individual's repertoire (Wallace, 1966). Skillful behavior further requires that the individual be capable of matching performance to the demands of the context. Although skills training is most often associated with behavior therapy, there is actually a fair amount of attention to increasing capabilities in most therapies. Giving advice and instructions, modeling new desired behaviors, suggesting new activities, and providing written materials and psychoeducational programs, for example, qualify as skills-acquisitions procedures. Pharmacotherapy also can be considered capability enhancing when it increases the capability of the system to regulate or self-regulate. Skills training and psychoeducational approaches are well-established drug abuse intervention procedures (Botvin, Dusenbury, Baker, & James-Ortiz, 1989).

Motivational Enhancement

Performance depends on more than capability: It requires motivation. Motivational enhancement can be thought of as requiring some variation of three different classes of intervention (contingency management, exposure-based procedures, cognitive modification) depending on the factors interfering with skillful, adaptive, and functional responses. When maladaptive–dysfunctional behavior (including emotional, cognitive, and overt–motor behaviors) is under the control of its contingencies, then an effective treatment will require that the therapist manage contingencies so that clinical progress is reinforced and clinical deterioration is not. The therapist must clarify or make salient the contingencies that are operating in the individual's life at the moment. The therapist also has to figure out a way to reduce other behaviors, such as emotions, overt behaviors, and cognitions, that interfere with or inhibit the desired behavior. Generally, some form of cognitive modification and/or exposure-based or other emotional processing procedures are required.

A focus on motivation is the hallmark of psychodynamic and psychoanalytic treatments. It is also, however, the hallmark of behavioral and cognitive–behavioral approaches (cf. Kazdin, 1993; Kohlenberg & Tsai, 1991). Both object-relations therapies (Kernberg, Selzer, Koenigsberg, Carr, & Appelbaum, 1989) and cognitive therapies (Beck, Rush, Shaw, & Emery, 1979; Ellis, 1987) focus on changing cognitive structures, schemas, underlying assumptions, and beliefs. Experiential and exposure-based treatments focus on reducing emotions that interfere with effective behavior. There are a number of substance abuse treatments that target motivation. Contingency management programs are best exemplified by the voucher system of Higgins (Higgins et al., 1993) and the community reinforcement approach (Azrin, Sisson, Meyers, & Godley, 1982; Higgins, 1997). In addition, there are aversive conditioning programs (McLellan & Childress, 1985), the extinction effect of naltrexone treatment (Brahen, Henderson, Capone, & Kordal, 1984; O'Malley, Jaffe, Rode, & Rounsaville, 1996), cognitive-restructuring treatments (Beck et al., 1979), and cue exposure

(Childress, 1991; Childress, Ehrman, McLellan, & O'Brien, 1988; Childress, McLellan, & O'Brien, 1988; McLellan, Childress, O'Brien, & Ehrman, 1986), to name just a few.

Generalization of Gains

Learning to be effective in a therapist's office or an inpatient or residential setting is useless if the new behaviors do not generalize to the patient's everyday life settings. Generalization of behavior learned in one context to another context cannot be assumed. The third task of therapy, therefore, is to actively ensure generalization of new behaviors to the natural environment. Activities can include homework practice assignments, in vivo interventions, coaching in the natural environment by means of telephone (or E-mail), and systems interventions either in the natural environment or by bringing the environment (e.g., the family) into the therapy office. There are any number of drug abuse treatments that focus on this aspect of treatment. Examples are active outreach to patients in their own environment (Henggeler & Borduin, 1990), drug hotlines, therapeutic communities, and milieu treatments.

Structuring the Environment

Maintenance of therapeutic gains is highly related to how supportive the environment is of new response patterns achieved in therapy. As with generalization of new behaviors, an environment that reinforces clinical progress rather than dysfunctional, disordered behavior cannot be assumed. The fourth function of treatment, therefore, is to ensure that the patient's natural environment is maximally supportive of progress achieved in treatment. Case management is the principal environmental intervention in most treatment programs. Drug abuse treatments have, as well, traditionally emphasized a number of other approaches to this function of treatment. The inclusion of family and friends in treatment programs (Santisteban et al., 1996), the community reinforcement program developed by Azrin (Azrin et al., 1996; Azrin, Donohue, Besalel, Kogan, & Acierno, 1994; Azrin, McMahon et al., 1994), Al-Anon, and other similar programs that coordinate with 12-step programs, as well as other systemic interventions, have their effect by structuring the environment. Not as much attention has been paid to structuring the treatment environment itself except in therapeutic communities.

Enhancing Therapists' Capabilities and Motivation

An effective treatment is of little value if the therapist is unable or unmotivated to apply the treatment when it is required. Enhancing therapists' capabilities and motivation to treat effectively should be an essential part of any treatment. It has, however, been a lost area of treatment development and research. I have been concerned about this particular problem in the treatment of borderline personality disorder, where patient dropout and therapist demoralization are both exceptionally high. In developing a treatment for this disorder, I ultimately redefined my own definition of psychotherapy itself to include the treatment of the therapist as an integral part of the therapy rather than as an ancillary activity (Linehan, 1993). The problem of community therapists not applying therapies that have been shown efficacious in academic setting is, of course, not new (Goldfried & Wolfe, 1996). The problem, however, is unlikely to be resolved as long as academic researchers put blame for the failure in generalization on the character, motivation, or previous training of the therapists. Such a stance is a bit like blaming the victim for not improving.

Especially with severe and complex diagnoses (Level 1 disorders), when patients are often in excruciating pain that therapy cannot immediately reduce, I have noticed that patients often reinforce therapists for providing ineffective treatments and punish them for providing effective treatments. This may be because effective treatments require exposure to painful stimuli, whereas ineffective treatments allow avoidance of these cues. In many service settings, there is precious little reinforcement for therapists adhering to efficacious treatments, and there is much that interferes with such treatment, especially the emotional stress of difficult patients. There is also often little support aimed at providing resources to therapists in need, so that they can stretch their limits when necessary. In short, we have paid very little scientific attention to the problem of dissemination, use of efficacious treatments, and reinforcement in the natural environment.

STAGES OF TREATMENT RESEARCH

On the way to effective treatments, development, validation, and dissemination each occur in somewhat ordered sequences, each having its own questions and its own range of appropriate methodologies. When there is a lack of clarity about where in this process one is and which questions can or ought to be asked (given the current information and development of a particular intervention), it is difficult to evaluate the appropriateness of any given research method. A research methodology is neither good nor bad on its own. A methodology is only good or bad for particular questions; if you're confused about the questions, you're necessarily going to be confused about the methodology (Koerner & Linehan, 1997).

The development, evaluation, and dissemination of new mental health treatments go through at least three stages (National Institute on Drug Abuse; NIDA, 1994), as outlined in Exhibit 2. The goal of Stage 1 is the development and pilot evaluation of new treatments. Research at this stage occurs within the context of discovery in scientific research. The main question addressed is the feasibility of the new treatment working for the intended problems, and the validity needed at this point is face validity. The treatment must appear to work, and evidence must be obtained showing the promise of the new treatment before proceeding to the next stage. Stage 2 is the stage of treatment validation and encompasses the context of verification in science. The main question is efficacy of the treatment, and one is concerned not only with whether the treatment works but also with whether it is working for the reasons one thinks. Internal validity is of primary importance at this stage. Satisfactory evidence for treatment efficacy should be the criterion for going to the next stage of treatment research. In the final stage, research focuses on dissemination of the treatment. Stage 3 addresses the clinical use of the treatment when applied in service (rather than research) settings. Taking the liberty to add a new context of research (to the contexts of discovery and verification commonly alluded to), Stage 3 can also be thought of addressing issues in the context of application. That is, questions have to do with application of treatments in contexts where they are needed. The primary question asks whether the treatment is feasible; useful, external validity is required.

Stage 1: Treatment Development

New treatments are needed when either we have no effective treatment for a particular disorder, problem, or patient population or when the treatments that we do have are not sufficiently effective and efficient. In Stage 1, the aim may be to develop a wholly new treatment from the ground up, to modify an already existing treatment to make it better, to take a treatment already established in clinical practice and subject it to empirical analyses, or to take a treatment that is effective for one problem area and modify it for use with another disorder or population. This stage corresponds to the development of new medications in biological research. However, as noted by Barlow (1994), whereas in biological treatments there is an enormous pharmaceutical industry supporting and profiting from the development of new drugs, there is no corresponding financial enterprise in the area of psychosocial interventions. Thus, as a research phase, the development of new treatments has historically not received very much attention, either theoretically or financially. This presents a serious problem in the field because without a steady influx of new and improved treatment

EXHIBIT 2
Stages of Treatment Development, Validation, and Dissemination

Stage 1: Development

Part A: Generation

Iterative, qualitative methodologies and content analyses:
   development of treatment manual(s)
Nonrandomized studies
   Case series
   Open trials, pre–post designs
   Comparisons with historical, treatment-as-usual, and standard, no-treatment
      controls

Part B: Standardization

Iterative, qualitative methodologies and content analyses:
   development of training plans
   Outcome, adherence, and competence measures
Correlational and between-groups designs
   Reliability of measures
   Validation of measures

Part C: Pilot tests of efficacy

Randomized pilot studies:
   comparisons to no-treatment, treatment-as-usual, standard controls
   Experimental $n = 1$ series

Stage 2: Validation

Part A: Efficacy

Randomized clinical trial comparing treatment with internal-validity controls:
   psychosocial "placebo" controls
Replication studies

Part B: Mechanisms

Component analyses—dismantling studies
Process-analyses studies
Analyses of response predictors

Part C: Utility

Comparisons with standard treatments
Comparisons with efficacious treatments: Horse race studies
Matching studies
   Level of disorder
   Status of mediating variables
   Participant characteristics
   Therapist characteristics

Table continues

EXHIBIT 2 *Continued*

Stage 3: Dissemination

Part A: Services Development

Iterative, qualitative methodologies and content analyses:
  adaptation to organizational structure
  Treatment manual, training plan, fidelity measures
  Development of services outcome measures
Nonrandomized program evaluation
  Open trials, pre–post designs
  Comparisons with historical, treatment-as-usual, standard treatment programs

Part B: Program Evaluation

Evaluation
  Fidelity to adapted treatment manuals
  Fidelity to efficacious treatments
  Accessibility and barriers to treatment
  Systemic problems of application
Consumer-satisfaction studies
Analyses of response predictors

Part C: Effectiveness

Experimental analyses of training plans for mental health professionals
Multicenter randomized trials, outcomes research
Analyses of cost-effectiveness
Analyses of cost benefit

procedures, it is impossible for the field as a whole to progress. The only way to get better than we are is to develop new treatments that, although perhaps built on old treatments, are, nonetheless, better than what we have now.

The methodologies relevant to Stage 1 are not the same methodologies as at later stages, so, when evaluating the rigor of Stage 1 research designs, it is not appropriate to apply methodological rules developed for other stages of research. At least three workshops have been sponsored by the National Institutes of Health in the last several years, bringing together researchers in treatment development and evaluation to discuss and hammer out strategies for developing new treatments for both mental disorders (National Institute of Mental Health; NIMH, 1991) and drug abuse (Moras, 1995; NIDA, 1996). In addition, several program announcements have been sent out by both institutes calling for proposals to develop, evaluate, and disseminate behavioral treatments (e.g., NIDA, 1994). My comments about Stage 1 are drawn heavily from these workshops and announcements. Development of new treatments can be broken down into three substages or parts: generation of new treatments, standardization, and pilot tests of efficacy.

Part A: Treatment Generation

The first task in developing a new treatment is the creation of the actual intervention and the writing of a treatment manual that comprehensively describes the specific intervention strategies used in the new treatment. Iterative, qualitative methodologies and content analyses are the primary methodologies at this first stage. Interestingly, although a substantial amount of work has been done developing very sophisticated qualitative research methods in other areas of research (e.g., Strauss, 1987; Strauss & Corbin, 1990), there has been very little application of these methods in treatment-development designs. There are four primary contexts of discovery for new treatments: (a) empirical research in relevant areas (e.g., epidemiology, basic behavioral, neurobiological, psychopathology research, longitudinal studies), (b) clinical practice, (c) personal experience of the investigator, and (d) information obtained in further stages of treatment research, which, in an iterative fashion, feeds new ideas and revisions of old ideas back into Stage 1. To the extent that these sources create a synergy, breakthroughs may emerge.

A central problem in the field at the moment is the paucity of communication venues between those researching new treatments and both basic scientists and applied practitioners. Although the NIMH and the NIDA have held workshops bringing together basic scientists and treatment researchers (1992; 1996), much more needs to be done. Ultimately, the principles of change used by the therapist in treatment are the same as those uncovered by the basic scientist. To the extent that these are thoroughly understood by those developing new treatments, we should be able to develop more effective interventions.

In addition to grounding in basic behavioral science, however, the treatment research also must be based on a fine-grained as well as a holistic understanding of the disorders, problems, and individuals in need of change. To date, we have not been able to develop effective methods of reciprocal interchange between scientist and practitioner. It is perhaps here, in the field of treatment development, that the model of scientist–practitioner is most essential. It takes both a scientist and a practitioner to develop a new treatment. It is interesting to note, however, how little attention is given to treatment-development methodology in standard texts on research design, clinical psychology, and psychiatry.

The appropriate studies in Part A are very small samples, well-documented case series, pre–post designs (open treatment trials in the parlance of pharmacotherapy), and nonrandomized comparisons with historical, treatment-as-usual, and waiting-list controls. In ongoing service settings, this is the place for organizing the best clinical data one can. As data emerge, the treatment can be revised and improved until the investigator is satisfied that the treatment is sufficiently promising to go on to the next step.

Part B: Treatment Standardization

Part A is followed by, evolves into, or may occur simultaneously with Part B. Part B is called for when you've established that you have a good, or at least promising, idea and now you want to standardize the good idea. Using the same iterative qualitative methodologies, the investigator develops and tests the plan for recruiting and training therapists and then constructs measures of adherence and competency to the treatment protocol. Essentially, you are standardizing not only your treatment but also your ability to measure fidelity to treatment. Outcomes measures also are put together here, and the reliability and validity of all measures and assessment procedures are established. Rigor at this stage of research is essential if outcomes from subsequent clinical evaluation studies are to be interpretable. The NIMH treatment study comparing interpersonal therapy, cognitive therapy, and pharmacotherapy for depression (Elkin et al., 1989) has provided both an impetus to research in this area and a lesson in the problems that can occur if this step is not taken seriously. In that study, exceptional care was taken in the development of measures of adherence to treatment. Yet when outcomes differed by site for one of the treatment modalities, these measures were not able to pick up the clinical differences in treatment delivery that clinicians listening to the tapes observed (Jacobson & Hollon, 1996). In Project MATCH (MATCH Research Group, 1996), the failure to find between-group differences in outcome when three very different treatments were compared has been interpreted as due to excessive hours of assessment swamping the effects due to treatment. This is the type of methodological error that should be ferreted out in Stage 1 of treatment research.

Part C: Efficacy Pilot Testing

The aim of Part C is to gather data sufficient to decide whether to proceed to Stage 2. There are diverse opinions on just what is needed at this step. To a certain extent, what is needed will depend on the state of existing treatment research in the area under consideration. In some cases, Part C may be skipped altogether if the investigator modifies an existing well-researched treatment or develops a relatively simple intervention, has the necessary measures already developed, and the Part A studies have been rigorously conducted and compelling when contrasted to other studies. If one developed a pretreatment intervention that reduced dropouts of crack addicts from treatment to 10% from a previous rate of 80% in the same clinic (and assuming tasks of Part B are completed), it might be reasonable to go directly to a Stage 2 clinical trial of the intervention. In most cases, however, small ($n = 20$ or so), randomized pilot trials of the new treatment are the next step and constitute Part C. The new treatment; the control condition; participant recruitment and screening procedures; the therapist-training plan; measures of fidelity, competence, and treatment outcome; data collection and recording forms, and so on are all piloted at this point. The idea here is to compare the new treatment with a theoretically specified control condition, with the goal of determining likely effect sizes of the new treatment. At a minimum, the treatment must be better than no treatment plus assessment alone. With very efficacious treatments, this pilot study may itself cross over to be a first Stage 2 study. A well-conducted, rigorous, small series of experimental single-participant designs would also be convincing here. Behavior analysts typically use single-participant designs, but otherwise, single-participant designs are rarely used.

Stage 2: Treatment Validation

The task of Stage 2 is to evaluate the efficacy of a new treatment and to develop some knowledge of the process whereby efficacious treatments work. Although it is not typical to do so, Stage 2 research, similar to Stage 1, can also be broken into parts testing efficacy, mechanisms of action, and utility.

Part A: Testing Efficacy

Once a new treatment is developed, the next task is to evaluate whether the treatment is efficacious. Ordinarily, this question is addressed by a randomized clinical trial. The central question at this point is what to compare the new treatment to. The answer depends on the state of research in the area targeted and the questions asked. If we are to progress scientifically, it is crucial that the comparison group be selected with great care. At a minimum, one wants to control for the eight factors listed by Campbell and Stanley (1963) as jeopardizing internal validity: history, maturation of participants, testing, instrumentation, statistical regression, selection, experimental mortality, and selection history and selection maturation. In addition, it is usual in current intervention trials to control for assessment bias, therapist expertise and experience, expectancy of improvement, and provision of a noncontingent warm and caring relationship. The design should be comparable to the placebo comparison in pharmacotherapy trials.

If the treatment is efficacious in the first trial, a replication study is the second step. Indeed, the importance of replication is so important that it would make sense to build it into the design at the beginning. As research is currently funded, it often takes years to get a treatment replication off the ground. If the new treatment is not more efficacious than the control condition, the investigative line should address reasons for the failure in efficacy and return in a recursive fashion to Stage 1.

Part A of Stage 2 is not the time to compare the new treatment with other standard treatments (i.e., "horse race" studies). The danger in these studies, from the point of view of treatment development, is that a new treatment with great, but as yet unrealized, promise may be prematurely discarded. For example, the principles underlying a new treatment may be such that over time and development, the new treatment will be vastly superior to anything yet developed or used. But in its infancy, the new treatment may not be sufficiently developed to produce better outcomes than an alternate treatment that, while better now, has no promise of improving.

Part B: Testing Mechanisms of Action

Once you know a treatment is efficacious, that is to say, it is helpful, you're still not ready for the horse race studies. Treatment development, which is to say, trying to get better than we currently are, is a very different endeavor than trying to find out if our new treatment is the best, or if it's better than everything else. Once it is known that a treatment has promise, then the next task is to improve it further, making it more efficient and efficacious. Tasks in Part B must be designed with this end in view and include component and process-analyses studies, dismantling studies, and studies designed to analyze response predictors. What is needed at this point is programmatic, theoretically driven research. The promise here is that if each promising treatment-development team focuses on ascertaining, building on, and improving the mechanisms of change in its own unique treatment approach, eventually the entire field will progress, and we will all find the same principles and truths of clinical change. It's as if treatment developers are each standing at a different place on a circle and in the middle of the circle are the efficacious, effective, efficient, and cost-beneficial treatments. If each team is working on making its own treatment better, modifying it as new data emerge (and revisiting Stage 1), all will get to the same middle. In the end, there will be a certain limited number of principles of change, and all of us will get there, sooner or later. Treatment-development methodology must be designed to get us there.

Part C: Testing Utility

The next step of treatment development, or Part C, can be thought of as the managed care stage of treatment validation. The question at this point is the usefulness of the new treatment. The basic question here is: Is this efficacious treatment better than something else? It's not a question of can I make it better? or why is it good? or how could I get it better? it's a question of, is it better than something else? Part C informs the practitioner of what treatment should be given by which mental health professional to which patient for what problem. It is an extremely relevant question from a services and consumer's point of view. In Part C, efficacious treatments are compared with standard treatments and/or to other efficacious treatments. The horse races make sense here. Also appropriate here are treatment-matching studies in which treatment conditions are matched on such variables as type, complexity, and severity of disorder; status of the hypothesized mediating variables; general participant characteristics; and therapist variables. A major point here is that these comparisons, or horse race studies should only be done with well-researched treatments that are already known to be efficacious in their own right.

Stage 3: Treatment Dissemination

Stage 3 in treatment development is the dissemination of efficacious treatment to the general public by means of practice settings. The task here is to take an efficacious treatment and do what is necessary to get that treatment working effectively in the real world. As noted by many (Barley, 1996; Newman & Tejeda, 1996), the transition from efficacy in the research setting to effectiveness in the services setting is fraught with difficulties that are often unrecognized by the academic researcher. Despite efforts on the part of the federal government to prioritize services research, there has been a tremendous failure in getting many of our efficacious treatments from Stage 2 through Stage 3. Many of our most important questions about treatment, especially those necessary for making treatment decisions in the individual case, require Stage 3 research. Once again, three parts can be considered: services development, program evaluation, and testing effectiveness.

Part A: Services Development

A treatment that is efficacious in a research setting may or may not translate easily to a service setting. Ordinarily, modifications must be made in the treatment itself (e.g., dropping some parts or integrating the protocol into other standard treatments), the method of delivery (e.g., shortening and lengthening, changing modes), the therapist-training program, the attention to supervision and monitoring of fidelity to treatment, the outcomes assessment, and/or the selection criteria for therapists. The task here is not unlike Stage 1, Part A, tasks when a treatment is adapted for a different patient population or a different disorder. What must be developed here can be thought of as the trappings of the treatment. Appropriate intake procedures, training and supervision programs for therapists, support services and incentives to maintain staff adherence to treatment and competency, treatment protocols, guidelines and reporting formats, reimbursement schedules, outcome-assessment methods, and consumer-satisfaction measures—all must be developed. Each of these has to be feasible in the services setting. The eight hours of assessment in some clinical research studies and the intensive monitoring and coding of therapy tapes typical of clinical trials are not going to be reasonable in the average service setting.

Similar to Stage 1, the appropriate methodologies here are iterative, qualitative methodologies and small-sample, single-group, nonrandomized program evaluation designs such as open-trial, pre–post designs. Training may, at first, be as simple as workshops, providing consultation to a service unit, or forming self-study groups. Outcome data may consist of evaluations that are routinely collected in the service setting, such as incident reports, number of sessions attended, other services obtained (including inpatient days), and consumer evaluations.

Part B: Program Evaluation

Once a treatment appears to be reasonably adapted for a service setting, the next step is formal program evaluation. The focus here is on accessibility and barriers to treatment, safety of the treatment (do people get worse?), fidelity of the delivered treatment to the treatment manual, and consumer satisfaction. In particular, the investigator needs to ferret out any system problems of application, particularly problems associated with recruitment, selection, education, and training of therapists; maintenance of treatment fidelity and competence over time and in various patient populations; and recruitment, triage, levels of care needed, and retention of appropriate patients. Although consumer satisfaction may or may not be related to actual clinical progress and outcomes, an efficacious treatment is not particularly useful if everyone hates the treatment or switches to another health care provider. It is extremely important, however, that it remain clear that no matter how well designed, a pre–post treatment evaluation study simply cannot answer the all important question of whether a particular treatment is actually effective. It only can address the question of whether it's feasible and whether it's safe. The major feasibility questions that can be answered have to do with the ability of the setting to actually deliver the treatment and the willingness and/or capability of patients to participate in the treatment. Safety has to do with whether people get worse in the treatment. These are not minor questions, but they are different from the question of effectiveness. If the treatment appears to be effective (i.e., participants are better at the end of it), one can't know what caused the improvement, and one certainly doesn't know if it was due to the treatment, unless program evaluation has been done properly.

Part C: Testing Effectiveness

Effectiveness of treatments, including cost-effectiveness and cost benefits, in service settings is the key question in Part C. The need for well-done studies at this stage cannot be overstated. Large, multicenter, randomized trials or well-designed and controlled nonrandomized comparison studies are appropriate here. Doing studies well at this point absolutely depends on research demonstrating that therapists in the relevant context can indeed be trained both to treatment adherence and to treatment competence. It is not uncommon in discussions of treatment effectiveness to routinely confound the training and expertise and competence of the therapists with the efficacy of the treatment. When efficacious treatments are provided by untrained professionals and nonefficacious treatments are provided by highly trained professionals, there is no way to evaluate effectiveness. Experience and training in doing some type of therapy are not necessarily the equivalent of training and competence in a specific treatment. In psychosocial treatments, individuals trained in one type of treatment occasionally attempt complex new treatments and procedures with only minimal training, sometimes as little as reading a treatment description or going to a 1- or 2-day workshop. I recently asked a prominent surgeon who specialized in facial reconstruction if he could learn to do heart surgery by going to a 1- or 2-day workshop, or even by going to visit someone's clinic for a few weeks of supervision. He replied (and remember he already was a trained surgeon) that he would have to do an entire several-year residency to learn it! Contrast this with the mental health professional trained in behavior therapy switching to psychodynamic therapy (or vice versa) after only a workshop or two. Even in major research studies, it is not uncommon to have research therapists with only minimal training and supervision of two or three training cases. Without treatment fidelity and competence, treatment studies at this level are somewhat pointless.

CONCLUSIONS

A number of conclusions about the development, evaluation, and dissemination of mental health treatments emerge from what I have said so far:

1. We must put a higher priority on improving mental health treatments than on proving the relative value of current treatments. Two patterns of psychosocial treatment development predominate in the mental health field. In the first, clinician investigators put a lot of effort and rigorous thought into the generation of new treatments (Stage 1, Part A) and

treatment manual writing, often in the form of clinical books (Stage 1, Part B), and, soon after, go to dissemination in the community (Stage 3, Parts A and B); without first conducting the clinical trials needed to justify the effectiveness and utility of the treatments (Stage 2, Parts A–C; Stage 3, Part C). In the second, enormous resources are used to conduct Stage 2 randomized clinical trials comparing the relative effectiveness of complex psychosocial interventions with each other or to biologic interventions (i.e., Part C horse race studies), and little attention is given either to circling back and using the results to further improve the treatments under study (Stage 1) or to develop a rigorous evaluation of training programs and feasibility of implementing those treatments in the community (Stage 3). Stage 2 horse race designs tell us little about how to improve the treatments investigated. For better or worse, most effective psychosocial interventions are exceedingly complex. When one treatment regime is found to be more useful than another, we have no idea of why that occurs or of what is the active factor in the superior treatment. Such designs are extremely inefficient for developing better treatments. Premature treatment comparisons also can impede progress. A treatment with greater eventual promise, for example, may be thrown out because at an early stage of development it is less effective than a competitor treatment. What is missing from our current research paradigms are the basic studies on specific change procedures from which more effective treatments can be built. Analogue studies with clinical populations are needed. Although there were compelling reasons for the fall from favor of analogue treatment research using college students and other less than optimal populations, we have perhaps thrown the baby out with the bathwater. Internal validity has been oversacrificed on the altar of external validity.

2. We must link basic behavioral science to the clinical situation when developing new mental health treatments. Development of new treatments needs to be clearly linked to basic research in the behavioral sciences. We need to find a way to get those who are primarily treatment researchers together with basic behavioral researchers. It is difficult to imagine what could be more relevant to developing more effective psychotherapies than basic research on social influence (social psychology), the role of experience on change (learning), individual differences and the organization of behavior (personality), the reciprocal influence of physiology and behavior

(neuropsychology), perception, cognition, emotions, and so on. The growing rift between clinical psychology and other fields of psychology is limiting the ability of psychologists to take the science of behavior and apply it to treatment problems. The parochial practice of trying to develop new treatments simply from research carried out on current treatments will not get us very far. The hit and miss strategy of empirically testing any idea, independent of sound scientific theory, will not get us where we need to go. We need to get our best and our brightest young clinical researchers, put them in the laboratories of our best basic behavioral researchers, and support them in translating behavioral and biological empirical findings into mechanisms of change that can be applied eventually in the clinical context.

3. We must break down divisions between biological and behavioral sciences if we are to find the best treatments for mental health disorders. Bias, politics, and guild interests not only take too much energy away from the pursuit of the knowledge that will allow us to build effective treatments but also interfere with our chances of developing effective treatments. The mental health field seems consistently caught up in rhetorical battles about what are essentially empirical questions. Unfortunately, the rhetoric also carries power, and advances are too often cut off for political and/or guild reasons. Battles about which variables are most important in the influence and change of mental disorder have no place outside of a rigorously empirical–theoretical context. The battles between the biological and behavioral sciences are particularly unfortunate given that the two are inextricably linked in practice. There is no doubt that all human behaviors are biological events. Similarly, all human biological processes are but behaviors of the organism taking place in a psychological and environmental context. Process research linking clinical change through behavioral–psychological treatments to corresponding biological changes is essential if we are to understand the final common pathways of clinical change. Just as we have learned much by observing behavioral–psychological change resulting from biologic interventions, we can also learn by observing biologic changes resulting from behavioral–psychological interventions.

4. We must intensively study both who and how we should train to implement new treatments (training research) as well as factors that impede, punish, encourage, and reinforce application of new treatments (systems and human factors re-

search), if we are to advance in the dissemination of efficacious treatments. The failure to transfer effective new treatments from the clinical research sites to the clinical practice sites has been a topic of much debate and very strong opinions. A lot of heat and not much light have been generated. Insufficient research has been done on how to train individuals in the delivery of effective treatments. We must find a way to get those who are primarily researchers together with those in service settings. There is perhaps no better way to do this than for researchers themselves to be in charge of dissemination of their own research. I am beginning to believe that we ought to think of Stage 3 dissemination of research as akin to a service obligation if one is funded for treatment development and evaluation research. If a treatment research grant is awarded and the new treatment is efficacious, then there should be some obligation or reward for the investigator to attend to dissemination. This practice is already starting in Great Britain, where in the initial grant proposals submitted to the Medical Research Council to develop or evaluate treatments, one must discuss how results of the research will be disseminated other than by publishing in academic journals.

5. Comparing apples to oranges will not get us very far. Both comprehensiveness of treatment and the level of individual mental disorder targeted by treatment are relevant in comparing treatment effectiveness and utility. Mental health treatments must be evaluated according to how well they (a) enhance patient capabilities, (b) strengthen motivation for clinical progress, (c) enhance generalization of gains to the natural environment, (d) structure the environment to support clinical progress, and (e) enhance therapist capabilities and motivation to implement the treatment. This is particularly true for severe and persistent mental disorders where more comprehensive treatments are needed. The very same mental disorder in individuals at different levels of overall disorder may require very different treatments. Although level of disorder is usually controlled for in randomized clinical trials, such is often not the case in reviews and public discourse about which treatments are effective for what. Decisions about what treatment is needed by whom must take the level of individual disorder into account when comparing effectiveness and utility of treatments.

6. We must develop a definition of optimal treatment-development stages and invest in the development of better

research methodologies. We must find ways to foster treatment research from start to finish. Together, researchers, practitioners, and policymakers need to hammer out some consensus on stages of treatment research and at least minimum expected methodologies. Because treatment research is so difficult without federal funding, the National Institutes of Health also must be included at every step of the way. It is critical that we publish widely any research criteria that are set, so that they are not secret. When they are secret, all but "insiders" are excluded from research. We need good ideas too badly to allow this. Finally, we need to influence reviewers of journals, of grants, of everything, to adopt some standards of treatment-development methodology. What I have offered may not be what is eventually agreed on, but it is a step.

REFERENCES

American Psychiatric Association. (1994). *Diagnostic and statistical manual of mental disorders* (4th ed.). Washington, DC: Author.

Azrin, N. H., Acierno, R., Kogan, E. S., Donohue, B., Besalel, V. A., & McMahon, P. T. (1996). Follow-up results of supportive versus behavioral therapy for illicit drug use. *Behavior Research and Therapy, 34,* 41–46.

Azrin, N. H., Donohue, B., Besalel, V. A., Kogan, E. S., & Acierno, R. (1994). Youth drug abuse treatment: A controlled outcome study. *Journal of Child and Adolescent Drug Abuse, 3,* 3–16.

Azrin, N. H., McMahon, P. T., Donohue, B., Besalel, V. A., Lapinski, K., Kogan, E. S., Acierno, R., & Galloway, E. (1994). Behavior therapy for drug abuse: A controlled treatment–outcome study. *Behavior Research and Therapy, 32,* 857–866.

Azrin, N. H., Sisson, R. W., Meyers, R., & Godley, M. (1982). Alcoholism treatment by disulfiram and community reinforcement therapy. *Journal of Behavioral Therapy and Experimental Psychiatry, 13,* 105–112.

Barley, W. D. (1996). Health care policy, psychotherapy research, and the future of psychotherapy. *American Psychologist, 51,* 1050–1058.

Barlow, D. H. (1994). Psychological interventions in the era of managed competition. *Clinical Psychology: Science and Practice, 1,* 109–122.

Beck, A. T., Rush, A. J., Shaw, B. F., & Emery, G. (1979). *Cognitive therapy of depression.* New York: Guilford Press.

Beutler, L. E., & Clarkin, J. F. (1990). *Systematic treatment selection: Toward targeted therapeutic interventions.* New York: Brunner/Mazel.

Botvin, G. J., Dusenbury, L., Baker, E., & James-Ortiz, S. (1989). A skills training approach to smoking prevention among Hispanic youth. *Journal of Behavioral Medicine, 104*, 573–582.

Brahen, L. S., Henderson, R. K., Capone, T., & Kordal, N. (1984). Naltrexone treatment in a jail work-release program. *Journal of Clinical Psychiatry, 45*, 39–41.

Campbell, D. T., & Stanley, J. C. (1963). *Experimental and quasi-experimental designs for research.* Boston: Houghton Mifflin.

Chambless, D. L., Sanderson, W. C., Shoham, V., Johnson, S. B., Pope, K. S., Crits-Christoph, P., Baker, M., Johnson, B., Woody, S. R., Sue, S., Beutler, L. E., Williams, D. A., & McCurry, S. (1996). An update on empirically validated therapies. *The Clinical Psychologist, 49*, 5–18.

Childress, A. R. (1991). Integrating cue exposure techniques with standard psychosocial treatments for cocaine dependence. In *Research and treatment: Alliance for the 21st century.* Symposium conducted at the meeting of the National Institute on Drug Abuse, Washington, DC.

Childress, A. R., Ehrman, R., McLellan, A. T., & O'Brien, C. P. (1988). Conditioned craving and arousal in cocaine addiction: A preliminary report. In L. S. Harris (Ed.) *Problems of drug dependence, 1987:* Proceedings of the 49th annual scientific meeting, the committee on Problems of Drug Dependence (NIDA Research Monograph 81, pp. 74–80). Rockville, MD: National Institute on Drug Abuse.

Childress, A. R., McLellan, A. T., & O'Brien, C. P. (1988). Classically conditioned responses in cocaine and opioid dependence: A role in relapse? In B. A. Ray (Ed.), *Learning factors in substance abuse* (NIDA Research Monograph 84, pp. 25–43). Rockville, MD: National Institute on Drug Abuse.

Elkin, I., Shea, M. T., Watkins, J. T., Imber, S. D., Sotsky, S. M., Collins, F. L., Glass, D. R., Pilkonis, P. A., Leber, W. R., Doherty, J. P., Fiester, S. J., & Parloff, M. B. (1989). NIMH Treatment of Depression Collaborative Research Program: I. General effectiveness of treatments. *Archives of General Psychiatry, 46*, 971–982.

Ellis, A. (1987). *Handbook of rational–emotive therapy.* New York: Springer.

Foa, E. B., Hearst-Ikeda, D. E., & Perry, K. (1995). Evaluation of a brief cognitive–behavioral program for the prevention of chronic PTSD in recent assault victims. *Journal of Consulting and Clinical Psychology, 63*, 948–955.

Foa, E. B., Jaycox, L. H., Meadows, E. A., Hembree, E., & Dancu, C. (November, 1996). Preliminary efficacy of prolonged exposure (PE) vs. PE and cognitive restructuring for PTSD in female assault victims. In P. A. Resick (Chair), *Treating sexual assault/sexual abuse pathology: Recent findings.* Symposium conducted at the meeting of the Association for the Advancement of Behavior Therapy, New York.

Garfield, S. L. (1994). Research on client variables in psychotherapy. In A. E. Bergin & S. L. Garfield (Eds.), *Handbook of psychotherapy and behavior change* (pp. 190–228). New York: Wiley.

Goldfried, M. R., & Wolfe, B. E. (1996). Psychotherapy practice and research: Repairing a strained alliance. *American Psychologist, 51*, 1007–1016.

Greenberg, L. S., Rice, L. N., & Elliott, R. (1993). *Facilitating emotional change: The moment-by-moment process*. New York: Guilford Press.

Henggeler, S. W., & Borduin, C. M. (1990). *Family therapy and beyond: A multisystemic approach to treating the behavior problems of children and adolescents*. Pacific Grove, CA: Brooks/Cole.

Herman, J. L. (1992). *Trauma and recovery: The aftermath of violence—From domestic abuse to political terror*. New York: Basic Books.

Higgins, S. T. (1997). Potential contributions of the community reinforcement approach and contingency management to broadening the base of substance abuse treatment. In J. A. Tucker, D. A. Donovan, & G. A. Marlatt (Eds.), *Changing addictive behavior: Moving beyond therapy assisted change*. New York: Guilford Press.

Higgins, S. T., Budney, A. J., Bickel, W. K., Hughes, J. R., Foeg, F., & Badger, G. (1993). Achieving cocaine abstinence with a behavioral approach. *American Journal of Psychiatry, 150*, 763–869.

Jacobson, N. S., & Hollon, S. D. (1996). Cognitive–behavior therapy versus pharmacotherapy: Now that the jury's returned its verdict, it's time to present the rest of the evidence. *Journal of Consulting and Clinical Psychology, 64*, 74–80.

Kazdin, A. E. (1993). *Behavior modification in applied settings* (5th ed.). Pacific Grove, CA: Brooks/Cole.

Kernberg, O. F., Selzer, M. A., Koenigsberg, H. W., Carr, A. C., & Appelbaum, A. H. (1989). *Psychodynamic psychotherapy of borderline patients*. New York: Basic Books.

Koerner, K., & Linehan, M. M. (1997). Case formulation in dialectical behavior therapy. In T. Eells (Ed.), *Handbook of psychotherapy case formulation* (pp. 340–367). New York: Guilford Press.

Kohlenberg, R. J., & Tsai, M. (1991). *Functional analytic psychotherapy: Creating intense and curative therapeutic relationships*. New York: Plenum.

Linehan, M. M. (1993). *Cognitive behavioral therapy of borderline personality disorder*. New York: Guilford Press.

Linehan, M. M. (1997). Theory and treatment development and evaluation: Reflections on Benjamin's "Models of Treatment." *Journal of Personality Disorder, 11*, 325–335.

MATCH Research Group. (1996, June). *Project MATCH: Treatment main effects and matching results*. In Ronald M. Kadden (Chair), Plenary session at scientific meeting of the Research Society on Alcoholism, Washington, DC.

McLellan, A. T., & Childress, A. R. (1985). Aversive therapies for substance abuse: Do they work? *Journal of Substance Abuse Treatment, 2*, 187–191.

McLellan, A. T., Childress, A. R., O'Brien, C. P., & Ehrman, R. (1986). Extinguishing conditioned responses during treatment for opiate dependence: Turning laboratory findings into clinical procedures. *Journal of Substance Abuse Treatment, 3*, 33–40.

Miller, W. R., & Rollnick, S. (1991). *Motivational interviewing: Preparing people to change addictive behavior*. New York: Guilford Press.

Moras, K. (January, 1995). Minutes of the National Institute on Drug Abuse Behavioral therapy development program workshop, Rockville, MD.

National Institute on Drug Abuse. (1994). *Behavioral Therapies Development Program* (Program Announcement No. PA-94-078).

Newman, F. L., & Tejeda, M. J. (1996). The need for research that is designed to support decisions in the delivery of mental health services. *American Psychologist, 51,* 1040–1049.

National Institute of Mental Health. (1991). *Proceedings of National Institute of Mental Health Psychotherapy and Rehabilitation Research Consortium.* Fairfax, VA: C.A.S.E.T. Associates.

National Institute of Mental Health. (1992). *National Institute of Mental Health treatment development workshop.* Washington, DC.

National Institute on Drug Abuse. (1996, May). *Proceedings of the National Institute on Drug Abuse Behavioral Therapy Development and Psychological Science Meeting,* Bethesda, MD.

National Institute on Drug Abuse. (1996, October). *Proceedings of the NIDA Stage I follow-up meeting,* Bethesda, MD.

O'Malley, S. S., Jaffe, A. J., Rode, S., & Rounsaville, B. J. (1996). Experience of a "slip" among alcoholics treated with naltrexone or placebo. *American Journal of Psychiatry, 153,* 281–283.

Santisteban, D. A., Szapocznik, J., Perez-Vidal, A., Kurtines, W. M., Murray, E. J., & LaPerriere, A. (1996). Efficacy of intervention for engaging youth and families into treatment and some variables that may contribute to differential effectiveness. *Journal of Family Psychology, 10,* 35–44.

Strauss, A. L. (1987). *Qualitative analysis for social scientists.* New York: Cambridge University Press.

Strauss, A. L., & Corbin, J. (1990). *Basics of qualitative research: Grounded theory procedures and techniques.* Newbury Park, CA: Sage.

Wallace, J. (1966). An abilities conception of personality: Some implications for personality measurement. *American Psychologist, 21,* 132–138.

16

THERAPEUTIC COMMUNITIES: RESEARCH AND APPLICATIONS

GEORGE DE LEON

Therapeutic communities have been treating substance abusers for three decades. Originating as an alternative to conventional medical and psychiatric approaches, the therapeutic community has established itself as a major psychosocial treatment modality for thousands of chemically involved individuals (Tims, De Leon, & Jainchill, 1994). The maturation of the therapeutic community as a sophisticated human services modality is evident in the broad range of programs that subscribe to the basic therapeutic community perspective and approach, serving an estimated 80,000 admissions yearly. These comprise a wide diversity of clients, who use an expanded cafeteria of drugs and present complex social psychological problems in addition to their chemical abuse.

The therapeutic community's basic social learning model has been amplified with a variety of additional services: family, educational, vocational, medical, and mental health. Staffing compositions have been altered to include increasing proportions of traditional mental health, medical, and

This chapter is based on an invited address presented at the 104th Annual Convention of the American Psychological Association, August 1996, Toronto, Ontario, Canada.

educational professionals to serve along with recovered paraprofessionals (e.g., Carroll & Sobel, 1986; De Leon, 1993c, 1997; Winick, 1991).

Correctional institutions, medical and mental hospitals, and community residence and shelter settings, overwhelmed with alcohol and illicit drug abuse problems, have implemented therapeutic community programs within their institutional boundaries (Galanter, Franco, Kim, Jamner-Metzger, & De Leon, 1993; Wexler & Williams, 1986). Therapeutic community agencies have incorporated basic elements of its drug-free philosophy and view of "right living" into education and prevention programs for schools and communities.

Therapeutic community research also has made significant strides in the years since 1976, when the National Institute on Drug Abuse (NIDA) supported the first Therapeutic Communities of America planning conference, which included a panel of just six researchers engaged in therapeutic community studies (De Leon & Beschner, 1977). Although not quantitatively analyzed, the rise in research is evident in several indicators: the number of published studies in American journals that have been collated in bibliographies (e.g., De Leon & Ziegenfuss, 1986) and reviews of therapeutic community research (e.g., De Leon, 1985); the number of federally funded therapeutic community grants and contracts; and the number of different therapeutic community agencies that are grant recipients. Perhaps the most convincing indicator of the developing status of therapeutic community research is a first-ever NIDA Technical Review for Therapeutic Community Research, which convened in mid May 1991 and resulted in NIDA Research Monograph 144 (Tims et al., 1994).

The present chapter provides an overview of the research on the therapeutic community approach to the treatment of chemical dependency and related problems. The initial section briefly outlines the therapeutic community approach, the essential elements of the method, and the components of a generic therapeutic community model. The second section summarizes key findings and conclusions from the past research–evaluation literature on traditional therapeutic communities. The third section provides a selective overview of the current applications of the therapeutic community model and approach for a diversity of clients and settings. The fourth section summarizes key findings and conclusions from recent and ongoing evaluation studies of modified therapeutic communities along with new research initiatives in treatment process. The final section reviews some implications for treatment planning and policy.

THE THERAPEUTIC COMMUNITY MODALITY

The therapeutic community is a drug-free modality that uses a social psychological, self-help approach to the treatment of drug abuse. Therapeutic community programs are most often community-based residences in urban and nonurban locales. However, therapeutic community programs have been implemented in a variety of other settings, including nonresidential sites (e.g., hospitals, jails, schools, halfway houses, day treatment clinics, and ambulatory clinics). Therapeutic communities typically offer a wide variety of services, including social, psychological, educational, medical, legal, and social advocacy. However, these components and services are coordinated in accordance with the therapeutic community's basic self-help model.[1]

The Traditional Residential Therapeutic Community

Much of research on the therapeutic community approach and its effectiveness has been based on the long-term residential model also termed the *traditional* therapeutic community. Traditional therapeutic communities are often similar in planned duration of stay (15 to 24 months), structure, staffing pattern, perspective, and rehabilitative regime but frequently differ in size (30 to 600 beds) and client demography. Staff are typically composed of therapeutic-community-trained clinicians and other human service professionals. Primary clinical staff are usually former substance abusers who themselves were rehabilitated in therapeutic community programs (De Leon & Rosenthal, 1989). Other staff consist of professionals providing medical, mental health, vocational, educational, family counseling, fiscal, administrative, and legal services.

Therapeutic communities accommodate the broad spectrum of drug abusers. Although they originally attracted narcotic addicts, a majority of their contemporary client populations are nonopioid abusers. Thus, this modality has responded appropriately to the changing trend in drug use patterns, treating clients with drug and psychological problems of varying severity, different lifestyles, and various social, economic, and ethnic–cultural backgrounds.

The therapeutic community views drug abuse as a deviant behavior, reflecting impeded personality development or chronic deficits in social, educational, and economic skills. Its antecedents lie in socioeconomic disadvantage, in poor family effectiveness, and in psychological factors (De Leon & Rosenthal, 1989). Thus, the principal aim of the therapeutic community is a global change in lifestyle: abstinence from illicit substances, elimination of antisocial activity, development of employability, and prosocial attitudes and values. The rehabilitative approach requires multidi-

[1]Therapeutic communities for addictions appeared a decade later than therapeutic communities in psychiatric hospitals, pioneered by Jones (1953) and others in the United Kingdom (see Kennard, 1983). Although the name *therapeutic community* evolved in these hospital settings, there is no clear evidence of direct influences of the Jones therapeutic community on the origins and development of addiction therapeutic communities.

mensional influence and training, which for most can occur only in a 24-hour residential setting.

Essential Elements of the Method and Model

The current diversity of programs within the therapeutic community modality has underscored the need to define, or at least characterize, a generic therapeutic community approach and model. In this regard, research and clinical practice have identified some essential elements of the theory, method, and model (see, e.g., De Leon, 1995b; De Leon, in press; De Leon & Rosenthal, 1989; De Leon & Ziegenfuss, 1986; Kooyman, 1993; Tims et al., 1994).

The therapeutic community can be distinguished from other major drug treatment modalities in two fundamental ways. First, it offers a systematic treatment approach that is guided by an explicit perspective on the drug use disorder, the person, recovery, and right living. Second, the primary therapist and teacher is the community itself, which consists of the social environment, peers, and staff, who, as role models of successful personal change, serve as guides in the recovery process. Thus, the community serves as both the context in which individual change occurs and the method for facilitating change.[2]

Perspective

Although expressed in a social psychological idiom, this perspective, evolved directly from the experience of recovering participants in therapeutic communities, has been organized in terms of four interrelated views: of the substance disorder, the person, recovery, and right living (see, e.g., De Leon, 1995b). Substance abuse is seen as a disorder of the whole person. For the therapeutic community, the fundamental problem is the person's behaviors, attitudes, and values—not the drug. Recovery is a self-help process of incremental learning toward a stable change in behavior, attitudes, and values of right living, which are associated with maintaining abstinence.

Elements of Community as Method

The quintessential element of the therapeutic community approach may be termed *community as method*. What distinguishes the therapeutic community from other treatment approaches (and other communities) is the purposive use of the peer community to facilitate social and psychological change in individuals (De Leon, 1995b). Thus, in a therapeutic commu-

---

[2]Comparative studies of inpatient and outpatient alcohol and cocaine treatment indicate no differences in outcomes (e.g., Alterman, O'Brien, & Droba, 1993). However, these do not refer to therapeutic-community-oriented residential treatment programs.

nity, all activities are designed to produce therapeutic and educational change in individual participants, and all participants are mediators of these therapeutic and educational changes.

The therapeutic community perspective on the disorder, the person, recovery, and right living and its distinctive approach—the use of community as method—provide the conceptual basis for defining a generic therapeutic community program model in terms of its basic components. They typically consist of a peer-managed work structure, a daily regime of therapeutic and educational groups, community meetings and seminars, and a stage and phase program format with peers and staff serving as role models and guides in the process. These components are adapted in different ways depending on the setting and the populations served (see De Leon, 1995b).

The Treatment Process

The process of change in the therapeutic community reflects its perspective and approach (see De Leon, 1995b). A disorder of the whole person means that change is multidimensional. Thus, change must be viewed along several dimensions of behavior, perceptions, and experiences. The main approach for facilitating change is the use of the community as method, which uses of all activities of community, life, and program components, as multiple interventions. Recovery unfolds as developmental learning that can be described in terms of stages of change.

THERAPEUTIC COMMUNITY RESEARCH

A considerable research literature on the therapeutic community has evolved since its inception over 30 years ago. The majority of the studies have focused on descriptions of the social and psychological profiles of therapeutic community admissions and evaluations of treatment effectiveness through assessment of posttreatment outcomes. A smaller number of studies have addressed treatment-retention and treatment-process issues. This section briefly and selectively summarizes key findings and conclusions in each of these research areas, drawn from a variety of reviews in the literature (e.g., Anglin & Hser, 1991; De Leon, 1984, 1985; Gerstein & Harwood, 1990; Hubbard et al., 1989; Simpson, 1997; Simpson & Sells, 1982; Tims et al., 1994; Tims & Ludford, 1984).

Social Profiles

Figures 1 to 3 display the sociodemographic characteristics of admissions to therapeutic communities. Clients in programs have been primarily

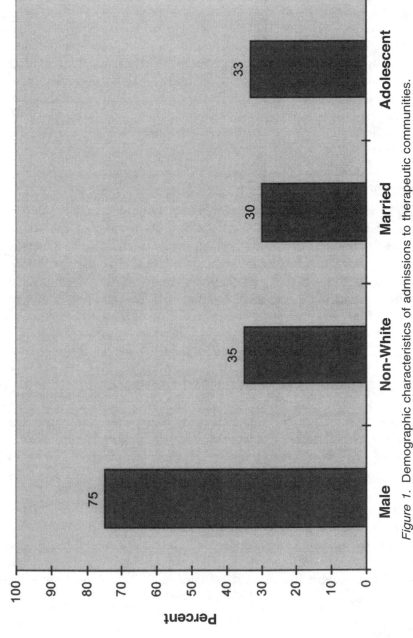

Figure 1. Demographic characteristics of admissions to therapeutic communities.
Note: Data used to construct this graph were compiled from various sources. See De Leon, G. (1994). Therapeutic communities. In M. Galanter & H. D. Kleber (Eds.), *The American psychiatric press textbook of substance abuse*, pp. 391–414. Chicago, IL: American Psychiatric Press.

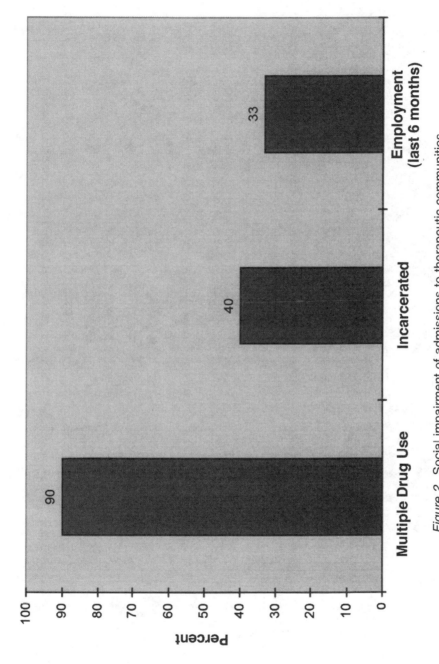

Figure 2. Social impairment of admissions to therapeutic communities.
Note: Data used to construct this graph were compiled from various sources. See De Leon, G. (1994). Therapeutic communities. In M. Galanter & H. D. Kleber (Eds.), *The American psychiatric press textbook of substance abuse*, pp. 391–414. Chicago, IL: American Psychiatric Press.

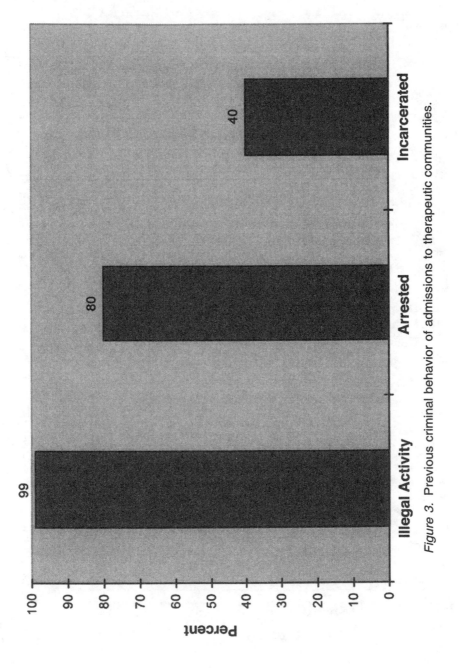

Figure 3. Previous criminal behavior of admissions to therapeutic communities.

male (70%–75%), but female admissions have increased in recent years. Most community-based therapeutic communities have an open admissions policy in respect to gender, race–ethnicity and age, although the demographic proportions differ by geographic regions and in certain programs. In general, Hispanics, Native Americans, and clients under 21 years of age represent smaller proportions of admissions (see Figure 1).

The majority of entries have considerable histories of multiple drug use, including marijuana, opiates, alcohol, and prescription medications, although in recent years, a majority report cocaine or crack as their primary drug of abuse. Most have poor work histories and have engaged in criminal activities at some time in their life. Less than a third have had full time jobs for more than 5 months, and more than two thirds have been arrested (e.g., De Leon, 1984; Hubbard, Valley Rachal, Craddock, & Cavanaugh, 1984; Simpson & Sells, 1982; see Figure 2).

About a fourth of admissions are adolescents (Pompi, 1994), although some programs serve adolescents exclusively. Over 70% of admissions have dropped out of school; more than 70% have been involved with the criminal justice system or have been arrested at least once (see Figure 3). Compared with adults, more adolescent clients have histories of family deviance, more have been treated for psychological problems, and more were legally referred to therapeutic community treatment (De Leon & Deitch, 1985; Holland & Griffen, 1984; Jainchill, Bhattacharya, & Yagelka, 1995; Pompi, 1994).

Social profiles of admissions to traditional therapeutic community programs are similar regardless of primary drug preference. They do not differ significantly from client profiles in special therapeutic community facilities implemented exclusively for certain populations, such as adolescents, mothers with their children, ethnic minorities, criminal justice referrals, or prison inmates. The profiles of these various special populations appear to be more homogeneous than heterogeneous.

Psychological Profiles

Clients differ in demography, socioeconomic background, and drug use patterns, but psychological profiles obtained with standard instruments appear remarkably uniform, as evident in a number of therapeutic community studies (e.g., Barr & Antes, 1981; Biase, Sullivan, & Wheeler, 1986; Brook & Whitehead, 1980; De Leon, 1989; De Leon, Skodol, & Rosenthal, 1973; Holland, 1986; Jainchill, 1994; Kennard & Wilson, 1979; Zuckerman, Sola, & Masterson, 1975). The psychological profiles reveal drug abuse as the prominent element in a picture that mirrors the features of both psychiatric and criminal populations. For example, antisocial personality disorder characteristics and poor self-concept of delinquent and repeated offenders are present, along with the dysphoria, depression, anxiety, and confused thinking of emotionally unstable or psychiatric populations (see Figure 4).

There are a few completed diagnostic studies of admissions to the therapeutic community using the National Institute of Mental Health's Diagnostic Interview Schedule (Robins, Helzer, Cottler, & Goldring, 1989). In these, over 70% of the admission sample revealed a lifetime nondrug psychiatric disorder in addition to substance abuse or dependence. One third had a current or continuing history of mental disorder in addition to their drug abuse. The most frequent nondrug diagnoses were phobias, generalized anxiety, psychosexual dysfunction, and antisocial personality. There were only a few cases of schizophrenia, but lifetime affective disorders occurred in over one third of those studied (De Leon, 1989, 1993b; Jainchill, 1994; Jainchill, De Leon, & Pinkham, 1986). Studies using the structured Diagnostic Interview for Children and Adolescents revealed comparable percentages of dual disorder among adolescent admissions (e.g., Jainchill, De Leon, & Yagelka, 1997; see Figure 5).

Psychological profiles vary little across age, sex, race, primary drug, or admission year and are not significantly different from drug abusers in other treatment modalities (Jainchill, 1994; Rounsaville et al., 1991). Thus, in addition to their substance abuse and social deviancy, drug abusers who enter therapeutic communities reveal a considerable degree of psychological disability, a conclusion confirmed in the diagnostic studies. Despite the common practice in standard therapeutic communities of excluding clients with serious psychological problems, the large majority of adult and adolescent admissions meet the diagnostic criteria for psychiatric disorders other than substance abuse.

Treatment Effectiveness

A substantial research–evaluation literature documents the effectiveness of the therapeutic community approach in rehabilitating drug abusers (e.g., Anglin & Hser, 1991; Condelli & Hubbard, 1994; De Leon, 1984, 1985; Gerstein & Harwood, 1990; Hubbard et al., 1984; Simpson & Sells, 1982; Tims et al., 1994; Tims & Ludford, 1984). The main findings on short- and long-term posttreatment follow-up outcomes from single-program and multiprogram studies are selectively reviewed in the following paragraphs.

Significant improvements occurred on separate outcome variables (e.g., drug use, criminality, and employment) and on composite indexes for measuring individual status or success. Maximum to moderately favorable outcomes (based on opioid, nonopioid, and alcohol use; arrest rates; retreatment and employment) occurred for more than half the sample of completed clients and dropouts (De Leon, 1984; Hubbard et al., 1989; Simpson & Sells, 1982).

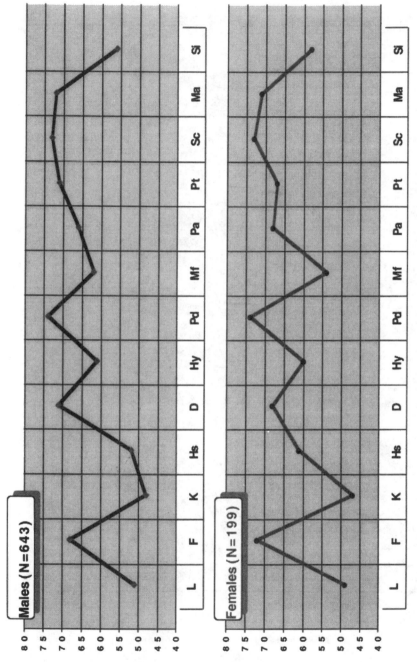

Figure 4. Minnesota Multiphasic Personality Inventory profiles for 1984–1985 admissions to a Northeastern therapeutic community. L = Lie; F = Frequency; K = Correction; Hs = Hypochondriasis; D = Depression; Hy = Hysteria; Pd = Psychopathic Deviate; Mf = Masculinity–Feminity; Pa = Paranoia; Pt = Psychasthenia; Sc = Schizophenia; Ma = Hypomania; Si = Social Introversion. Source: De Leon, G. (1989). Psychopathology and substance abuse: What we are learning from research in therapeutic communities. *Journal of Psychoactive Drugs, 21*, 177–188. Reprinted with permission of Haight Ashbury Publications, 612 Clayton St., San Francisco, CA 94117.

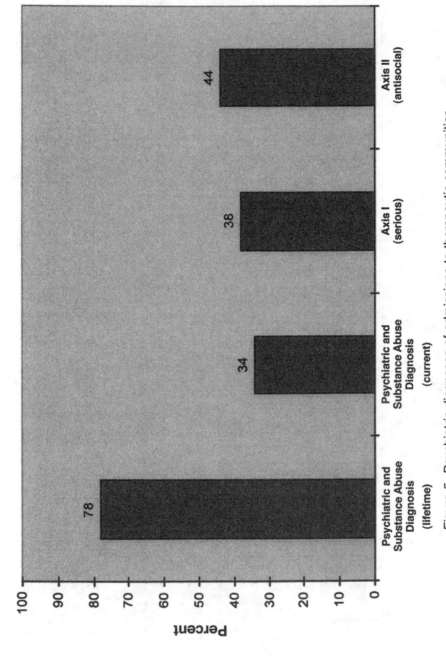

Figure 5. Psychiatric diagnoses of admissions to therapeutic communities.

Source: De Leon, G. (1993a). Cocaine abusers in therapeutic community treatment. In F. M. Tims (Ed.), *Cocaine treatment: Research and clinical perspectives,* (NIDA Research Monograph No. 135, NIH Publication No. 93–3639, pp. 163–189). Rockville, MD: National Institute on Drug Abuse.

Research documents a consistent positive relationship between time spent in residential treatment and posttreatment outcome status (e.g., De Leon, 1984; Hubbard et al., 1984, 1989; Kooyman, 1993; Simpson, 1997). In Figure 6, for example, success rates (based on composite indexes of no drug use and no criminality) at 2 years posttreatment approximate 90% for graduates–completees. Success rates are 50% for dropouts who remain more than 1 year in residential treatment and 25% for those who drop out in less than a year. Improvement rates over pretreatment status approximate 100%, 70%, and 40%, respectively, for graduates, long-term, and short-term dropouts (De Leon, Wexler, & Jainchill, 1982).

In the few studies that have investigated psychological outcomes, results uniformly show significant improvement at follow-up (e.g., Biase et al., 1986; De Leon, 1984; Holland, 1983). A direct relationship has been suggested between posttreatment behavioral success (i.e., reduced drug use and criminality) and psychological adjustment (De Leon, 1984; De Leon & Jainchill, 1981–1982).

Dropout is the "rule" for all drug treatment modalities. For therapeutic communities, retention is of crucial importance because research has established a firm relationship between time spent in treatment and successful outcome. However, most admissions to therapeutic community programs leave too soon—many before treatment influences are presumed to be effectively rendered. Research on retention in therapeutic communities has increased in recent years, and reviews have appeared in the literature (e.g., De Leon, 1985, 1991; Lewis & Ross, 1994). Studies focus on several issues: retention rates, client predictors of dropout, and attempts to enhance retention in treatment.

Retention Rates

Dropout is highest (30% to 40%) in the first 30 days of admission but declines sharply thereafter (De Leon, 1985). This temporal pattern of dropout is fairly uniform across therapeutic community programs. In long-term residential therapeutic communities, completion rates average 10% to 20% of all admissions. One-year retention rates range from 15% to 30%, although trends suggest gradual increases in 12-month retention compared with the period before 1980 (De Leon, 1991; see Figure 7).

Predictors of Dropout

Reliable client characteristics that predict retention have been identified, with the exception of severe criminality and severe psychopathology, which are correlated with earlier dropout. Recent studies point to the importance of dynamic factors (i.e., changing characteristics) in predicting retention in treatment, such as perceived legal pressure, motivation, and readiness for treatment (e.g., Condelli & De Leon, 1993; De Leon, 1988;

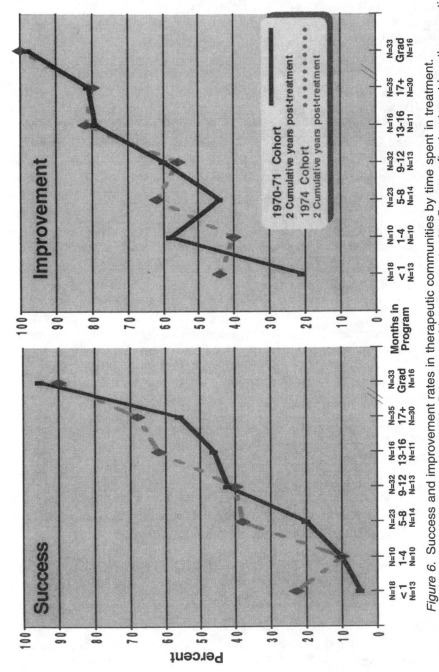

Figure 6. Success and improvement rates in therapeutic communities by time spent in treatment. Success and improvement rates 5 years after treatment in a therapeutic community. *International Journal on the Addiction, 17,* 703–747. Reprinted courtesy Marcel Dekker, Inc. from 98–8.

Source: De Leon G., Wexler, H. & Jainchill, N. (1982).

Therapeutic Community Research

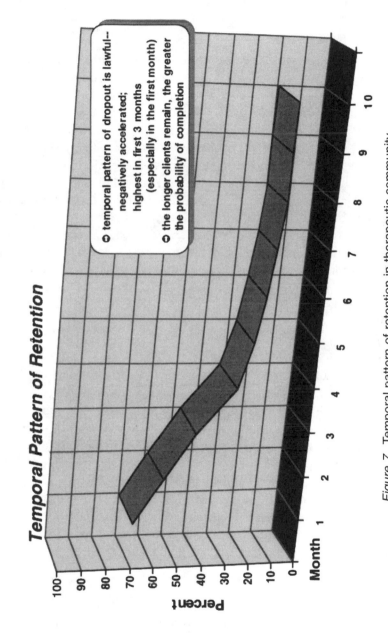

Figure 7. Temporal pattern of retention in therapeutic community.

Source: De Leon, G. (1991). Retention in drug free therapeutic communities. In R. W. Pickens, C. G. Leukenfeld & C. R. Schuster (Eds.), *Improving drug abuse treatment*, (NIDA Research Monograph No. 106, DHHS Publication No. ADM 91–1754, pp. 218–244). Rockville, MD: National Institute on Drug Abuse.

THERAPEUTIC COMMUNITIES   409

De Leon, Melnick, Kressel, & Jainchill, 1994; Hubbard et al., 1989). The specific contribution of motivational factors to retention and outcomes is discussed in the Current Research and Evaluation Initiatives section later in this chapter.

Enhancing Retention

Some experimental attempts to enhance retention in therapeutic communities have used supportive individual counseling, improved orientation to treatment by experienced staff ("senior professors"), and family alliance strategies to reduce early dropout (e.g., De Leon, 1988, 1991). Other efforts provide special facilities and programming for mothers and children (Hughes et al., 1992; Stevens, Arbiter, & Glider, 1989; Stevens & Glider, 1994) and curriculum-based relapse-prevention methods (Lewis, McKusker, Hindin, Frost, & Garfield, 1993) to sustain retention throughout residential treatment. Results from these efforts did not present firm conclusions, but indications were promising.

Although a legitimate concern, retention should not be confused with treatment effectiveness. Therapeutic communities are most effective for those who remain long enough for treatment influences to occur. Obviously, however, a critical issue for therapeutic communities (and drug treatments in general) is maximizing retention to benefit more clients.

MODIFICATIONS AND ADAPTATIONS OF THE THERAPEUTIC COMMUNITY MODEL AND APPROACH

Currently, a wide variety of drug abuse treatment programs self-identify as therapeutic communities. Today, the therapeutic community modality consists of multiple types of programs serving a diversity of clients who use a variety of drugs and present complex social psychological problems in addition to their chemical abuse. Client differences, as well as clinical requirements and funding realities, have encouraged the development of modified residential therapeutic communities with shorter planned durations of stay (3, 6, and 12 months) as well as therapeutic community-oriented day treatment and outpatient ambulatory models.

Current Modifications

Most community-based traditional therapeutic communities have expanded their social services or incorporated new interventions to address the needs of diverse admission cohorts. In some cases, these additions enhance but do not alter the basic therapeutic community regime; in others, they significantly modify the therapeutic community model itself.

Family Services Approaches

The increased participation of families or significant others has been a notable development in therapeutic communities for both adolescents and adults. Some therapeutic communities offer programs in individual- and multiple-family therapy as components of their adolescent programs, nonresidential modalities, and (more recently) short-term residential modalities. However, most traditional therapeutic communities do not provide a regular family therapy service because the client in residence is viewed as the primary target of treatment rather than the family unit.

Experience has shown that beneficial effects can occur with forms of significant-other participation other than family therapy. Seminars, support groups, open houses, and other special events focus on how significant others can reinforce the client's staying in treatment. They teach the therapeutic community perspective on recovery and provide a setting for sharing common concerns and strategies for coping with the client's future reentry into the larger community. Thus, family-participation activities may enhance the rehabilitative process for the residential client by establishing an alliance between significant others and the program.

Primary Health Care and Medical Services

Although funding for health care services remains insufficient for most therapeutic communities, these public health agencies have expanded services for the growing number of residential clients with sexually transmitted and immune-system-compromising conditions, including HIV seropositivity, AIDS, syphilis, hepatitis B, and, recently, tuberculosis. Screening, treatment, and increased health education have become more sophisticated and effective, both on site and through linkages with community primary health care agencies.

Aftercare Services

Currently, most long-term therapeutic communities have well-established linkages with other service providers and 12-step groups for their graduates. Therapeutic communities with shorter term residential components, however, are now instituting well-defined aftercare programs both within their systems and through linkages with other non-therapeutic community agencies. There are limits and issues concerning these aftercare efforts and discontinuities between the perspectives of the therapeutic community and other service agencies. These are outlined in the final section of this chapter (see also De Leon, 1990–1991).

Relapse Prevention Training

On the basis of its approach to recovery, the traditional therapeutic community has always focused on the key issues of relapse prevention. The

24-hour communal life fosters a process of learning how to resist drug taking and other negative behaviors. In the therapeutic community's social learning setting, the individual engages many of the social, emotional, environmental, and circumstantial cues for, and influences on, drug use that exist in the larger macrosociety. This broad context of social learning essentially provides a continual relapse-prevention training program (De Leon, 1991).

A number of therapeutic communities include special workshops on relapse-prevention training, using a curriculum, expert trainers, and formats developed outside the therapeutic community area (e.g., Marlatt & Gordon, 1985). These workshops are offered as formal additions to the existing therapeutic community protocol, usually in the reentry stage of treatment. However, some programs incorporate relapse-prevention training workshops in earlier treatment stages. In a few other therapeutic communities, relapse-prevention training is central to the primary treatment protocol (e.g., Lewis et al., 1993). Clinical impressions supported by data of the efficacy of relapse-prevention training within the therapeutic community setting are favorable, although rigorous evaluation studies are still in progress (McKusker et al., 1995).

Twelve Step Components

Historically, therapeutic community graduates were not consistently integrated into Alcoholics Anonymous meetings for a variety of reasons (De Leon, 1990–1991). In recent years, however, there has been a gradual integration of Alcoholics Anonymous, Cocaine Anonymous (CA), or Narcotics Anonymous (NA) meetings during and following therapeutic community treatment, given the wide diversity of users socially and demographically and the prominence of alcohol use regardless of the primary drug of choice. The common genealogical roots found in therapeutic communities and 12-step groups are evident to most participants, and the similarities in the self-help view of recovery far outweigh other differences in specific orientation. Today, 12-step groups may be introduced at any stage in residential therapeutic communities, but are considered mandatory in the reentry stages of treatment, that is, in the aftercare or continuance stages of recovery after leaving the residential setting.

Mental Health Services

Among those seeking admission to therapeutic communities in recent years, increasing numbers have documented psychiatric histories (e.g., Jainchill, 1994; Jainchill et al., 1986). Certain subgroups of these clients who are treated within the traditional therapeutic community model and regime require some modification in services and staffing. For example, psychopharmacological adjuncts and individual psychotherapy are used for selected clients at appropriate stages in treatment. Nevertheless, traditional community-based therapeutic community models are limited in accommodating the substance abuser with a serious psychiatric disorder. As described below in the section on mentally ill chemical abusers, the primary psychiatric substance abuser requires specially adapted forms of the therapeutic community model.

The Multimodal Therapeutic Community and Client–Treatment Matching

Traditional therapeutic communities are highly effective for a certain segment of the drug abuse population. However, those who seek assistance in therapeutic community settings represent a broad spectrum of clients, many of whom may not be suitable for long-term residential stay. Thus, today, many therapeutic community agencies are multimodality treatment centers that offer services in their residential and nonresidential programs, depending on the clinical status and situation needs of the individual. Modalities can include short-term (under 90 days), medium-term (6–12 months), and long-term (1–2 years) residential components and drug-free outpatient services (6–12 months). Some operate drug-free day treatment and methadone maintenance programs. Admission assessment attempts to match the client to the appropriate modality within the agency. For example, the spread of drug abuse in the workplace, particularly in cocaine use, has prompted the therapeutic community to develop short-term residential and ambulatory models for employed, more socialized clients (Saler, 1988).

As yet, the effectiveness of therapeutic-community-oriented multimodality programs has not been systematically evaluated. The comparative effectiveness and cost benefits of long- and short-term residential treatment is of great interest. However, convincing evidence supporting the effectiveness of short-term treatment in any modality, residential or ambulatory, is not yet available.

Given what is known about the complexity of the recovery process in addiction and the importance of length of stay in treatment, short-term residential treatments alone will not likely be sufficient to yield stable positive outcomes. In the multimodal therapeutic communities, combinations of residential and outpatient services appear to be needed to provide a long-term treatment involvement and impact.

Current Applications for Special Populations

The evolution of the therapeutic community is most evident in its application to special populations of substance abusers treated in various settings. It is beyond the purview of the present chapter to detail all of the many modifications of these adapted models. In general, these models retain the focus on mutual self-help and the essential elements of the community approach—the meetings, groups, work structure, and the perspective on recovery and right living. This section highlights some of the key applications of the therapeutic community treatment approach for different client populations in different settings.

Adolescents

The prominence of youth drug abuse and the unique needs of the adolescent have led to adaptations of the traditional therapeutic community approach that appear more appropriate for these youthful clients. These include age-segregated facilities with considerable emphasis on management and supervision, educational needs, family involvement, and individual counseling. More extensive accounts of the treatment of adolescents in therapeutic communities and effectiveness of these adapted therapeutic communities are contained in other writings (e.g., De Leon & Deitch, 1985; Jainchill et al., 1995; Pompi, 1994).

Addicted Mothers and Children

Several therapeutic communities have adapted the traditional model for chemically dependent mothers living in residential treatment with their children. The profile of the addicted mother in residence is generally not different from that of other abusers, although it reflects more socially disadvantaged clients with poor socialization skills and a predominance of crack cocaine abuse. It is clear that these women require a lifestyle with changes and opportunities for personal maturation. Thus, within the context of the basic therapeutic community regime, additional child care and administrative and therapeutic services and modifications are provided to address these clients' specific needs and promote their recovery. These include family-unit housing for mothers and children, medical and psychological care, parental training, and child care. Further accounts of clinical issues in therapeutic community programs for females in general, and addicted mothers, in particular, are contained in other writings (e.g., Coletti et al., 1997; De Leon & Jainchill, 1981–1982; Hughes et al., 1992; Stevens et al., 1989; Stevens & Glider, 1994).

Incarcerated Substance Abusers

In recent years, therapeutic community models have been adapted for incarcerated substance abusers in prison settings. This development has been fostered by overcrowded prisons, the influx of drug offenders, and the documented success of an early therapeutic community prison model in reducing recidivism to crime and relapse to drug use (Lockwood & Inciardi, 1993; Wexler & Williams, 1986). Modifications of the traditional model are shaped by the unique features of the individual correctional institution (e.g., its focus on security, its goal of early release, its limited physical and social space, and the prison culture itself).

A prominent feature of the modified prison model is the mutual involvement of correctional officers, prison administrators, and mental health and therapeutic community treatment paraprofessionals. For inmates who leave these prison therapeutic communities, models for continuance of recovery have recently been established outside the walls in therapeutic-community-oriented halfway houses (e.g., Graham & Wexler, 1997; Knight, Simpson, Chatham, & Camacho, 1997; Lockwood & Inciardi, 1993; Wexler & Love, 1994)

Mentally Ill Chemical Abusers

Special therapeutic community-adapted models have been developed to exclusively treat the more seriously disturbed mentally ill chemical abusers. Several of these have been developed by community-based therapeutic community agencies as special programs in separate facilities; others have been implemented as innovative research demonstration projects in the mental hospitals (e.g., Galanter et al., 1993), and in community-residence settings for the homeless mentally ill chemical abuser (e.g., De Leon, 1993b; Rahav et al., 1994; Sacks, De Leon, Bernhardt, & Sacks, 1997).

In these models for the dually disordered, the basic peer orientation and elements of the daily therapeutic community regime are retained, although there is more focus on adapting to individual differences and greater flexibility in planned duration of stay, as well as in the phase format. Specific modifications include the inclusion of a standard psychotropic medication regime, moderated intensity of groups, a less rigid and demanding work structure, significant use of individual psychotherapy, case management, and skills training (e.g., Sacks et al., 1997; Silberstein, Jamner-Metzger, & Galanter, 1997).

AIDS- and HIV-Seropositive Clients

Therapeutic communities have evolved a compassionate and sophisticated response to the HIV/AIDS epidemic since its identification in the early and mid 1980s. HIV/AIDS oriented special programs are now the rule in most well-managed therapeutic communities. These integrate AIDS- and HIV-seropositive clients into the regular daily regime and address the special issues of HIV, including education, pre- and posttest counseling for HIV testing, confidentiality concerning disclosure, and support through medical crises. These special programs are directed to the target residential clients, their families, and significant others. Programs include individual and group formats for counseling on sexual practices and on drug and alcohol use behavior and procedures for contact notification. Some therapeutic communities have innovated special residential models serving AIDS clients exclusively (Brown & McLellan, 1996; De Leon, 1997; McKusker & Sorensen, 1994).

CURRENT RESEARCH AND EVALUATION INITIATIVES

Two major areas of inquiry that constitute the current research–evaluation agenda for the therapeutic community modality are (a) the diversity of programs and clients and (b) the treatment process. This section briefly summarizes key findings and conclusions from evaluation studies on the effectiveness of modified therapeutic communities and research initiatives in process-related studies.

Effectiveness of Modified Therapeutic Communities

The effectiveness (and cost-effectiveness) of modified therapeutic communities for special populations and in nontraditional special settings were evaluated in a number of single-program and multisite studies. Many of these studies were funded by NIDA (see the Appendix). They generally describe program elements and client profiles and assess retention during treatment and posttreatment outcomes. This section summarizes key findings and conclusions in published papers or research reports from illustrative studies on the diversity of clients treated and settings for modified therapeutic communities.[3]

- Profiles of admissions indicate that contemporary modified therapeutic communities are serving individuals who reveal a considerable degree of social and psychological dysfunction in addition to their substance abuse.
- Client improvements are obtained in the domains of drug use, criminality, and psychological status during treatment and at posttreatment follow-up. The improvements are most consistent for treatment completers; among dropouts, they are generally related to length of stay in treatment.
- Planned duration of residential treatments is generally shorter than in earlier years. However, outcomes are still favorable among the clients who complete or stay longer in treatment. Differential effects of longer and shorter planned durations of residential stay remain to be clarified.
- The therapeutic community model and method can be successfully adapted for a wide diversity of substance abusers and feasibly implemented in a variety of community-based and

---

[3]Program descriptions and preliminary evaluation data for a number of these applications are provided in De Leon (1997).

institutional settings. The robust generalizability of the therapeutic community approach across these clients and settings is a consistent finding.

- Aftercare services are a necessary condition for maintaining stable outcomes. Thus, regardless of planned duration of primary treatment, individuals must continue in the treatment process for some undetermined time beyond the residential phase.

- Aftercare models must be integrated with the primary treatment model in terms of philosophy, methods, and relationships, to provide effective continuity of care. Controlled studies will assess therapeutic-community-oriented versus non-therapeutic-community-oriented aftercare models on samples leaving therapeutic-community-oriented primary treatment.

- Although still ongoing, fiscal studies indicate that therapeutic-community-oriented programs provide favorable cost–benefit gains, particularly in reduction of expenditures associated with criminal activity and mental health services. In short, therapeutic community treatment appears to reduce the social costs of drug abuse.

Advances In Treatment Process

Until recently, the treatment process in the therapeutic community has been a "black box" that has remained well hidden from clinical inquiry or research investigation. The link between treatment services, treatment experiences, and treatment outcomes must be explicated to substantiate conclusions concerning effectiveness and to improve treatment itself. However, the study of treatment process in the therapeutic community goes much beyond the listing of various services rendered and monitoring client participation in these services. As described earlier, therapeutic communities are community milieus that consist of a daily regime of structured and unstructured interactions and activities occurring in formal and informal ways in the program. These interact in complex and subtle ways as global social and interpersonal interventions.

Thus, the area of treatment process presents a most formidable evaluation challenge for therapeutic community research investigators. It requires, at a minimum, a theoretical formulation of recovery (e.g., the characteristic stages of client change in the therapeutic community), operational definitions of the therapeutic community active treatment elements, appropriate assessment measures, feasible methods of data collection, and multivariate analytic statistical models for capturing the effects of global interventions in dynamic interaction with a changing client during the process. Although still in the initial stage of sophistication, developing treatment-process research has produced preliminary findings in theory and measurement that also have clinical use in therapeutic communities (Melnick, De Leon, Thomas, Kressel, & Wexler, in press; Simpson, Joe, Rowan-Szal, & Greener, 1995).

Therapeutic Community Treatment Elements

A theoretical framework organizing the essential elements of the therapeutic community has been formulated (e.g., De Leon, 1995b); initial empirical studies support the validity of these elements. For example, the Survey of Essential Elements Questionnaire (SEEQ) provides a standardized description of the current diversity of therapeutic community programs in terms of their adherence to the therapeutic community approach (e.g., De Leon & Melnick, 1992). Domains and items have been formulated based on the theoretical framework of the essential elements of the therapeutic community (see Melnick & De Leon, 1999). Criterion validity for the domains and the items were obtained with a national panel of therapeutic community experts. Studies with the SEEQ, involving therapeutic community programs, provide impressive quantitative validation of the instrument, which is designed to provide a high–low index of therapeutic community orientation on the basis of scored elements (Melnick & De Leon, 1999; Melnick, De Leon, Hiller, & Knight, in press).

Studies in Motivation and Readiness for Treatment

Unlike fixed client characteristics, such as social background or demography, dynamic variables, such as client perceptions, continually interact with the treatment and nontreatment influences in the change process. Studies have been conducted using the Circumstances, Motivation, Readiness Scales. This instrument measured four dimensions of the motivational construct—circumstances (external pressures), internal motivation (intrinsic pressures), readiness for treatment, and suitability for the therapeutic community treatment. These studies have focused on two broad issues: differentiating motivational levels across subgroups of substance abusers and motivation as a predictor of retention and outcomes (e.g., DeLeon et al., 1994; Melnick, De Leon, Hawke, Jainchill, & Kressel, 1997).

BROADER IMPLICATIONS FOR TREATMENT AND POLICY

The findings and conclusions from the advances in therapeutic community research highlight three major implications for treatment:

- The weight of the evidence from controlled and comparative studies indicated that modified therapeutic communities provided effective treatment for substance abusers, including those who reveal a wide range of social and psychological problems. Therefore, the therapeutic community approach can be suitably adapted for treating special populations of substance abusers.
- Because of their unique self-help perspective, therapeutic communities provide an extremely favorable cost–benefit alternative to traditional institutional-based treatments in mental health, hospital, correctional, and community-based settings.[4]
- Advances in therapeutic community research have contributed to the development of a theoretical framework to guide clinical practice, program planning, and treatment improvement.

With respect to policy issues diversity in clients, services, and staffing, along with conservative funding policies, have surfaced complex issues for therapeutic communities. Modifications of the model, shorter planned durations of treatment, managed care, and welfare reform continually challenge the therapeutic community to retain the essentials of its drug-free treatment approach and its self-help perspective. However, these issues also underscore the unique contribution that therapeutic communities can make to mainstream health care perspective and policy.

Increasing numbers of special populations are entering therapeutic communities with social deficits and medical and psychological problems. Thus, therapeutic communities are implementing residential programs in collaboration with other human services systems, such as child care, mental health and social service agencies, and the more recent homeless shelter system. Traditionally these agencies have had primary treatment and management responsibility for the clients served. Their inability to provide effective substance abuse services has forged new relations with therapeutic community agencies. However, the policies and practices of these agencies often appear contrary to therapeutic community perspective and method. This can be illustrated in three distinctions concerning treatment and social service needs of special populations. These examples are drawn from mental health and shelter populations, although they also highlight policy and practice conflicts involving other populations, such as criminal justice, adolescents, and mothers and infants.

---

[4]A number of these issues are discussed in De Leon (1995a).

Housing versus Treatment

The fundamental distinction of the therapeutic community is that it uses "community as method" in addressing substance abuse, social, and psychological problems of the individual. It is a special challenge to develop a community dynamic in populations that are largely socially disaffiliated, such as homeless, mentally ill chemical abusers. These subgroups are generally intolerant of demands and structure and are often itinerant. On a pragmatic level, it is essential to limit resident access to the macrocommunity for a period of time until the resident completely affiliates with the microcommunity of peers.

The therapeutic community's psychological view of limited access contradicts policy concerning the mentally ill, homeless substance abusers, who view community residences as housing rather than treatment settings. Residents in these facilities are tenants, free to come and go and optionally use professional and social services available to them in the outside community. Often their freedom as tenants may be counter to their actual therapeutic needs. Thus, the roles of tenant and of participant in a residential treatment community must be further clarified.

Client's Rights and the Self-Help Community

Basic elements of the therapeutic community approach and model would appear to contradict policy concerns about client rights. Examples of these are the therapeutic community's privilege–sanction system—the need for disciplinary measures that may involve discharge, mutual peer self-help versus treatment provider, unpaid peer job functions, and urine testing. These elements derive from therapeutic community self-help recovery perspective, which empowers the peer community to regulate and teach its members. In the therapeutic community view, the health, safety, and integrity of the peer community must be maintained to assure its capability to address the needs and welfare of individuals who are the central focus. Thus, potential conflicts must be resolved between the traditional human services view of client rights and the view that to foster individual recovery, the peer community must be responsible for its own health and safety.

Entitlements and the Self-Help Ethic

In the therapeutic community perspective, recovery is maintained by a value system that guides right living, which emphasizes the work ethic, honesty, personal responsibility, accountability, and self-reliance. Efforts to teach these values can be inadvertently undermined by the existing social service entitlement system, which provides the recipient with unrestricted access to unearned income. Mentally ill chemical abuser residents, for example, and those in homeless shelters who have ready access to their monthly allowances are free to purchase drugs or alcohol even if these are used off premises. On a clinical level, they can misuse their entitlements to resist the demands of therapeutic community treatment, which focuses on preparing individuals to manage their lives.

Recent changes in welfare policy also can impede and potentially subvert the integrity of the drug-treatment system. Therapeutic community research has shown that a critical threshold level of treatment impact must be achieved to assure that individuals can continue their recovery on their own and function as productive and independent participants in society. Thus, wise policy must be balanced with respect to limiting entitlement and fostering self-help recovery. Funding levels have to be sufficient, and administrative procedures for accessing these funds must be feasible, to assure that effective treatment impacts can occur.

Some Resolutions

The experience of the standard therapeutic community with substance abusers is that these issues are readily resolved when approached from a recovery perspective. For example, in standard therapeutic communities publicly subsidized residents voluntarily agree to turn their welfare checks and food stamps over to the program. Residents provide informed consent to comply with program rules and regulations at the risk of discharge and to accept the personal limits, restrictions, and social demands imposed by the therapeutic community. Indeed, the demands of a self-help-oriented treatment present continuing motivational issues for the individual. These are effectively and humanely addressed in a self-help peer community whose credibility has been firmly supported by substance abuse treatment policy. Treatment in emerging modified residential therapeutic communities will require similar support from mental health and social service policy that is enlightened by a self-help recovery perspective.

CONCLUSION

The evolutionary changes of the therapeutic community reveal the vigor, resourcefulness, and flexibility of the modality to adapt to growth and change. Movement into mainstream health care has brought not only challenges to the therapeutic community to retain its unique identity but also opportunities to influence health care itself through its perspective on treating the whole person and its self-help approach. Research has been a force in this evolution, documenting the effectiveness and validity of the therapeutic community. Current advances in research promise to further illuminate the essential nature of the therapeutic community: the use of community as a potent and humane method for positively changing individual behaviors, attitudes, and values. What began as an alternative treatment for substance abuse is developing into a significant approach toward impacting a wide range of social psychological problems.

REFERENCES

Alterman, A. I., O'Brien, C. P., & Droba, M. (1993). Day treatment vs. inpatient rehabilitation of cocaine abusers: An interim report. In F. M. Tims & C. G. Leukefeld (Eds.), *Cocaine treatment: Research and clinical perspectives* (NIDA Research Monograph No. 135, NIH Publication No. 93-3639, pp. 150–162). Rockville, MD: National Institute on Drug Abuse.

Anglin, D. M., & Hser, Y.-I. (1991). Treatment of drug abuse. In M. Tonry & N. Morris (Eds.), *Drugs and crime: Crime and justice: A review of research* (pp. 393–460). Chicago: The University of Chicago Press.

Barr, H., & Antes, D. (1981). *Factors related to recovery and relapse in follow-up* (Final report of project activities, Grant No. 1H81 DA01864). Washington, DC: National Institute on Drug Abuse.

Biase, V., Sullivan, A. P., & Wheeler, B. (1986). Daytop miniversity—Phase 2. College training in a therapeutic community: Development of self-concept among drug-free addicts/abusers. In G. De Leon & J. T. Ziegenfuss (Eds.), *Therapeutic communities for addictions: Readings in theory, research and practice* (pp. 121–130). Springfield, IL: Charles C Thomas.

Brook, R. C., & Whitehead, I. C. (1980). *Drug-free therapeutic community.* New York: Human Science Press.

Brown, B., & McLellan, A. T. (Eds.). (1996). HIV/AIDS and drug abuse treatment [Special Issue]. *Journal of Substance Abuse Treatment, 13*(5).

Carroll, J. F. X., & Sobel, B. S. (1986). Integrating mental health personnel and practices into a therapeutic community. In G. De Leon & J. T. Ziegenfuss (Eds.), *Therapeutic communities for addictions: Readings in theory, research, and practice* (pp. 209–226). Springfield, IL: Charles C Thomas.

Coletti, S. D., Schinka, J. A., Hughes, P. H., Hamilton, N. L., Renard, C. G., Sicilian, D. M., & Neri, R. L. (1997). Specialized therapeutic community treatment for chemically dependent women and their children. In G. De Leon (Ed.), *Community as method: Therapeutic communities for special populations and special settings* (pp. 115–128). Westport, CT: Greenwood Publishing.

Condelli, W., & De Leon, G. (1993). Fixed and dynamic predictors of client retention in therapeutic communities. *Journal of Substance Abuse Treatment, 10,* 11–16.

Condelli, W., & Hubbard, R. L. (1994). Client outcomes from therapeutic communities. In F. M. Tims, G. De Leon, & N. Jainchill (Eds.), *Therapeutic community: Advances in research and application* (NIDA Research Monograph No. 144, NIH Publication No. 94-3633, pp. 80–98). Rockville, MD: National Institute on Drug Abuse.

De Leon, G. (1984). *The therapeutic community: Study of effectiveness* (DHHS Publication No. ADM 84-1286). Rockville, MD: National Institute on Drug Abuse.

De Leon, G. (1985). The therapeutic community: Status and evolution. *International Journal of Addictions, 20,* 823–844.

De Leon, G. (1988). Legal pressure in therapeutic communities. In C. G. Leukefeld & F. M. Tims (Eds.), *Compulsory treatment of drug abuse: Research and clinical practice* (NIDA Research Monograph No. 86, DHHS Publication No. ADM 88-1578, pp. 160–177). Rockville, MD: National Institute on Drug Abuse.

De Leon, G. (1989). Psychopathology and substance abuse: What we are learning from research in therapeutic communities? *Journal of Psychoactive Drugs, 21,* 177–188.

De Leon, G. (1990–1991). Aftercare in therapeutic communities. *International Journal of Addictions, 25,* 1229–1241.

De Leon, G. (1991). Retention in drug free therapeutic communities. In R. W. Pickens, C. G. Leukefeld, & C. R. Schuster (Eds.), *Improving drug abuse treatment* (NIDA Research Monograph No. 106, DHHS Publication No. ADM 91-1754, pp. 218–244). Rockville, MD: National Institute on Drug Abuse.

De Leon, G. (1993a). Cocaine abusers in therapeutic community treatment. In F. M. Tims & E. G. Leukefeld (Eds.), *Cocaine treatment: Research and clinical perspectives* (NIDA Monograph Series No. 135, Publication No. 93-3639, pp. 163–189). Rockville, MD: National Institute on Drug Abuse.

De Leon, G. (1993b). Modified therapeutic communities for dual disorder. In J. Solomon, S. Zimberg, & E. Shollar (Eds.), *Dual diagnosis: Evaluation, treatment, training, and program development* (pp. 147–170). New York: Plenum.

De Leon, G. (1993c). What psychologists can learn from addiction treatment research. *Psychology of Addictive Behaviors, 7,* 103–109.

De Leon, G. (1995a). Residential therapeutic communities in the mainstream: Diversity and issues. *Journal of Psychoactive Drugs, 27,* 3–15.

De Leon, G. (1995b). Therapeutic communities for addictions: A theoretical framework. *International Journal of the Addictions, 30,* 1603–1645.

De Leon, G. (Ed.). (1997). *Community as method: Therapeutic communities for special populations in special settings.* Westport, CT: Greenwood Press.

De Leon, G. (in press). *The therapeutic community: Theory, model, and method.* Norwell, MA: Klewer Academic.

De Leon, G., & Beschner, G. (Eds.). (1977). The therapeutic community. *In proceedings of therapeutic communities of America planning conference.* Washington, DC: Department of Health, Education, and Welfare.

De Leon, G., & Deitch, D. (1985). Treatment of the adolescent substance abuser in a therapeutic community. In A. Friedman & G. Beschner (Eds.), *Treatment services for adolescent substance abusers* (DHHS Publication No. ADM 85-1342, pp. 216–230). Rockville, MD: National Institute on Drug Abuse.

De Leon, G., & Jainchill, N. (1981–1982). Male and female drug abusers: Social and psychological status 2 years after treatment in a therapeutic community. *American Journal of Drug and Alcohol Abuse, 9,* 465–497.

De Leon, G., & Melnick, G. (1992). *The therapeutic community scale of essential elements questionnaire (SEEQ).* New York: Community Studies Institute. 2 World Trade Center, 16th floor, NY.

De Leon, G., Melnick, G., Kressel, D., & Jainchill, N. (1994). Circumstances, Motivation, Readiness and Suitability (The CMRS scales): Predicting retention in therapeutic community treatment. *American Journal of Drug and Alcohol Abuse, 20,* 495–515.

De Leon, G., & Rosenthal, M. S. (1989). Treatment in residential therapeutic communities. In T. B. Karasu (Ed.), *Treatments of psychiatric disorders* (Vol. 2, pp. 1379–1396). Washington, DC: American Psychiatric Press.

De Leon, G., Skodol, A., & Rosenthal, M. S. (1973). The Phoenix House therapeutic community for drug addicts: Changes in psychopathological signs. *Archives of General Psychiatry, 28,* 131–135.

De Leon, G., Wexler, H., & Jainchill, N. (1982). Success and improvement rates 5 years after treatment in a therapeutic community. *International Journal of the Addictions, 17,* 703–747.

De Leon, G., & Ziegenfuss, J. T. (Eds.). (1986). *Therapeutic communities for addictions: Readings in theory, research and practice.* Springfield, IL: Charles C Thomas.

Galanter, M., Franco, H., Kim, A., Jamner-Metzger, E., & De Leon, G. (1993). Inpatient treatment for the dually diagnosed: A peer-led model. In J. Solomon, S. Zimberg, & E. Shollar (Eds.), *Dual diagnosis: Evaluation, treatment, training, and program development* (pp. 171–192). New York: Plenum.

Gerstein, D. R., & Harwood, H. (Eds.). (1990). *Treating drug problems: A study of the evolution, effectiveness, and financing of public and private drug treatment systems.* (Report by the Institute of Medicine Committee for the Substance Abuse Coverage Study, Division of Health Care Services). Washington, DC: National Academy Press.

Graham, W. F., & Wexler, H. K. (1997). The Amity therapeutic community program at Donovan Prison: Program description and approach. In G. De Leon (Ed.), *Community as method: Therapeutic communities for special populations and special settings* (pp. 69–86). Westport, CT: Greenwood Press.

Holland, S. (1983). Evaluating community based treatment programs: A model for strengthening inferences about effectiveness. *International Journal of Therapeutic Communities, 4,* 285–306.

Holland, S. (1986). Mental health and the TC. In A. Acampora & E. Nebelkopf (Eds.), *Proceedings of the 9th World Conference of Therapeutic Communities of America: Bridging Services* (pp. 122–131). San Francisco: Walden House.

Holland, S., & Griffen, A. (1984). Adolescent and adult drug treatment clients: Patterns and consequences of use. *Journal of Psychoactive Drugs, 16,* 79–90.

Hubbard, R. L., Marsden, M. E., Valley Rachal, J., Harwood, H. J., Cavanaugh, E. R., & Ginzburg, H. M. (1989). *Drug abuse treatment: A national study of effectiveness.* Chapel Hill: University of North Carolina Press.

Hubbard, R. L., Valley Rachal, J., Craddock, S. G., & Cavanaugh, E. R. (1984). Treatment Outcome Prospective Study (TOPS): Client characteristics and behaviors before, during, and after treatment. In F. M. Tims & J. P. Ludford (Eds.), *Drug abuse treatment evaluation: Strategies, progress, and prospects* (NIDA Research Monograph No. 51, DHHS Publication No. ADM 84-1329, pp. 42–68). Rockville, MD: National Institute on Drug Abuse.

Hughes, P., Starr, C. L., Urmann, C. F., Williams, K. M., Coletti, S. D., Neri, R. L., Landress, H. J., & Sicilian, D. M. (1992, September). Evaluating a therapeutic community for cocaine abusing women and their children. In P. A. Vamos & P. J. Corriveau (Eds.), *Proceedings of the XIV World Conference of Therapeutic Communities, Drugs and Society to the Year 2000* (pp. 935–938). Montreal, Quebec, Canada: Portage Program for Drug Dependencies.

Jainchill, N. (1994). Co-morbidity and therapeutic community treatment. In F. M. Tims, G. De Leon, & N. Jainchill (Eds.), *Therapeutic community: Advances in research and application* (NIDA Research Monograph No. 144, NIH Publication No. 94-3633, pp. 209–231). Rockville, MD: National Institute on Drug Abuse.

Jainchill, N., Bhattacharya, G., & Yagelka, J. (1995). Therapeutic communities for adolescents. In E. Rahdert, Z. Sloboda, & D. Czechowicz (Eds.), *Adolescent drug abuse: Clinical assessment and therapeutic interventions* (NIDA Research Monograph No. 156, NIH Publication No. 95-3908, pp. 190–217). Rockville, MD: National Institute on Drug Abuse.

Jainchill, N., De Leon, G., & Pinkham, L. (1986). Psychiatric diagnoses among substance abusers in the therapeutic community. *Journal of Psychoactive Drugs, 8,* 209–213.

Jainchill, N., De Leon, G., & Yagelka, J. (1997). Ethnic differences in psychiatric disorders among adolescent substance abusers in treatment. *Journal of Psychopathology and Behavioral Assessment, 19*(2), 133–147.

Jones, M. (1953). *The therapeutic community: A new treatment method in psychiatry.* New York: Basic Books.

Kennard, D. (1983). *An introduction to therapeutic communities.* London: Routledge & Kegan Paul.

Kennard, D., & Wilson, S. (1979). The modification of personality disturbance in a therapeutic community for drug abusers. *British Journal of Medical Psychology, 52,* 215–221.

Knight, K., Simpson, D. D., Chatham, L. R., & Camacho, L. M. (1997). An assessment of prison-based drug treatment: Texas' in-prison therapeutic community program. *Journal of Offender Rehabilitation, 24*(3–4), 75–100.

Kooyman, M. (1993). *The therapeutic community for addicts: Intimacy, parent involvement, and treatment success.* Rotterdam, The Netherlands: Erasmus University.

Lewis, B. F., McKusker, J., Hindin, R., Frost, R., & Garfield, F. (1993). Four residential drug treatment programs: Project IMPACT. In J. A. Inciardi, F. M. Tims, & B. W. Fletcher (Eds.), *Innovative approaches in the treatment of drug abuse: Program models and strategies* (pp. 45–60). Westport, CT: Greenwood Press.

Lewis, B. F., & Ross, R. (1994). Retention in therapeutic communities: Challenges for the nineties. In F. M. Tims, G. De Leon, & N. Jainchill (Eds.), *Therapeutic community: Advances in research and application* (NIDA Research Monograph No. 144, NIH Publication No. 94-3633, pp. 99–116). Rockville, MD: National Institute on Drug Abuse.

Lockwood, D., & Inciardi, J. A. (1993). CREST Outreach Center: A work release iteration of the TC model. In J. A. Inciardi, F. M. Tims, & B. W. Fletcher (Eds.), *Innovative approaches in the treatment of drug abuse: Program models and strategies* (pp. 61–69). Newport, CT: Greenwood Press.

Marlatt, G. A., & Gordon, J. R. (Eds.). (1985). *Relapse prevention*. New York: Guilford Press.

McKusker, J., & Sorensen, J. L. (1994). HIV and therapeutic communities. In F. M. Tims, G. De Leon, & N. Jainchill (Eds.), *Therapeutic community: Advances in research and application* (NIDA Research Monograph No. 144, NIH Publication No. 94-3633, pp. 232–258). Rockville, MD: National Institute on Drug Abuse.

McKusker, J., Vickers-Lahti, M., Stoddard, A., Hindin, R., Bigelow, C., Zorn, M., Garfield, F., Frost, R., Love, C., & Lewis, B. (1995). The effectiveness of alternative planned durations of residential drug abuse treatment. *American Journal of Public Health, 85*, 1426–1429.

Melnick, G., & De Leon, G. (1999). Clarifying the nature of therapeutic community treatment: The Survey of Essential Elements Questionnaire (SEEQ). *Journal of Substance Abuse Treatment, 16*(4), 307–313.

Melnick, G., De Leon, G., Hawke, J., Jainchill, N., & Kressel, D. (1997). Motivation and readiness for therapeutic community treatment among adolescents and adult substance abusers. *American Journal of Drug and Alcohol Abuse, 23*, 485–506.

Melnick, G., De Leon, G., Hiller, M. L., & Knight, K. (in press). Therapeutic communities: Diversity in treatment elements. *Substance Use and Misuse*.

Melnick, G., De Leon, G., Thomas, G., Kressel, D., & Wexler, H. K. (in press). Inmate motivation and participation in prison treatment programs. In D. D. Simpson, H. K. Wexler, & J. Inciardi (Eds.), *Prison Journal* [Special Issue].

Pompi, K. F. (1994). Adolescents in therapeutic communities: Retention and post treatment outcome. In F. M. Tims, G. De Leon, & N. Jainchill (Eds.), *Therapeutic community: Advances in research and application* (NIDA Research Monograph No. 144, NIH Publication No. 94-3633, pp. 128–161). Rockville, MD: National Institute on Drug Abuse.

Rahav, M., Rivera, J. J., Collins, J., Ng-Mak, D., Sturz, E. L., Struening, E. L., Pepper, B., Link, B. G., & Gross, B. (1994). Bringing experimental research designs into existing treatment programs: The case of community-based treatment of the dually diagnosed. In B. W. Fletcher, J. A. Inciardi, & A. M. Horton (Eds.), *Drug abuse treatment: The implementation of innovative approaches* (pp. 79–93). Westport, CT: Greenwood Press.

Rahav, M., Rivera, J. J., Nuttbock, L., Ng-Mak, D., Sturz, E. L., Link, B. G., Streuning, E. L., Pepper, B., & Gross, B. (1995). Characteristics and treatment of homeless, mentally ill, chemical abusing men. *Journal of Psychoactive Drugs, 27*, 93–103.

Reich, W., Shayka, J. J., & Taibson, C. (1991). *Diagnostic interview for children and adolescents, DICA-R-A.* St Louis, MO: Washington University.

Robins, L. N., Helzer, J. E., Cottler, L. B., & Goldring, E. (1989). *NIMH diagnostic interview schedule: Version III revised. (Dis-M-R).* St Louis, MO: Department of Psychiatry, Washington University.

Rounsaville, B. J., Anton, S. F., Carroll, K., Budde, D., Prusoff, B. A., & Gawin, F. (1991). Psychiatric diagnoses of treatment-seeking cocaine abusers. *Archives of General Psychiatry, 48*, 43–51.

Sacks, S., De Leon, G., Bernhardt, A. I., & Sacks, J. (1997). Halsey House: A modified therapeutic community for homeless MICA clients. In G. De Leon (Ed.), *Community as method: Therapeutic communities for special populations in special settings* (pp. 19–38). Westport, CT: Greenwood Press.

Saler, G. (Ed.). (1988, Spring). *Therapeutic community research facts: What we know.* (Available from TCA News, Therapeutic Communities of America, National Office, P.O. Box 6037, Washington DC 20005)

Silberstein, C. H., Jamner-Metzger, E., & Galanter, M. (1997). The Greenhouse: A modified therapeutic community for mentally ill homeless addicts at New York University–Bellevue Medical Center. In G. De Leon (Ed.), *Community as method: Therapeutic communities for special populations in special settings* (pp. 53–65). Westport, CT: Greenwood Press.

Simpson, D. D. (1997). Effectiveness of drug abuse treatment: A review of research from field settings. In D. M. Fox & J. A. Egertson (Eds.), *Treating drug abusers effectively* (pp. 41–73). Cambridge, MA: Blackwell.

Simpson, D. D., Joe, G. W., Rowan-Szal, G., & Greener, J. (1995). Client engagement and change during drug abuse treatment. *Journal of Substance Abuse, 7*, 117–134.

Simpson, D. D., & Sells, S. B. (1982). Effectiveness of treatment for drug abuse: An overview of the DARP research program. *Advances in Alcohol and Substance Abuse, 2*, 7–29.

Stevens, S., Arbiter, N., & Glider, P. (1989). Women residents: Expanding their role to increase treatment effectiveness in substance abuse programs. *International Journal of the Addictions, 24*, 425–434.

Stevens, S., & Glider, P. (1994). Therapeutic communities: Substance abuse treatment for women. In F. M. Tims, G. De Leon, & N. Jainchill (Eds.), *Therapeutic community: Advances in research and application* (NIDA Research Monograph No. 144, NIH Publication No. 94-3633, pp. 162–180). Rockville, MD: National Institute on Drug Abuse.

Tims, F. M., De Leon, G., & Jainchill, N. (Eds.). (1994). *Therapeutic community: Advances in research and application* (NIDA Research Monograph No. 144, NIH Publication No. 94-3633). Rockville, MD: National Institute on Drug Abuse.

Tims, F. M., & Ludford, J. P. (Eds.). (1984). *Drug abuse treatment evaluation: Strategies, progress and prospects* (NIDA Research Monograph No. 51, DHHS Publication No. ADM 84-1329). Rockville, MD: National Institute on Drug Abuse.

Wexler, H. K., & Love, C. T. (1994). Therapeutic communities in prison. In F. M. Tims, G. De Leon, & N. Jainchill (Eds.), *Therapeutic community: Advances in research and application* (NIDA Research Monograph No. 144, NIH Publication No. 94-3633, pp. 181–208). Rockville, MD: National Institute on Drug Abuse.

Wexler, H. K., & Williams, R. (1986). The Stay'n Out therapeutic community: Prison treatment for substance abusers. *Journal of Psychoactive Drugs, 18,* 221–230.

Winick, C. (1991). The counselor in drug abuse treatment. *International Journal of the Addictions, 18,* 221–230.

Zuckerman, M., Sola, S., & Masterson, J. (1975). MMPI patterns in drug abusers before and after treatment in therapeutic communities. *Journal of Consulting Clinical Psychology, 43,* 286–296.

APPENDIX
CURRENT APPLICATIONS OF MODIFIED THERAPEUTIC COMMUNITIES FOR SPECIAL POPULATIONS AND IN SPECIAL SETTINGS

LITERATURE RESOURCES

THERAPEUTIC COMMUNITIES IN JAILS–PRISONS

Jainchill, N. (1999). *Creating an environmental risk index for adolescent TCs.* Final report of project activities (NIDA Grant #R01 DA09896). New York: Center for Therapeutic Community Research at NDRI, Inc., 2 World, Trade Center, 16th floor, New York.

Knight, K., Simpson, D. D., Chatham, L. R., & Camacho, L. M. (1997). An assessment of prison-based drug treatment: Texas' in-prison therapeutic community program. *Journal of Offender Rehabilitation, 24,* 75–100.

Inciardi, J. A., Martin, S. S., Butzin, C. F., Hooper, R. M., & Harrison, C. D. (1997). An effective model of prison-based treatment for drug-involved offenders. *Journal of Drug Issues, 27,* 261–278.

Wexler, H. K., De Leon, G., Thomas, G., Kessler, D., & Peters, J. (1999). The Amity Prison therapeutics community evaluation: Reincarceration outcomes. *Criminal Justice and Behavior, 26,* 144–167.

MENTALLY ILL AND HOMELESS CHEMICAL ABUSERS

Galanter, M., Franco, H., Kim, A., Jamner-Metzger, E., & De Leon, G. (1993). Inpatient treatment for the dually diagnosed: A peer-led model for acute and intermediate care. In J. Solomon, S. Zimberg, & E. Shollar (Eds.), *Dual diagnosis: Education, treatment, training, and program development* (pp. 171–192). New York: Plenum.

Liberty, H. J., Johnson, B., Ryder, J., Messina, M., Reynolds, S., & Hossain, M. (1998). Dynamic recovery: Comparative study of therapeutic communities in homeless shelters for men. *Journal of Substance Abuse Treatment, 15,* 401–423.

Rahav, M., Rivera, J. J., Nuttbock, L., Ng-Mak, D., Sturz, E. L., Link, B. G., Streuning, E. L., Pepper, B., & Gross, B. (1995). Characteristics and treatment of homeless, mentally ill, chemical abusing men. *Journal of Psychoactive Drugs, 27,* 93–103.

Sacks, S., De Leon, G., Bernhardt, A. I., Sacks, J., Staines, G., Balistreri, E., & McKendrick, L. (1998). Modified therapeutic community for homeless MICAs: Socio-demographic and psychological profiles. *Journal of Substance Abuse, 15,* 545–554.

Westreich, L., Galanter, M., Lifschutz, H., Metzger, E. J., & Silberstein, C. (1996). A modified therapeutic community for the dually diagnosed: Greenhouse program at Bellevue Hospital. *Journal of Substance Abuse, Treatment 13,* 533–536.

WOMEN WITH CHILDREN

Hughes, P. H., Coletti, S. D., Neri, R. L., Stahl, S., Urmann, C. F., Sicilian, D. M., & Anthony, J. C. (1995). Retention of cocaine abusing women with children in a therapeutic community. *American Journal of Public Health, 85,* 1149–1152.

Hughes, P. H., Starr, C. L., Urmann, C. F., Williams, K. M., Coletti, S. D., Neri, R. L., Landress, H. J., & Sicilian, D. M. (1992). Evaluating a therapeutic community for cocaine-abusing women and their children. In P. A. Vamos & P. J. Corriveau (Eds.), *Drugs and society to the year 2000* (pp. 935–938). Montreal: Portage Program for Drug Dependencies.

Stevens, S. T. & Patton, T. (1998). Residential treatment for drug addicted women and their children: Effective treatment strategies. *Drugs and Society, 13*, 235–249.

DAY TREATMENT AND SHORT-TERM RESIDENTIAL THERAPEUTIC COMMUNITIES

De Leon, G., Staines, G., Perlis, T. E., Sacks, S., Hilton, R., Brady, R., & Melchionda, R. (1995). Therapeutic community methods in methadone maintenance (Passages): An open clinical trial. *Journal of Drug and Alcohol Dependence, 37,*45–57.

McKusker, J., Vickers-Lahti, M., Stoddard, A., Hindin, R., Bigelow, C., Zorn, M., Garfield, F., Frost, R., Love, C., & Lewis, B. (1995). The effectiveness of alternative planned durations of residential drug abuse treatment. *American Journal of Public Health, 85,* 1426–1429.

17

SCIENTIFIC BASIS FOR TOBACCO POLICY: NICOTINE RESEARCH TRAVAILS

JACK E. HENNINGFIELD AND CHRISTINE R. HARTEL

One of the best and most recent examples of scientific research having a direct effect on public policy is that of nicotine and tobacco research, which has informed United States policy on tobacco control, in particular, the tobacco regulation issued by the Food and Drug Administration in 1996 (Regulations restricting sale of cigarettes, 1995, 1996; Kessler et al., 1996). Nicotine research is also a notable scientific success story in that it has made rapid and significant progress in an area that poses major theoretical questions and substantial methodological challenges.

The research literature on tobacco and nicotine documents much of what we now understand to be the behavioral and biological basis for tobacco use. Scientists now understand the pathogenesis of tobacco addiction, as well as cancer researchers understand the pathogenesis of tobacco-caused cancer and as well as pulmonary specialists understand the pathogenesis of many tobacco-caused lung diseases. Moreover, research on

We express our great appreciation to Geoffrey Mumford for his invaluable editorial guidance in the development of this manuscript.

tobacco and nicotine has contributed to our ability to treat tobacco addiction with greater effectiveness and at a lower cost than treating cancer, emphysema, and many other tobacco-caused diseases (Warner, 1997).

The tobacco and nicotine research literature consists of several thousand publications on the physical and psychological origins of, and the prevention and treatment of, tobacco addiction. This literature is described briefly in the latter part of this chapter, after the discussion of its effects on changes in public policy.

PUBLIC POLICY IMPLICATIONS

That nicotine is addictive was clear to scientists by 1982, when the then-director of the National Institute on Drug Abuse (NIDA), William Pollin, testified before the U.S. Congress that cigarette smoking was a form of drug dependence and that nicotine met all the criteria for a dependence-producing drug (U.S. Department of Health and Human Services [DHHS], 1983). These conclusions were based on research findings from around the world, including the United Kingdom (e.g., Russell, 1978), Sweden (e.g., Fagerstrom, 1978), and Japan (Ando & Yanagita, 1981). But most of the definitive research that supported these conclusions was accomplished in the United States with direct support from NIDA. Much of this early research can be found in NIDA's research monographs (e.g., Grabowski & Hall, 1985; Jarvik, Cullen, Gritz, Vogt, & West, 1977; Krasnegor, 1979), the 1988 Report of the U.S. Surgeon General (DHHS, 1988), and in NIDA's Triennial Reports to Congress (e.g., DHHS, 1991).

Tobacco Regulation by the Food and Drug Administration (FDA)

In August 1995, the FDA proposed its tobacco regulation based on its conclusion that nicotine in cigarettes and smokeless tobacco products was a drug and that cigarettes and smokeless tobacco products were drug delivery devices. Whereas it may seem obvious that nicotine is a drug in the broadest sense of a chemical that affects the processes of living tissue (Hardman, Gilman, & Limbird, 1996), the criteria for classifying a drug under the provisions of the U.S. Federal Food, Drug, and Cosmetic Act are much more demanding (Regulations Restricting Sale of Cigarettes, 1995, 1996; Kessler et al., 1996; Page, 1998). There must be findings that a chemical is used to the affect the structure and function of the body and that this is understood and intended by its manufacturer (Kessler et al., 1996). When a manufacturer makes a specific medical claim for a substance, determination that the chemical is a drug subject to FDA regulation is generally straightforward. Failure to make an explicit claim complicates the process but does not preclude the classification of the substance as a drug. Thus manufacturers could not, for example, sell bottles of aspirin devoid of claims and thereby avoid FDA oversight, because it would be possible to establish that users of this product used it for the intended purpose of producing a pharmacological effect and that manufacturers could reasonably be assumed to be aware of such a basis for use.

The FDA allowed public comment on its proposed regulation of tobacco for approximately five months, until January 1996, during which time it received more than 750,000 comments from individuals and from organizations such as the American Medical Association and the American Psychological Association, as well as from the tobacco industry. After considering and addressing all the comments that it received, the FDA modified and formalized its position in its final tobacco regulation. The final regulation was published on August 28, 1996, in the *Federal Register* (Regulations, 1996).

The purpose of FDA's regulation is to reduce the death and disease caused by tobacco. The basis for the regulation includes several important research findings: (a) Tobacco use produces pharmacological effects that are critical incentives for people to use tobacco (e.g., weight and mood control); (b) these pharmacological effects cause nicotine addiction; and (c) the tobacco industry intended its products to have these effects. The strategy of the regulation is to reduce the appeal and to make scientifically based efforts to reduce the ease with which young people can procure adequate quantities of tobacco to cause and sustain addiction. This regulation was implemented in stages beginning in February 1997 (Kessler et al., 1996; Regulations, 1996). In addition, the FDA has coupled its regulatory efforts to protect the public from tobacco toxins with treatment efforts. This includes making lifesaving medications like nicotine gum and the nicotine patch more readily available by approving over-the-counter marketing and by moving rapidly in other areas of the evaluation of nicotine-dependence-treatment medication. The regulation has been challenged by the tobacco industry resulting in mixed Federal Court decisions; the U.S. Supreme Court took the case under consideration in 1999 (Biskupic, 1999).

Tar and Nicotine Ratings: A Bogus Pipeline?

In another area of regulation, the conclusion that tar and nicotine ratings assigned to individual cigarette brands did not predict human exposure under actual smoking conditions (National Cancer Institute [NCI], 1996), was based solidly on research findings (Benowitz et al., 1983; Henningfield, Kozlowski, & Benowitz, 1994; Kozlowski, Frecker, & Lei, 1982). Even tobacco industry research, kept secret until the mid-1990s, came to these same basic conclusions (Henningfield & Schuh, 1996; Hurt & Robinson, 1998; Slade, Bero, Hanauer, Barnes, & Glantz, 1995). However, due to significant opposition by the tobacco industry (Freedman, 1995), little headway was made in changing the system of cigarette dose estimation until 1994.

In hearings held by the U.S. Congress in the spring of 1994, the FDA testified that the ratings were seriously deficient and contended that the tobacco industry had known that this was the case (Regulations, 1995). Moreover, the FDA alleged that tobacco companies had apparently designed cigarettes that would deliver certain doses to the Federal Trade Commission (FTC) measuring machines but at the same time ensured that these cigarettes had sufficient "flexibility" in their delivery characteristics to enable consumers to extract the levels of nicotine that their bodies needed to sustain addiction (Regulations, 1995, 1996; Slade et al., 1995). In fact, under closer examination it became apparent that the engineering of many cigarettes actually fostered inadvertent self-administration of higher than advertised tar and nicotine dosages (Brandt, 1998; Miletich, 1998).

In 1994, Henningfield, Kozlowski, and Benowitz proposed a method for providing for cigarettes the equivalent of the labeling system for food. This proposal included a means to stratify cigarettes based on their maximum nicotine yields. It also included a category for cigarettes that contained and delivered insufficient nicotine to sustain addiction readily. A complementary paper suggested that over a period of one or two decades, all cigarettes be reduced in nicotine deliveries to meet those levels (Benowitz & Henningfield, 1994). This position was more thoroughly developed and proposed by the Council on Scientific Affairs of the American Medical Association (Henningfield et al., 1998).

In 1995, the National Cancer Institute (NCI), NIDA, and the FTC convened an expert meeting to review the existing cigarette-dose-rating system. Research data were pivotal in the committees' final conclusions, which included the following: "Actual human smoking is characterized by wide variations in smoking patterns, which result in wide variations in tar and nicotine exposure. Smokers who switch to lower tar and nicotine cigarettes frequently change their smoking behavior, which may negate potential health benefits" (NCI, 1996, p. vi). In early 1997, the state of Massachusetts held public hearings on a new cigarette-labeling approach that included the key recommendations of the NCI expert committee (Phillips, 1997).

The FTC has the ultimate responsibility for making the rules that will govern cigarette labeling, although FDA might ultimately assume this role if its regulation is upheld by the U.S. Supreme Court. Because the current rules were considered deficient by so many scientists and others, the FTC proposed new rules for discussion and comment. The rule-making process will undoubtedly be protracted, containing as it does opportunities for comment (FTC, 1997) and redrafting and then additional comment.

The FDA's efforts and the mounting pressure of litigation by state attorneys general to recover tobacco-disease-related health care costs from the tobacco companies brought a legal settlement with government agencies that would ultimately result in adoption of greater restrictions on tobacco marketing and compensation for diseases caused by tobacco. In November 1998, 46 state attorneys general and 4 tobacco companies settled the largest civil lawsuit in history for $206 billion dollars in an effort to resolve remaining state claims for the health care costs of treating sick smokers. Payments were scheduled to begin in 2000 and continue for 25 years, in exchange for an agreement that the states would drop any remaining lawsuits against the industry. The settlement also requires the industry to fund a foundation with $250 million over 10 years to support the study of programs to reduce underage tobacco use and the prevention of diseases associated with tobacco use. Some of the stated goals of that foundation are consistent with elements of the national tobacco settlement that failed in Congress during the summer of 1998, including counteradvertising campaigns, research to reduce underage tobacco use, and epidemiology studies to track youth smoking. In addition, the settlement will provide $1.45 billion for a national public education fund for tobacco control and place a variety of restrictions on advertising and marketing to youth (Greyelin, 1998).

However, public health advocates noted that the settlement was not necessarily a substitute for a comprehensive national tobacco control policy. It was missing several critical elements, including FDA authority to regulate tobacco products, adequate youth-access restrictions to tobacco, "look-back" penalties to hold industry accountable for the implementation of effective prevention programs, and restrictions of tobacco advertising in magazines with significant youth readership and marketing at retail outlets near schools. These deficiencies would severely limit the public health benefit of the settlement (Burns et al., 1997). Furthermore, the failure of the settlement to require states to fund their own tobacco control programs was viewed by many as a mechanism for the industry to sidestep the intent of a comprehensive tobacco control plan. Nevertheless, the very existence of the current settlement is certainly a harbinger of change and a testimony to the strength of the scientific basis of the conclusions drawn by public health policymakers.

Public health leaders are now urging states to enact legislation that would include state-specific countermarketing campaigns, including paid advertising; treatment for smokers, including underage smokers; community-based programs to prevent and reduce tobacco use; school-based programs; enforcement of laws that prohibit sale of tobacco to minors; and evaluation and monitoring to ensure that the programs are working effectively (e.g., Ad Hoc Group, 1998; National Center, 1997). It is clear that advocacy efforts on these topics must continue in the years to come, as the tobacco industry continues to exploit loopholes in regulatory oversight to unlease new marketing campaigns similar to those previously shown to be aimed at undermining cessation efforts to "keep them [smokers] in the franchise for as long as possible" (Slade & Henningfield, 1998).

TOBACCO AND NICOTINE RESEARCH

The scientific contributions to public policy in the area of tobacco regulation were significant. But this research did not emerge accidentally or piecemeal from the scientific community. Research on nicotine and tobacco has been heavily supported by NIDA and other government agencies as a matter of both policy and science. Effective leadership at many levels of government provided early financial support for research, and government dissemination of research results provided a wealth of reference material, insight, and direction that was invaluable to researchers who were conducting research on nicotine pharmacology and tobacco self-administration (e.g., Grabowski & Hall, 1985; Jarvik et al., 1977; Krasnegor, 1979).

The research discipline of behavioral pharmacology faced significant methodological challenges in its early work on nicotine and tobacco. Some initial studies, for example, focused on developing valid approaches to quantifying tobacco smoke self-administration in controlled environments with objective measures of puffing and expired air carbon monoxide assessment (Henningfield, Stitzer, & Griffiths, 1980). It then took several years of research to conclude solidly that cigarette smoking was an orderly form of drug self-administration controlled by many of the same factors that control other forms of drug self-administration. These factors included the amount (dose) of nicotine self-administered at a given time (e.g., Griffiths, Henningfield, & Bigelow, 1982), the time since the last opportunity to self-administer (deprivation; e.g., Griffiths & Henningfield, 1982), and the effects of other drugs on cigarette smoking (Mello, Mendelson, Sellers, & Kuehnle, 1980; Spealman & Goldberg, 1982).

It was also necessary to define the topography of cigarette-smoking behavior and the subtle changes in puffing and inhalation patterns critical to the individual's control over the actual level of nicotine self-administration (Gritz, Rose, & Jarvik, 1983; Herning, Jones, Bachman, & Mines, 1981; Kozlowski, Jarvik, & Gritz, 1975; Nemeth-Coslett & Griffiths, 1985). This work provided a rational basis for evaluation and application of nicotine-replacement medications. The first nicotine-replacement medication, nicotine polacrilex ("gum"), was developed by the Swedish drug company A. B. Leo and is currently marketed in the United States by SmithKline Beecham Consumer Healthcare. Basic researchers made many of the discoveries that led to the more efficacious use of nicotine gum (DHHS, 1991; Grabowski & Hall, 1985; Henningfield, Radzius, Cooper, & Clayton, 1990; Lucchesi, Schuster, & Emley, 1967; Sachs, 1995).

Research progressed rapidly on the characterization of nicotine's pharmacokinetics and pharmacodynamics (e.g., Benowitz, 1993). This work was critical not only in facilitating our understanding of the pharmacological basis of tobacco self-administration but also in providing tools for other investigators to use in their nicotine research. Useful nonhuman primate models of nicotine self-administration were developed and proved invaluable in the following decades of nicotine research (Rose & Corrigall, 1997). Meanwhile, Murray Jarvik and his colleagues laid the foundation for the modern era of studies of nicotine withdrawal, its treatment with nicotine medications, and the importance of combining behavioral strategies to enable the potential pharmacological benefits of nicotine-delivering medications to occur (Gritz et al., 1983; Rose, Jarvik, & Rose, 1984; Shiffman & Jarvik, 1976).

Over the years, the main focus of tobacco research has been on cigarette smoking, but some research also has been carried out on smokeless tobacco (e.g., Benowitz, Porchet, Sheiner, & Jacob, 1988; Fant, Henningfield, Nelson, & Pickworth, in press) and on cigars. Some of the currently popular hand-rolled, large cigars can contain more tobacco than a package of cigarettes and as much nicotine as two packages of cigarettes (Henningfield & Fant, in press; Henningfield, Hariharan, & Kozlowski, 1996).

CURRENT RESEARCH

Today, research on nicotine continues to press the frontiers of knowledge with new technologies and new strategies for making discoveries that will contribute to developing more effective prevention and treatment strategies. This includes studies of specific brain mechanisms and genetic determinants of the behavioral effects of nicotine administration, metabolism, and withdrawal in animals and humans (Perez-Stable, Herrera, Jacob, & Benowitz, 1998; Picciotto et al., 1998; Tyndale, Pianezza, & Sellers, 1998). Such research also provides the scientific basis for policy development and contributes to our general understanding of the nervous system and behavior as well.

Other areas of current research interest include the study of the reinforcing effects and mechanisms by which nicotine affects metabolism, performance, and mood (e.g., Epping-Jordan, Watkins, Koob, & Markou, 1998; Fowler, Volkow, Wang, Pappas, Logan, & MacGregor, 1996; Fowler et al., 1996; Perkins, Grobe, Caggiula, Wilson, & Stiller, 1997). Research continues on the characteristics of different nicotine delivery systems that affect the toxicity and cardiovascular effects of nicotine and how these factors add to the tobacco-dependence process (e.g., Benowitz, 1993). The interaction between the peripheral, sensory and centrally modulated pharmacological effects of nicotine and tobacco smoke are being explored to develop more effective treatments for nicotine-dependent smokers (Rose et al., 1994). Other efforts continue to refine our ability to diagnose nicotine dependence, thereby enabling effective individualized treatment (Hughes, 1994). Still other scientists are exploring applications of existing and new medications for the more efficacious treatment of nicotine dependence and withdrawal (Dewey et al., 1998; Hatsukami, Skoog, Allen, & Bliss, 1995; Henningfield & Slade, 1998). Finally, scientists are using a pocket-size computerized monitoring system to measure nicotine withdrawal, craving, and other behavior in the natural environment of cigarette smokers (Shiffman, Paty, Gnys, Kassel, & Elash, 1995).

This summary only scratches the surface of nicotine research. But it illustrates the rich diversity of the present nicotine research effort, and it brings to light the contributions that these investigators are making to further our understanding of nicotine addiction.

CURRENT PUBLIC HEALTH AND RESEARCH CHALLENGES

Increasing Tobacco Prevalence

Despite our increased understanding of nicotine dependence, the number of children and adolescents who have started smoking increased rapidly throughout the 1990s (Centers for Disease Control and Prevention, 1998). Already this has led to increased prevalence of smoking among young adults (age 18–25). This means that the overall adult prevalence of cigarette smoking, which has been relatively flat at about 25% to 26% since 1993, could begin its first solid increase in decades. This has occurred despite enormous efforts to help people quit smoking and the improved accessibility of medications to aid in those efforts.

The factors in this increase undoubtedly include effective youth-targeted marketing, such as R. J. Reynold's Joe Camel campaign, the relative price decline of cigarettes led by Philip Morris's discounting of its Marlboro brand in 1992, and the proliferation of even lower cost generic brands (Lynch & Bonnie, 1994; DHHS 1994). Another contributor is the remarkably easy access to cigarettes by youth enabled by lax regulations and enforcement before the 1997 implementation of the FDA tobacco regulation (Regulations, 1995, 1996). The FDA's proposal to reduce access to and cut the appeal for tobacco products among youth has substantial long-term promise, but many challenges remain both for those pursuing basic research and for those attempting to apply scientific findings at the public health level.

Pediatric Nicotine Dependence: Treatment and Prevention Efforts Are Lagging

One of the many challenges facing researchers and policymakers alike is the problem of pediatric nicotine dependence (Kessler, 1995; Slade, 1993). For example, we now understand that youths smoke not only to be "cool" but also because they frequently have made the transition to some level of nicotine addiction before adulthood (Lynch & Bonnie, 1994; DHHS, 1994). Unfortunately, these observations are yet to be matched by a comprehensive effort to develop and evaluate youth-targeted treatment programs, although the National Cancer Institute announced a request for research applications to stimulate research in this area in 1997. The oft-heard conclusion that kids don't want to quit smoking and will not accept treatment should be taken as a challenge for public-health-minded researchers to develop treatment approaches that will be both acceptable and effective. It should certainly not be a reason to give up. Almost certainly our efforts to develop treatments for nicotine-addicted youth would be enhanced through the increased involvement of psychologists with experience in child development, early learning, and child disabilities.

With respect to prevention and education efforts, it appears that marketers of tobacco and other consumer products have kept abreast of how to reach today's (and probably tomorrow's) young people, whereas research on the etiology of nicotine dependence and how to effectively intervene has lagged far behind. Also, behavioral and pharmacological treatments that have proven effective are out of the reach of many American citizens most in need of them (Centers for Disease Control and Prevention, 1991; Henningfield & Slade, 1998; Slade & Henningfield, 1998). The demographics show that tobacco dependence has become most prevalent among lower income Americans, who frequently have little or no health care coverage. Yet, until recently, one needed a prescription to obtain nicotine-replacement medications. Additionally, the cost of the smallest package of such medications was more than that of a carton of cigarettes. Such economic barriers have contributed to a situation in which it has been much easier to obtain the cigarettes that cause disease rather than the potentially lifesaving medications (Henningfield & Slade, 1998; Schuh & Henningfield, 1995; Slade & Henningfield, 1998). This situation was significantly altered by FDA's approval of nicotine gum and two of the nicotine transdermal patches for over-the-counter sales in 1996 (Shiffman et al., 1995, 1997). But we still have a long way to go before these medicines are as easily obtainable as cigarettes.

BASIC RESEARCH

Figure 1. The interrelationship among basic research, public health, and treatment access.

Marriage Proposal: Basic Research, Public Health, and Treatment Access

Figure 1 illustrates our conceptualization of the interrelationship among basic research, public health, and treatment access. Basic research is the foundation for much of what we do in the public health policy and medical care arenas. This has taken us far, but we must consider the fact that even if we had unlimited funds for treatment and prevention, limitations in our basic knowledge still leave us with treatment and prevention approaches that are ineffective or unacceptable to many individuals. Furthermore, even if effective, acceptable treatments are developed, if they can't be obtained by those who need them, then these treatments might as well not have been developed. Clearly, as a society, we need to devise creative ways to make it easier to obtain lifesaving behavioral and pharmacological treatments than it is to acquire the disease-causing substances. Finally, public health approaches are the key to motivating people to change their behavior, as well as to establish environments that support behavior change.

THE SCIENTIST'S ROLE

It can be very exciting for a scientist to have the opportunity to contribute to public health policy while attempting to meet the challenges posed by a difficult research area. There is clearly a lot yet to be accomplished. Over the past few decades, we have progressed from a rather crude understanding that tobacco use was probably motivated by various but poorly defined pharmacological actions of nicotine to our current understanding of the behavioral pharmacological interactions that lead to nicotine dependence, as well as the identification of specific receptors and endogenous neurotransmitters that underlie nicotine tolerance, physiological dependence, reinforcement, and other behavioral effects (Henningfield, Schuh, & Jarvik, 1995).

Research has brought us a long way, but there are still many challenges to face. With the increasing progress of research worldwide, we might be able to turn the tide on the most disastrous and preventable cause of death and disease facing us as we enter the twenty-first century. Basic research will continue to be critical and should remain the foundation of our treatment and prevention strategies, as well as for public health policy development.

REFERENCES

Ad Hoc Group. (1998). *Treating tobacco dependence in the U.S.: Ad hoc findings and recommendations*. Washington, DC: Center for the Advancement of Health.

Ando, K., & Yanagita, T. (1981). Cigarette smoking in Rhesus monkeys. *Psychopharmacology, 72*, 117–127.

Benowitz, N. L. (1993). Nicotine replacement therapy: What has been accomplished—Can we do better? *Drugs, 45*, 157–170.

Benowitz, N. L., Hall, S. M., Herning, R. I., Jacob, P., III, Jones, R. T., & Osman, A. (1983). Smokers of low-yield cigarettes do not consume less nicotine. *The New England Journal of Medicine, 309*, 139–142.

Benowitz, N. L., & Henningfield, J. E. (1994). Establishing a nicotine threshold for addiction. *The New England Journal of Medicine, 331*, 123–125.

Benowitz, N. L., Porchet, H., Sheiner, L., & Jacob, P. (1988). Nicotine absorption and cardiovascular effects with smokeless tobacco use: Comparison with cigarettes and nicotine gum. *Clinical Pharmacology and Therapeutics, 44*, 23–28.

Biskupic, J. (1999, April 27). Justices to decide FDA's role over tobacco. *The Wall Street Journal*, p. A4.

Brandt, A. L. (1998, October 9). Expert dissects cigarette for state's case. *The News Tribune*, p. B3.

Burns, D., Benowitz, N., Connolly, G. N., Cummings, K. M., Davis, R. M., Henningfield, J. E., Shopland, D. R., & Warner, K. E. (1997). What should be the elements of any settlement with the tobacco industry? *Tobacco Control, 6*, 1–4.

Centers for Disease Control and Prevention (1998). Selected cigarette smoking initiation and quitting behaviors among high school students—United States, 1997. *Morbidity and Mortality Weekly Report, 47*, 386–389.

Dewey, S. L., Morgan, A. E., Ashby, C. R., Jr., Horan, B., Kushner, S. A., & Logan, J. (1998). A novel strategy for the treatment of cocaine addiction. *Synapse, 30*, 119–129.

Epping-Jordan, P. P., Watkins, S. S., Koob, G. F., & Markou, A. (1998). Dramatic decreases in brain reward function during nicotine withdrawal. *Nature, 393*, 76.

Fagerstrom, K. O. (1978). Measuring degree of physical dependence to tobacco smoking with reference to individualization of treatment. *Addictive Behaviors, 3*, 235–241.

Fant, R. V., Henningfield, J. E., Nelson, R. A., & Pickworth, W. B. (in press).

Pharmacokinetics and pharmacodynamics of moist snuff in humans. *Tobacco Control*.

Federal Trade Commission. (1997). Cigarette testing: Request for public comment. *Federal Register, 62,* 48157–48163.

Fowler, J. S., Volkow, N. D., Wang, G. J., Pappas, N., Logan, J., & MacGregor, R. (1996). Inhibition of monoamine oxidase B in the brains of smokers. *Nature, 379,* 677–678.

Fowler, J. S., Volkow, N. D., Wang, G. J., Pappas, N., Logan, J., & Shea, C. (1996). Brain monoamine oxidase A inhibition in cigarette smokers. *Proceedings of the National Academy of Sciences, USA, 93,* 14065–14069.

Freedman, A. M. (1995, December 28). FTC will overhaul tar and nicotine ratings. *The Wall Street Journal,* pp. B1, B5.

Grabowski, J., & Hall, S. M. (Eds.). (1985). Pharmacological adjuncts in smoking cessation, (NIDA Research Monograph No. 53, DHHS Publication No. ADM 85-1333). Washington, DC: U.S. Government Printing Office.

Greyelin, M. (1998, November 16). Top tobacco firms agree to pay states up to $206 billion in 25 year settlement. *The Wall Street Journal,* p. A3.

Griffiths, R. R., & Henningfield, J. E. (1982). Experimental analysis of human cigarette smoking behavior. *Federation Proceedings, 41,* 234–240.

Griffiths, R. R., Henningfield, J. E., & Bigelow, G. E. (1982). Human cigarette smoking: Manipulation of number of puffs per bout, interbout interval and nicotine dose. *Journal of Pharmacology and Experimental Therapeutics, 220,* 256–265.

Gritz, E. R., Rose, J. E., & Jarvik, M. E. (1983). Regulation of tobacco smoke intake with paced cigarette presentation. *Pharmacology Biochemistry and Behavior, 18,* 457–462.

Hardman, J. G., Gilman, A. G., & Limbird, L. E. (Eds.). (1996). *Goodman and Gilman's pharmacological basis of therapeutics* (9th ed.). New York: McGraw-Hill.

Hatsukami, D., Skoog, K., Allen, S., & Bliss, R. (1995). Gender and the effects of different doses of nicotine gum on tobacco withdrawal symptoms. *Experimental and Clinical Psychopharmacology, 3,* 163–173.

Henningfield, J. E., Benowitz, N. L., Slade, J., Houston, T. P., Davis, R. M., & Deitchman, S. (1998). Reducing the addictiveness of cigarettes. *Tobacco Control, 7,* 281–293.

Henningfield, J. E., & Fant, R. V. (in press). Nicotine concentration, smoke pH and whole tobacco aqueous pH of some cigar brands and types popular in the United States. *Nicotine & Tobacco Research*.

Henningfield, J. E., Hariharan, M., & Kozlowski, L. T. (1996). Nicotine content and health risks of cigars. *Journal of the American Medical Association, 276,* 1857–1858.

Henningfield, J. E., Kozlowski, L. T., & Benowitz, N. L. (1994). A proposal to develop a meaningful labeling for cigarettes. *Journal of the American Medical Association, 272,* 312–314.

Henningfield, J. E., Radzius, A., Cooper, T. M., & Clayton, R. R. (1990). Drinking coffee and carbonated beverages blocks absorption of nicotine from nicotine polacrilex gum. *Journal of the American Medical Association, 264*, 1560–1564.

Henningfield, J. E., & Schuh, L. M. (1996). Pharmacology and markers: Nicotine pharmacology and addictive effects. In National Cancer Institute (Ed.), *The FTC cigarette test method for determining tar, nicotine, and carbon monoxide yields of U.S. cigarettes: Report of the NCI ad hoc committee* (NIH Publication No. 96-4028, pp. 113–126). Bethesda, MD: National Institutes of Health.

Henningfield, J. E., Schuh, L. M., & Jarvik, M. E. (1995). Pathophysiology of tobacco dependence. In F. E. Bloom & D. J. Kupfer (Eds.), *Psychopharmacology: The fourth generation of progress* (pp. 1715–1729). New York: Raven Press.

Henningfield, J. E., & Slade, J. (1998). Tobacco dependence medications: Public health and regulatory issue. *Food and Drug Law Journal, 53*, 75–114.

Henningfield, J. E., Stitzer, M. L., & Griffiths, R. R. (1980). Expired air carbon monoxide accumulation and elimination as a function of number of cigarettes smoked. *Addictive Behaviors, 5*, 265–272.

Herning, R. I., Jones, R. T., Bachman, J., & Mines, A. H. (1981). Puff volume increases when low-nicotine cigarettes are smoked. *British Medical Journal, 283*, 1–7.

Hughes, J. R. (1994). An algorithm for smoking cessation. *Archives of Family Medicine, 3*, 280–285.

Hurt, R. D., & Robinson, C. R. (1998). Prying open the door to the tobacco industry's secrets about nicotine. *Journal of the American Medical Association, 13*, 1173–1181.

Jarvik, M. E., Cullen, J. W., Gritz, E. R., Vogt, T. M., & West, L. J. (Eds.). (1977). *Research on smoking behavior* (NIDA Research Monograph No. 17, DHEW Publication No. ADM 78-581). Washington, DC: U.S. Government Printing Office.

Kessler, D. A. (1995). Nicotine addiction in young people. *The New England Journal of Medicine, 333*, 186–189.

Kessler, D. A., Witt, A. M., Barnett, P. S., Zeller, M. R., Natanblut, S. L., & Wilkenfeld, J. P. (1996). The Food and Drug Administration's regulation of tobacco products. *The New England Journal of Medicine, 335*, 988–994.

Kozlowski, L. T., Frecker, R. C., & Lei, H. (1982). Nicotine yields of cigarettes, plasma nicotine in smokers, and public health. *Preventive Medicine, 11*, 240–244.

Kozlowski, L. T., Jarvik, M. E., & Gritz, E. R. (1975). Nicotine regulation and cigarette smoking. *Clinical Pharmacology and Therapeutics, 17*, 93–97.

Krasnegor, N. A. (Ed.). (1979). *Cigarette smoking as a dependence process.* (NIDA Research Monograph No. 23, DHEW Publication No. ADM 79-800). Washington, DC: U.S. Government Printing Office.

Lucchesi, B. R., Schuster, C. R., & Emley, G. S. (1967). The role of nicotine as a determinant of cigarette smoking frequency in man with observations of certain cardiovascular effects associated with tobacco alkaloid. *Clinical Pharmacology and Therapeutics, 8,* 789–796.

Lynch, B. S., & Bonnie, R. J. (Eds.). (1994). *Growing up tobacco free: Preventing nicotine addiction in children and youths.* Washington, DC: National Academy Press.

Mello, N. K., Mendelson, J. H., Sellers, M. L., & Kuehnle, J. C. (1980). Effects of heroin self-administration on cigarette smoking. *Psychopharmacology, 67,* 45–52.

Miletich, S. (1998, October 9). A prof and his cigarette butts. *Seattle Post-Intelligence,* p. B1.

National Cancer Institute. (1996). *The FTC cigarette test method for determining tar, nicotine, and carbon monoxide yields of U.S. cigarettes: Report of the NCI ad hoc committee* (NIH Publication No. 96–4028). Bethesda, MD: National Institutes of Health.

National Center for Tobacco-Free Kids. (1997). Campaign for Tobacco Free-Kids. Contact Congress. Washington, DC: Author. Retrieved July 12, 1999 from the Worldwide Web: http://www.tobaccofreekids.org.

Nemeth-Coslett, R., & Griffiths, R. R. (1985). Effects of cigarette rod length on puff volume and carbon monoxide delivery in cigarette smokers. *Drug and Alcohol Dependence, 15,* 1–13.

Page, J. A. (1998). Federal regulation of tobacco products that treat tobacco dependence: Are the playing fields level? *Food and Drug Law Journal, 53,* 11–42.

Perez-Stable, E. J., Herrera, B., Jacob, P., III, & Benowitz, N. L. (1998). Nicotine metabolism intake in Black and White smokers. *Journal of the American Medical Association, 280,* 152–156.

Perkins, K. A., Grobe, J. E., Caggiula, A., Wilson, A. S., & Stiller, R. L. (1997). The reinforcing effects of low-dose nicotine nasal spray in humans. *Pharmacology Biochemistry and Behavior, 56,* 235–241.

Phillips, F. (1997, January 30). "Light" cigarette claims challenged. *The Boston Globe,* pp. B1, B9.

Picciotto, M. R., Zoli, M., Rimondini, R., Lena, C., Marubio, L. M., Pich, E. M., Fuxe, K., & Changeux, J.-P. (1998). Acetylcholine receptors containing the Beta-2 subunit are involved in the reinforcing properties of nicotine. *Nature, 391,* 173–177.

Regulations Restricting the Sale and Distribution of Cigarettes and Smokeless Tobacco to Protect Children and Adolescents; Final Rule, 21CFR & 801, et al. (1996).

Regulations Restricting the Sale and Distribution of Cigarettes and Smokeless Tobacco to Protect Children and Adolescents; Proposed Rule, 21CFR & 801, et al. (1995).

Rose, J. E., Behm, F. M., Westman, E. C., Levin, E. D., Stein, R. M., & Lane, J. D. (1994). Combined effects of nicotine and mecamylamine in attenuating smoking satisfaction. *Experimental and Clinical Psychopharmacology, 2,* 328–344.

Rose, J. E., & Corrigall, W. A. (1997). Nicotine self-administration in animals and humans: Similarities and differences. *Psychopharmacology, 130,* 28–40.

Rose, J. E., Jarvik, M. E., & Rose, K. D. (1984). Transdermal administration of nicotine. *Drug and Alcohol Dependence, 13,* 209–213.

Russell, M. A. H. (1978). Cigarette smoking: A dependence on high-nicotine boli. *Drug Metabolism Reviews, 8,* 29–57.

Sachs, D. P. L. (1995). Effectiveness of the 4-mg dose of nicotine polacrilex for the initial treatment of high-dependent smokers. *Archives of Internal Medicine, 155,* 1973–1980.

Schuh, L. M., & Henningfield, J. E. (1995). Nicotine replacement treatment and public health interventions: Toward a marriage of two approaches. In K. Slama (Ed.), *Tobacco and health: Proceedings of the Ninth World Conference on Tobacco and Health.* New York: Plenum.

Shiffman, S. M., Gitchell, J., Pinney, J. M., Burton, S. L., Kemper, K. E., & Lara, E. A. (1997). Public health benefit of over-the-counter nicotine medications. *Tobacco Control, 6,* 306–310.

Shiffman, S. M., & Jarvik, M. E. (1976). Smoking withdrawal symptoms in two weeks of abstinence. *Psychopharmacology, 50,* 35–39.

Shiffman, S. M., Paty, J. A., Gnys, M., Kassel, J. D., & Elash, C. (1995). Nicotine withdrawal in chippers and regular smokers: Subjective and cognitive effects. *Health Psychology, 14,* 301–309.

Slade, J. (1993). Adolescent nicotine use and dependence. *Adolescent Medicine: State of the Art Reviews, 4,* 305–320.

Slade, J., Bero, L. A., Hanauer, P., Barnes, D. E., & Glantz, S. A. (1995). Nicotine and addiction: The Brown and Williamson documents. *Journal of the American Medical Association, 274,* 225–233.

Slade, J., & Henningfield, J. E. (1998). Tobacco product regulation: Context and issues. *Food and Drug Law Journal, 53,* 43–74.

Spealman, R. D., & Goldberg, S. R. (1982). Maintenance of schedule-controlled behavior by intravenous injections of nicotine in squirrel monkeys. *Journal of Pharmacology and Experimental Therapeutics, 223,* 402–408.

Tyndale, R. F., Pianezza, M., & Sellers, E. M. (1998). Genetically deficient CYP2A6 provides protection against tobacco dependence and lowers cigarette consumption. Paper presented at the College on Problems of Drug Dependence 1998 Annual Meeting: Scottsdale, AZ.

U.S. Department of Health and Human Services. (1983). *Why people smoke cigarettes* (PHS Publication No. 83-50915). Rockville, MD: Author.

U.S. Department of Health and Human Services. (1988). *The health consequences of smoking: Nicotine addiction. A report of the surgeon general.* Washington, DC: U.S. Government Printing Office.

U.S. Department of Health and Human Services. (1991). *Drug abuse and drug abuse research: The third triennial report to Congress* (DHHS Publication No. ADM 91-1704). Rockville, MD: Author.

U.S. Department of Health and Human Services. (1994). *Preventing tobacco use among young people: A report of the surgeon general.* Washington, DC: U.S. Government Printing Office.

Warner, K. E. (1997). Cost effectiveness of smoking cessation therapies—interpretation of the evidence and implications for coverage. *Pharmacoeconomics, 11,* 538–549.

AUTHOR INDEX

Numbers in italics refer to listings in the reference sections.

Abbott, P. J., 267, *277*
Abbott, R. D., 230, *241*
Abelson, H., 54, *61*
Abelson, M. L., *183*
Aboagye, K., *212*
Abrahms, J. L., 261, *277*
Abramowitz, R. H., 339, 340, 346, *360*
Abrams, D., *280*
Abrams, E. J., *328*
Abrams, K., 195, *210*
Abumrad, N. N., *44*
Acierno, R., 376, *391*
Ackerman, S. P., 205, *211*
Ad Hoc Group, 435, *441*
Adalf, E. M., 74, *77*
Adams, E. H., 54, *61*
Adams, S. L., 83, *95*
Addalli, K., *41*
Adler, M.W., *324*
Ager, C. R., *145*
Ageton, S. S., 347, *360*
Aggleton, P., 310, 321, *325*
Agrawal, K. C., 351, *361*
Aguilar-Gaziola, S., *42*
Alberts, J. L., *283*
Alcoholics Anonymous, 252, 253, 254, *277*
Alheid, G., 179, *183*
Allan, L. G., 127, 129, 138, 143, *147*
Allen, L., 195, *210*
Allen, M. W., *320*
Allen, Susan, 315, *324, 327*
Allen, Sharon, 438, *442*
Allsop, S., 265, *277*
Alpert, R., *44*
Alterman, A. I., 171, *189, 263, 281, 422*
Altman, J., 227, 236, 246, 250, *277*
Amalric, M., 164, 168, *185*
Amaro, B. S., *212*
Amaro, H., 199, *210*
Amass, L., 156, *156*
American Psychiatric Association, 6, *35*, 161, 162, 173, *180, 201, 210, 369, 391*
Ames, L. B., 75, *76*
Amezucua, C., 205, *210*

Amit, Z., 151, *159*
Anda, R. F., 249, *277*
Anden, N.-E., 164, *183*
Anderson, E., *364*
Andersson, T., 336, *362*
Ando, K., 432, *441*
Andrews, D. W., 230, 238, 356, *359*
Andrews, J. A., 14, *41*
Angelo, W. A., 77, *83*
Anglin, D. M., 200, 202, 203, 207, *210, 213, 214, 399, 404, 422*
Angst, J., *43*
Anisman, H., *184*
Annis, H. M., 264, 265, *279*
Annon, J. J., 202, *213*
Annon, T. A., 203, *214*
Anslinger, H. J., *68*
Anstine, P. S., *158*
Antes, D., 403, *422*
Anthony, J. C., 8, *35, 44, 203, 214*
Anton, R. F., 337, *361*
Anton, S. F., 30, *41, 43, 427*
Appelbaum, A. H., 375, *393*
Appletree, R. L., 51, *62*
Arbiter, N., 410, *427*
Arendt, R., 200, *216*
Arkin, R. M., 290, 292, *303*
Arndt, I. D., 156, *158*
Arthur, M. W., 290, *308*
Asarnow, J. R., *145, 359*
Ase, J. M., *78*
Ashby, A. E., *441*
Ashby, C. R., Jr., *278*
Asher, S. R., 351, *357*
Astin, J. A., 128, *147*
Auerbach, J. D., 194, 209, *210*
Aultman, T. V., 311, *329*
Austin, G. A., 82, *95*
Ayllon, T., 257, *277*
Aytaclar, S., 22, *35*
Azrin, N. H., 154, *159, 257, 266, 277, 283, 376, 391*

Babor, T. F., *280*
Bachman, J., *443*

Bachman, J. G., 48, *61*, 131, *144*, 226, 227, *236*, *237*, *239*, 286, 295, 306, 308, 361

Badger, G. J., 156, *156*, *158*, 279, 280, 305, 393

Bain, G., *185*

Baker, A., 321, *324*

Baker, D. P., 347, 348, 357, *364*

Baker, E., 228, *237*, 289, 291, 293, 295, 296, 303, *304*, 375, 391

Baker, L., 333, *362*

Baker, S., 254, *281*

Baker, T. B., 138, 144

Balistreri, E., *429*

Ball, J. C., 321, *324*

Ball, S. A., *43*, 263, 278

Balshiem, M., 195, *210*

Balster, R. L., 163, *183*

Baltes, P. B., 337, *357*

Bamji, M., *328*

Bandura, A., 228, *237*, 257, 258, 277, 300, 303

Bane, A. L., *239*, 305

Banys, P., *283*

Baquet, C., 205, *213*

Barchas, J., 102, 109, *116*

Bardo, M. T., 23, *35*

Barkley, R. A., 18, *35*

Barley, W. D., 385, *391*

Barlow, D. H., 378, *391*

Barnes, D. E., 433, *445*

Barnes, G. M., *303*

Barnett, S. P., *443*

Barnhart, W. J., 175, *188*

Barocas, R., 335, *364*

Baron, R. M., 106, *113*

Barr, H., 403, *422*

Barr, H. M., 78, 83, *216*

Barrera, M., 25, *37*

Barrett, M. E., 202, *211*

Bartolo, R. D., 224, *241*, 287, *307*

Bass, A., 260, *279*

Bassford, T. L., 205, *211*

Bast, C. P., *306*

Bates, M. E., 126, *146*

Batson, H. W., 296, *303*

Baucher, H., *212*

Bauco, P., *180*

Baum, A., 191, 192, 194, 208, *210*

Bauman, K. E., 83, *95*, 226, *237*

Bavelas, A., 50, *61*

Baxter, R., 321, *328*

Beauvais, F., 295, 300, *307*

Beck, A. T., 261, 262, *277*, 284, 375, *391*

Becker, D. M., 192, *214*

Beckman, L. J., *210*

Beckwith, J. B., *200*, 210

Beel, A. J., 82, *95*

Befort, K., *186*

Behm, F. M., *282*, *444*

Belding, M. A., 260, *280*

Belknap, J. K., 31, *38*, 178, *186*

Bell, C., 205, *210*

Bell, R. M., 290, 292, 293, 294, 295, 303, 305

Bendriem, B., *44*, *242*

Benowitz, J. E., *433*

Benowitz, N. L., 434, 437, 438, *441*, *442*, 444

Bentler, P. M., 33, *41*, 131, *146*, 225, *241*, 295, 297, 306, 307, 335, 362

Bergman, J., 164, *180*

Bergman, L., 103, *113*

Berkanovic, E., 192, 193, *210*

Berke, J. D., *36*

Bernhardt, A. I., 415, *427*, *429*

Bero, L. A., 433, *445*

Berry, E., *238*

Berry, J. W., 199, *217*

Besalel, V. A., 376, *391*

Beschner, G., 396, *423*

Bess, V., *303*

Bessler, A., 18, *41*

Best, J. A., *305*

Bettes, B. A., 295, *303*

Beutler, L. E., 368, *391*

Beyer, C., *328*

Bhat, R. V., 176, *181*

Bhattacharya, G., 403, *425*

Bhave, G., 314, *324*

Bhavnagri, N., 349, *357*

Biase, V., 403, 407, *422*

Bickel, W. K., 153, 156, *156*, *158*, 260, 267, *279*, 280, *393*

Bickley, P. G., *364*

Biederman, J., 16, 18, 19, *35*, 36, *39*, *44*

Bigelow, C., *426*, 430

Bigelow, G. E., *36*, 149, *157*, 260, *283*, 436, 442

Bijil, R., *42*

Binson, D., 314, *325*

Biro, E., *187*

Bishop, E. S., 65–66, 66–67, 76
Bisighini, R. M., 278
Biskupic, J., 433, 441
Black, S. A., 198, 210
Blackson, R., 242
Blackson, T. C., 9, 23, 24, 25, 36, 43, 225, 240
Blaine, J., 278, 284
Blazer, D. G., 40
Bliss, R., 438, 442
Block, J., 25, 36, 100, 107, 109, 113, 116, 229, 241, 347, 364
Block, J. H., 25, 36, 113
Bloom, F. E., 99, 101, 109, 111, 114, 115, 163, 164, 168, 169, 173, 182, 185, 186, 189
Blossoman, J. B., 185
Blower, S. M., 321, 324
Bobat, R., 327
Bogaerts, J., 324
Bohman, M., 337, 358
Bolan, G., 327
Bonagura, N., 41
Bone, L. R., 192, 214
Bonnie, R. J., 438, 439, 443
Booth, C. L., 349, 358
Booth, M. W., 200, 202, 203, 206, 210, 213
Booth, R., 321, 324
Borduin, C. M., 273, 279, 337, 361, 393
Borges, G., 42
Botvin, E. M., 228, 237, 286, 289, 291, 293, 295, 296, 297, 303, 304
Botvin, G. J., 21, 43, 223, 226, 228, 237, 286, 288, 289, 291, 293, 294, 295, 296, 297, 303, 304, 305, 307, 375, 391
Bourdin, C. M., 376
Bowser, B., 201, 212, 328
Boyd-Franklin, N., 353, 358
Bozarth, M. A., 27, 36, 99, 101, 117, 172, 190
Brady, R., 430
Brahen, L. S., 376, 392
Branch, J. D., 351, 361
Brandt, A. L., 434, 441
Breese, G. R., 169, 182
Breiter, H. C., 29, 36
Bresford, S., 213
Breslau, N., 18, 37
Brett, P. J., 265, 279
Brigham, J., 25, 43, 226, 242

Britt, M. D., 168, 181
Britton, K. T., 169, 177, 184, 187
Bromberg, W., 69, 76
Bromet, E., 194, 211
Brondino, C. M., 273
Brondino, M. F., 279
Bronfenbrenner, U., 333, 336, 337, 338, 339, 345, 358
Brook, D. W., 25, 36, 229, 237, 341, 358
Brook, J. S., 14, 22, 25, 36, 38, 131, 144, 226, 229, 237, 341, 347, 351, 358
Brook, R. C., 403, 422
Brooks-Gunn, J., 19, 39
Brooner, R. K., 15, 20, 36, 159, 260, 280, 283
Brown, B., 416, 422
Brown, B. B., 348, 349, 358, 360, 364
Brown, B. S., 50, 62
Brown, C. H., 23, 40, 109, 115, 197, 212, 341, 361
Brown, D. R., 199, 211
Brown, J., 280
Brown, K. S., 305
Brown, S. A., 83, 95, 96
Brown, S. L., 185
Brown, Z. A., 216
Brown-Bryant, R., 191, 193, 211
Brownstein, J. N., 205, 211
Brunaghim, J., 112, 116
Brunn, J., 81, 95
Bry, B. H., 33, 36, 226, 230, 237, 335, 347, 351, 358
Bucholz, K. K., 43
Buck, K. J., 31, 38
Buck v. Bell, 72, 76
Buckley, P. F., 19, 37
Budde, D., 427
Budney, A. J., 158, 260, 266, 267, 273, 277, 279, 280, 393
Buis, M., 198, 214
Bukstein, O. G., 16, 37
Bullough, B., 195, 211
Bulterys, M., 320, 324
Burack, J., 107, 110, 116
Burdine, J. N., 192, 215
Burleson, J. A., 280
Burnam, A., 199, 199, 212
Burns, D., 435, 441
Burton, S. L., 445
Busch, M. P., 318, 329
Butchart, A. T., 293, 308

Butler, W. T., 320, *326*
Butzin, C. F., *429*
Byck, R., 255, *278, 279*

Cabral, H., *212*
Cacciola, J. S., 263, *281*
Cadoret, R. J., 9, 10, 16, 26, *37,* 101,
    114, 229, *237, 238*
Caetano, R., 198, *211*
Caggiula, A., 437, *444*
Caine, S. B., *41,* 164, 165, 166, 167,
    179, *181, 184, 185*
Cairns, R. B., 342, 344, *358*
Callahan, L., 208, *215*
Callan, A., 192, *212*
Calnan, M., 191, 194, *211*
Camacho, L. M., 415, *425, 429*
Cameron, T., 84, *95*
Campanelli, P. C., 293, *308*
Campbell, D. T., 382, *392*
Campbell, U. C., 151, *157*
Campos-Outcalt, D., 205, *211*
Canby, C., 230, *237*
Canino, G. J., *43*
Capaldi, D. M., 16, *37,* 349, 352, 354,
    359
Caplan, M. Z., 293, 304, 335, *359*
Capone, T., 376, *392*
Cappell, H., 130, 136, *147*
Caprara, G. V., 25, *43,* 226, *242*
Carael, M., *324*
Caravevo-Anduaga, J., *42*
Carboni, S., 177, *181*
Cardwell, J., 296, *303*
Carlson, J. N., 151, *158*
Carmelli, D., *37*
Carmona, G. N., 153, *157*
Carpenter, C. C. J., 318, *325*
Carr, A. C., 265, 277, 375, *393*
Carr, G. D., 163, *181*
Carr, J. N., 192, 200, *211*
Carran, D., *327*
Carroll, J. F. X., 396, *422*
Carroll, K. M., 254, 257, 263, *278, 280,*
    281, 427
Carroll, M. E., 151, 152, 153, 155, 156,
    157, 158, 159
Carseldine, D., 82, *96*
Carter, R., 195, *211*
Carter, V. A., 172, *185*
Caspi, A., 22, 24, *37*

Cassel, J., 231, *238*
Castanon, N., *43*
Castro, F. G., 200, *210*
Catalano, R. F., 131, 224, 230, 239, *241,*
    297, 306, 332, *361*
Catania, J. A., 311, 314, *325, 328*
Cauce, A. M., 340, 348, *359, 362*
Cavanaugh, E. R., 321, *327,* 403, *425*
Ceci, S. J., 337, 345, *358*
Celetano, D. D., *328*
Cellucci, T., 201, *213*
Centers for Disease Control and Preven-
    tion, *201, 211,* 310, 322, *325,*
    438, 439, *441*
Chamberlin, R., 343, *362*
Chambless, D. L., 368, *392*
Champion, L., 336, *363*
Chandler, M. J., 108, *116,* 342, *364*
Chang, G., *186*
Chappel, J. N., 253, *278*
Charlton, M., *42*
Chasnoff, I. J., 202, *211*
Chassin, L., 25, *37*
Chatham, L. R., 415, *425, 429*
Cheal, N., 205, *211*
Chen, D., *328*
Chen, K., 125, 126, 131, *145, 146*
Chesney, M., *323*
Chess, S., 23, 24, 26, *37, 43*
Chevron, E., 257, *280*
Chiauzzi, E. J., 25, *37*
Chilcoat, H. D., 18, *37*
Childress, A. R., 29, *37,* 227, *238,* 258,
    278, 376, *392, 393*
Chipman, S., 195, *215*
Choquette, K. A., 265, *282*
Christenson, B. A., 83, *95*
Christie, N., 81, *95*
Christman, D., *44*
Chu, S. Y., 317, *326*
Churgin, S., 224, *241,* 287, *307*
Chyao, A., *324*
Cicchetti, D., *37,* 98, 99, 100, 102, 103,
    105, 106, 107, 108, 109, 110,
    111, 112, *114, 116,* 332, 342,
    344, *359*
Claiming our Rights, *325*
Clark, D. B., 16, 17, *37*
Clarke, C., 260, *281*
Clarke, P. B. S., 172, *181*
Clarkin, J. F., 368, *391*
Clarren, S. K., *78*

Clayton, R., 229, *238*
Clayton, R. R., 437, *443*
Cleary, S. D., 24, *44*
Cloninger, C. R., 23, *38*, 337, *358*
Coates, T. J., 310, 311, 316, 318, 321, 323, *325, 327, 329*
Coatsworth, J. D., 333, 337, *359, 364*
Coen, K. M., 172, *181*
Coffin, V. L., 164, 167, *181*
Cohen, B., 322, *326*
Cohen, D. J., 332, *359*
Cohen, J., *38*, 131, 229, *238, 326*
Cohen, P., 14, 25, 36, *38, 144*, 194, *211*, 226, 229, 237, *238*, 341, 351, *358*
Cohen, R., *365, 366*
Cohen, S., 192, 194, 195, 197, *206*
Coie, J. D., 131, *145*, 332, 351, *357, 359*
Cole, M., 172, 179, *187, 188*
Cole, R., 350, *362*
Coletti, D., 295, *306*
Coletti, S. D., 414, *422, 425, 430*
Collins, A. C., 28, *41*, 176, *181*
Collins, F. L., 195, *214, 392*
Collins, J., *426*
Collins, R., 192, *216*, 295, *304*
Collins, R. J., 163, 168, *189*
Colliver, J., 11, *38*
Colon, H. M., 321, *326*
Comer, J. P., 346, 347, 348, *359*
Comer, S. D., 155, *157*
Compas, B. E., 131, *145*
Condelli, W., 404, 407, *422*
Cone, E. J., *159, 283*
Connolly, G. N., *441*
Connor, E. M., 320, *326*
Conrad, D. L., *185*
Cook, L., 169, *188*
Cooney, N., *280*
Cooper, M. M., 163, *181*
Cooper, T. M., 437, *443*
Coovadia, H. M., *327*
Cope, N., 192, 193, *211*
Corbin, J., 381, *394*
Corey, L. A., *40*
Corrigall, W. A., 172, *181*, 437, *444*
Costa, F. M., 13, 14, *38, 39*, 109, *115*, 131, *145*
Costa, M. S., 14
Costello, E. J., 342, *358*
Cottler, L. B., 404, *427*
Coustsoudis, A., *327*

Cox, W. M., 130, 131, *145, 147*
Crabbe, J. C., 31, *38, 43*
Craddock, S. G., 403, *425*
Cramer, J. C., 202, *211*
Crane, L., 198, *214*
Crawford, J. L., 287, *308*
Crawley, J. N., *189*
Creese, I., 164, *184*
Crick, N. R., 335, *360*
Crits-Christoph, P., 257, 263, 272, 278, *392*
Crouch, J. L., 273, *279*
Cullen, J. W., 432, *443*
Cummings, E. M., 112, *114*
Cummings, K. M., *441*
Cunningham, J. S., 172, *185*
Curran, D., *328*
Curran, J. W., 311, 327, *329*
Curran, P., 25, *37*
Curtis, S., *35*
Curtiss, M. A., 192, 201, *211*
Cushing, G., *116*
Cushing, J., *98*
Cutter, H. S., 265, *282*

Daghestani, A., 53, *62*
Dakof, G. A., 230, *241*
D'Amicao, E., *187*
Dancu, C., 372, *392*
Dani, J. A., 171, 176, *181*
Darling, L., *348*
Darling, N., 226, *242*, 349, *360, 364*
David, S. L., 233, *242*
Davies, M., 225, 226, *239*, 311, *328*
Davies, W. H., 97, *115*
Davis, J. M., 77, *83*
Davis, R. M., *441, 442*
Davis, W. M., 164, *181*
Davis-Hearn, M., 294, *307*
Dawes, M. A., 21, 22, *38, 238*
Dawson, D. A., 8, *39*
Day, L. E., 230, *241*
Dayan, P., 27, *43*
De La Rosa, M. R., 202, *211*
De Leon, G., 395, 396, 397, 398, 399, 403, 404, 407, 410, 411, 412, 414, 415, 418, *422, 423, 424, 425, 426, 427, 429, 430*
De Zoysa, I., *326*
DeCarlo, P., *329*
Deckel, A. W., 22, *38*

Deffenbacher, J. L., 226, *241*
DeGrandpre, R. J., 153, 156, *156*
Deitch, D., 254, *278*, 403, 414, *423*
Deitchman, S., *442*
Delaney, D. D., 280
Delaney, H. D., 267, *277*
DelBoca, F. K., 280
Demarsh, J., 229, *238*
Dembo, R., 229, *238*
Deminiere, J. M., 151, *158*, *189*
Deneau, G., *181*
Dennison, J., 312, 313, 329
Dent, C. W., 290, *308*
Des Jarlais, D. C., 310, *324*, *326*
Desai, S., *324*
Deshotel, K. D., *185*
Devor, E. J., 337, *359*
DeVry, J., 151, *157*
Dewey, S. L., *44*, *242*, 250, *278*, 438,
        441
deWitt, H., 153, *159*, 164, 172, *181*, *188*
Dexter, L. A., *61*
DeZoysa, I., *326*
DiAmico, D., 249, *282*
Diana, M., 177, *181*
Diaz, J., 179, *181*
Diaz, T., 228, *237*, 293, 295, 296, 297,
        303, *304*, *305*, 317, 321, *326*
Diaz, Y. E., *327*
DiChiara, G., 27, *42*, *43*, 169, 179, *182*,
        187
Dicker, B. J., 232, *238*
DiClemente, C. C., 193, 206, *212*, 272,
        273, *281*, *282*
DiClemente, R. J., 311, *326*
Dielman, T. E., 293, *308*
Dierich, A., *186*
DiGiuseppe, R., 261, *279*
DiMarco, A., 249, *282*
Dinges, M. M., 226, *238*
Dinwiddie, S. H., *43*
Dishion, R. J., *359*
Dishion, T. J., 226, 229, 230, *238*, 335,
        349, 350, 352, 354, 356, *363*
Divane, W. T., 153, *159*
Dixon, J., 321, *324*
Dixon, R. D., 84, *95*
Dodge, K. A., 335, 350, *360*
Doherty, W. J., 229, *241*
Dolcini, M. M., 314, *325*
Dole, V. P., 246, 248, *278*
Dolle, P., *186*

Donaldson, R. V., 292, 304
Dondero, T. J., *327*
Donham, R., *158*, 280
Donnermeyer, J. F., 226, *241*
Donohew, R. L., 23, *35*
Donohue, B., 376, *391*
Donovan, D., 280
Donovan, J. E., 13, 14, *38*, *39*, 109, *115*
Donovan, W. J., 68, *77*
Donselaar, I., 151, *157*
Dorn, N., 224, *238*, 287, *304*
Dornbusch, S. M., 335, 348, *364*
Douglas, J. M., *327*
Droba, M., *422*
Drucker, E., 316, 321, *326*, *328*
Drug Enforcement Administration, *61*
Dryfoos, J. G., 294, *304*
Duman, R. S., *42*
Dunkel-Schetter, C., 198, *217*
Dunn, G., *283*
Dunne, M. P., *43*
DuPont, R. L., 50, *61*, *62*
Durbin, D., 349, *360*
Dusenbury, L., 228, *237*, 289, 295, 296,
        303, *304*, *305*, 375, *391*
Dushiminimana, A., *324*
Dwyer, J. H., 240, *241*, 306, *363*

Eaves, L., *43*
Ebert, L., 206, *215*
Eckhardt, M. J., 171, *182*
Eddy, N. B., 64, 67, *77*
Edelbrock, C. S., 18, *35*
Edlund, M. J., 14, 15, 16, 17, *40*
Egeland, B., 99, *117*
Eggert, L. L., 232
Ehrhardt, A. A., 322, *326*
Ehrman, R., 376, *392*, *393*
Ehrman, R. N., 258, *278*
Eikelboom, R., 172, *188*
Eisen, S. A., *43*
Eisenberg, L., 109, *115*
Eiumtrakol, S., *328*
Elash, C., 438, *445*
Elder, G. H ., 342, *358*
Elderton, E. M., 72, *77*
Eliany, M., 85, *95*
Elkin, I., 382, *392*
Ellickson, P. L., 290, 292, 293, 294, 295,
        303, *305*
Elliott, D. S., 13, *38*, 347, 351, *360*

Elliott, R., 371, *393*
Ellis, A., 261, 262, *279, 392*
Emery, G., 375, *391*
Emley, G. S., 437
Enerback, C., *182*
Eng, A., 291, 293, 304, *304*
Eng, E., 192, *212*
Eng, T. R., 320, *326*
Engel, J. A., 169, 171, *182, 185*
English, C., 260, *281*
Engstrom, J., 198
Ennett, S. T., 226, *237*
Ensminger, M., 23, 40, 109, 115, 197,
     212, 341, 351, 361
Enstrom, J., *214*
Epping-Jordan, P. P., 437, *441*
Epstein, J. A., 226, 237, 293, 295, 296,
     297, *304*
Epstein, J. L., 347, 348, *360*
Erickson, D. J., 17, *41*
Erickson, P. G., 74, *77*
Esch, R. A., 156, *156*
Escobedo, L. G., *277*
Eshleman, S., *40, 115*
Espinoza, R., 205, *210*
Esposito, R. U., 172, *182, 185*
Estey, J., *327*
Ettenberg, A., 168, 169, *182, 184, 186*
Etz, K., 11, *38*
Evans, J., 195, *216*
Evans, R. I., 228, *239*, 288, 289, 290,
     305
Everingham, S. M. S., *282*
Everitt, B. J., 180, *182, 277*
Exner, T. M., 322, *326*

Fabsitz, R. R., *37*
Fagerstrom, K. O., 432, *441*
Fahlke, C., *182*
Fainsilber-Katz, L., 349, *361*
Fairhurst, S. K., *212*
Falciglia, G., 192, *216*
Fant, R. V., 437, *441, 442*
Faraone, S. V., 16, 18, 19, *35, 36, 39, 43*
Farge, E., *212*
Farkas, K., 200, *216*
Farmer, M. E., *42*
Farquhar, J. W., 231, *239*
Farrington, D., 13, *41*
Farris, B., 195, *212*
Federal Trade Commission, *442*

Fehrs, L. T., *326*
Feinberg, M. B., *326*
Felch, L. J., 260, *283*
Felix-Ortiz, M., 10, *42*, 300, *307*
Fenton, B., *42*
Ferguson, P., 197, *212*
Fernandez, T., *365*
Ferraro, K. R., 84, *95*
Ferrence, R. G., 199, *212*
Ferrer, H. P., *145*
Ferris, J., 85, 86, 87, 88, 91, *95*
Fibiger, H. C., 163, 164, 181, *187*
Figert, A. E., 194, 209, *210*
Filazzola, A. D., 291, 293, *303*
File, S. E., *182*
Fillmore, K. M., 85, *95*, 131, *145*
Fischer, M., 18, *35*
Fischl, M. A., *325*
Fischman, M. W., 44
Fishbein, M., 290, *305, 327*
Fisher, K., 206, *215*
Fisher, L. A., 83, *95*
Fishman, H. C., 333, 337, *362*
Fitzgerald, H. E., 34, 45, 97, 98, 101,
     106, 108, *115, 117*
Fitzgerald, J., *37, 238*
Fitzgerald, L. W., *42*
Fitzpatrick, M. L., 203, *212*
Flay, B. R., 131, *146*, 241, *288*, 294,
     305, 363
Fletcher, A. C., 226, *242*, 348, *364*
Fletcher, B. W., 424, *427*
Flora, J. A., 231, *239, 242*
Florscheim, P., 348, *360*
Flygaare, B., 153, *158*
Flynn, B. S., *305*
Foa, E. B., 371, *392*
Foerg, F., *158*, 260, 267, 280, *393*
Foerg, J. R., *158*
Fogg, C. P., 335, 341, 347, *364*
Foley, J., *328*
Foltin, R. W., 44, *157*
Fong, G. T., 311, *327*
Ford, D. H., 128, 129, 130, 135, *145*,
     342, *360*
Fortenberry, J. D., 14, *38*
Fortmann, S. P., *239*
Foster-Johnson, L., 14, *39*
Fountain, D., preface
Fowler, D. E., *185*
Fowler, J. S., 44, *242*, 437, *442*
Franco, H., 396, *424, 429*

Frank, A., 278
Frank, D. A., 200, 201, *212*
Frank, R. A., *182*
Frank, R. G., 40
Franklin, K. B. J., 172, *181*
Frecker, R. C., 433, *443*
Freedman, A. M., 434, *442*
Freeman, R. G., 72, 77
Frei, N. R., 192, *211*
Freimuth, V., 195, *212*
French, D. C., 335, *359*
Freud, S., 255, 279
Fried, V. M., 191, 195, *214*
Friedle, N. M., 164, *185*
Friedman, A. S., 230, *239*
Friedman, P., *326*
Friedman, S. R., 321, 324, *326*
Frisher, M., *326*
Fritschi, O., 260, *281*
Froehlich, J. C., 171, *182*
Fromme, K., 84, 95
Frost, R., 410, *426*
Frye, G. D., 169, *182*
Fullilove, M. T., 201, 207, *212*
Fullilove, R. E., 201, *212*

Gable, R. S., 122, 133, *145*
Galanter, M., 273, *279*, 396, 415, *424*,
    427, 429
Galavotti, C., *327*
Gallagher, P. E., 20, 43
Gamshadzahi, A., 205, *213*
Garbarino, J., 339, 340, 346, *360*
Garcia, M., 229, *238*
Garcia-Jetton, J., 18, 39
Gardi, J., *187*
Gardner, C. O., 40
Garfield, F., 410, *426*
Garfield, S. L., 368, *392*
Garmezy, N., 108, 110, *114, 115*, 332,
    333, 334, *360, 362, 363*
Garrett, C., 260, *281*
Gary, L. E., 199, *211*
Gastfriend, D. R., 36
Gatley, S. J., 44
Gawin, F. H., 250, 257, 263, 278, 279,
    427
Gawin, R. M., 278
Gelber, R., *326*
Geller, B. M., *305*
Genevie, L., *211*

Genung, L., *238*
George, J. R., *327*
Gerard, K., 203, *212*
Gerhardt, C. A., 131, *145*
Gerkin, A. E., 84, 95
Gerstein, D. R., *424*
Gessa, G. L., 175, 177, *181, 182, 187*
Getreu, A., *238*
Gfroerer, J. C., 38, 54, 61, 229, *239*
Giampino, T., *41*
Giancola, P. R., 38
Giesbrecht, N., 85, 95
Gilchrist, L. D., 291, 293, *305, 308*
Gilman, A. G., 432, *442*
Ginacola, P. R., 21, 22
Ginzburg, H. M., 321, *327, 425*
Giovino, G. A., *277*
Gitchell, J., *445*
Glancy, L. J., 16, 37
Glantz, M. D., 9, 10, 11, 14, 23, 24, 38,
    98, 101, 102, 107, *115*, 120, 131,
    226, 227, 239, 261, 262, 263,
    279, 281
Glantz, R. S., *145*
Glantz, S. A., 433, *445*
Glass, S., 319, *329*
Glautier, S., *277*
Glenn, N., 195, *212*
Glick, M., 104, *117*
Glick, S. D., 151, *158*
Glider, P., 410, 414, *427*
Glowa, J. R., *189*
Gnys, M., 438, *445*
Goddard, H. H., 72, 77
Godley, M., 257, *277*, 376, *391*
Goeders, N. E., 151, *157*, 163, 168, *182*,
    184
Goehl, L., 260, *281*
Gold, L. H., 172, *185, 188*
Goldberg, C. J., 295, *304*
Goldberg, D., *326*
Goldberg, J., 43
Goldberg, S. R., 168, *182*, 436, *445*
Goldfried, M. R., 377, *392*
Golding, J., *199, 212*
Golding, J. M., *145*
Goldman, A. I., 294, *307*
Goldman, M. S., 83, 95
Goldring, E., 404, *427*
Goldstein, R., 287, *308*
Gollub, R. I., 36
Golub, A., 11, 39

Gomberg, E. S. L., 33, *45*, 105, 108, *117*
Gombeski, W., 195, *212*
Gonzalez, N., 340, *362*
Good, P. I., 163, *181*
Goodman, J. M., 36
Goodman, R. M., 192, *215*
Goodstadt, M. S., 286, 287, *305*
Goodwin, F. K., *42*, *116*
Gordon, A. S., 25, 36, 71, 72, 77, 226, 229, *237*, 341, 351, *358*
Gordon, J. R., 253, 264–265, *281*, *426*
Gordon, L. T., 263, *278*
Gorman, K., 151, *159*
Gorman-Smith, D., 348, *360*, *366*
Gorski, T. T., 264, *279*
Gottfredson, D., 347, 351, 355, *360*, *361*
Gottlieb, N. H., 192, 194, 195, 197, 206, *213*
Gottman, J. M., 349, *361*
Goulet, J., *42*
Grabowski, J., *282*, 432, 436, 437, *442*
Grady, D. K., 178, *186*
Grady, K., 293, *304*, 335, *359*
Graham, J. M., 264, *277*
Graham, J. W., 228, *239*, 292, *304*
Graham, K., 265, *279*
Graham, S., 205, *217*
Graham, W. F., 415, *424*
Grant, B. F., 8, *39*
Grant, K. A., 171, *183*
Grant, T. M., *216*
Gray, J., 195, *210*
Green, L., 192, 194, 195, 197, 206, *213*
Green, P., 84, *95*
Greenbaum, P. E., 14, *39*
Greenberg, L. S., 371, *393*
Greene, A. D., 199, *211*
Greene, M. H., 51, *62*
Greene, R. W., *39*
Greener, J., 418, *427*
Greenfield, A. D., 67, *78*
Greenspan, S., 335, *364*
Grella, C. E., 202, *213*
Greylin, M., 435, *442*
Griffen, A., 403, *424*
Griffin, K. W., 226, *237*
Griffin, M. L., 201, *213*
Griffiths, R. R., 149, *157*, 436, *442*, *444*
Griffon, N., *181*
Grisel, J. E., 178, *186*
Gritz, E. R., 432, 436, 437, *442*, *443*
Groat, H., 202, *213*

Grobe, J. E., 249, *282*, 437, *444*
Grober, J. S., 293, *304*
Groseclose, S. L., 316, 321, 326, *329*
Gross, S., 201, *212*
Grosskurth, H., 320, *326*
Grove, K., 340, *362*
Gruber, V., *324*
Gruenwald, A. B., 321, *326*
Grunberg, N., 191, 192, 194, 208, *210*
Guerin, G. F., 151, *157*
Guerra, N. G., 335, 353, *361*, *366*
Guerri, C., *182*
Guitart, X., *42*
Gustafson, R., *95*
Gutzwiller, F., *325*
Guydish, J., *328*

Habinmana, P., *324*
Haefely, W., *187*
Hagan H., *326*
Haggard, H. W., 75, *77*
Haggerty, K. P., 231, *240*
Haggerty, R. J., 108, *115*, 236, *240*
Hahesy, T., *44*
Haignere, C., 311, *328*
Hall, H., 192, 193, *211*
Hall, S. M., 260, *279*, *281*, *283*, 432, 436, 437, *441*, *442*
Hall, W., 94, *96*
Hamaidan, Y., 175, *187*
Hamburg, B. A., 11, *39*
Hamilton, N. L., *422*
Hammer, S., *325*
Hammond, M. C., *185*
Hanauer, P., 433, *445*
Hand, T. T., *189*
Haney, M., 151, *158*
Hanoune, J., *186*
Hansen, J. J., 156, *159*
Hansen, T., 53, *62*
Hansen, W. B., 228, *239*, *240*, *241*, 290, 292, 297, *304*, *305*, *306*, *363*
Hard, E., *182*
Hardman, J. G., 432, *442*
Hargreaves, M. K., 205, *213*
Hargreaves, W. A., 260, *279*
Hariharan, M., 437, *442*
Harle, M., *429*
Harrell, J. P., 199, *216*
Harrington, N. G., 23, *35*
Harrison, C. D., *429*

Harrison, D., 195, *213*
Harrison, E. R., 294, *303*
Harrison, I., 195, *213*
Hartmark, C., *38*
Harts, J., 171, *182*
Harwood, H. J., preface, *425*
Haskell, W. L., *239*
Hatch, J., 192, *212*
Hatch, M., 195, *215*
Hatsukami, D. K., 153, *158*, 438, *442*
Haughton, E., 257, *277*
Hausam, D. D., *185*
Hauth, A. C., *327*
Havis, J., *239*
Hawke, J., *418*
Hawke, M. L., *426*
Hawkins, J. D., 131, 135, *145*, 226, 230,
    231, *239*, *240*, *241*, 297, *306*,
    332, *334*, *335*, *359*, *361*
Hayashida, M., 171, *189*
Haynes-Sanstad, K., *329*
Hays, R., *327*
Hays, S., *316*
Hayward, W., 67, 77
Health Canada, 83, *96*
Hearst, N., *325*
Hearst-Ikeda, D. E., 371, *392*
Heath, A. C., *43*
Heather, N., 321, *324*
Hebert, K. M., *185*
Heckhausen, J. D., 128, *145*
Hegedus, A. M., 17, *38*
Heidbreder, C., 174, *188*
Heimer, L., 179, *183*
Heinemann, S., 171, 176, *181*
Heinrichs, S. C., 164, 167, 177, 178,
    179, *181*, *183*, *184*, *187*
Helzer, J. E., 404, *427*
Hembree, E., 372, *392*
Hen, R., *43*
Henderson, C. R., 343, 350, *362*
Henderson, D., 198, *216*
Henderson, R. K., 376, *392*
Henggeler, S. W., 273, 279, 282, 337,
    361, 376, *393*
Henn, F., *44*
Henningfield, J. E., 149, *157*, 434, 436,
    437, 438, 439, 440, *441*, *442*,
    445
Henningfield, L. T., *433*
Henriksen, S. J., *186*
Hepler, N. A., 295, *306*

Herman, J. L., 372, *393*
Herman-Shipley, N., 198, *214*
Hernandez, M., 198, *217*
Herning, R. I., *441*, *443*
Herrera, B., 437, *444*
Herting, J. R., 232, *238*
Hervis, O. E., 340, *365*, *366*
Hesselbrock, V., 22, *38*
Heyser, C. J., 171, 179, *183*, *188*
Heywood, E., 229, *238*
Hibbard, J., 195, 206, *213*
Higgins, D. L., 318, *327*
Higgins, G. A., 171, *188*
Higgins, S. T., 153, 154, 156, *156*, *158*,
    159, 260, 266, 267, 273, 277,
    279, 280, 283, 376, *393*
Hill, D. R., 194, 195, *216*
Hiller, M. L., 418, *426*
Hilton, M. E., 86, 89, *96*
Hilton, R., *430*
Hinde, R., 106, *115*
Hinden, B. R., 131, *145*
Hindin, R., 410, *426*, *430*
Hines, M. H., 224, *240*, 288, *306*
Hinson, R. E., 127, *147*
Hintzen, P., 317, *328*
Hiraga, Y., 340, *362*
Hirky, A. E., 25, *44*
Hiroi, N., *43*
Hirsch, B. J., 206, *213*
Hirsch, M. S., *325*
Hirschi, T., 229, *240*
Hitzemann, R., *44*, *242*
Hoerger, B. A., *158*
Hoffman, A., 287, *308*
Hoffman, P. L., 171, *182*, *183*
Hohenstein, J. M., *281*
Holderness, C. C., 19, *39*
Hole, A. V., 258, *278*
Holland, S., 403, 407, *424*
Hollander, J. R., 260, *280*
Hollon, S. D., *393*
Holmberg, S. D., 321, *327*
Holmes, O. W., 72
Holt, P., 321, *324*
Homel, R., 82, *96*
Hooper, R. M., *429*
Hoover, D. R., *328*
Hope, B. T., 129, *146*
Hops, H., 14
Horan, B., *278*, *441*
Horger, B. A., 151

Horton, A. M., 424, *427*
Hossain, M., *429*
Hough, R., 199, *217*
Houston, T. P., *442*
Hovland, C. I., 223, *239*
Hser, Y.-I., 200, 202, 203, 206, *210, 213,*
    399, 404, 422
Hsieh, S., 203, *214*
Hu, D. J., 320, *327*
Huang, S. C., *41*
Hubbard, R. L., 321, *327, 399, 403, 404,*
    407, 410, 422, 425
Hubbell, C. L., 171, *183*
Hubner, C. B., *183*
Hudes, E. S., *324*
Hughes, J. R., 156, *158, 280, 393, 438,*
    443
Hughes, M., 8, *40, 44, 115*
Hughes, P. H., 414, *422, 425, 430*
Hughes, W. K., *158*
Huizinga, D., 13, *38, 347, 360*
Hulthe, P., *182*
Humfleet, G. L., *281*
Humphrey, R. H., 225, *237*
Hunt, L. G., 62
Hunter, G. A., 177, *187*
Hurd, P., 290, 292, *306*
Hurd, Y. L., 164, 166, 171, *183, 189*
Hurt, R. D., 433, *443*
Husband, S. D., 260, *280, 321, 328*
Huston-Lyons, D., *183*
Hyman, S. E., 28, *36, 39, 99, 109, 115,*
    175, 178, 183
Hyytia, P., *41, 169, 170, 171, 179, 183,*
    189

Ickovics, J., 192, 193, 194, 208, 209, *216*
Ifill-Williams, M., 296, *304*
Iguchi, M. Y., 260, *280, 283, 321, 328*
Imber, S. D., *392*
Imperato, A., 169, *182*
Inciardi, J. A., 414, 415, *424, 426, 427,*
    429
Inderbitzin, L. B., 19, *43*
Inguar, D. H., *185*
Institute of Medicine, 97, 99, *115, 128,*
    145, 172, 183, 332, 361, 399,
    404
Irwell, L., 72, *77*
Israel, B. A., 205, 206, *213*

Jacks, S. D., *282*
Jackson, B. B., 194, 195, 198, *216*
Jackson, J. S., 206, *215*
Jacob, P. III, 437, *441, 444*
Jacobs, D., *306*
Jacobsen, D. M., *325*
Jacobson, N. S., *393*
Jacoby, C., 293, *304, 335, 359*
Jaffe, A. J., *186, 394*
Jaffe, H., *327*
Jaffe, J. H., 129, 131, *145*
Jaggi, J., *238*
Jahnke, W., 11, *39*
Jainchill, N., 395, 403, 404, 407, 410,
    411, 412, 414, 418, *423, 424,*
    425, 426, 427, 429
James, S., 195, *213*
James-Ortiz, S., 295, 296, 303, *304, 375,*
    391
Jamner-Metzger, E., 396, 415, 424, *427,*
    429
Janis, I. L., 223, *239*
Jarvik, M. E., 432, 436, 437, 440, *442,*
    443, 444, 445
Jatlow, P., *278*
Jatlow, P. I., *279*
Jauregui, J., *189*
Jaycox, L. H., 372, *392*
Jellinek, E. M., 74–75, *77*
Jemmott, J. B., 311, *327*
Jemmott, L. S., 311, *327*
Jenkins, E., 205, *210*
Jessor, J., *347*
Jessor, R., 13, 14, *38, 39, 107, 109, 115,*
    132, 145, 228, 229, 239, 300,
    306, 341, 347, 361
Jessor, S. L., 13, *39, 107, 115, 228, 229,*
    239, 300, 306
Jetton, J. G., *35*
Jimenez, A., *329*
Joe, G. W., 418, *427*
Johannessen, K., *182*
Johanson, C. E., 163, *183, 188*
Johnson, B., 191, 194, *211, 429*
Johnson, B. D., 11, *39*
Johnson, C. A., 240, *241, 290, 303, 306*
Johnson, J., 38, 199, *210*
Johnson, J. L., 110, *115*
Johnson, L. D., *361*
Johnson, R. S., 201, *213*
Johnson, S. B., *392*

Johnson, V., 25, 42, 125, 127, 131, *145,*
     146, 229, *241*
Johnson, W., *329*
Johnston, L. D., 48, *61,* 131, *144,* 225,
     227, *236, 237, 239,* 286, 295,
     306, 308
Jolliffe, N., 74–75, *77*
Jones, E., 246, *280*
Jones, M., *425*
Jones, R. T., *441, 443*
Jones, T. S., 317, *326, 329*
Jops, H., *41*
Jovanovic, B., *329*
Judd, L. I., *42*
Julesz, J., *187*
Justice, J. B., Jr., 164, 175, *186*

Kadden, R. K., 263, *280*
Kadlec, K., 171, *186*
Kagan, J., 105, *115*
Kahen, V., 349, *361*
Kahn, J. G., 310, 311, *327*
Kalichman, S. C., *327*
Kalish, M. L., *327*
Kamb, M. L., 311, 320, *327*
Kamenga, M. C., *326*
Kamien, J. B., 164, *180*
Kaminer, Y., 16, *37*
Kandel, D. B., 11, *39,* 97, 98, 99, 109,
     115, 125, 126, 131, *145, 146,*
     225, 226, 229, *239, 240,* 335,
     351, *361*
Kantor, J. M., *36*
Kaplan, B., 105, *117*
Kaplan, D., 84, *95*
Kaplan, E. H., 321, *327*
Kaplan, H. B., 14, *40,* 132, *145, 146,*
     229, *240,* 300, *306*
Kaplan, J., 81, *96*
Kaplan, S., *211*
Karp, R. J., *77, 83*
Kasckow, J. W., 19, *43*
Kaskutas, L., 86, 89, *96*
Kassel, J. D., 438, *445*
Kassen, S., *38*
Kassler, S. W., *329*
Kassler, W. J., *326*
Katon, R. N., *61*
Katori, R. N., 50
Katzenstein, D. A., *325*
Kautz, J., *212*

Kavaliers, M., 178, *183*
Kavanaugh, K., 230, *238*
Kazdin, A. E., 375, *393*
Kearney, A. L., 224, *240,* 288, *306*
Kearns, I., 82, *96*
Kegeles, S. M., 316, 324, *327*
Keith, S. J., *42*
Keith, T. Z., *364*
Kelder, S. H., 294, *307*
Kellam, S. G., 23, *40,* 109, *115,* 197,
     212, 341, 351, *361*
Keller, R. W., 151, *158*
Kelley, H. H., 223, *239*
Kelly, J. A., 311, 315, *327*
Kelly, L. M., 199, *216*
Kemper, K. E., *445*
Kendall, P. C., 353, *366*
Kendler, K. S., 30, 31, *40*
Kennard, D., 403, *425*
Kennedy, D. N., *36*
Kenny, D. A., 106, *113*
Kernberg, O. F., 375, *393*
Kerner, J., 295, 296, *303, 304*
Kerr, J. S., 25, *40*
Kerrigan, J., 53, *62*
Kessler, D., *429*
Kessler, D. A., 431, 432, 433, 439, *443*
Kessler, R., *42*
Kessler, R. C., 8, 14, 15, 16, 17, *40, 43,*
     44, 103, 107, *115,* 229, *240,*
     335, *361*
Keyes, S., 25, 36, 98, *113*
Keynes, J. M., *77*
Khalsa, J. H., 202, *211*
Khantzian, E. J., 15, 24, *40,* 257, *280*
Kidorf, M., 15, 36, 260, *280*
Kieffer, B. L., *186*
Kiely, K., *35*
Kihara, M., *325*
Killen, J., 290, 293, 306, 307, *308*
Kim, A., 396, *424*
Kim, S., 224, *240,* 288, 295, *306*
Kin, A., *429*
Kinder, B. N., 287, *306*
King, O. E., 340, *366*
King, R., 320, *327*
King, V. L., 15, 36, 260
Kippax, S., *325*
Kirisci, L., 21, 22, 35, *38,* 226, *238*
Kiseler, P., *326*
Kitchen, I., *186*
Kitchen, S., 53, *62*

Kitzman, H., 350, *362*
Klassen, A. D., 197, *217*
Kleber, H. D., *279*
Kleigman, R., 200, *216*
Klein, R. G., 18, 19, *40, 41*
Kleinbaum, D., *213*
Kleinman, J., 191, 195, *214*
Kleinman, S. H., 318, *329*
Klerman, G. L., 257, *280*
Kliegman, R., 201
Klinger, E., 130, *145*
Klinger, M., 97, *115*
Klokke, A., *326*
Klonoff, P., 164, *187*
Klorman, R., 112, *116*
Knight, K., 415, 418, *425, 426, 429*
Koch, G. G., 83, *95*
Koenigsberg, H. W., 375, *393*
Koepke, D., *305*
Koerner, K., 377, *393*
Kogan, E. S., 376, *391*
Kohlenberg, R. J., 375, *393*
Kokkinidis, L., *184*
Kolody, B., *42*, 199, *217*
Komro, K. A., *158*
Konde-Lule, J. K., 310, *327*
Koob, G. F., 26, 27, 28, *40*, 101, 109,
        115, 162, 163, 164, 165, 168,
        169, 170, 171, 172, 173, 174,
        175, 176, 177, 178, 179, 180,
        *181, 182, 183, 184, 185, 186,
        187, 188, 189, 437, 441*
Koopman, C., 311, *328*
Kooyman, M., 398, 407, *425*
Kopstein, A., *38*
Kordal, N., 376, *392*
Korelitz, J. J., 318, *329*
Korenman, S., 102, 109, *116*
Korner, P., *280*
Kornetsky, C., 163, 172, *182, 183, 185*
Kosten, T. A., 30, *41*
Kosten, T. R., *43, 279*
Kosterman, R., 231, *240*
Kozel, B. A., 54
Kozel, N. J., 50, 51, *61, 62*
Kozlowski, L. T., 434, 437, *442, 443*
Kozlowski, N. L., *433*
Kraemer, H. C., 11, *39*, 231, *242*
Krank, M. D., 127, *147*
Kranzler, H. R., 250, 280, 337, *361*
Kranzler, T. R., *43*
Krasnegor, N. A., 432, 436, *443*

Kressel, D., 410, 418, *424, 425, 426*
Kreutzer, T., 99, *117*
Krieger, N., 195, 199, 209, *214*
Kuehnle, J. C., 436, *443*
Kuhn, L., 320, *327*
Kuig, V. L., *280*
Kumpfer, K. L., 229, 231, 232, *238, 240*
Kurawige, J. B., *324*
Kurtines, W. M., 230, 242, 268, 283,
        333, 337, 340, 357, 359, 364,
        365, 366, 394
Kushner, M. G., 17, *41*
Kushner, S. A., 278, *441*
Kwapil, T. R., 19

Labouvie, E. W., 13, 25, *42, 44*, 126,
        127, 131, 140, *146*
Lac, S. T., 151, 152, 155, *157*
Lacan, G., *41*
Lacelle, G., 151, *159*
Lacey, L., 198, 205, *214*
Ladd, G. W., 349, *362, 363*
LaDue, R. A., 78
Lake, J. R., 172, 178, *185*
Lamb, R. J., 260, *280*
Lambert, G., *328*
Lamborn, S. D., 335, 349, 358, *364*
Lammers, C. H., *181*
Lampinen, T., *329*
Landress, H. J., 202, 211, *425*
Lane, J. D., 168, *182, 444*
Lane, S., 42
Lange, U., 201, *213*
Lange, W. R., 321, *324*
LaPadula, M., 18, *41*
LaPerriere, A., 364, *394*
Lapinski, K., *391*
Lara, E. A., *445*
Last, J. M., 48, *62*
Latham, C. J., *283*
Latkin, C. A., *328*
Lawless, B. A., *185*
Le, H. T., 164, *184*
Leacock, S., 70, *77*
Leaf, P. J., *40*
Lee, S., 347, *360*
LeFevour, A., 174, *188*
LeFevre, R., 151, *158*
Leftwich, M. J. T., 195, *214*
Legault, M., *185*
Lehman, D. A., 175, *188*

Lei, H., 433, *443*
Leigh, B. C., 83, 84, 96
Leigh, W. A., 192, 199, *214*
Leino, E. V., *145*
Le Meur, M., *186*
Le Moal, M., 129, 137, *147*, 151, *158*, 175, *189*
Lemon, J., 94, 96
Lena, C., *444*
Lennox, T., 197, *212*
Lenz, K. M., 192, *211*
Lerner, J. V., 23, 25, *41*, *43*, 351, *362*
Lerner, R. M., 342, *360*
Leshner, A. I., xiii, 332, *362*
LeSieur, K., 349, *362*
Lesnick, L., 17, *38*
Lettieri, D., 197, *212*
Lettieri, D. J., 120, 131, *146*, 197, *212*
Leutz, W. A., 206, *214*
Lévesque, D., *181*
Levin, E. D., *282*, *444*
Levine, D. M., 192, 205, *214*
Levy, D. E., 84, 95
Lewin, K., 50, 62
Lewis, B. F., 407, 410, 411, 412, *426*
Lewis, R. A., 230, *240*
Lewisohn, P. M., 14, *41*
Lex, B. W., 197, 200, *214*
Li, F., 349, *359*
Li, T.-K., 171, *182*
Liberty, H. J., *429*
Liddle, H. A., 230, *241*
Liebson, I., 260, 260, *283*
Liese, B. S., 261, *277*
Lifschutz, H., *429*
Liljegren, S., 25, *37*
Liljequist, S., 169, *185*
Lillie-Blanton, M., 203, 207, *214*
Limbird, L. E., 432, *442*
Lin, N., *43*
Lindan, C. P., *324*
Linehan, M. M., 369, 377, *393*
Link, B. G., *426*, *429*
Liu, J., 17, *40*
Livermore, G., Preface
Locke, B. Z., *42*, *116*
Lockwood, D., 414, 415, *426*
Loeb, P., 260, *279*
Loeber, R., 13, *41*
Logan, J., *44*, *278*, 437, *441*, *442*
London, J., 321, *329*
Long, B., 145

Longshore, D., 204, 206, *214*
Lorang, M. T., 164, 175, *186*, *189*
Love, C. T., 415, *428*
Lovinger, D. M., *185*
Lovinger, P. L., 171
Lowe, R. A., 317, *328*
Lowery, R. C., 84, 95
Lown, E. A., 201, *212*
Lu, S., 22, 35
Luborsky, L., 257, 260, *278*, *281*, *284*
Lucas, J. J., *43*
Lucchesi, B. R., *437*
Ludford, J. P., 399, 404, *428*
Luepker, R. V., 290, 292, 293, 294, *303*, *306*, *307*
Lumeng, L., 171, *182*
Lundy, B. Z., *305*
Luo, C.-C., 327
Lurie, P., 316, 317, 321, *328*
Luthar, S., 98, 107, 110, 111, *114*, *116*
Lynch, B. S., 438, 439, *443*
Lynch, M., 108, 110, *114*
Lyness, W. H., 164, *185*
Lyons, M. J., *43*

Maccari, S., 151, *158*
Maccoby, N., 290, 293, *306*, *308*
MacGregor, R., 437, *442*
MacKinnon, D. P., 230, 232, *240*, *241*, 297, *306*, *363*
MacNicholl, T. A., 71, 78
Maddahian, E., 33, *41*, 295, *306*, *307*, *362*
Madden, G. J., 156, *156*
Madden, P. A. F., *43*
Maddhian, E., 335
Magnusson, D., 103, *113*, 336, 345, *362*
Majumdar, S. K., *283*
Makadon, H. J., *329*
Makris, N., *36*
Makuc, D. M., 191, 195, *214*
Maldonado, R., *186*
Malgady, R. G., 226, *237*
Malin, D. H., 172, 178, *185*
Malloy, P., 18, *41*
Mancilla, Y., 337, *365*
Mandel, W., *328*
Manderscheid, R. W., *116*
Manfredi, C., 198, 205, *213*, *214*
Mann, B. J., 273, *279*
Mannuzza, S., 18, *41*

Marcus, A., *198*, *214*

Mardsen, M. E., *326*, *425*

Marglin, S. H., *183*

Margolis, R. D., *268*, *269*, *271*, *271*, *272*, *280*

Margulies, R. Z., *229*, *240*, *335*, *361*

Marihuana Problems, *68*, *78*

Marin, B. V. O., *197*, *215*

Marin, G., *198*, *215*

Markides, K. S., *198*, *210*

Markman, H. J., *145*, *359*

Markou, A., *41*, *162*, *164*, *172*, *175*, *179*, *180*, *184*, *185*, *188*, *189*, *277*, *437*, *441*

Marks, M. J., *28*, *41*, *176*, *181*

Marlatt, G. A., *84*, *96*, *253*, *257*, *261*, *262*, *263*, *264*, *280*, *281*, *426*

Marquis, P., *199*, *215*

Marsden, M. E., *321*, *327*

Martes, M.-P., *181*

Martin, A. C., *25*

Martin, C. S., *21*, *25*, *36*, *38*

Martin, J. C., *216*

Martin, N. G., *43*

Martin, S. S., *429*

Martz, K. A., *182*

Marubo, L. M., *444*

Mason, C. A., *340*, *350*, *362*

Masse, L. C., *23*, *24*, *41*

Mast, E. E., *277*

Masten, A. S., *109*, *116*, *334*, *362*

Masterson, J., *403*, *428*

MATCH Research Group, *382*, *393*

Matheson, P. B., *328*

Mathew, R. T., *36*

Matos, T. D., *321*, *326*

Matthes, H. W. D., *168*, *186*

Mattheson, P. B., *320*

Mattox, A. J., *155*, *159*, *186*

Maude-Griffin, P. M., *272*, *281*

Maughan, B., *336*, *363*

May, S., *153*, *157*

Maynard, J., *72*

Mayor's Committee on Marihuana, *68*, *78*

Mayrock, D. E., *216*

McAdoo, H. P., *353*, *362*

McAlister, A. L., *205*, *210*, *290*, *292*, *293*, *306*, *307*, *308*

McCance, E., *263*, *278*

McClary, A., *71*, *78*

McCord, J., *23*, *24*, *41*, *229*, *240*

McCord, W., *229*, *240*

McCourt, W., *261*, *263*, *279*, *281*

McCully, J., *127*, *147*

McCusker, J., *410*

McElgin, W., *37*

McGee, L., *131*, *146*

McGlothlin, W. H., *202*, *210*

McGonagle, K. A., *14*, *15*, *16*, *17*, *40*, *115*

McGrath, J. E., *50*, *62*

McGue, M., *337*, *362*

McGuigan, K., *294*, *305*

McGuire, W. J., *228*, *240*, *289*, *300*, *306*, *307*

McInerney, J. F., *261*, *279*

McKay, J. R., *263*, *281*

McKendrick, L., *429*

McKeon, P., *33*, *36*, *226*, *237*, *335*, *358*

McKinnon, J. A., *358*

McKinnon, M. A., *349*

McKusker, J., *411*, *412*, *426*, *430*

McLean, A. R., *321*, *324*

McLellan, A. T., *156*, *158*, *257*, *260*, *281*, *284*, *376*, *392*, *393*, *416*, *422*

McLeroy, K. R., *192*, *193*, *207*, *215*

McMahon, P. T., *376*, *391*

McMahon, R. J., *226*, *229*, *230*, *238*, *351*, *363*

McMahon, T., *98*, *116*

McNamara, G., *23*, *25*, *44*

McNeil, D. W., *83*, *95*

Meadows, E. A., *372*, *392*

Meek, P., *283*

Mehta, R., *17*, *42*

Meisch, R. A., *153*, *157*

Melaga, W. P., *28*, *41*

MeLeroy, K. R., *214*

Mello, N. K., *436*, *443*

Melnick, G., *410*, *418*, *424*, *426*

Melton, G. B., *273*, *279*, *337*, *361*

Menard, S., *13*, *38*

Mendelsohn, J. H., *436*

Mendelson, J. H., *443*

Menzaghi, F., *177*, *179*, *183*, *184*

Merikangas, K. R., *17*, *29*, *42*, *43*

Messina, M., *429*

Metcalf's Coca Wine (Advertisement), *64*, *78*

Mettzger, W., *195*, *212*

Metzger, D., *156*, *158*

Mewcomb, M., *33*

Meyer, J. M., *43*
Meyer, R. E., *186*
Meyers, C. P., *324*
Meyers, R., 257, 277, 376, *391*
Mezzich, A. C., 21, 24, 36, 38, 109, *117*
Michael, R. P., *188*
Mick, E., 16, 19, 35, *36*
Milberger, S., *35*
Milburn, N. G., 199, *211*
Miletich, S. A., 434, *444*
Millby, J. B., 260, *281*
Miller, J., 54, *61*
Miller, J. G., 128, *146*
Miller, J. Y., 131, 226, 239, 297, 306,
    332, *361*
Miller, T. Q., 131, *146*
Miller, W. R., 272, 273, 281, 373, *393*
Millman, R. B., 291, *303*
Mills, F. G., 169, *187*
Mills, T., 311, *328*
Millstein, R., *44*
Mines, A. H., *443*
Minnes, S., 200, *216*
Minuchin, S., 333, 337, *362*
Mirin, S. M., 201, *213*
Mittlemark, M. B., 239, *305*
Moffitt, T. E., 22, *37*
Mogil, J. S., 178, *186*
Mokotoff, E., 317, *326*
Molina, B. S. G., 18, 25, 37, *42*
Moller, K. A., 77, *83*
Molnar, B., *42*
Molraard, V., *240*
Montague, P. E., 27, *43*
Montgomery, E., 205, *217*
Monti, P., *280*
Montoya, I. D., 159, *283*
Moodley, D., *327*
Moolten, M., *185*
Moore, B. A., 267, *277*
Moore, K. E., 164, *185*
Moore, M., *327*
Moore, T., *212*
Mora, E. M., 198, *211*
Morales, E. S., 321, *329*
Moras, K., *394*
Morgan, A. E., *278*
Morles, E. S., *321*
Morral, A. R., 260, *280*
Morris, J. A., *217*
Morris, K. A., 180, *182*
Morris, N., 195, *215*

Moses, F., 171, *183*
Moses, H. D., 34, 45, 98, *117*
Mosha, F., *326*
Mosher, W., 205, *217*
Moskowitz, J., 224, 241, 287, *307*
Moss, H. B., 21, 25, 36, 38, 43, 226, *242*
Motola, A. H. D., *182*
Motoyoshi, M., *145*
Mounts, N., 335, 349, 358, *364*
Mozley, D., *238*
Mozley, P. D., *37*
Mrazek, P., 236, *240*
Mueller, C. W., 23, *35*
Muhlin, G., *211*
Munford, M., 195, *215*
Murray, D. M., 290, 294, 303, 306,
    307
Murray, E. J., 365, *394*
Murray, G. F., 74, *77*
Musto, D. F., 62, 65, 66, 68, 69, *78*
Mwijarubi, E., *326*
Myers, C. P., *321*

Nadaud, D., *189*
Nader, M. A., 153, 155, *158*
Nader, P. R., *217*
Naranjo, C., 171, *186*
Narrow, W. E., *116*
Natanblut, S. L., *443*
Nathan, P. E., 25, 26, *42*
National Cancer Institute, 433, 434, 439,
    444
National Center for Tobacco-Free Kids,
    435, *444*
National Commission on AIDS, 321, *328*
National Institute on Drug Abuse, 48,
    50, 54, 55, 62, 192, 215, 225,
    226, 240, 378, 380, 381, 394,
    396, 416, *432*
National Institute of Mental Health, 380,
    381, 382, 394, *404*
National Institutes of Health, 310, 320,
    328
National Institutes of Health Consensus
    Development Program, 248, *281*
Nawrocki, P., *324*
Neal, A., 202, *213*
Neale, M. C., *40*
Needle, R. H., 228, *241*
Negus, S. S., 168, *186*
Neighbors, B., 16, *37*

Neighbors, H. W., 194, 195, 206, *215*
Neiss, R., 140, *146*
Nelson, C. B., 14, 15, 16, 17, 40, *44,*
    115
Nelson, K. E., *328*
Nelson, M., 85, 95
Nelson, R. A., 437, *441*
Nemeth-Coslett, R., 436, *444*
Neri, R. L., 425, *430*
Nesselroade, J. R., 337, *357*
Nestler, E. J., 28, *42, 43,* 99, 109, *115,*
    129, 136, *146,* 174, 175, 178,
    186, *188*
Newcomb, M. D., 10, *41, 42,* 131, *146,*
    147, 225, 226, *241,* 295, 297,
    300, *306, 307,* 335, 341, 347,
    358, 362
Newman, C. F., 261, *277*
Newman, D. L., 22, *37*
Newman, F. L., 385, *394*
Ng-Mak, D., 426, *429*
Nich, C., 263, *278*
Nicholas, L. J., 232, *238*
Nomura, C., 226, *237*
North, R. A., 169, *182*
Nowinsky, J., 254, *281*
Nsengumuremyi, F., *324*
Nuechterlein, K., *116*
Nutlock, L., 426, *429*
Nutt, D., *277*
Nygaard, S. L., 152, *157*
Nyswander, M., 246, 248, *278*

O'Brien, A., 180, *182*
O'Brien, C. P., *37,* 171, *189,* 238, 246,
    257, 263, *281, 282,* 284, 376,
    392, 393, 422
O'Donnell, J., 230, *241*
Oetting, E. R., 226, *238, 241,* 295, 300,
    307
O'Farrell, T. J., 265, *282*
Office of National Drug Control Policy,
    244, 274, 275, *282*
Ogborne, A. C., 70, *78*
O'Gorman, T. W., 229, *238*
Oldham, J. M., 20, *43*
Olds, D. L., 343, 350, *362*
O'Malley, P. M., 48, *61,* 131, *144,* 225,
    227, *237, 239,* 286, 295, *306,*
    308, 361
O'Malley, S. S., *42,* 177, *186, 394*

Onken, L. S., *278*
O'Reilly, K. R., 317, *327, 328*
Oreland, L., *185*
Oretti, R., *277*
Orlandi, M., *286*
Ortiz, J., 28, *42*
Orzi, F., 27, *42*
Osman, A., *441*
O'Sullivan, M. J., *326*
Oswald, L. M., *282*
Otero-Sabogal, R., 197, *215*
Ouellet, L., *329*
Oziemkowska, M. J., *328*

Padian, N., 319, *329*
Page, J. A., 432, *444*
Palley, C. S., 224, *241,* 287, *307*
Pandina, R. J., 25, 33, 36, *42,* 123, 126,
    127, 131, 135, *146,* 226, 229,
    237, *241,* 335, *358*
Pantin, H. M., 335, 353, 355, 356, 363,
    365
Pape, N. E., 287, *306*
Pappas, N., *44,* 437, *442*
Parke, R. D., 349, *357, 363*
Parkinson, D., 194, *211*
Parsons, C. H., 175, 176
Parsons, L. H., *41,* 186, *189*
Paschall, M., 202, *215*
Pasternak, G. W., *186*
Patterson, G. R., 229, *241,* 335, 349,
    350, 351, 352, *359, 363*
Patterson, T. L., *217*
Patton, T., *430*
Paty, J. A., 438, *445*
Pau, C.-P., *327*
Paul, S. M., *189*
Pauls, D., *43*
Paulson, S. E., 348, *363*
Pauly, J. R., 176, *181*
Payza, K., *185*
Pearson, H. W., 120, 131, *146*
Pearson, J., *305*
Pearson, K., 72, *77*
Pechacek, T. F., 290, *306*
Peck, H., *211*
Pedraza, M., 335, *358*
Pelham, W. E., 18, 21, 38, *42*
Pellborn, L. A., *185*
Pellini, E. J., 67, *78*
Pentel, P. R., 153, *158*

Pentz, M. A., 228, 231, 232, 240, 241, 293, 306, 307, 335, 363
Perez-Stable, E. J., 195, 198, 215, 437, 444
Perez-Vidal, A., 340, 364, 365, 366, 394
Perkins, K. A., 249, 282, 437, 444
Perlis, T. E., 430
Pernow, B., 185
Perry, C. L., 152, 158, 290, 292, 293, 294, 306, 307, 308
Perry, K., 371, 392
Peters, J., 429
Peters, R., 351, 363
Peterson, J., 325
Petraitis, J., 131, 135
Petrila, A., 14, 39
Petronis, K. R., 8, 35
Pettit, H. O., 168, 169, 182, 184, 186, 189
Pfeffer, A. O., 169, 171, 186, 187
Pfister, K., 35
Phelps, M. E., 41
Phillips, A. G., 163, 181
Phillips, F., 434, 444
Phillips, K. A., 318, 326, 328
Phillips, M., 265, 277
Phinney, J., 196, 215
Pianezza, M., 437, 445
Piazza, P. V., 129, 137, 147, 151, 158
Picciotto, M. R., 437, 444
Pich, E. M., 177, 179, 184, 186, 444
Pickens, R. W., 9, 39, 120, 131, 145, 226, 239, 337, 362
Pickles, A., 336, 363
Pickrel, S. G., 273, 279, 282
Pickworth, W. B., 437, 441
Piemme, T. E., 50, 61
Piercy, F. P., 230, 240
Pillow, D., 25, 37
Pincus, T., 208, 215
Pinkham, L., 404, 425
Pinney, J. M., 445
Piot, P., 317, 328
Piotrowski, N. A., 283
Pirie, P., 294, 307
Pistis, M., 177, 181
Platt, J. J., 321, 328
Pliner, V., 328
Plotsky, P. M., 189
Poling, J., 43
Pollak, S., 112, 116
Pommering, T., 182

Pompi, K. F., 414, 426
Pontieri, F. E., 27, 42, 43, 179, 187
Pope, K. S., 392
Porchet, H. L., 437, 441
Portoghese, P. S., 186
Poulos, C. X., 130, 136, 147
Predy, P. A., 184
Preisig, M. A., 42
Prescott, C. A., 30, 40
Price, R. H., 332, 335, 336, 363
Prochaska, J. O., 212, 272, 282
Profilet, S. M., 349, 362
Project MATCH Research Group, 254, 263, 282
Prusoff, B. A., 43, 427
Przybeck, T. R., 8, 42

Quan, J., 319, 329
Quazi, Q. H., 77, 83
Quinton, D., 336, 363

Rabe, C., 171, 183
Raber, J., 186
Rachal, J. V., 321, 327
Radzius, A., 437, 443
Rae, D. S., 42, 116
Rahav, M., 415, 426, 429
Rakowski, W., 192, 215
Raleigh, M. J., 41
Ramey, S. L., 145
Ramirez, A., 205, 210, 212
Ramsay, D. S., 129, 131, 138, 139, 143, 147
Ramsey, N. F., 158, 159
Randels, S. P., 78
Rassnick, S., 169, 171, 177, 178, 179, 184, 187
Raucci, J., 151, 158
Rawleigh, J. M., 156, 159
Rayfield, M. A., 327
Reedt, l., 328
Reese, H. W., 337, 357
Regier, D. A., 14, 15, 17, 19, 42, 103, 116
Regulations Restricting the Sale and Distribution of Cigarettes and Smokeless Tobacco, 432, 433, 434, 438, 444
Reich, W., 427

Reid, J. B., 229, *241*, 349, 350, *363*
Reid, L. D., 177, *183*, *187*
Reilly, P. M., *281*, *283*
Reingold, A. L., 321, 328
Reiss, D., 332, 335, 336, *363*
Reivich, M., *37*, *238*
Remington, P. L., 277
Renard, C. G., *422*
Renick, N. I., 291, 293, 303, 304
Resnicow, K., 294, 307
Reynolds, S., *429*
Rhoades, H. M., 282
Rhodes, F., *327*
Rhodes, J. E., 206, *215*
Rice, L. N., 371, *393*
Richards, G., 169, *187*
Richards, L. G., 287, 307
Richters, J. E., 98, 109, *116*
Riley, E., *187*
Rimondini, R., *444*
Ring, J., 199, *215*
Ringwalt, C., 202, *215*
Rio, A., *365*, *366*
Rioden, D. R., *36*
Ripka, G. V., 282
Risch, N., *42*
Rivas-Vasquez, A., *365*, *366*
Rivera, J. J., *426*, *429*
Rizley, R., 109, *114*
Robbins, S. J., 258, 278
Robbins, T. W., 180, *182*
Roberts, A. J., *41*, 171, 179, *183*, *187*
Roberts, C. S., 164
Roberts, D., 350, *366*
Roberts, D. C. S., *187*
Roberts, R. E., 14, *41*
Robertson, E., 11, *38*
Robinette, D., *37*
Robins, L. N., 8, 13, *42*, 341, *363*, 404, *427*
Robinson, C. R., 433, *443*
Robinson, J., 350, *362*
Robledo, P., 179, *184*
Robles, R. R., 321, *326*
Rocha, B. A., 28, *42*
Rode, S., *394*
Rodefer, J. S., 153, 155, 156, 157, *159*
Rodin, J., 192, 193, 194, 208, 209, *216*
Rodriquez deFonseca, F., *186*
Roemhild, H. J., 290, *303*
Rogers, J., *327*
Rogers, T. C., 69, 76

Rogillio, R. B., *185*
Rogosch, F. A., 102, 110, 111, *114*
Rohsenow, D. J., 96
Roizen, R., 84, 96
Rojas, M., *38*
Rolf, J., 109, *116*
Rolfs, R., *329*
Roll, S., 272
Rollnick, S., *281*, 373, *393*
Rompre, P. P., 27, *45*
Room, R., 96
Roques, B. P., 186
Rose, J. E., 247, 249, 282, 436, 437, 438, *442*, *444*
Rose, K. D., 437
Rose-Krasnor, L., 349, *358*
Rosen, B. R., *36*
Rosenthal, M. S., 397, 398, 403, *424*
Rosett, H. L., 70, 75, 78
Rosman, B. L., 333, *362*
Ross, R., 407, *426*
Rossetti, Z. L., 175, 177, *181*, *187*
Rossi, J. S., *212*
Rossner, S., 185
Rotgers, F., 282
Rotheram-Borus, M. J., 311, 328
Rounsaville, B. J., 20, 30, *41*, *42*, *43*, 186, 257, 263, 278, 279, 280, 394, 404, *427*
Rouse, B. A., *61*, 202, *211*
Rowan-Szal, G., 418, *427*
Rozelle, R. M., *238*, 305
Rubin, B. R., 23, 40, 109, *115*, 341, *361*
Rubin, K. H., 349, *358*
Rubio-Stipec, M., *43*
Rugg, D. L., *327*
Rupp, J. W., *217*
Rush, A. J., 375, *391*
Russell, M. A. H., 172, *187*, 432, *445*
Russell, R. R., 163, *181*
Russo, N. F., 199, *210*
Rustin, T., 282
Rutherford, M. J., 263, *281*
Rutter, M., 98, 105, 108, 111, *115*, *116*, *117*, 332, 335, 336, 344, *363*, *364*
Ryan, T. M., 203, *210*
Rychtarik, R. G., 273, *281*
Rydell, C. P., 282
Ryder, J., *429*

Sabogal, F., 198, *215*

Sachs, D. P. L., 437, *444*
Sacks, J., 415, *427, 429*
Sacks, S., 415, *427, 429, 430*
Sadeghi, K. G., 169, *187*
Sahai, H., 321, *326*
Salber, E., 205, 206, *216*
Saler, G., *427*
Salgado de Snyder, V. N., 199, *216*
Sallis, J. F., *217*
Sameroff, A. J., 108, *116*, 335, 342, 363, 364
Sampson, P. D., 78, *83*
Samson, H. H., 169, 171, *186, 187*
Sanchez-Craig, M., 261, *282*
Sanders, M., 249, *282*
Sanderson, W. C., *392*
Sanders-Phillips, K., 192, 196, 205, *216*
Sanhueza, P., 171, *186*
Santi, S., *305*
Santisteban, D. A., 333, 340, 357, *359, 364, 365, 366, 376, 394*
Sarnyai, Z., 178, *187*
Saunders, B., 265, *277*
Sayers, M., 120, 131, *146*
Scearce-Levie, K., *43*
Schable, C., *327*
Schaefer, G. J., *188*
Schaefer, N., 192, *216*
Schafer, J., 83, *96*
Schaps, E., 224, *241*, 287, *307*
Scheier, L. M., 21, *43*, 131, *147*, 226, *237, 238*, 300, *307*
Scheller-Gilkey, G., 19, *43*
Schenk, S., 151, *158, 159*
Schinka, J. A., *422*
Schinke, S. P., 286, 291, 293, 295, 296, *297, 304, 305, 307*
Schlyer, D., *44*
Schmeidler, J., *238*
Schmidt, C. W. Jr., 15, *36*
Schmidt, S. E., 230, *241*
Schmitz, J. M., 265, *282*
Schneider-Rosen, K., 103, 106, *114*
Schnell, D. J., *327*
Schnoll, S., 53, *62*
Schoch, P., 169, *187*
Schochetman, G., *327*
Schoenwald, S. K., 273, *282*
Schopen, C. K., *185*
Schorr, L. B., 205, *216*
Schotz, W. E., 205, *217*
Schramm, W., 50, *62*

Schreiber, G. B., 318, *329*
Schroeder, R. L., 168, *188*
Schuh, L. M., 433, 439, 440, *443, 445*
Schulenberg, J. E., *144*, 227, *237*
Schulteis, G., *41*, 162, 163, 171, 172, *179, 183, 184, 185, 188, 189*
Schultz, W., 27, *43*
Schulz, R., 128, *145*
Schumaker, S. A., 194, *216*
Schuster, C. R., 159, 163, 168, 182, *188, 203, 214, 237, 283*
Schwartz, C. E., 128, *147*
Schwartz, D., 348, *359*
Schwartz, J., 194, *211*
Schwartz, J.-C., *181*
Schwartz, R. D., *189*
Scierka, A., 249, *282*
Scopetta, M. A., 340, *365, 366*
Scott, G., *326*
Scottenfeld, R. S., *186*
Scrimshaw, S. C. M., 198, *217*
Seal, D. W., *326*
Sechrest, L., 231, *241*
Secker, W. S., *305*
Seeley, J. R., 14, *41*
Seeman, M., 195, *216*
Seeman, T., 195, *216*
Sees, K., *283*
Seever, M. H., *181*
Seifer, R., 335, *364*
Self, D. W., 175, *188*
Sellers, E. M., 171, *186, 188*, 437, *445*
Sellers, M. L., 436, *443*
Sells, S. B., 399, 403, 404, *427*
Selzer, M. A., 375, *393*
Senkoro, K., *326*
Sepinwall, J., 169, *188*
Serufilira, A., *324*
Shadish, W. R., 270, *283*
Shaefer, N., *205*
Shapiro, D. H., 128, *147*
Shaw, B. F., 375, *391*
Shaw, G. K., 250, *283*
Shayka, J. J., *427*
Shea, C. E., *44, 442*
Shea, M. T., *392*
Shedler, J., 100, 109, *116*, 229, *241*, 347, *364*
Sheiner, L., 437, *441*
Shelton, K., 151, *158*
Sher, K., 99, 106, *116*
Sher, K. J., 17, *41*

Sherrod, L., 108, *115*
Shiffman, S. M., 438, 440, *445*
Shippenberg, T. S., 174, *188*
Shiue, C. Y., *44*
Shoemaker, W., *42*
Shoham, V., *392*
Shope, J. T., 293, *308*
Short, P. E., *185*
Shriver, M., *329*
Shumaker, S. A., 195, *216*
Shure, M. B., 145
Sicilian, D. M., *422, 430*
Sidney, S., 195, *214*
Siegel, R., 53, *62*
Siegel, S., 127, 129, 138, 143, *147*
Sienna, M., 18, *39*
Sieur, K., *361*
Sigvardsson, S., 337, *358*
Silberstein, C. H., 415, *427, 429*
Silva, P. A., *37*
Silverman, K., 154, *159*, 260, 267, 280, *283*
Simon, H., 151, *158*
Simonin, F., *186*
Simpson, D. D., 399, 404, 407, 415, 418, *425, 427, 429*
Simpson, S. S., 403
Singer, L., 200, 201, *216*
Singh, K., 348, *364*
Singleton, E. G., 199, *216*
Siqueland, L., *278*
Sisson, R. W., 154, *159*, 257, 266, 277, *283*, 376, *391*
Sivo, P., 293, *304*
Skager, R., 295, *307*
Skinner, M., 352, *359*
Skodol, A. E., 20, *43*, 403, *424*
Skolnick, P., *189*
Skoog, K., 438, *442*
Slaby, R. G., 335, *361*
Slade, J., 433, 434, 436, 439, *442, 443, 445*
Slaughter-Defoe, D. T., 347, 348, *364*
Slinkard, L. A., 290, 293, 306, *307*
Sloboda, R. W., 227
Sloboda, Z., 14, *39*, 233, *239, 242*
Slowe, S., *186*
Slutske, W. S., 32, *43*
Smallish, L., 18, *35*
Smart, R. G., 70, 74, *77, 78*
Smith, A. D., 175, *186*
Smith, B. H., 18, *42*

Smith, E. D., *78*
Smith, G. M., 335, 341, 347, *364*
Smith, G. T., 83, *95*
Smith, J. E., 168, *182*
Smith, L. A., 337, *361*
Smith, S. G., 164, *181*
Snow, D. L., 290, 292, *308*
Sobel, B. S., 396, *422*
Sobell, L. C., 257, *283*
Sobell, M. B., 171, *188*, 257, *283*
Soberman, L. H., 230, *238*
Sola, S., 403, *428*
Solomon, R. L., 130, *147*
Solowij, N., 94, *96*
Song, L., 201, *216*
Sorenson, J. L., 321, *329, 426*
Soriano, J., *35*
Sotsky, S. M., *392*
Spanagel, R., 249, *283*
Spealman, R. D., 164, *180*, 436, *445*
Spencer, T., 36, *44*
Sperling, R. S., *326*
Spitalnic, S. J., *183*
Spitzer, R. J., 82, *96*
Spoth, R., 231, *240*
Spracklin, K. M., 349, *359*
Sprendle, D. H., 230, *240*
Sroufe, L. A., 98, 99, 103, 105, 106, 107, *116, 117*, 332, 344, *359, 364*
St. Lawrence, J. S., 327
Stacy, A. W., 83, 84, *96*, 290, *308*
Stahl, S., *430*
Staines, G., *429, 430*
Stall, R., 311, 325, *328*
Stanley, J. C., 382, *392*
Stanton, M. D., 270, *283*
Starr, C. L., *425*
Statham, D. J., *43*
Steckler, A. B., 192, *215*
Stein, R. M., *282, 444*
Steinberg, L., 226, *242*, 335, 348, 349, *358, 360, 364*
Stevens, D. E., 17, *42*
Stevens, S. T., 410, 414, *427, 430*
Stevenson, D. L., 347, 348, *357, 364*
Stevenson, L. Y., 327
Stewart, J., 172, 180, *188*
Stewart, M., 9, *37*, 101, *114*
Stiller, R. L., 249, *282*, 437, *444*
Stinus, L., 171, 172, 175, 179, *183, 187, 189*
Stitzel, J. A., 28, *41*

Stitzer, M. L., 131, *147*, 153, *157*, 260,
    266, *283*, 436, *443*
Stockard, C. R., 71, *71–72*, 74
Stockard, R. G., 78
Stockwell, T., 82, *95*
Stoddard, A., 426, *430*
Stokols, D., 205, 209, *216*
Stolar, M., 29, *42*
Stone-Washton, N., 271, *283*
Stoolmiller, M., 16, *37*, 352, *359*
Stout, D. B., *41*
Stouthamer-Loeber, M., 13, *41*, 335, 349,
    363
Strain, E., 153, *157*
Strauss, A. L., 381, *394*
Streissguth, A. P., 78, 83, 200, *216*
Streuning, E. L., *38*
Strogatz, D., *213*
Stroot, E., 84, *95*
Struening, E. L., *211*, 426
Stryker, J., 323, *329*
Sturz, E. L., 426, *429*
Su, S., 229, *241*
Substance Abuse and Mental Health Ser-
    vices Administration, 4, 5, 6, 7,
    58, 192, *217*, 225, 240, 244, *283*
Suikis, D. S., *362*
Sullivan, A. P., 403, *422*
Sullivan, P., *40*
Sun, P., 290, *308*
Suprasert, S., *328*
Sussman, S., 290, 292, 293, *308*
Suzdak, P. D., 169, *189*
Svikis, D. S., *337*
Swan, G. E., *37*
Swapil, T. R., *41*
Swartz, M., *40*
Sweat, M. D., 312, 313, 326, *329*
Swendsen, J. D., 17, *42, 43*
Swinson, R. P., 197, *217*
Swisher, J. D., 287, 288, *308*
Swofford, C. D., 19, *43*
Szapocznik, J., 230, *242*, 268, *283*, 331,
    333, 335, 337, 340, 353, 355,
    356, 357, 359, 363, 364, 365,
    366, 394

Tabakoff, B., 171, *183*
Taibson, C., *427*
Takemori, A. E., *186*
Tanaka, F. M., 131

Tanaka, J. S., *144*
Tanda, G., 27, *42, 43*, 179, *187*
Tapasak, R. C., 290, *308*
Tarter, R. E., 21, 22, 24, 25, 35, 36, 38,
    43, 101, 102, 105, 106, 109, *117*,
    226, 238, *242*
Tate, C., 74, *78*
Tatelbaum, R., 343, *362*
Taylor, C. B., *239*
Taylor, J., 198, 199, 206, 207, *216*
Taylor, R. D., 340, 350, *366*
Tebes, J. K., 290, *308*
Tejeda, M. J., 385, *394*
Telch, M. J., 290, 292, 293, *308*
Telegdy, G., *187*
Templeton, L., 85, 86, 87, 88, 91, *95*
Tennen, H., *43*
Tevisan, L., *42*
Thomas, A., 23, 24, 26, *37, 43*
Thomas, G., 426, *429*
Thomas, P. A., *328*
Thomas, S. B., 205, *216*
Thompson, A., 224, *238*, 287, *304*
Thompson, E. A., 232, *238*
Thompson, S. S., 151, 155, *157, 159*
Thompson, T., 153, *158, 188*
Thomson, S. J., *305*
Thornell, A., *35*
Tiffany, S. T., 138, *144*
Tims, F. M., 395, 398, 404, *427, 428*
Tobin, J. W., 201, *213*
Todd, J., *326*
Tolan, P. H., 348, 353, *360, 366*
Tolliver, G. A., 169, *187*
Tonigan, J. S., 272, *281*
Toomey, R., *43*
Toomey, T. L., *158*
Torestad, B., 336, *362*
Tortu, S., 289, 291, *303*
Toth, S. L., 100, *114*
Toth, V., *305*
Tremblay, R. E., 23, 24, *41*
Trepper, T. J., 230, *240*
Triffleman, E., *43*
Trimble, J. E., 295, *308*
Tripathi, S. P., *324*
Trivette, P., *364*
Troughton, E., 9, *37*, 101, *114*, 229, *238*
True, W., *43*
Trussell, J., 322, *326*
Tsai, M., 375, *393*
Tsaid, W.-Y., *327*

Tsuang, M. T., 30, 31, *43*
Tubman, J. G., 25, *43*
Tucker, D., 99, 103, 105, 109, 112, *114*
Turbin, M. S., 14, 39, 131, *145*
Turkheimer, E., 120, *147*
Turner, H., *325*
Tusel, D. J., 267, *281, 283*
Tyndale, R. F., 437, *445*
Tzavara, E., *186*

Ungerstedt, U., 164, *183, 189*
University of Michigan, 7, *44*
Urmann, C. F., *425, 430*
U.S. Department of Health and Human Services, 432, *445*
U.S. Public Health Service, *217*
U.S. *vs.* Jin Fury Moy, 65
U.S. vs. Doremus, 66

Vaccarino, F. J., 164, 168, *185, 189*
Vaccaro, G., 23, 25, *44*
Vaillant, G. E., 26, *44*, 131, *147*, 254, *283*
Vakassian, L., *188*
Valadez, A., 151, *159*
Valdiserri, R. O., 311, *329*
Valentine, C., *327*
Valle, R., 199, *217*
Valleroy, L. A., 316, 326, *329*
Valley Rachal, J., 403, *425*
Valverde, O., *186*
Van de Perre, P., *324*
Van Den Bos, J., 14, 39, 131, *145*
Van der Stratten, A., 319, *329*
Van Kammen, W. B., 13, *41*
van Ree, M., 151, *157, 158, 159*
Vanderryn, J., 39, 131, *145*
Vanyukov, M., 101, 102, 105, 106, 109, *117*
Vaskassian, L., 168
Veblen-Mortenson, S., *158*
Vecsernyes, M., *187*
Vega, W., *42*, 199, 205, *217*
Velasquez, M. M., *212*
Velez, C. N., 38, 229, *238*
Velicer, W. F., *212*
Venderryn, F. M., 14
Venesoen, P., 265, *279*
Vicary, J. R., 23, 25, *41, 43*, 351, *362*

Vickers-Lahti, M., *426, 430*
Virus, R. M., 164, *190*
Vitkun, S., *44*
Vittinghoff, E., 319, *329*
Vlahov, D., *328*
Vogt, T. M., 432, *443*
Volkow, N. D., 28, 29, *44*, 227, 242, 437, *442*
Volpicelli, J. R., 171, 177, *189*
von Bertalanffy, L., 102, *117*
von Eye, A., 25, *43*
von Knorring, A.-L., 337, *358*

Wadsworth, K. N., 131, *144*, 227, *237*
Wagle, U., *324*
Wagner, E., *213*
Wakefield, J., 101, *117*
Walfish, S., 287, *306*
Wallace, J., 374, *394*
Wallace, J. M., Jr., 295, *308*
Waller, S., *283*
Walters, E., *42*
Wang, E. Y. I., *241, 363*
Wang, G. J., *44*, 437, *442*
Ward, D. M., 273, *282*
Warnecke, R. B., 198, 205, 206, *213, 217*
Warner, K. E., 432, *445*
Warner, L. A., 8, *44*
Warner, R. H., 70, 75, *78*
Warren, M. P., 19, *39*
Warshawsky, L., 201, *216*
Washton, A. M., 271, *283*
Watkins, J. T., *392*
Watkins, S. S., 437, *441*
Watt, N. F., *145, 359*
Weaver, F., *212*
Webb, H., 195, *217*
Webb et al v. U.S., 66, *78*
Weber, W., 35
Webster-Stratton, C., 230, *242*
Weeks, J. R., 163, 168, *181, 189*
Weight, F. F., 171, *185*
Weinger, M. B., 168, *188*
Weinstein, B., *329*
Weinstein, N. D., 192, 193, *217*
Weintraub, S., 109, *116*
Weiser, J., 110
Weiss, F., *41*, 162, 164, 166, 171, 175, 176, 177, 179, *183, 184, 185, 186, 189*

Weiss, R. D., 201, *213*
Weissberg, J. S., 293
Weissberg, R. P., 293, *304*, 335, *359*
Weisskoff, R. M., 36
Weissman, M. M., *43*, 257, *280*
Weisz, J., 107, 110, *116*
Weller, S. B., 267, *277*
Wellman, B., 85, 95
Welte, J. W., *303*
Weniger, B. G., 327
Werner, A., 105
Werner, H., *117*, 342, 344, 366
West, L. J., 432, *443*
West, S. G., *145*, *359*
West, T. E., *189*
Westman, E. C., 282, *444*
Westreich, L., *429*
Wexler, H. K., 396, 407, 414, 415, 418, *424*, *426*, *428*, *429*
Wheeler, B., 403, *422*
White, C., 171
White, D. M., *61*
White, G., *185*
White, H. R., 13, *44*, 131, *146*
White, R. A., *326*
Whitehead, I. C., 403, *422*
Whiteman, M., 14, 25, 36, 131, *144*, 226, 229, 237, 341, 351, *358*
Wickelgren, I., 27, *44*
Widaman, K. F., 84, *96*
Widnell, K. L., 129, *146*
Wiebel, W. W., 321, *324*, 329
Wikler, A., 161–162, 163, *189*
Wild, K. D., *183*
Wilden, A., 102, *117*
Wilens, T. E., 16, 19, *35*, 36, *44*
Wilkenfeld, J. P., *443*
Williams, C., *213*, 295, 306
Williams, C. L., *158*, 199, *217*, 293, 304, *304*
Williams, K. M., 396, *425*
Williams, L., *238*
Williams, P. T., *239*
Williams, R., 396, 414, 415, 428
Williams, R. A., 331, *366*
Williamson, D. F., *277*
Wills, T. A., 23, 24, 25, *44*
Wilsnak, R. W., 197, *217*
Wilson, A. S., 249, 282, 437, *444*
Wilson, D. D., *425*
Wilson, O. B., 172, *185*
Wilson, S., 403

Windle, M., 18, 22, 23, 24, *44*
Windle, R. C., 18, 22, 23, 24, *44*
Wingood, G. M., 206, *212*, 311, *326*
Winick, C., 396, *428*
Winkleby, M. A., 231, *242*
Winstein, B., 317, *326*
Wirtz, P. W., *278*
163, 172, *189*
Wise, R. A., 27, 36, *45*, 99, 101, *117*, 129, 131, 137, *147*, 163, 164, 168, 172, *180*, *181*, *185*, *190*
Witherspoon, W. E., *185*
Witt, A. M., *443*
Wittchen, H. U., *40*, *42*
Witts-Vitale, S., *303*
Wodak, A., 321, *324*
Wolf, A. P., *44*, *242*
Wolf, W., *327*
Wolfe, B. E., 377, *392*
Wolkenstein, B. H., *305*
Wong, S., 85, 86, 87, 88, 91, 95
Wood, G. R., 64, 78
Wood, W., 58
Woodley-Remus, D., 171, *186*
Woods, J. H., 168, *182*
Woods, S. C., 129, 131, 138, 139, 143, *147*
Woods, S. W., *42*
Woodworth, G., 9, *37*, 101, *114*
Woody, G. E., 156, *158*, 257, 260, 263, *281*, *284*
Woolverton, W. L., 153, 155, *158*, 164, *190*
Worden, J. K., *305*
World Conference of Therapeutic Communities of America, *424*
World Health Organization, 161, *190*
Wortley, S., 85, 95
Wozniak, J., *44*
Wright, D., 38
Wright, F. D., 261, *277*
Wright, S. I., 197, *217*
Wyvell, C. L., 155, *157*

Yaeger, R. J., 261
Yaganeh, M., *186*
Yagelka, J., 403, 404, *425*
Yamaguchi, K., 11, *40*, 125, 126, *146*, 225, 240
Yanagita, T., *181*, 432, *441*

Yates, W. R., 9, 37, 101, *114*
Yeager, R. J., *279*
Yura, M., 287, *308*

Zacharko, R. M., *184*
Zacny, J. P., 153, *159*
Zambrana, R. E., 198, 202, *217*
Zax, M., 335, *364*
Zeller, M. R., *443*
Zhang, H., *42*
Zhangs, G., 178, *186*
Zhao, S., *40*
Zhu, K., 231, *240*

Ziegelsberger, W., *187*
Ziegenfuss, J. T., 396, 398, *424*
Zieglgansberger, W., 249, *283*
Zigler, E., 103, *117*
Zoli, M., *444*
Zorn, M., 426, *430*
Zucker, R. A., 33, 34, *45*, 97, 98, 100,
    105, 106, 108, 109, *115*, *117*
Zuckerman, B. S., *212*
Zuckerman, M., 300, 308, 403, *428*
Zweben, A., 273, *281*
Zweben, J. E., 268, 269, 271, *271*, 272,
    280
Zweifel, M., 171, *182*

SUBJECT INDEX

Abstem. *See* disulfiram (Abstem)
abstinence syndrome, 163
abstinence violation effect, 264, 265
abstinence vs. controlled use, 275–276
abuse. *See also* use, dependence, abuse
    disease models of, 97–98
    individual differences in, 9
    interactions in, 9–10
acamprosate
    for alcohol craving, 249
adaptation
    enduring protective factors in, 109–
        110
addiction
    affective habituation and withdrawal
        in, 172
    components, operational construct,
        treatment focus in, 162t
    corticotropin-releasing factor in, 178–
        179
    dopamine system and, 28
    dynorphin in, 178
    in mothers and children
        therapeutic communities for, 414
    neuropeptide FF in, 178
    neuropharmacological elements in,
        177–179
    reinforcement in, 162t, 162–163
    serotonin system and, 28–29
    temporal phases of ontogenesis in, 111
ADHD. *See* attention deficit hyperactiv-
        ity disorder
adolescent transitions program, 230
adolescent use, 130
    competence-enhancement approach to,
        291–292, 293
    increase in, 286
    initiation of
        psychosocial factors in, 286
    mediating mechanisms in, 297–301
        conceptual framework for study of,
            297, 298f, 299–300
adolescent use prevention
    educational approach to, 287–288
    effectiveness of
        implications for, 294–295
        long-term, 293–295

with minority populations, 295–297
    short-term, 292–293
impact on health problems, 301–302
long-term effects of, 293–295
    program deficiencies and, 294
mediating mechanisms research in
    conceptual framework, 297, 298f,
        299f, 299–300
    implications of, 300–301
principles for, 231–232
psychosocial approaches to, 288–292
in racial-ethnic minorities, 295–297,
        301
research needs in, 301
school-based programs for, 287–288
    affective educational, 288
    effectiveness of, 292–297
    informational, 287–288
    limitations of, 301
    psychosocial approach in, 288–292
short-term effects of, 292–293
social influence approach to, 289–291
social resistance skills training for,
        290–291
adolescents
    alcohol use by, 296
    with dual disorder, 404
    initiation in, 225, 295, 299f, 299–300
    minority
        smoking in, 296–297
    prevention principles for, 233–234
    sequencing in, 225
    therapeutic communities for, 414
affective prevention programs, 224
affectivity
    substance abuse disorders and, 25
aftercare
    in therapeutic community model, 411
agonists
    in treatment, 248–249
agonists as substitution therapy, 248–249
agoraphobia
    addictive disorders and, 17
AIDS. *See* HIV/AIDS
alcohol
    availability of
        approval of, 91, 92t, 93

alcohol (*continued*)
consumer sovereignty vs. control, 81
control of
attitudes about and expectancies,
90–91, 91t
control vs. consumer sovereignty, 82
craving for, 249
expectancies and
alcohol-control attitudes and, 90–
91, 91t
of effect on others, 88t, 90
of effect on self, 87t, 89–90
neurotransmitter effects of, 246
nondrug alternatives to, 154
prohibition of, 69–70
in Canada, 70
national, 69
state, 69
withdrawal criteria for, 173
alcohol and drug policy attitudes study
measurement in, 85–86
alcohol research
animal embryo studies, 74
fetal alcohol damage
early studies, 71–72
fetus and, 70, 71, 72–75
public vs. scientific opinion on, 69–75
Women's Christian Temperance Union
and, 70–71
alcohol use
by adolescents, 130
by Black women, 198–199
initiation of, 225, 299f, 299–300
compared in Mexican and Black
women, 201–202
by minority adolescents, 296
sequencing from, 225
social influence prevention model and,
293
stressful life events and, 196–197
in women, 196–199
community norms and, 203
alcohol withdrawal
corticotropin-releasing factor in, 177
Alcoholics Anonymous (AA), 252, 254,
277. *See also* 12-step programs
alcoholism
cognitive-behavioral model of, 261,
262
cognitive-behavioral therapy for, 261–
262
alternative rewards

dose effect of
in animals and humans, 153–154
drug type and route of administration
and, 154
with medication
animal studies of, 155–156
human studies, 156
nondrug
in animals, 150–152
in clinical setting, 154–155
in humans, 152
in prevention, 150–152
in reduction, 152–153
unit price of drug and, 153
Amazing Alternatives program, 152
amphetamine. *See also* psychomotor stimulants
dopamine receptor antagonist effect
on, 164, 166
animal models
of abuse, 149
generality to humans
concordance in, 149–150
lack of, 150
anslinger, H. J., 68
Antabuse. *See* Disulfiram (Antabuse)
antagonists
in treatment, 247–248
antisocial personality disorder
and abuse, 15–16
anxiety disorders
addictive disorders and, 17
attention deficit hyperactivity disorder
(ADHD)
substance use disorders and, 18–19
attitude(s)
alcohol and drug policy
measurement of, 85–86
study results, 88–90
drug policy
prediction with expectancy and experience measures, 91, 92t, 93
public, 63–64
aversion therapy, 250–251

behavior
from dyscontrol to control of, 369–371
behavioral disinhibition
substance abuse disorders and, 22–23
behavioral therapies
contingent punishments in, 259, 260

cue extinction techniques in, 258
incentives in, 259, 260
operant behavior theory in, 257
operant conditioning techniques in, 258–259
reinforcement in, 260–261
social learning in, 258, 259–260
structured, 259
beliefs
drug use and, 64
biological factors
in initiation, 299
biopsychosocial criteria
for drug use behavior, 135–142
biopsychosocial paradigm
brain responses and, 129–130
motivational processes in, 130, 130f
neural capacity and, 129–130
bipolar disorder
and substance use disorders, 16
Bishop, Ernest, 65–66
on addiction maintenance, 66
antidotal toxic substance theory of, 66
mechanism of addiction and, 65–66
on opiate addiction treatment, 65–68
Black women
alcohol use by, 198–199
drug use by, 199
risk for high blood pressure, 195
smoking behavior in, 197–198, 199
blunts
abuse pattern with, 57
usage trend for, 54
Botvin, G. J., 223–224
Bromberg, Walter
cannabis research, 69
Bronfenbrenner, U., on sets, 337
buprenorphine
in heroin treatment, 249
with nondrug-alternative reinforcers, 155–156
Buspirone
in alcoholics, 250

Calcium carbamide (Abstem). See Disulfiram (Antabuse)
California Drug and Alcohol Treatment Assessment (CALDATA), 275
Canadian Opium and Drug Act, 1911, 73

cannabis
Bromberg research on, 69
capability enhancement, 375. See also competence-enhancement prevention
model
of therapists, 377
CEWG. See Community Epidemiology Work Group
child development
exosystem in, 339–340
macrosystems in, 337, 340
mesosystems in, 337, 338f, 339
microsystems in, 337, 338f, 339
children
nicotine dependence in, 439
prevention principles for, 233–234
prevention programs for, 232–233
use prevalence in, 225
children of alcoholics and substance abusers
prevention research for, 235
cigarette labeling
for tar and nicotine content, 433–434
cigarette smoking
compared Mexican and Black women, 201–202
research on, 436–437
Cloud 9 (herbal stimulant)
abuse pattern with, 58
cocaine. See also Psychomotor stimulants
abuse pattern with, 55–56
dopamine receptor antagonist effect on, 164, 166, 167f
nondrug alternatives to, 154
usage of
National Household Survey on Drug Abuse data, 54
withdrawal criteria for, 173
cocaine addiction
desipramine in, 250, 251
Cocaine Anonymous (CA), 252
cocaine craving
gamma vinyl-GABA in, 250
cocaine dependence
nondrug alternatives to, 154
Cocaine Papers, Freud, 255
cocaine use
depression and, 201
reduction of
buprenorphine with saccharin in, 155–156

cognitive and cognitive-behavioral therapy, 261–263
  components of, 262–263
  effectiveness of, 263
  Marlatt model in, 261, 262
cognitive-behavioral theory
  in relapse prevention, 263, 264
coherence
  in structural ecodevelopmental preventive intervention, 355
Committee on Problems of Drug Dependence, 67
Community Epidemiology Work Group (CEWG). *See also* State Epidemiology Work Group
  dissemination of meeting reports, 5959
  evolution of, 40–52, 49–52
  indicator data in, 50, 51
  international organizations and, 59
  membership in, 54–55
  methodological issues in, 51–52
  as network of experts, 50
  participants in, 49
  reporting in, 51
  trend reports of
    for blunts, 54
    for crack cocaine, 53–54
    for methaqualone, 52–53
community reinforcement approach (CRA), 266
community reinforcement approach (CRA) + vouchers
  effectiveness of, 267
  techniques in, 266–267
community reinforcement approach (CRA) + vouchers, 266–267
community-based treatment
  vouchers in, 266–267
comorbidity, 14–15
  targeting of underlying, 251
compensatory factors
  in development of abuse, 112
compensatory protective factors
  influence on abuse development, 108, 109–110
competence-enhancement prevention model, 291–292, 293
  life skills training in, 292
  self-management and social skills in, 291
  verbal and nonverbal skills in, 291
compulsion, 161

conduct disorder
  and abuse, 15–16
  social ecology, development and interactions in, 350–351
consumer sovereignty
  drug-control policies and, 80–81
contexts
  of drug abuse research, 63–64
contingency management, 266–267
contingent punishments, 259, 260
corticotropin-releasing factor
  in addiction, 178–179
crack cocaine
  usage trend for, 53–54
craving. *See also* relapse
  brain regions in, 29
  and relapse, 180
cue extinction, 265
cultural context
  of drug abuse research, 63–64
cultural factors
  in initiation, 299

Dederich, Charles, 254
demographic factors
  in initiation, 299
dependence. *See also* use, dependence, abuse
  by and age, 7t, 7–8, 8t
  corticotropin-releasing factor activation in, 179
  defined, 161, 162
  gender and, 9
  molecular, cellular, system adaptations in, 174–177
  motivational view of, 172, 174t
  neuroadaptations in, 173–174
  by sex and age, 7t, 7–8, 8t
dependence syndrome
  reinforcement in, 162
depression
  alcohol and tobacco use in, 197, 198, 199
  in Black and Latino women, 199
  smoking and, 249–250
depressive disorders
  and substance use disorders, 16–17
desipramine
  for cocaine craving, 250, 251
detoxification
  Bishop on, 66

development. *See also* developmental psychopathology
  incoherent organization of domains and, 106–107
  maladaptive, 106, 107
    plasticity and, 106
  meaning of term, 342
  organizational perspective on, 105–108
  probabilistic model of, 105, 106
  prototypic organization and later drug abuse, 107–108
  social ecology theory in, 337, 338f, 339–340
  in structural ecosystems theory, 342
  transactional model of, 108–110
developmental psychopathology. *See also* development
  adaptation in, 103, 104
    effect on outcome and, 99
  capacity-mechanism interaction in, 98–99
  covariance of internal processes in, 100–101
  description of, 98, 111
  diversity of process and outcome in, 101, 102
  equifinality in, 102, 103
  individual differences in, 100
  interrelated influences in, 100–101
  multifinality in, 102, 103
  pathways of, 103
  perspective of, 98–100
  principles of, 100–105
  progression of influences in, 99
  research and, 111–113
  research directions from, 111–113
    attachment theory on internal representation, 111–112
    avoidance, 112
    cessation of abuse, 112
    compensatory factors, 112
    designs and strategies in, 113
    potentiating factors, 112
  variations along continuum of, 101
deviance model, abuse and, 13–14
deviance syndrome, 13
difficult temperament
  substance abuse disorders and, 23–24
disulfiram (Antabuse), 250–251
Dole, Vincent, methadone treatment, 246, 248

dopamine
  extracellular in nucleus accumbens after cocaine self-administration, 175, 176f
  opiate release and, 169
dopamine receptor subtypes
  functional classification of, 164, 166, 166t
dopamine reward system
  addiction and, 28
dopamine system
  in addiction, 28
  in amphetamine reinforcement, 164
  in cocaine reinforcement, 163
  in ethanol reinforcement, 170–171
  mesolimbic
    in drug action, 178
  midbrain, 164, 165f
  nicotine activation of, 172
  nicotine stimulation of, 176
Drug Abuse Reporting Program (DARP), 275
drug policy
  attitudes and, 85–86, 88–90
  and HIV prevention, 320–322
drug properties
  dependence and, 120–121
drug use. *See* use; use, dependence, abuse
drug use behavior
  factors in, integrated domain model of, 297, 298f, 299
  initiation model of, 299f, 299–300
drug-control policies
  consumer sovereignty and, 80–81
  options for, 81–82
  public opinion and, 81–83
dynorphin
  in addiction, 178

eating disorders
  substance use disorders and, 19
education
  alcohol and tobacco use and
    in Black women, 197–198
    in Latinas, 198
Eddy, Nathan, 64
emotion
  from quiet desperation to emotional experiencing, 370, 371–372
emotional pain disorders, 371
  treatment of, 371–372

environment
in animal vs. human use, 150
drug use
assumptions in, 133
generalized, 133–134
stages in, 133
opportunistic, 142
respondent-operating
definition of, 135
generic properties of, 135–136
structuring of
in psychosocial treatment, 376–377
use behavior and, 127–128
environmental factors
in initiation, 299
epidemiology
trends in, 48
ethanol
neuroadaptation and motivational effects of, 177
ethnic identity
definition of, 196
influence on health and risk behaviors, 196
ethnic minority groups
adolescent
drug prevention in, 295–297, 301
risk factors for drug use by
importance of, 203–204
ethnic minority women
drug use by, 201–204
intervention programs for, 204–207
ethnicity
in treatment response, 203
etiology
comorbidity in, 14–20
concurrent behavior in, 13–14
co-occurring behavior in, 13–14
developmental, 34–35
of drug use
in adolescent minority populations, 295–296
epidemiology in, 4–9
executive cognitive function in, 21–22
gateway hypothesis of, 11–13
genetics in, 29–32
interactive systems in, 33
intermediation characteristics in, 26
multifactorial influences in, 33
neurobiology in, 26–29
personality in, 25–26
progression in, 10–11

temperament in, 22–25
eugenics
alcohol use and, 73
executive cognitive function deficiency
drug dependence and, 21–22
exosystems
influence on child, 339–340
influence on structural ecosystems theory, 349–350
expectancies. See also drug-control policies
alcohol control and, 90–91, 91t
for alcohol effect
on others, 87, 87t
on self, 87t, 89–90
attitudes for public policy and use and, 84
drug, 86–87
effect of, 80
effect on others, 87, 88t
for tobacco use, 87, 88t
experience
drug-related, 87–88
extended amygdala
in motivation, 179–180

family
iatrogenic effects of intervention, 356–357
models of, 268
as risk and protective factor, 334
Strengthening Families Program for, 232
in structural ecodevelopmental preventive interventions, 353–354
in structural ecosystems theory, 337, 353
therapist's tasks with
analysis of structures and systems, 269
joining, 269
relapse prevention, 270
stabilization, 269
teaching coping strategies, 270
family services
in therapeutic community model, 411
family studies
of substance use disorders, 30, 31
Federal Bureau of Narcotics
vs. Mayor LaGuardia, New York, 68

Federal Drug Administration (FDA)
    tar and nicotine rating and, 434
    tobacco regulation by, 431, 432–433
    treatment efforts of, 433
Federal Trade Commission (FTC)
    on cigarette labeling, 433
    tar and nicotine ratings and, 434
fentanyl
    abuse pattern with, 58
fetal alcohol syndrome, 72–73. *See also*
        fetus
Fetus
    alcohol effect on
        early research on, 70, 71, 72–73
Freeman, R. G., on prenatal alcohol use,
        71–72
Freud, Sigmund, on addiction, 255, 279

gamma vinyl-GABA (GVG)
    as craving suppressant, 250
gamma-aminobutyric acid (GABA) an-
        tagonists
    ethanol effects and, 169, 170f
gamma-aminobutyric acid (GABA) sys-
        tem
    in dependence, 179
    sedative-hypnotic potentiation of, 169
gateway hypothesis, 11–13
    implications of, 12–13
gender differences
    in depression and cocaine use, 201
    drug dependence and, 8t, 9
    in drug use, 191, 199–200
    in Latino drug use, 202–203
    in treatment response, 203
generalization of gains
    in psychosocial treatment, 376
genetics. *See also* heritability
    in etiology, 29–32
    substance use disorders and, 29
glutamate systems
    in alcohol reinforcement, 171
Goddard, H. H., 72
Gordon, Alfred, on alcoholism, 72
Gordon, J. R.
    on relapse prevention, 263–265
group therapy
    confrontation in, 271–272
    rules for, 271
    vs. 12-step programs, 270–271

Harrison Anti-Narcotic Act, 1915, 65,
        73–74
Hayward, W., 67
health behaviors
    in Black women, 196
    in Latinas, 196
    promotion of positive, 223
health care services
    in therapeutic community model, 411
health problems
    adolescent use and prevention and,
        301–302
health promotion programs
    for women
        combination approaches to, 206–
            207
        ecological approach to, 204–205,
            207
        lay health advisors in, 205–206
herbal stimulants
    abuse pattern with, 58
heritability
    of alcohol damage, 71–72
    of mental retardation, 72
    of substance use disorders, 30–32
heroin use
    abuse pattern with, 55, 56–57
    black tar, 56
    buprenorphine for, 249
    contaminated, 56–57
    LAAM for, 248
    methadone for, 246, 248
    reinforcement of, 168
        neurobiological substrates for, 168–
            169
    white, 56
heuristic model
    of use, abuse, 119–144
HIV/AIDS
    in therapeutic community clients,
        415–416
    in United States
        incidence of, 310
        prevalence of, 310–311
        vs. other countries, 310
    in women
        drug-related, 201
HIV/AIDS prevention, 311–320
    cause and change levels in, 311, 312t,
        313t
    at community-level, 316
    counseling and testing in, 318–320

HIV/AIDS prevention (*continued*)
drug policy and, 320–322
at dyadic-familial level, 314–315
at individual level, 311, 312t, 313t,
314, 322
at institutional-community level, 315–
316
medical-technological, 318, 322
multiple levels of intervention, 311,
314–320
policy-legal interventions in, 316–317,
322
research questions concerning, 319
research recommendations for, 323–
324
research vs. drug policy and, 320–321
sexually transmitted disease treatment
in, 319
at superstructural level, 317
targeting of resources for, 310–311
vaccines for, 320
of vertical transmission, 319–320
in women, 314–315, 322–323

illegal drug use
comparing Mexican and Black women,
201–202
prevalence of, 4–6, 5t
in 8th through 12th grades, 6
incentives, 259, 260
incidence
trends in, 48
indicator data
community epidemiology work group
use of, 50, 51
information-dissemination prevention
programs, 224
inhibition
substance abuse disorders and, 24–25
initiation
in adolescents, 299f, 299–300
age and, 225
discontinuance and maintenance following, 226–227
family and peers in, 226
family processes in, 229
hypothetical model for, 299f, 299–300
implications for prevention, 300–
301
theories of, 299–300
International Epidemiology Work Group
(IEWG), 59, 60

intervention
for HIV/AIDS prevention
multiple levels of, 311, 314–320
for special populations, 276
in women
ecological approach to, 204–205
lay health advisors in, 205
intracranial self-stimulation (ICSS) behavior
reward value of, 172–173
intravenous drug use
HIV/AIDS and, 301–310, 311
Irwell, L., on maternal alcohol use, 72

Jellinek, E. M.
on alcohol use in pregnancy, 74–75

Kallikak family study, 72, 73
Kandel, D., 97

LAAM (L-alpha-acetylmethadol)
as substitution therapy, 248
LaGuardia committee, *The Marihuana
Problem in the City of New York*,
68
Latinas
depression in, 199
drug use by
comparison, Black women, 202
narcotic use by
comparison, white women, 202–203
smoking behavior in, 198
Latinos
gender differences in use by, 202–203
Leacock, Stephen, on alcohol use, 70
life events
alcohol and tobacco use and, 196–197
and risk behaviors in women, 194–195
Life Skills Training (LST)
study of, 228
Life Skills Training (LST)
in adolescent drug use prevention, 292
effectiveness of, 296
in minority adolescents, 296
life space conditions, 135
opportunistic, 142
supportive, 141–142, 144
sustaining, 142

limit setting, 259
living-systems models, 128–129, 129f

macrosystems
    ideological and cultural, 337, 340
mandrax. methaqualone (quaalude)
Marihuana Problem in the City of New York, The, 68
marijuana use
    abuse pattern with, 55, 57
    availability for
        approval of, 91, 92t, 93
    dependence on, 8–9
    expectancies with, 87, 88t
    by minority adolescents, 296
    social influence approach to, 293
    trends in, 225
Marlatt, G. A.
    cognitive-behavioral model of, 261, 262
    on relapse prevention, 263–265
mecamylamine
    in smoking cessation, 247
media influence
    in initiation, 299
men
    influence on women's drug use, 200
mental health services
    in therapeutic community model, 412–413
mental health status
    and alcohol and tobacco use in women, 197
mental retardation
    from alcohol use, 72
mesolimic dopamine reward system
    addiction and, 28
mesosystem(s)
    in child development, 337, 338f, 339
    family-peer, 349
    family-school, 347–348
    influence on structural ecosystems theory, 347–348
Metcalf's CocaWine (Advertisement), 64
methadone
    as substitution therapy, 246, 248
methamphetamine
    abuse pattern with, 57
methaqualone (quaalude; mandrax)
    abuse/usage trend with, 52–53

Mexican American women
    alcohol, cigarette, illegal drug use by, 201–202
Mexican immigrant women
    alcohol, cigarette, illegal drug use by, 201–202
microsystems
    in child development, 337, 338f, 339
Miller, W., 272
monitoring systems, 48
Monitoring the Future Study (MFS), 6, 48, 225
motivation
    dependence and, 172–177
    extended amygdala in, 179–180
    in use, dependence, abuse, 126–127
motivation enhancement
    in psychosocial treatment, 375–376
    of therapists, 377
motivational interviewing, 272
mu receptor
    in opiate use reinforcement, 168
multisystemic therapy (MST), 273

Naloxone
    alcohol use reduction with, 171
    in opiate addiction, 247
naltrexone
    for alcohol craving, 249
    alcohol use reduction with, 171
    in opiate addiction, 247
Narcotic Drug Problem, The, Ernest Bishop, 65–66
narcotics
    Latino use of, 202–203
    neurotransmitter effects of, 246
Narcotics Anonymous (NA), 252
National Cancer Institute (NCI)
    on cigarette dose-rating, 434
    on cigarette labeling, 433, 434
National Clearinghouse for Alcohol and Drug Information
    disemination of Community Epidemiology Work Group and International W G reports, 59
National Comorbidity Survey, 15
National Household Survey on Drug Abuse, 48
National Household Survey on Drug Abuse Main Findings 1997, 5t, 5–6

National Institute of Drug Abuse
(NIDA)
Community Epidemiology Work Group
establishment by, 50
monitoring and surveillance systems of,
224
on therapeutic communities, 396
National Institutes of Health Development Program, 248
neighborhood
as risk and protective factor, 334
network therapy, 273
neural capacity
stimulation of, 142–143
neural reward circuit, 164, 165f
neuroadaptation
addiction and, 28
with- and between-system, 173–174
neurobiological substrate(s)
extended amygdala, 179–180
mesocorticolimbic dopamine system,
164, 169
midbrain dopamine system, 164
neurobiology
dopamine reward system and, 27–28
in etiology, 26–29
neuroadaptive brain changes and, 28
serotonin system and, 28–29
neuropeptide FF
in addiction, 178
nicotine
behavioral effects of, 437
delivery characteristics of, 438
dopamine reward system and, 246
neuroadaptation and motivational effects of, 176–177
neurotransmitter effects of, 246
reinforcement effects of, 437
replacement therapy for, 248–249,
436–437, 439
research on, 436–437
current, 437–438
withdrawal criteria for, 173
nicotine acetylcholine receptors
in nicotine reinforcement, 171–172
nicotine and tobacco research
public policy implications of, 432–436
tar and nicotine ratings
Federal Trade Commission and, 434
Food and Drug Administration and,
434
National Cancer Institute and, 433

nicotine craving
gamma vinyl-GABA in, 250
nicotine dependence
in children
treatment and prevention of, 439
pediatric, 439
research findings for, 432–433
scientist's role in public health policy,
440–441
vulnerability to, 31
nicotine gum
origin of, 436–437
nicotine patch, chewing gum and nasal
sprays
as substitution therapy, 248–249
nicotine replacement medication, 436–
437, 439
availability of, 433
nicotinic acetylcholine receptors
molecular action of nicotine at, 176
NIDA. *See* National Institute on Drug
Abuse
nineteenth century
drug development in, 65
novelty-sensation seeking
substance abuse disorders and, 23
Nyswander, Marie, methadone treatment,
246, 248

Office of National Drug Control Policy
(ONDCP)
on benefits of drug treatment, 244
on treatment effectiveness, 274–275
operant behavior therapy, 257–258
operant conditioning
in treatment, 248–249
opiate addiction
physical mechanisms of, 65–66
treatment of
scientific research vs. public opinion,
65
opiate addition
substitution therapy for, 246, 248
opiate receptors
in heroin reinforcement, 168
opiate withdrawal
corticotropin-releasing factor for, 178–
179
opiates
neuroadaptation and motivational effects of, 174–175

positive reinforcement of
dopamine-independent and dependent mechanisms in, 169
opioid maintenance
federal government and, 65
opioid peptide system
in alcohol reinforcement, 171
nicotine activation of, 172
within-system neuroadaptation in, 178
opioid use
nondrug alternatives to, 154–155
opioids
withdrawal criteria for, 173
opium
abuse pattern with, 58
Oregon Social Learning Center
on integration of social, ecological, developmental elements, 351, 352
organismic status, 135, 139–141
motivated, 140–141
performance capable, 139–140
response ready, 139
outcomes
of drug use, 121–123, 123f
health and racism, 199
of treatment, 244

parents
monitoring in prevention, 229–230
parenting practices of, 230
Patterson, G. R., 351–352
pediatric nicotine dependence, 439
peers
influence in initiation, 299
as risk and protective factor, 334
Students Taught Awareness and Resistance program for, 231–232
personality. See also temperament
substance abuse disorders and, 25–26
personality disorders
substance use disorders and, 19
political context
of drug abuse research, 64
positive reinforcement, 162t, 162–163
neurobiological substrates of, 163–172
posttraumatic stress disorder
substance use disorders and, 17–18
potentiating factors
in development of abuse, 112
pregnancy

health behaviors and, 202, 204
prevalence
trends in, 48
prevention
Center for Substance Abuse Prevention violence network of, 58
epidemiologic, etiologic, research findings for, 228–233
family in, 229–230
of HIV/AIDS, 311–320
nondrug-alternative rewards in, 150–152
in animals, 150–152
in humans, 152
principles of, 233–234
in women
ecological approach to, 204
health programs for, 204–207
prevention programs
affective, 224
brain mechanisms illustrations in, 227
community, 231, 234
comprehensive family, school, peer, 230–231
information-dissemination, 224
school setting for, 234
STAR (Students Taught Awareness and Resistance), 231–232
prevention research
in children of alcoholics and substance abusers, 235
in communication techniques, 235
future needs and directions in, 234–235
history of, 223–224
markers for problem behaviors, 235
national program outcomes and, 224
replication studies, 235
risk and protective factors model of, 332
school environment and outcomes, 235
prison settings
therapeutic communities for, 414–415
problem behavior theory
in Life Skills Training, 228
problems in living
restoration to tolerable, 373
self-respect and, 370, 372–373
progression
in substance abuse, 10–11

prohibition, 82
   amendment to the U.S. Constitution, 74
   in Canada, 70
   national, 69
   repeal of, 74
   state, 69
Project MATCH
   on motivational interviewing, 273
Project MATCH research group, 254,
      263
Project Northland, 152
Project RESPECT Study Group
   for HIV prevention, 311, 314
protective factors
   compensatory, 108, 109–110
   enduring, 109–110
   in prevention, 228–229
   research in, 334, 336
psychiatric disorders
   comorbid, 14–15, 19
      models for, 15
         therapeutic communities for, 415
      targeting of, 251
psychoactive substances
   control of, 82
psychodynamic therapies
   theories of, 256
psychological factors
   in initiation, 299
psychological status
   and risk behaviors in women, 195
psychomotor stimulants. See also amphet-
      amine; cocaine
   dopamine levels in nucleus accumbens
      and, 164, 166f, 167f
   neuroadaptation and motivational ef-
      fects of, 175–176, 176f
   neurobiological substrates for, 163–167
psychopharmacological treatment, 245–
      252. See also psychosocial treat-
      ment
   agonist-antagonist combinations in,
      249
   agonists in, 246, 248–249
   antagonists in, 247–248
   aversion in, 250
   concept of, 246
   craving suppressants in, 249–250
   current, 252
   history of, 246
   vaccines in, 241
psychosocial treatment. See also psycho-

pharmacological treatment; treat-
      ment
   from behavior dyscontrol to control,
      369–371
   behavioral, 257–261
   cognitive and cognitive-behavioral,
      261–263
   community-based, 265–267
   disorder levels and treatment stages in,
      368–374
   family approach in, 267–270
   flexibility of, 369
   group therapy, 270–272
   from incompleteness to capacity for
      joy, 373
   level of care and functions of, 374–
      377, 390–391
      capability enhancement, 375
      enhancement of therapists' capability
         and motivation, 377
      generalization of gains, 376
      motivational enhancement, 375–376
      structuring the environment, 376–
         377
   motivational interviewing, 272
   multisystemic therapy, 273
   network therapy, 273
   pretreatment stage of, 373–374
   from problems in living to ordinary
      happiness and unhappiness, 372–
      373
   psychodynamic, 255–257
   from quiet desperation to emotional
      experiencing, 371–372
   relapse prevention in, 263–264
   12-step programs in, 252–254
   therapeutic communities in, 254–255
public health policy
   scientist's role in, 440–441
public opinion
   drug-control policies and, 81–83
   vs scientific research, 65
      Ernest Bishop and, 65–68
public policy
   nicotine and tobacco research and,
      432–436

quaalude. See methaqualone

racism
   alcohol use and, 198

effect on health outcomes, 199
smoking and, 198–199
Reconnecting Youth program, 232–233
recovery groups, 270–272
reduction
nondrug-alternative rewards in, 152–153
behavioral economics of, 153–154
Regulations Restricting Sale of Cigarettes, 1995, 1996, 431, 432, 438–439
reinforcement
in addiction
positive and negative, 162t, 162–163
reinforcer
defined, 162
relapse. See also craving
abstinence violation effect and, 264, 265
in alcohol use, 263
vulnerability to, 180
relapse prevention
cognitive-behavioral theory in, 263, 264
cue extinction in, 265
in family therapy, 270
training in therapeutic community model, 411–412
reliability measures
in treatment standardization, 382
research
political context of, 64
science vs. public and, 64–65
resistance skills
in prevention, 228
risk and protective factors
across domains, 340–341
classification of, 334–335
contextual, 334
identification of, 334–335
individual and interpersonal, 334–335
multiple-risk indexes and, 335–336
as processes, 336
reorganization in categories and domains, 334–335
research in, 332, 333–336
in school setting, 230
risk behaviors
ethnic identity and, 196
factors related to, 199–204
in women, 192, 193, 194–195

Ritalin
abuse pattern with, 58
rohypnol
abuse pattern with, 58

schizophrenia
substance use disorders and, 19
school
as risk and protective factor, 230, 334, 335
sedative-hypnotics
positive reinforcement of
neurobiological substrates for, 169, 170f, 171
Self-respect
problems in living and, 372–373
sequencing
in use, 225
serotonin
in nucleus accumbens
after cocaine self-administration, 175, 176f
serotonin system
addiction and, 28–29
alcohol effect on, 246
in alcohol reinforcement, 171
Services Research Outcomes Study on treatment, 244
SET. See Structural Ecosystems Theory (SET)
Sexually transmitted disease (STD), co-factor in HIV transmission, 319–320
Skinner, B. F., 257
smokeless tobacco use
social influence approach to, 292
smoking
in adolescent minority populations, 296–297
in Black women, 196–199
depression and, 249–250
life skills training and, 296
social influence approach to, 292–293, 294
social ecology theory
child in, 337, 339
exosystems in, 337, 339–340
macrosystems, 440
mesosystems in, 337, 339
microsystems, 337, 339
systems in, 337, 338f, 339–340

social factors
  in initiation, 299
social influence prevention model
  normative education in, 290
  psychological inoculation in, 289–290
  short-term effects of
    on alcohol use, 293
    on cigarette smoking and smokeless
      tobacco use, 292–293
    on marijuana use, 293
  social resistance skills training in, 290–
    291
  verbal and nonverbal skills in, 291
social inoculation
  in prevention, 228
social learning theory
  in Life Skills Training, 228
  in treatment, 257–260
social resistance skills training
  for adolescent drug use prevention,
    290–291
  STAR program in, 231–232
social support
  tobacco use and, 197
SOCRATES (Stages of Change Readi-
      ness and Treatment Eagerness
      Scale), 272–273
sponsorship
  in 12-step programs, 253–254
Stages of Change Readiness and Treat-
      ment Eagerness Scale (SOCRA-
      TES), 272–273
STAR (Students Taught Awareness and
      Resistance)
  description of, 231
  results of, 231–232
State Epidemiology Work Group, 58. See
      also Community Epidemiology
      Work
  Group (CEWG)
state legislation
  for tobacco use control, 435–435
Stockard, C.
  animal embryo studies, 74
  genetic effects of alcohol, 71
Strengthening Families program, 232
structural ecodevelopmental preventive
      intervention (SEPI), 353–356
  coherence in, 355–356
  cross-domain effects of, 353–354
  family in, 353
  iatrogenic effects of, 356–357

targeting to developmental moment,
    354
Structural Ecosystems Theory (SET),
    331–332, 336–357
  development in, 342
  developmental focus in, 341–344
  developmental systems theory and, 342
  ecodevelopment in, 342
  evidentiary support of, 346–352
    cross-domain influence in, 348
    exosystem in, 349–350
    family-peer system in, 349
    family-school mesosystem influence,
      347–348
    social ecology model in, 347
  features of, 337
  as guide to intervention design, 353–
    357
  historical perspective on, 336–337
  intervention design and, 353–357
  mesosystem interactions in, 346
  risk and protection across domains in,
    340–341
  social ecology, development and inter-
      actions in
    coercion model in, 351–352
    conceptual model in, 350–352350–
      351
  social ecology paradigm in, 337, 338f,
    339–340
  social interactions in, 344–345
  spatial dimensions in, 344–345
  transactional development model and,
    342, 344
Substance Abuse and Mental Health Ser-
      vices Administration (SAMSHA)
  Services Research Outcomes Study on
      treatment benefits, 244
substance abuse disorders (SUDs). See
      also use; use, dependence, abuse
  age and, 7t, 8, 8t
  internalizing and externalizing co-oc-
      currence in, 23
  prevalence of, 8, 8t
  problems associated with, 6–8, 7t
substitution pharmacotherapy
  for cigarettes, 248–249
  for heroin use, 246, 248
  LAAM in, 248
  methadone in, 246, 248
  nicotine patch, chewing gum and nasal
      sprays, 248–249

public health benefits of, 248
surveillance
    Community Epidemiology Work Group
        and, 49–52
    of trends, 52–54
surveillance system(s)
    Community Epidemiology Work
        Group, 49–59
        indicator data sets in, 48–49
    International Epidemiology Work
        Group, 59
    State Epidemiology Work Groups, 58
syringe and needle acquisition
    HIV reduction with, 316–317

temperament. *See also* personality
    difficult
        substance abuse disorders and, 23–24
    substance abuse disorders and, 22–25
therapeutic communities
    collaboration with human services sys-
        tems, 419
    community as method in, 398–399
    as method and model, 398
    as modality, 396–399
    modifications of
        evaluation of effectiveness of, 416–
            417
    motivation and treatment readiness re-
        search in, 418
    origin and concept of, 254
    perspective of, 398
    residential settings for, 396
    for special populations
        client's rights and self-help commu-
            nity, 420
        entitlements and self-help ethic,
            420–421
        housing vs. treatment and, 420
    stages of treatment in, 255
    traditional residential, 396, 397–398
    treatment elements of
        Survey of Essential Elements Ques-
            tionnaire and, 418
    treatment process in, 399
        advanced research in, 417–418
    vs. other modalities, 398
    welfare reforms impact on, 421
therapeutic communities research, 399–
    416
    criminal behavior and, 402f, 403

demographics of, 400f, 403
Minnesota Multiphasic Personality In-
    ventory admission profile in, 405f
in motivation and treatment readiness,
    418
policy implications of, 419–421
psychiatric diagnoses and, 404, 406f
psychological profiles in, 403–404,
    405f
social impairment and, 401f, 403
social profiles in, 399, 400f, 401f, 402f,
    403
treatment effectiveness in, 404, 405f,
    407
    dropout predictors, 407, 409f
    retention rates and, 407, 408f, 409f,
        410
treatment implications of, 419–420
treatment process advances in, 417–
    418
therapeutic community model
    in addicted mothers and children, 414
    in adolescents, 414
    in AIDS and HIV-seropositive clients,
        415–416
    in mentally ill substance abusers, 415
    modifications of, 410–413
        aftercare services in, 411, 416
        family services approach, 411
        mental health services in, 412–413
        multimodal and client–treatment
            matching in, 413
        primary health care and medical ser-
            vices in, 411
        relapse training in, 411–412
        12-step components in, 412
    in prisons, 414–415
    in special problems, 413–416
tiapride
    for alcohol craving, 250
tissue capacity, 136–137, 143
    conditionally responsive, 137–138
    controlling of critical circuits, 137
    sensitive, 137
tobacco
    availability of
        approval of, 91, 92t, 93
tobacco policy–nicotine research
    interrelationship of basic research, pub-
        lic health, treatment access, 440,
        440f
tobacco use

expectancies for, 87, 88t
health care costs from
    industry-government agency compensation settlement for, 435
initiation of and sequencing from, 225
prevalence increase in, 438–439
regulation by Federal Drug Administration, 431, 432–433, 438–439
state legislative control of, 435–436
stressful life events and, 196–197
in women, 196–197
tramadol hydrochloride
    abuse pattern with, 58
transactional model of development
    bidirectionality of developmental domains and environment, 108
    potentiating factors in, 110
    protective compensatory factors in, 108, 109–110
    vulnerability factors in, 109
transient influences
    on abuse, 110
trauma
    substance use disorders and, 17–18
treatment. *See also* psychopharmacological treatment; Psychosocial treatment
    abstinence or controlled use in, 275–276
    effectiveness of, 274–275
    goals of, 245
    multimodal and client-matched, 413
    psychopharmacological, 245–252
    psychosocial, 252–273
    response to
      gender and ethnicity in, 203
    social benefit of, 243–244
    social learning theory in, 257–258
    social techniques in, 259–260
    of special populations, 276
Treatment Outcome Prospective Study (TOPS), 275
treatment research. *See also* psychosocial treatment
    basic science and, 381, 388–389
    bridging between biological and behavioral science and, 389
    development of, 378–383
      contexts for, 381
      efficacy pilot testing in, 382–383
      generation in, 381–382, 388–389, 391

nonrandomized studies in, 381–382
standardization of, 379, 382
treatment manual in, 382
dissemination of, 379
    effectiveness of, 387
    program evaluation in, 386–387
    services development in, 385–386
in level of disorder and comprehensiveness of treatment, 390
stages of, 377–387
in training issues, 390
validation of, 379, 383–385, 390–391
    efficacy studies and trials in, 383–384
    mechanisms of action analyses, 384
    utility in, 384–385, 388
trends
    detection of, 52–54
    Monitoring the Future Study and, 225
    in selected drugs, 52–58
Twelve(12)-step programs, 252–254
    concept of, 252–253
    current status of, 254
    group therapy vs., 270–271
    history of, 252
    in therapeutic community model, 412
twin studies
    of substance use disorders, 30, 31

U.S. v. Doremus, 66, 67
U.S. v. Jin Fury Moy, 65
use. *See also* substance abuse disorders; use, dependence, abuse
    consumer sovereignty vs. control policies and, 81
    controlled vs. abstinence from, 275–276
    effect on tissue and individual, 146
    expectancies and, 86–88, 87t, 88t, 89–91, 91t
    experience of, 84–85
    gender differences in, 191, 199–200
    initiation of. *See* Initiation
    monitoring systems for, 48
    nondrug-alternative rewards to
      in prevention, 150–152
      in reduction, 152–153
    risk factors in women, 200
    surveillance systems for, 48
    transition into dependence, 172
use, dependence, abuse

biopsychosocial criteria for, 135–142.
    See also named criteria, e.g.
    Life space conditions
    life space conditions, 141–142
    organismic status, 139–141
    tissue capacity, 136–139
biopsychosocial paradigm, 128–132
common-factors theories of, 131–132
dimensions of
    generalized environment, 133–134
    respondent-operating environment,
        134–142
environment and, 127–128
individual factors in, 226
origins of
    implications of, 142–144
stage-phase sequences in, 123–126,
    126f
    acquisition, 124
    control-extinction, 124, 125
    dynamic and developmental, 1264
    habit formation, 124–125
    transitions across, 125–126
taxonomy of root questions in, 120–
    128
    dynamics of use behavior, 123–126
    individual differences in vulnerabili-
        ties, 126–127
    life space structure and dynamics,
        127–128
    outcomes of use, 121–123
    properties of drugs, 120–121, 122

vaccines
    for drugs of abuse, 251
validation measures
    in treatment standardization, 382
violence
    network for, 58
vouchers

in community-based treatment, 266
vulnerability
    in adolescents, 299
    developmental transitions in, 227
    individual differences in, 126–127
    to relapse, 180
    to substance use disorders, 31, 32
vulnerability factors
    in maladaptation, 109
    in transactional model of abuse, 109

Webb et al. v. U.S., 66, 67
Wikler, A., on biochemical-neurophysio-
        logical mechanisms, *161–162*
withdrawal
    agents for early, 66
    diagnostic criteria for, 173
    emotional aspects of, 162
withdrawal syndrome, 161
women. *See also* Black women; Ethnic
        minority women; Latinas
    alcohol use by, 196–199
    drug abuse by
        risk factors for, 200, 203–204
    drug-using
        health problems in, 201
        vs. nondrug-using, 200
    health behaviors of, 192–193
        factors influencing, 194
        psychosocial variables in, 195–196
    health promotion programs for, 204–
        207
    HIV prevention in, 314–315, 321–323
    risk behaviors in, 192, 193
        factors influencing, 194–195
    risk factors for use/abuse by, 200
        importance of, 203–204
    tobacco use by, 196–199
Women's Christian Temperance Union
        (WCTU), 70–71
    Committee of Fifty and, 71

ABOUT THE EDITORS

Meyer D. Glantz, PhD, is the associate director for science and acting deputy director of the Division of Epidemiology and Prevention Research of the National Institute on Drug Abuse (NIDA), National Institutes of Health. At NIDA, Dr. Glantz has previously served as the chief of the Epidemiology Research Branch and the director of the Etiology Research Program. Prior to coming to NIDA he worked as a researcher and clinician at the Veterans Administration Clinic in Boston.

Dr. Glantz is a Fellow of the American Psychological Association and serves as a consultant to and board member of a variety of scientific and professional organizations and publications. He is the author of numerous articles and chapters on substance abuse, drug abuse etiology, cognitive therapy, and the elderly and has edited several volumes including *Vulnerability to Drug Abuse, Biobehavioral Research Approaches to Drug Abuse Etiology,* and *Resilience and Development: Positive Life Adaptations.* In addition, he maintains a private clinical practice in the Washington, DC area, supervises other clinicians, and is a lecturer for the Montgomery County Adult Education program. Dr. Glantz received his doctorate from Harvard University in 1979.

Christine R. Hartel, PhD, is associate executive director for science at the American Psychological Association, where she represents the scientific and science policy interests of the association to federal and state agencies, other scientific and professional organizations, and APA governance groups. She was elected a Fellow of the Association this year. Dr. Hartel worked for six years at the National Institute on Drug Abuse, awarding grants and contracts for basic and clinical research on drug abuse in the fields of neuroscience, behavior, pharmacology, and chemistry. She has written many articles, technical reports, and book chapters on drugs and the brain, amphetamine research, and the medical uses of marijuana. She also edited the book *Biomedical Approaches to Illicit Drug Demand Reduction*. Dr. Hartel has been a consultant to the World Health Organization on the effects of marijuana. As a research psychologist at the U.S. Army Research Institute for the Behavioral and Social Sciences, she studied the cognitive effects of drugs and other stressors on soldier performance, as well as their implications for the design of weapons systems. In 1985, Dr. Hartel received the Army's Research and Development Award, the highest civilian honor conferred by the Army for technical excellence. Dr. Hartel received her PhD in biopsychology from the University of Chicago in 1985.